MW00775159

*Traditions in*
# Turmoil

# Traditions in
# Turmoil

## Mary Ann Glendon

EX CORDE
ECCLESIAE

VERITATIS SPLENDOR

·AVE·
MARIA

UNIVERSITY

*Sapientia* Press
of Ave Maria University

Copyright © 2006 by Mary Ann Glendon. All rights reserved.
No part of this publication may be reproduced or transmitted in any form or means, electronic or mechanical, including photography, recording, or any other information storage or retrieval system, without permission in writing from the publisher.

Requests for permission to make copies of any part of the work should be directed to:

Sapientia Press
of Ave Maria University
24 Frank Lloyd Wright Drive
Ann Arbor, MI 48106
888-343-8607

*Cover Design:* Eloise Anagnost
*Cover Photo:* Elizabeth Glendon Lev

Printed in the United States of America
Library of Congress Control Number: 2005929011
ISBN 1-932589-24-4

# Table of Contents

Foreword by Richard John Neuhaus ............................. ix

Author's Preface................................................. xi

## SECTION I: Law and the Human Sciences

Chapter 1   Tradition and Creativity in Culture and Law ...................... 3

Chapter 2   Why Cross Boundaries? ........................................ 15

Chapter 3   Max Rheinstein: Pioneer in Legal Sociology ...................... 23

Chapter 4   Rousseau and the Revolt Against Reason ......................... 33

Chapter 5   John Paul II's Challenge to the Human Sciences................... 45

Chapter 6   The First Ten Years of the Pontifical Academy of Social Sciences....... 49

## SECTION II: The Ecology of Freedom

Chapter 7   The Moral Structure of Freedom ................................ 55

Chapter 8   The Cultural Underpinnings of America's Democratic Experiment..... 61

Chapter 9   Traders and Raiders .............................................. 77

Chapter 10  Villages and Virtues............................................. 83

Chapter 11  Cities and Civil Society ......................................... 91

Chapter 12  Suburbs and the Seedbeds of Democracy.......................... 99

Chapter 13  Feminism and the Family ....................................... 105

Chapter 14  Who's Afraid of Tom Wolfe?..................................... 115

Chapter 15  William Galston's Communitarian Liberalism...................... 119

Chapter 16  Michael Sandel's Liberal Communitarianism ...................... 125

Chapter 17  Religion and Democratic Society ................................ 131

Chapter 18  In the Country of Old People .................................... 137

## SECTION III: Law and Culture

Chapter 19    Human Personhood in the Federalist Papers........................145

Chapter 20    Reflections on the Flag-Burning Case ............................153

Chapter 21    Laurence Tribe on Abortion ......................................157

Chapter 22    When Words Cheapen Life..........................................165

Chapter 23    Family Law and Popular Culture ..................................167

Chapter 24    A Nation Under Lawyers...........................................177

Chapter 25    Legal Ethics: Worlds in Collision ...............................191

Chapter 26    Classical and Romantic Judges....................................203

Chapter 27    Carl Rowan's Thurgood Marshall ..................................213

Chapter 28    Clarence Thomas: Postmodern Judge ...............................219

Chapter 29    The Continental Advantage in Interpretation .....................223

Chapter 30    Family Law in a Time of Turbulence...............................237

## SECTION IV: Human Rights

Chapter 31    Rights in Twentieth-Century Constitutions .......................255

Chapter 32    Law, Communities, and the Religious Freedom
              Language of the Constitution.....................................269

Chapter 33    The Illusion of Absolute Rights..................................279

Chapter 34    John Paul II, Letter to Mary Ann Glendon and Holy See's
              Delegation to the Fourth World Conference on Women...............287

Chapter 35    Advancing Women's Freedom and Dignity ...........................291

Chapter 36    The Unfinished Journey...........................................299

Chapter 37    What Happened at Beijing ........................................301

Chapter 38    Knowing the Universal Declaration of Human Rights ...............315

Chapter 39    Foundations of Human Rights: The Unfinished Business ............335

Chapter 40    Catholic Thought and Dilemmas of Human Rights ................349

Chapter 41    Charles Malik and the Universal Declaration......................363

Chapter 42    John P. Humphrey and the Universal
              Declaration of Human Rights .....................................371

Chapter 43    The Forgotten Crucible: The Latin American
              Influence on the Universal Human Rights Idea.....................383

## SECTION V: Catholicism in a Time of Turmoil

Chapter 44   Why I'm Still a Catholic ..........................................399

Chapter 45   Contrition in the Age of Spin Control ...........................409

Chapter 46   Witness to Hope...................................................415

Chapter 47   The Hour of the Laity ............................................421

Chapter 48   A Generation Searching ..........................................433

Index.......................................................441

# Foreword

THIS IS NOT MERELY a collection of random pieces: This is a book. It is all of a piece, and that is because Mary Ann Glendon—her life, her work, and her thought—is all of a piece. The book displays the myriad angles of vision and arenas of commitment from which and in which Glendon has developed important themes that have a powerful bearing on how we think and live at the beginning of the third millennium.

The title is the key to what follows. That ours is a time of intellectual, cultural, moral, and religious turmoil does not need to be argued. What does need to be argued, and what Glendon argues with force and freshness, is that our response to turmoil requires a greater honesty in coming to terms with tradition, and with traditions in conflict. There can be no creativity without tradition, Glendon convincingly contends in her Erasmus Lecture of 1992, which is included in this book.

That is little understood, she writes in her introduction, by many on both the left and right. Quoting one of her favorite thinkers, the theologian Bernard Lonergan, she urges us to be "big enough to be at home in both the old and new; and painstaking enough to work out one at a time the transitions to be made." Make no mistake: Mary Ann Glendon is not a "beyondist"—one of those people who claim their positions are beyond liberal and conservative but reliably end up being one or the other. Nor is she a "centrist," who carefully navigates between opposing views lest she be dubbed "controversial."

Working within the capacious structure of the Christian intellectual tradition, most reflectively and generously articulated in Catholic teaching, Glendon constructively engages alternative ways of thinking about what it means to be human and what is required to nurture a society worthy of human beings. As the reader will see, her work ranges far and wide, and it goes deep. There is hardly a subject she addresses that does not change the way we think about it.

In her book by that title, Glendon made "rights talk" part of our public vocabulary. In the present book she further explores the indispensability of the idea of human rights, and the impossibility of sustaining that idea without an adequate anthropology, that is, what it means to be human. She here makes important advances on my own writing about "mediating structures" in society, analyzing what she calls the "seedbeds" of memory, virtue, and caring. As a Harvard professor, she is more than a match for the brightest and best, sometimes erudite and sometimes simply pretentious, who have, she believes, betrayed the university's responsibility to students and society. Moreover, she has not held herself aloof from frays in the public square, as witness her vivid writing on the 1995 United Nations conference on the family in Beijing where she led the Vatican delegation.

Always and in all she does, Mary Ann Glendon is a woman. Charmingly and vivaciously so. Also relentlessly and uncompromisingly so. She is a teacher, writer, wife, and mother; and she is a feminist who sees through the delusional feminisms that claim a woman can "have it all." Decisions must be made. Opportunities are embraced and opportunities are declined. Not young women alone, but young women in particular, will discover in her life and thought a way of being in the world as a whole person. In each part of this wonderful book the discerning reader will discover more fully what it means to be a person "big enough to be at home in both the old and new; and painstaking enough to work out one at a time the transitions to be made."

—Richard John Neuhaus
*New York City*

# Author's Preface

**A** LIVING TRADITION is always a system on the move. By the late 1960s, when I began teaching and writing about law and social institutions, there was no doubt that western liberal democracies were on the brink of transformations as profound as those that had accompanied the industrial revolution. For a time it seemed as though the changes might proceed incrementally, maintaining substantial continuities with the past while adjusting to new circumstances. It soon became apparent, however, that western societies, and their legal systems, had entered a period of exceptional turmoil. Customs and understandings in every sphere of human activity were unsettled, with far-reaching consequences for family life, relations between men and women, the world of work, business and commerce, schools and universities, religious groups, and, of course, the study and practice of law. The old order was falling apart, and the shape of things to come was far from clear. It was a time of risk, a time of challenge, and a time of promise.

Most of the essays in this collection were written from the vantage point of the law, which Oliver Wendell Holmes, Jr., once likened to a magic mirror in which one could see all the triumphs and tragedies, struggles and routines of the human race.[1] Someday, perhaps, that mirror will reveal clear directions and patterns in the maelstrom of interests, beliefs, and hopes through which we have recently passed. Already, the major demographic indicators—marriage, divorce and birth rates—have begun to stabilize at their new high or low levels. Nearly all of these essays, however, were written when demographic turbulence was at its height. The pieces in Part I, "Law and the Human Sciences," ponder, from various angles, the challenges and the rewards of scholarship in such an era. Gathered in Part II, "The Ecology

---

[1] Several of the essays in this volume appeared in *First Things*, the interfaith journal of religion and public life on whose board I have happily served for many years. With a view toward the general reader, essays that were prepared for law reviews or other specialized publications have been lightly edited, and most footnotes have been omitted.

of Freedom," are a series of reflections on how changes in the mediating structures of civil society have affected the cultural underpinnings of America's democratic experiment. Part III, "Law and Culture," contains writings concerned with the relation of law to behavior and ideas. The essays and speeches in Part IV, "Human Rights," recall the remarkable achievements of the post-World War II human rights movement and analyze the contests currently raging over its future direction. Included in this section, as a preface to my speeches at the 1995 Beijing Women's Conference, is one item not authored by me: the letter written by Pope John Paul II to me and the Holy See Delegation on the eve of our departure for China. Finally, in Part V, "Catholicism in a Time of Turmoil," are collected some essays on Catholic traditions in the eventful pontificate of John Paul the Great.

During the waning years of the twentieth century, the traditions discussed in these essays—legal, social, and religious were in a state akin to that which students of complex adaptive systems call "the edge of chaos." Relatively stable systems erupted into turbulence; settled arrangements came apart, components flying off in all directions. From some angles, the systems seemed to be collapsing; from others, to be crucibles of creativity. The edge of chaos is a scary place, but it is also charged with potency. A time of turmoil is a time of testing and responsibility if one believes, as I do, that the course of human events can be influenced to some extent by human intelligence, cooperation, determination, and good will.

As a living tradition moves forward, it is laden with the accumulated accidents and inventions of the men and women who have gone before—a cargo of useful ideas and practices that await development, and a jumble of outworn artifacts that might well be left behind. Future generations will judge whether our own period of stewardship has burdened or enriched their inheritance, whether we have advanced or hindered the conditions for human flourishing. It seems to me that no one has better suggested the spirit in which citizens, scholars, and members of a pilgrim Church should confront the challenges of traditions in turmoil than the philosopher Bernard J. F. Lonergan: "There is bound to be formed a solid right that is determined to live in a world that no longer exists. There is bound to be formed a scattered left, captivated by now this, now that new possibility. But what will count is a perhaps not numerous center; big enough to be at home in both the old and new; and painstaking enough to work out one at a time the transitions to be made." That is the spirit in which I have tried to work, and I hope it is reflected in these essays.

—Mary Ann Glendon
*Chestnut Hill, Massachusetts*
*July 2005*

# Law and the Human Sciences

# CHAPTER I

# Tradition and Creativity in Culture and Law

This essay was the 1992 Erasmus Lecture,
sponsored by the Institute on Religion and Public Life.[1]

A WELL-KNOWN ACCOUNT of creativity sets the scene for a celebrated act of creation, and a bleak scene it was: "In the beginning . . . the earth was without form and void, and darkness covered the face of the abyss." On that occasion, creativity consisted in bringing something out of nothing—a feat so remarkable that the Hebrew verb used to describe it *(barah)* refers exclusively to divine activity. In the English language, the words "create" and "creative" long had a similar connotation. It was not until the Renaissance that they began to be used in the way that we now take for granted, referring to the work of human minds or hands. That change in linguistic usage was just one sign of a new way of thinking about the place of man in the universe. Central to that new world-view was an exhilarating vision of human potency—a vision that we English speakers associate with Shakespeare's ode to humanity in *Hamlet*: "How noble in reason! How infinite in faculty! In form and movement how express and admirable! In action how like an angel! In apprehension how like a God!"

With that heady estimation of human capacities came a certain sense of liberation from tradition, custom, and the group. Still, it was not until the Romantic era that creativity came to be identified in many quarters with individual originality, and later yet that disdain for tradition became a tradition in itself. At the extreme, in our time, the tradition of anti-traditionalism would have it that *homo sapiens sapiens* can cancel its debts to the past, and that we too can bring wonders out of the void.

The idea that tradition is antithetical to creativity of the human sort is what I propose to examine and challenge—along with its usual underlying assumptions that tradition is necessarily static, and that the essence of creativity is originality. To anyone with a scientific bent, my project will seem to be an exercise in the obvious. For in the history of science, as Stephen Toulmin, Thomas Kuhn, and others have made clear, nearly every great advance has

---

[1] Mary Ann Glendon, "Tradition and Creativity in Culture and Law," *First Things* 27 (November 1992): 13–19.

been made by persons (typically, groups of persons) who simultaneously possess two qualities: a thorough grounding in the normal science of their times, and the boldness to make a break with the reigning paradigm within which that normal science takes place. My concern, however, is the progress of anti-traditionalism in the human sciences, where what counts as an advance, or creativity, is more contestable, and where many eminent thinkers now devote much of their energy to attacking the traditions that have nourished their various disciplines. Several of these literary legionnaires have crossed academic boundaries to join forces in a kind of holy war against "Western civilization."

I shall confine my attention here to the field with which I am most familiar, namely the law—though this may vex the spirit of Erasmus, who seems to have had a rather low opinion of lawyers, calling them "among the silliest and most ignorant of men." Erasmus might have been amazed, however, if he could have known the degree to which lawyers themselves, and especially teachers of lawyers, would one day come to exhibit disdain for their own craft, and to disavow openly the ideals of their traditions. I say traditions, for, where Americans are concerned, three traditions are involved: the common law tradition that we inherited from England, the tradition of American constitutionalism, and the craft tradition of the profession.

Roberto Unger, a guru of the Critical Legal Studies movement, came uncomfortably close to the mark in his much-quoted description of the legal world he entered in the late 1960s. Most professors then, he wrote, "dallied in one more variant of the perennial effort to restate power and preconception as right. In and outside the law schools, most jurists looked with indifference or even disdain upon the legal theorists. . . . When we came, they were like a priesthood that had lost their faith and kept their jobs. They stood in tedious embarrassment before cold altars." To the extent that Unger's portrait captures something of the current self-understanding of lawyers, it points to a state of affairs that cannot help but have implications for our law-saturated society. Thus it seems worthwhile to inquire into the extent, causes, and consequences of a widespread loss of confidence among lawyers themselves concerning legal traditions that have been intimately bound up with our historic experiment in ordered liberty.

The legal tradition we inherited from England is almost a textbook example of what Alasdair MacIntyre has called a living tradition, one that is "historically extended" and "socially embodied," whose development constantly points beyond itself.

In taking up the tradition of the common law, we are faced first with a matter of terminology. The term "common law" refers to the type of law, and lawmaking, that historically distinguished the English legal system from the legal systems of continental Europe. The common law is an evolving body of principles built by accretion from countless decisions in individual lawsuits. Because it emerges from practice rather than theory, its principles are highly fact-sensitive and not too general. Continental law, by contrast, had, as they say, the smell of the lamp—it was developed by scholars, and was further rationalized and systematized by comprehensive legislative codifications.

Two remarkable features of the common law tradition need to be emphasized here. The first is its continuity. Over centuries that saw the rise and fall of feudalism, the expansion of commerce, and the transition to constitutional monarchy, the common law of England adapted to each new circumstance without abrupt change or any root-and-branch reorganization of the sort represented by the European codifications. Statutes in England, for the most part, were like patches here and there against the background of the common law, and judges tried to construe them so as to blend them, as far as possible, into the fabric of the case law. Thus in 1894 the great English legal historian F. W. Maitland could look back on centuries of legal evolution and say: "When we speak of a body of law, we use a metaphor so apt that it is hardly a metaphor. We picture to ourselves a being that lives and grows, that preserves its identity while every atom of which it is composed is subject to a ceaseless process of change, decay, and renewal." Lest the reader surmise that that sort of thinking was confined to armchair types, or to the other side of the Atlantic, consider that at just about the same time in Boston a judge named Oliver Wendell Holmes, Jr., was likening the law to a "magic mirror" in which a suitably trained observer could see a "mighty princess" eternally weaving into her tapestry "dim figures of the ever-lengthening past."

The second feature of the common law that must be stressed is the distinctive methodology that enabled it to adapt and grow while maintaining its continuity. To try to describe that method is a bit like trying to describe swimming or bicycle riding, for it consists of a set of habits and practices that are acquired only by doing. But the conventional understanding goes something like this: The common law judge is supposed to be a virtuoso of practical reason, weaving back and forth between facts and law, striving not only for a fair disposition of the dispute at hand, but to decide each case with reference to a principle that transcends the facts of that case, all with a view toward maintaining continuity with past decisions, deciding like cases alike, and providing guidance for parties similarly situated in the future. It was those sorts of operations that Lord Coke had in mind in the seventeenth century when he famously said: "Reason is the life of the law; nay, the common law itself is nothing else but reason." To Coke, "reason" did not mean deductive reason (as it did for Descartes), nor self-interested calculation (as it did for Hobbes). It was, rather, an extended process of collaboration over time. Or, as he put it himself, it was a kind of group achievement, "gotten by long study, observation, and experience, . . . fined and refined over centuries by generations of grave and learned men. . . ."

To be a traditionalist in such a tradition seems pretty clearly not to be frozen in the past or mired in the status quo, but rather to participate, as

MacIntyre puts it, in a community of intense discourse about what it is that gives the tradition in question its point and purpose. It is a fair question whether one can really speak of creativity, as distinct from mere inventiveness or successful problem-solving, in the common law tradition. On this point, I would like to suggest that the American Founding was a classic instance of the kind of creativity that emerges from, and is deeply rooted in, the very tradition that it irrevocably transforms. The Declaration of Independence, the Constitution, the Federalist Papers, and the landmark early decisions of the Supreme Court could only have been produced by statesmen who were steeped in the English legal heritage. True, the Founders varied considerably in the degree of regard they had for that tradition. But all of them fully understood the role the common law had played in safeguarding the lives, liberties, and property of Englishmen through civil war and social upheaval. When the American colonists came into conflict with their royal governors, they claimed that same common law as their birthright. They broke with the mother country, but they did not reject their own past. Rather, their English legal inheritance was taken up, transformed, and made into the basis of a new order.

Another type of legal creativity—the everyday creativity of judges and lawyers—is of a more modest sort, but should not be underrated. It is the creativity of the artisan rather than the architect, but the same observation holds regarding the importance of being grounded in tradition for any significant advance. Think of the preventive law handed down through generations of practitioners—the well-wrought agreements, bylaws, contracts, deeds, leases, wills, and trusts that at their best aid human beings to carry on mutually beneficial relations with a minimum of friction, to make reliable plans for the future, and to avoid unnecessary disputes by anticipating and providing for contingencies. What lawyer could responsibly draw up such a document without consulting the experience of bench and bar embodied in the humble form book? And when preventive law fails, creativity of a modest sort is involved in dispute settlement as well.

At this point, an inquisitive person might ask why, if the common law tradition had such a robust capacity for creative development, it has fallen into disrepute among many of its inheritors.

It seems relevant, to begin with, that the tradition is one whose participants were never much given to introspection. Legal knowledge for most of our history was, after all, passed on through apprenticeship. And because its methodology was latent, our continental friends, with their strong suit in theorizing, often assumed that we had no method worthy of the name. Erasmus was characteristically blunt on this subject: "The study of English law," he said, "is as far as can be from true learning." And, in a similar vein, Tocqueville, on his visit to the United States in 1831, remarked on how "strange" it was that such a legalistic society had not yet produced "any great writers inquiring into the general principles of the laws."

A mere decade after Tocqueville penned those words, however, the man who was to bring fancy theory to American law was born in Boston, Massachusetts. As fate would have it, he devoted much of his prodigious talent to debunking the roles of tradition and reason in the law. It would be hard to exaggerate the impact of Oliver Wendell Holmes, Jr. on American legal culture. His life was literally the stuff of which legends are made. He was the gifted son of a famous father, and he was a genuine Civil War hero, wounded at Ball's Bluff, Antietam, and Fredericksburg. By the time of his death in 1935 at age 93, he had distinguished himself in every role the legal profession had to offer. As a young practitioner in a busy Boston firm, he spent his evenings writing a treatise on the common law that revolutionized the way American lawyers write and speak about law. He then taught briefly at Harvard Law School before his appointment to the Massachusetts Supreme Judicial Court in 1882. After twenty years on that bench (three of them as Chief Justice), he was named, at the age of 61, to the United States Supreme Court, where he served for another 29 years. He left his stamp on nearly every area of law—as much through his fluent literary style as through his innovative theories or his decisions and dissents in landmark cases. Where legal theory is concerned, Holmes's writings set the scholarly agenda for the entire twentieth century: Legal realism, pragmatism, sociological jurisprudence, law and economics, and critical legal studies are all little more than elaborations of themes announced by Holmes. As a leading Legal Realist wrote in the 1930s, "Holmes was the daddy of us all."

This "daddy," however, inadvertently hindered his progeny from building on his own achievements. Consider how he taught them to view tradition. Wherever one looks in the law, Holmes complained in 1897, in what is still the most widely quoted law review article ever published, one sees "tradition" getting in the way of "rational policy." But the "tradition" against which he railed was just the dead hand of the past, as witness another well-known statement: "It is revolting to have no better reason for a rule of law than that it was laid down in the time of Henry IV."

This reductionist assault on tradition was combined with an attack on traditional legal reasoning. The opening sentence of his 1881 treatise, *The Common Law*, was a thinly veiled challenge to Lord Coke's dictum that "Reason is the life of the law." Holmes wrote: "The life of the law has not been logic: it has been experience." One interesting fact about that famous aphorism is that even at the height of nineteenth-century legal formalism, American lawyers were not making such an extreme claim as that the life of the law was logic. As for Coke, he would have agreed wholeheartedly with Holmes on the priority of experience over logic. A second interesting fact about Holmes's formulation is that it closely resembles a statement in a German legal treatise that we now know Holmes checked out of a Boston library in 1879. I mention this not to impugn Holmes's originality but to call attention to a point that is more important: The criticism in question was directed by its German author at the rigid conceptualism of scholars who *did* believe that logic was the life of the law. The German academics who were then engaged in drafting the German Civil Code of 1896 envisioned that code as ideally possessing "logical closedness" *(logische Geschlossenheit)*. It was highly inappropriate for Holmes to apply the same criticism to Coke, or even to more formalistic nineteenth-century writers on the judge-made, open-textured, common law.

But Holmes was a man on the move. With the same fast shuffle that he used to convert "tradition" into fossilized "history," he reduced "reason" to dry "logic"—a collection, as he put it, of syllogisms, axioms, and deductions. That took the whiskey out of the highball. And there was more. For Holmes announced, as though it were a discovery, what lawyers have always known: that there are many times when the law is silent, obscure, or incomplete, and that judges often do not simply find and apply the law, but actually exercise a limited lawmaking function. In a passage meant to shock, Holmes offered his theory of what judges were making law from. Expediency, opinion, and even prejudice, he said, had all played a greater role "than the syllogism" in fashioning the rules by which we are governed. One might think that it would not take a Sherlock (or an Oliver Wendell) Holmes to discern that judges, being human, display the usual human flaws in the exercise of their rational faculties.

But Holmes pressed the point further. Revisiting the subject at the height of the blunt macho style that was his trademark, Holmes told an audience of law students: "You will find some text writers telling you that [law] . . . is a system of reason." That, according to the great man, was obfuscation. Laws were nothing more or less than "commands" backed up by the armed might of the state. The aim of legal study was simply the science of prediction, prediction of "where the axe will fall." And in words that are still engraved on the mind of every law student, he said that if you want to know the law, "you must look at it as a bad man does." He exhorted his youthful listeners to use "cynical acid" to wash away all the moralizing language of right and wrong so that they could see the law as it truly is. But don't think I mean any disrespect for the law, he hastened to add, "I *venerate* the law." Why such piety toward mere command? Because, he said, "it has the final title to respect that it exists."

In the same speech, later published under the title *The Path of the Law*, Holmes said that his "ideal" was to put the law on a more modem and scientific basis through clear thinking about means and ends, costs and benefits. "Reason" might be out, but what Holmes approvingly called "rationality" was in. Accordingly, in a passage that has become sacred scripture in some quarters, he advised that every lawyer acquire a knowledge of economics, for the "man of the future is the man of statistics and the master of economics."

By thus bracketing tradition and reason, Holmes helped to prepare the way for the carnival of twentieth-century American legal theory. For many of his successors, tradition took on a pejorative sense—it became the debris of old errors, power relations, and prejudices. His critique of reason laid the foundation for the fact-skeptics and the rule-skeptics of the 1930s who called themselves Realists, and for their successors, the critical theorists, who came on the scene in the 1960s.

With hindsight, though, it is remarkable how deeply Holmes himself drew from the springs of the very tradition he was engaged in disparaging. In this respect, he bears a striking resemblance to those of his contemporaries whom Hilton Kramer calls the great "tradition-haunted" artists—Picasso and Matisse, Eliot and Yeats, Schoenberg and Stravinsky. With his vision of the "mighty princess," with his mastery of his craft, and with his vaulting ambition, Holmes was a Picasso-like figure—larger than life, boldly iconoclastic, yet mindful of his lineage and of the continuity of culture. *The Path of the Law* was his *Demoiselles of Avignon*.

Now what is very important to acknowledge at this point is that Holmes was far ahead of most of his contemporaries in his perception that the common law tradition was in a period of crisis. He was right on the mark in his understanding of the way in which the American constitutional tradition represented an important break, as well as continuity, with the common law tradition. To borrow Thomas Kuhn's terminology again, trouble spots had appeared in the reigning paradigm, and the normal legal science of the turn of the century was not handling them well.

What was the nature of the crisis? The Anglo-American legal system, not for the first time in its long history, was confronted with major social, economic, and political changes, but this time they were occurring with unprecedented rapidity. I will mention just three major sources of difficulty.

Consider first that when Holmes was a young lawyer in the 1870s, legislatures had begun producing a new type of statute—primitive regulatory legislation, much of it addressed to conditions in factories. Those whose interests were adversely affected by these laws took their complaints to the courts, with the result that the Supreme Court embarked on its first sustained adventure with the power of judicial review, a power that it had possessed for nearly a century, but which it had exercised sparingly. The behavior of the Supreme Court and other courts in that period (striking down much early social legislation as infringing on economic rights) is now frequently treated in law school classes as showing that the judiciary was in the service of the dominant classes. But there was another dimension to the story. When late nineteenth-century judges entered the still relatively uncharted areas of statutory interpretation and constitutional review, they really did not know how to handle the new situation. It is helpful to keep in mind that as late as 1875, nearly half of the United States Supreme Court's case load was still pure common law litigation.

By 1925, however, statutes figured importantly in all but about 5 percent of the cases. Most judges during those years of transition tended to proceed in the way they knew best—by falling back on their practice of construing enacted law (including the Constitution) in such a way as to blend in with, rather than displace, the common law background where, as it happened, freedom of contract was ensconced as a leading principle. In a series of famous dissents, Holmes, to his credit, tried to point out to his fellow judges that the rules of the game had changed in 1787. But that point seldom got across until the 1930s, and even then it was not fully absorbed.

A second source of strain on the customary ways of doing things, down in the capillaries of the legal system, was the rapid development of industry and commerce. Pre-industrial property, tort, and contract principles were often poorly suited to the new problems generated by urbanization, industrialization, and the rise of the large business corporation.

Third, by the end of Holmes's long life in the 1930s, the American experiment had moved into yet another phase as the federal government vastly expanded its activities through legislation which the Court, in a stunning about-face, upheld against constitutional attack. Among the New Deal lawyers who had broken ground by producing the Social Security Act, the securities laws, and the national labor relations legislation, there were some eminent academics. They called attention to an urgent problem: the need to begin the study of legislative drafting and interpretation in the nation's law schools. Remarkably, however, to this day that call has gone largely unheeded.

In sum, it seems fair to say that the stresses and strains on the legal system that appeared during Holmes' lifetime called for a high degree of juristic skill, imagination, and creativity. How did the legal profession respond?

To begin with the obvious, lawsuits have to be decided. Judges on the front lines cannot decline to render a decision just because the problems brought to them are new and the law is unclear. So judges in state courts duly began to try to adapt the principles of pre-industrial personal injury law, face-to-face sales law, and agrarian land law to the circumstances of an industrialized and urbanized society. Often expressing their impatience with the failure of legislatures to resolve the larger policy conflicts implicit in that enterprise, some of these judges moved boldly and openly into rulemaking and policymaking. The purported discovery that judges had always engaged in "creative" activity was taken by some as legitimating a more ambitious concept of the judicial role, and by a few as a sign that all bets were off. Contrary to what many people believe, the Warren Court of the 1950s did not initiate, but simply took to new heights, this movement by judges into areas where their legitimacy is weakest—finding broad social and economic facts (as opposed to facts based on the evidence in the case before them) and adjudicating between conflicting and competing interests in society (as opposed to resolving the particular dispute at hand).

What about the call of scholarly New Dealers like James M. Landis and Felix Frankfurter for more attention to the study of legislation? Non-lawyers may be surprised to learn that even now American law schools devote practically no systematic attention to the drafting or interpretation of statutes, and very little to empirical study of how various regulatory arrangements work out in practice. In the spring of 1992, a committee appointed to review the curriculum at Harvard Law School reported that Harvard, like most other law schools, was still teaching the basic required first-year program "almost without regard to the coming of the regulatory state, and without recognition that statutes and regulations have become the predominant legal sources of our time."

An interested citizen, learning of this state of affairs, might be forgiven for wondering what American law schools *have* been doing all this time. Part of the answer is that prosaic regulatory law never really had a chance once constitutional law became the "glamour subject" of legal education in the 1950s and 1960s. The constitutional law that took center stage, moreover, sloughed off its old preoccupations with federalism and the separation of powers to concentrate its main attention on the court-centered jurisprudence of the rights revolution. The old, instinctive preference for judge-made over enacted law that had shaped constitutional interpretation at the turn of the century enjoyed an Indian summer among majorities on the Warren and Burger courts as they embarked on this second exciting adventure with judicial review. That same preference persists today among many law professors who teach that the Constitution is just a "text" whose various provisions are mere starting points for freewheeling judicial development, as if the people of the United States had not established a regime that places important limits on both judicial and legislative lawmaking.

Meanwhile, a new generation of tradition- and reason-bashers appeared in the legal academy. The law-and-economics school took up Holmes's "ideal" of instrumental rationality, while the critical theorists gave his skepticism a new postmodern twist with the aid of French literary criticism and neo-Marxist social thought. It is a big step, for example, from observing that there are certain leeways inherent in fact finding and rule application, to asserting that there is no such thing as a fact and that all rules are radically indeterminate and manipulable. It is another major leap from being realistic about the difficulties of disinterested decision making to a condemnation of the entire legal system as fatally tainted with racism, sexism, and other forms of hegemony. There is a world of difference between the lawyerly reformism of the New Dealers and the view that law is nothing more than concentrated politics—between, one might say, Felix Frankfurter and the Frankfurt School.

Noticeably less interested than Holmes and the Realists in law as such, the "crits" have borrowed the main elements of their critical theory from France, Italy, and Germany—countries that had never had experience with anything like the common law, where reason too often meant *raison d'état,* and which historically had difficulty establishing regimes in which the rule of law is respected. But many critical scholars had absorbed so little "normal science" that they could not see the problems in transferring a critique of continental law to their own system. In the dark, all law looks the same.

The work of many of these legal avant-gardists thus reminds one of Marx's dictum that history repeats itself, first as tragedy, then as farce. They have added only marginally to the critical insights of their "tradition-haunted" predecessors, for their wholesale rejection of the past has left them with a rather flimsy conceptual apparatus. By opting out of the ongoing argument embodied in living legal traditions, they are left to commune disjointedly with one another or with themselves. Many of them, like their counterparts in the art world, are attracted by violence and destruction. One legal Dadaist, for example, has written exuberantly in the *Yale Law Journal* that "trashing is fun." "Context-smashing" is central to the program advocated by Unger, who criticizes "eighteenth-century constitutionalism" for the drag that its checks and balances impose on the pace of social change. He envisions future governments with "ministries of destabilization" to promote ferment and creative disarray.

After suggesting a comparison between avant-gardism in the law and in the arts, I must admit that I am more uneasy about the cultural effects of this phenomenon in law than in, say, painting. I also believe that, unfortunately for us Americans, bashing legal traditions is a graver matter for our society than it is for the continental countries from which American critical legal theorists have drawn their inspiration. More homogeneous nations have many sources of social cohesion other than their legal systems: in shared customs, history, religion, song, and poetry. But for a people as diverse as ours, the law has had to bear more cultural weight. In the United States, for better or worse, law has become a principal carrier of those few values that our heterogeneous citizenry holds in common—freedom, equality, and inclusiveness of the community for which we accept common responsibility. Law is one of the chief means through which we order our lives together. The attack on reason and tradition in law thus strikes at the heart of our version of the democratic experiment.

I would not wish to be understood to be saying that the legal profession has entirely capitulated to the tradition of anti-traditionalism. The bar still contains a fair number of men and women who take pride in their craft, and who endeavor to follow Abraham Lincoln's advice to lawyers to be peacemakers among neighbors. On the bench there are still many independent judges who are not afraid to exercise judgment, and who endeavor to do so modestly and objectively. Such judges, as Paul Carrington has observed, are in an important sense models for the functioning of the rest of government, beacons by which public servants of all sorts "are led in the direction of restrained adherence to principle." Even in the legal academy, one can still find an occasional figure like Archibald Cox, who dared to speak recently of his "deep belief that judges and academic scholars have an obligation to put aside all private predilections, commitments, self-interest, using only the most disinterested and detached reason they can bring to bear."

But the legal profession is changing. Many practitioners are now more accurately described as businessmen and -women than as members of a liberal profession. And certain other developments in the practice cannot be entirely unrelated to the atmosphere in the academy. The teaching that all rules are indeterminate includes the rules of ethics that were once thought to impose limits on what a lawyer might or might not do. One may surmise—though this would be hard to prove—that years of portraying legal reasoning as mere window dressing may have contributed to a certain neglect of craftsmanship.

All this is beginning to sound as though, in the legal world, darkness is once again creeping over the abyss where our old enemy chaos lies waiting. Certainly our three American legal traditions—each in its way representing a human effort to hold the chaotic forces of power, passion, and self-interest in check—are not enjoying their finest hour. If I were to try to imagine one of today's students updating Roberto Unger's description of the elite academy, it might go something like this: "When we came, most professors had ceased even to pretend that law was anything other than power and preference. Their legal apostasy often coexisted, however, with a fervent devotion to this or that new cause or dogma. Disdaining their ancestors, they did not hesitate to live off the inheritance amassed by the labor of others. Turning their backs on the laity (who still naively looked to law for justice), they decked their altars with mirrors—into which they gazed long and attentively, self-made men worshipping their creators."

The bleakness of this picture is mitigated, however, by the reminder that other legal dark ages have passed away. After a copy of the *Corpus Juris Civilis* was rediscovered at Amalfi in the eleventh century, it took only a few hundred years for Europeans to build up an impressive legal system.

Then, too, in theology—as Avery Dulles has pointed out—the sources continue to radiate great liberating power. They provide each new generation with "a platform from which we can see and judge the present differently from the way in which the present sees and judges itself." There is an analogous platform in law, but a shakier one. What provides it, I believe, is not some particular source or sources, but the distinctive common law method of reasoning. The platform is shaky because common law reasoning has to start from premises that are doubtful or in dispute, and because it does not aim at certainty, but only at determining which of opposing positions supported by strong evidence and convincing reasons should be accepted. We may concede to Holmes & Co. that the open texture of this sort of reasoning does permit bias to creep in, and that its reliance on precedent can preserve not only the wisdom, but also the sins and ignorance and power relations of the past. We must admit as well that its conclusions are flawed, due to our own limitations and the limitations of those upon whose accomplishments we build.

But when all that is conceded, the fact remains, as Aristotle pointed out long ago, that dialectical reasoning is the only form of reasoning that is of much use in "the realm of human affairs," where premises *are* uncertain, but where, though we can't be sure of being right, it is crucial to keep trying to reach better rather than worse outcomes. It is time for lawyers and philosophers alike to recognize that common law reasoning is an operating model of that dialectical process, and that its modest capacity to guard against, and correct for, bias and arbitrariness is no small thing. Over time, the recurrent, cumulative, and potentially self-correcting processes of experiencing, understanding, and judging enable us to overcome some of our own errors and biases, the errors and biases of our culture, and the errors and biases embedded in the data we receive from those who have gone before us. As Benjamin N. Cardozo once put it, "In the endless process of testing and retesting, there is a constant rejection of the dross."

And so, by a long and circuitous route, I come back to the proposition with which I began: that human creativity is inescapably dependent on what has gone before. This is not a very remarkable proposition. Perhaps what ought to seem remarkable is only the extent to which so many practitioners of the human sciences seem to want to ignore it.

As for what might emerge if legal theorists were to turn back to law, and to consciously appropriate their own tradition of open-ended, dialectical, probabilistic reasoning, who knows? Creativity is mysterious not only in its origins but also in its outcome. An Eskimo creation myth makes this point in a charming way. At the beginning of the world, the story goes, Raven the Creator planted a seed. From the seed came a vine, and on the vine in time there grew a pod. One day the pod ripened and fell to the ground and out of it climbed the first man. Raven, the great black bird, walked round and round the man, inspecting him from top to toe, and finally asked, "What are you?" "How should I know," said the man, "you were here first." "Well," said Raven, "I planted that seed, I created that vine and that pod, but I never thought something like you would come out of it!"

# CHAPTER 2

# Why Cross Boundaries?

*This reflection on the joys and perils of comparative and interdisciplinary studies was prepared for a symposium at Washington and Lee University Law School called "Writing Across the Margins."*[1]

**W**HAT MADE THE INVITATION to participate in this symposium irresistible was not only the prospect of swapping tales with fellow trespassers, but the spirit of risk-taking that seems to have animated the conference plan. Even the word "margins," which ordinarily would connote more or less fixed bounds, becomes elastic in the lexicon of the organizer, Professor Lash LaRue. "Come to Lexington," he said, "and talk about the rhetoric of authority in constitutional law, or about the difficulties and rewards of cross-disciplinary or cross-national research, or any or all of the above."

That was an offer I couldn't refuse. I will confine myself to just one aspect of the topic: the question of why anyone engages in comparative legal studies, given the formidable practical difficulties and the high risk of error or failure.

I will be brief about the difficulties, for they are fairly obvious. The major problem is that if cross-disciplinarians waited to know as much as we feel we ought before writing, we could never put pen to paper. The same may be said, of course, of any researcher in the natural or human sciences, because the horizon of human knowledge recedes as the mind approaches it. But the risks of error, oversight, and misunderstanding increase exponentially if one combines disciplines, legal systems, and languages.

Some might include on the list of disadvantages the risk of being regarded by one's peers with a certain amount of suspicion. Consider the pioneers of the new science of complexity, formerly known as chaos science. They are mathematicians, physicists, and biologists who suffered considerable professional disadvantages in their respective disciplines. Because they strayed across the margins of several fields, they were regarded as neither fish nor fowl. They were treated as outsiders for many years by math, physics, and life science departments.

---

[1] Mary Ann Glendon, "Why Cross Boundaries?" *Washington and Lee Law Review* 53 (3; 1996): 971–80.

Fortunately, the field of law has been relatively hospitable to cross-disciplinary work, in part because law students arrive with such varied educational backgrounds, and because so many lawyers have to be generalists. Lawyers have learned that what begins as trespass can become possession if the poacher settles down and cultivates the area. And, as property students know, the right sort of possession kept up for a sufficient length of time may end in ownership. The law and economics movement, which was just getting started when I was a student at the University of Chicago, affords a striking example of how scholars who began by writing across the margins could ultimately rewrite the page and relocate the margins.

Some interdisciplinary projects, however, remain outside the legal mainstream. In the United States that has been the case with comparative law. American comparatists, in fact, often find that our enterprise is more welcome among colleagues abroad than at home. To many American lawyers, an interest in other legal systems is something like an interest in wines: A little knowledge about them is a sign of good taste and sophistication, but a serious dedication may be evidence of waste or luxury or even worse.

Sometimes it is just old-fashioned chauvinism that causes American lawyers to resist cross-national studies. But more often their skeptical attitudes reflect the same doubts that comparatists themselves entertain. As the domestic legal environment becomes ever more complex and specialized, it is hard enough to keep abreast of even one corner of our own legal system. The more areas, systems, and approaches one tries to cover, the greater the likelihood of becoming a Jill of all trades who is mistress of none. We become vulnerable to the charge, leveled by Judge Harry Edwards, of producing work that is neither useful to the legal community nor a significant contribution to other fields of human knowledge. It is difficult to deny that Judge Edwards has a point when he complains that: "Our law reviews are now full of mediocre interdisciplinary articles. Too many law professors are ivory tower dilettantes, pursuing whatever subject piques their interest, whether or not the subject merits scholarship, and whether or not they have the scholarly skills to master it."

With comparative law, the difficulties escalate. We not only must become familiar with the technical aspects of another legal system, we also have to assess how the law on the books actually operates in its own social context. In other words, we must become comparative social scientists. Often we must learn another language.

The harder we try to avoid the pitfalls identified by Judge Edwards, the more likely we are to become mired in an even more intractable problem: The field of human knowledge is vast, and life, alas, is short. On one side of our path, then, is the swamp of superficiality; on the other, the lime-pit of limitless learning. The path itself is slippery, and we can never see more than a few paces ahead.

Why, then, would anyone undertake comparative legal studies? For most of the American comparatists of the previous generation the answer was easy: They had no choice. Nearly all were European-born lawyers forced to emigrate and start over from scratch in the 1930s. Some, like my teacher Max Rheinstein, were already comparatists; but the majority had comparison thrust upon them.

For most of the current generation, I venture to guess that the first steps were not taken pursuant to any plan, but rather involved some casual trespass that led to an "aha" experience—an experience so pleasurable we are impelled to try to repeat it. A good example is David Currie, who taught and wrote about environmental and constitutional law at the University of Chicago for many years before his dean, Gerhard Casper, encouraged him to take a research leave in Freiburg. Currie was attracted to the idea because he had always enjoyed studying languages.

I suppose he must have embarked on the experience as something of a lark, a vacation from his multi-volume history of the Constitution in the United States Supreme Court. In Freiburg, he began looking into how Germany was dealing with problems of pollution, and he made, as he put it to me in a recent conversation, "a series of minor discoveries." They seem to have affected him like eating peanuts. He turned his attention next to German constitutional law, where he came upon the notion of "positive rights" (the idea that the State must not only refrain from infringing certain rights, but must affirmatively promote them, even to the point of setting conditions for their effective exercise). He describes his encounter with that concept as "eye-opening," because it enabled him to notice aspects of American constitutional law that he had never considered before.

Out of Currie's margin-crossing came several important writings, including an essay on positive and negative rights in American law and books on constitutional law in both German and English. He has gone on to learn Italian and is currently planning a book on Italian constitutional law.

What gets a scholar hooked on comparative legal studies, I believe, are not the usual pragmatic justifications that can be given for cross-national research. Whatever prompts one's initial step across the margins, what grips and holds people, is one of the most powerful drives known to the human species: the unrestricted desire to know. If hauled before Judge Edwards and charged with trespassing, the only honest defense most comparatists could offer would be, "I couldn't help it."

I would like, therefore, to focus on the question whether there is some reason why trespass should be especially productive of fertile insights. That question falls somewhere within psychology, philosophy, and history, but has received relatively little attention from any of those disciplines.

By insight, I mean the "aha" experience—the major and minor flashes of understanding that seemingly pop into one's mind from nowhere. The classic instance is the tale of Archimedes, who became discouraged while trying to devise a method for measuring the proportion of gold in a crown. He betook himself to the public baths, where, as legend has it, he was idly noting the displacement of water by his body, when he had an idea so powerful that he ran naked into the street shouting a "Eureka" that has echoed through the centuries.

Modern firsthand accounts of pathbreaking discoveries suggest that there may well be a connection between important insights like Archimedes's and the crossing of boundaries.[2] A common thread in these stories is a complete inability on the part of some of the most brilliant people who have ever lived to explain just how they reached the breakthrough in question. It is significant that they characteristically insist the insight was not achieved through long study—although long study is a prerequisite, for as Louis Pasteur put it, "Fortune favors the prepared mind."

A typical account is that given by the mathematician Karl Friedrich Gauss to a friend of how he finally found the solution to a problem with which he had been struggling for four years. "At last," wrote Gauss, "I succeeded, not by dint of painful effort, but so to speak by the grace of God. As a sudden flash of light, the enigma was solved. . . . For my part I am unable to name the nature of the thread which connected what I previously knew with that which made my success possible."

It is noteworthy that Gauss and others have stressed that their breakthroughs did not emerge from logical, systematic processes of induction or deduction. In fact, it was only some time later that Gauss logically worked out the proof to validate his discovery. The sequence of proof following discovery is easy to overlook because when we read about the solution of a mathematical or scientific problem in a textbook, the order is always reversed: We are shown the proof as though it had led to the solution.

Students of cognitive theory (philosophers and psychologists writing across the margins of their disciplines) situate such episodes within the dynamic structure of human knowing: the cumulative processes through which all of us attend to the world around us, reflect on our experiences, get ideas about them, and use reason to sort the good ideas from the duds. That recurrent process of experiencing, understanding, and evaluating regularly generates insights—not only great ideas on rare occasions in the minds of geniuses, but little bright ideas in the minds of all of us every day.

In the recurrent mental operations that we collectively refer to as "knowing," the insight part is the most mysterious. If it is not the crowning step in a chain of logical reasoning—if it requires preparation, but preparation alone can't make it happen—where does it come from? What makes

---

[2] Many such stories are collected in Arthur Koestler, *The Act of Creation: A Study of the Conscious and Unconscious Processes of Humor, Scientific Discovery, and Art* (London: Hutchinson & Co, 1964).

insight more or less likely? What conduces to insights of high quality, the kind that stand up to logical scrutiny and open new vistas?

Some who have speculated about these questions suggest that there are conditions that affect the frequency and quality of creative mental activity in individuals and in groups. The science historian Thomas Kuhn contends that significant advances in the natural sciences have generally been made by people who combine two qualities that do not always sit easily with one another: mastery of the normal science of their times plus the boldness to break with the intellectual framework within which that normal science takes place.[3] A leading example would be Charles Darwin who was fully immersed in the biological science of his day before he got the ideas that utterly transformed it.

Arthur Koestler's studies of artistic and scientific creativity point to another condition that seems to be closely associated with the kinds of insights that change the way we understand the world. Koestler noticed that transformative breakthroughs have often been sparked by what he called "bisociation." Bisociation was his name for what happens when two or more well-developed but relatively autonomous matrices of thought and experience come into contact. Such encounters across disciplinary or cultural boundaries, according to Koestler, seem to trigger a fertile process of uncovering, selecting, reshuffling, combining, and synthesizing data, ideas, and skills.

What do those accounts of great moments of intellectual history have to do with our homely discipline of law? They are like a photographic enlargement of the very same mental operations that take place in our minds from infancy onward. The insights of a lawyer or a toddler may be less momentous than those of a Gauss, but the process is the same.

A few years ago I came across a passage in an essay by a French historian that comes as close as anything I have seen to specifying the kind of "aha" that legal comparatists regularly experience. Fernand Braudel put it this way: "Live in England for a year and you will not learn much about the English. But when you return to France you will see, in the light of your surprise, that which had remained hidden to you because it was so familiar."[4] That is precisely what happened to David Currie when he went to Freiburg. And that is what kept great comparatists like Max Rheinstein and John P. Dawson enthusiastic and productive right up to the end of their lives. There is something compelling about the experience of seeing something about our own legal system "in the light of [our] surprise," something that would probably have remained invisible to us without the perspective from another country, or culture, or from other disciplines such as literature, history, and

---

[3] Thomas Kuhn, *The Essential Tension: Selected Studies in Scientific Tradition and Change* (Chicago: University of Chicago Press, 1977), 225.
[4] Fernand Braudel, "Histoire et Sciences Sociales: La Longue Durée," *Annales: Economies, Sociétés, Civilisations* 725, 737 (1958).

economics. Then, as we reason about, and critically evaluate, what we have seen, we are off to the races: the recurrent steps in the dynamic, cumulative processes of human knowing. Those processes of experiencing, understanding, reasoning, and judging in turn lead to cognitive restructuring, higher viewpoints, and fresh insights. And so it goes.

Like Currie, I stumbled into comparative law through language: Max Rheinstein recruited me for the University of Chicago's Foreign Law Program because of my schoolbook French. When I became a law professor, it seemed natural to me, when dealing with problems our legal system doesn't handle very well, to look around to see how those problems were dealt with in the legal systems of other liberal democracies. I began to realize, through comparative constitutional studies, that the post-World War II language of human rights, like other languages, is spoken in different dialects. That led to the recognition that our American form of rights talk is quite distinctive.[5] It differs in significant respects from the discourse embodied in the United Nations Universal Declaration of Human Rights and in many continental European legal systems. That realization in turn led me into problems of cultural and legal hermeneutics. More recently, it has drawn me into the study of the migration of legal ideas, of legal syncretism, and of the way in which differing rights ideas can merge with, colonize, displace, or be displaced by one another.

To return to the question I posed at the outset: Can one say any more about the conditions that promote fertile ideas? This is not just a matter of interest to scholars. When longtime practicing lawyers are asked what qualities they value in an associate, they often say that a pearl beyond price is the associate who, in addition to possessing all the usual legal skills, is able to regularly come up with problem-solving ideas.

But good ideas cannot be produced on demand. Nor can we do much to upgrade the mental equipment we received at birth. We can, however, cultivate the "prepared mind" of which Pasteur spoke; we can be attentive to experience; and we can develop our reasoning skills. Beyond that, cognitive theory suggests that confrontation or comparison of different spheres of meaning increases the probability of insights, and opens up previously unrecognized avenues of inquiry. Legal sociologist Gunther Teubner refers to such encounters as "shocks" that promote transformative restructuring by shaking up the categories within which we habitually work. But "triggers" and "shocks" are metaphors, not explanations. Perhaps the most one can say is that "bisociation" seems to work even though we don't know why or how.

Let me now return to two points I mentioned earlier: the facts that many "bright ideas" are duds; and that most paradigm-transforming achievements have not been produced by rebels who scorned the work of their predecessors, but by innovators who respected and mastered a tradi-

---

5 Mary Ann Glendon, *Rights Talk: The Impoverishment of Political Discourse* (New York: The Free Press, 1991).

tion. Think here not only of Darwin, but Picasso, Stravinsky, and T. S. Eliot. For those of us who labor at less exalted levels, does that not condemn us to the slippery slope of superficiality or the hopelessly long march toward the book we will never be quite ready to write?

In facing that dilemma, legal scholars would do well to ponder Thomas Kuhn's observation that, more often than not, it is the community of specialized knowers, rather than any single individual, that possesses the requisite combination of a rigorous grounding in tradition with an innovative spirit. When both qualities are well-represented in the professional mix, and when both traditionalists and innovators are well-grounded in normal science, you have what Kuhn calls the "essential tension" that promotes creativity. The tension benefits the entire group by pulling all of its members in both directions. The stage is then set for collective achievements like quantum theory, or the American Founding, or, at a more modest level, law and economics.

Kuhn's observations are especially pertinent to a field like comparative law. European comparative law institutes have tackled the problem of amassing the requisite languages and technical legal knowledge by fostering scholarly collaboration. Thirty years of collaborative effort on the *International Encyclopedia of Comparative Law* under the direction of Ulrich Drobnig at Hamburg's Max Planck Institute for Foreign and International Law provide eloquent testimony both to the difficulties and rewards of teamwork.

In the light of Thomas Kuhn's research, however, I cannot help wondering about the implications for our own legal system of the fact that so many American legal scholars currently are disdainful of our own equivalent of normal science, namely the study and practice of law. The American legal academy seems to be well-supplied with iconoclasts, but these daring individuals often have a shallow understanding of their own legal traditions and of the nuts and bolts of the legal system. A related concern is that so many legal scholars work in relative isolation, and as a result lose the benefits that can attend more self-consciously collaborative enterprises.

On the other hand, one need not find one's intellectual companions in one's own discipline, or one's own nation-state, or even in one's own time. In fact, the most moving account of reaching across margins that I have ever seen is about friendship with the dead. I would like to close, therefore, with a few lines from a letter by a thinker who initiated a great transformation in political philosophy. He had just been released from prison, and was keeping, as we would say, a low profile, working outdoors on his estate, with few opportunities for intelligent conversation. In the evenings, however, he writes:

> I return to my house and go into my study. At the door I take off my clothes of the day, covered with mud and mire, and I put on my regal and courtly garments; and decently reclothed, I enter the ancient courts of ancient men, where, received by them lovingly, I feed on the

food that alone is mine and that I was born for. There I am not ashamed to speak with them and to ask them the reasons for their actions; and they in their humanity reply to me. And for the space of four hours I feel no boredom, I forget every pain, I do not fear poverty, death does not frighten me. I deliver myself entirely to them.[6]

The letter is dated December 10, 1513. The writer was that tradition-haunted paradigm breaker Niccolò Machiavelli.

It is worth recalling that Machiavelli would not have located himself within the then-unknown discipline of "political science" any more than Adam Smith would have called himself an economist. The freedom to roam among fields of knowledge that they enjoyed has been lost to us with the increasing fragmentation and specialization of the human sciences. From that perspective, the act of writing across margins can be viewed as an act of faith in the unity of knowledge. In that sense, we who cross borders are not trespassers at all. We are more like voyagers drawn by the eros of the mind toward the destination for which we were born.

---

[6] Letter from Niccolò Macchiavelli to Francesco Vettori of December 10, 1513, in Niccolò Macchiavelli, *The Prince,* trans. Harvey C. Mansfield (Chicago: University of Chicago Press, 1985), Appendix at 107–8

# CHAPTER 3

# Max Rheinstein:
# Pioneer in Legal Sociology

*In 1991, the University of Bonn held a symposium to remember and honor the German-born lawyers who had achieved distinction abroad after having fled from National Socialist Germany. For each figure so honored, an American and a German scholar presented an evaluation of that person's "influence" in American and German law, respectively. As Rheinstein's student and, later, co-author, I was invited to present the American perspective on the work of my large-souled and learned mentor. The essay appeared in Der Einfluß deutscher Emigranten auf die Rechtsentwicklung in den USA und in Deutschland (Tübingen: J.C.B. Mohr, 1993).*

IN HER 1968 BOOK, *Illustrious Immigrants: The Intellectual Migration from Europe 1930–41,* Laura Fermi chronicled the lives and careers of several of the most distinguished Europeans who sought refuge in the United States during the National Socialist period. Many of her subjects were leading scientists like Albert Einstein and her own Nobel-prize-winning husband, Enrico Fermi, or well-known figures in the arts such as Thomas Mann and Bela Bartok. Her principal focus, however, was on the diaspora of dozens of less celebrated doctors, artists, musicians, scientists, mathematicians, economists, and lawyers, and on how they began their lives anew under difficult circumstances. Of all the professionals, lawyers reported the most serious obstacles in pursuing their chosen career in the new country. Not only did they find small resemblance between their own practices and those of American jurists, they received little assistance in resettlement from professional organizations in their field. According to Mrs. Fermi, of the two thousand or so lawyers who immigrated during the period in question, relatively few were able to regain the professional standing that they had achieved in their countries of origin.

My teacher and mentor Max Rheinstein was described by Mrs. Fermi as one of the most fortunate, as well as one of the most eminent, in the lawyer group. Born in 1899 to Christian parents of Jewish ancestry, he was still relatively young when he arrived in the United States in 1933. To his great advantage, he was already a specialist in comparative law and well acquainted with the common law. He had written his doctoral thesis on tortious interference with economic relations in English law, and his postdoctoral book on "The Structure of Contractual Obligation in Anglo-American Common Law." Within two years after leaving Germany, he had secured a position on the faculty of the prestigious University of Chicago Law School.

Still, when I accepted this assignment to assess the influence of Max Rheinstein on American law, it seemed to me doubtful whether he had achieved the influence he might have had if his career had not been brutally interrupted. But as I pondered the matter, I had the same experience that often befell me as Rheinstein's student: I began to suspect that I was asking the wrong question. For Max Rheinstein's life and achievements call into question the notion that greatness for a lawyer resides in having left an identifiable personal mark on a particular nation's law.

By some standards, the "influence" of Max Rheinstein on American law might not appear substantial. He was a private law expert whose career spanned the years when public law gained and held the center stage in the United States. He was a comparatist whom fate had thrust into one of the most insular of developed nations. When one rereads today the articles he wrote many years ago, one is struck by how many current developments were prefigured in his ideas on the administration of estates, on interpretation of texts, and on the adaptation of family law to a changing society. Still, it is difficult in most instances to say whether and how these writings influenced the law whose course they often anticipated. He did not found a school of thought, or write a leading treatise. Most of his many books and articles are not now widely cited or consulted.

But I am fairly sure that Max himself did not measure influence in those ways. Nor did he appear to seek that sort of influence. The four hundred and some entries in his bibliography are a record of the byways, detours, and principal stopping places of a restless and inquiring mind on its journey through a fascinating and ever-changing world. What seems to have drawn him on and sustained him through good times and bad, despite the physical infirmities that beset him in his later years, was his unrestricted desire to know, his thirst for understanding, the excitement of intellectual discovery. Compared to that excitement, I believe, the question of influence was incidental to him. Some evidence that this was so appears in one of his essays on a perennial theme of comparatists: the aims and uses of comparative law. After dutifully listing all of the many purposes comparative legal studies have been said to serve, Rheinstein spoke for himself:

> Being a professor, I would state first the usefulness our insights have in and by themselves. They are answers, mostly tentative ones, to man's insatiable quest for knowing his world. They are as valuable or as useless as the insights obtained in such sciences as comparative religion, comparative linguistics, biology, or physics. They satisfy our curiosity.

Despite his passionate interest in the "law-in-action," Max was first, last, and always, a scholar.

He was well-equipped for that vocation, being possessed of immense learning of a kind that has almost disappeared from our busy twentieth-century world. And he was not above showing it off. That endearing weakness of his was once captured by a Chicago student cartoonist who portrayed Max standing beside a blackboard on which he had written a series of hieroglyphics. The balloon over his head showed him asking the bewildered students, "Doesn't *anyone* know what happened in that horrible case of 11 Ramses 3, Tablet 70, where a scrivener cut the bird facing Northeast, rather than Northwest, and the son, according to the 'clear meaning', was cut off pyramidless?" *Wissenschaft* was Max Rheinstein's vocation. He preached it, he practiced it, and he inspired others—we will never know how many—to do the same.

Let me now turn, pursuant to my assignment, to areas where Rheinstein's influence, in the conventional sense, is more readily discernible. The place where that influence seems to have been the strongest is in divorce law reform. Through essays, studies, and speeches beginning in the 1940s, Rheinstein played an important role in preparing the way for the introduction of non-fault divorce in the United States. His work advanced the divorce reform movement mainly by (though he would not have put it this way) delegitimating the then-predominant legal pattern of exclusively fault-based divorce. In historical essays, he showed how startling an innovation the Christian ideal of marital indissolubility had been in the ancient world. He traced the ancestry of modern divorce laws to ecclesiastical separation norms that had been converted to divorce grounds when jurisdiction over matrimonial causes passed from church courts to the secular state in the post-Reformation era. Drawing upon sociological research, he demonstrated that there was no simple correlation between strict or easy divorce and the incidence of marriage breakdown in a given country. Taking a comparative approach, he showed that non-fault divorce grounds were not so novel or radical as many Americans believed. By contrasting the law on the books in the United States with the law in practice, he showed that by the 1950s what appeared to be fault divorce had been converted nearly everywhere into mutual consent divorce by collusion, migration, and liberal judicial construction. No one made these sorts of demonstrations more effectively than Rheinstein.

Yet, when non-fault divorce began to spread in the United States, Rheinstein was not among its enthusiastic proponents. Indeed, he stated in his best-known book *Marriage Stability, Divorce, and the Law* (1972), that although at one time he had been a critic of the old "hypocritical" system in which collusion made a mockery of strict divorce laws, he had come to see the matter in a different light. There was much to be said, he argued, for the "democratic compromise" that was in force in most places until the 1970s: relatively strict law on the books and relatively lenient divorce in practice. The chief opponents of that system, he pointed out, were academics. What he thought they had over-looked in their desire for a tidy solution was that what appeared to them to be hypocrisy was, from another point of view, an enlightened way of accommo-dating the ideals of a large part of the population with their frequent inability to live up to those ideals under particular circumstances. Moreover, by the early 1970s, when non-fault grounds were sweeping the Western world, Rheinstein had already gone on to what he considered to be more important issues in the area of the economics of divorce. He was one of the first persons to point out the key role that the grounds for divorce play in setting the background against which negotiation takes place. Long before most of the architects of non-fault divorce had made the connection between marriage breakdown and the poverty of women and children, he was pointing out the unsuitability of bas-ing support and marital property law on the notion that self-sufficiency would ordinarily be attainable by both ex-spouses.

Rheinstein's family law work was but one application of his lifelong inter-est in legal sociology. Though his influence in that field is more difficult to trace, his writings illustrate his own concept of "legal influence." In a tribute to Ernst Rabel, he spoke of the limits of a single individual's range of knowl-edge, and of the way in which advances in the human sciences, as in the nat-ural sciences, required the pooling and coordination of individual talents and efforts. "Influence" for Rheinstein seems to have been a cultural term, signi-fying the radiating effects of groups and movements rather than individuals. This was the sense in which he employed the word in his memorable opening speech at the 1969 meeting of the Deutsche Gesellschaft für Rechtsvergle-ichung in Regensburg. His speech, titled "Die Rechtshonoratioren und ihr Einfluß auf Charakter und Funktion der Rechtsordnungen," drew attention to the influence of certain types of legal actors. Later, he published an English version which he titled simply "Leader Groups in American Law." "Recht-shonoratioren" was a term coined by Max Weber to designate that group of "law notables" who in a given culture enjoy such prestige and power that they decisively determine the characteristic features of the legal order of their soci-ety. In the twentieth century, Rheinstein argued, scholars had achieved "co-leader" status in the United States. Scholars, no less than judges and eminent practitioners, were shaping American law, with the result that the law of the United States was developing traits similar to those "well known in the classi-cal professorial law of the European continent, especially Germany."

How should one situate Max Rheinstein in those intellectual move-ments that have helped to shape twentieth-century law? It seems to me that his place is with those who pioneered the multidisciplinary study of law. The founder and the greatest practitioner of that method was Rheinstein's own teacher, Max Weber. The leading figures in the United States were Roscoe Pound, Karl Llewellyn, Rheinstein himself, and the anthropologist Clifford

Geertz. Rheinstein, Llewellyn, and others made the Chicago Law School of the 1950s and 1960s hum with interdisciplinary activity. Numerous important cross-national, anthropological, and sociological studies were carried out there in that period. Law-and-economics, for which Chicago is now famous, was but one aspect of this intellectual ferment.

Most Chicago scholars in those days insisted on examining any given legal problem against its historical background, and with a view toward ascertaining its practical dimensions. In Rheinstein's case, that intense interest in the relevance of law to practical problems and their solution owed much to another emigré lawyer, Ernst Rabel. Rheinstein had been Rabel's *Assistent* at the University of Munich in 1922, and later followed Rabel to the newly founded Kaiser-Wilhelm-Institut in Berlin. The curiosity Weber had inspired about the mutually conditioning relations between legal and social institutions, and Rabel's insistence on discerning how legal norms function in their practical context, seem to have been the chief determinants of Rheinstein's own scholarly interests. His wide-ranging knowledge of, and meticulous labors in, many different areas of substantive law (particularly obligations, succession, and private international law) gave depth and credibility to his sociological and comparative work. Conversely, his comparative, historical, and sociological perspective enriched all of his studies of positive law. The qualities Rheinstein once attributed to Weber are the qualities one came to associate with Rheinstein: "universality of knowledge together with the gift of penetrating analysis, objectivity, passion for accurate formulation, and genius for recognizing the essentials, and the relations between seemingly remote phenomena."

All of Rheinstein 's "family law" studies were the work of Rheinstein the legal sociologist and comparatist, in collaboration with Rheinstein the private-law scholar, persistently asking "How does it work in practice?" and "What do people really do?" In 1949, at the request of the Social Science Research Council, he investigated the state of legal studies relating to the family. Finding that family law had been shockingly neglected by the profession, he outlined a research agenda.

> What ought to be undertaken is an intensive, systematic, and complete inquiry into all those needs which the family law is meant to satisfy, the extent to which these needs are satisfactorily taken care of at present, and the probably much greater extent to which the present law is unsatisfactory. We ought to know the underlying facts; we must try to find out the impact, desirable or undesirable, of present and proposed legislation: we must find out how identical needs are taken care of in those foreign countries which have given more attention to them in the past than has this country; and, on the basis of all such inquiries, there should be elaborated a set of model laws to be recommended to the states for adoption. Finally, if and when this work has been done, a

powerful organization should be created for the educational and other efforts necessary to secure adoption of such legislation.

That was Rheinstein's idea of a research program. As to who might carry it out, he suggested that perhaps the American Law Institute "might lend its well-established organization for the new task." Forty years later, for the first time in its history, the American Law Institute embarked on a modest project in the area of family law. Influence? Doubtful. Prescience? It will be another forty years, at least, before the American Law Institute catches up with him.

Rheinstein's most significant personal contribution to the multidisciplinary study of law was to make available in English Max Weber's pioneering work on the sociology of law. Rheinstein had been a student in a course called "General Economic Theory" that Weber taught at the University of Munich. In this course, shortly before his death, Weber presented the distillation of his life's research and thought. Rheinstein, then a 21-year-old, was so deeply impressed that years later he described as a "labor of love" the prodigious work he did in translating, editing, and explaining Weber's theory of law.

It is said that Weber himself considered the sociology of law, together with his presentation of the basic forms of domination and his political writings, to be the most original part of his great unfinished systematic treatise, *Economy and Society*. The service that Rheinstein performed for legal sociology, however, went far beyond making this important work available in English. The complexity and subtlety of Weber's thought, as is well-known, have often caused it to be misunderstood, oversimplified, or ignored. The difficulties of substance have been compounded by the impenetrability (even for Germans) of Weber's writing style. Max Rheinstein and Edward Shils, working together on the translation, rendered the text more understandable by including translations of other, related, parts of *Economy and Society*. They devised English equivalents for German words that were artificially coined by Weber. Rheinstein's many footnotes and annotations explained those frequent passages where Weber's remarks were cryptic but dense with meaning.

These notes, a delight to read in themselves, take the reader through Hohfeldian analysis, courtly love, the lost civilization of the Khazars, the disrepute of Roman Law studies under National Socialism (as a "product of the Jewish mind"), the Albigensian and Waldensian heresies, and on, and on. Rheinstein checked Weber's sources, and even furnished missing references for Hindu, Chinese, Jewish, Islamic, and primitive legal systems, as well as for Roman, English, and medieval European law, and the laws of Germany, America, and France. He explained technical terms from each of these systems, and indicated where later research or new discoveries had altered the views of the generation of scholars on whose works Weber had relied.

This annotated translation alone would have been a monumental contribution to sociology in general, and legal sociology in particular. But Rheinstein did more. In one of his finest essays, a 48-page introduction to the Weber translation, Rheinstein in his own systematic and concise style, so different from Weber's, set forth an authoritative explanation of Weber's sociology. This essay brought order and clarity into the rich material that was buried in sentences where every proposition is narrowed by a qualifying proposition, which in turn is repeatedly qualified, and where (still in the same sentence) the main proposition is combined with its set of qualifiers and subqualifiers. Weber wrote in this fashion, apparently, because of his intolerance for overgeneralization, and because (according to his widow),

> He was entirely unconcerned with the form in which he presented his wealth of ideas. So many things came to him out of that storehouse of his mind, once the mass was in motion, that many times they could not be readily forced into a lucid sentence structure.

Rheinstein shared Weber's obsession with keeping generalizations tailored close to the facts, but he went into Weber's "storehouse" and put the wares in order. Only someone with Rheinstein's learning and intellectual gifts could have succeeded at such a task. He succeeded so well, in fact, that many legal writers freely borrow from that essay, apparently not realizing the extent to which it represents original work rather than common knowledge. Or perhaps Rheinstein made it common knowledge. If so, that would be an example of another kind of "influence": that of the authoritative explanations that enable the human sciences to absorb the hard-won insights of each passing generation. In any event, there is little doubt that Rheinstein helped Weber's ideas about legal sociology gain a significantly wider audience among Americans.

It is harder to trace Rheinstein's influence on comparative law in the United States, for comparative law there, regrettably, remains rather underdeveloped. For Max himself, comparative law seems mainly to have been a window onto the complex interaction among law, behavior, and ideas; a potent generator of new insights; and an aid to understanding. The most important of his essays relating to comparative law have been gathered by Reimer von Borries into an *Einführung in die Rechtsvergleichung*, where no doubt they exert a beneficial effect on the formation of German law students. On the other side of the Atlantic, however, conditions are still less hospitable to comparative legal studies. For some forty-two years at Chicago, Rheinstein strove to broaden the horizons of American lawyers. But most of his American students simply did not yet feel the need to deal with the fact of interdependence in a shrinking world, much less to acknowledge that we might have something to learn from another country's legal system. The Chicago Foreign Law Program which he founded was probably more appreciated by its European exchange students than by its American participants. The American law students who passed through Chicago in Rheinstein's time would be more apt to recall other sorts of influence—such as the example of his work habits and his great personal kindness. The door of his office at the law school was always open, and the busy man inside would always put aside his pen or his book for a visitor. He shared his encyclopedic knowledge, his good judgment, and his sympathetic understanding with deans and dunces, radical students and eminent foreigners. His genuine liking for, interest in, and curiosity about people enabled him to bridge generational, cultural, racial, gender, or religious differences with what seemed to be not only ease but enthusiasm.

Finally, a word should be said on this occasion concerning Max Rheinstein's role as an important intermediary between the United States and Germany in the years immediately after World War II. He was one of the first Americans to travel to Germany after the war ended. For eighteen months, from the fall of 1945 to the spring of 1947, he served as a member of the Legal Division of the American Military Government. His first duties were to assist with the reopening of the German courts and the reconstitution of the law faculties of the universities in the American zone of occupation. Later, he was a member of the Allied Control Council's Committee on the Revision of German Law. We have a glimpse of him in that period from an English lawyer, a man who had encountered Max at the Kaiser-Wilhelm-Institute before the war, and who was himself sent to Berlin in 1946 as a British military representative. One day, the British officer spotted a notice of a chamber music concert to be held that evening. Seeking relief from a mood of depression which had settled on him from the moment of his arrival in Berlin, he set out to locate the event, walking through the streets of the war-torn city. When he found the makeshift concert hall, there he also found Max Rheinstein. As the Englishman recalled the moment years later, it was the sight of that benevolent figure, sitting among the ruins, waiting for the music to begin, that awakened in him the first rays of hope for the future.

Konrad Duden, a German law professor who had been a member of the old Kaiser-Wilhelm-Institute cadre, wrote this about Max in the postwar period:

> He was and is unbelievably generous toward the Germans who expelled him. Before and after the end of the war he fought with all his might against equating Germans with Nazis and for a reasonable peace. One cannot read what he said and wrote at that time without being moved.

Malcolm Sharp, a Chicago colleague, from an American point of view, recalled at the time of Rheinstein's death in 1978: "Max's efforts contributed to softening asperities due to the War of 1939 and to seeing in perspective the vicissitudes of denazification. He seems to have foreseen at an early time the cooperation of the present American and German governments."

Upon his return to the United States in 1947, Rheinstein did not hesitate to speak out forcefully against the abuses and excesses of military government in occupied Germany. He also cautioned against disguising what in reality were political judgments as legal judgments in connection with the prosecution of war criminals. He pointed out that disrespect for law on the part of those who portrayed themselves as champions of democracy might discourage "the promising beginnings of a revival of the feeling for law in a country which, whatever plans one may hold today, will one day again occupy an influential place in the world."

Today, when one reads what Rheinstein wrote in those years, his counsels of moderation and his warnings about victors' justice and ex post facto punishment may seem so reasonable as to be obvious. But it took great courage, charity, and humanity to say and write such things in 1947. Max's advocacy of just treatment for the citizens of a recently defeated enemy nation was not without personal cost in terms of his relations with some of his American colleagues who were less prepared than he to distinguish between Germans and Nazis. What he had to say about the future of Germany back then was at long distance from what many Americans, not to mention the French and Soviet governments, were ready to hear. Shortly after his return from serving in the Military Government, Rheinstein gave a speech, reprinted in the *Congressional Record*, in which he criticized proposals then under discussion for partitioning Germany into two halves, or into a group of independent states. The long-term interests of democracy would be much better served, he vainly argued in that 1947 speech, if Germany were preserved, or re-established, as a unified country.

Max's foresight in this, I think, is a vivid reminder of his character and wisdom.

Some years after Max's death, his son John Rheinstein, a retired physicist, told me that his father had always felt proud that he had been able to help in the postwar years, that he believed that he had had some success in making the denazification process less harsh than it might have been, and that he was pleased with what he had done for the reorganization of German law, and for the restoration of American–German relations in general. In the same conversation, John brought me up to date concerning yet another way in which Max Rheinstein's influence continues to radiate. I am sure it would have warmed Max's heart to know that one of his grandsons and his only granddaughter became lawyers. John Rheinstein confirmed Laura Fermi's impression that Max was one of the most fortunate of the emigre lawyers. According to John, that was the way Max saw it, too. "My father," John said, "thought that he had a wonderful life."

# CHAPTER 4

# Rousseau and the Revolt Against Reason

*This essay was part of First Things magazine's "Millennium Series" which explored the religious and social development of the West during the Second Millennium through ten essays, each taking a particular historical figure as the prism through which to view the century in which he lived. As I had proposed Rousseau for the eighteenth century, I received the assignment to write about this towering and troubling figure.*[1]

IN 1749 THE ACADEMY OF DIJON offered a prize for the best essay on the question, "Has the restoration of the sciences and the arts contributed to the improvement of the mores?" Most of the contestants must have vied in counting the ways "enlightenment" had raised the level of culture. By the middle of the eighteenth century, advances in science and technology had fueled faith in progress. It was widely believed that the human race was emerging from a long night of ignorance and superstition into an era when Reason at last would conquer age-old social and political problems. It was something of a sensation, therefore, when the palm went to a self-taught 38-year-old who answered the question with a resounding "No."

In the essay now known as his *First Discourse*, Jean-Jacques Rousseau argued that manners and morals had been corrupted as the arts and sciences had advanced. The arts had encouraged sensuality and license, while science had set up strange gods against true religion. Reason had been elevated over feeling, learning over plain goodness and honesty. City people looked down on country folk, and the rich more than ever lorded it over the poor. Political writers spoke less of virtue than of commerce. Society was overrun with scribblers who "smile contemptuously at such old names as patriotism and religion, and consecrate their talents and philosophy to the destruction and defamation of all that men hold sacred." Echoing pietistic warnings about vain learning, Rousseau asked: What is learning without virtue? What progress can there be without progress in goodness?

The *First Discourse* was followed by a cascade of writings in which Rousseau challenged the scientific rationalism of Voltaire and other well-known

---

[1] Mary Ann Glendon, "Rousseau & the Revolt Against Reason," *First Things* 96 (November 1999): 42–47.

intellectuals who immodestly called themselves *les Lumières*, the enlightened ones. In the space of twelve years, the eccentric outsider produced a stream of work that made him the preeminent critic of modernity. Yet he was no traditionalist. Through his elevation of feeling over reason, he became the leading prophet of the ultramodern era that would succeed the so-called age of reason.

Rousseau was born in Calvinist Geneva in 1712, the son of a watchmaker and a mother who died from complications of childbirth. When the boy was ten, his father placed him in the care of an uncle who in turn sent him to live with a country pastor. These men provided him with a haphazard education, but the precocious youth never received any formal schooling. At fifteen, after an unhappy apprenticeship to an engraver, he struck out on his own for the nearby Duchy of Savoy. There, a parish priest commended the wandering lad to the hospitality of a woman of good works in Annecy.

Warmhearted Madame de Warens, the estranged wife of a landowner, was not your usual church lady. Though a convert to Catholicism and pious in her way, she did not believe in original sin, or Hell, or that it could be sinful to follow one's natural impulses. She took a fancy to the clever, awkward boy, and he developed an enduring attachment to her. Rousseau spent several formative years as a sort of cavalier-servant, and occasional sexual partner, to this woman, whom he called *Maman*. Under her protection, he read voraciously, gained a sense of his extraordinary mental powers, and learned enough about music to support himself as a copyist and teacher.

In 1744, after holding various menial positions—footman, tutor, secretary—in well-to-do households here and there, Rousseau settled in Paris, determined to be independent. There he became friendly with Diderot, and began his lifelong liaison with Thérèse Le Vasseur, a laundry maid in his residential hotel. According to the well-known story in Rousseau's *Confessions*, each of the five children born of this union was abandoned to a foundling home shortly after birth. The writer whose works had extolled the child-centered family explained to posterity that he had insisted on this "solution," over Thérèse's tearful protests, because he was too poor to provide for children, and that, besides, they would have interfered with his study and work.

(Rousseau's biographers, though skeptical of much of his autobiographical material, have always taken that tale at face value. There is reason to suppose, however, that the long-suffering Thérèse may not have complied with her consort's wishes. She and her ever-present mother treated their brilliant patron, in many respects, like a child or ward. They did not hesitate, for instance, to make financial arrangements with Rousseau's friends behind his back. It would have been quite in character for them, faced with his refusal to accept parental responsibility, to have placed the babies with members of their large, extended Catholic family.)

Rousseau's circumstances improved greatly after he won the Dijon prize. His cheeky, contrarian *First Discourse* brought him not only literary fame, but an entrée into polite society where, however, he would never be at ease. That essay was followed by his discourses on *Inequality* (the *Second Discourse*) and *Political Economy*, both destined to be landmarks in political philosophy. *Julie, ou la Nouvelle Héloïse,* which appeared in 1761, became the best-selling novel of the eighteenth century. The *Social Contract,* with ideas and phrases that would capture the imaginations of revolutionaries, and *Émile*, his enormously influential work on education, were both published in 1762.

That extraordinary burst of creativity was followed by a long period of physical and mental decline, the former mostly due to an agonizing disorder of the urinary tract, and the latter aggravated by persecution for the blasphemies that Catholics and Calvinists alike discerned in his work. Despite the sufferings, real and imagined, of his later years, Rousseau managed to produce the *Confessions, Dialogues,* and *Reveries of a Solitary Walker,* all published posthumously.

After his death in 1778, Rousseau's popularity soared to new heights. *Julie* and *Émile* continued to attract a wide readership, especially among women, while his political writings made him a cult hero to the leaders of the French Revolution. The century was one in which rulers and politicians were particularly open to the ideas of philosophers. Frederick II of Prussia, Catherine the Great, and Joseph II of Austria considered themselves enlightened monarchs and took pride in being advised by the likes of Voltaire. The American Founders were much influenced by the thinking of Locke and Montesquieu.

When the French Revolution entered its radical phase, it was the ideas and catchphrases of Rousseau, more than any other thinker, that dominated the thinking and speaking of the insurgents.

Even today, Rousseau remains the preeminent expounder of challenging ideas about human beings, nature, politics, and history that must be reckoned with one way or another. Whether one finds him disturbing or stimulating, it is nearly impossible to remain unaffected by him. Like Plato and Nietzsche, he saw deeply into the most important questions and wrote about them so beautifully that, love him or hate him, we all stand in his shadow. As Allan Bloom once wrote, "His influence was overwhelming, and so well was it digested into the bloodstream of the West that it worked on everyone almost imperceptibly."

Rousseau's influence on political thought extended far beyond France and its Revolution. His early modern predecessors—Machiavelli, Hobbes, Locke, and Spinoza—had broken with the virtue-based political theories of the ancients and developed theories of government based on human nature as they thought it really was, rather than as it ought to be. Rousseau attacked this "new science of politics" at its foundations. He began his *Discourse on Inequality* by scoffing at previous attempts to account for the origins of government by describing what human beings must have been like in the "state of nature." The mythic tales told by Hobbes and Locke had recounted the progress of mankind from "a horrible state of war" (Hobbes) or from a "very precarious, very unsafe" existence (Locke) into a more secure way of life in organized society. According to Rousseau, such accounts had it backwards. Prior writers had failed to understand the natural condition of man, he claimed, because they "carried over to the state of nature ideas they had acquired in society; they spoke about savage man but they described civilized man." The complex fears and desires they attributed to our early ancestors could only have been produced by society.

Rousseau then presented his own version of prehistory as universal truth: "O man, of whatever country you are, and whatever your opinions may be, listen: behold your history as I have thought to read it, not in books written by your fellow creatures, who are liars, but in nature, which never lies." The earliest human, as Rousseau imagined him, was a simple, animal-like creature, "wholly wrapped up in the feeling of [his own] present existence." He was not inherently dangerous to his fellows as Hobbes had it. But neither was he fallen as the biblical tradition teaches. Rather, he must have led a "solitary," "indolent" life, satisfying his basic physical needs, mating casually without forming ties. He possessed a "natural feeling" of compassion for the suffering of other sentient beings that made him unwilling to harm others, unless (a big unless) his own self-preservation was at stake. He was not naturally endowed with reason, but existed in an unreflective state of pure being. The transition from this primitive state into civil society represented a "loss of real felicity," in Rousseau's view, rather than an unambiguous step forward.

Rousseau next took aim at the social contract theories of his predecessors. As he saw it, what drew human beings out of their primeval state was not rational calculation leading to agreement for the sake of self-preservation (as Hobbes and Locke thought), but rather a quality he called "perfectibility." Previous thinkers, he claimed, did not pay sufficient attention to the distinctively human capacity to change and develop, to transform oneself and to be transformed. In other words, they failed to consider the implications of the fact that human nature itself has a history. Or that human beings, through their capacity to form ideas, can to some extent shape that history. These were the insights of the *Discourse on Inequality* that won the admiration of such a dissimilar personality as Immanuel Kant and stirred the historical imaginations of Hegel and Marx.

With the development of human faculties, Rousseau continued, came language, family life, and eventually an era when families lived in simple tribal groups. That centuries-long stage of communal living, succeeding the state of nature and preceding organized society, he wrote, "must have been the happiest and most stable of epochs" which only a "fatal accident" could have brought to an end. That accident was precipitated by the ever-restless human mind that invented agriculture and metallurgy, which led in turn to the state of affairs where human beings lost their self-sufficiency and came to depend on one another for their survival. ("It is iron and wheat which have civilized men and ruined the human race.")

In contrast to Locke, who taught that property was an especially important, prepolitical right, Rousseau wrote:

> The first man who, having enclosed a piece of ground, bethought himself of saying This is mine, and found people simple enough to believe him, was the real founder of civil society. From how many crimes, wars and murders, from how many horrors and misfortunes might not any one have saved mankind by pulling up the stakes, or filling up the ditch, and crying to his fellows, "Beware of listening to this imposter, you are undone if you once forget that the fruits of the earth belong to us all, and the earth itself to nobody."

Contrary to Hobbes and Locke, Rousseau contended that it was civil society, not nature, that gave rise to a state of affairs that was always in danger of degenerating into war. Civil society begat governments and laws, inequality, resentment, and other woes. Governments and laws "bound new fetters on the poor, and gave new powers to the rich; which irretrievably destroyed natural liberty, eternally fixed the law of property and inequality, converted clever usurpation into unalterable right, and, for the advantage of a few ambitious individuals, subjected all mankind to perpetual labor, slavery and wretchedness." It would be absurd to suppose, he went on, that mankind had somehow consented to this state of affairs where "the privileged few . . . gorge themselves with superfluities, while the starving multitude are in want of the bare necessities of life."

Though Rousseau's evocative imaginary depictions of primitive societies were to swell the tide of nineteenth-century romantic "nostalgia" for the simple life, he himself insisted that there was no escape from history. There was no going back, he explained, because human nature itself had changed: "The savage and the civilized man differ so much . . . that what constitutes the supreme happiness of one would reduce the other to despair." Natural man had been sufficient unto himself; man in civil society had become dependent on his fellows in countless ways, even to the point of living "in the opinions of others." Reprising the theme of his Dijon essay, Rousseau concluded that modern man, though surrounded by philosophy, civilization, and codes of morality, had little to show for himself but "honor without virtue, reason without wisdom, and pleasure without happiness."

The radical character of Rousseau's political thought is nowhere more apparent than in his treatments of reason and human nature. Together with early modern and Enlightenment thinkers, he rejected older ideas of a natural law discoverable through right reason. But by insisting that human beings are not naturally endowed with reason, he struck at the very core of the Enlightenment project, subordinating reason to feeling in a move that would characterize the politics of a later age. Like others within the modern horizon, he rejected the older view that human beings are naturally social or political. But by exalting individual solitude and self-sufficiency, he set himself apart from his fellow moderns, anticipating the hyper-individualism of a much later age—our own.

Not without justification, then, did Bloom call the *Discourse on Inequality* "the most radical work ever written, one that transformed the way people thought about the world." This one essay contained the germs of most of the themes Rousseau would develop in later works, and that would be further elaborated by others who came under his spell. Rousseau's lyrical descriptions of early man and simple societies fueled the nineteenth-century popular romantic revolt against classicism in art and literature. His criticism of property, together with his dark view of the downside of mutual dependence, made a deep impression on the young Karl Marx.

The thesis of the *Second Discourse*, that the most serious forms of injustice had their origins in civil society rather than in nature, foreshadowed Rousseau's famous charge at the beginning of *The Social Contract* that virtually all existing governments were illegitimate: "Man is born free; and everywhere he is in chains." Having raised the explosive issue of legitimacy, and sensing that Europe's old regimes were about to crumble, Rousseau turned to his most ambitious project to date: the question of how better governments might be established. "I want to see," he wrote, "if, in the civil order, there can be some legitimate and solid rule of administration, taking men as they are and the laws as they can be."

Like many critical theorists before and since, Rousseau was less successful at developing a positive political vision of his own than he had been at spotting flaws in the theories of others. In *The Social Contract*, he framed the problem of good government as that of finding a form of political association which would protect everyone's person and property, but within which each person would remain "as free as before." The solution he devised was an agreement by which everyone would give himself and all his goods to the community, forming a state whose legislation would be produced by the will of each person thinking in terms of all (the "general will"). The state's legitimacy would thus be derived from the people, who, in obeying the law, would be obeying themselves.

That solution to the problem of legitimate government would obviously require a special sort of citizen, a "new man" who could and would choose the general will over his own interests, or the narrow interests of his group. The concept of the general will thus links *The Social Contract* to Rousseau's writings on nurture, education, and morals, particularly *Émile*, which contains his program for forming the sentiments of the young so that they will retain their natural goodness while living in civil society.

The legitimate state, as Rousseau imagined it, would need not only virtuous citizens, but an extraordinary "Legislator" who could persuade people to accept the rules necessary for such a society. Law in the properly constituted state would be, among other things, an instrument of transformation: "He who dares to undertake the making of a people's laws ought to feel himself capable of changing human nature." Rousseau had learned from the classical philosophers, however, that good laws can take root only amidst good customs. It was thus implicit in *The Social Contract* that many existing societies were already beyond help. "What people," Rousseau asked, "is a fit subject for legislation?" His answer was not encouraging to revolutionaries bent on overthrowing unjust regimes: "One which, already bound by some unity of origin, interest, or convention, has never yet felt the real yoke of law; . . . one in which every member may be known by every other, and there is no need to lay on any man burdens too heavy for a man to bear; . . . one which is neither rich nor poor, but self sufficient. . . . All these conditions are indeed rarely found united, and therefore few states have good constitutions."

Once a legitimate state is established, it needs to be maintained and defended. Thus, according to Rousseau, there should be no "particular associations" competing for the loyalty of citizens; religion should not be left independent of political control; and those who refuse to conform to the general will would have to be "forced to be free."

The contrast between Rousseau's program and the practical ideas that guided the American Founders could hardly be more striking. The legacy of the most influential political *thinker* of the eighteenth century is thus at odds with the era's greatest political *achievement*—the design for government framed by men who believed that good governments could be based on reflection and choice. The pragmatic authors of *The Federalist* had their own clear-eyed understanding of human nature with its potency and its limitations. They knew that human beings are creatures of reason and feeling— capable of good and evil, trust and betrayal, creativity and destruction, selfishness and cooperation. In Madison's famous formulation: "As there is a certain degree of depravity in human nature which requires a certain degree of circumspection and distrust, so there are other qualities in human nature which justify a certain portion of esteem and confidence."

As it turned out, Rousseau and his most discerning readers, especially Tocqueville, served the world's democratic experiments well as sources of constructive criticism. They were instrumental in keeping alive the classical insight that a healthy polity cannot be sustained without virtuous citizens and good customs. They have been among the main contributors to the classical critique of liberalism that has sustained, enriched, and corrected the excesses of democratic states. At the same time, however, liberal democracy has been menaced by Rousseau's most illegitimate offspring—not the Le Vasseurs who, God willing, are still thriving somewhere, but practitioners of the politics of feeling who bridle at authority themselves, but advocate authoritarian measures to force others to be free.

Generations of scholars have attempted to resolve the seeming contradictions in Rousseau's political writings, notably between his passionate attachment to natural freedom and his complacency about the state that forces non-conformists to be free. Biographers have pointed out that Rousseau himself was against revolution; that he thought the ideas in *The Social Contract* could work only in a small homogeneous polity like Geneva; and that he was generally pessimistic about the possibility of changing bad institutions.

But in the worlds of politics and culture, what Rousseau actually said or meant was of less consequence than the emotional responses his writings stirred. Rousseau's critique of existing governments was heady stuff. The difficulty and subtlety of his political thought were masked by his fluid, seductive literary style. His writings thus became a reservoir of ideas and slogans from which individualists and communitarians, revolutionaries and conservatives, moralists and bohemians, constitutionalists and Marxists drew freely and selectively. Vulgarization of his thought sheared off his deep historical pessimism, with the result that his influence at the popular level was overwhelmingly to the left where, ironically, it fed the nineteenth-century cult of progress.

Though Rousseau can fairly be regarded as the leading secular thinker of the Counter-Enlightenment, his "defense" of religion shows how firmly he stood within the modern horizon of his antagonists, and how he extended that horizon. Voltaire and others, much impressed by the natural science of their day, mounted an offensive against what they called clericalism but by which they meant Christianity in general and Catholicism in particular. They portrayed organized religion as an impediment to progress and a bastion of bigoted ignorance. Rousseau gained more credit than he deserved for reproving their contempt of religion in his *First Discourse*, for he was no friendlier to traditional religion than they. His childhood Calvinism and his brief, later passage through Catholicism left him with a vocabulary and a critical stance, but little more. Where Christianity was concerned, he seems to have unquestioningly accepted the reigning opinion among the secular learned men of his time.

He made his own views about organized religion clear in *Émile* and *The Social Contract*, so clear in fact that he was forced to flee from both Swiss and French authorities. The Savoyard vicar in *Émile* sounded much like Rousseau himself. He argued that the presence of religion in society should be welcomed, but not the religion of the day. Rejecting both reason and revelation, he proclaimed that, "The essential worship is that of the heart. God does not reject its homage, if it is sincere, in whatever form it is offered to him." The religion that Rousseau "defended" was a radically subjective one based on inner sentiment—a belief system rooted in being true to one's own feelings. It was the religion of Madame de Warens—the same religion that a

U.S. Supreme Court plurality would one day attempt to establish when it announced a "right to define one's own concept of existence, of meaning, of the universe, and of the mystery of human life" (*Casey* v. *Planned Parenthood*, 1992).

That private, inner religion was well-suited for the ideal polity outlined in the *Social Contract*. Once a truly legitimate state has been constructed, Rousseau argued, religion would be helpful in shoring it up—ideally, a patriotic "civil religion." Sharing Hobbes's fear of competitors for loyalty with the state, Rousseau held that a well-constituted state could be tolerant of other sorts of religious activity so long as they remained inward and private. Unlike Luther and other reformers, he was uninterested in correcting the defects of institutional religion. He came not to support their critique, but to push it to the limit.

Morality, in Rousseau's view, was rooted in neither reason nor revelation, but in the natural feeling of compassion. Indeed, he is in an important sense the father of the politics of compassion. As we now know, however, compassion is a shaky foundation on which to build a just society. Compassion, unlike charity, is not a virtue acquired by self-discipline and habitual practice. It is only a feeling, and a fleeting one at that. It yields not only to self-preservation, but to self-interest.

Rousseau's thought won admiration from a surprising assortment of readers. *Julie* marked the rise of the romantic literary genre that celebrates the primacy of feeling and the beauties of nature, while the *Confessions* did the same for the modern literature of self-revelation. Taken out of context, his passages on the communal existence of peoples, his evocation of a lost happy childhood of the human race, and his stress on the importance of religion found wide and disparate audiences, as did his critiques of the commercial mentality, the institution of private property, and the conquest of nature. The new human sciences of anthropology and psychology and the modern understanding of history are all in his debt.

Yet not all of his insights were original. He borrowed heavily, though haphazardly, from classical and biblical sources to criticize the reigning dogmas of his age. The extent of his debt was not always apparent, for he was adept at "translating" traditional wisdom into language that appealed to secular intellectuals. Though his skepticism about the benefits of progress in the arts and sciences was at odds with widely held views among educated men of his time, such attitudes would have been common among the women who were his closest friends, and in popular devotional literature.

Madame de Stael once remarked of Rousseau, "He had nothing new, but he set everything on fire." Though exaggerating his lack of originality, she did not overestimate the magic of his prose. Rousseau was a consummate stylist, the father of the soundbite, a phrasemaker par excellence. Moreover, he gave many different kinds of readers the impression that he understood and empathized with their deepest concerns. Above all, he tapped into *ressentiment* as no writer had done before. All the humiliations he had suffered in his life, all the pettiness and vice he had observed in the households of the ruling classes, lent power to his prose. Many before and since have written about the plight of the disadvantaged and the injuries of class, but Rousseau remains, as Judith Shklar neatly put it, the "Homer of the losers."

By Rousseau's own lights, however, his influence was different from, even opposite to, what he had hoped. His philosophical ideas, he frequently insisted, were only for the few, and the writings containing them could not be understood unless read in relation to one another—and more than once. The teaching of the *First Discourse*, for instance, is not that the sciences and the arts are unworthy pursuits, but that their spread to the public at large, their vulgarization, had had a corrupting effect—by destabilizing customary morality and fostering skepticism. The best education for ordinary folk, Rousseau held, was education aimed at the formation of healthy sentiments.

But no writer can control how and by whom his works are read. Discerning readers like Tocqueville and Kant were stimulated by Rousseau. To them, his writings were sources of enrichment and challenge, not least because, in his borderline mystical way, he carried forward to the new science of politics important insights from classical and biblical thought. Many activists who were "influenced" by Rousseau's political ideas, however, probably never read even one of his works in its entirety. More often than not, Rousseau's writings seem to have affected the emotions of his readers more than their intellects. Even Jacques Maritain, who detested Rousseau, conceded that, more than any other writer, Rousseau gave voice to the longings of his times:

> Such men are prophets of the spirit of the world, prophets of below, who concentrate in their heart the influences which work in the deeps of wounded humanity during a whole epoch. They then proclaim the age which is to follow them, and at the same time discharge on the future with prodigious strength those influences which have found their unity in them. They act on men by an awakening of emotional sympathies. . . . They spread around them the contagion of their self, the waves of their feelings and their instincts, they absorb people into their temperament.

What is one to make of a body of thought so ambiguous and so influential as that of Rousseau? Rousseau's native genius enabled him to acquire a good grasp of one of the two great premodern intellectual traditions. He learned enough from the ancient Greeks to mount a powerful critique of narrow scientific rationalism, but not enough to appreciate the more capacious form of reason that gave the classical and biblical traditions alike their dynamism. Like the Enlightenment thinkers he criticized, Rousseau rejected the moral and intellectual traditions that had nourished his own genius, throwing out the *ratio* of natural law along with modern scientific reason. He thus failed to see that what he called "perfectibility" was rooted in man's innate desire to know, the desire that gives rise to the never-ending, recurrent operations of questioning, experiencing, understanding, and choosing.

This prodigiously gifted, gravely flawed genius of the eighteenth century was at his best when he reminded his proud contemporaries of the limitations of science and politics. He sounded an early, much needed warning that material progress does not necessarily bring moral progress. He helped to keep alive the classical insight that good government requires moral foundations. He gave vivid expression to the plight of the poor and marginalized. But Rousseau's most problematic legacy, the one that bedevils us today, has been his elevation of sincerity over truth, and feeling over reason. Ironically, philosophical works he meant for the few fostered popular skepticism and relativism, while his writings addressed to the many promoted a revolt against reason even among philosophers.

# John Paul II's Challenge to the Human Sciences

This comment was delivered at a 1991 symposium on Pope John Paul II's Centesimus Annus, issued on the 100th anniversary of Pope Leo XIII's landmark social encyclical Rerum Novarum.[1]

IF WE THINK OF *Centesimus Annus* merely as the new encyclical on economic issues, we gloss over one of its most significant aspects—its appreciation of the unity that underlies the fragmented human sciences. There is an "of-courseness" about Pope John Paul II's assertion that "in order to better incarnate the one truth about man in different and constantly changing social, economic, and political contexts, the Church's social teaching enters into dialogue with the various disciplines concerned with man." But this forward-looking interdisciplinary approach to social questions is by no means the one that is taken for granted in most of the world's great research institutions. The methodology of *Centesimus Annus* in fact runs counter to, and challenges, deeply entrenched tendencies toward separation, specialization, and autonomous development of the human sciences of politics, economics, law, theology, history, philosophy, and sociology.

In this "economic" encyclical, John Paul II reminds us that economics—like all the other social sciences—is ultimately concerned with the human person and with culture. Indeed, the bulk of the document discusses economics only to place that aspect of human life in a proper perspective. That perspective (equally applicable to politics, law, and the other disciplines relating to man) is rooted in what the Holy Father calls "a correct view of the human person." It is a point of view that treats each individual as uniquely valuable in himself, yet takes account of our social nature, which finds its expression in the complex networks of groups and associations—familial, juridical, economic, social, political—that compose society.

---

[1] Mary Ann Glendon, "A Challenge to the Human Sciences," in *A New Worldly Order*, ed. George Weigel (Washington, DC: Ethics and Public Policy Center, 1992), 79–83.

But that does not exhaust the subject, though many social scientists would be content to end there. Man is not only a doer and a chooser, alone and in association with others: He is also a knower. "Above all," the new encyclical reminds us, "man is a being who seeks the truth and strives to live in that truth, deepening his understandings of it through a dialogue which involves past and future generations."

Since the events of 1989, if not before, we citizens of the liberal democracies have had little difficulty perceiving the errors about the person inherent in socialist thought, with its subordination of the individual to the group, its denial of the role of free choice in individual and collective moral decision, and its constriction of the sphere of human freedom. Yet if we view our own familiar economic, political, and legal structures through the lens John Paul provides, we can see that they, too, are deeply affected by a faulty anthropology—denying our social nature by treating the individual as radically autonomous, and exalting choice for its own sake, without reference to responsibility for its ends. As for truth, it seems that, to the extent that our fragmented human sciences are beginning to find common ground, it is on the killing fields of nihilism, where force is elevated over reason, and truth is said to be unknowable, variable, or entirely subjective.

John Paul II is fully aware of the problem: "Nowadays there is a tendency to claim that agnosticism and skeptical relativism are the philosophy and the basic attitude which correspond to the democratic forms of life." He reminds us that those attitudes toward reason and truth, as history shows, lead easily to totalitarianism. If there is no transcendent truth, there is no sure principle for justly ordering social relations. The "force of power takes over, people become means and objects to be exploited, there is no basis for human dignity, and no basis for human rights."

Having made this point, the Holy Father is careful to emphasize that the Christian response is not a religious "fundamentalism that claims the right to impose its concept of what is true or good on others." In a firm reminder that in this world we see only as through a glass darkly, he writes, "Christian truth is not of this kind. . . . [It] does not presume to imprison changing sociopolitical realities in a rigid schema, and it recognizes human life is realized in history in conditions that are diverse and imperfect."

What, then, can it mean to "live in truth" under imperfect conditions in a constantly changing world? In words that challenge every practitioner of the human sciences, the Holy Father responds that it means "paying heed to every fragment of truth" that one's faith and reason have enabled one to gain from one's own "life experience and in the culture of individuals and of nations." It means affirming all this in dialogue with others. It means verifying our heritage of values existentially, testing those values in our own lives, striving to "distinguish the valid elements in the tradition from false and obsolete ones or from obsolete forms which can usefully be replaced by others more suited to the times."

John Paul II's epistemology contrasts sharply with the attitudes toward human reason that are now prevalent among the American knowledge class, attitudes that, in the form of a vulgar relativism, are increasingly pervasive in American popular culture. Among the more worldly of our opinion leaders it is widely held that "reason" is but self-interested calculation in furtherance of one's own preferences or interests. Many of our academic pundits disdain reason altogether, yet—in a strange loop—are often quite dogmatic about their rigorous skepticism. The degree to which these attitudes have, in one form or another, penetrated our culture poses a serious threat to our ongoing democratic experiment. For they sap our will and capacity to engage in rational discourse about the ordering of our lives together. In practical terms, they come to the same conclusion: Politics is the mere clash of power and interests.

Against these irresponsible and debilitating attitudes, John Paul II sets the transformative politics of 1787 and 1989—a politics in which citizens are able to transcend, or even sacrifice, in some measure, what they perceive to be their private interests for the sake of the common good. It is a politics founded on a more capacious vision of the human person—a being flawed, to be sure, but capable through reason and dialogue of devising institutions and structures that permit imperfect men and women to work together for their own and the common good. John Paul II does not pretend it will be easy to discern the common good in modern pluralistic societies. But he does insist on our responsibility to use our rational faculties to the fullest, bringing our beliefs and opinions ever closer to such moral knowledge as is available to human beings.

The charge to economists, lawyers, philosophers, theologians, sociologists, psychologists, and students of politics is thus a weighty one. The challenge of *Centesimus Annus* to the human sciences is to assume responsibility for their part in contributing to the formation of culture—with an adequate conception of human personhood, and with due respect for human environments, those social arrangements that either "help or hinder [our] living in accordance with truth." The unity that underlies the Holy Father's interdisciplinary approach is the ongoing process of human knowing: the experiencing, understanding, and judging through which we attempt to discern the operation of divine grace, and to cooperate with it.

CHAPTER 5 • John Paul II's Challenge to the Human Sciences

# The First Ten Years of the Pontifical Academy of Social Sciences

*Shortly after I was appointed President of the Pontifical Academy of Social Sciences, the Academy marked its tenth anniversary. The following remarks were delivered in May 2004 at the anniversary celebration held in the Casina Pio IV, the Academy's headquarters in Vatican City.*[1]

*Presidents of Sister Academies, Honorable Ambassadors, Esteemed Guests, and Dear Colleagues:*

ON BEHALF of the members of the Pontifical Academy of Social Sciences, it is a great pleasure to welcome you to this celebration of the tenth anniversary of our founding, and to thank our distinguished visitors for honoring us with their presence here.

Shortly after Pope John Paul II established the Pontifical Academy of Social Sciences in January 1994, he welcomed the original members of this group with the exhortation to "Be not afraid" in the quest for knowledge. He urged us to search for "all the grains of truth present in the various intellectual and empirical approaches" of the disciplines gathered under this roof. As a model, he held up St. Thomas Aquinas whose unrestricted desire to know led him to seek dialogue with the most advanced natural and human science of his time, and to engage the ideas of the great minds of antiquity.

On that occasion, he also reminded us that we must not be content merely with harvesting the wisdom of the social sciences. He made clear that we were not to regard the secluded and beautiful Casina Pio IV as an ivory tower where scholars commune only with each other. As might be expected from the philosopher-pope who has traveled the world speaking truth to power for the past twenty-five years, John Paul II enjoined us to bring the wisdom of the social sciences to bear on human realities "with a view to finding solutions to people's concrete problems, solutions based on social justice."

---

[1] Mary Ann Glendon, "The First Ten Years of the Pontifical Academy of Social Sciences," presented at the Tenth Plenary Session of the Pontifical Academy of Social Sciences, Casina Pio IV, Vatican City, 30 April–3 May 2004.

Since then, in each meeting with our young academy, he has asked us to stretch our capacities, to be bold and creative in deploying the resources of our disciplines. In his 1998 address, he told us to keep in mind that sometimes we would be called to play the role of "pioneers . . . to indicate new paths and new solutions for solving in a more equitable way the burning issues of today's world."[2]

The pope also expressed his hope that the relationship between Catholic social thought and the social sciences would be a two-way street. Quoting from his social encyclical *Centesimus Annus*, he said that by entering into dialogue with the disciplines concerned with the human person, the Church not only "assimilates what these various disciplines have to contribute," but also "helps them to open themselves to a broader horizon."[3]

In his 1994 Apostolic Letter establishing the Academy, John Paul II recalled the remarkable flourishing of Catholic social thought in the century following Pope Leo XIII's path-breaking 1891 encyclical on labor questions, *Rerum Novarum*. He wrote that, "Over the last century the Church has strengthened her 'citizenship status' by perfecting her social doctrine . . . [in] close collaboration, on the one hand, with Catholic social movements, and on the other, with experts in the social sciences." He recalled how Pope John XXIII had stressed, in *Pacem in Terris* and *Mater et Magistra*, "that the social doctrine must always strive to take into account 'the true state of affairs' by maintaining a constant dialogue with the social sciences." Then, citing "the great tasks the future has in store," John Paul II said the time had now come to give "new expression" to this long-standing interdisciplinary dialogue. Accordingly, he created a body to study social science alongside the 400-year-old Pontifical Academy of Science. He charged the new academy with the task of "promoting the study and progress of the social, economic, political, and juridical sciences, and of thus offering the Church the elements which she can use in the study and development of her social doctrine."[4]

In some ways, the Pontifical Social Science Academy is like its sister academies all over the world, and in some ways it has a distinctive character. Like other learned academies, the Pontifical Academy of Social Science is dedicated to the pursuit of knowledge, but a distinctive feature that influences our choice of subjects is that we are expected to provide the Church with useful material to aid in the continuing "development of her social doctrine." In that sense, we are something like the Councils that governments appoint when expert knowledge on such matters as, for example, biotechnology, is required. Like such advisory bodies, our role is not to announce or develop doctrine, but to make sure that those who do explain, announce, and develop doctrine have the best possible information and the most promising ideas at their disposal.

---

[2] Address to the Pontifical Academy of Social Sciences, 23 April 1998, (2).
[3] *Centesimus Annus*, 59
[4] Statutes of the Pontifical Academy, Article 1.

But unlike governments, who seek expert opinion to aid in the formulation of policy, the Church does not make policy prescriptions, nor does she offer technical solutions to specific problems. As John Paul II has put it, "The Church has no models to present; models that are real and truly effective can only arise within the framework of different historical situations, through the efforts of all those who responsibly confront concrete problems in all their social, economic, political and cultural aspects, as these interact with one another" (CA, 43).

The aim of the social doctrine, as the pope put it in his encyclical *Solicitudo Rei Socialis*, is to offer "principles for reflection, criteria of judgments and directives for action" showing that the Gospel message in all its richness and newness applies "to people's lives and the life of society" (*SRS*, 8). As he elaborated in an address to our Academy four years ago, the social doctrine is meant to be "a vehicle though which the Gospel of Jesus Christ is brought to bear on the different cultural, economic and political situations facing modern men and women. . . . The Church's task—her right and her duty— is to enunciate those basic ethical principles forming the foundation and proper functioning of society, within which men and women make their pilgrim way to their transcendent destiny."[5] To promote the building up of a society that enables each man and woman to perfect his or her own nature, the Holy Father urged the Academicians to "help to insure that social doctrines do not ignore the spiritual nature of human beings, their deep longing for happiness and their supernatural destiny which transcends the merely biological and material aspects of life."

Over the past ten years, under the inspiring leadership of President Edmond Malinvaud, we Academicians have tried to live up to the confidence reposed in us. We have made what we believe are important contributions to the understanding of the changing world of work, the risks and opportunities presented by globalization, the dilemmas of democracy, and the consequences of changing relations among the generations. Our members, emblematic of the universal concerns of the Church, come from all continents of the world, and each is a specialist in at least one of the human sciences. It has not been easy for this diverse group of men and women to learn to communicate across disciplinary, cultural, and linguistic boundaries. But in ten years we have made great progress, educating and being educated by each other in this multinational, multidisciplinary setting. All would agree, I believe, that it has been an extraordinarily enriching experience to be able to hear such a wide range of thoughtful perspectives on the problems we have studied. We look forward to ever greater progress in fulfilling our mission to the Church, the social sciences, and to humanity.

---

[5] Address to the Pontifical Academy, 23 February 2000, No. 1.

CHAPTER 6 • The First Ten Years of the Pontifical Academy of Social Sciences

# The Ecology of Freedom

# The Moral Structure
# of Freedom

*In 1996, the Path of Peace Foundation sponsored a symposium at the
United Nations on Pope John Paul II's 1995 Address to the U.N. General Assembly:
"The United Nations: A Family of Nations?" Each speaker at the symposium was asked
to comment on a different section of the text. My assignment was to reflect
on the passages where the Pope discussed the nature of freedom.[1]*

IN THE SPEECH we have gathered here to discuss, Pope John Paul II pays
eloquent tribute to the "quest for freedom," which he describes as "one of
the great dynamics of human history." He affirms "a legitimate pluralism of
forms of freedom," yet cautions that the banner of freedom is often raised
over activities that are destructive of the liberty of individuals and nations.

The question arises, then: How can one recognize authentic forms of
freedom, and distinguish them from dangerous counterfeits? In the para-
graphs upon which I have been asked to comment, the Pope suggests that
freedom is distinguished by a "moral structure," an "inner logic" that is
"ordered to the truth." But since both freedom and truth are notoriously
elusive, that leads to another question: How does one reconcile a legitimate
plurality of freedoms with the notion of objective truth?

The existence of multiple conceptions of freedom is a fact that sometimes
escapes notice. It was quite striking at the 1995 Beijing conference, for example, how many of the participants seemed to believe they were communicating
with one another in a kind of Esperanto of human rights—as though the ordinary obstacles to cross-cultural communication had been somehow suspended. But if one listened closely, it was clear that words like "rights" and
"freedom" were being used in vastly different senses by various participants.

It is easy to see how the illusion of a universal rights language arose. In
the contemporary world, the "longing for freedom" most commonly finds

---

[1] Mary Ann Glendon, "Freedom and Moral Truth," in "The United Nations: A Fam-
ily of Nations?" A seminar on the Address of His Holiness John Paul II to the United
Nations Organization, Path to Peace Foundation, Trustee Council Chambers at U.N.
Headquarters, New York, 8 May 1996.

expression in terms of human rights. And since 1948, the nations of the world have been committed to the idea that certain basic rights are universal. But as that idea has taken root and flourished, we seem to be in the presence of a phenomenon something like what language teachers call "false friends." Most of us can remember how grateful we were, when we began studying foreign languages, for the existence of cognates. But no sooner does one discover those friendly words that mean the same thing in two languages than one encounters the treacherous "faux amis"—words that sound familiar, but have quite a different meaning.

Not only do parties to contemporary debates about rights often mean quite different things by the word "rights," they often have very different understandings of what freedom is, in particular its relation to truth and responsibility. If you dig a little deeper, you will usually find different assumptions about the nature of the human person.

Take the two main forms of political discourse that are predominant at the transnational level in the world today. We may call them the libertarian and the dignitarian dialects of rights.

As early as the eighteenth century, there was already a discernible divergence within the common horizon of modern thinking about rights. The Anglo-American tradition has long emphasized political and civil liberties, framed as "negative rights" (for example, restraints on governments), while the countries more influenced by the Romano-Germanic tradition have typically accompanied those political and civil rights with certain positive obligations on the part of the state toward citizens, and on the part of citizens toward each other.

Later, in the wave of constitution-making and international human rights that followed World War II, there were marked differences between older, more libertarian ideas about rights, and the way rights were formulated in the newer, post-1945 national constitutions and supranational instruments. To be sure, these differences are ones of degree and emphasis, but that does not diminish their significance. Indeed, the spirit of these differences penetrates every corner of the respective legal systems and their surrounding cultures.

The main points of contrast can be briefly summarized. Rights discourse of the type commonly found in countries influenced by English common law confers its highest priority upon individual freedom from governmental constraint. Rights tend to be formulated without mention of their limits, their relation to responsibilities, or to other rights. Freedom, in such a context, has a procedural framework, but lacks an explicit normative structure. Rather than aiming at the common good, it tends to become an end in itself.

The dignitarian rights language that one finds in, say, the Universal Declaration of Human Rights, in several postwar constitutions, and in the social doctrine of the Catholic Church, is characterized by a more nuanced dialect of freedom and responsibility. In both the U.N. tradition and in many modern constitutions, rights are envisioned not only as protected by fair procedures, but as grounded and situated in a normative framework based on human dignity. Specific rights are typically formulated so as to make clear that they are related to one another, that certain groups as well as individuals have rights, and that political entities, as well as citizens, have responsibilities. For example, the Universal Declaration and many dignitarian constitutions provide that the family is under the special protection of society and the state.

Underlying these different concepts of rights and freedom are somewhat different notions about the person who is endowed with rights and freedoms. John Paul II has always made a point of emphasizing that it is helpful to search for the conception of the person that underlies competing ideas about politics, economics, and culture. That search in the present context leads us to another "false friend": the "individual," who, within the libertarian tradition, tends to be imagined as an independent, radically autonomous, self-determining being. Dignitarian personhood, by contrast, pays tribute to the unique worth of each individual, but also recognizes that we are constituted, in important ways, by and through our relations with others.

American and German constitutional court decisions provide vivid illustrations of these contrasting anthropologies. The U.S. Supreme Court has said, for example, that the "most comprehensive of rights and the right most valued by civilized men" is "the right to be let alone." That idea, which would sound very strange in many parts of the world, belongs to an entirely different universe of discourse from the German Court's repeated emphasis that "the image of man in the Basic Law is not that of an isolated, sovereign individual. [T]he tension between the individual and society [is resolved] in favor of coordination and interdependence with the community without touching the intrinsic value of the person."

Many practical effects of these contrasting anthropologies can be traced in the day-to-day workings of the respective legal systems, especially where laws and policies relating to the family, or to religious associations, are concerned.

I must stress that neither libertarian nor dignitarian constellations exist in a pure form anywhere, but each set of ideas does give a distinctive cast to the polity where it prevails. And each is subject to deformation. As we look around today, libertarian notions of freedom seem to be advancing at the expense of more complex dignitarian ideas. For one thing, libertarian ideas are easy to sloganize. They are "built to travel," tailor-made for the "sound bite." Their individualism appeals to men and women "on the way up" in business and government—the modernizing, mobile elites who predominate in the First World and who constitute a kind of First World within the Third World.

It is cause for concern, I believe, that the ideas that travel fastest are mere abstractions—ideas about rights that have been detached from the

CHAPTER 7 • The Moral Structure of Freedom

social and political contexts that moderate them in the countries where they have traditionally had their homes. In the United States, for example, a variety of political checks, positive laws, and customs can and do limit individual liberties. Without such cultural checks, libertarian freedom can quickly degenerate into mere license.

That unhappy prospect brings us to the Pope's admonition that: "The basic question which we must all face today is the responsible use of freedom, in both its personal and social dimensions." The danger of confusing freedom with the absence of restraint is well-known. It has been captured in the saying: "A man has as many masters as he has vices." In public life, when freedom unravels into license, politics becomes a war of all against all.

But legitimate forms of freedom can also be derailed in ways that are more modern. The Pope mentions, for example, utilitarianism, the selfish instrumental politics of short-term profit maximization, based on a materialistic view of the human person. Equally insidious is the spreading influence of extreme forms of skepticism and relativism. By denying the existence of any common truths to which citizens of all nations can appeal, they corrode the very foundation of universal rights.

These newer types of threats to freedom help us to understand why John Paul II stresses that responsible use of freedom requires a concern for truth. As he has written elsewhere, when freedom is detached from truth "it becomes impossible to establish personal rights on a firm rational basis; and the ground is laid for society to be at the mercy of the unrestrained will of individuals or the oppressive totalitarianism of public authority" (*Evangelium Vitae*, 96).

In other words, unless freedom is connected to a common conception of truth, it becomes impossible to have an intelligible debate about how we are to live our freedom together on spaceship earth. Human rights deliberations degenerate into cacophony. Human rights declarations will tend to become mere bulletin boards where this or that interest group strives to post its favorite new right—with little concern for how it may undermine the conditions for effective freedom. The dream of universal human rights, paid for with the blood of freedom's martyrs, risks dissolving into scattered rights of personal autonomy. It does not seem fanciful to think that if such trends continue, a range of novel sexual liberties might one day become the bread and circuses of modern despots—consolation prizes for the loss of effective political and civil liberties, and for the denial of economic and social justice.

But the question persists: How can one tell if the quest for freedom is on the right path, given that human access to truth is imperfect, and nearly every proposition about truth and freedom is vigorously contested? Here the Pope's precise choice of words seems significant. By stating that "the inner logic of freedom is fulfilled in man's quest for truth," he reminds us that truth, like freedom, is the object of a continuing search.

Because the quest for freedom must be accompanied by the quest for truth, there is an important connection between "the moral structure of freedom" and the dynamic structure of human knowing. We humans move toward the goals of freedom and truth through experiencing, reflecting upon experience (others' experience as well as our own), and making choices based on experience and reflection. Those recurrent processes have the potential to be self-correcting—if one is attentive, intelligent, reasonable, and responsible. And because that sequence of experiencing, understanding, and choosing is a recurrent set of operations, there is nothing rigid or static about the structures of freedom and knowing. They are structures on the move throughout the whole of human history. The universal longing for freedom, like the unrestricted desire to know, involves all men and women. There is no map for the journey, only a method that is hard-wired, so to speak, in the human mind.

The method—experiencing, understanding, and judging—flourishes in an atmosphere of intellectual freedom and respectful dialogue. It follows that sharing information and ideas among the participants in the quest is of crucial importance. Hence the Pope's stress on the "politics of persuasion" and on the notion of a common moral order to which all can appeal. Hence, too, his description of his speech as a meditation on the role of the United Nations. How ironic, if in our age of rapid communication, deliberation about the most important questions—such as "how ought we to live together?"—were to break down. How tragic, if, at the end of this violent century, men and women of different nations were to deny the common humanity that makes such communication possible.

But dialogue does have conditions. Hence the Pope's insistence on the importance of culture, the moral traditions, and moral communities where we first learn about self-restraint and respect for others. And hence his stress on the human person as a creature "endowed with the ability to reflect and the ability to choose" (par. 4). In this vision of the person, there is an echo of the American Founders who in *Federalist* No. 1 posed the fateful question of whether good government can be established by reflection and choice, or whether the political fate of humanity must forever be determined by force and accident.

Like the architects of the American democratic experiment, Pope John Paul II has faith in the God-given capacity of human beings for reflection and choice. Like the American Founders, he urges "the risk of freedom." But in the speech we ponder today, he makes explicit what friends of liberty in former times thought they could take for granted: that authentic freedom cannot be severed from responsibility, from the quest for truth, or from "the risk of solidarity." As our own troubled century draws to a close, who can doubt that we need to be reminded from time to time of the eternal golden braid that links freedom to truth, and all human beings to one another in the family of man and the city of God?

CHAPTER 7 • The Moral Structure of Freedom

# The Cultural Underpinnings of America's Democratic Experiment

*This essay grew out of my seminar on the Foundations of Western Legal Thought. It appeared in* Building a Healthy Culture, *edited by Don Eberly.*[1]

IF HISTORY TEACHES US ANYTHING, it is that constitutional democracy cannot be taken for granted. There are conditions that are more or less favorable to liberty, self-government, and the rule of law, and those conditions involve the character and competence of citizens and public servants. But character and competence have conditions, too, residing in nurture and education. The American version of the democratic experiment leaves it primarily up to families, schools, religious groups, and a host of communities of memory and mutual aid to promote the republican virtues of self-restraint, respect for others, and sturdy independence of mind—and to transmit them from one generation to the next. Thus, the deteriorating health of these groups has grave implications for a regime of ordered liberty.

The stakes are high, for as Alexis de Tocqueville pointed out long ago, if democratic nations should fail "in imparting to all citizens those ideas and sentiments which first prepare them for freedom and then allow them to enjoy it, there will be no independence left for anybody."[2] The American Founders seem simply to have taken for granted that the requisite habits and beliefs would be taught and transmitted within families and the institutions that surrounded and supported them. To them, the young United States must have seemed blessed with an abundance of social, as well as, natural resources. Today, however, families, neighborhoods, religious groups, and communities are showing signs of exceptional stress. We have begun to realize that we cannot indefinitely consume our social capital without replenishing it.

What lends particular poignancy to the present situation, though, is that—as with the natural environment—many threats to the social environment are the byproducts of genuine improvements in the general standard of

---

[1] Mary Ann Glendon, "The Cultural Underpinnings of America's Democratic Experiment," in *Building a Healthy Culture*, ed. Don Eberly (Grand Rapids, MI: Wm. B. Eerdmans Publishing, 2001), 41–58.

[2] Alexis de Tocqueville, *Democracy in America* (Garden City, NY: Doubleday, 1969), 315.

living—technological advances, social welfare programs, and increased opportunities for individual fulfillment. The crucial question is this: How can we preserve and pursue the social, economic and political goods of a democratic republic without eroding its cultural foundations? This essay traces some key shifts in the relation between democracy and its culture-forming institutions and argues for a more "ecological" approach to politics.

## DEMOCRACY AND CULTURE AT THE DAWN OF THE DEMOCRATIC ERA

*Democracy* generally connotes a range of *political structures* through which popular consent may be expressed and related freedoms (especially of speech and association) may be protected. But it is important to keep in mind that democracy is also a set of ideas about equality, freedom, and popular sovereignty that have transformed the political and social landscape of the world. Those ideas came to the fore, and modern democracy was born, in the struggle to replace hereditary monarchies with representative governments. In France, that struggle involved an all-out attack on culture-forming institutions—a move that, paradoxically, endangered democracy. Under the slogan, "there are no rights except those of individuals and the State," French revolutionaries targeted not only the feudal statuses of the Old Regime, but also the Church, the craft guilds, and many aspects of family organization. They saw civil society as a bastion of inequality, a source of oppression to individuals, and a competitor with the State for the loyalty of citizens. One consequence of that revolutionary zeal to abolish the old *corps intérmédiaires* between citizen and state was that "civil society" became a major subject in continental European political thought throughout the nineteenth century. Tocqueville, Hegel, Marx, Durkheim, and others wrote at length about what the relations were, or should be, among individuals, the institutions of civil society, and the state.

Tocqueville, in particular, speculated about what might ensue if the institutions of civil society, once regarded as too powerful, became too weak. He pointed out that, with increasing centralization of political power, the very same groups that had once seemed to stifle individual development and to obstruct national consolidation, might turn out to be essential bulwarks of personal freedom and to provide useful checks on majoritarian rule. He speculated further that growing individualism, together with excessive preoccupation with material comfort, might weaken democracies from within by rendering their inhabitants susceptible to new forms of tyranny: "Habits form in freedom," he warned, "that may one day become fatal to that freedom." As the bonds of family, religion, and craft fraternities loosened, he feared that men would become feverishly intent on making money or dangerously dependent on "a powerful stranger called the government." That state of affairs, he surmised, could foster the emergence of new forms of despotism:

Far from trying to counteract such tendencies, despotism encourages them, depriving the governed of any sense of solidarity and interdependence, of good-neighborly feelings and desire to further the welfare of the community at large. It immures them, so to speak, each in his private life and, taking advantage of the tendency they already have to keep apart, it estranges them still more.[3]

Tocqueville was no reactionary. He was convinced that nothing could halt the advance of the democratic principle. Indeed, he described himself as "constantly preoccupied by a single thought: the thought of the approaching irresistible and universal spread of democracy throughout the world." The only question, so far as he was concerned, was whether it would produce free democratic republics or tyrannies in democratic form. In the first volume of his book on American democracy (an instant best-seller that went through twelve editions by 1848), he urged Europeans not to resist the inevitable, but rather to work with all their might to assure that freedom was preserved in the coming regimes. From his observations in the United States, he was persuaded that everything depended on whether the citizens possessed the habits and attitudes needed to sustain liberty within democracy. To those who shared that way of thinking, civil society—as the locus of the groups where the requisite habits and attitudes are formed—became a matter of crucial political importance.

Though the cultural foundations of democracy were of great interest to many nineteenth-century continental thinkers, matters were different in the United States. At the time of the American Revolution, land ownership was more evenly distributed than anywhere in Europe, and most Americans lived in self-governing towns and cities. About four-fifths of the (non-slave) population were independent farmers, small businessmen, and artisans. The American insurgents had no interest in radically restructuring society; their aim was to achieve independence from England. Strictly speaking, theirs was a secession rather than a revolution. As soon as they were free of the colonial yoke, the Founders concentrated on producing an ingenious design for a republic with democratic elements, a Constitution with vertical and horizontal separation of powers, and a system of checks and balances. The design was for a *federal* system that left authority over matters that immediately touched the lives of citizens mainly in the hands of state and local governments. Except for the Founders' concern to control the power of "factions" (special interests), civil society received relatively little attention in American political thought until the twentieth century—when it became apparent to writers like Robert Nisbet, Nathan Glazer, and Robert Bellah that large corporations were acquiring sovereignlike power, and that many of the mediating structures of civil society were in distress.

---

[3] Ibid.

CHAPTER 8 • The Cultural Underpinnings of America's Democratic Experiment

The chief interest of the American experiment, in Tocqueville's view, was not as a model for any other nation to copy, but rather that it afforded concrete evidence that the benefits of democracy need not be purchased at the price of liberty. To those of his readers who were fearful that democracy meant mob rule (tyranny by the majority), he said: "American laws and mores are not the only ones that would suit democratic peoples, but the Americans have shown that we need not despair of regulating democracy by means of laws and mores *(les moeurs)*."[4]

What did Tocqueville mean when he wrote of "regulating" democracy by laws and mores? He described with admiration how the American Constitution and federal system provided structural checks on pure majoritarianism. But he saw the small self-governing townships of New England as furnishing an equally important kind of check, an internal check within the citizenry itself. By affording many opportunities for participation in government, they permitted citizens to acquire "clear, practical ideas about the nature of their duties and the extent of their rights." "Local institutions are to liberty," he wrote, "what primary schools are to science; they put it within the people's reach; they teach people to appreciate its peaceful enjoyment and accustom them to make use of it. Without local institutions a nation may give itself a free government, but it has not got the spirit of liberty."[5]

The French visitor was even more impressed by the vigor and variety of the *social* groups that stood between the individual and government. He saw a country where most men, women, and children lived on farms or were engaged in running a family business (both forms of livelihood involving intense cooperation among the participants). These families—the first and most important teachers of the republican virtues of self-restraint and respect for others—were surrounded by a myriad of religious, civic, and social associations. Those latter groups provided settings where "every man is daily reminded of the need of meeting his fellow men, of hearing what they have to say, of exchanging ideas, and coming to an agreement as to the conduct of their common interests."

Thus, though he had high praise for the U.S. Constitution, he insisted repeatedly that the success of the American version of the democratic experiment was due less to the laws than to their culture or, as he put it, their "mores"—the widely shared habits and beliefs that constituted the true and invisible constitution of the republic. "Laws," he wrote, "are always unsteady when unsupported by mores; mores are the only tough and durable power in a nation."[6] In this respect, he was reminding his contemporaries of older classical and biblical traditions that stressed the importance of "laws written on the heart." The Athenian Stranger in Plato's *Laws*, for example, says of

4 Ibid., 311.
5 Ibid., 63.
6 Ibid., 274.

unwritten customs: "[W]e can neither call these things laws, nor yet leave them unmentioned . . . for they are the bonds of the whole state, and . . . if they are rightly ordered and made habitual, shield and preserve the . . . written law; but if they depart from right and fall into disorder, then they are like the props of builders which slip away out of their place and cause a universal ruin—one part drags another down, and the fair superstructure falls because the old foundations are undermined."[7]

Undergirding both laws and mores in America, Tocqueville discerned the influence of religion. "Religion," he wrote, "is considered as the guardian of mores, and mores are regarded as the guarantee of the laws and pledge for the maintenance of freedom itself."[8] His message was clear—culture is prior to politics and law, and religion is at the heart of culture. The health of the structures of civil society would be decisive in determining whether future citizens of emerging democracies would enjoy equality in liberty or endure equality in servitude.

## DEMOCRACY AND CULTURE IN THE INDUSTRIAL ERA

As Tocqueville predicted, the democratic principle spread. In the latter half of the nineteenth century, it showed its strength in the legislatures of the industrialized republics. Universal (male) suffrage brought a steady increase in legislation aimed at improving conditions in factories and tenements, and establishing rudimentary protections for the poor and unemployed. In Europe, this legislation laid an early foundation for modern "social" democracies. In the United States, however, the Supreme Court, in its first vigorous exercise of the power of judicial review, held many of these laws unconstitutional as violations of property rights and freedom of contract. In Russia, revolution set in motion a chain of events that simultaneously foreclosed the development of democracy there for nearly a century and corroded the substance of civil society.

Meanwhile, the Industrial Revolution was producing momentous transformations in civil society. It would be hard to say which of these related changes was more consequential for the future—the movement of most remunerative work outside the home, urbanization, the rise of large market actors whose power rivaled that of governments, the bureaucratization of both political and economic structures, and the development of mass communications.

Much has been written about political implications of most of these developments, but too little attention has been paid to the political consequences of the transformation of family life that took place when most men became wage earners. The separation of home and work ushered in a wholly new way of life—that modern phenomenon known as the homemaker–breadwinner

---

[7] Plato, *The Laws*, 793b, c.
[8] Tocqueville, 47.

family. It represented an advance over the age-old family division of labor in farming and fishing villages: If the man's salary was large enough, his transition to wage work brought relief for his wife and children from the hard life of the family farm or other family enterprise. But this new sort of family turned out to be less secure for women and children. Their economic welfare now depended entirely on the husband and father, while he was no longer so dependent on them. The divorce rate began slowly to climb. A telling shift took place in child custody law: As children became liabilities—in the economic sense—rather than much-needed assets, the traditional legal presumption in favor of fathers was replaced by a presumption in favor of maternal custody.

Tocqueville saw the expansion of business enterprise, even in its early phase, as posing a new threat of minority tyranny. He noted that the rising entrepreneurial class, unlike the aristocracies of old, did not seem to feel obliged by custom to come to aid of its servants or relieve their distress:

> The industrial aristocracy of our day, when it has impoverished and brutalized the men it uses, abandons them in time of crisis to public charity to feed them. . . . I think that generally speaking the manufacturing aristocracy which we see rising before our eyes is one of the hardest that have appeared on earth. . . . [T]he friends of democracy should keep their eyes anxiously fixed in that direction. For if ever again permanent inequality of conditions and aristocracy make their way into the world, it will have been by that door that they entered.[9]

By the early twentieth century, it was apparent—even to friends of capitalism—that large-market actors had acquired a great deal of influence over the political process and everyday life. In a 1927 essay, an American philosopher, later associated with the political thought of Franklin Roosevelt's New Deal, suggested that the powers of large property owners over persons who are not economically independent approached what historically has constituted political sovereignty. "It may well be," Morris Cohen wrote, "that compulsion in the economic as well as the political realm is necessary for civilized life. But we must not overlook the actual fact that dominion over things is also dominion over our fellow human beings."[10]

The centralization and bureaucratization of government meant that politics and economic life were increasingly dominated by large, impersonal organizations. The family home came to be regarded by many as a "haven in a heartless world." That haven, however, was coming under siege.

---

[9] Ibid., 557–58.
[10] Morris Cohen, "Property and Sovereignty," *Cornell Law Quarterly* 13 (1927): 8.

## DEMOCRACY AND THE FREE MARKET ADVANCE: THE CULTURAL SUPPORTS FALTER

In the aftermath of World War II, the democratic principle again extended its reach. New nations emerged with constitutions in democratic form, and, together with mature republics, pledged themselves in the Universal Declaration of Human Rights to the goal of realizing "better standards of life in larger freedom." To the demands that democracy itself places on civic competence and character, many countries had added the demands of the welfare state. The countries that embarked on these ambitious ventures seemingly took for granted that civil society would continue to supply the habits and attitudes required by democracy, the economy, and the expanding welfare system. Meanwhile, however, the institutions upon which republics had traditionally relied to foster republican virtues and to moderate greed were falling into considerable disarray.

Nowhere is this more apparent than in the case of the family. Even the farsighted Tocqueville did not foresee how deeply the ideas of equality and individual liberty—and even the market ethos—would affect relations among family members. He understood that tyranny could be accomplished softly, working on the mind rather than the body, but he could not have imagined the technological revolution that would put immense culture-shaping power in the hands of the media. Confident that "democracy loosens social ties, but it tightens natural ones," he believed that "orderly and peaceful" homes could be depended upon to produce self-reliant citizens who knew how to respect others, to compromise differences, and to restrain their own tendencies toward selfishness. Habits acquired in the home would provide the foundation for developing further skills of communal living in other sites such as schools, workplaces, and towns. Women, as the first and main teachers of children, were key to the whole system:

> There have never been free societies without mores, and . . . it is woman who shapes these mores. Therefore everything which has a bearing on the status of women, their habits, and their thoughts is, in my view, of great political importance.[11]

Who could have foreseen the series of turbulent changes that, beginning in the mid-1960s, shook up the roles of the sexes, transformed family life, and wrought havoc with the cultural foundations of democratic republics? The sexual revolution and sudden shifts in birth rates, marriage rates, and divorce rates caught professional demographers everywhere by surprise. In 1985, French demographer Louis Roussel summed up the developments of the preceding two decades: "What we have seen between 1965 and the present,

---

[11] Tocqueville, 590.

CHAPTER 8 • The Cultural Underpinnings of America's Democratic Experiment

among the billion or so people who inhabit the industrialized nations, is . . . a general upheaval across the whole set of demographic indicators, a phenomenon rare in the history of populations. In barely twenty years, the birth rate and the marriage rate have tumbled, while divorces and illegitimate births have increased rapidly. All these changes have been substantial, with increases or decreases of more than fifty percent. They have also been sudden, since the process of change has only lasted about fifteen years. And they have been general, because all industrialized countries have been affected beginning around 1965."[12] Several other developments also had serious implications for society's seedbeds of character and competence—an unprecedented proportion of mothers of young children began to work outside the home; an unprecedented proportion of children were spending all or part of their childhood in fatherless homes; institutions outside the home were playing an ever-greater role in the formation of children; the mass media were gaining ever-more direct access to children; and no society had yet come up with an adequate replacement for the unpaid labor of women. The societies affected had, in fact, embarked on a vast social experiment.

At about the same time, there were signs of disturbance in schools, neighborhoods, churches, community and workplace associations—institutions that traditionally depended on families for support, and that in turn served as important resources for families. That was no coincidence. Not only had urbanization and geographic mobility taken their toll, but many of the institutions of civil society had relied heavily on women, who were now in short supply, as volunteers and caregivers.

The movement of most women into the work force deprived many groups of unpaid staffers; removed the informal law enforcement system (the "eyes and ears") from many neighborhoods; and precipitated a caretaking crisis. The traditional pool of family caretakers for the very young, the disabled, and the frail elderly was drying up, with no real replacement in sight—an ominous development for the most vulnerable members of society. The extent of the crisis can be appreciated when one takes account of the fact that the proportion of the population that cannot be self-sufficient (very young children, the ill, and the frail elderly) has hardly changed in the past hundred years. The *composition* of that population has shifted (with fewer children and more elderly in the mix than a century ago), but their *proportion* to the whole has remained relatively steady.

In the late 1980s, the rates of demographic change slowed in the more affluent democracies. They have stabilized, but at new high or low levels, leaving a set of problems that no society has ever before had to confront on such a scale. In the United States, for example, divorce and non-marital

---

[12] Louis Roussel, "Démographie: deux décennies de mutations dans les pays industrialisés," in *Family, State, and Individual Economic Security*, ed. M.-T. Meulders-Klein and J. Eekelaar (Brussels: Story Scientia, 1988), I, 27–28.

births have brought about a situation where between one-fifth and one-quarter of young children currently live in single-parent homes, and over half spend at least part of their childhood in such households. The great majority of these homes are headed by women, and their economic circumstances are precarious: Nearly half of all female-headed families with children under six live in poverty. The schools, churches, youth groups, neighborhoods, and so on that once provided assistance to such families in times of distress are in trouble, too. They not only served as reinforcements for, but also depended on, families, neighborhoods, and each other for personnel and reinforcement.

Whatever else may be said about these new conditions, they have impaired civil society's capacity for fostering the habits and practices that make for democratic citizenship. As an insightful journalist observed, we are experiencing a "fraying of the net of connections between people at many critical intersections. . . . Each fraying connection accelerates the others. A break in one connection, such as attachment to a stable community, puts pressure on other connections: marriage, the relationship between parents and children, religious affiliation, a feeling of connection with the past—even citizenship, that sense of membership in a large community which grows best when it is grounded in membership in a small one."[13]

Observers across the political spectrum have expressed concern about the implications of these developments for the quality of the work force, the fate of the social security system, and the incidence of crime and delinquency. Less attention has been paid, however, to the *political* implications—the likely effect upon the world's democratic experiments of the simultaneous weakening of child-raising families and their surrounding and supporting institutions. Not only have the main institutions that fostered non-market values in society become weaker, but values promoted by the market and the media seem to be penetrating the very capillaries of civil society.

Surely Tocqueville would have asked: Where will modern republics find men and women with a grasp of the skills of governing and a willingness to use them for the general welfare? Where will your sons and daughters learn to view others with respect and concern, rather than to regard them as objects, means, or obstacles? What will cause most men and women to keep their promises, to limit consumption, to stick with a family member in sickness and health, to spend time with their children, to answer their country's call for service, to reach out to the unfortunate, to moderate their own demands on loved ones, neighbors, and the polity? Where will a state based on the rule of law find citizens and statesmen capable of devising just laws and then abiding by them?

The findings of surveys of the political attitudes of young Americans are disquieting. In 1999, over one-third of high school seniors failed a national

[13] William Pfaff, "Talk of the Town," *New Yorker* (August 30, 1976): 22.

civics test administered by the U.S. Department of Education, and only 9 percent were able to give two reasons why it is important to be involved in a democratic society.[14] Another study found a sense of the importance of civic participation almost entirely lacking: "Consistent with the priority they place on personal happiness, young people reveal notions . . . that emphasize freedom and license almost to the complete exclusion of service or participation. Although they clearly appreciate the democratic freedoms that in their view, make theirs the 'best country in the world to live in,' they fail to perceive a need to reciprocate by exercising the duties and responsibilities of good citizenship."[15] When asked to describe what makes a good citizen, only 12 percent mentioned voting. Fewer than one-quarter said that they considered it important to help their community to be a better place. When asked what makes America special, only 7 percent mentioned that the United States was a democracy. Such attitudes cannot be dismissed simply as a function of immaturity, for a comparison with earlier public opinion data revealed that the 1990 cohort knew less about civics, cared less, and voted less than young people at any time over the preceding five decades.[16]

## THE ECOLOGY OF FREEDOM
## IN THE ERA OF GLOBALIZATION

At first glance, democracy appears triumphant at the dawn of the twenty-first century. Republics in democratic form have spread across Eastern Europe and Latin America and into many parts of Asia and Africa. A majority of the world's countries, over one hundred nations, now call themselves democratic, though "democratizing" would be a more accurate term in some cases. Scholars tell us that democracies are disinclined to go to war with one another, and that no famine has ever occurred in a democracy.[17] Democratic principles and ideas are increasing urged upon, and have been adopted by, many institutions of civil society.

But governments in democratic form can mask an undemocratic reality. The future of the world's democratic experiments appears clouded by several overlapping developments.

In the first place, there has been a *certain atrophy of the democratic elements in modern republics*. The *centralization of government* has drawn decision-

---

[14] Chris Hedges, "35% of High School Seniors Fail National Civics Test," *New York Times* (November 21, 1999): 16.

[15] People for the American Way, *Democracy's Next Generation* (Washington: People for the American Way, 1989), 27.

[16] Michael Oreskes, "Profiles of Today's Youth: They Couldn't Care Less," *New York Times* (28 June 1990): A1, D21.

[17] Francis Fukuyama, *The End of History and the Last Man* (New York: Free Press, 1992); Amartya Sen, *Development as Freedom* (New York: Knopf, 1999).

making power away from local governments that once served as "schools for citizenship" and afforded average citizens the opportunity to participate in public life. *Globalization* has drained power from the nation-state. Non-representative *special interest groups* and lobbies often play the decisive role in shaping legislation and administrative action. A development in some countries, which could spread to supranational tribunals, is the overly *ambitious exercise of judicial power* to invalidate popular legislation, as well as to use hyper-individualistic interpretations of rights to undermine the institutions of civil society. All in all, it is increasingly difficult for most men and women in today's democratic regimes to have a say in framing the conditions under which they live, work, and raise their children.

As discussed above, democratic experiments are also threatened by *the decline of their seedbeds of civic virtue*. Character and competence do not emerge on command. They are acquired only through habitual practice. Those habits will either be sustained or undermined by the settings in which people live, work, and play. Democracies therefore cannot afford to ignore nurture and education, or the social and political institutions where the qualities and skills that make for good citizenship and statesmanship are developed and transmitted from one generation to the next.

Third, the megastructures of civil society have acquired such power as to raise *the spectre of new forms of oligarchy*. In terms of economic resources and ability to shape policy and events, the influence of some market actors, foundations, and special interest organizations exceeds that of many nation-states. Indeed, nation-states have limited power to affect the large economic forces that shape the lives of their citizens. The status and security of most people are increasingly dependent upon large corporate employers or government. Routines of family life have been adjusted to conform to the demands and timetables of the economy. The general standard of living has risen in many places, but at the same time disparities have widened between rich and poor. Troubling questions arise: Has "emancipation" from the oppressive aspects of older ways of life merely afforded men and women the opportunity to develop their talents to fit the needs of the market? Have women been freed from one set of rigidly bounded roles only to become unisex hominids whose family life must regularly be subordinated to the demands of the workplace?

And what will the new oligarchs be like, if the democratic elements in modern republics should one day become mere empty forms? The men and women who hold key positions in governments, political parties, corporations, mass media, foundations, and so on are often quite remote from the concerns of the average citizen. Strong ties to persons and places, religious beliefs, attachment to tradition, and even family life are apt to be less important to those at the top than to the men and women whose lives they affect. Decision makers already have tended to be rather free in adopting measures that undermine the delicate communities on which others depend for practical and emotional support—as witness the organization of work and schooling, the planning of cities, programs for public assistance, all too frequently designed without considering the impact on families and neighborhoods.

If that were not cause enough for concern, modern mass media render the problem of "soft tyranny," identified by Tocqueville, more acute than in his day. Modern tyrannies, he predicted, would prefer the kind of power that acts upon the will, rather than the crude use of force. Unlike ancient despots who frequently resorted to physical oppression, new forms of despotism would "leave the body alone and go straight for the soul"—to the point that "even desires are changed."[18]

*Materialism, extreme individualism, and hedonism* have taken their toll—and perhaps have even set the stage for regimes where individual liberty will be lost, or confined to matters that distract from politics. As Tocqueville wrote, "What can even public opinion do when not even a score of people are held together by any common bond, when there is no man, no family, no body, no class and no free association which can represent public opinion and set it in motion? When each citizen being equally impotent, poor, and dissociated cannot oppose his individual weakness to the organized force of the government?" In a country which permits its fonts of public virtues to run dry, he warned, there would be "subjects" but no "citizens."[19] One wonders: Is the unlimited sexual liberty so relentlessly promoted on all fronts today a kind of consolation prize for the loss of real liberty in the political and economic sphere? A kind of latter-day bread and circuses?

Finally, there is the corrosive effect on the polity of a *spreading lack of confidence that there are any common truths* to which men and women of different backgrounds and cultures can appeal. Many serious twentieth-century thinkers argue that tyrannies, old and new, whether majoritarian or of minorities, are rooted in nihilism. Hannah Arendt, for example, wrote: "The ideal subject of totalitarian rule is not the convinced Nazi or the convinced Communist, but people for whom the distinction between fact and fiction (for example, the reality of experience) and the distinction between true and false (for example, the standards of thought) no longer exist."[20] Pope John Paul II, reflecting on the experience of totalitarianism in Eastern Europe, put it this way:

> [T]otalitarianism arises out of a denial of truth in the objective sense. If there is no transcendent truth, in obedience to which man achieves his full identity, then there is no sure principle for guaranteeing just relations between people. Their self-interest as a class, group or nation would

---

[18] Tocqueville, 255 and 434–35.
[19] Ibid., 314, and 93–94.
[20] Hannah Arendt, *The Origins of Totalitarianism* (New York: Meridian, 1958), 474.

inevitably set them in opposition to one another. If one does not acknowledge transcendent truth, then the force of power takes over, and each person tends to make full use of the means at his disposal in order to impose his own interests or his own opinion, with no regard for the rights of others.[21]

In view of the atrophy of democratic participation, the disarray among the small structures of civil society, the menace of oligarchy, and the spread of materialism, hyper-individualism, and popular relativism, what can one say about the prospects for renewing American culture?

## WHITHER DEMOCRACY AND THE SOCIAL ENVIRONMENT?

At the dawn of the democratic era, it seemed to Tocqueville that the irresistible advance of democracy was leading to only two possible outcomes—democratic freedom or democratic tyranny. Today, with the democratic nation-state and its cultural supports weakened, the market seems to be about where democracy was then. The market is both a set of institutions and a powerful idea, fate-laden and irresistible, with the potential to improve the lives of men and women everywhere or to subject them to new forms of tyranny. The great challenge is to shift probabilities in the first direction.

This overview of democracy's ever-changing relationship to its cultural supports suggests four tentative conclusions:

1. For the benefits of democratic society and the free market to be realized and their destructive potential minimized, the explosive energies of free politics and free economics must be disciplined and directed by a vibrant moral culture.

2. The moral culture depends, in turn, on the health of society's main culture-forming institutions.

3. Paradoxically, liberal democracy and free markets pose threats, not only to each other, but to the seedbeds of the very qualities and institutions both need in order to remain free and function well.

4. The corrective may lie in another paradox: Democratic states and free markets may need to refrain from imposing their own values indiscriminately on all the institutions of civil society. They may even need, for their own good, to be actively solicitous of groups and structures whose main loyalty is not to the state and whose highest values are not efficiency, productivity, or individualism.

---

[21] *Centesimus Annus,* 44.

Could law and policy help to revitalize, or at least avoid further harm to, families and other fragile institutions upon which political freedom and economic vitality depend? Unfortunately, we do not know very much about how to encourage, or even to avoid damage to, the social systems that both undergird and buffer the free market and the democratic polity. In fact, we probably know even less about the dynamics of social environments than we do about natural environments.

One thing we have learned through trial-and-error is that intervention, even with the most benign motives, can have unintended and harmful consequences. In an address to the French National Assembly, anthropologist Claude Lévi-Strauss called attention to the endangered state of social environments, but cautioned at the same time against regulatory hubris. Two hundred years after the French Revolution attacked civil society, he told the legislators that the problem today is to restore civil society:

> Notwithstanding Rousseau, who wanted to abolish any partial society in the state, a certain restoration of partial societies offers a final chance of providing ailing freedoms with a little health and vigor. Unhappily, it is not up to the legislator to bring Western societies back up the slope down which they have been slipping. . . . [But] the legislator can at least be attentive to the reversal of this trend, signs of which are discernible here and there; he can encourage it in its unforeseeable manifestations, however incongruous and even shocking they may sometimes seem. In any case, the legislator should do nothing that might nip such reversal in the bud, or once it asserts itself, prevent it from following its course.[22]

It may well be that the idea of "regulating" complex social systems (in the sense of controlling their development or ensuring desired outcomes) is an illusion. Interventions can shift probabilities, but often in unanticipated ways. Prudence thus suggests proceeding modestly, preferring local experiments and small-scale pilots to broad, standardized, top-down programs. Often, the principle of "do no harm" will be the best guide. At a minimum, that would require attention to the ways in which governmental or business policies may be undermining fragile social structures, or discouraging persons who devote time and effort to the nurture of future citizens.

Is there reason to hope that the fine texture of civil society can be reinvigorated? One close observer of changes in the political capillaries of democracies finds hope in the fact that many kinds of micro-governments are spontaneously emerging at the neighborhood and community level in Europe and the United States. George Liebmann, whose three densely

---

[22] Claude Lévi-Strauss, "Reflections on Liberty," in *The View From Afar* (New York: Basic Books, 1985), 288.

packed monographs on civil society deserve to be better known,[23] has studied the emergence of such phenomena as *woonerven* (residential street control regimes) in The Netherlands, neighborhood councils in the Nordic countries, local law enforcement in the 25,000 communes of France, and business improvement districts and residential community associations in the United States. He found that many of these groups have evolved from small spontaneous cooperative endeavors into responsive and effective "sub-local" governments. Though some of these associations are controversial, Liebmann contends that they are spreading and are likely to spread further, as a reaction to the centralization and bureaucratization that have dominated political and social life for most of the century. Such bodies may become "schools for citizenship" in the twenty-first century.

Another promising sign is experimentation with the delivery of social services such as education, health care, and child care through smaller seedbed institutions (religious groups, workplace associations) rather than state-run bureaucracies.[24] Yet another positive development is increasing interest in the principle of subsidiarity: the idea that no social task should be peformed at a higher level or by a larger institution than can perform that task adequately. The editor of a journal that follows such developments, predicts that the most important political issues in the twenty-first century will be either global or local:

> Problems are migrating up and down all over government, in search of the appropriate place for solution. . . . Citizens are essentially looking for two forms of public authority: intimate ones in their community that can deal with their needs in a humane way, and regional ones big enough to impose some order and stability on economic life. The governments they have are mostly too remote and bureaucratic for the first job and too small and weak for the second one.[25]

Ultimately, what will be decisive for democracy and the free market alike is not the seedbeds of civil society (which can produce weeds as well as flowers), but the seed itself. The seed is the human person, uniquely individual, yet inescapably social; a creature of unruly passions who nevertheless possesses a certain ability, individually and collectively, to create and abide by systems of moral and juridical norms.

---

23 George Liebmann: *The Little Platoons: Sub-Local Governments in Modern History* (Westport, CT: Praeger, 1995); *The Gallows in the Grove: Civil Society in American Law* (Westport, CT: Praeger, 1997); *Solving Problems Without Large Governments* (Westport, CT: Praeger, 1999).

24 Peter L. Berger and Richard John Neuhaus, *To Empower People: From State to Civil Society* (Washington, DC: American Enterprise Institute, 1996).

25 Alan Ehrenhalt, "Demanding the Right Size Government," *New York Times* (October 4, 1999): A33.

CHAPTER 8 • The Cultural Underpinnings of America's Democratic Experiment

# Traders and Raiders

*This review of one of the great Jane Jacobs' lesser-known books,*
Systems of Survival: A Dialogue on the Moral Foundations
of Commerce and Politics, *appeared in the*
*December 1993 issue of First Things.*[1]

IN HER LATEST BOOK, Jane Jacobs trains her genial, sparkling intelligence on a subject that is much neglected in our law-saturated society: the great webs of manners, customs, social sanctions, and informal understandings that undergird economic and political life. As Judith Martin (Miss Manners) has had occasion to point out in the pages of *First Things*, members of a society without well-developed systems of informal social regulation will tend to resort too often and too quickly to law, a crude, incomplete, and expensive substitute. With *Systems of Survival*, Jacobs becomes an eloquent contemporary proponent of Tocqueville's view that manners and mores are much more important than laws in sustaining the world's democratic experiments.

Jacobs makes a surprising claim that has been misunderstood by some reviewers. She contends that human beings have developed two and only two basic "systems of survival": a "commercial syndrome" and a "guardian syndrome." Each of these survival strategies has arisen and persisted, she argues, because it promotes material success in the way of life with which it is associated. Like the other animals, we find and pick up what we can use, and appropriate territories. But unlike the other animals, we also trade and produce for trade. Because we possess these two radically different ways of meeting our basic needs, we also have two radically different systems of morals and values—both systems valid and necessary. The two systems differ because the qualities that are conducive to the flourishing of traders are different from the qualities that are conducive to the successful acquisition, exploitation, or protection of territories.

The "commercial syndrome" has its principal home among peoples who trade or produce for trade (though it is not co-extensive with, or limited to, the world of business). The linchpin of the commercial syndrome is honesty,

---

[1] Mary Ann Glendon, review of *Systems of Survival: A Dialogue on Moral Foundations of Commerce and Politics* by Jane Jacobs, *First Things* 38 (December 1993): 50–53.

for the very good reason that trading systems don't work without a good deal of trust, even among strangers. Because traders' prosperity depends on making reliable deals, they set great store by policies that tend to create or reinforce honesty and trust: respect contracts; come to voluntary agreements; shun force; be tolerant and courteous; collaborate easily with strangers. Because producers for trade thrive on improved products and methods, they also value inventiveness, and attitudes that foster creativity, such as "dissent for the sake of the task."

"Guardians" are modern versions of the raiders, warriors, and hunters who once made their livings through sorties into unknown or hostile territories. Today's guardians (usually more concerned with administering or protecting territories than acquiring them) are found in governmental ministries and bureaucracies, legislatures, the armed forces, the police, business cartels, intelligence agencies, and many religious organizations. Guardians prize such qualities as discipline, obedience, prowess, respect for tradition and hierarchy, show of strength, ostentation, largesse, and "deception for the sake of the task." The bedrock of a guardian system is loyalty. It not only promotes their common objectives, but it keeps them from preying on one another. They are wary of, even hostile to, trade, for the reason that loyalty and secrets of the group must not be for sale.

Ideally, says Jacobs, the commercial and guardian syndromes in a given society should co-exist in separate, symbiotic relationships. Why separate? Because, according to Jacobs: "[C]razy things happen systematically when either moral syndrome . . . embraces functions inappropriate to it." It is as though each system has its own moral ecology that can be fatally disrupted by the introduction of foreign elements. Jacobs fears that the guardian syndrome may be gaining ascendancy in inappropriate places and that "systemic corruption" of both syndromes may be spreading. Systemic corruption, more intractable than random individual corruption, frequently takes the form of breakdown, with each system losing the ability to discipline its members or to check its own extreme proclivities. But it may also produce "monstrous hybrids"—like the Sicilian mutual defense societies that applied raiding methods to trading (Mafia), the Ik of southern Uganda who began raiding each other when they were forced from hunting into farming, or American investment bankers in the takeover era.

I must now briefly digress to explain why summarizing Jacobs' ideas, as I have just done, can easily lead to misconstruing her enterprise. Any summary, no matter how carefully done, comes out sounding a bit like the horoscopes on the placemats in a Chinese restaurant. (Guardians respect tradition and authority. They can't stand criticism, even from their mother. If you are a guardian, you are apt to be a politician, a bishop, or a prison warden.) In Jacobs' book, however, the idea of two basic systems of survival emerges gradually from conversations among characters in a dialogue. It is clear that the relationship between style and substance is not accidental. A remark toward the end of the book by Kate, a biologist with an interdisciplinary bent, probably represents Jacobs' own reflection on her method. Kate says: "[T]ruth is made up of many bits and pieces of reality. The flux and change in itself is of the essence. Change is so major a truth that we understand process to be the essence of things."

In reading *Systems of Survival*, however, I was often reminded of another reason some writers have chosen the dialogue form. In Plato's *Seventh Letter*, he reveals why he never wrote any treatises or lectures on the questions to which he had devoted his life. Those great subjects, Plato explained, "cannot be put into words like other studies. Acquaintance with them must come rather after a long period of attendance on instruction in the subject itself and of close companionship, when, suddenly, like a blaze kindled by a leaping spark, it is generated in the soul and at once becomes self-sustaining." It is because Jacobs' book harvests the fruit of her lifelong reflection on human ingenuity (and on the settings that are conducive to human flourishing) that one keeps on thinking about her ideas in a way that one doesn't keep thinking about zodiac categories. But the fruit is not there for the picking. Her book is rather an invitation to participate in the conversation.

A misunderstanding of that fundamental point has led most reviewers to treat Jacobs' book as a kind of social horoscope, overlooking her Tocquevillean call to reflection on the present condition of our economic and political mores. What is the current state of the great web of understandings that undergirds relations among those who trade and produce for trade in our society? How well are we doing at restraining force, fraud, and unlimited greed in commercial life? What is the current state of America's guardian cultures? How can the persons who perform those essential roles be kept from running rampant over personal plans, property, and freedoms?

Another misunderstanding, perhaps arising from Jacobs' use of the ambiguous word "moral," concerns the scope of her inquiry. Thus, Alan Wolfe, writing in the *New York Times*, takes Jacobs to be arguing that "there are no more than two moral systems." Early in the book, however, Kate explains that, in addition to the two clusters of traits characteristically associated with the two different ways of making a living, there are several "universal values" such as cooperation, faith, mercy, patience, and wisdom that are prized in all sorts of settings. And, Kate adds, "in conduct of personal life, too, for that matter, not just in working and public life." But the discussion leader, a publisher named Armbruster, requests the group to concentrate on economic and political life. They agree to leave to one side those moral systems that are about making a life, as distinct from making a living. In the domains to which they devote their attention, what is striking is that, when the "universals" are subtracted from the qualities prized in different occupational specialties, one is left with two remarkably different lists of qualities.

The conversation meanders toward a conclusion that seems to belong to the domain of practical epistemology. In complex modern societies, the discussants agree, raiders and traders cannot simply go their symbiotic respective ways in their separate spheres. Since interaction is unavoidable, contemporary liberal democracies need more individuals who are "morally flexible enough to adapt to either syndrome as need be, and knowledgeable enough to know the difference." The participants note that this is not an impossible feat—lawyers, for example, often shift from guardian roles in adversarial situations to trader roles in other facets of legal work. (The idea that lawyers might be intelligently ethically ambidextrous, rather than merely ethically versatile, is one that should endear Jacobs to members of the legal profession.)

Those who are interested in "first-order" questions, though, may be disappointed in Jacobs' book, for her characters are resolutely concerned with second-order problems. Their questions are not about the good life and how to live it; they are about comfortable self-preservation and what sorts of strategies have historically been effective in promoting it. Still, if mere life in reasonable comfort is not the *summum bonum*, neither is it to be scorned. In illuminating the informal understandings upon which we all unconsciously rely, Jacobs reminds us of the fragility of much that we take for granted. The question that will occur to readers of *First Things* is: What is the condition of the first-order moral foundations that undergird the second-order guardian and commercial syndromes?

Jacobs brushes up against that question occasionally, as when Jasper, a writer of crime novels, warns that neither honesty nor loyalty comes naturally; both depend on constant inculcation and watchfulness. But who is doing the inculcating, and who is watching? Jacobs' own confessed partiality for trader values seems to incline her toward a universalistic individualism that makes it hard for her to carry through on the full implications of her own argument that the trader cultures she admires are at risk without the presence in society of groups that exalt qualities she really doesn't like at all. Guardians aren't particularly tolerant, egalitarian, or much interested in dissent.

So we have in *Systems of Survival* a conversation among a group of likeable, intelligent, sociologically minded, modern men and women, who arrive at, and shrink from, the disturbing and paradoxical insight of the great social thinkers: that trader (liberal democratic) society may be dependent on the maintenance in its midst of some very non-liberal institutions—such as religious groups with strong truth claims. Yet if her main thesis is correct, it is highly relevant to current controversies over the family and the military, for her message is that to reorganize these irritating (to traders), but necessary, groups on liberal principles may be to destroy them, and to undermine liberal society in the process.

One matter this reader would have liked Jacobs' discussants to address is the role that such processes as rationalization, bureaucratization, and the "liberation" of the individual from family and group ties have played among the deep causes of what Jacobs calls systemic corruption. The guardian and trader syndromes described by Jacobs are above all social and relational phenomena, dependent on widely shared understandings. A lone raider is no raider; a lone trader is no trader. Thus, what Jacobs describes as the spread of the guardian syndrome may be something worse: the spread of individual raiding behavior unchecked by informal social constraints of any sort. Perhaps that is what she means by systemic corruption. But if so, the causes may be more directly traceable to the above-mentioned features of modernity than to the careless mingling of guardian and trader cultures.

Jacobs' approach to the riddle of social causation, however, is of less importance than her elaboration of the point that "the great web is in a deplorable state." Of course, if she is right about the persistence of survival strategies, new guardian and trader cultures are probably already forming somewhere. But what rough beasts are slouching toward New York, Tokyo, and Brussels to be born?

CHAPTER 9 • Traders and Raiders

# Villages and Virtues

*This essay reviews two books about rural and village life that raise hard questions about how a vibrant democracy can be sustained through periods of profound social change: Richard Critchfield's* The Villagers: Changed Values, Altered Lives, the Closing of the Urban-Rural Gap *and Charles K. Fish's* In Good Hands: The Keeping of a Family Farm. *The essay appeared in the October 1995 issue of First Things.[1]*

SITTING IN THE BRITISH MUSEUM, amidst a great, grimy, bustling city, Karl Marx wrote that the bourgeoisie should be thanked for at least one accomplishment: rescuing a large part of the European population from "the idiocy of rural life." Over a century later, it is still open season for intellectuals on villagers and their values. In American universities, on the rare occasions when small towns are discussed at all, they are typically portrayed as hotbeds of intolerance, hypocrisy, and oppression.

Not even the New England town meeting can count on the benefit of the doubt. In a lecture on the tension between judicial review and democratic decisionmaking, Archibald Cox once innocently remarked that he would be vexed if the Supreme Court were to overturn an ordinance adopted in the open meeting of his town. That smacked of heresy to Cox's colleague Laurence Tribe who warned that to praise the town meeting form of government "ignores the danger of small-town oppression." Casual identification of small towns with oppression is not confined to the leftward range of the political spectrum. Charles Fried, Solicitor General under President Reagan, wrote in 1990: "What moves me is my attachment to human liberty, liberty of spirit, liberty from the crowd, and even from . . . the community (or, less charitably, the petty impositions of village tyrants)."

Caricatures of community by the knowledge class, of course, bear no closer relation to reality than rosy-hued postcard pastoral scenes. But such negative stereotypes play into the hands of those eager to entrust fundamental questions of how we should order our lives together to judges rather than

---

[1] Mary Ann Glendon, "Villages and Virtues," review of *The Villagers, Changed Values, Altered Lives, the Closing of the Urban-Rural Gap* by Richard Critchfield, and *In Good Hands: The Keeping of the Family Farm* by Charles K. Fish, *First Things* 56 (October 1995): 39–42.

to local self-determination and ordinary politics. The waters of opportunism have closed over the efforts of the civil rights movement of the 1950s and 1960s to open political processes to broader participation through education and voting. The rights revolution that took rise in the 1970s came not to strengthen politics, but to bury—or at least to bypass—it. Would-be oligarchs of the right and left seize any pretext to delegitimate the democratic elements in our republican experiment. In their book, the failures of local government in the segregated South provide an excuse for reading the Ninth and Tenth Amendments out of the Constitution.

Excellent antidotes to sentimental, as well as to disparaging, views of village life are two recent thick descriptions by Richard Critchfield and Charles Fish. Critchfield's portraits of eight peasant villages and Fish's story of a family farm in Vermont also prompt reflection on the question whether stable regimes of individual rights, complex economies, and modern welfare states can be sustained without the habits of cooperation and self-restraint that are nurtured in the world's communities of memory and mutual aid.

Critchfield, a journalist who died suddenly in December 1994, shortly after the publication of *The Villagers*, began to study and write about villages in the late 1960s, using the "participant-observer" method favored by many anthropologists. A village, as he defines it, is a settlement ranging from a few households to a few thousand inhabitants who subsist by farming or fishing. For over a quarter century, he lived for periods ranging from three months to more than a year in rural communities in many parts of the world, including India, Korea, Java, Kenya, Egypt, Mexico, and Poland. His early reports on these sojourns won him one of the first MacArthur "genius" awards. His legacy is a remarkable collection of stories and essays where the sights, sounds, and rhythms of village life are portrayed through the eyes of the men and women the author came to know over the years.

The importance of Critchfield's work is heightened by the fact that village life underwent a momentous historic transformation during the years he was visiting and revisiting his village friends. As late as the 1970s, about two-thirds of the world's population still lived in villages where modes of life and work had changed little since agriculture was invented. By the year 2000, for the first time in human history, a majority of the earth's inhabitants would be living in urban areas. The significance of that shift is rivaled only by humankind's transition from hunting and gathering into settled farming many thousands of years ago.

Critchfield's early works emphasized the continuities between village life today and ancient human settlements. One of his central theses was that villagers everywhere, across space and time, share something like a common culture—characterized by the habits, routines, and outlooks associated with agriculture; by respect for religion, family ties, and property; and by habits of subordinating self-interest to family and community solidarity.

Over the 1970s and 1980s, when Critchfield revisited villages where he had once lived, he was astonished to see how profoundly those continuities had been disrupted, and how rapidly those habits and attitudes had unravelled. Not only were rural folk flocking to cities, but technology had been transforming every detail of farm and family life. Along with the tractor, television had arrived, and so had the birth control pill and the IUD. The most radical change took place in ways of imagining reality. "Among the village people I knew personally, there was a marked difference: something had happened in their minds. They felt that the future would no longer simply repeat the past, as it had always done, but could be radically improved by all the new western technologies."

The excellence of Critchfield's last book, *The Villagers,* consists in his vivid depictions of people and communities caught up in the sweep of profound political, economic, and social movements: Polish villagers adjusting to the collapse of state socialism; a Mexican village losing many of its inhabitants through emigration to the United States; an Indian village that went from subsistence to commercial farming between 1965 and 1970; Muslim villages in Egypt and Java and Confucian villages in China and South Korea undergoing modernization.

When Critchfield attempted to assess the significance of what he had observed, however, he was at something of a loss. His generally fine writing falters as he tries to move from description to explanation. Resorting to assertion rather than analysis, he categorically announces that "rural life is the source, and the only source, of such aspects of our culture as religious beliefs, the agricultural moral code, the institutions of family and property, and the work ethic." That dubious premise leads him to predict that if the common culture of villages collapses, the rest of the world will suffer dire consequences, because "the way and view of life in villages like Ghungrali and Popowlany, so little changed from the day agriculture was invented ten, twelve thousand years ago until just the last twenty-five or thirty years, gave our unstable human society much of what stability it had."

Charles Fish does not attribute such culture-saving importance to country ways in his evocative memoir, *In Good Hands.* One reason is that he appreciates more fully than Critchfield what is gained, as well as what is lost, when the agricultural way of life disappears. *In Good Hands* is neither history nor reportage. It is to *The Villagers* as a painting is to a documentary film. From memory and empathetic imagination, plus a few family documents and his boyhood diary, Fish recreates the story of "The Farm" near Rutland, Vermont, where his mother was raised and his relatives have lived for six generations. A town boy who summered with his maternal kin, Fish had a certain emotional distance from the Farm and its ways, even at the age of eight. His book both interrogates and celebrates the tradition from which he sprang.

In the United States, from the very beginning, there was a closer relationship between farm villages and nearby towns than in the developing countries where Critchfield did most of his work. Most of our farmers were not isolated from town life, and our townspeople long remained on intimate terms with the countryside. Hard as it is to imagine today, nearly one-third of the American population was still engaged in farming on the eve of World War II. And, despite many earlier labor-saving improvements, it was only in the 1920s and 1930s that the farming way of life in this nation was radically transformed by technology.

Like Critchfield (and this reviewer), Fish was born in the 1930s "into the thinnest shadows of the vanishing era" of rural America. Critchfield's recollection of his native North Dakota could apply as well to the New England dairy country of Fish's Vermont, or of Granby, Massachusetts, where my great-uncle Lyman Gallup kept sixteen Jersey cows until the late 1950s. "There is just the faintest memory of village-like dirt roads, horse-drawn farm wagons, threshers pitching bundles by hand and small farms where cows were milked, pigs fed, bread baked, vegetables canned, and chickens ran about underfoot." By the 1940s, that world was already coming to an end. Agribusiness was just around the corner; the days of the family farm were numbered. Today, the proportion of Americans who live on farms is a mere 2 percent.

Charles Fish's relatives on his mother's side are among that dwindling band. Since 1836, when their "Founder," Henry Lester, moved to Rutland, members of the Lester clan have continuously worked and raised their families on the same 80 acres, converting from dairy farming to market gardening only in the 1960s. Critchfield would have recognized the Lesters as partakers of universal village culture. Their world, as portrayed by a wandering son, was one where childhood was not clearly separated from adulthood; where work, play, and moral education tended to blend and merge; where sexuality was regarded as a powerful, unsettling force that needed to be tamed by manners and marriage; where "manly and womanly characteristics were sharply distinct in some respects"; where the connection between a family and its land lent meaning and dignity to the humblest tasks; and where there was much to remind the farmer that nature was not under his control. Henry Lester, like Critchfield (and Thomas Jefferson), believed there was a special relation between farming and upright living. In an essay written in 1833, the Founder opined that agriculture, more than any other occupation, "tends to lead the mind to religion, morality, and virtue."

Fish's love for the Farm did not blind him to the shortcomings of the way of life under which it prospered, nor to the price it could exact from individuals. It struck him, in particular, that reason and spiritedness had to be kept in harness to the service of the Farm. Given free rein, those qualities, so essential to science and politics, could easily threaten the whole enterprise—by "changing the farmer into something else." Fish came to realize that the Farm cannot be home to people for whom the deepest satisfactions are in the search for knowledge. He came to admire men and women whose ambitions were devoted to larger and more public purposes: "[T]hey, too, plant, harvest, and preserve—[though] their efforts are more ambiguous and debatable."

In the end, Fish embraces an understanding of the Farm as an impressive example of humankind's brave and transient efforts to achieve order. He probably owes to the Farm his vivid apprehension of a truth that city cousins can easily forget: "[A]ll stability is an artful imposition of uncertain duration." In that light, "the farm, where peaceful people could live and work, was a remarkable achievement of wisdom and will, an island in the ebb and flow of history. . . . Measured against the common operations of our nature over time—lust, laziness, bloodshed, indifference—the higher forms of civil and domestic order are almost radiant."

Reflecting on the Farm and the fragility of order, Fish came to understand something else as well: That no way of life can endure without cultivating the qualities of character upon which it depends. Yet he concludes his gracefully written book with an image of religion in the scrapheap. On a recent visit to the Farm, Fish found in a storage barn, amidst the odds and ends of former times, a wooden signboard from the now-defunct community chapel where he had attended Bible school as a boy. This prompts his concluding reflections: "These things pass: the separate world, the divine mission. These endure: love, friendship, work, the land, a neighbor's helping hand. These lie in darkness: the fate of the republic, the shape of souls to come."

Though both Fish and Critchfield effectively rebut crude stereotypes by portraying country life in all its complexity, they both seem to accept an unduly simplistic attitude toward religion as an artifact that is passing away with the ways of life that supposedly gave rise to it. Critchfield, unlike most historical materialists, found that prospect alarming, because he viewed religion as useful to the maintenance of social stability. Fish, for his part, records the passing of the faith of his forbears with apparent equanimity. He tells the reader that the church bell no longer rings for him. "Choices are made. There is always a price."

Fish's portrait of the life and times of the Farm suggests, however, that what has passed away is merely a sort of religion that was sustained by little except habit and compatibility with a certain way of life. As Fish describes the religion of the Lesters, it endured without explicit theology, without ritual, and without durable institutions. The non-denominational chapel where Fish's grandmother took him in the summers was, like my mother's small-town Congregational church, "short on doctrine and ritual, long on biblical stories, devotion, morality, and good works." As Fish recognizes, no way of life that diverges significantly from the general drift of the greater society can survive without an articulated vision of itself and without institutions to sustain its vision through changing circumstances.

CHAPTER 10 • Villages and Virtues

In that connection, one of Critchfield's major contributions is to describe how the disintegration of an entire world of meaning—so unsettling for the men and women who experience it—has opened fertile ground for fundamentalism in the developing world. Closer to home, Fish's chronicle provides a glimpse into the process through which American liberal Protestantism has lost ground both to fundamentalism and secularism. For a religion to avoid those twin hazards in the turbulence of transition from one era to the next, it helps to possess an intellectual tradition to articulate and reflect on religious teachings, as well as durable institutions to make those teachings fresh for each new generation.

The human sciences and institutional frameworks, though, are the creations of city dwellers. It is no accident that "cities" and "civilization" have the same root. Thus Critchfield had it exactly backward: Stability, in the sense of capacity to maintain coherence and identity over time, depends heavily on urban human achievements. He was prevented from seeing this by the same bias that led him to suppose that religion is born with and dies with rural life. Like many intellectuals, Critchfield simply supposed that religious faith is incompatible with a vigorous intellectual life.

Critchfield was right, though, to be worried about the condition of the world's seedbeds of character and competence, even if he was mistaken in locating them exclusively in rural settings. The political, scientific, economic, and social goods that Americans and many others have come to cherish depend, today more than ever, on certain qualities that once were reliably cultivated in the polis (ideally around 5,000 citizens according to Plato) and in urban neighborhoods, as well as in villages. It is hard to imagine how a regime favorable to individual liberty, the work ethic, security of transactions, equal opportunity, and relief of misery can be sustained without a goodly supply of citizens who are prepared to restrain their own appetites, plan for the future, render community service, provide for themselves and their dependents, and reach out to the needy.

In the United States, we have traditionally left it primarily up to families, schools, religious groups, workplace associations, and local communities, to teach and transmit republican virtues and the skills of self-government from one generation to the next. Deprived of continuity by the mobility of our population, and of their mainstays by women's massive entry into the paid labor force, all of those mediating structures are in disarray. As for local governments, these little "schools for citizenship" as Tocqueville called them, have become ghosts of their former selves, with their powers siphoned off to distant capitals. The storied New England town meeting has been reduced, in Fish's words, to a place where "selectmen and school directors are fighting over the remnants of a vanishing domain, for much of what they do is to administer the increasingly detailed agendas of the state and federal governments."

This is hardly the moment, therefore, to lightly dismiss the small building blocks of civil society as intolerant, hypocritical, and oppressive. As one who has lived in a small town, a large city, and a suburb, my own experiences lead me to agree with Michael Sandel that "intolerance flourishes most where forms of life are dislocated, roots unsettled, traditions undone." A certain degree of "hypocrisy" may be the price that must paid for a strong system of moral teachings that are difficult to live up to. As for oppression, let it be noted that those who label communities oppressive are often quite ready to permit distant apparatchiks to dictate the conditions under which we live and work. Oppression, to many who came of age in the sixties, is just another name for authority.

The generation that collapsed the distinction between authority and authoritarianism is now struggling to raise its children in a society where the former is collapsing and the latter is gaining ground. To save their children, they must save the culture. That will require these busy people to find time for intelligent and active involvement in the activities and institutions through which we order our lives together. As Fish says, "These lie in darkness: the fate of the republic and the shape of souls to come."

CHAPTER 10 • Villages and Virtues

# Cities and Civil Society

*The years I spent in Chicago from 1957 to 1968 as a student,*
*newspaper reporter, and lawyer gave me a special interest in Alan Ehrenhalt's*
*The Lost City: The Forgotten Virtues of Community in America.*
*This review appeared in the November 1995 issue of First Things.* [1]

Y̶OU HAVE TO GIVE Alan Ehrenhalt, the editor of *Governing* magazine, credit for a lot of nerve. It is one thing to take on the job of sympathetically interpreting the 1950s, but *Chicago* of the 1950s? *Virtue* in the stormy, husky, brawling city of big shoulders and big payoffs? Come to think of it, Basic Books is pretty adventurous, too. Many a publisher might have passed on a book extolling the virtues of urban life under the reign of Richard the First (Daley, of course). There just aren't that many potential readers like Andrew Greeley, who once told an interviewer he imagined heaven as being something like Chicago in the time of "The Mayor."

To avoid misunderstanding, I must make clear that *The Lost City* does not portray the fifties as a golden age. But it does provide a wholesome corrective to accounts that dwell exclusively on the defects of that decade, with its lack of opportunities for women and minorities, and its cult of bourgeois domesticity. Ehrenhalt wisely observes:

> In drawing up our balance sheet for 1950s America, assessing the values and the costs, we do need to examine the holes in its assumptions of contentment. But that the contentment was real—and widespread—is a truth that needs to be remembered as well. . . . It does a disservice for the historian and the critic to mock the comforts of ordinary people.

Social critics have devoted much energy to exposing the ways in which elements of the fifties ethos may have fostered future adolescent rebellion. What they have overlooked, Ehrenhalt claims, were "the small but hard-won satisfactions of grownups who were grateful for a modicum of physical comfort after

---

[1] Mary Ann Glendon, "Lost in the Fifties," review of *The Lost City: The Forgotten Virtues of Community in America* by Alan Ehrenhalt, *First Things* 57 (November 1995): 46–49.

two rough decades." He seems right on the mark in his analysis of what the fifties meant to the generation that struggled through the Depression and survived World War II. For them, the period was one "when life as it was seemed so much better than life as it might have been."

Though Ehrenhalt greatly adds to the understanding of a much-maligned city and decade, that is not his main aim. His voyage in time was undertaken primarily in quest of political knowledge. He returned to the fifties in search of insight regarding some urgent contemporary questions about how human beings order their lives together: What conditions are necessary in order to have such minimum elements of dignified living as safe streets, classrooms conducive to learning, and a reasonable degree of social stability? How are social cohesion (community) and legitimate leadership (authority) gained and lost?

Since Aristotle, those who ponder such questions have often looked to the past, or to the experience of other cities and states, for clues to what works, what fails, and what side-effects are associated with this or that arrangement. History and comparison are the laboratories of the social scientist. Faulty as that equipment is, we haven't got much else. Ehrenhalt, in that tradition, takes as his theater of observation three communities in the Chicago area as they were forty years ago and as they are today. The result is a deeply challenging work of social criticism that, with the help of well-chosen photographs, vividly evokes a time and place.

If you have ever entered Chicago at Midway Airport, chances are your taxi took you through the first of these neighborhoods—St. Nicholas of Tolentine Parish. St. Nick's lies in the "bungalow belt" on Chicago's Southwest Side, a vast expanse of low, solid, bay-windowed brick dwellings in shades of beige and ochre. In the 1950s, these were the dream houses of a diverse mixture of working-class Bohemian, German, Irish, Italian, Lithuanian, Polish, and Slovak families. Outwardly, the bungalows look much the same today as they did forty years ago, even to the ornamental lamps and plants in their front windows. What has vanished is the neighborhood-centered life that once buzzed around them—the shops where merchants and customers knew one another; the comings and goings between adjacent back yards; the activity in the streets that was "monitored during all the waking hours of the day by the informal law enforcement system of the neighborhood, the at-home mothers." The mothers had an important ally in watchful Monsignor Fennessy, who, for decades, "walked the neighborhood day and night, . . . greet[ing] people on their front stoops, and hand[ing] out dimes to children." St. Nick's Church itself was mother to a host of associations and activities for men, women, and children. Its pre-Vatican II liturgy was richly ceremonial; its masses well-attended; its parish school staffed with a full complement of nuns.

As it happens, I knew that neighborhood well. During the academic year 1956–57, I was a part-time reporter for its gung-ho weekly paper, the

*Southwest News-Herald.* Five days a week, after classes at the University of Chicago, I took the bus to 59th and Kedzie, journeying, as through a space warp, from the Great Books to the great bake-offs. I spent many hours covering events in neighborhood churches, gymnasiums, and schools; recording the births, weddings, achievements, mishaps, and deaths of Southwest-siders. Across the street from the *News-Herald* was a union hall where the Mayor himself would sometimes make a brief appearance, flanked by burly men in Robert Hall suits. The engines that kept that way of life humming were the churches, the unions, the locally owned businesses, and the unpaid labor of women. So far as I can see, there is not a single false note in Ehrenhalt's re-creation of that place and time.

Today, the Southwest Side is a shell of its former self—with few stay-at-home parents, most of its local businesses bought up by distant corporations, and not one nun left in St. Nick's struggling parish school. Plant closings took their toll on the economic life of the community; divorce took its toll on families; and women's increased labor force participation deprived the schools and churches not only of volunteers, but of interested close observers of their missions. Community seems to have evaporated. As for authority, Ehrenhalt writes, "Outside the province of the individual family, there are no noticeable figures of authority at all."

Eastward of St. Nick's, and centered on 47th and South Park Way, was the neighborhood once called Bronzeville. In the fifties, it was the heart of Chicago's South-Side ghetto, where most of the city's African-American population was crowded and kept in by de facto segregation. Ehrenhalt does not gloss over the conditions of squalor and limited opportunity that prevailed there. The fact that it was so difficult for blacks to move to other parts of the city, however, meant that middle-class people, "church ladies," stable families, and skilled and white-collar workers remained in the population mix. Bronzeville was the diverse, vibrant, suffering, struggling world whose pains and joys were portrayed by Lorraine Hansberry in her 1959 Broadway play, *A Raisin in the Sun.* In Ehrenhalt's book, as in that memorable play, Bronzeville of former times is presented as a place where, "however difficult the present might be, the future was worth thinking about and planning for in some detail."

The churches were Bronzeville's "most uniformly successful and self-reliant social institutions." Besides five churches with a seating capacity of two thousand or more, and two with over ten thousand members on their rolls, there were dozens of little store-fronts. The larger churches fostered elaborate networks of social groups and activities, and their ministers were the community's preeminent leaders. The leading clergymen, because they were beholden to no outside interests, were even more respected than the businessmen, the editor of the *Defender,* and William Dawson, the machine boss. Says Ehrenhalt, "They were the indispensable coordinators of the community."

Today, the physical structures of the Bronzeville neighborhood no longer exist. Most of its buildings were leveled—so that some of the country's worst public housing could be erected on the sites of what had been some of its worst slums. Like many other American cities, Chicago learned the hard way that bulldozed communities could not simply be "renewed." But even if urban renewal had not taken its toll, other social forces were irrevocably transforming the ghetto. For, as opportunities for better jobs and housing opened up, the black middle class moved away. Hardly anything now remains of the community whose "uniqueness depended on the presence of people from all classes with all sorts of values" living and working side by side. Only the churches survive in anything close to recognizable form, "struggling hero-ically against the social disorganization that is all around them." But, without the middle-class families and other community pillars, the churches have lost much of their authority. Their songs still ring out on Sunday, but their teach-ing voices have become fainter.

On the western outskirts of Chicago stands Elmhurst, the third and last stop in Ehrenhalt's quest. In the 1950s, many white middle-class families succumbed to the allure of the new, affordable homes that were sprouting in pastel profusion in places like Elmhurst. Returning veterans, salesmen, engi-neers, office managers—many of them the first in their families to attend college or have white-collar jobs—liked the idea of raising their children outside the city. They and their wives were attracted by the light, airy open spaces built into the modern split-level and ranch-style construction. As Ehrenhalt puts it, they moved "into houses and lives that seemed, even to them, almost too good to be true."

With hindsight, however, the dreams of those hopeful, mobile men and women of the fifties were constructed on exceptionally shaky foundations. The new arrivals, having left their roots and extended families behind, naively believed "that community was something they could simply recreate in the place they were moving to." *The Lost City* recounts the frenetic efforts they made to jumpstart social life and to foster neighborliness among people who happened to have bought houses next-door to one another. One group banded together to form a church that, like Baby Bear's bed, was not too hard, not too soft, but just right for the lifestyles suburbanites were in the process of inventing. The new church was long on social life, short on doc-trine, and for a while it flourished.

Community, however, is as hard to create as it is to renew. The newcom-ers to Elmhurst had no shared memories. Indeed, their chief common char-acteristic was being a newcomer. In the beginning, they were aided by the presence in their midst of many men who had served in World War II. That experience made the veterans "almost a fraternal group," and gave them "con-fidence and authority as community leaders." But, as the country is now dis-covering, that kind of authority expires with the generation that earned it.

Today, Elmhurst's busy two-job families have little time to nurture the structures and institutions of community. The church that figured so importantly in their lives forty years ago has suffered a massive membership decline.

As for authority in the family and the schools, Ehrenhalt makes a convincing case that it was already on the wane in the middle-class enclaves of the 1950s. Popular magazines like *McCall's* and *Parents* were exhorting fathers to be friends and companions to their kids, not just distant breadwinners. Parents' lives revolved around children to an unprecedented degree. The ideal of "family togetherness" was symbolized by the architecture of the new homes with their large living rooms. Fathers still imposed rules and exercised discipline, but, Ehrenhalt observes, "they were beginning to doubt their own legitimacy in doing it, and they betrayed those doubts, and that made their efforts at authority seem all the more arbitrary and capricious." In that light, the generation that came of age in the 1960s was not rebelling against domestic tyranny (as they claimed), so much as exploiting the vulnerability of a soft regime. Their parents undermined their own governments with good intentions.

Ehrenhalt's analysis of authority in the schools is similar. The Elmhurst teachers he interviewed remember feeling that their authority over what they saw as pampered kids was precarious. Former students, for their part, recall the school atmosphere as intimidating. No contradiction, says Ehrenhalt. Insecurity will often cause a teacher, or a parent, to step up the volume. Today, he reports, the high school has abandoned the discipline that its students once resented, but it has also abandoned the belief in character-building that once gave educators their sense of purpose. Teachers, like many other authority figures, "not only have lost the ability to enforce standards of conduct, but any clear sense of what standards to enforce."

Even the yellow, pink, and aqua dream houses had a drawback. They were small structures whose vaunted living spaces were achieved at the price of cramped, thin-walled bedrooms. Suburban babyboomers thus had little privacy at home, were crowded together in schools, yet were treated as "special" by their earnest parents. Ehrenhalt sees in that state of affairs some of the "roots of hyper-individualism in the age that followed."What does Ehrenhalt make of all this? His conclusions, like his descriptions, deserve to be read and pondered carefully. In brief, the main lesson he draws from his visits to St. Nick's, Bronzeville, and Elmhurst is this: In the moral, as in the economic, realm, there is no free lunch. The gains of the past forty years have been real, in terms of personal freedom, choice, and job opportunities, especially for women and minorities. But the losses have been real, too. In developing this theme, Ehrenhalt makes an important contribution to the understanding, not only of the fifties, but of the conditions for community and authority. He recognizes that many readers will balk at his emphasis on the importance of "authority"—a word that to his generation (he was born in 1947) has sinister connotations of arbitrariness and oppression. Nevertheless, he insists, "there is no easy way to have an orderly world without somebody making the rules by which order is preserved. Every dream we have about recreating community in the absence of authority will turn out to be a pipe dream in the end."

A major reason authority is currently such a bad odor, of course, is that the distinction between authority and authoritarianism was lost in the sixties. Since many readers will not appreciate that distinction, and because authority is such a key concept for Ehrenhalt, I wish he had devoted some attention to the question of how power earns and maintains its claim to acceptance and legitimacy. On the other hand, the strength of the book is in its finely drawn observations. The author was probably wise in his decision to keep explicit theorizing to a minimum.

*The Lost City* does, moreover, make a significant contribution to the understanding of one of the most perplexing problems of contemporary political theory: Can liberal democratic experiments sustain a shared culture that will restrain human appetites without using oppressive force? His answer, though he does not put it quite this way, is affirmative—provided that liberalism does not attempt to transform every institution of civil society in its own image. As he sees it, the adults of the 1950s—a critical mass of them—lived by an implicit bargain by whose terms lasting relationships were given priority over unfettered personal freedom and choice. "People stayed married to their spouses, to their political machines, to their baseball teams. Corporations also stayed married—to the communities they grew up with." That bargain gave us "communities that were, for the most part, familiar and secure; stable jobs and relationships whose survival we did not need to worry about in bed at night; rules that we could live by, or, when we were old enough, rebel against; and people known as leaders who were trusted with the task of seeing that the rules were enforced."

The price of that bargain was substantial: "a whole network of restrictions on our ability to do whatever we liked." But in repudiating the deal, we sacrificed many things that Americans still rightly regard as essential to the good life. We need to realize, he writes, that "privacy, individualism, and choice are not free goods and that the society that places no restrictions on them will pay a high price for that decision."

Ehrenhalt neither wishes, nor believes it is possible, to restore the families, neighborhoods, patterns of work and investment, schools, politics, and religion of a former time. The key question for him is whether we can "rebuild some anchors of stability" to help us through times of turbulence. Can we, he asks, "develop a majority culture strong enough to tell its children there are inappropriate ways to behave in a high school corridor? Is there a way to relearn the simple truth that there is sin in the world, and that part of our job in life is to resist its temptations?" To do so would require us to correct for the excesses of "a generation determined to keep permissiveness and unfettered self-expression at the top of its list of values—long after they ha[ve] turned into corrosive forces for the society as a whole."

That is a tall order, but Ehrenhalt is cautiously sanguine about the answers to the questions he poses. He draws comfort from two other historical moments when community and authority were in crisis. The 1920s, he points out, were characterized by a vivid sense of lost community and authority, yet were followed by the extraordinary social cohesion and common effort of the Depression and war years. An even more interesting case, he argues, is England in the 1820s, a time of notorious disrespect for authority, with manners and beliefs profoundly unsettled by revolutionary ideas from France. Who could have foreseen, he asks, the Victorian era of reform and the revitalization of religion that followed?

But as Ehrenhalt surely knows, English and American civil society in the nineteenth and early twentieth centuries was thick with the sorts of communities of memory and mutual aid whose present decline he has so well documented. The social networks that sustained earlier generations are now hanging in shreds. The fact is that our current situation is historically unprecedented in ways that make it fanciful to look for a swing of the historical pendulum to restore conditions of orderly, dignified living. No solution is on the horizon, to take the most troubling example, for the socialization of what is very likely a critical mass of children, rich and poor alike, being raised in transient neighborhoods, with little parental supervision, in broken and reconstituted families where no arrangements or commitments seem permanent or reliable.

Ehrenhalt thus seems to be resisting his own data when he pins his hopes on "what the next generation grows up believing—the generation being raised by the creators of the deluge." The generation now coming of age faces a future in which their prospects—as a group—are worse than those of their parents and grandparents. Ehrenhalt insists that to dismiss the idea that they will restore community and authority is to show "too little respect for the natural desire of any generation to correct the errors and excesses of the generation before." Desire, however, is one thing, ability another. And if the generation that has known so little order should move, as Ehrenhalt hopes, to reimpose it, there is another question to be asked. What sort of authority will they be able to imagine?

CHAPTER 11 • Cities and Civil Society

# Suburbs and the
# Seedbeds of Democracy

*Long an admirer of Christopher Lasch, I felt a great sense of loss
when his unique voice was stilled by death in 1994. This review
of his posthumous* Women and the Common Life: Love, Marriage,
and Feminism *appeared in the February 1997 issue of First Things.*[1]

HISTORIAN AND CULTURAL CRITIC Christopher Lasch occupied a peculiar niche in contemporary social thought. His books, especially *Haven in a Heartless World* and *The Culture of Narcissism*, were widely reviewed, yet his name is better-known than his ideas. (Lasch could only shake his head with bemusement when *Haven in a Heartless World*, with its heavily ironic title, was repeatedly labeled a sentimental tract on the family.) Fellow scholars cited him often, but few actually grappled with his challenges to their reigning paradigms. Except for a brief stint advising President Jimmy Carter, Lasch was never taken into the corridors of power. His critique of the nanny state made him useless to the liberal left; his jeremiads on consumer capitalism alienated the economic right; and his tirades against "elites" made him persona non grata to much of the knowledge class.

Unforgivably in the eyes of these latter, he was an unapologetic defender of the lower middle-class moral traditions from which many knowledge workers of his generation had emerged and escaped. To make matters worse, he was a leading champion of the good sense of the citizenry as against the nostrums of bureaucrats and so-called experts.

In 1993 and 1994, while battling the cancer that claimed his life at the age of sixty-one, Lasch completed both *The Revolt of the Elites and the Betrayal of Democracy*, and, with the help of his daughter, this collection of essays on women, love, the family, and feminism. Elisabeth Lasch-Quinn writes in her introduction that her father regarded these essays (all but one previously published) as steps in a longstanding search for connections

---

[1] Mary Ann Glendon, "Women and the Common Life: Love, Marriage, and Feminism," review of *Women and the Common Life: Love, Marriage, and Feminism* by Christopher Lasch and Elisabeth Lasch-Quinn, *First Things* 70 (February 1997): 40–43.

between feminism and the modern ideals of intimacy and domesticity. Their chief value, however, may well lie in the way Lasch relates women's history to his lifelong concern with the conditions for democratic self-government.

Long before women's studies became a field unto itself, Lasch was writing about women's roles in history. Like Fernand Braudel and others who ventured into the long-neglected territory of the history of ordinary life, Lasch pioneered in connecting the history of everyday things to larger economic developments. But his own work was distinguished by a passionate interest in the lives of women and the firm conviction that neither cultural history nor women's history can be understood apart from one another. At a time when leading historians of the family were concentrating on the English and French aristocracy, Lasch focused on marriage and family life among ordinary Americans. His historical vantage point yielded fruitful insights into contemporary American life which he presented in a highly readable series of books, articles, and review essays for *The New York Review of Books*.

The overarching concept that, for Lasch, links changes in women's roles and the family to the cultural history of the West in general is the rationalization of everyday life. Lasch-Quinn summarizes his thesis succinctly:

> Much of modern life . . . rests on the assumption that all realms of activity should come under intense scrutiny, that science and rationality can best lead to an understanding of human experience, and that only trained experts can direct the conduct of daily existence. The reordering of life according to such principles of rationalization resulted from the tendency of corporate capitalism and the modern liberal state to expand their power, which they accomplished by means of a bureaucratic structure and paternalistic ethos. The service professions, acting on behalf of the state, intruded into the private domain, helping to replace habit and custom with esoteric techniques for addressing everyday problems, causing a situation of dependence on elites that is antithetical to democracy.

There, in a nutshell, is the line of thinking that made Lasch such a blister to many liberals and conservatives: his condemnation of corporate and governmental power grabs; his attachment to a robust vision of democratic citizenship; and his conviction that the social work establishment, educators, therapists, and other semi-skilled technocrats had undermined the competence of the middle class, while subjecting the poor to "new controls sincerely disguised as benevolence."

Also central to Lasch's thought, and to these essays, is the belief that a vibrant civil society (the "common life" of his title) is both a prerequisite for, and a goal of, democracy. In the centerpiece of the collection, "The Sexual Division of Labor, the Decline of Civic Culture, and the Rise of the Suburbs," Lasch postulates that changes in women's roles were importantly linked to the decline of communities of memory and mutual aid.

The essay begins by challenging a standard historical narrative according to which industrialization forced middle-class women into the role of full-time housewives, a prison from which they were freed only by the glorious revolution of the 1960s. In reality, Lasch claims, the misnamed "traditional" household, where the wife is a full-time homemaker, is of much more recent date. It was "a mid-twentieth century innovation," appearing on a broad scale only in connection with the rapid growth of suburbs after World War II.

Lasch supports his contention with evidence that the period from 1890 to 1920 was a time of intense participation by middle-class women in civic life. Homemakers and single women alike devoted much of their time and energies to charitable activities, religious groups, and reform movements, from the township and village level to the state and national arenas. So why did the myth take hold that most women were isolated in the home once their husbands became wage earners? Lasch plausibly speculates that many historians overlooked "women's contribution to an intermediate realm of civic culture that belongs neither to the family nor the market" because of a mindset in which the only work that counts is work for pay.

The era of middle-class women's busy and important civic service, however, wound down as domestic helpers grew scarce, and as professional social workers and administrators took over many of the activities that had previously been controlled by unpaid volunteers.

It is Lasch's contention that when one takes all this civic activity into account, and adds the wage work of lower-class women, one has to move the appearance of full-time homemaking on a broad scale from the late nineteenth century to the post-World War II period. To my mind, however, Lasch's emphasis on community service underrates the importance of the earlier shift from the interdependent family farm or shop to the wage-earner's household where women and children became much more dependent economically on the husband-father than he was on them. That momentous transition had at least as much influence on the dynamics of family life and the shape of twentieth-century feminism as the later move to the suburbs. Lasch is certainly correct, though, that the homemaker–breadwinner household was far from being "traditional." Its rise to predominance was historically unprecedented.

Lasch is also right to emphasize that women's roles did change significantly with the exodus to the suburbs in the 1940s and 1950s. The small, child-raising family became more inward-turning, and the bonds between husband and wife and parent and child were forced to bear more emotional weight. Moreover, when upwardly mobile men and women shook the dust of villages and urban neighborhoods from their feet, they left behind the civic cultures that had flourished in such places, along with the old informal, support systems among relatives and neighbors that everyone had taken for granted. The homemaker was far more on her own in the domestic sphere than she had ever been—and far more dependent on her husband.

**CHAPTER 12** • Suburbs and the Seedbeds of Democracy

Of course, as Lasch points out, that very "privacy" was part of the appeal of the suburb. Along with advice comes nosiness; material and emotional support from neighbors and relatives entails expectations of reciprocity. The suburb offered an escape from external obligations, interference, and constraints:

> [Suburbs] were designed to exclude everything not subject to choice—the job, the extended family, the enforced sociability of the city streets. Americans hoped to put all that behind them when they headed for the seclusion of the suburbs, where they were accountable it seemed to no one.

Ironically, just when women found themselves with unprecedented amounts of time for, and control over, the internal affairs of the household, they began to feel less competent in child-raising and other tasks which their predecessors from the beginning of time had handled with aplomb. The shortage of informal sources of advice and support made itself felt. Barely having emerged from older forms of subordination, middle-class women thus fell into "a new kind of dependence, the dependence of the consumer on the market, and on the providers of expert services, not only for the satisfaction of their needs but for the very definition of their needs." In this way, Lasch connects women's history to the erosion of the conditions for democratic self-government.

Lasch finds support in Betty Friedan's *The Feminine Mystique* (1963) for his contention that the loss of common life, and the decline in women's civic roles, fueled the frustration that gave rise to the feminism of the 1960s. Friedan's book was, he points out, chiefly addressed to concerns of educated suburban women. The feminism of such women, he argues, was bedeviled from the start by their dependence on "experts"—doctors, counselors, educators, child-raising specialists.

Respecting women too much to see them as passively carried along on the wave of events, Lasch insists that women themselves bear a share of the responsibility for the replacement of patriarchal authority with new forms of social discipline. While homemakers were ceding power in their own domains to experts, the feminist revolution, he charges, was "hijacked by new economic and social elites."

This is consistent with Elizabeth Fox-Genovese's account of how official feminism bought into the same disrespect for unpaid work that Lasch criticizes in family historians. The feminist movement's chief prescription for women's emancipation was market work. Official feminism embraced a male model for advancement in which family responsibilities were subordinated to the demands of the world of work. As Betty Friedan concedes in the June 3, 1996, *New Yorker* magazine, feminists thus distanced themselves from the concerns of the great majority of women who were and are trying to juggle work and family life under difficult circumstances.

What Lasch adds to this picture is that married women's large-scale entry into the workplace coincided with the shift to an economy that "depended on work that had no other object than to keep people at work and thus to sustain the national capacity to consume which in turn sustained production, which sustained . . . an approximation of full employment—all without reference to the intrinsic quality of the goods and services produced or the intrinsic satisfaction of the work that went into them."

Regarding the view that religion perpetuates false consciousness, male domination and female dependency, Lasch observes:

> [Religion] is a challenge to self-pity and despair, temptations common to all of us, but especially to those born into the wrong social class. . . . Submission to God makes people less submissive in everyday life. It makes them less fearful but also less bitter and resentful, less inclined to make excuses for themselves. Modern social movements, on the other hand, tend to rely on resentment. . . . They distrust any understanding that would seem to "blame the victim." In this way they discourage the assumption of personal responsibility.

Unlike more timid male academics, Lasch does not hesitate to offer his thoughts concerning a better approach to women's issues. A feminism "worthy of the name," he says, would seek to remodel the workplace around the needs of the family, rather than acquiesce in the opposite situation; it would cease disparaging unpaid work; and, above all, it would "insist that people need self-respecting, honorable callings."

This concern with the human need for decent, useful work is a recurrent theme in Lasch's later writings. In some respects, his thoughts are reminiscent of Freud's apostrophe to work in *Civilization and its Discontents*. Like Freud, Lasch seems to write from the very core of his being on this subject. "The only escape from the polarity of egoism and altruism," he says, "lies in the selflessness experienced by those who lose themselves in their work, in the effort to master a craft or a body of knowledge, or in the acceptance of a formidable challenge that calls on all their resources." Lasch describes those fortunate enough to have such work as "blissfully self-forgetful."

But while Freud regarded such satisfactions as beyond the scope and ken of mere common folk, Lasch railed against a social order where opportunities for useful work are widely unavailable. His writing on this subject has many affinities in substance, though not in tone, with the social encyclicals of John Paul II who consistently insists on the importance of the non-economic aspects of work, the dignity of unpaid labor, and the priority of human over economic values.

From glimpses provided in his daughter's introduction, it seems that Lasch himself found "blissful self-forgetfulness" in his work up to the very end of his life. Lasch-Quinn writes:

CHAPTER 12 • Suburbs and the Seedbeds of Democracy

[I]ncreasingly we worked every possible hour of the day, my father making an adjusted routine according to each stage of his illness. The sweatshop's compulsion, though, was absent. Instead there was the strangest exhilaration. This was confusing; we seemed to be so content, even joyful at times, yet my father was dying.

Somehow, between frightening medical emergencies and worries, my parents created a space of peace and calm. That living room became for me a haven. . . . Sometimes it seemed almost sacred.

Lasch may not have been a prophet in his own land, but he seems to have been happier than prophets of antiquity. He was blessed with a joyous family life, a deeply satisfying vocation, and a sober sense of hope that he always carefully distinguished from optimism.

These essays are among the best contemporary writing in their field, not only because their author was a fine historian, but because he was a man who loved women. He loved them enough to cherish the details of their everyday lives, to listen to their voices past and present, and to believe that they themselves can shift the probabilities toward a different and better future.

# Feminism and the Family

*In October 1996, the year after I represented the Holy See at the U.N.'s Beijing Women's Conference, I was invited to give a talk at a fund-raiser for a pregnancy support group in Western Massachusetts where I grew up. It was a special joy for me that my sixth-grade teacher, Mary Flynn, was in the audience. Miss Flynn was a great, selfless educator who introduced generations of Berkshire County kids to the intellectual and artistic treasures of Western civilization. An abridged version of this talk was published in the February 14, 1997 issue of* Commonweal.

I AM HONORED TO BE HERE on behalf of Berkshire County Pregnancy Support Services. When I look at the people who organized this event, I can't help regretting that the media so seldom lets us see this kind, loving face of the pro-life movement. Day in and day out, they offer a helping hand to women facing what is often the worst crisis of their lives. They show in a practical, concrete way how being pro-life means being pro-woman and pro-child.

Berkshire County is an especially appropriate place to think about women's issues, because, as we all know, one of the best-known figures of nineteenth-century feminism, Susan B. Anthony, was a Berkshire native, born in Adams. Another pioneering feminist, Elizabeth Cady Stanton, grew up not far away from here in Johnstown, New York.

My remarks today will be under four headings. First, I am going say a few words about the Beijing conference, to show why so many women were alienated by the approach to women's issues that was dominant there. Then I want to turn to some of the problems that were not adequately addressed at Beijing, particularly the problems of juggling work and family responsibilities. Third, I am going to suggest that today's women's issues are, in an important sense, everybody's issues. Finally, I will offer some observations about how we might begin to regain some control over the conditions under which we live, work, and raise our children.

As news reports indicated, there were actually two women's conferences in China in September 1995: the official U.N. conference where delegates and negotiators from 181 member states produced the final version of the document known as the Beijing Program of Action, and a larger, more colorful, unofficial conference held several miles away. This second conference was a parallel meeting sponsored by non-governmental organizations (NGOs). The official conference was attended by 5,000 persons; the NGO conference was attended by 30,000.

The word "conference" in both cases is somewhat misleading. U.N. conferences would be more accurately described as dispersed negotiating sessions. Their main aim is to put the final touches on a document that has been circulating for years in draft form. To do this, the delegates split up into groups to go over different sections of the document, paragraph by paragraph, trying to reach consensus on the final text that will be submitted for approval when the whole group comes together on the last day. As for the NGO conference with its 30,000 participants, you wouldn't go far wrong if you translated "conference" in that setting as "lobbyists' headquarters" and "NGO" as "special interest group."

Like most U.N. conference documents, the Beijing document that emerged after two weeks of negotiations was a set of non-binding guidelines for future action. This one set a U.N. record for length at 125 pages, single-spaced. The document contains many very fine proposals regarding women's access to education and employment, and the feminization of poverty. But it is marred by two serious defects.

The first is that the best parts of the Beijing program—especially the ones I just mentioned—are the most likely to remain dead letters because they require funding. If there was anything that united the rich countries at Beijing it was was their successful fight to keep out any language that would commit them in any way to back up their promises with material resources.

The second defect also involves something that was left out. It is nothing short of amazing, in a world where over eight out of ten women have children, that a 125-page program of action produced at a women's conference barely mentions marriage, motherhood, or family life!

The reaction of most women to this document, I suspect, would be similar to that of a young Nigerian law student who wrote me recently. She couldn't afford to go to the conference, but she tried to follow it closely from afar. She was disappointed, she said, that the conference had paid so little attention to the problems that the majority of the world's women struggle with on a daily basis. She was surprised, for example, that the section on women's health was focused almost entirely on women's reproductive systems. She wondered why it didn't address the health of the whole woman, particularly the problems of poor nutrition, sanitation, and tropical disease that have a disproportionate impact on women. (Keep in mind that women and girls compose 70 percent of the world's poverty population.)

Even the treatment of reproductive health in the document is strange, since it focuses almost entirely on birth control and abortion, as though reproductive health did not include pregnancy and childbirth.

How are these omissions to be explained? For the answer, one has only to look at the original draft document prepared by the U.N. Committee on the Status of Women. In the few places where the drafting committee mentioned marriage, motherhood, or family life, these aspects of women's lives were described in a negative way—as sources of oppression, or as obstacles to women's progress. In other words, what we had to work with in Beijing was a document whose defects corresponded rather closely to the defects of old-line 1970s feminism. A negative attitude toward men and marriage and the same lack of attention to the problems of women who are mothers were starkly evident.

The conference document is not legally binding. It is in the form of "international standards" against which U.N. member states are supposed to measure their conduct. So why all the fuss and lobbying about a set of non-binding guidelines?

The main reason is this: Government agencies and private foundations tend to use these U.N. documents (I should say, selected parts of these documents) to justify the way they run their foreign and domestic programs. That means that when they announce policies and set conditions, they don't have to invoke the modern version of the golden rule ("We've got the gold, so we make the rules"). It sounds so much better to say: "We follow guidelines established by international consensus." But the bottom line is that millions of people's lives are affected by a kind of rulemaking as far removed as possible from public scrutiny and democratic participation.

That fact makes these U.N. conferences magnets for all sorts of special interest groups, especially those who want to do an end run around ordinary political processes. It is tempting for them to try to plant their agendas in a long, unreadable document, behind closed doors at a conference held in some faraway place. (When I say closed doors, I mean that literally. All the negotiating sessions in Beijing were closed to the public and the press.)

The Beijing conference offers two main lessons for those of us who are concerned with women's issues. First, beware of policies manufactured far away from public scrutiny, and without input from the people most concerned. (That point hardly needs mention here in the Berkshires. Here in Western Massachusetts we know what it is like to have our hash settled by distant legislators in Boston and Washington.)

Second, it is increasingly obvious that old-line feminist ideology has little to offer where today's issues are concerned. Beijing was sort of like a Woodstock reunion. It showed that the handwriting is on the wall for the peculiar form of feminism that held sway in the 1960s and 1970s. And the message on the wall is the same that was written there in the Book of Daniel: "You have been weighed in the balance and found wanting."

That point was reinforced for me by the conversations I had with my students when I returned from Beijing. The very first question the women

CHAPTER 13 • Feminism and the Family

law students asked was one that had never occurred to me. It was: "What was the average age of the women at the conference?" Looking back, I realized that there was almost no one there under 40. Most were in their late 40s, 50s, or 60s. Many, like Bella Abzug and Betty Friedan, were older.

The attitudes of my women students toward legendary figures like Abzug and Friedan are similar to the way my generation thought about Susan B. Anthony and the suffragettes. We admired them for securing the vote for women, but we didn't identify with them. To us they seemed quaint, and a bit strange. Similarly, my students seem grateful to the second-wave women's movement for the educational and employment opportunities they now enjoy, but they are ready to move on to new frontiers. In opinion polls in the 1990s, when women are asked the question, "Do you consider yourself a feminist?" two-thirds of American women answer no. What is even more striking is the response of younger women. Among college women in their twenties, four out of five say they do not consider themselves feminists.

What is the message that large majorities of women are sending to organized feminism? Betty Friedan herself, I believe, has read it correctly. The message seems to be that official feminism hasn't been listening to the women who are too busy to be in movements; that it is out of touch with the real-life concerns of most women today. In a recent *New Yorker* magazine article, Friedan urges feminists to wake up to the fact that "the most urgent concerns of women today are not gender issues but jobs and families." And whom did we see on the cover of *Time* magazine as the key voter in the 1996 elections? An exhausted, frazzled working mother. The issue on her mind? Job and family.

I have observed a similar shift in attitude even among my career-oriented law students. Law schools were strongholds of feminism in the late 1970s when women were a minority. But now that women make up nearly half the student body (and are more representative of the female population), I hear much more concern about how one can have a decent family life without suffering excessive career disadvantages. Most significant of all, in my view, is that this worry now seems to be bothering the young men almost as much as the women.

The signs of shifting attitudes among men lead to a point I will discuss later: the sense in which today's women's issues are everybody's issues. But first, it needs to be said that many issues confront men and women in significantly different ways, especially where the women concerned are, or hope to be, mothers. Let me give you some examples of that differential impact.

A major issue for the women's movement of the 1970s was the "gender gap" between men's and women's wages. We used to hear that for every dollar earned by a man, a woman made sixty cents. Today, women's opportunities have improved to the point where there is virtually no gender gap between the earnings of women and men *who have made similar life choices.*

Among young adults who have never had children, women's earnings are now nearly 98 percent of men's earnings.

But something is wrong with that picture. Why do we talk about women in the abstract when the great majority of women are mothers? The women who are disadvantaged in the workplace are not women in the abstract, but women who are raising children. The real income gap in this country is between child-raising families and other types of households.

Another good example of the different form that the work-family dilemma takes for men and women is what happens when a child-raising family is broken by divorce. (Keep in mind here that the majority of all divorces involve couples with children under sixteen.) There is no doubt that the rise in divorce has had a disproportionate effect on women. After divorce it is nearly always the mother who remains primarily responsible for the physical care of young children; the father's standard of living typically rises, while that of the mother and children declines—in all too many cases to below the poverty line.

To put it another way, motherhood in our society is a pretty risky occupation. Ironically, women in the abstract have never had more rights, but rarely has the position of mothers been more precarious. Women have tried to protect themselves and their children against the risks they face in two ways: They are having fewer children, and they are maintaining at least a foothold in the labor force even when their children are very young. But that strategy still does not protect them very well against the four deadly Ds: disrespect for unpaid work in the home; disadvantages in the workplace for anyone who takes time out for family responsibilities; divorce; and the destitution that afflicts so many female-headed families.

As if that were not enough, many women now find themselves facing "Work-Family Dilemma II": No sooner has the last child left home, than the needs of aging parents start the process of juggling job and family responsibilities all over again.

The fact is that we are in a situation where the experience of past generations gives little guidance. Now that most women are in the labor force, no one has yet come up with a good solution to the problem of who performs the caretaking work for children and the elderly that women used to do for free. The idea of some social conservatives is that women should "just stay home" (unless they are welfare mothers in which case off to work they must go.) I can't help thinking that the "just stay home" idea is a bit like what the chicken said to the pig when they were trying to think what they could give to Old MacDonald for a birthday present. The chicken said: "How about a nice breakfast of bacon and eggs—I'll provide the eggs and you give the bacon." You can see why the pig was not enthusiastic about that division of labor.

Another set of problems that will have a disparate impact on women is just beginning to come into view. Thanks to medical advances, we have never had such a large elderly population. As you know, that group is composed of more women than men. At the same time, we know that much of the burden of supporting that population will fall on the shoulders of a labor force that is growing proportionately smaller.

Against that background, a real concern about the assisted suicide movement is the pressure that is going to be exerted on elderly people in failing health to cease using up scarce resources. When you consider that three out of four poor Americans over 65 are women, you can see that this is yet another issue that is everybody's issue, but that will affect women in a special way. It is sobering to think that more than two-thirds of the people Dr. Jack Kevorkian has helped to die are women.

Assisted suicide also involves the question of who settles whose hash. The "right to die" (like the right to abortion) is being pushed mainly by people who are accustomed to having a lot of control over their lives. The outcome of the debate over this issue is likely to be determined by judges—who are also people who are used to having a lot of control over their lives.

To privileged folks, the right to die may look like an aspect of personal freedom—a way of feeling in control until the very end. In the case of such people, it may well work out that way. But here is my question: How is it going to work out for the less fortunate, the people who are in the most danger of being regarded as burdensome to their families and a drag on the taxpayers of the welfare state? What is a "right to die" for some may well become a "duty to die" for others. If that happens, women, again, will be most affected.

Let's consider the ways in which, despite the disparate impact on women, all these problems are everybody's problems. One of the main sources of discontent with the old feminism was the way it set women and men at odds with one another. But the fact is that we are all in this together. In the world of work, men as well as women are increasingly chafing under pressures to put the demands of the job ahead of the needs of their families. Both men and women are increasingly realizing that feminists have always had a strong point when they complained that society gives little respect or security to people who make sacrifices for their children and families. Ironically, the 1970s feminists bought into that same disrespect. By treating marriage and motherhood as obstacles to women's progress, they actually helped to reinforce the idea that the only work that counts is work for pay outside the home!

But while feminists were maintaining, correctly, that society doesn't respect work in the home, things were changing in the workplace outside the home. In too many ways, as Berkshire residents know all too well, the new globalized economy is sending the same message to many working men and women that society once sent to homemakers: that they and the work they do are not worthy of much respect.

Here are some questions posed by Msgr. George Higgins, a longtime advocate of the rights of workers, in a recent speech. When a profitable company "downsizes," doesn't that tell dedicated employees that their years of service don't really count for much? When employees' wages stagnate while their companies prosper, aren't working people being told that their effort and skill aren't valued? And when benefits like health insurance and pensions are cut back, doesn't that tell working people that nobody cares what happens when they get sick and old? To those questions, one might add: What scale of values rewards some CEOs to the tune of hundreds of millions a year while moms and dads must work harder than ever to counter a relative decline in real family income?

These are men's *and* women's issues. They are family issues. They are issues about what kind of society we want to try to hand on to future generations.

Something is wrong when most jobs are too rigidly structured to accommodate family responsibilities. Something is wrong when we frame laws and policies as though human beings existed to serve the economy, rather than the other way around. In the long run, that is not even good for the economy. To spell out the obvious: A healthy economy requires a certain kind of work force, with certain skills and qualities of character. And those qualities—honesty, work ethic, ability to cooperate with others—are going to be acquired, for the most part, in the nation's families or not at all.

Having said that, it is not easy to imagine what can be done about all this. Some factors, such as worldwide economic developments, may be outside the control of any one country. Other factors, let's admit it, are in ourselves. Some of the extra work we do is more related to the lifestyle of a consumer society than to basic family needs. We Americans do have a tendency to want to "have it all." But anyone who has tried to combine work and family life knows that we can't have it all. You are always shortchanging somebody somewhere—one day it's the job, the next it's your spouse, or your children. The grown-up question is not, can all our dreams come true. It is whether we can do better than we are doing now. Is it possible to harmonize women's and men's roles in social and economic life with their desires (and their children's needs) for a decent family life?

I would say it is possible—but that the prospects are dim, unless society as a whole is prepared to recognize that when mothers and fathers raise their children well, they are not just doing something for themselves and their own children, but for all of us. Governments, private employers, and fellow citizens would all have to recognize that we owe an enormous debt to parents who do a good job raising their children under today's difficult conditions. There is something heroic about the everyday sacrifices that people have to make these days just to do the right thing by their nearest and dearest.

Those observations bring me back to politics. Here I want to focus on one basic problem: the problem of how American men and women can gain a say in the decisions that shape their lives and livelihoods—a voice in our jobs, in our children's education, in our communities, and in the direction our country is taking.

CHAPTER 13 • Feminism and the Family

Is that problem soluble? A glance around the social landscape is not particularly reassuring. Something is terribly wrong when Americans from every viewpoint and every walk of life are beginning to feel that the forces that govern our economic and political lives have spun out of control; and when parents feel that they are losing the struggle for the hearts and minds of their own children.

There has been much speculation about why many Americans seem uninterested in voting and in the electoral process generally. That disaffection just might have something to do with the perception that both political parties are out of touch with citizens' deepest concerns. Reporting on political party finances shows that that common perception isn't crazy. Both political parties are heavily financed by big business—the Democrats by the kinds of businesses that make their livings from government, and the Republicans by the kinds of businesses who just want government to butt out. Yes, the Democrats throw a few crumbs to working men and women. Yes, the Republicans throw a few crumbs to those who are concerned about the moral fabric of society. But it has been a long time since either party in office has done much for constituents whose main concerns are decent jobs and decent conditions for raising a family.

My one suggestion for a way to overcome these problems is likely to make people groan, but I can see no alternative. Simply put, more of us have to take a more active role in politics. If these old Berkshire hills of ours could speak, they would remind us that frustration with a distant, unresponsive government is nothing new here in Shays' Rebellion country. A recent book by Edward Countryman on our ancestors' uprising says: "It took Shays' Rebellion in 1786 to show what was at stake. Coastal merchants, Harvard graduates, and Boston professional men put themselves in charge of the commonwealth." Even then, the courts were perceived as in the service of the elites.

Noting that, in the end, Daniel Shays' violent protest was futile, Countryman went on to point out that Americans had to learn to organize themselves in a new society that was necessarily complex—a society where commerce could not be ignored, but where the voice of the people had to be heard.

The following year, the constitutional convention in Philadelphia produced an ingenious design for a republic with democratic elements. To protect those democratic elements, the Bill of Rights specified that all powers not expressly delegated to the federal government, or forbidden to the states, are reserved to the states and the people. That's a forgotten part of the Bill of Rights—the 10th amendment. We hear little about the powers reserved to the people from the groups that are self-appointed defenders of our civil liberties. Yet what liberty is more basic than the freedom to participate in setting the conditions under which we live, work, and raise our families?

Here, in Berkshire County, those powers reserved to the people were long exercised in our town meetings. In fact, if these old hills of ours could speak, they might recall the fall of 1831 when a stranger passed through our towns on his way from Albany to Boston. The French traveler, Alexis de Tocqueville, admired our town meeting form of government so much that he immortalized it as the very essence of good government in his *Democracy in America*. (He envied us because local government in his own country had been intentionally destroyed by a revolution, followed by a dictatorship.)

If these old hills of ours could speak, what stories they could tell about the women and men who have lived here. They led hard lives, in the beginning, wresting a living from stony soil. Later, many led hard lives in the textile mills, the paper mills, and still later at GE. But they always had a sense that they were making things better for the next generation. When industries left, life became hard in another way.

Now it seems that many people are tempted to give up on the idea that we can help to make things better. They are tempted to give up on the idea that we could ever take back democratic institutions; that we could ever restore decisionmaking power to the many who have the most to lose from the few who have the most to gain.

But if these old hills of ours could speak, wouldn't they remind us that the women and men who have gone before us often faced greater challenges than we do now? If that is right, then do we really want to be the generation who didn't even try to turn things around? After all, this isn't Eastern Europe where the men and women who toppled authoritarian regimes are now struggling to build democratic government from scratch. We have the machinery here at hand. We've had it for over 200 years. It's rusty, but it's there.

CHAPTER 13 • Feminism and the Family

# CHAPTER 14

# Who's Afraid of Tom Wolfe?

*Tom Wolfe's sprawling social realist novel,* A Man in Full, *made most literary critics uncomfortable. This review, which appeared in the August/September 1999 issue of* First Things, *explains why.*[1]

W HY DOES TOM WOLFE'S LATEST BOOK make the mandarins of taste so uncomfortable? John Updike took a good deal of space in the *New Yorker* to declare that *A Man in Full* was "entertainment, not literature." Norman Mailer in the *New York Review of Books* dismissed the novel as an "adroit commercial counterfeit." Martin Amis and others fell into line, all seemingly intent on assuring that no one took the book's position at the top of the best-seller list as evidence of literary merit. When Wolfe's work was passed over for last year's Pulitzer and other awards, J. Bottum noted in the *Weekly Standard* that, "There's something about his sprawling brand of social realism that makes our literary professionals purse their lips in disapproval."

T. S. Eliot once told us that "Humankind cannot bear very much reality." Perhaps that is why so many literary professionals not only disapproved of but misread Wolfe's book. What, for example, is one to make of the capsule description of *A Man in Full* that ran week after week on the *New York Times* best-seller list: "Life in Atlanta on the cusp of the millennium, as Old South values collide with a new world." The Old South? Wolfe makes clear in his very first chapter that, for him, Atlanta is emblematic of modern American mobility. The self-made real estate tycoon Charlie Croker muses: "Atlanta had never been a true Old Southern city like Savannah or Charleston or Richmond, where wealth had originated with the land." Atlanta was "the offspring of the railroad business," a place where "people had been making money on the hustle ever since." Nor is *A Man in Full* about a collision of values. It's a portrait of a society where values other than sheer self-interest are difficult to discern.

Strangely, most reviewers (John Podhoretz was an exception) overlooked the extent to which *A Man in Full* is about masculinity. The book is densely

---

[1] Mary Ann Glendon, "Who's Afraid of Tom Wolfe?" review of *A Man in Full* by Tom Wolfe, *First Things* 96 (August/September 1999): 13–14.

populated with male characters from diverse ethnic and economic back-grounds, each struggling in his way with the question of what it is to be a man in a world where masculine roles entrenched for centuries have all but disappeared. Women and children are very much in the background. For most of the men, sexual conquest and various forms of imitation warfare have immense importance; fatherhood barely figures among their preoccupations.

Another curious feature of the reviews is that nearly all of them take for granted that the book's "hero" is the flamboyant, aging Charlie Croker who, when we meet him, is on the brink of a financial disaster precipitated by a foolish investment in a 40-story office building named after himself. Yet the book has another protagonist. In fact, the action of the plot involves the convergence of Croker's journey through life with the odyssey of 24-year-old Conrad Hensley, who has a menial job in a California frozen food ware-house owned by Charlie. When we meet Conrad, he, too, is on the brink of a fall—precipitated by a foolish, or at least inexpedient, refusal to escape imprisonment by pleading guilty to a crime he did not commit.

Conrad, like nearly half the members of his generation, spent much of his childhood without a father. His hippie parents openly disdained such bourgeois values as "order, moral rectitude, courtesy, cooperation, education, financial success, comfort, respectability, pride in one's offspring, and, above all, domestic tranquillity." The boy, for his part, dreamed of a more orderly life, a college education, and a happy family. But the dream became difficult to realize when, at age eighteen, he married his pregnant girlfriend Jill and soon thereafter had a second child. Nevertheless, Conrad took a dangerous job so as to save for a condo, tried hard to be a good father to his bratty chil-dren, and, despite temptations, remained faithful to his nagging wife Jill. His progress toward these modest goals is interrupted when he is falsely accused of aggravated assault.

Things really take a turn for the worse when Conrad refuses the prose-cutor's offer of probation in exchange for a guilty plea. He is convicted and sentenced to two years in prison. To his uncomprehending and infuriated wife, he tries to explain: "But I kept something, Jill. I kept my honor, and I didn't bargain away my soul. When the time comes I wanna be able to look Carl and Christy in the eye and say, I was innocent. I was falsely accused. I refused to compromise with a lie. I went into prison, but I went into prison a man, and I came out of prison a man."

It is far from clear, however, that Conrad will be able to emerge from the Santa Rita Correctional Facility with his manliness or anything else intact. Lying on his bunk in this terrifying place, Conrad lets his thoughts wander. "He had grown up associating religion with the self-delusion and aimlessness of adults. But now he thought about the soul, *his* soul. Or he tried to. But it was only a word! He didn't know how to give it any meaning! . . . And yet there was something . . . that caused him to care whether he lived or died and to worry about Jill and Carl and Christy. Perhaps that was his soul. Whatever it was it was not confined within his body and his mind."

Through a mix-up, Conrad receives an anthology of writings by Stoic philosophers instead of the mystery thriller he was eagerly awaiting, *The Stoic's Game*. In this strange tome, he finds passages that seem addressed directly to him. He is intrigued by Epictetus's idea of a divinity who gives mankind "a spark of his own fire." He tries to open himself up to this divine energy. "Having never believed in a god, and having never prayed before, he didn't even know that this was prayer."

Though Conrad finds much sustenance in the book, he is no Stoic. He becomes a more self-aware version of the same Conrad who had risked death in the Croker warehouse to save his buddy Ken from the path of a careening forklift. In jail, Conrad invites deadly retaliation when he comforts a hapless newcomer who has been sodomized and beaten by members of the vicious gang that rules the cellblock. When he is delivered from that peril by an earthquake that destroys the prison (shades of St. Paul!), Conrad puts his life in jeopardy yet again to extricate a cellmate from the rubble. He realizes that if he followed Epictetus's counsel, he would not get involved in the problems of others, but he doesn't feel able "to be that heartless."

Updike, one of the few reviewers to understand that the book in an important way was "all about religion," got the religion wrong. No Stoic ever taught that a man should lay down his life for his brother. Critical of the book as culminating "in renunciation and non-attachment," Updike completely lost sight of Conrad who, at story's end, heads home to the wife and children he has never ceased to think about and love through all his wanderings. To Updike, the book's "most sympathetic" character is a 42-year-old African-American lawyer who over the course of the book gradually sheds his refined tastes, regular habits, and moral scruples. Is it possible that Updike simply cannot imagine a good family man as the hero of a novel?

For many reviewers, I suspect, Wolfe has penetrated American reality too deeply for comfort. His portrait of fin-de-siecle America is unsettling, in some ways reminiscent of Rome in the time of Nero and his Stoic tutor Seneca. There is more wealth and social mobility than in the Republic, especially for men who know how to seize the main chance. There is also more equality. Citizens of many different languages and origins mingle on an equal footing. And what liberty! Behavior formerly frowned upon is now tolerated. Marriage is easily terminated. Pleasures once reserved to the wealthy are now within the reach of persons of modest means. Games and spectacles abound. The poor are in a separate world, but kept from destitution by the dole. The affluent ape the speech, dress, and manners of the lower classes.

Artists, of course, are supposed to see more deeply than the rest of us. But that gift does not always earn admiration for those who possess it. Wolfe forces us to contemplate what happens when a whole society begins to reject the habits and virtues that are necessary to sustain dignified life in a democratic polity (and what happens to writers who buy into the values of such a society).

It is said that *A Man in Full* has contributed to a revival of interest in the Stoics. How intriguing if that is indeed the case. In an increasingly chaotic Rome, the teachings of the Stoics offered people support in times of trial and lent dignity to the humblest life. But we know now that their philosophy of renunciation and non-attachment was a forerunner to a more complete answer to the question of what it is to be "a man in full."

# CHAPTER 15

# William Galston's
# Communitarian Liberalism

*In the early 1990s, with William Galston, I assisted Amitai Etzioni in drafting
a "Communitarian Platform," and for a number of years I served on the editorial board of
The Responsive Community, the magazine of Etzioni's communitarian movement.
This review of Galston's* Liberal Purposes: Goods, Virtues, and Diversity in the
Liberal State *appeared in 61* George Washington University Law Review *1955 (1993).*[1]

LAWYERS WHO WISH TO SAMPLE the current academic debate between liberalism and its critics could do no better than to begin with William Galston's spirited attempt to raise out of that discussion a chastened vision of liberalism made sturdier through honest confrontation with its own strengths and weaknesses. Galston's defense of liberal democracy against its triumphalist friends, as well as an assortment of communitarian, classical, and neo-Marxist critics, is particularly interesting because of the variety of hats he wears. He is both an unapologetic liberal and a prominent communitarian, a university professor and a long-time activist in Democratic presidential politics, a reflective political philosopher and an ex-Marine. Currently, he is President Clinton's Deputy Assistant for Domestic Policy. In *Liberal Purposes*, it is mainly the philosopher who speaks—the kind of philosopher who goes about the city seeking conversation on the fundamental issues behind the issues of the day.

Galston's starting point is that the American experiment "is in trouble because it has failed to attend to the dependence of sound politics on sound culture." The problem he sets for himself is whether a diverse polity dedicated to liberty and equality can remain true to its highest ideals without inadvertently destroying the foundations on which it ultimately rests. Or, conversely, whether the liberal state can become (as Galston says it must) "far more actively involved in reproducing the conditions necessary to its own health and perpetuation" without undermining liberal institutions or "the capacious tolerance that gives liberal society its special attraction." Galston defines the liberal

---

[1] Mary Ann Glendon, review of *Liberal Purposes: Goods, Virtues, and Diversity in the Liberal State* by William Galston, *George Washington Law Review* 61, (6; August 1993): 1955–60.

polity as a community characterized by "popular-constitutional government; a diverse society with a wide range of individual opportunities and choices; a predominantly market economy; and a substantial, strongly protected sphere of privacy and individual rights." The communitarian in Galston recognizes that delicate task as of the utmost importance; the can-do Marine in him claims the mission can be successfully accomplished.

Galston is in good company when he asserts the close connection between politics and culture. The American Framers knew that republican governments, more than any other form, would require certain kinds of excellence in citizens and public servants alike. It follows that friends of liberal democracy cannot remain indifferent to the institutions—families, neighborhoods, workplace, and religious associations—that are the seedbeds of character and competence. As Tocqueville pointed out, if democratic nations should fail in "imparting to all citizens those ideas and sentiments which first prepare them for freedom and then allow them to enjoy it, there will be no independence left for anybody. . . ." The only wonder is that so many political theorists still have not come to terms with the fact that America's social resources, like its natural resources, can no longer simply be taken for granted.

The chapter on "Liberal Virtues" spells out with more precision why liberal regimes must grapple with the problem of how to foster the skills and virtues that are essential to the maintenance of democratic government. A liberal polity, Galston points out, needs the general virtues required by every political community (courage, law-abidingness, loyalty), but in addition it requires certain kinds of excellence specific to itself. Because the American regime emphasizes individual liberty, we need citizens who are independent, moderate in their demands, and able to discern and respect the rights of others. Our great heterogeneity places a special premium on tolerance. Our economic system relies on the work ethic and the ability to postpone gratification.

Since these skills and virtues do not arise naturally, liberal communities must be attentive to the processes by which they are engendered, strengthened or eroded. Galston considers three possibilities: liberal culture may tend to undermine the very traits that it requires; life in a liberal polity may in itself suffice to habituate citizens to the liberal virtues; liberal virtues must be actively fostered by the institutions of liberal society. The pessimistic view that liberalism is inherently destructive of its own foundations is associated with certain communitarian critics of liberalism like Alasdair MacIntyre, while the faith that liberalism can be self-sustaining has been ably defended by Stephen Macedo. Though Galston finds the empirical evidence mixed, he takes seriously the possibility that liberal principles of individual liberty, equality, and tolerance may so structure and dominate society that they corrode the communities of memory and mutual aid that undergird the liberal project. He is concerned that liberalism is not especially hospitable to "ways of life that require self-restraint, hierarchy, or cultural integrity."

It seems to this reviewer that the problems identified by Galston may not be intrinsic to liberalism. The question, at bottom, may be the one to which the old political philosophers gave a negative answer: Can there be a republic in an extended territory? The American Founders wagered that the answer could be yes. Today, with increasing heterogeneity and the institutions of civil society in some disarray, that wager is still open. Galston, taking a philosophical rather than a sociological tack, suggests that American political life suffers from having accepted a skimpy version of liberalism—a vision of the Constitution as a kind of elaborate traffic system that permits individuals to pursue to pursue their diverse ideas of the good life with as few collisions as possible. In this vision, the State remains rigorously neutral among conceptions of the good, confining itself mainly to making and enforcing the rules for the pursuit of self-interest and self-actualization.

Discussing and distancing himself from many of liberalism's leading defenders (Bruce Ackerman, Ronald Dworkin, Charles Larmore, and John Rawls), Galston points out that official "neutrality" unavoidably results in privileging some conceptions of the good over others, notably secular over religious ways of seeing the world. He is equally critical of prominent theorists like Alasdair MacIntyre and Roberto Unger who, from different vantage points, regard the liberal project as fatally flawed.

His own position, which he presents as a defense of liberalism, has much in common with the views of such classical critics as Harvey C. Mansfield, Jr., and Thomas Pangle, and such communitarian critics as Michael Walzer and Michael Sandel. Like them, he comes not to bury but to save the liberal polity. The main difference is that friendly classical and communitarian critics have provided a vantage point outside the liberal tradition from which to view the best and worst features of liberalism, while Galston maintains that "Liberalism contains within itself the resources it needs to declare and defend a conception of the good and virtuous life that is in no way truncated or contemptible."

In the end, though, Galston's insistence that the liberal virtues require "the rejection of any comprehensive egoism" brings him close to classical and communitarian positions. Comprehensive egoism, after all, is one of the passions that liberalism liberates. For that reason, the American Founders and Tocqueville counted heavily on families and religion to help moderate individual greed, selfishness, and ambition. Galston makes the same implicit judgment when he adopts the position that liberalism needs to actively tend to its religious underpinnings and its child-raising families. It matters less whether the resources for discerning and correcting the excesses of liberalism are to be found within or outside the liberal tradition itself, than whether they can be found and deployed at all.

Galston's recognition that the seedbeds of civic virtue must be actively cultivated brings him to the edge of a thicket of paradoxes. Liberalism, in order to flourish, may need to refrain from imposing its own image on all the institutions of civil society. Democratic experiments may actually depend on preserving here and there within the liberal polity certain familial and religious structures that are not necessarily democratic, egalitarian, or liberal, and whose highest loyalty is not to the state. That is a hard nut for liberalism to crack. How can one be sure that non-democratic plants would not take over the democratic garden? And how would one distinguish the flowers of civic virtue from the weeds of civil strife?

Some indication of Galston's thinking on these matters is given in his sketch of a proposed reorientation of church–state law. "I have come to believe," he states, "that the understanding of the public role of religion, morality, and excellence developed by the figures of the founding period and by Tocqueville offers insights that present-day liberals can ignore only a great cost." Galston maintains (and the experience of other liberal democracies like Canada and Germany supports him) that the relation between liberalism and religion need not be one of unremitting hostility. He finds that a certain blindness toward religion is inherent in the liberal project, but he attributes its presence to historical rather than philosophical reasons. Nothing in liberalism (or the American Constitution), as Galston sees it, requires the strict mechanical separationism that has marked American Supreme Court opinions since the 1940s. That rigorous posture, in fact, would seem to be inconsistent with liberal tolerance.

To show how liberalism might better promote religious tolerance and freedom, Galston offers the example of laws mandating a period of silence in public schools for meditation or voluntary prayer. The Supreme Court's invalidation of one of these statutes in *Wallace* v. *Jaffree*, 472 U.S. 38 (1985), Galston believes, blocked an intelligent, democratic, compromise that would have promoted legitimate parental concerns without advancing any particular religion and without encouraging "antireligious ire."

Further light on the practical implications of Galston's proactive liberalism is shed by his recent communitarian writings and activities. His brand of liberal philosophy in practice translates not into liberal (in the sense of leftward) politics, but communitarianism. In a recent article, Galston writes, "Communitarianism is a movement that seeks to balance rights and responsibilities and to nourish the moral ties of family, neighbourhood, workplace and citizenship as a basis for innovative public policy. . . . All in all, I believe that communitarianism represents the most promising basis so far for muting the left/right divisions that have shaped (and stalled) so much public-policy debate over the past generation. It offers the most hope for building on widely shared moral sentiments—concerning family, neighborhood, work, and citizen responsibility—not to justify the status quo, but rather to mobilize a broad coalition in the cause of long-overdue reform of our society as well as of our government." Galston the communitarian has long been an energetic advocate of proactive family policy. The bare outlines of his approach are set forth in *Liberal Purposes*, but readers interested in his specific proposals should consult his "Liberal-Democratic Case for the Two-Parent Family" in *The Responsive Community*.

Toward the end of *Liberal Purposes*, Galston the philosopher writes, "My thesis is that principled grounds exist for reconciliation between the combatants in the cultural wars of our generation, but that if a cease-fire is to be effected, each side will have to moderate its most extreme (and least defensible) claims." It is heartening to know that the professor who proclaims that belief, and who exemplifies in himself the liberal virtues of tolerance and moderation, is now Galston the statesman. Philosophers have not always fared well among politicians, but friends of self-government can rejoice that Galston's calm, reasonable voice will be heard in the councils of state. That voice in essence is neither liberal nor communitarian. It is the ancient voice of dialectical reason, loyal to the regime, yes, but seizing every opportunity, by questioning, probing, praising, and criticizing, to assist that regime in living up to its highest potential. What can one say but "Semper Fi" and good luck!

# CHAPTER 16

# Michael Sandel's
# Liberal Communitarianism

*This review of my colleague Michael Sandel's* Democracy's Discontent:
America in Search of a Public Philosophy *appeared in the
April 1, 1996 issue of* The New Republic.[1]

**W**E ARE ALL CIVIC REPUBLICANS NOW. Or so it might seem, given the
widespread absorption of the criticisms of liberalism launched by Michael
Sandel and others in the 1970s. Who would have guessed then that Republican and Democratic candidates alike would be humming the same tunes of
responsibility, virtue, and character? That students of politics would be
exploring the nooks and crannies of "civil society"? That lawyers and judges
would be rediscovering a design for government as well as a charter of rights
in the Constitution?

As these ideas have moved into mainstream American political discourse,
the various criticisms of liberal theory are best understood as attacks on its
excesses (social or economic libertarianism), or on the blind spots of its egali-
tarian-redistributionist strands. For none of the major players in the debate
seriously contests the liberal project of government based on consent and limited by certain inalienable rights. Their main focus is rather on the scope of the
democratic elements in our political arrangements, and on the hierarchy of
rights. Whether rooted in classical, biblical, communitarian, or civic republican perspectives, liberalism's gadflies come not to bury it, but to save it.

Sandel's latest contribution to this discussion, like his previous works, is
notable for its seriousness, its intelligence, and its illuminating excursions
into constitutional law. The book begins with a reprise of his analysis of the
theory of liberalism that until recently seemed dominant in the academy and
the Supreme Court, if not in the larger society. That set of ideas found concrete expression in what Sandel calls the "procedural state," in which selected
rights are treated as trumps; government is supposed to be neutral toward
competing values; and human beings are envisioned as independent, freely
choosing, self-constituting individuals. All those ideas, he contends, are deeply

---

[1] Mary Ann Glendon, review of *Democracy's Discontent: America in Search of a Public
Philosophy* by Michael J. Sandel, *The New Republic* 214 (14; 1 April 1996): 39–41.

flawed. Giving highest priority to individual liberty to choose one's values for oneself neglects the freedom of citizens to shape the forces that govern their lives. The fiction of the freely choosing self fails to respect persons who are "encumbered by moral or civic obligations they have not chosen." As for neutrality, it is a lie, favoring hyper-liberal concepts of liberty over all rivals.

Building on these concepts, which will be familiar to readers of his earlier work, Sandel devotes the bulk of his new book to a demonstration that a more robust political vision has long played an important role in American political life. In constitutional law, for example, the traditional rationale for free speech connected it to effective participation in self-government and the pursuit of truth, rather than, as in recent years, self-expression. Where Sandel breaks new ground is in a series of chapters under the heading of "The Political Economy of Citizenship." In these, he shows that the civic consequences of economic policy loomed large in political discourse from the years of the Founding through the early years of the labor movement and the Progressive era to the presidential campaign of Hubert Humphrey, who was one of the last defenders of local communities, family farms, and small businesses against massive concentrations of political and economic power. It was only in the 1970s, according to Sandel, that public debate on the economy moved so decisively toward a preoccupation with how to promote growth and redistribution. He sees the Keynesian revolution as the economic counterpart of the rights revolution in constitutional law, the economic expression of the procedural republic.

The vitality of the "civic strand" in legal, political, and economic thinking leads Sandel to believe that the republican vision remains a viable basis for a renewal of the democratic experiment. That vision, as he presents it, is at odds with several tenets of unreconstructed liberalism. Since the essence of freedom in the "civic republic" is participation in "a political community that controls its own fate," political power must be dispersed. Since self-government depends on informed deliberation among citizens who share a concern for the public good, the polity cannot be indifferent to the character and values of its citizens. Nor can it ignore the health of the communities of memory and mutual aid in which civic skills and virtues are acquired and nurtured.

Now that concerns about liberalism's extremes, the retrieval of its republican strand, and the rediscovery of the intermediate institutions of civil society have been widely assimilated, we are back to the two questions that have dogged the American version of the democratic experiment from the beginning: Can there be a republic in an extended territory with a heterogeneous population? (The classical political philosophers doubted it.) Can good government be established by "reflection and choice" (as the authors of *The Federalist* wagered), or must our political fate be determined by "accident and force"?

A problem for champions of a republican vision is that many Americans seem to have silently given up on both propositions. After all, the demands of a republic on citizens and public servants are immensely difficult to meet. Self-government not only requires certain civic skills (deliberation, compromise, consensus-building, civility, reason-giving), but theaters in which those arts can be meaningfully exercised. A regime of ordered liberty demands certain character traits—self-restraint, respect for others, public spiritedness, and sturdy independence of mind. Our egalitarian and welfare aspirations require a modicum of fellow-feeling, as well as a certain disposition to assume responsibility for oneself and one's dependents.

But where do such qualities come from? That question has sent civic republicans and chastened liberals, those fraternal twins, back to Tocqueville. What other schools for citizenship or seedbeds of civic virtue are there besides families, educational institutions, neighborhoods, workers' associations, religious groups, town governments, and the myriad other social subsystems that fill the space between individuals and the megastructures of state and market? Civil society, long neglected in political theory and practice, is back in vogue.

Unfortunately, the mediating structures of civil society are not in peak condition. Centralization of power has lessened opportunities for political participation; and changes in the economy have curtailed the ability of employees to have a say in the government of the workplace. The travail of groups such as families, neighborhoods, and churches also reflects a deep ambivalence in the American soul. It is true that we are always forming associations, but we are always dissolving them, too: cashing out, moving on, starting over. The United States has long had the highest marriage rate in the Western world—and the highest divorce rate. A part of the challenge for civic republicans, as Michael Walzer once remarked, is that "there's nobody here but us Americans." Indeed, as innumerable national surveys show, we place an extraordinary value on several freedoms that are in tension with republican aspirations.

It was easy at first to shrug off the erosion of the republican elements in the polity, Sandel says, since most of it occurred in the postwar years when the economy was strong, the United States enjoyed primacy in the world, and a majority of citizens had realized the dream of home-ownership. It is only as we enter the season of what he calls "democracy's discontent" that the full extent of our disempowerment becomes apparent, and troubling. Americans, he says, are increasingly afflicted with the sense that "we are losing control of the forces that govern our lives" and that "the moral fabric of community is unraveling around us." That diagnosis seems to be widely shared. When Robert Reich speaks of "a profound sense that economic forces are out of control—that neither hard work nor general economic improvement will lead to higher incomes," he chants in unison with Pat Buchanan. And when Ellen Goodman laments that parents have to spend more and more time "doing battle with our own culture," her sisters in woe include Phyllis Schlafly.

That spreading uneasiness might be the beginning of wisdom if it moved policymakers away from their customary preoccupation with the short term and the quick fix. But if, by some miracle, that were to occur, they would need to raise politics above its current level. For the fact is that no one has much of an idea of how to reinvigorate civil society or to jumpstart self-government. It is one thing to understand that it takes a village to raise a child, but quite another to know what it takes to raise and maintain the village-like institutions that sustain families and the larger polity alike. It is one thing to say that the era of big government is over, but another—as Eastern Europeans have found—to call into being a vibrant democracy. Thus far, the populist energy in current politics seems aimed more at the replacement of current policies and programs at the national level than at the task of rebuilding self-government from the grassroots up. And no wonder, for the centralization of power has caused the skills of self-government to atrophy.

An encouraging sign in political theory is the remarkable reawakening of interest (here and in Europe) in the nitty-gritty of federalism; subsidiarity (the principle of leaving social tasks to the smallest social unit that can perform them adequately); and modes of legal ordering other than direct, top-down regulation. Sandel emphasizes the need to encourage the sorts of institutions that aid citizens to deliberate well about the common good, and to consider the "civic consequences of economic arrangements." The hope for self-government, he writes in his conclusion, "lies not in relocating sovereignty, but in dispersing it, exploring the unrealized possibilities in federalism and in the institutions such as schools, workplaces, churches and synagogues, trade unions and social movements."

Politically, the stage is set for creative experiments with ideas like the one advanced by Peter Berger and Richard Neuhaus in the 1970s—that the state can promote the delivery of services such as health, education, and child care more economically, efficiently and humanely through the mediating institutions of civil society than through state-run agencies. A beneficial side effect would likely be to boost the vitality of the organizations concerned. Consider the innovative approach to daycare authorized by Congress in the child welfare legislation of 1990. That statute, with broad bipartisan support, gives the states discretion to issue vouchers that permit working parents to choose their own daycare providers, expressly including centers run by religious groups that take religious affiliation into consideration in their hiring practices. Low-income housing is another area where non-governmental organizations (especially trade unions and black churches) have already demonstrated their potential.

But in moving from theory to practice, born-again republicans quickly stop twittering in concert like birds on a New Hampshire morning. One contingent regularly celebrates family, neighborhood, and religion (never mentioning workers' associations), while others praise family, neighborhood, and unions (with nary a word for churches). For some, "community" primarily means the nation; for others, the states; for still others, the town, tribe, or coven. An especially hard nut for chastened liberals to crack is the likelihood that liberal regimes in order to survive may need to refrain from imposing their own image on all the institutions of civil society.

Anticipating what is likely to be an important objection to his thesis, Sandel acknowledges that communities can be narrow-minded and exclusive. "Republican politics," he concedes, "is risky politics." But he argues that a politics that brackets morality is at least as risky, for it has caused "the yearning for a public life of larger meaning [to find] undesirable expression. Fundamentalists step in where liberals fear to tread." His principal response to champions of full-bore liberalism is that the procedural republic "cannot secure the liberty it promises, because it cannot inspire the moral and civic engagement self-government requires." Elsewhere Sandel has written that "intolerance flourishes where forms of life are dislocated, roots unsettled, traditions undone."

Sandel recognizes that the obstacles to his lofty republican vision are many and formidable. Its prospects will depend to a great extent on the fragile seedbeds of civic virtue, and thus on culture. Still, he is right to emphasize the role of law and the Constitution, because no other country's culture is so permeated by legal ideas, and because juridical frameworks powerfully influence the relationships among government, markets and the structures of civil society. If those frameworks are restructured (or reinterpreted) with economic man, unencumbered man, or other sociopaths in mind, we should not be surprised to find ourselves increasingly surrounded by such creatures. Nor should we be surprised to see our society becoming less hospitable to the weak, the vulnerable, and dependent.

It is to be regretted that Sandel does not press his case for transformative politics further into the realms of practical political science, for the country desperately needs a discussion of the nitty-gritty of federalism, of the appropriate, or optimal, relations among state, market, and civil society under modern conditions. What does each do best? How can the harmful tendencies of each be checked without stifling their beneficial functions? What level of decisionmaking is best? What about indirect effects, long-term consequences, and sensitive dependence on initial conditions? It is time, in short, for a more ecological approach to the relations among law, economy, and the structures of civil society. Addressing such issues in depth would help Sandel make clear that his brand of soulcraft is not about soul-engineering, but about protecting social environments that are conducive to the development of the habits and the virtues upon which all liberal welfare states finally depend.

But the key to the fate of the republic is not in the seedbeds but in the seeds, the men and women in whose minds and hearts the tensions between individual rights and the common good are first felt and resolved. In this connection, Sandel's best-known contribution to the criticism of contemporary liberalism has been his attack on its implicit vision of the person: "By insisting that we are bound only by ends and roles we choose for ourselves, it denies that we can ever be claimed by ends we have not chosen—ends given by nature or God, for example, or by our identities as members of families, peoples, cultures, or traditions." But overemphasis on "encumbered selves" carries risks for republicanism. After all, encumbrances (the baggage we all inherit and acquire) may or may not be conducive to human flourishing. As for choice, it is unavoidable. The hope (and the danger) for the democratic experiment lies in the way in which we continuously constitute ourselves, for better or worse, individually and collectively, through large and small decisions.

More than any other form of government, a democratic republic depends on the capacity of men and women to reflect upon their existence, to make judgments concerning the good life, to devise norms and, to abide by those norms most of the time. Those decisions, of course, can be powerfully influenced (and not only for the better) by cultural conditioning and social environments. But those encumbrances and settings in turn can be affected to some degree by "reflection and choice." Indeed, the success of the recent critiques of liberalism is a tribute to that ongoing process of experiencing, understanding, and judging.

Thanks to Sandel and others, the "search for a new public philosophy" seems less urgent now than the search for a new political practice. Meanwhile the eyes of the real enemies of liberalism are upon the United States. They are betting that it is too late for liberalism's friendly critics to halt the relentless march of historical processes. Let us hope that they have underestimated our system's openness to self-correction through reflection, deliberation and, yes, choice.

# Religion and Democratic Society

When this 1996 Notre Dame commencement speech was chosen for inclusion in
Go Forth and Do Good: Memorable Notre Dame Commencement Addresses (2003),
I was especially pleased to find myself in the company of one of my heroes, Charles Malik,
a principal framer of the Universal Declaration of Human Rights,
who had addressed the graduating class in 1952.[1]

BISHOP D'ARCY, President Malloy, reverend clergy, honored guests, and faculty, I am delighted to join you in offering congratulations to the families, friends, and most especially the members of the Notre Dame Class of 1996. I can well imagine the happiness and pride that you parents and graduates are feeling today. And I am deeply grateful to have been invited to share this special occasion with you.

As a token of my gratitude, I am going to make you a gift of the most important lesson I have learned from all the graduation ceremonies I have attended over the years as a student, a parent, and a teacher. I can put it in the form of a beatitude: Blessed is the commencement speaker who keepeth it short, and who delayeth not the party.

One of the reasons I am so pleased to be here today is that it gives me a chance to acknowledge a gift I once received from Notre Dame. Many years ago, when I was a high school student in a small town in Western Massachusetts, I began to have difficulty putting together what I had been taught in Sunday school with the world of ideas I was encountering in the public library. Then one day I came across an essay in our local newspaper by a Father Theodore Hesburgh. One sentence jumped out at me, and it is no exaggeration to say that it had a profound effect on my life from then on. "When you encounter a conflict between science and religion," Father Hesburgh wrote, "you're either dealing with a bad scientist or a bad theologian."

---

[1] Mary Ann Glendon, "Religion and a Democratic Society," in *Go Forth and Do Good: Memorable Notre Dame Commencement Addresses*, ed. Wilson D. Miscamble (Notre Dame, IN: University of Notre Dame Press, 2003): 254–61.

That characteristically blunt Hesburgh-ism not only helped me on the perilous journey from childhood beliefs to adult faith, but it helped to channel my adolescent rebelliousness toward a critical engagement with the natural and human sciences.

The members of the Class of 1996 have had the good fortune of being steeped in the tradition in which Father Ted's insight was grounded. As I read in *Domers*, you were initiated into it four years ago when Vice-President O'Hara welcomed you with the words: "We don't apologize for being different here. We proclaim it. . . . We believe a true education integrates both faith and reason."

As you know, that enlightened approach to faith and reason is not new. You are have the good fortune to be among the heirs of what Chicago's Robert Maynard Hutchins enviously referred to as "the longest intellectual tradition of any institution in the contemporary world." You are the heirs of the same fearless approach to knowledge that enabled Thomas Aquinas to commune with the ancient Greeks without the slightest worry that his faith would be unsettled. Why not? Because Thomas understood the intellect as a great gift from God, a gift that not only does not threaten faith, but advances the ability of each new generation to know, love, and serve God in this world.

A very different set of attitudes prevails in some other parts of the American educational landscape. There, one dogma holds that faith and reason are enemies, and that science has made religion obsolete. Another accords a place to religion as a kind of private, leisure-time activity, but insists that religiously grounded viewpoints are out of bounds in the public square. In many institutions supposedly devoted to free inquiry, those views are held with fundamentalist fervor, and propagated with missionary zeal.

The idea that religion ought to be kept private has even attracted a certain following among religious Americans, including Catholics. The reasons are understandable. Just as it is not easy for an individual to grow from childhood to adult faith, it wasn't easy for American Catholics to make the transition from the immigrant church to the position in American society they now enjoy. On that rocky road, many people chose to follow what one might call "the way of the turtle." The turtle keeps her religion inside her shell. She remains silent on many issues of the day, lest she be accused of trying to "impose" her views on her fellow citizens.

Other Catholics, eager to make their way in the world, chose what one might call "the way of the chameleon." The chameleon tries to blend in with established patterns of secular culture. When parts of their heritage didn't lend themselves to blending, chameleon theologians appeared to help make doctrine fit more comfortably with the attitudes and lifestyles of the upwardly mobile. The turtle generation so feared rejection by mainstream culture that it hid its light under a bushel. The chameleon generation so craved acceptance by elite culture that it sold its own birthright.

Fortunately for our beloved republic, religious Americans of all persuasions are beginning to reject those choices. They have begun to let their light shine. They are taking their rightful places in the public discussion of where we are as a society and where we are headed. Americans of diverse faiths have begun to discover that they often have more in common with one another than with the secularized rank-and-file of what my fellow honoree Professor Stephen Carter calls the "Culture of Disbelief."

When this new generation of unapologetically religious Americans brings its own insights and wisdom to bear on the issues of the day, they are not seeking to *impose* their views on anyone, but they will no longer be denied their right to *propose* their ideas along with everyone else's.

And just in time, because public deliberation has been greatly impoverished by the absence of this kind of diversity. It was troubling at the U.N.'s recent Beijing conference on women, for example, to see how few voices other than religious voices were raised on behalf of the world's poorest and most marginalized women. It is alarming how many political and economic decisions here at home are taken without a care for their long-term consequences or indirect effects. As the American Founders well knew, a democratic society without the influence of religion can easily consume its own cultural foundations. It can easily fall into a selfish materialism and a brutish indifference about the future. To meet the challenges our polity will face in the years to come, America needs *all* her voices, now more than ever.

But here is a key point: Religious participants in public debates will not be effective unless they can speak in terms that are persuasive to men and women of good will—of diverse faiths and no faith. They will get nowhere if they just preach to the converted. Or if they behave like the Dublin man who went to London and saw a terrible brawl going on in the street. He went up to one of the participants, tapped him on the shoulder, and asked, "Excuse me, is this a private fight, or may I join in?" In the "politics of persuasion," it is intelligence and skill in dialogue that will count.

That is where the education that dares to be different can make a difference. You have perhaps heard Father Hesburgh say: "The worst heresy is that one life cannot make a difference." But you may wonder: Just how might a Domer's education make a difference?

Well, first, don't be surprised if ideas and habits of thinking you picked up here keep coming back to you, taking on deeper meanings, and radiating outward to unexpected places—like Father Ted's throw-away line years ago on science and religion. Don't be surprised if one day you find yourself quoting Patty O'Hara to your own children. An education like yours tends to be a "gift that keeps on giving."

Then, too, unlike the chameleons who tend to blend into the dominant culture just where it needs to be challenged, you Domers are more likely to be the kind of independent-minded citizens that our nation's Founders counted on.

You will have a headstart on bridging differences in our pluralistic society, because you know that tolerance doesn't consist merely in putting up with those who disagree with us. It means engaging them—because they are just as much creatures of God as we are; and because we know, alas, that our own access to truth is imperfect.

Finally, since your parents and I are veterans of the 1960s, I cannot resist adding that you are also well-equipped to be radicals—in the sense of getting to the root of things. Many people who take lofty moral positions on economic and social justice have sloughed off several other moral teachings that are hard to follow in our permissive society. Novelist Saul Bellow calls such persons practitioners of the "easy virtues." He compares them to a man who rides into a ghost town and declares himself sheriff. On the other hand, many staunch defenders of traditional personal morality and the protection of life falter when it comes to social justice. They can't quite wrap their minds around the preferential option for the poor.

But there are good reasons why the Catholic Church consistently warns not only against putting "profits ahead of people," but also against putting "self-indulgence ahead of our responsibilities to our families and the common good." There is a growing realization, across the political spectrum and among persons of all faiths, that materialism, present-mindedness, and carelessness about life at its frail beginnings and endings are creating a culture that corresponds to *nobody's* vision of the good society. There is a growing appreciation of the essential connection, the seamlessness, if you will, between the duty to respect every human being wherever he or she is on life's journey, and the duty to respond with compassionate justice to all who are in need. Here is where Judaeo-Christian traditions of responsibility and solidarity intersect with the great American traditions of hospitality and generosity, of welcome to the stranger and lending a helping hand to the person in need.

Now, speaking of hospitality reminds me of my promise not to delay the festivities. So let me speed you on your way with a blessing attributed to a woman who understood and responded to the radical message of the Gospel in all its fullness: St. Brigid of Kildare. Brigid's abbey in sixth-century Ireland was a haven for needy strangers and a hospice for the dying. And Brigid seems to have loved a good party. At least that is the impression one gets from her blessing which begins: "Lord, I would have a lake of the finest ale!" Brigid goes on:

> I would welcome the poor to my feast
> For they are God's children
> I would welcome the sick to my feast
> For they are God's joy
> Let the poor sit with Jesus at the highest place

And let the sick dance with the angels.
God bless the poor,
God bless the sick
And bless our human race
God bless our food
God bless our drink
All homes, O God, embrace.

If Brigid were here today, she would surely add: God bless the Notre Dame Class of 1996!

CHAPTER 17 • Religion and Democratic Society

# In the Country
# of Old People

*In May 2004, the Pontifical Academy of Social Sciences devoted its annual
plenary meeting to "Intergenerational Solidarity, Welfare, and Human Ecology."
As coordinator of that program, I prepared a final report, synthesized
in this essay for the October 2004 First Things.[1]*

OTTO VON BISMARCK NEVER DREAMED, when he established the world's
first social security system, that a large proportion of the populace would live
long enough to draw pensions. With a tight grip on the public purse, the
Iron Chancellor set age 65 as an eligibility threshold that few could be
expected to cross. When the U.S. version of the welfare state came into
being fifty years later, the labor force was still relatively large in comparison
to the population of those receiving benefits. Few could have anticipated, in
the New Deal era, the demographic developments that have brought all of
the institutions on which people rely for support and security to the brink of
crisis. Impeding any easy solution is the fact that many of the pressures on
families, welfare systems, and benevolent associations are the byproducts of
genuine advances in health and opportunity.

Longer life spans have expanded the population of frail elderly persons,
including victims of dementias characterized by lengthy periods of disability.
Changes in women's roles have greatly reduced the traditional pool of caregivers for the very young and the very old alike. Low birth rates are decreas-
ing the ratio of active workers to pensioners and persons requiring social
assistance. In combination, declining birth rates and improved longevity
mean that the dependent population now includes a much smaller proportion of children and a much larger proportion of disabled and elderly persons than ever before. But with increased divorce and unwed parenthood,
the poverty population is now composed largely of women and children.

The building pressure on economic and human resources from both ends
of the life cycle has received remarkably little attention from policymakers,

---

[1] Mary Ann Glendon, "Discovering Our Dependence," *First Things* 146 (October
2004): 11–13.

despite a warning from the Senate Special Committee on Aging in a 2002 report that, without significant reform, "the United States could be on the brink of a domestic financial crisis." The issues cannot be ignored much longer, however, for the first wave of the nation's 77 million babyboomers will reach age 65 in 2011. According to Alan Greenspan, the country "will almost surely be unable to meet the demands on resources that the retirement of the babyboom generation will make."

The pinch is already provoking generational conflict in the ambitious welfare states of northern Europe, where birth and immigration rates are lower than in the United States and where the elderly wield considerable political clout. Modest proposals to cut back on pensions or to raise the retirement age in France and Germany have met with strikes and protests from the groups affected. At the same time, young Europeans are complaining about the high cost of health care for the elderly, and resentful of fees that are eroding the tradition of free university education. (One German youth leader gained notoriety by suggesting that old folks should use crutches rather than seeking expensive hip replacements).

That the coming economic crunch is only one aspect of the dilemmas our aging society will confront was emphasized at two recent interdisciplinary meetings. It was the sense of the President's Council on Bioethics, after hearing testimony at its June meeting on aging, dementia, and caregiving, that discussions of these matters tend to neglect important medical, psychological, ethical, and social issues. The Council is currently in the process of deciding whether to explore the area further with a view toward producing a report that might aid in the search for practices and ideals adequate to the new culture of longevity.

That such investigations are urgently needed was one conclusion of the Pontifical Academy of Social Sciences after devoting its annual spring meeting in Rome to a conference on the ways that changing relations between generations have affected the very young, the frail elderly, and the severely ill or disabled—both in welfare states and in places where the welfare state is minimal or non-existent. The Academy, established in 1994 by Pope John Paul II, was charged by him with the task of contributing to the advance of the social sciences while helping to find "solutions to people's concrete problems, solutions based on social justice." Its membership, drawn from five continents, is composed of experts in the social sciences, including two American Nobel laureates in economics, Kenneth Arrow and Joseph Stiglitz. Like the U.S. President's Council, the Academicians were of the view that underlying the welfare crisis is a deeper crisis involving changes in the meanings and values that people attribute to aging and mortality, sex and procreation, marriage, gender, parenthood, relations among the generations, and life itself.

The papers presented to the Academy and its conclusions, soon to be published by Libreria Editrice Vaticana, should be of wide interest since several were based on cross-national studies. The speakers included, for example, Francis Fukuyama, whose book *The Great Disruption* treats the late twentieth-century revolution in behavior and ideas in affluent nations, and Jacques Vallin, the Director of the French National Demographic Institute, who has studied the changing age structure of populations on a worldwide basis.

The presentations led to much discussion of the implications for the dependent population of the dramatic alterations in social norms that took place in many countries in recent decades. Where children are concerned, changes in the sexual and marriage behavior of large numbers of adults have altered the very experience of childhood. Moreover, as the proportion of child-less households has grown, and societies have become more adult-centered, the general level of concern for the well-being of children has declined. As the saying goes, out of sight, out of mind. Cambridge economist Partha Dasgupta noted an interesting "free rider" problem: Childless individuals (who as a group enjoy a higher standard of living than child-raising persons as a group) expect to be cared for in old age through benefits financed by a labor force they did not help to replenish.

With widespread acceptance of the notion that behavior in the highly personal areas of sex and marriage is of no concern to anyone other than the "consenting adults" involved, it has been easy to overlook what should have been obvious from the beginning: Individual actions *in the aggregate* exert a profound influence on what kind of society we are bringing into being. Eventually, when large numbers of individuals act primarily with regard to self-fulfillment, the entire culture is transformed. The evidence is now over-whelming that affluent Western nations have been engaged in a massive social experiment—an experiment that brought new opportunities and lib-erties to adults, but one that puts children and other dependents at consid-erable risk.

Disarray in one sustaining cultural institution, moreover, weakens the others. The spread of family breakdown has been accompanied by distur-bances in schools, neighborhoods, churches, local governments, and work-place associations—all of the structures that have traditionally depended on families for their support and that in turn have served as important resources for families in times of stress. The law has changed rapidly, too, becoming a testing ground for various ways of re-imagining family relations and an arena for struggles among competing ideas about individual liberty, equality between men and women, human sexuality, marriage, and family life. It does not seem an exaggeration to speak, as some at the Rome conference did, of a breakdown in social norms.

Perhaps no single development, apart from the epidemic of fatherless-ness, has had more impact on the environment of childhood, the care of dependents, or the health of the mediating institutions of civil society than the mass movement of women, including mothers of young children, into the paid labor force. It is a mark of great progress that we now live in a world where women have more opportunities than ever before in history. No society, however, has yet figured out how to assure satisfactory conditions for child-raising when both parents of young children work outside the home. No society has yet found a substitute for the loss of other types of caregiving previously provided mainly by women.

For many women, moreover, the picture of progress is ambiguous. Though birth rates are declining, the majority of women still become mothers. When mothers of young children enter the labor force, whether because of necessity or desire, they tend to seek work that is compatible with family roles. That usually means jobs with lower pay, fewer benefits, and fewer opportunities for advancement than those available to persons without family responsibilities. So, ironically, the more a woman foregoes advancement in the workplace for the sake of caring for her own children, the more she and her children are at risk if the marriage ends in divorce. On the other hand, the more she invests in her work, the greater the likelihood her children will have care that is less than optimal. It is not surprising therefore that women are hedging against these risks in two ways: by having fewer children than women did in the past, and by seeking types of labor force participation that are compatible with parenting. In so doing, they often sacrifice *both* their child-raising preferences and their chances to have remunerative, satisfying, and secure employment.

Thus, while enormous advances have been made by women without children, mothers face new versions of an old problem: Caregiving, one of the most important forms of human work, receives little respect and reward, whether performed in the family, or for wages outside the home. Despite these risks, most married women still accept primary responsibility for child care, thereby incurring disadvantages in the labor force. If divorce or separation occurs, most mothers seek and accept primary responsibility for the care of children even when they are not well-equipped financially to do so. Indeed, if women did not continue to shoulder these risks and burdens, it is hard to see how any social institution could make up for the services they now provide.

The main solutions proposed by the feminism of the 1970s (at the zenith of the welfare state) were the socialization of caregiving and the equalization of child care responsibilities between fathers and mothers. But those ideas have not had broad appeal—either for parents or for taxpayers. They ignore that for many women, caring for children and other family members is central to their identity, sustaining the relationships that make their lives meaningful.

What makes the dependency-welfare crisis so confounding is that all of society's sources of support and security are implicated. Families, still the central pillar of our caregiving system, are losing much of their capacity to care for their own dependent members, just when government is becoming less capable of fulfilling the roles it once took over from families. Ironically, the ambition of welfare states to free individuals from much of their dependence on families, and to relieve families of some of their most burdensome responsibilities, may have succeeded just well enough to put dependents at heightened risk now that welfare states are faltering.

At the Rome meeting, the British social theorist Margaret Archer pointed out a curious fact that may have impeded reform efforts: The overemphasis on self-sufficiency in contemporary political thought coexists with an approach to welfare that underrates human capacities and ignores important dimensions of personhood. Social policy, she noted, has been influenced by mindsets that treat human beings as passive subjects or instrumental rationalists rather than as active agents whose decisions are influenced not only by calculation of self-interest but by strongly held values. In a similar vein, the Italian sociologist Pierpaolo Donati pointed out that prevailing concepts of society also inhibit constructive solutions: Society is not just a collection of self-seeking individuals, but "a fabric of relationships, to a certain extent ambivalent and conflicted, in need of solidarity."

Perhaps the most important conclusion reached by the Pontifical Academy was that if political deliberation about the impending dependency-welfare crisis proceeds within a framework based solely on the idea of competition for scarce resources, the outlook for dependents is grim. As noted, divisive intergenerational conflict is already observable in Europe. The most ominous development, of course, is the growing normalization of the extermination of persons who become inconvenient and burdensome to maintain at life's frail beginnings and endings.

To state the obvious: If the outlook for dependents is grim, the outlook for everyone is grim. Despite our attachment to the ideal of the free, self-determining individual, we humans are dependent, social beings. We still begin our lives in the longest period of dependency of any mammal. Almost all of us spend much of our lives either as dependents, or caring for dependents, or financially responsible for dependents. To devise constructive approaches to the dependency-welfare crisis will require acceptance of those simple facts of life. And it will require a certain tragic sensibility, for there is no solution that will not entail striking balances among competing goods.

CHAPTER 18 • In the Country of Old People

# Law and Culture

# Human Personhood
# in the Federalist Papers

*In 1992, the Federalist Society held a symposium
on the philosophical foundations of* The Federalist. *My contribution
was this talk on the authors' concept of the person. A version of the talk
appeared in 16* Harvard Journal of Law and Public Policy *1301 (1993).*[1]

**S**CHOLARLY DISCUSSION OF THE FOUNDATIONS of *The Federalist Papers* typically takes the form of speculation about the relative significance of one or another strand among its many and varied philosophical sources. The authors of two 1992 books critiquing the Framers' assumptions about human nature, however, do not tarry in the garden of influences. Francis Fukuyama in *The End of History and the Last Man*[2] and Thomas Pangle in *The Ennobling of Democracy: The Challenge of the Postmodern Age*,[3] do, however, regard *The Federalist* as primarily, though not exclusively, grounded in the new science of politics of Machiavelli, Hobbes, Locke, and Montesquieu. Of particular relevance to the present symposium is that both authors find *The Federalist*'s vision of human nature to be incomplete in certain key respects. For Fukuyama, it is the human desire for recognition, that has been slighted; for Pangle, it is the erotic thirst for knowledge. Moreover, both authors trace the Framers' alleged neglect to the view of human nature elaborated in the principal foundational works from which the Framers drew.

Fukuyama and Pangle see Madison, Hamilton, and Jay as accepting from Hobbes and Locke a conception of the human person as a being driven primarily by fear and desire, who is enabled, through the faculty of reason, to escape from a precarious existence in the state of nature and to form societies with a modicum of order, liberty, and security. Unlike the classical

---

[1] Mary Ann Glendon, "Philosophical Foundations of The Federalist Papers: Nature of Man and Nature of Law." *Harvard Journal of Law and Public Policy* 16 (1; Winter 1993): 23–32.

[2] Francis Fukuyama, *The End of History and the Last Man* (New York: Free Press, 1992).

[3] Thomas Pangle, *The Ennobling of Democracy: The Challenge of the Postmodern Age.* (Baltimore: Johns Hopkins, 1992).

political philosophers, these early modern political theorists and statesmen tended to understand "reason" simply as calculation in the service of self-preservation and self-interest. Reason, on this understanding, is the servant of the passions, rather than the means through which the passions may on occasion be mastered.

Fukuyama contends that the image of the human person as a creature of appetite and aversion led the architects of American constitutionalism to underestimate the power of another aspect of human nature which frequently outweighs material self-interest, and which is, therefore, a political force of no small consequence. This other "part of the soul," as Fukuyama (following Plato) puts it, is *thymos*. *Thymos* is what Plato called "spiritedness," and what Fukuyama himself (following Hegel) calls the "desire for recognition"—recognition of one's own worth and dignity, and of the worth of the persons and principles that one values. Good *thymos*, with its associated sentiments of shame, honor, and righteous anger, is the source of political virtues like courage and public spiritedness, while bad (or frustrated) *thymos* has been known to precipitate individuals and whole nations into the deepest of trouble.

Fukuyama does not claim that the authors of *The Federalist* were unaware of *thymos*. As he recognizes, Hamilton and Madison held that it was the dangerous propensities of human nature, with pride and ambition prominent among them, that give rise to the need for government, and that pose a constant threat to peace and order. To neutralize these passions, the Framers devised strategies for holding them in check, or channeling them into the private pursuit of wealth, comfort, and security. Fukuyama's contention is that because the Framers regarded pride and ambition in such a negative light, they erred on the side of caution in checking and countervailing the desire for recognition in public life. As a result, he argues that the Framers did not take full advantage of the opportunity to harness the positive aspects of *thymos* in the service of the democratic experiment, and that they may even have increased the risk to the polity of the sentiments of anger and resentment that arise when *thymos* is not properly satisfied. Even worse, their new-fangled institutional contrivances to suppress the desire for recognition or to direct it away from public life may have helped to bring into being men and women like Nietzsche's "last men," fit only to be subjects rather than citizens.

Fukuyama effectively exposes a paradox at the heart of the Anglo-American version of liberal democracy. The political theory on which the liberal state is founded provides no particular reason why talented people should choose public service over other pursuits, or why men and women in private life should perform community service—or even conduct themselves responsibly in everyday life. Yet the success of liberal democratic experiments is crucially dependent on their ability to produce virtuous and public-spirited citizens and statesmen. To Fukuyama this leads to yet another paradox:

Liberal democracies . . . are not self-sufficient: the community life on which they depend must ultimately come from a source different from liberalism itself. The men and women who made up American society at the time of the founding of the United States were not isolated, rational individuals calculating their self-interest. Rather, they were for the most part members of religious communities held together by a common moral code and belief in God. The rational liberalism that they eventually came to embrace was not a projection of that pre-existing culture, but existed in some tension with it. . . . [I]n the long run those liberal principles had a corrosive effect on the values predating liberalism necessary to sustain strong communities, and thereby on a liberal society's ability to be self-sustaining.

Pangle, in *The Ennobling of Democracy*, arrives at a strikingly similar conclusion: "Did not theorists like Hamilton . . . depend upon, and yet inadequately account or provide for, certain absolutely crucial moral and educational foundations of civic republican culture. . . ?" Like Fukuyama, Pangle comes not to denigrate but to shore up American constitutionalism. In that spirit, he is concerned about the tension between the philosophical foundations on which American constitutionalism was constructed and the cultural foundations that are necessary to sustain it. "[H]as modern theory," he asks, "in its successful attempt to clarify and satisfy the most basic legitimate demands of political life, obscured the clear view of human excellence that is required in order to shape a public life that reflects the whole of the common good?" Pangle's thoughts then turn, as Fukuyama's do, to whether the liberal political vision could be strengthened by incorporating a fuller conception of the human person.

Though Pangle's criticism of the anthropology of *The Federalist* consists merely of a few passing observations in a book primarily devoted to the challenge of postmodernism, it provides an illuminating complement to the tack taken by Fukuyama. For Pangle, what was slighted in the Framers' understanding of human nature were the higher forms of reason and desire that enable us to master the lower passions, as well as the role of nurture and education in cultivating those higher faculties. The desire for knowledge and the love of truth, Pangle argues, are particular forms of *eros*. Those passions, he contends, not only could serve as the foundation for the firmest personal and political attachments, but could undergird a sense of common humanity in our increasingly diverse society. Like the positive aspects of *thymos*, though, the eros of the mind requires cultivation. Pangle observes that the framework of American constitutionalism "makes very little provision for the inculcation, fostering, or even preservation of [the] crucial excellences of character" on which the Founders relied to keep unruly lower passions in check.

Pangle and Fukuyama share the apprehension that structures, laws, and institutions designed a certain way will tend over time to produce a certain kind of individual. Paradoxically then, on their view, the culture that the Founders helped to bring into being may have rendered it less likely that that their descendants would be virtuous citizen-statesmen like themselves (fewer George Washingtons, more hollow men). To Fukuyama, contemporary preoccupation with private satisfactions evokes Nietzsche's "last men":

> Throwing themselves into essentially unpleasant or stultifying work with a view to the accumulation of greater material satisfactions and petty signs of prestige . . . may not future generations of Americans lead increasingly fragmented and purposeless existences in a world of unprecedented materialism, desperate personal isolation, and inner psychological weakness verging on collapse?

Pangle is prompted to wonder about if the capacity for citizenship can be sustained:

> [T]he question that has bulked ever larger as our constitutional system has evolved . . . , is whether and how the system provides for the moral and civic education of a people that becomes more fragmented in every sense as it is given more and more power and responsibility.

Both Fukuyama and Pangle render an important service to students of law and politics by forcing their readers to confront a fact vividly present to the authors of *The Federalist*, but which modern Americans all too easily forget. The fact is that the regime explained and defended by Madison, Hamilton, and Jay was and remains an experiment, one that depends heavily on certain cultural foundations. The experiment, moreover, is a test of two great perennial questions about politics: Whether there can be a democratic republic in an extended territory with a heterogeneous population. And whether, as Hamilton put it in *Federalist* No. 1, human beings are really capable of devising good governments by "reflection and choice, or whether they are forever destined to depend for their political constitutions on accident and force."

I am less convinced than Fukuyama and Pangle, though, that the authors of *The Federalist* overlooked the higher forms of reason and desire. The forgetfulness of the classical, biblical, and republican strands of our heritage to which *The End of History* and *The Ennobling of Democracy* call attention seems to me to be more characteristic of our own times than of the cultural milieu of eighteenth-century America. The view of human nature in the pages of *The Federalist* is a complex one, informed not only by the new science of politics, but by classical and biblical ideas, as well as by antebellum notions of what a gentleman is and does. Consider, for example, John Jay's discussion in *Federalist* No. 64 of the way that honor, oaths, reputations, conscience, love of country, and family affections and attachments influence the human mind. It is true that if one merely canvasses the passages where human nature is discussed, one finds the authors fairly consistently presenting a rather somber account of human nature that goes something like this: Human nature is a mixture of base and virtuous elements. "Just as there is a certain degree of depravity in human nature which requires a certain degree of circumspection and mistrust, so there are other qualities which justify a portion of esteem and confidence. Republican government requires the latter in a higher degree than any other" (No. 55, Madison). But one cannot count on the virtuous parts to come though in the clutch: "If impulse and opportunity be suffered to coincide, we well know that neither moral nor religious motives can be relied on as an adequate control" (No. 10, Madison). It is precisely because men are not angels, that we need government.

Suppose, though, that instead of just asking what the text says about human nature, we ask some other questions, such as: (1) To what qualities of the reader do Madison, Hamilton, and Jay appeal in their effort to be persuasive? (2) How do they have "Publius" present *himself* to his readers? and (3) What sort of relationship do they try to establish between Publius and the reader? The answers to those questions, I suggest, disclose a kind of "strange loop" in *The Federalist*. That is, although Publius keeps insisting that it is unrealistic to count on human reason (e.g., "It is probably more to be wished than expected that the plan will receive dispassionate consideration," No. 2), the ultimate success of his argument depends to a considerable degree on the will and ability of the readers (and other Americans) to transcend the passions of the moment and to heed his exhortations to be an example to all nations. The success of the argument also depends on convincing the reader that Publius himself and the delegates to the constitutional convention were able to do this too!

Over and over, Publius appeals to the prideful qualities that Fukuyama calls *thymos* and to the disinterested form of reason that Pangle sees as grounded in a kind of *eros*, for example, "Happy will it be for ourselves and honorable for human nature if we have wisdom and virtue enough to set so glorious an example to mankind!" (No. 36). *The Federalist* is not just an appeal to reason over passion. It is also a shrewd appeal to certain kinds of passion. Much of its persuasive power comes from the way it speaks directly to what Lincoln in his *First Inaugural* was to call "the better angels of our nature." Consider the passage in which Madison describes his ideal readers: "These papers are not addressed to persons who are without a spirit of moderation or to biased minds. They solicit the attention only of those who add to a sincere zeal for the happiness of their country a temper favorable to a just estimate of the means of promoting it" (No. 37). Though Madison, Hamilton, and Jay repeatedly profess their skepticism about the ability of human reason to master passion, they frame their arguments so as to appeal to the human capacity to do precisely that. They call for "correct and unprejudiced minds" and they reach out to "sincere and disinterested advocates of good government."

CHAPTER 19 • Human Personhood in the Federalist Papers

The best evidence on this point is the structure and style of the papers themselves—the way they state the questions, weigh the evidence, and seriously consider arguments pro and con. The papers are a virtuoso performance of the exhortation in *Federalist* No. 71 to consider the ideas in all their aspects, and to trace them out to all their consequences. Thus, the human person, as envisioned by Hamilton, Jay, and Madison, seems to me to be much more than just a rational calculator. He is also a knower and a chooser, the kind of person who might just possibly be capable of "establishing good government through reflection and choice."

Fukuyama and Pangle might respond to the foregoing observations in this vein: "Naturally, the Framers, with their classical educations, knew about the higher forms of reason and desire, and no doubt they strategically deployed this knowledge in their argumentation. Our contention is that they did not sufficiently attend to these aspects of human nature in their design for government."

But where does that response lead? Fukuyama is not very specific concerning what the Framers should have done to keep us all from turning into the civic equivalent of 90-pound weaklings. It is true that our constitutional design for government includes a variety of devices meant to keep individual and group passions under control. Fukuyama seems to suggest that these checks have gone too far. But without some indication of what institutional corrections he proposes, the critique has a disconcerting resemblance to Roberto Unger's attack in his 1987 book, *False Necessity*, on checks and balances as inhibitors of "creative" social ferment. I am sure Fukuyama would not join in Unger's call for governmental "ministries of destabilization," but it is hard to know what to make of his apparent lament that Hegel was born too late to inspire the founders:

> Hegel gives us the opportunity to reinterpret modern liberal democracy in terms that are rather different from the Anglo-Saxon tradition of liberalism emanating from Hobbes and Locke. This Hegelian understanding of liberalism is at the same time a more noble vision of what liberalism represents, and a more accurate account of what people around the world mean when they say they want to live in a democracy.

Pangle's observation that the authors of *The Federalist* depended upon, yet did not adequately provide for, certain moral and educational foundations seems well-grounded. But I do not think the Framers are to be greatly faulted for this oversight. They were well aware that their enterprise required certain kinds of excellence on the part of both citizens and statesmen. Indeed, Madison specifically acknowledged that republican government required a higher degree of virtue in its citizens than any other form (No. 55). They knew that their experiment depended in crucial ways on "the general spirit of the people" (No. 84). Accordingly, their federal design for government provided for and protected much free space within which they expected families, churches, and townships to enable citizens to learn the skills of cooperative living and self-government, as well as to acquire the republican virtues of self-restraint and concern for the common good. When one reflects on the social conditions of that time, it is hard to blame eighteenth-century statesmen for leaving such matters in local hands, and for devoting most of their energy and attention to problems that must have seemed to be much more urgent.

Nevertheless, Pangle is right to remind contemporary Americans that we ignore at our peril the classical teachings that a republic must attend to the conditions—especially nurture and education—that are required to produce the kind of citizens who can rise to the high demands of a republican form of government. Fukuyama may well be right to sound an early warning that the remarkable advance of liberal democracy in the world carries risks of a kind that would have been a luxury to contemplate in the years before the fall of communism. However one evaluates the political theory of the Founders and their philosophical antecedents, the inescapable fact is that responsibility for the fate of their innovative political experiment has now devolved to their successors. Madison, aware of the changes that time might wreak, declined to pronounce on what might become of the American project with the passage of the years and with increase in the size of the population (No. 55). That would left to the political imaginations of future generations. Pangle and Fukuyama, then, should not be taken as visiting the failings of the sons upon the fathers, but as inviting serious reflection by contemporary men and women on latent possibilities and perennial questions.

CHAPTER 19 • Human Personhood in the Federalist Papers

# Reflections on the
# Flag-Burning Case

*The U.S. Supreme Court majority's 1989 decision in* Texas v. Johnson *that flag burning was constitutionally protected expressive activity was controversial among legal scholars and unpopular with the public. It prompted this reflection on the state of our civic culture, published in the March 1990 issue of* First Things.[1]

O NE OF MY JOBS as a summer reporter for the *The Berkshire Eagle* during my college and law school years was to cover the Fourth of July parade in Pittsfield, Massachusetts. This day-long assignment in stifling heat was not coveted by the regular newsroom staff, and so it routinely fell to me as low person on the totem pole.

In my memory, all of these occasions now are blended into one big parade, except for the time I sat next to Norman Rockwell in the reviewing stand. When the head of the procession, American flag held high, passed in front of us, Rockwell, himself already a national symbol of sorts, leaped to his feet, placed his hand over his heart, and called out, "Long may she wave!" The rest of us rose too as the first flag passed by. What we did not anticipate was that our illustrious neighbor would stand to salute the flag every single time one passed. There were a lot of American flags in a Fourth of July parade in those days. But, after some initial confusion, we all followed suit. The old man gave us quite a workout.

With nearly thirty years distance from that event, what strikes me now is that Rockwell's feeling about the flag, or at least his way of expressing it, was even then out of synch with the sentiments of most of his fellow Berkshire County residents. All in the reviewing stand were slightly discomfited by Rockwell's repeated manifestations of civic piety. I am sure that what drove most of us to our feet after the initial salute had less to do with the flag than with the concern of some of us that Rockwell should not be left standing

---

[1] Mary Ann Glendon, "Reflections on the Flag-Burning Case," *First Things* (March 1990): 11–13.

alone and of others that they should not be embarrassed by remaining seated once nearly everyone else was standing.

This is not to say we were indifferent to the flag. Still, as I recall all those parades, it seems to me that the things that moved us were rather more personal. Besides the stirring martial music and the fun of seeing friends and relatives marching, there was the serious part of the parade—groups of veterans in uniform, middle-aged and elderly survivors of the nation's wars and military adventures whose justice we did not then question. The Fourth of July, marking the beginning of a war of independence, belonged in an important way (as did Memorial Day) to our local American Legionnaires and the Veterans of Foreign Wars. Of all the people who have been distressed by the Supreme Court's decision in the flag-burning case, the most deeply and personally aggrieved are probably the nation's veterans and their families. Yet, even for these, it has been a long, long way from Iwo Jima to Saigon and beyond.

Now, in the new post-Vietnam America, there comes before the nation's highest court a case involving sacrilege against the principal symbol of our civil religion. The legal issue, strictly speaking, was a rather narrow one. Several years ago, the Court had decided that civil blasphemy was protected by the First Amendment (for example, that the state could not constitutionally punish *verbal* disrespect for the flag). It had also extended constitutional protection to certain disrespectful *behavior* toward the flag (for example, wearing the flag on the seat of one's pants). Was burning the flag in a different category? In deciding that it was not, the majority made clear that flag burning that tended to provoke an immediate breach of the peace would still be punishable under state laws.

Something more profound than distinctions among various ways of expressing contempt must account for the emotion elicited by the Court's decision that flag burning, too, was within the scope of protected freedom of expression. Yet it is hard to zero in on what that something is. The four judicial opinions in the case, the arguments of the state of Texas and of the defendant, Gregory Johnson, as well as press reports of the reactions of the citizenry to the decision reveal a remarkable lack of consensus on what the flag means. To the defendant it is a symbol of oppression and evil ("Red, white, and blue, we spit on you"). To the State of Texas, it is a symbol of "nationhood and national unity." To constitutional law scholar Laurence Tribe, it is an "emblem of unity *and* diversity." To Justice Brennan, writing for the majority, it symbolizes our principles of freedom, inclusiveness, and tolerance of dissent, and thus protects the very behavior that defiled it. But Justice Stevens, in a strange-loop dissent, also saw the flag as a symbol of freedom and tolerance, yet considered that was precisely why it should be protected from "desecration."

The range of popular reactions was even wider. One witness to the flag burning reverently collected its remains and buried them in his backyard. Another bystander, interviewed on National Public Radio, said, "The way I see it, I buy a flag, it's my property. I can burn it." An American Legion spokesman who opposed the decision, when asked on the *Today Show* to say precisely what the flag symbolized, replied, in a simplified version of the Stevens strange loop, "It stands for the fact that this is a country where we can do what we want, where we have the right to do what we want."

What is one to make of the degree to which those who would make flag burning a crime resort to religious language in describing the flag and the offense against it? The section of the Texas Penal Code under which the defendant was prosecuted is titled "Desecration of a Venerated Object." The venerated objects protected by the statute include not only the national flag, but also the Texas flag, public monuments, and places of worship and burial. In his dissent, Chief Justice Rehnquist referred to the "almost mystical reverence" and "the uniquely deep awe and respect for our flag felt by virtually all of us."

Not everyone is comfortable with speaking about the flag in terms usually reserved for religious matters, or with according "mystical reverence" to secular symbols. Johnson's lawyer pointed out that in National Socialist Germany, the swastika was protected from desecration. Is it possible that what is disturbing to devotees of civil religion about the flag-burning decision is that we are increasingly aware of the difficulty in specifying any meaningful shared content to the symbol? Despite the spectacle of politicians falling over themselves to rally 'round the flag, it is doubtful that there is any substantial American consensus on what the flag symbolizes, because it is becoming hard to specify in what sense this increasingly heterogeneous country is a "nation."

Further, it is unlikely that a contrary decision in the flag case, or the passage of a statute, or adoption of a constitutional amendment could ever settle these matters. A shared sense of the meaning of the flag has vanished from the national scene along with the township life that Norman Rockwell knew, idealized, and immortalized. Civil society has become more complex, with national political boundaries becoming less relevant to economic activity and the flow of commerce, and with many Americans defining themselves in relation to a region, a race, a religion, or other group before identifying with the nation.

The civil religion is in a period of upheaval. Whether the outcome is to be reformation or decline, no one can say. The crisis of faith has brought forth many who are attached to a past that can never be retrieved, or that perhaps never was—at least not in quite the way they imagine it. It has brought out others who delight in destruction and irreverence for their own sake. At best, it has given rise to civil conversation about the goals our society is to pursue.

Meanwhile, the job of protecting the national symbol has been shifted from law to other social norms: custom, convention, disapproval. As the pub philosopher Andy Capp once remarked, "The difference between law and custom is that it takes a helluva lot more nerve to violate a custom."

CHAPTER 20 • Reflections on the Flag-Burning Case

# CHAPTER 21

# Laurence Tribe on Abortion

*I was disappointed in my colleague Laurence Tribe's book*
*Abortion: The Clash of Absolutes, for it seemed to me a partisan brief*
*in the guise of a scholarly analysis of the U.S. Supreme Court's abortion decisions.*
*This review appeared in the August/September 1990 issue of First Things.[1]*

*A*BORTION: *THE* C*LASH OF* A*BSOLUTES* is an expert brief on behalf of strict adherence to the terms of the abortion liberty granted in *Roe* v. *Wade*, no matter how much leeway the Supreme Court may give to legislatures in the post-*Webster* era. The renown of its author, Harvard Law Professor Laurence Tribe, is such that the book bids fair to become the official handbook of abortion rights advocates for the next several years. In ten concise, clearly written chapters, he canvasses the current legal situation, the history of abortion, the problem of finding abortion rights in the Constitution, the question of the personhood of the fetus, the politics of abortion, and the possibility of a new approach to this most divisive of political issues.

Tribe's announced purpose is a constructive one: to challenge the inevitability of permanent conflict on abortion policy; to examine critically the arguments on both sides of the debate, identifying areas of common ground and disagreement; and "to lay the groundwork for moving on." He hopes, he says, to persuade his readers "that we need not cling so fiercely to one or the other extreme, that there is room for movement toward healing our divisions over the abortion question based on shared values and goals."

This introductory statement might lead one to suppose that Tribe is about to endorse the sort of accommodation currently proposed by moderate abortion-rights supporters like Daniel Callahan. These compromises seek to safeguard unborn life in early pregnancy (where empathy with the fetus is more difficult) chiefly by creating opportunities for advice and help to the pregnant woman, but would increase protection for the fetus as its development progresses. Most of Tribe's book, however, is aimed at countering the growing consensus that some sort of political middle ground must be found between a total ban on abortions and the abortion license of *Roe* v. *Wade*. He

---

[1] Mary Ann Glendon, "Intra-Tribal Warfare," review of *Abortion: The Clash of Absolutes* by Laurence Tribe, *First Things* 5 (August/September 1990): 55–59.

puts his very considerable legal and rhetorical talents in the service of shoring up the crumbling doctrine of *Roe*—if not by court decision, then by legislation, and if not by state legislation, then by a pre-emptive federal freedom-of-choice act. Though the book is in the form of a search for accommodation, the search leads Tribe to the position currently taken by the pro-choice leadership: not the slightest legal interference with the abortion rights granted by *Roe* v. *Wade* should be tolerated.

One by one, Tribe considers and rejects the major proposals for reform of abortion law. He cannot even approve bans on sex-selection abortions, for he sees no evidence that sex-selection abortion is a problem in the United States, and forbidding them could be the camel's nose under the tent, leading to further erosion of abortion rights. Proposals for notification of parents of minors, mandatory counseling and information about alternatives to abortion, regulation of abortion clinics, or limits on the reasons for which abortions may be performed are labeled as pseudo-compromises that "offer only an illusion of reasonable accommodation." Such proposals are "cruel" because, to the extent that some women seeking abortions are denied or delayed, "we will still be faced with the disruptions of life and the unwanted children. . . ." The truly moderate position, Tribe explains, is *Roe* itself, which wisely leaves the decision to the woman herself but permits some regulation in the interest of the fetus after viability—so long as that regulation does not interfere with the woman's "health."

The attempt to portray *Roe* as moderate is not the most convincing part of Tribe's book. Since the Court has defined "health" as "well being," *Roe* leaves virtually no room for protection even of viable fetuses from abortion. This was made abundantly clear in the cases that followed *Roe* where the Court struck down nearly every legislative attempt to regulate late abortions. Even *Webster* merely permits a state to require a test for viability. The post-*Roe* cases reveal how little regulation in the interest of protecting unborn life the Court has been willing to tolerate. In 1979, for example, the Court struck down a legislative attempt to require that postviability abortions be performed using methods that would give the fetus a chance to be born alive. If *Roe* and its progeny are not extreme, one must wonder why no country other than China has gone so far in exempting abortion from legal regulation.

Although he defends the broad abortion rights granted in *Roe*, Tribe does suggest, with hindsight, that it would have been wiser for the Court to have decided the case on narrower grounds. He explains that the abortion right could then have been expanded slowly in later cases, so as to get the public used to it bit by bit, rather than shocking and galvanizing pro-life sentiment with one sudden dramatic decision. (There is a certain tension between these strategic considerations and Tribe's effort to portray *Roe* as moderate.)

After learning that the author approves of no compromise where *Roe*'s abortion liberty is concerned, the reader's curiosity is piqued. What is the new approach that will aid us to transcend conflicts over the abortion issue? Stated in the most general way, Tribe's proposal is one that virtually all pro-life and pro-choice partisans have already accepted: "We must reduce the number of situations in which women are pregnant but do not want to be." Tribe would proceed toward this common ground mainly on two fronts: social programs and technology. Like most pro-life supporters who share his unexceptionable goal, Tribe favors efforts to make our society more hospitable to children, supportive of motherhood, and encouraging to child-raising families. To accomplish these ends, he looks mainly toward governmental initiatives through parental leaves, maternity benefits, day care, and so on. He does not mention the large part of pro-life activity and resources devoted to some 3,400 local organizations that afford financial and other assistance to enable women to continue with their pregnancies.

The social welfare side of Tribe's new approach will appeal to many pro-lifers, especially those Catholics who see abortion as part of the "seamless garment" of life issues. But it is disappointing that Tribe cites with approval a *New York Times* Op-Ed piece by President Carter's former counsel, Lloyd Cutler, arguing that the state has a moral obligation to provide for pregnant women and children if it denies poor women free access to abortions. Tribe praises the article without mentioning the sinister reason Cutler gives for insisting on our social duties to the poor: "The moral zeal of the right-to-life movement ought to be tempered by the realization that for every unwanted child they force into this world, they may be piling huge future obligations on all of us that our Government would be bound to satisfy." There is a world of difference between the preferential option for the poor advocated by many Catholics and Cutler's constricted vision of the human community, reinforced as the latter is with a stern warning about a potential "sharp growth of the underclass." In the former view, public and private social assistance are expressions of neighborliness; in the latter, increased spending for the poor is presented as a punishment for heedless pro-lifers and a warning to taxpayers.

A Nobel prize will surely be in order for the man or woman who figures out how to bring forth Tribe's (and pro-life's) ideal society where abortions will no longer be sought. So far, however, the common goal seems elusive, and the question therefore becomes: What do we do in the meantime? In a section titled "Using Technology to Circumvent Destiny," Tribe speculates that scientific advances may soon render both birth control and abortion safer, simpler, and less physically intrusive.

An absolutely safe, highly effective, nonintrusive contraceptive could prevent an enormous number of unwanted pregnancies. Even slightly improved contraceptives would reduce the demand for abortions.

Several alternatives to available contraceptive technologies are in effective use in some parts of Europe or are at least being examined seriously. For women these include: contraceptive implants placed under the skin; injectable microspheres and micro-capsules that provide a constant dose of a contraceptive hormone over several months; monthly injectables; vaginal rings that release hormones; nasal sprays that prevent ovulation; and, apparently, intracervical implants to neutralize sperm by using an electrical current to deter migration across the cervix and toward the fallopian tubes.

Near-perfect control of procreation, Tribe hopes, may be within our grasp. But how perfect will it be? Most, though not all, birth control innovations are meant to be used by women. Reactions to such matters are subjective, of course, but I must confess that to me this array of implants, injections, rings, sprays, and electric currents does not sound "absolutely safe" or even "non-intrusive." Would many men use the male counterparts to these devices that Tribe dutifully lists in another passage?

When contraception fails, Tribe seems to pin great hopes on RU-486. Referring to its relative safety and ease of use, he finds it hard to see why it should be "denied" to women. As with contraceptives that act upon the woman's body chemistry, however, it is not clear that high-tech is really the safe way to go. The RU-486 method requires the patient to take three doses of this synthetic steroid, followed by an injection or suppository of the hormone prostaglandin. As a contemporary of many women who were told that another steroid, DES, was a simple, safe precaution against miscarriage, I cannot help wondering whether an abortifacient whose long-term effects are unknown is so much a boon to women as to the next generation of tort lawyers.

The main flaws in Tribe's "new" approach, then, are two. Its first prong implies that we should not ask people to respect the lives of unwanted or inconvenient humans as long as we do not have in place a social-welfare state so perfect that pregnancy and child-rearing are no longer burdensome. The second, despite a nod in the direction of male contraception, keeps the main costs of the sexual revolution right where they have always been—on the bodies of women.

Fortunately, there *is* a large middle ground on which moderate pro-choice and pro-life supporters seem tentatively to be staking out positions. Contrary to stereotypes, and unlike the pro-choice leadership, many thoughtful choice supporters are concerned not only with "who decides" but with what is decided. For this reason, abortion-rights proponent Daniel Callahan has concluded in a recent essay that the hostility of pro-choice leaders to any and all compromise is a tactical mistake. Polls show that most pro-choice supporters are troubled by certain grounds for abortion, and that they have a gradualist view of personhood.

Callahan warns that pro-choice loses support among its own ranks when it insists that discretionary abortions, for reasons such as sex selection, must be tolerated in order to protect "necessary" abortions. In a revealing passage of his chapter on the politics of abortion, Tribe shows that he knows this too:

> Polling data suggest that, if the pro-choice movement is to maintain its momentum, it cannot let the prolife side shift the debate to why a woman wants any given abortion. The movement's current popularity clearly depends on keeping the question focused on *who* will make the decision.

Much of the pro-life leadership has already approached the middle ground that Callahan and other pro-choicers have sighted. While insisting on the principle of protection for innocent unborn human life, many pro-life leaders have accepted that under current conditions that goal must be pursued incrementally: by seeking the maximum legal protection for unborn life that is legally and culturally sustainable, and continuing to work for the transformation of individuals and society on which all "rights" ultimately depend.

In Tribe's concluding chapter, he too calls for introspection and conversion. He asks pro-life and pro-choice sympathizers to look deeply within themselves and confront honestly the possibility that their "real" motives may be different from their "professed" ones. The pro-life movement, he suggests at several points, is animated "in part" by a reluctance to see women play roles more equal to those of men and by harsh attitudes toward sexual morality. Theories that any significant part of pro-life is anti-woman, however, are hard put to explain why women are significantly more pro-life than men. It does not take Sherlock Holmes, on the other hand, to discern why the strongest supporters of elective abortion are young men.

The corresponding sin of pro-choice, Tribe suggests, may be a certain contempt for the "recent immigrants" and "lower-status religious groups" from which pro-life draws disproportionate support. In his speculation about the silent motives of pro-choicers, there is no mention of the profit-making abortion industry, or of the social attitudes that occasionally surface in statements like NARAL director Kate Michelman's:

> It's terrible to reduce such an important social issue to this, but the truth is that prenatal care, delivery, and the first year of life on welfare cost taxpayers $4,000 a year compared with $250 for an abortion.

My own view is that searches for hidden reasons are not very useful. Any coalitions as diverse as the pro-life and pro-choice movements will have some members who are animated by base and unworthy motives. After many years of watching the fray, I see no reason not to accept the accounts given by both sides as substantially accurate descriptions of what is most important to most of their supporters. After all, both sets of values *are* important. Women are entitled to equal respect, dignity, and personal liberty. But a society that establishes a constitutional right to dispose of unwanted unborn life may have implicitly adopted the principle that burdensome human beings can be sacrificed at the request of those on whom they depend.

Where the important values of women's liberty and protection of innocent life clash, countries all over the Western world have worked out political accommodations. These compromises do not avoid pain and tragedy—how could they? But they do try to balance compassion for pregnant women and concern for unborn life, sometimes by emphasizing the former in the early stages and the latter as the pregnancy advances. Imperfect? Yes. Unsatisfactory to practically all determined activists on both sides? Yes. But in a democratic and pluralistic society, as Tribe so rightly observes, education, dialogue, persuasion, and, ultimately, voting are "all we've got."

Lest any reader suppose that this review is a disinterested appraisal of Tribe's book, I should clarify my own position. Not only are the author and I friendly colleagues whose views on the abortion issue differ, but Tribe has strongly expressed his disagreement with me in the very book that is here under review. While these circumstances may render me somewhat less "objective" than the usual book reviewer, they also perhaps confer certain advantages, as I will endeavor to show by briefly relating the positions in the current book to the main themes of my colleague's life work.

Though *Abortion: A Clash of Absolutes* is an uncompromising defense of the extreme pro-choice position, it is a book shot through with questioning and self-doubt. Tribe's honesty and scientific sophistication compel him to face squarely what some pro-choice advocates deny: that the fetus is a developing human life. He is critical of Justice Blackmun in *Roe* and of those pro-choice supporters who avoid or deny this simple fact. Just how critical is demonstrated in a 1985 *Harvard Law Review* article where Tribe criticized the Court in *Roe* for "reaching beyond the facts of the case to rank the rights of the mother (sic) categorically over those of the fetus, and to deny the humanity of the fetus (even denying that a *viable* fetus is a 'person' prior to the 'moment' of birth). . . ." Like virtually all constitutional law specialists, regardless of their views on abortion, Tribe has found Justice Blackmun's opinion in *Roe* to be deeply flawed. Tribe's own idea of a better course to have pursued in that case is signaled in the 1985 article where he chides the Court for its failure to show "a more cautious sensitivity to the *mutual* helplessness of the mother and the unborn that could have accented the need for affirmative legislative action to moderate the clash between the two."

The Larry Tribe whose career as a constitutional lawyer has been largely devoted to protecting the rights of the weakest and most vulnerable members of society does not coexist comfortably with the Tribe who reluctantly defends the right to abort what he recognizes as a human person. Nor does the rhetoric of privatization come naturally to a man who espouses an active role for government in enlarging the community of those for whom we assume common responsibility, and who has so effectively shown why private choice must sometimes bow before important social interests such as equal opportunity in employment and equal access to accommodations.

I thus discern that within *The Clash of Absolutes* there is another clash, a sort of intra-Tribal struggle. It is a struggle between two good guys—the Larry Tribe who is compassionate toward the weak, vulnerable, and disenfranchised against the pioneering feminist Larry Tribe. Like many thoughtful men in the academic world, Tribe seems to feel that, as a male, he cannot appear to be siding with the enemies of feminism. His avowed ambivalence, however, together with the tension between the views expressed in this book and the general development of Tribe's other work, leads me to believe that Tribe will come, as most women do, to accord more weight to the value of protecting human life than is here expressed. His sincere empathy with women will lead him to see that women are not well served by a movement that makes the right to abortion paramount to all others, or which implies that women are so weak that they need not be held morally responsible. His concern for constructing an abortion-free society will lead him to see that *Roe*'s abortion license itself promotes a climate where too many decisions are weighted in favor of abortion. Most important of all, his concern for the oppressed and endangered will lead him to see that none of us, men or women, can afford to let our legal system lapse into careless delegation of decisions about what life is worthy to live.

One of the many qualities that lifts Larry Tribe above the ranks of lesser legal scholars is his willingness to reexamine his positions and change his mind. Given the far-reaching implications of this important contemporary civil rights issue, it seems likely that while this book may appear to some abortion rights proponents to be the last word on the subject, it will not be so for its ambivalent author. It is my confident hope that, over time, in *Tribe* v. *Tribe* the better man will win.

# CHAPTER 22

# When Words Cheapen Life

*Bostonians were shocked on December 30, 1994, by news that a gunman had killed two employees at local abortion clinics. The war of words that followed prompted these reflections on rhetoric, published as an op-ed piece in the New York Times after a lengthy argument with editors who wanted to change "pro-life" to "anti-abortion".* [1]

**A**FTER MONTHS OF RELATIVE CALM in the abortion debate, the shootings in Brookline, Massachusetts, on December 30, 1994, have unleashed yet another volley of bitter recriminations between activists. A Planned Parenthood newspaper ad with the headline "Words Kill" blamed pro-life rhetoric for the deaths of two clinic receptionists.

This charge deserves to be taken seriously, for how we name things determines to a great extent how we think, feel, and act regarding them. Words can kill; but it's not so simple as pro-choice leaders would have it. Words kill by creating a climate where life is cheap; they can stifle the inner voice that reminds us that evil can never be overcome by evil. From abortion rights to euthanasia to indifference to the plight of the poor, the road has been paved with soothing words chosen to harmonize conscience with convenience. Consider how brutal regimes of chattel slavery and apartheid were legitimated by the notion that blacks weren't fully human. The Supreme Court endorsed that view in 1857 when Dred Scott came before the Court as a man, only to be dismissed as a piece of property.

In *Roe* v. *Wade*, the Court again made a fateful semantic choice. By refusing to acknowledge the developing fetus as either human or alive, it entered into complicity with advocates' deceptive phrases like "clump of tissue" and "product of conception." Even those who would distinguish between the born and the unborn should be nervous when the state dissembles about the definition of life.

In the two decades after it handed down its decision, the Court foreclosed most opportunities for influencing abortion law through legislative politics. Courts have also sanctioned the use of injunctions, buffer zones,

---

[1] Mary Ann Glendon, "When Words Cheapen Life," *New York Times* (10 January 1995): A19.

and organized crime statutes to keep pro-life demonstrators away from clinics. The danger of such measures was summed up last week by the pro-choice civil rights lawyer Harvey Silverglate, who said that if such techniques had been used against civil rights protesters in the 1960s "you can be assured there would have been a lot more violence."

Now, Planned Parenthood seeks to silence even "verbal attacks" against abortion rights. What it really wants is to suppress the pro-life movement's insistence—so hurtful to the clinic business—that abortion destroys developing life. To banish opponents of abortion and their deeply held beliefs from public life, however, would be unwise and undemocratic.

This is not to claim that the language of dehumanization alone has been responsible for increasing violence and waning compassion in these troubled United States. Or that Government approval of abortion has been the only factor promoting acceptance of brutal quick fixes for a range of social problems. But how can the pro-choice movement's rhetoric fail to promote a coarsening of spirit, a deadening of conscience, and a disregard for the humanity of one's opponents—as well as for those who seem to us to be less than full-fledged "persons"?

That is why the late Walker Percy, physician and novelist, deplored "the chronic misuse of words" to disguise what takes place during abortion. It is an ominous sign, as artists are often the first to realize, when a society begins to manipulate the concept of humanity.

In the wake of the Brookline tragedies, are there any words of hope? Perhaps. The Massachusetts news media have begun to cover those services that make the pro-life movement more than just anti-abortion—financial aid to single mothers, shelters for mothers and children with AIDS, parenthood classes. This has put into focus the common task to which the overwhelmingly female rank-and-file of both movements have always been committed: building a culture that is respectful of women, supportive of child-raising families, and protective of the weak and vulnerable.

# Family Law and Popular Culture

*In 1990, to commemorate the life and work of Haskell Freedman,
a respected Boston trial court judge, the Flaschner Judicial Institute
established an annual lecture in his name. I was deeply honored
to have been asked to give the inaugural lecture which was
published in the September/October 1990 Boston Bar Journal.[1]*

**W**HEN I WAS INVITED TO DELIVER this first annual lecture in memory of Judge Haskell C. Freedman, it seemed to me that the subject matter ought to pay tribute to Judge Freedman's important contributions to family law reform and to continuing legal education. The idea I would like to develop, therefore, is that all family lawyers—and family law itself—are engaged in education. Whether or not members of the family law bar embrace this role, they cannot help but have an influence on ordinary Americans' impressions concerning family law, family life, and the legal system in general. In a broad sense, of course, this assertion could be made about the entire legal profession. That great French observer of early American democracy, Alexis de Tocqueville, did, in fact, make such a claim. As he traveled about the territories of the United States in 1831 and 1832, Tocqueville heard people in all walks of life using legal language. He attributed this tendency of Americans to borrow so much of their discourse from legal phraseology and concepts to the fact that most public men here, unlike those in France, were lawyers. Whatever the cause, Tocqueville found that a legalistic spirit "infiltrates through society right down to the lowest ranks," and "enwraps" the whole body social, "penetrating each component class and constantly working in secret upon its unconscious patient, till in the end it has molded it to its desire."

Tocqueville's observations are even more pertinent to contemporary popular culture than they were to that of Jacksonian America. Not everyone would agree with the legal historian Lawrence Friedman that "life in modem

---

[1] Mary Ann Glendon, "Family Law and Popular Culture," *Boston Bar Journal* 34 (5; September/October 1990): 4–8.

America is a vast, diffuse school of law," but it would be hard to deny that we are presently living in one of the most legalistic societies that has ever existed on earth. There are two major reasons why the influence of law on popular culture has increased since Tocqueville's time. Most obviously, a great communications and entertainment industry has arisen. Movies, radio, television, and the print media circulate a good deal of information about law, sometimes in frankly dramatic or fictional form, sometimes in the form called reporting. They surround us with ideas and images of law and lawyers.

Secondly, ordinary Americans have many more personal contacts with the legal system than their ancestors did. In historical times, if you were not wealthy, and if you were able to refrain from committing acts of violence, you could live your whole life without ever seeing the inside of a courtroom or lawyer's office. In the late nineteenth century, though, things began to change rapidly. The middle class entered the market for testation. By the middle of the twentieth century, the achievement of the American dream of home ownership brought many working-class families as well as middle-income families into brief contact with the law. Then, when divorce became a mass phenomenon, many Americans (as parties or witnesses) had more extended (and less pleasant) contacts with lawyers.

The first point I would like to make here is that, in this deluge of impressions about law and lawyers, not all areas of law are equally represented. The Sherman Act and the percentage depletion allowance, for example, do not figure prominently in the plots of television dramas or on the front pages of the daily papers. Crime, family discord, and inheritance have been regular staples of entertainment, though. When modern authors treat these subjects, they often dramatize their legal aspects, too. If we turn from the mass media to the other major source of popular information about law—the lawyer's office—we can make similar observations. Most Americans will never have occasion to consult a lawyer except in connection with family disputes, or the preparation of a will or estate plan, or the purchase of a dwelling. Thus one can say that family lawyers are more engaged in mass education than most other lawyers, today more than ever before.

If it is correct to say that the family lawyer's office is a little law school, it is appropriate to ask what lessons it is teaching. A recent law review article by two prominent legal sociologists has proposed some interesting answers to this question. Austin Sarat and William Felstiner in a symposium issue of the *Yale Law Journal* on popular legal culture start with an assumption similar to mine:

> Much of the conversation between lawyers and their clients is educational: lawyers provide knowledge of how particular legal processes work and introduce their clients to ways the law might be used in their favor. Practicing lawyers thus play an important role in shaping mass legal consciousness and in promoting or undermining the sense of legitimacy that the public attaches to legal institutions.

In order to "assess the implications of what lawyers actually tell their clients about the legal process," the two researchers obtained permission to follow forty divorce cases from beginning to end. Over a period of 33 months, Sarat, a chaired professor of political science, and Felstiner, the director of the American Bar Foundation, sat in on 115 lawyer–client conferences in all, listening to 20 different lawyers interacting with their clients. They conducted the study in two states, chosen because their divorce laws differed in significant ways and because, in the authors' view, the states represented "very different legal cultures."

The first interesting finding was that the "law talk" they heard from lawyers in these sessions was much the same everywhere. Contrary to what one might expect, they found no significant variations between male and female lawyers, between large firms and small ones, between specialists and non-specialists, or between experienced lawyers and beginners. The main lesson divorce clients are learning from their lawyers is that outcomes are determined not by legal rules and rights but by capricious judges. According to Sarat and Felstiner, the lawyers rarely attempted to defend the rationality of the legal norms involved in the cases they were handling. They placed much greater emphasis on the personalities of the judges and the other lawyers involved than on the background law. With respect to judges, "the clear tendency of lawyers' talk about judges is to call into question their skill, dedication, and concern." The lawyers' message about judges was that one can rely on neither their technical competence nor their good faith. The most common word used in connection with judges was *arbitrary*. Their message about the law was that it has no inherent rationality and that it has little to do with how a case will be likely decided. Many lawyers implied that only their own personal connections and special inside knowledge of the local system would carry the day.

Sarat and Felstiner's judgment about what they heard is rather harsh: They claim that divorce lawyers introduce their clients into a "chaotic 'anti-system'" in order to create client dependence and to portray themselves as lone warriors who will champion the client's cause in a world that is neither equitable, reasonable, nor just. The researchers offer a surprise conclusion: Divorce lawyers are engaged in the same educational project as the group of legal academics known as the critical legal studies movement! Both groups, Sarat and Felstiner claim, are devoted to proving that legal rules are indeterminate, to debunking the myth that law is a search for justice, and to promoting distrust of the entire legal order.

There are many ways we might respond to the claims advanced in this study. If we wanted to deny that it has any validity whatsoever, we might start by questioning whether the researchers had accurately reported and correctly interpreted what they heard. We would not be able to tell for sure whether the study was indeed vulnerable in this way, though, unless we went over the entire manuscripts of the 115 interviews ourselves. The record of these interviews might be susceptible of alternative and more benign interpretations. We might come away with a quite different notion from that of the researchers about the lessons that divorce lawyers were teaching their clients. We would no doubt find that much time was taken up with the kind of amateur psychiatric social work that all divorce lawyers must practice whether they want to or not. We might find, too, that many clients at this stressful time in their lives were uninterested in discussions of law and that some were only too apt to perceive the legal world as topsy-turvy and only too eager to cast the lawyer in the role of gladiator against injustice and irrationality. Sometimes a lawyer might emphasize the chanciness of litigation in order to deal tactfully with what he or she perceives as a credibility problem of the client. Such emphasis might also help the client overcome emotional obstacles to a settlement that would be to his or her own advantage. I do find it significant that while, on the whole, the text of this study paints a rather unflattering picture of divorce lawyers, a footnote mentions that, "contrary to some images in popular culture, the divorce lawyers we observed are overwhelmingly pro-settlement."

We might pursue the question of the validity of the study along another line by querying whether the sample was indeed representative. After all, only twenty lawyers were included, and the authors admit (again, in a footnote) that there are some biases in their small sample. For one thing, the sample group involved a higher proportion of women than there is among divorce lawyers overall. For another, most of the lawyers did not represent wealthy clients and would not have been ranked at the top of the local divorce bar in terms of income and prestige. Thus, the authors concede (still in fine print) that "the findings of this project should not be considered representative of all divorce lawyers." What they *do* claim is that their sample "is characteristic of lawyers that most people with ordinary financial resources are likely to consult." This, of course, is the basis of their contention that their findings are relevant to the effect of law on popular culture. We might imagine another kind of response to the study in more pragmatic terms. We might point out that, after all, the lawyer is not there to give the client a lesson in civics. The lawyer's main job is to get the best possible result for his or her client. Furthermore, it is safe to assume that most clients have no wish to spend their money to acquire tutoring in law or to impress social scientists who happen to be sitting in on the conference.

There are, no doubt, other ways we might challenge this article, but let us now move directly to the heart of the matter—the authors' claim that divorce lawyers, like some critical legal studies proponents, are preaching the radical indeterminacy of all legal rules and the futility of any search for justice through law. It seems to me that this claim overlooks an elementary distinction between legal roles: the distinction between preventive law and litigation. When a client comes to a lawyer for planning advice, whether in connection with taxes, drafting a long-term contract, or setting up a real estate transaction, the lawyer is going to take the relevant body of law very seriously indeed. To be sure, the client will be told where there seems to be some flexibility in the rules and where one might prudently take a risk, but the overall impression the lawyer gives is *not* going to be one of indeterminacy. The very same body of law will look quite different, however, if the client comes in for advice after the IRS has challenged his tax deductions, after she learns she has been disinherited by her father, or after another party has repudiated a twenty-year lease in the third year. The same rules that were *properly* regarded for planning purposes as fairly clear and hard-edged are (again properly) regarded as less clear and more indeterminate in a settlement context. They are up for grabs if the situation should come to litigation, where fact-finding and credibility come into play.

To make the same point somewhat differently, we might ask what lessons about law Sarat and Felstiner would have heard if they had listened to lawyer–client conferences in estate planners' offices. I imagine that they would have heard legal rules presented as clear, fairly rational, and involving a reasonable degree of predictability if ever litigation should ensue. I speculate further that they would have found lawyers taking justifiable pride in helping people to provide for spouses, children, friends, and charity.

I have introduced the subject of estate planning partly to further this discussion of indeterminacy, but also to point up certain special characteristics of divorce law. The same legal rules will indeed, and properly should, look less clear and certain to a litigator whose client is already in the soup, than they will or should to a counselor whose job is to keep the client as far away from the soup as possible. There are, of course, important differences in legal rules in this respect, though. Thus, we now need to consider that bright-line rules predominate in some areas of law (like tax, real property, and wills), while other areas are characterized by flexible standards and by opportunities for the exercise of judicial discretion and the lawyer's art.

This observation suggests yet another take on the Sarat-Felstiner thesis: Since divorce law, in particular, has become so loaded with legislative grants of open-ended discretion, Sarat and Felstiner's lawyers were probably telling their clients no more than the plain, honest truth when they characterized the rules on property division, support, and custody as not particularly rational, fair, or predictable! Not only is divorce an area in which the law often does not govern outcomes, it is an area in which much of the law is not even *meant* to do so, as the law is in the form of rather vague guidelines for the exercise of discretion. Thus, assuming for the moment that this study of what lawyers tell their clients did indeed uncover a problem, a major part of that problem may reside not so much in lawyers and judges as in the law itself.

I am skeptical, however, about Sarat and Felstiner's further inference that encounters with arbitrariness and unpredictability in divorce law settings may cause people to become cynical about the entire legal system and tend therefore to "delegitimate" the administration of justice. People are capable of making distinctions. Sarat and Felstiner may have underestimated people's intelligence and good sense. Another contributor to the Yale symposium on law and popular culture was closer to the mark when he observed that, "the public seems, in fact, to have a love-hate relationship with the law." For most Americans, law is a "bag of tricks" *and* "a shining sword of justice," a "bottomless pit of artifice" *and* a powerful force for reason. It does not take an Oliver Wendell Holmes to understand that law can be an instrument of oppression under some circumstances, but a bulwark of liberty under others.

In consequence, I do not fully share Sarat and Felstiner's concern about what divorce lawyers teach us about the legal system in general. I am uneasy, however, about what divorce *law* may be communicating about some equally important things: family life and personal responsibility.

A study of the divorce process in England in the 1970s produced some findings that may be relevant to our situation in the United States. Bristol University investigators discovered that the majority of divorcing husbands and wives were very surprised and disappointed at how little attention was paid all along the line to the welfare of their children. This neglect of such an important concern was one of the main reasons why the Bristol researchers concluded that divorce hearings in that country "did not command the confidence and respect" of the parties. Here in the United States, to the extent that divorce law has failed to make clear that while one can terminate a marriage, one cannot terminate responsibilities to his or her children, it *has* been a school for scandal.

Fortunately, however, a new curriculum appears to be emerging for the divorce lawyer's law school. There are many scattered signs that we are on the threshold of an era of legal changes that cumulatively and gradually are introducing more rationality, predictability, good sense, and fairness into divorce law. Let us consider how these currents of change may bear on the matters that seemed to Sarat and Felstiner particularly troublesome.

Chief among the researchers' concerns was the fact that divorce lawyers frequently tell their clients that outcomes depend on the whim of the judge and the personal skill or contacts of the lawyer. Very often this is indeed no more than the unvarnished truth. Many currently pending and proposed law reforms, however, tend in the direction of reducing the degree of discretion and the element of chance in divorce law. Ongoing reforms in child support law, for example, are slowly but inexorably moving toward a system that will produce fewer disparities among outcomes of cases in which the parties are similarly situated. Perhaps we will never reach (or desire to reach) the point that many other countries have reached, the point at which a client can ask how much child support he or she can expect to pay or receive, and the lawyer can run a finger down a chart and give an exact figure. We are moving away, though, from the old situation in which the amount depends on which judge one draws, and in which the amount will not be much in any event. The new child support norms are also sending out a better message about personal responsibility for procreation and child-raising. The message has a ripple effect. Some high schools, for example, are now teaching young men about the new child support rules in a very down-to-earth way: "This is the weekly take-home pay of a bus driver. This is the amount that can be automatically deducted from that paycheck for the support of one child, for two children, and so on." This teaching represents quite an advance from the situation of only a few years ago in which an unwed or divorced father could be fairly sure that child support would be assessed at a token level and that it would be rather easy to evade collection of it.

Another trend that will diminish the appearance of irrationality is the increasing differentiation among divorce cases that require very different treatment, procedurally as well as substantively. This trend is less advanced, at present than some others, but there are many indications of it nonetheless: First, there is an increasing legislative consensus that a significant proportion of divorces do not require, and should not receive, a great deal of lawyer-time or court-time. This consensus is embodied in the summary dissolution statutes that have been adopted in a rapidly growing number of jurisdictions to permit short, childless marriages of couples with no significant property to be wound up with as little expense and delay as possible. Just as the small probate estate has long been spared protracted procedures of administration, so has a sizable category of divorces been exempted from big-time divorce law. There will be little indeterminacy for couples who opt for such procedures.

Another even larger category of divorces that is beginning to receive special treatment is the category comprising couples with minor children. Just as commercial law has had to develop special rules for consumer law, and just as corporation law has had to develop a separate body of law for close corporations, so the time has come for family law to distinguish between childless and child-raising marriages. It is time to recognize that divorcing couples and their minor children are not well served by property rules that treat the interests of husband and wife as central and relegate the needs of children to the margins.

Here are some of the signs that a special body of rules for such situations is developing within the framework of existing property division and support law: There is a great and continuing surge of activity in the area of child support. Less visibly, there is much evidence that many judges in divorce cases already do give special attention to the needs of children; they piece together as best they can from the income and property of the parents a basis for the subsistence of the custodial household. Here and there, divorce statutes are gradually being amended to codify and to reinforce this emerging judicial practice. This new legislation should have a beneficial effect on the processes of negotiation and settlement through which the overwhelming majority of divorce cases are resolved. England, for example, amended its financial provision statute (which closely resembles Ch. 208 §34 of the Massachusetts General Laws) in 1984 to provide that the welfare of minor children should be given first priority in allocating support and property. In 1989, Governor Dukakis signed into law an amendment to Ch. 208 §34 that though more modest in scope will at least require judges to make special findings on the present and future needs of children when allocating property in divorce cases. Such changes, minor though they may seem, will tend to dispel the impression that so many divorce litigants have gained in the past that divorce law is indifferent to the interests of children and that it systematically undervalues the costs of raising children and the lost opportunities of custodial parents.

These observations about divorce law also apply to many other areas of family law in which legal rules are in flux. Much of the current disarray in the law pertaining to marital contracts and informal cohabitation results from a failure to distinguish between child-raising couples and other situations. Judges must use a great deal of discretion in departing from the terms of private agreements according to which the parties to these arrangements are raising or have raised children together. There could still be much more scope for fixed rules and private autonomy, and thus less uncertainty about outcomes, in cases in which the contract or cohabitation concerns only two adults.

Another recent development that may prove to have a significant rationalizing effect on these areas of law is the decision in 1989 of the American Law Institute to take up, for the first time in its history, a project in the area of family law. As described by the Director of the A.L.I., Geoffrey Hazard, "the project will focus on problems growing out of the dissolution of families, both formal and informal ones. It will give particular emphasis to the substantive standards that guide decision makers in determining child support, property division, maintenance and custody, and to an assessment of the role of the courts in monitoring the negotiated settlements that comprise the vast bulk of family dissolution cases." The American Law Institute historically has had a great influence on American law and policy formation.

I have saved for the last consideration one other conclusion that Sarat and Felstiner arrived at on the basis of their licensed eavesdropping. The researchers found that divorce lawyers "do not take seriously" their obligation under various canons and rules of professional responsibility to maintain respect for law, courts, and judicial officers. This aspect of the study recalls an original and penetrating discussion of professional responsibility by the former Dean of Notre Dame Law School, Thomas L. Shaffer. Shaffer postulates that there is a tension within the legal profession between two quite different visions of what constitutes ethical behavior. One of these visions, the one he calls "the old WASP professional consensus," is the adversary ethic enshrined in our codes and canons of professional responsibility. Shaffer associates the other vision, which he calls an "old world ethic," with the ethical systems of the immigrants who came to America after 1850 from Ireland, Russia, Poland, and Italy. This old world ethic assumes that "making an idol" of American governmental institutions is "both inappropriate and ridiculous," that clients are more important than institutions, that relationships are more significant than rules, and it entails an attitude of "gentle cynicism" toward law and its officers. Shaffer points out that in present-day America each of these worldviews has been modified through contact with the other. Nevertheless, he contends, a certain tension remains, a tension that is now no longer ethnic or denominational. Rather, it is now a part of all of us in varying degrees. Shaffer deems this a healthy tension. An ethic for the professions, he posits, should not be completely personalistic, but it cannot be completely abstract and impersonal either. Thus, when Sarat and Felstiner report that divorce lawyers place people over rules and that they are constantly emphasizing the difference the personality of the judge makes, the authors may be a little hasty in attributing such statements to insensitivity to ethics. It may be that an ethical system is actively at work in what they observed, but that it is an ethical system that they did not recognize as such.

What would Haskell Freedman have had to say about all this? What I know of Haskell Freedman leads me to believe that if he were asked about the relative importance of the canons of ethics and more personalistic alternative ethical views, or if he were asked, more generally, about the pros and cons of the Sarat-Felstiner research, he would have reacted like the rabbi in a story my colleague Martha Minow likes to tell: The rabbi was asked to resolve a dispute between two members of his congregation. After the first man explained his grievance, the rabbi said to him, "You're right." Then the second man told his side of the story. The rabbi said, "You're right." The rabbi's wife, who had been in the kitchen listening to all this, called out to her husband, "What are you talking about, you fool? They can't both be right!" The rabbi said to her, "You know, you're right, too."

CHAPTER 23 • Family Law and Popular Culture

# A Nation
# Under Lawyers

*This talk on the uses and misuses of law in a democratic republic*
*was presented at the American Enterprise Institute, and later published*
*in the November/December 1994 issue of* The American Enterprise.[1]

*The spirit of the law, born within schools and courts, spreads*
*little by little beyond them; it infiltrates through society right*
*down to the lowest ranks, till finally the whole people have*
*contracted some of the ways and tastes of a magistrate.*

—ALEXIS DE TOCQUEVILLE

ONE FINE EVENING in the early spring of 1978, Tom Horsley, a San Jose accountant, was looking forward to a date with Alyn Chesslet, a San Francisco waitress. That night, countless young men the world over must have been in a similar frame of mind, sprucing themselves up for the initial step in the age-old minuets of courtship. Some set out on foot, some on bikes, and many, like Tom, in automobiles. Some had no farther to travel than the house next door; for others, like Tom, the meeting place was many miles away. Many had no definite program in mind; some, like Tom, had made more or less elaborate arrangements. In his case, the plan was for a classic American date: He would take Alyn to dinner and a show. Most of the evening's swains, we may assume, rendezvoused successfully with the women they had arranged to meet. But some, like Tom, found no one at the appointed spot. In many of these situations, the problem was a simple mistake concerning day, time, or place. But some unlucky suitors, like Tom, were well and truly stood up.

One may imagine various reactions to such a setback. Some men would have shrugged, made a date with another girl, and chalked the disenchanted evening up to life's inevitable disappointments. Others might have felt the

---

[1] Mary Ann Glendon, "A Nation Under Lawyers," *American Enterprise* (November/December 1994): 42–51.

need to protest to the woman herself, and perhaps even to complain to her friends and family. Some might have spread the word of her inconsiderate behavior. What seems almost inconceivable is that any of these young men would have taken their grievance to court—except, that is, in the United States of America. In May 1978, Tom Horsley filed an action against Alyn, claiming compensation for the time and expense involved in his futile trip to and from San Francisco.

Suits like Tom's, less of a novelty now than in the 1970s, are a bizarre contemporary offshoot of the legalism that has long been a hallmark of our national identity. In no other country has "the spirit of the law" penetrated so deeply into popular culture. Today, as in Tocqueville's times, to live in the United States is to be a pupil, willing or not, in a vast, bustling school of law. The curriculum of that institution, however, has undergone some startling changes, and the students are displaying some odd behavior.

The legalistic spirit today has taken far different forms from the sober legalism that our nineteenth-century visitor regarded as one of the sturdiest bulwarks of the democratic experiment. Where Tocqueville saw a people with "the ways and tastes of a magistrate," one is now more likely to encounter popular imitations of the language and attitudes of adversarial advocates. In American workplaces, schools, shops, streets, playgrounds, and homes, men, women, and even children caricature the behavior of hardball litigators. Consider what happened when a lower school principal recently dealt with a third-grade "riot" by requiring all members of the class to write statements of apology. The pupils who had not participated in the disorder were understandably offended, but their complaints had a strange sound. As one mother recounts the incident, one pint-sized prosecutor asked his parents, "Should we sue her?" "Isn't it illegal for her to punish those of us who did nothing?" demanded another prepubescent pettifogger. Where do eight-year-olds learn to talk this way?

Law is the silver chain that links contemporary Americans of all ages and origins to eighteenth-century revolutionaries and seventeenth-century colonists. Much of America's uniqueness, in fact, lies in the degree to which law figures in the standard accounts of where we came from, who we are, and where we are going. Unlike those of older nations, our origins are not shrouded in myth or legend. Our country's birthday commemorates the formal signing of a real document—a bill of grievances in which rebellious but fussily legalistic colonists recited their complaints, claimed that they had been denied "the rights of Englishmen," and officially pronounced the severance of their ties with the mother country. Tocqueville marveled at the contrast between the American struggle for independence and the French Revolution: "No disorderly passions drove it on; on the contrary, it proceeded hand in hand with a love of order and legality." Eventually, those law-struck rebels opted for a single-document constitution, rejecting the

English model of an "unwritten" charter resting on customary understandings. The design for government that emerged from the convention held in the summer of 1787 was a masterpiece not only of statesmanship but of juridical art. And no wonder, for 31 of the 55 delegates were lawyers.

A singular role for courts in the new regime was assured with Chief Justice Marshall's landmark decisions filling out the contours of federalism and his fateful assertion of judicial authority to review governmental action for conformity to the Constitution. No other country's judiciary had ever possessed such independence or exerted such power. Over the years, as in no other liberal democracy, lawyers garnered the lion's share of starring roles in the national drama. Among the marble busts in the French Pantheon or Germany's Walhalla, a tourist finds only a scattering of jurists. The National Portrait Gallery in Washington, by contrast, is crowded with men of law.

As for the citizenry, there was something peculiar about us from the beginning. Even when lawyers were scarce, historians say, the early settlers possessed a turn of mind that was decidedly legalistic. To Tocqueville, that odd trait seemed to augur well. It not only promoted the aptitude for self-government but also fostered the reverence for the Constitution and laws on which, according to the authors of *The Federalist*, the freedom of a democratic people depends. During the French uprisings of 1848, Tocqueville's troubled thoughts turned back to the continent he had visited in his youth: "The principles on which the constitutions of the American states rest, the principles of order, balance of powers, true liberty, and sincere and deep respect for law, are indispensable for all republics; they should be common to them all; and it is safe to forecast that where they are not found the republic will soon have ceased to exist."

The legalistic spirit that Tocqueville admired has shown itself at many crucial junctures when the mighty and the lowly alike abided by legal rulings that seemed to them disadvantageous, wrong, or even dangerous. During the Korean War, President Truman relinquished control of the steel industry when the Supreme Court told him to—even though he feared the impending strike would interfere with the flow of supplies to the front. President Nixon complied with the Court's command to turn over his "smoking gun" tapes to the Watergate special prosecutor, although it was far from clear how the Court would have been able to enforce its order had he chosen to defy it. And countless black and white parents nervously submitted to having their young children transported to schools in distant neighborhoods when federal courts ordered busing in an attempt to achieve school desegregation.

What keeps a measure of hardy legalism alive in our turbulent country? Tocqueville speculated that the mere presence of great numbers of lawyers in the population had a significant influence on the habits and attitudes of their fellow citizens. The courthouse in every county seat was like a "free school" where "every juror is given practical lessons in the law." Local government was a sort of lab school with a variety of opportunities for active participation, ranging from the town meeting to numerous elective offices. By taking an active role in local affairs, he wrote, an American "gets to know those formalities without which freedom can advance only through revolutions, and becoming imbued with their spirit, develops a taste for order, understands the harmony of powers, and in the end accumulates clear, practical ideas about the nature of his duties and the extent of his rights."

Today, the good news is that those free schools are open to all adults, including many who could not have voted, held office, or served on juries in Jacksonian America. The bad news, however, is that top-down regulation of various sorts reaches deeply into every town and hamlet, drastically reducing opportunities for citizens to participate in making the decisions that affect their own families and communities. With more law came still more lawyers, their influence magnified by newspapers, magazines, television shows, and films that report on and dramatize their doings. Bureaucrats grew plump with power and briefcase-toting litigators replaced Western gunslingers as popular heroes and villains. The country's legal education shifted to different sorts of classrooms. Alongside the old teachings, a new curriculum emerged with a more ambiguous relationship to the democratic enterprise. The legal teachings of the jury room and town hall were eclipsed by lessons absorbed passively from the communications and entertainment industries. A contemporary citizen's direct contacts with the legal system are apt to be passive too. Americans learn more about law and government in the toils of the tax, welfare, or Social Security System than in the jury room, town meeting, or party precinct organization. Such experiences tend to engender feelings of frustration and helplessness, rather than a sense of empowerment. Any parent who has dealt with the educational bureaucracy knows firsthand how it feels to be treated like a subject rather than a citizen. We are encountering law more, but participating less in its creation and administration. Frustration with normal politics has fueled resort to a poor substitute: litigation aimed at bringing about social change. Curiously, widespread popular discontent with the law's daily operation coexists with an exaggerated confidence in its power to cure social and economic ills. The same citizens who want to get annoying regulations out of their own lives often believe that the way to deal with a broad range of social problems is to bring a lawsuit, to criminalize unwanted activity, or to augment the power of police and prosecutors.

One of the most striking elements of the new legalism is its adversarial nature. Filmmakers, journalists, novelists, and television programmers are fascinated with the activities of the minority of lawyers who are engaged in courtroom work. Don't look soon for a TV sitcom on "Eleanor the Estate Planner," or real-life episodes from "Judge Wapner's Conciliation Clinic." Ratings thrive on crime, conflict, and courtroom drama. As a legal adviser to the popular *L.A. Law* show put it, to depict what most lawyers do most of the time would violate media "rules" against complexity and detail: "Transactional work is intellectually fascinating, but dramatically deadly." Of the forces that are contending for the soul of the legal profession, only a select few will be seen on prime time.

The overdramatized antics of lawyers in perpetual attack mode, though, are unfortunately models for handling routine disputes and disappointments, whether in the capillaries of the social system or in its political and commercial arteries. The fact is that everyone usually loses when rigid positions are taken too quickly, harms exaggerated, and claims made in all-or-nothing terms. Consider the escalation of the argument that developed between 12-year-old Kimberly Broussard and her homeroom teacher when Kimberly wore a T-shirt reading "Drugs Suck" to the Blair Middle School in Norfolk, Virginia. The teacher was adamant that the shirt not be worn in the school. Kimberly was equally insistent on her right to express herself. The teacher held to the view that displaying vulgar language violated the decorum necessary for the educational enterprise. Kimberly was suspended. But backed by the American Civil Liberties Union, she sued the school district, claiming a First Amendment right to wear the shirt to school. Eventually, a federal district judge ruled in a 26-page opinion that school officials had acted reasonably in barring her display of an offensive word. The dispute was resolved, but not without serious cost to the school district, to the taxpayers, to other litigants in the crowded federal courts, and to human relations in the Blair Middle School.

Inevitably, as systems of informal social regulation lose their effectiveness, new and greater demands are made on a judicial system that was designed primarily to be a last resort for the settlement of disputes. Americans are learning, painfully, that law is not well suited for all the tasks it is now being asked to perform. In 1978, when Tom Horsley's courtship wound up in court, the story was so unusual that it was prominently featured in the national press.

The suit over a broken date was, in fact, a law professor's farfetched hypothetical case come to life. For generations, beginning students of contract law had cut their teeth on versions of an imaginary "invitation to dinner" case where a guest reneged on a promise to attend a friend's dinner party even though he knew his host was counting heavily on his presence to help close a business deal, and was well aware that certain expenses had been incurred in reliance on his agreement. In the classroom exercise, students are expected to see why there are some promises that the law will not enforce even though all the elements of a legally binding contract are technically present. The exercise affords one of those all too rare occasions in the legal academy for teachers and students to remind themselves that the law has limits; that there are aspects of life that the state wisely refrains from regulating; that not every injustice can or should be adjudicated; and that few people would enjoy living in a society where every insult or injury gave rise to legal remedies. The San Francisco judge said as much when he threw out Tom's claim. This type of suit, according to Judge Richard Figone, "should never have been in court."

In the 1980s and 1990s, however, suits over the disappointments of everyday life have become more common and judges somewhat more receptive. No one suggests that these freakish lawsuits are statistically significant or a major cause of congestion in our overcrowded courts. They are extreme, cartoonlike manifestations of a growing problem—the breakdown of non-legal constraints on behavior and of informal methods of handling disputes. What has happened to the apparatus of custom, convention, etiquette, religion, and ethics?

In 1978, the same year that Tom Horsley sued Alyn Chesslet, journalist Judith Martin began to address herself to the poor condition of American manners and mores. Since then, as "Miss Manners," Martin has waged a spirited crusade to regenerate a workable ethics of everyday life. Her task has been an arduous one, for many men and women in our increasingly individualistic, highly mobile society have had little practice in the skills of associating. We are not born with those skills, she points out. We learn them, beginning in the family, where we first learn to consider the feelings and needs of others, to accommodate differences, and to assume responsibilities.

It cannot be coincidence that over the same thirty years that saw the legal profession shedding many traditional constraints, families and their surrounding communities have been undergoing upheavals too. Daniel Yankelovich sums up changes in our culture since the 1960s in this way: "The quest for greater individual choice clashed directly with the obligations and social norms that held families and communities together in earlier years. People came to feel that questions of how to live . . . were a matter of individual choice not to be governed by restrictive norms. . . . Commitments were loosened."

In other words, the very mobility, opportunity, and diversity that make American society so exciting and attractive render us prone to fragmentation and anomie. It is our national version of the Midas touch. Our social controls are relatively weak and shared understandings about proper behavior relatively thin. And as Miss Manners points out, this state of affairs fosters unhealthy forms of legalism: "A declining belief in etiquette as a legitimate force in regulating social conduct has prompted American society to try to get along without it. People who find rude but legally permitted behavior intolerable have attempted to expand the law to outlaw rudeness." But the attempt to "legalize" areas once regulated by informal understandings is not only ineffective at restoring civility, it is itself a symptom of disorder in the body social.

A certain amount of strife is unavoidable between people who do not grasp each other's expectations concerning right conduct—between country folk and city folk, knowledge class and working class, newcomers and established residents, as well as among members of differing ethnic and religious groups. Consider the squabbles that provide the daily grist of *The People's Court*. This popular television program, which first appeared in 1981, closely resembles the actual proceedings of a small claims court. A huge audience watches in fascination as retired judge Joseph A. Wapner, in his shrewd, no-nonsense way, sifts fact from opinion, winnows truth from falsehood, and dispenses rough justice in disputes of a kind that everyone has experienced at one time or another.

If you look closely, though, at Judge Wapner's courtroom, you will observe that in a hefty proportion of the cases the parties appear to be from different generations or different ethnic and social backgrounds. The elderly landlady has an Italian surname; her youthful lodger wears a turban. The black shopkeeper speaks standard English; his irate customer's speech is halting and heavily accented—he has brought a friend along to help. The hairdresser is Asian; his client Puerto Rican. The quarreling ex-lovers come in all assortments. Listen to them carefully, and you will notice how often the source of the difficulty seems to have been a misunderstanding—how frequently both parties seem to have placed entirely different interpretations on the same words and events. The landlady finds it incredible that her lodger assumed he could cook aromatic meals on a hot plate in his room; the roomer is outraged that he is not allowed to prepare his food where he lives.

Judge Wapner's court is a microcosm of a land of strangers; an America where opportunity lies just around the corner, but next-door neighbors do not know each other; where disputing parties often recognize no common source of authority (other than the law) and have no mutually respected umpire to consult (other than a judge); where people pack up their belongings and move to a new home over and over again in the course of a lifetime, often spending most of their lives far away from the communities in which they were raised; and where many parents are trying to hold full-time jobs while raising children without the support, interference, advice, criticism, nosiness, care, or concern of relatives, friends, and neighbors.

The spreading erosion of unofficial social controls is also apparent in American business and economic life. A classic study of commercial disputes in the early 1960s documented the existence of a well-established and extensive pattern of reliance on informal norms and sanctions to deal with problems that arose among competitors, suppliers, and buyers. Like many useful sociological studies, that one delivered no great surprises. It served, rather, to confirm what anyone familiar with the role of custom in the history of commerce would have expected. Over the past thirty years, however, there has been a marked turn in the commercial world from social methods of dispute resolution to law and the courts. Corporations that once shunned litigation are now regular and aggressive users of the legal system. Many are going to court as an early, rather than a last, resort. Some, abetted by changes in the legal profession, deliberately use lawsuits for harassment and coercion, rather than to pursue legitimate claims. Though big business has been the source of many of the loudest complaints about growing litigiousness, recent research reveals that contract suits brought by companies against one another comprise the largest single category of federal cases.

In sum, the heavy machinery of law is being wheeled out to deal with a growing array of personal, economic, and political matters to which it is poorly suited. As economic reporter Robert J. Samuelson has written, the law's all-or-nothing approach to right and wrong virtually guarantees unhappy results in the vast numbers of conflicts where there are gradations of blameworthy conduct on both sides. "We . . . are gradually turning every bad judgment, indiscretion or even honest mistake into a potential suit or crime." The result of such overuse, needless to say, is to undermine the respect for law that the Founders rightly saw as a vital pillar of the democratic experiment.

Law has begun to extend its cultural empire beyond customs and manners to popular speech. Law talk has become part of the lingua franca that we use to make ourselves understood, or at least heard, across a great variety of generational, linguistic, social, and ethnic divides. The language of rights is the most obvious example. On the benign side, concepts like individual liberty, privacy, evenhandedness, egalitarianism, and fair procedures probably have exerted a salutary unifying influence in our heterogeneous society. But legalese can also have a corrupting effect on everyday discourse in a country where many people take their moral bearings to some extent from law.

When "no fault" divorce was proposed in the 1960s, for example, law reformers did not mean to imply that no one is ever to blame when a marriage breaks up. But they failed to reckon with the common American propensity to equate legality with morality. The no-fault tag thus came in handy for those who were using divorce, not to escape physically and mentally injurious situations, but to pursue dreams and upgrade choices. Blending all too readily with the no-guilt language of psychotherapy, legal "no fault" provided a shield against moral evaluation and helped to justify decisions that might otherwise be viewed as self-indulgence at the financial and emotional expense of others. One began to hear parents of young children discussing their divorces in terms that would have aroused considerable skepticism a generation earlier. The breakup was "no one's fault"; like a natural disaster, it "just happened"; the spouses "grew apart"; their needs changed, and so on. (Rarely do *both* ex-spouses, or children of divorced couples, talk this way.)

The mannerisms of adversarial advocates, as portrayed in films and television, can also exert an unwholesome influence on everyday human relations. Outside the courtroom, few causes are advanced by a selective and self-serving presentation of facts and issues, by the artful use of epithet and innuendo, by avoiding the slightest concession that the other person might be partly right, or by the strident assertion of rights. Many laypeople do not realize what all real-life litigators know: Adversarial tactics in court are rigorously policed by a system of formal pleadings and answers, the supervision of a judge, canons of relevance, burdens of proof, the existence of a written record, the law of evidence, and so on. Liberated from such constraints and transplanted to homes, schoolrooms, and workplaces, the advocate's winning ways are apt to leave a fair amount of social wreckage in their wake.

The compulsory legal schooling to which Americans currently are subjected is a bewildering welter of contradictory impressions and experiences. Sometimes law appears to us as a powerful tool for social change; yet just as frequently it seems to pose irrational obstacles to common sense approaches to concrete problems. Bar leaders like to portray lawyers as champions of liberty, equality, and justice for all. Yet few Americans can have such a champion unless they are very poor or very rich. One day we complain of suffocating in a regulatory miasma; on the next we ransack the legal cupboard for nostrums to rectify every wrong, to ward off every risk, and to cure every social and economic ill.

Much of the responsibility for promoting exaggerated and simplistic notions of the saving power of law lies with the legal profession itself. Lawyers, to be sure, have good reason to take pride in their contributions to protecting political and civil rights. And they can justly claim to have made some modest contributions to improving the quality of our social, economic, and political life. When the nation made discernible progress in race relations, it was understandable that lawyers would place greater emphasis on the role of celebrated court cases like *Brown* v. *Board of Education* than on the gradual alteration of American sentiments or on legislative achievements like the Civil Rights Act and the Voting Rights Act. That natural professional pride became dangerous hubris, though, when reform-minded lawyers ignored the important openings to political participation afforded by the landmark civil rights decisions and turned them into launching pads for a series of evermore audacious flights from ordinary politics.

Premature and excessive resort to the courts, however, has been a disaster for the political health of the country. By politics here I mean the nearly forgotten activity now being revived and put into practice by men and women like Texas community organizer Ernesto Cortes. Cortes's multiracial, multidenominational Industrial Areas Foundation is dedicated to training citizens to organize their community groups, to initiate action about matters that are important to them, and, in general, to renew their interest in public life. "Politics, properly understood," says Cortes, "is about collective action which is initiated by people who have engaged in public discourse. Politics is about relationships which enable people to disagree, argue, interrupt one another, clarify, confront and negotiate, and, through this process . . . forge a compromise and a consensus which enables them to act. . . . In politics, it is not enough to be right . . . one also has to be reasonable, that is one has to be willing to make concessions and exercise judgment in forging a deal." To regain the ability to engage in politics in that sense, Cortes rightly insists, Americans must also regenerate the decaying civic, religious, and cultural organizations where people can learn how to engage others constructively in argument, to reflect upon their actions, and to make informed judgments. Sadly, court decisions have gone beyond addressing failures of politics to displacing politics altogether—and, often, to undermining the groups where political skills are acquired and nurtured.

Ironically, these unintended effects have often outweighed the courts' power to achieve specific results, particularly when judges have aimed beyond settling the dispute at hand. Gerald Rosenberg's study of the aftermaths of Supreme Court rulings reveals that even spectacular courtroom successes have had only a limited capacity to bring about broad changes sought by the winning side.

Ten years after the historic 1954 *Brown* v. *Board of Education* ruling, for example, the proportion of African-American children who attended integrated schools in the South had hardly budged; it was a mere 1.2 percent. The southern officials who had simply ignored *Brown* and its sequels did not stop dragging their feet until faced with congressional withdrawal of federal funding for their schools. But with passage of the Civil Rights Act of 1964, the proportion of southern black children attending schools with whites increased rapidly and impressively—jumping to 16.9 percent by the end of 1967 and to 85.9 percent in 1971. It was legislative rather than judicial action, Rosenberg concludes, that prompted concrete and substantial steps toward desegregation. Rosenberg may have underestimated the long-term influence of *Brown* in the many-stranded process of shaping attitudes that led to the Civil Rights Act and other advances, but his research casts serious doubt on the power of litigation and court decisions to effect significant social change.

While some lawyers were touting litigation as a quick fix for social ills, others were teaching that for nearly every injury suffered by a private individual there is someone with deep pockets—the government or a large corporation—who can be sued and made to pay. Several unusual features of American law—the use of juries in civil cases, the wild card of damages for emotional distress, the legality of arrangements under which the lawyer agrees to be paid only if successful—helped to foster the impression that litigation could be a profitable gamble. As Lawrence Friedman has observed, a "total justice" mentality emerged: "If a person feels wronged or injured, she feels that there must be a remedy, somewhere in the system."

In the wake of a nation frenzy of blaming and claiming, however, it is far from clear that the benefits (to persons other than lawyers) have outweighed the costs. While spellbinding lecturers on national platforms extol the lawsuit as a potion for social change or a passkey to corporate and governmental treasuries, many Americans are learning different, and harder, lessons in one-to-one tutorials with their own lawyers. There is little talk of "total justice" in these private sessions with the meter running. Even rough justice is elusive, especially when one is neither in the lowest nor in the highest income brackets. That lesson has been learned the hard way by countless homemakers in divorce cases.

Many small-business people have also been dunked in the legal reality tank. What would the owners of a Brooklyn sports bar have done, for example, if a lawyer customer had not donated his services when they were sued by the mighty Los Angeles Dodgers? In 1988, when Richard Picardi, Kevin Boyle, and David Senatore opened the Brooklyn Dodger, the L.A. team's owner wished them good luck in their new venture. Shortly thereafter, though, someone in the Los Angeles organization had a change of heart. Their next communication to the tavern owners was transmitted by a Wall Street law firm: Change the name or face a trademark infringement suit. Picardi said, "They thought they would just grind us down. They figured we were little guys in Brooklyn."

After four years of litigation, federal district judge Constance Baker Motley held that the big guys' suit was without merit. The former Brooklyn Dodgers gave up their name long ago, when they left for the West Coast in "one of the most notorious abandonments in the history of sports." The California organization, she said, was free to use the Brooklyn Dodgers name in marketing sports paraphernalia, but the bar owners were at liberty to continue their use of it in the restaurant business. That David and Goliath story would almost certainly have had a different outcome had it not been for Ronald Russo, a former criminal defense lawyer who represented the tavern owners free of charge for the entire four years. Middle-class men and women are no less vulnerable when they need to file suits themselves than when they are on the receiving end of a complaint. Ask any small-time landlord who has been up against a tenants' advocacy organization or a zealous rent-control board—say, one of the thousands of taxi drivers, school teachers, or retirees who own a three-decker and rent out two units.

With such a crazy curriculum in our vast law school, it is small wonder that Americans lash out at lawyers, bridle under laws that seem to make no sense, and deplore the "litigation explosion"—even as they demand legal remedies for virtually every type of personal or social problem. Common sense suggests, however, that what is disrupting this law-saturated society is not too much law, too many lawyers, or too much litigation. As a society becomes larger and more complex, its needs for law and lawyers will inevitably increase. What is problematic is not the amount so much as the quality of the new law that is being produced; not the number of lawyers so much as the way they imagine their roles; not the rise in litigation so much as the peculiar uses to which the courts are being put.

CHAPTER 24 • A Nation Under Lawyers

Law, as Tocqueville taught, is not the most important of "the causes that tend to maintain a democratic republic." But it is second only to what he called the "mores," by which he meant the "whole moral and intellectual state of a people." One prominent member of the legal profession who did not hesitate to admit the priority of culture over law was Judge Learned Hand. Hand's sober warning against expecting law to substitute for active citizenship was delivered in New York City at a celebration of "I Am an American" day during World War II. To a large audience in Central Park, including 150,000 newly naturalized citizens, he said, "I often wonder whether we do not rest our hopes too much upon constitutions, upon laws, and upon courts. These are false hopes; believe me, these are false hopes. Liberty lies in the hearts of men and women; when it dies there, no constitution, no law, no court can save it; no constitution, no law, no court can even do much to help it. While it lies there it needs no constitution, no law, no court to save it."

The country was receptive then to straight talk about civic responsibilities. The radio broadcast of Hand's address prompted so many requests for the text that it was printed, reprinted, and anthologized many times under the title "The Spirit of Liberty." Hand's message is incomplete, however, without the recognition that law has a certain power to affect "the hearts of men and women," especially in a country like the United States. It is true that law is unsteady if not supported by habits and beliefs. But it is also the case that habits and beliefs can benefit from legal reinforcement; and that the seedbeds of civic virtues can be trampled by clumsy governmental feet. That is one reason why law is too important to be left entirely up to lawyers.

The moment is long overdue for a realistic appraisal of what a democratic republic should and should not expect of law and lawyers, of what courts and legally trained individuals can do especially well, and of what tasks are better left to other institutions and people. With every passing day, the limits of law loom larger, and new adverse side effects of well-intentioned measures come to light. Problems that cannot be whisked away by judicial fiat or resolved by the invention of new rights and crimes continue to fester. In peddling an idea of law that promised too much, legal opinion leaders for the past thirty years set the stage for disappointment, disillusion, and disrespect. Consider Judge Richard Posner's dispiriting litany of recent reforms that have proved ineffective or counterproductive:

> [A] bankruptcy code that has led to a large and unanticipated increase in the number of filings coupled with the disappointing results (and lethal side effects) of the no-fault automobile compensation movement; a no-fault divorce movement that has boomeranged against the women's movement that urged its adoption; the creation of a system of environmental regulation at once incredibly complex and either perverse or ineffective in much of its operation; . . . the rather hapless

blundering of the federal courts into immensely contentious, analytically insoluble ethical–political questions such as capital punishment, prison conditions (how comfortable must they be?), sex and the family, and political patronage; the accidental growth of the class action lawsuit . . . into what many observers believe is an engine for coercing the settlement of cases that have no real merit yet expose defendants to astronomical potential liabilities; the flood of one-way attorney's fee-shifting statutes, which over-encourage litigation; and the creation of an intricate code of federal criminal procedure . . . in the name of the Constitution, and the wholesale imposition of the code on state criminal proceedings.

In many of the instances cited by Posner, lawmakers could have made more constructive contributions if they had tested their ideas in pilot programs before embarking on wholesale reforms. There are few other ways to increase our limited store of knowledge concerning such matters as: What are the actual effects of legal measures? How can law help to maintain a beneficial balance in the constantly shifting ecology of state, market economy, mediating structures of civil society, and individual rights? How can government regulate without co-opting or destroying what it touches? How can one foresee and avoid unintended consequences or harmful side effects of regulation? How can lawmakers determine the optimal proportion between fixed rules and individualized discretion in various concrete situations?

It is disheartening that in such a legalistic country we know so little about how law works, what it can do well, and what it cannot accomplish at all. In the vast law school we all attend, there is a growing sense that something has gone deeply wrong. As in the nation's primary and secondary schools, that realization is attended by much finger pointing and recrimination. Just as teachers blame parental irresponsibility for disorderly classrooms, it is common for lawyers to blame professional ills on client demands and conditions in the general culture. And just as parents complain that the schools are undercutting their efforts to instill good habits at home, Americans have the sense that the legal system often operates against the general welfare.

To some extent, popular discontent with the law and its minions seems to be a case of the mirror despising its own reflection. Lawyers, after all, represent their fellow citizens. But it is also the case, in our legalistic country, that the ways of lawyers exert a powerful effect on culture, as well as on political and economic life. At one time, Americans formed their impressions of law and lawyers mainly through direct experience and observation. Now those impressions are increasingly gained from images presented through the news and entertainment. Through the filters of the media, the rise in adversarial legalism within the profession is magnified manyfold to the outside world. The lawyer as peacemaker and problem solver is rarely newsworthy, rarely entertaining, and rarely glimpsed. A troubling synergy is set in motion between the most visible segment of the profession and a diverse popular culture short on unifying influences. Small wonder that increasingly adversarial forms of legalism have cropped up alongside the old magisterial spirit that Tocqueville admired. What does it mean, though, for our experiment in ordered liberty when legalism, instead of helping to harness the passions, is increasingly pressed into their service?

What does it mean for our vast law school when the instructors leave their customary posts? When practitioners forsake the business of representation to become operators on their own account—pursuing the rewards of the marketplace, but evading the market constraints to which most other businessmen are subject? When office lawyers behave like litigators—without the discipline of procedural rules and courtroom protocol? When judges mimic executives and legislators—without the accountability or checks by which those officials are restrained? When law professors begin to profess everything but law—without peer review or advanced training in other fields? Socrates, in *The Republic*, took a dim view of craftsmen who did not perfect their own arts and stick to them. It is not so terrible, he said, if a cobbler tries to be a carpenter, or a carpenter tries to make shoes, but "men who are not guardians of the laws and the city but only seem to be, utterly destroy a city." Injustice is certain to run rampant in a polity where the guardians of the laws seek forms of happiness that "will turn them into everything except guardians."

While it may be excessive to claim that the very survival of the republic is at stake, it seems clear that the internal struggles currently roiling the American legal profession have far-reaching political implications. Although these struggles are taking place largely out of public view, every citizen has a stake in the accommodations that are being struck among the many competing claims on the allegiance of individual lawyers and among the order-affirming and order-challenging activities of the profession as a whole. The arrangements that are emerging will not represent the total victory of one set of ideals and habits over others. Rather, it will be a matter of proportion and emphasis.

Several nice issues of balance, then, confront the profession and the citizenry it serves: balance between liberty and order; balance among the branches of government; balance among the conflicting loyalties that tug at every individual lawyer; balance between traditionalism and iconoclasm in the law; balance between artisans of order and connoisseurs of conflict in the profession as a whole. How will those delicate accommodations be made?

# Legal Ethics:
# Worlds in Collision

*This essay, a reflection on Jane Jacob's work on ethics
as applied to law, appeared in the
March 1995 issue of First Things.[1]*

CHICAGO'S FINANCIAL DISTRICT and the seat of its city government are only a few blocks apart, yet they belong to two different worlds. I learned this in my first few months of law practice in 1964 when, as the new kid on the block, I had to handle routine motions in both state and federal courts. There was scarcely any difference in atmosphere between my firm's sedate quarters in the Continental Bank building and the austere federal court-house just around the comer. An aura of solemnity surrounded the federal judges in their courtrooms, as it did our senior partners in their spacious but simply furnished offices. Lawyers exchanged pleasantries and conversed genially in the hallways of both places.

To walk from lower LaSalle Street to the municipal and county courts on Washington between Clark and Dearborn, however, was to pass through a culture warp. From the outside, Chicago's Civic Center on its massive concrete plaza was no less imposing than the federal building. Inside was bedlam. The Civic Center was filled with everything that made Chicago such an exhilarating and alarming city—jostling, shouting, joking, cajoling, back-slapping, backstabbing, bargaining, dealing, favors granted, grudges paid with interest, intimidation, bribery, conciliation, grand gestures, obscene remarks, and the occasional spontaneous act of generosity.

In the courtrooms, protocol was more or less observed, but the strain was often too much for the regulars. One young litigator from my firm never forgot his first appearance in municipal court. Full of himself, he stepped up when his case was called, and began, as we were taught to do in law school: "May it please the court, my name is Edward R. Lev and I represent the Continental Illinois National Bank and Trust Company of Chicago." The judge

---

[1] Mary Ann Glendon, "Legal Ethics—Worlds in Collision," *First Things* 41 (March 1994): 21–27.

glared down at the unfortunate newcomer and remarked (to the delight of seasoned hands): "Well, bully for you!"

Another of my colleagues reported hearing the following exchange in open court one day while waiting for his own case to be heard:

"Counsel, the Court believes it smells alcohol on Counsel's breath."
"Is that so, your Honor? Well, Counsel believes he smells garlic on the Court's breath."

The separate spheres of Chicago's legal universe generally kept to their own orbits. Large-firm attorneys had few dealings with small-time lawyers, and relatively little business in the county or municipal courts. However, Steven Lubet, who was a Chicago legal services lawyer in the 1970s, has recorded a rare occasion when the worlds of LaSalle Street and the Civic Center intersected in a dramatic way.

On the day in question, Lubet was waiting for his case to be called in one of the most disorderly courtrooms in the city. To his amazement, when the clerk bawled out the name of the next matter, a well-dressed lawyer approached the bench and said, "Your Honor, I would like to present Mr. Albert Jenner." Jenner was one of the city's most respected lawyers. He had been a member of the Warren Commission and minority counsel to the Senate committee investigating the Watergate affair. Lubet recalls: "Once Mr. Jenner's presence was announced, the entire courtroom suddenly metamorphosed. The muttering plaintiffs' bar fell silent. Clerks began answering inquiries from unrepresented defendants. The judge actually asked questions about the facts and the law. . . . Furthermore, this effect lasted for the entire day, long after Mr. Jenner left."

Jenner's appearance (apparently as a favor to a friend) was like a visitation from another planet. Long afterward, Lubet recounts, the regulars would talk of the time when "Bert Jenner handled a case in our courtroom."

Why do corporate lawyers and lawyers for "people" move past each other in the legal system like bishops of different colors on a chessboard? To many, the answer might seem obvious: "It's social class, stupid!" The most recent work of Jane Jacobs, however, reveals that there is more to the story. In *Systems of Survival* (reviewed in *First Things*, December 1993), Jacobs maintains that human beings have basically only two ways of making a living, one concerned with acquiring or protecting territories, and the other with trading or producing for trade. By a process resembling natural selection, humankind has developed two basic approaches to the ethics of making a living, each system perfectly calibrated to promote success and survival in the way of life it grounds. Though the two ethical survival strategies are strikingly different from one another, they are symbiotic—for modern societies need traders to produce and market goods and services, and we also require raiders to maintain order and stability. Raiders and traders are almost inevitably uncomprehending or disdainful of one another, but Jacobs argues that from a global point of view, each system is valid on its own terms and each promotes the general welfare.

Today's police officers, soldiers, and politicians (like their hunter-gatherer forerunners) flourish when certain qualities are in good supply among them: cunning, prowess, show of force, obedience, respect for hierarchy, readiness to take vengeance, and, above all, loyalty. The loyalty that is the bedrock of their relationships not only advances their common aims but keeps these dangerous people from harming one another. They are rightly suspicious of trading, for raiders' loyalty to each other and to their tasks must not be for sale.

Among traders, the central value is honesty, for the very good reason that commerce cannot be sustained for long without a good deal of trust. Traders prize such qualities as industriousness, thrift, inventiveness, tolerance, and ability to compromise. Unlike the clannish raiders, traders collaborate easily with strangers. They are rightly wary of force and deception (despite the tempting short-term benefits of such tactics), for trader prosperity in the long run depends on stable social conditions and reliable relationships.

Lawyers presented Jacobs with a puzzle, for they are associated with both raider and trader ethics, often switching from one role to another depending on the task. A certain tension is built into their official canons of ethics, for example, "A lawyer is a representative of clients, an officer of the legal system, and a public citizen having special responsibility for the quality of justice." In some legal contexts, an honesty-based ethic seems to prevail; in others, loyalty seems to be the highest value.

Jacobs noted with interest, though, that the culture of English barristers, historically at least, had a strong raider cast. Endowed with a virtual monopoly on the most raider-like legal activity—the planning and conduct of courtroom battles—barristers went to great lengths to shun trading. They did not discuss payment for their services, and would not sue to collect their fees. On the back of the barrister's gown there is still a little pocket that once enabled him to be paid without actually seeing or handling money. Unlike solicitors, barristers in former times chiefly belonged to social circles where it was considered disgraceful to be "in trade."

American conditions, however, were different from the beginning. Lawyers often had to be barristers and solicitors rolled into one. Abraham Lincoln's legal career, to take one famous example, involved him in the roles of zealous advocate one day and wise counselor or peacemaker the next. Legal education in the United States still purports to be a foundation for all types of legal work. To Jacobs, it seemed that lawyers might be carriers of a valuable new survival trait, one that might be especially useful in complex modern societies where raiders and traders cannot simply go their symbiotic separate ways. In many respects, everyone's life is becoming complicated in the way that lawyers' lives have always been. So if lawyers have really mastered the art of

CHAPTER 25 • Legal Ethics: Worlds in Collision

recognizing the different ethical systems and adapting appropriately to either one, depending on the task at hand, they ought to be handy people to have around. In other words, where many people see lawyers as, to put it politely, ethically challenged, Jacobs thinks they might be ethically ambidextrous.

Jacobs thus becomes one of the few people since Louis D. Brandeis to propose that the legal profession might have something to teach other occupational groups about ethics. Her theory is so endearingly contrarian that one wants it to be true. But generalist lawyers, for whom the case is strongest, are in increasingly short supply. Two momentous changes long ago transformed the legal world that Lincoln knew: increased specialization, prompted by the rise of corporate firms at the turn of the century, and a large influx of new lawyers from relatively unassimilated ethnic groups at about the same time. The profession began to develop more of a separation between legal raiders and traders, but not along neat English lines. The split reflected the growing social stratification of the bar, the increasing division of labor between litigators and office lawyers, and the development of a wide range of specialized fields of practice.

Once the dust settled after the robber baron era, trader values were in clear ascendancy among the establishment lawyers who dominated early professional organizations and wrote the first codes of ethics. This was only to be expected, since they and their corporate clients stayed away from courtroom confrontation as much as possible, and concentrated mainly on what Jacobs would call trading activities. Many other segments of the practice were trader strongholds as well: small-town counselors and specialized areas like conveyancing, estate planning, and most aspects of business law.

In a few areas, however, a number of factors combined to push raider values to the foreground. Litigation was a major specialty of many small firms and solo practitioners. Some low-status fields—plaintiffs' personal injury suits, domestic relations cases, and criminal defense work—revolved around raider fortresses. The clients in such matters, men and women in acute personal crises, were apt to regard the lawyer (and he was apt to see himself) as a champion, a special friend in need. Ethnic lawyers, even when engaged in traderlike activities, tended to regard themselves, and to be perceived by establishment lawyers, as outsiders. Whether fighting for their clients, or struggling for their own economic survival, they often had to operate in strange or hostile territory. They were at home in a milieu where favors were an important currency—where clients were friends, and friends were clients.

To elite lawyers, the legal world outside the financial district looked like a hotbed of sharp practice, hustling, ambulance-chasing, and generally deplorable ethical standards. Legal ethicists Thomas and Mary Shaffer, however, have convincingly demonstrated that two quite different ethical systems were operating side-by-side in the profession: an "old WASP" or "gentlemen's" ethic among small-town and establishment lawyers, and an "old world" ethic among lawyers from communities formed by immigrants from Ireland, Italy, Poland, and Eastern Europe. The "old world" ethic stressed loyalty to the client, even at some cost to the legal system; the "old WASP" ethic emphasized fidelity to legal institutions and their improvement, even at the cost of sometimes having to say no to clients.

The Shaffers' old world and old WASP ethics correspond at many points with Jacobs' loyalty-based and honesty-based systems. What they add, however, are the dimensions of ethnicity and religion. The old WASP ethics were rooted in Protestant rectitude and a well-understood gentlemen's code. The ethics of old world Jews and Catholics reflected a worldview that placed clients ahead of institutions, and treated relationships as more important than rules. From the old world vantage point, the gentlemen's way often seemed harsh, flinty-hearted, even inhuman. To establishment lawyers, the immigrants' irreverence toward the law and its minions looked more like cynicism than a way of keeping the things of the world in their proper place. Human nature being what it is, ample support could be found in either camp for the most negative interpretations. Still, both ethical systems reflected a coherent vision of the virtuous life. And both contained the seeds of corruption.

Ask any lawyer who complains about a supposed decline in the ethical tone of the legal profession to name the beast, and the answer is apt to be "commercialization." If there is one dogma to which high-minded lawyers cling more tenaciously than any other, it is that the legal profession ought to be above the "morals of the marketplace." It should give one pause, however, that Abraham Lincoln was quite comfortable with the idea that law is a business as well as a profession, and that his idea of virtue in a lawyer was not much different from common decency in any other occupation. The conceit that law is not a business, or only incidentally so, seems connected with the efforts of elite lawyers in the early years of this century to distance themselves from the buccaneer-founders of their own firms and from "hustling" immigrant lawyers, as well as to assert their independence from their own clients.

Many old school lawyers still chant the refrain. The "most serious threat to the legal profession" at the present time is "commercialism," former Solicitor General and Harvard Dean Erwin Griswold recently wrote. Albert Jenner, in his final public appearance, told a gathering of Chicago lawyers: "We need to reorient our thinking away from the legal marketplace and law firms as profit centers and revenue producers, and law as a business."

That careless use of "commercial" as an epithet is mischievous. Lawyers' stubborn refusal to recognize their affinities with other highly skilled, well-educated sellers of services seems to rest either on the arrogant assumption that businesspeople have fewer ethics, or the dubious proposition that businesspeople invariably place short-term profit maximization ahead of all other considerations. Those cramped ideas of business ethics, however, are widely recognized in the business world as signs of economic and moral pathology.

Unfortunately, as lawyers increasingly accept that law is, among other things, a profit-making business, many seem to believe that means all ethical bets are off.

If Jane Jacobs is right, the high-minded lawyers who look down on the morals of the marketplace have got it exactly backward. There was a joker in the pack of "gentlemen's ethics." The English gentry were pluperfect raiders who had nothing but contempt for shopkeepers and merchants. Old school American lawyers seem to have unwittingly imported the old barristers' disdain for trade into a legal world where most lawyers, most of the time, regardless of social standing, are engaged in trading activities. In recent years, again unwittingly, trader-lawyers have permitted their everyday ethics to be infiltrated and undermined by raider values that should have been reserved for special occasions.

To see why that is a plausible diagnosis, one must distinguish, as many ethicists do, between random individual corruption and the structures of sin that create an ethos in which it is exceptionally difficult for any individual to walk the paths of righteousness. What Jacobs calls systemic corruption is more serious than plain old sin, for it poisons the entire moral ecology of a community. Jacobs' original contribution to the understanding of the sources of systemic corruption is her theory that one cause is inadvertent. With a series of arresting examples, she shows how the introduction of trader values in a raiding system, or vice versa, can often change things just enough to shatter the old system, to "literally de-moralize" it. The host system breaks down, losing its ability to discipline its members. Virtues convert to vices. Honesty and loyalty take a back seat to greed and force, as traders indulge extreme proclivities for acquisitiveness, and raider destructiveness runs amok.

Thus, in one of Jacobs' illustrations, it was disastrous for the hunter-gatherer Ik tribe of southern Uganda when they were forcibly resettled from hunting into farming. The Ik had no difficulty learning how to farm, but they were unable to make the mental adjustments necessary to sustain a trading way of life. Holding on to their old ways while adopting the new manner of making a living, they turned their force and cunning on each other.

Closer to home, we can observe more familiar forms of raider corruption when our police officers and public officials traffic in what should not be for sale. Chicago, in the years I practiced there, was governed by one of the great raiders of all time, Richard J. Daley. Chicagoans still argue over the personal probity of the late mayor, but there is no doubt that the Democratic machine he headed, and the Cook County government—which was sometimes controlled by Republicans—were theme parks of raider culture gone bad. A federal investigation in the 1980s confirmed what every Chicago lawyer already knew or suspected: It was not only clerks, but certain judges, who were on the take. "Operation Greylord" made clear that the rot was deep and systemic.

Systemic corruption can wear pinstripes as well as polyester. As her prime example of what happens when traders take up raiding, Jacobs points to investment banking in the takeover era. The experience of large law firms in the same period provides a parallel illustration. Into the risk-averse worlds of corporate lawyers and bankers in the 1970s came a new generation of raiders, a mogul horde the likes of which had not been seen since the days when Jay Gould and other grandees of greed held sway. The corporate raiders' business was at first turned away by established firms. This was partly out of concern not to offend existing clients, but also because the raiders' tactics (such as using lawsuits for pure harassment) were so repugnant. That opened a legal niche to be quickly filled by younger, more aggressive, firms formed (as Lincoln Caplan points out in his chronicle of the rise of the Skadden firm) by Catholics, Jews, and non-Ivy Leaguers who had been snubbed by old-line firms.

The established firms soon found themselves forced to defend their clients against hostile takeovers. Eventually, most began to represent raiders as well. Louis Auchincloss, who retired from a Manhattan firm in 1987 to devote himself to fiction, observed sadly, "There was a time when you brought a suit only to right a wrong or collect an obligation. That all the finest firms [now bring takeover suits] is the single most corrosive factor in the ethics of the bar." Transactional lawyers (who used to be litigation-shy) joined forces with courtroom lawyers in the exciting new work. Together they hunted enterprises ripe for capture. They jointly plotted acquisitions and lawsuits. The workaholic Rambo was born.

Listen to how Lawrence Lederman, in his *Tales from the Takeover Era*, described what drew him from ordinary corporate law to takeover work: "Besides agility, attempting a takeover requires craft and the willingness to take risks." "Given a choice I preferred representing raiders. Besides enjoying the planning, as an outsider I was attracted to the entrepreneurial clients, interesting men with a sense of themselves who were trying to make their mark and didn't mind challenging and dismantling rigid corporate empires." "[L]ittle else in business galvanized people and brought them together as cohesively as organizing an attack that would require speed, surprise, and precision timing." "I found that all the mystery and excitement of sex, of breaking down resistance, of scoring and conquest, were associated with a takeover. Manliness was at stake, and measured." "[T]he takeover told of cunning and daring and the power to take what you wanted."

No sooner had the takeover frenzy begun to subside when the professional world was rocked by the savings and loan debacle. When, in 1986, federal agents began their investigation of Lincoln Federal Savings & Loan, the regulatory audit quickly escalated into a no-holds-barred adversarial battle. Lincoln's lawyers in the New York firm of Kaye, Scholer, Fierman, Hays &

Handler fought the government's requests for information every step of the way. Government attorneys struck back in kind, filing a suit that charged Kaye, Scholer attorneys with lying to regulators, obstructing the investigation, and remaining passive while Charles Keating provided false information. The government's hardball tactics included an administrative order freezing the partnership's assets, a move that brought Kaye, Scholer quickly to its knees. The firm paid $41 million dollars for a no-fault settlement of the charges.

Shaken by that unprecedented settlement, lawyers began to debate such questions as whether Kaye, Scholer attorneys had simply been helping their client in time-honored fashion to do what it wanted to do within limits of the law. Was a hostile regulatory audit the equivalent to litigation for ethical purposes? Did lawyers for publicly regulated clients have a special duty to the public? What ethical constraints should government attorneys observe? Should an administrative agency be allowed to freeze a firm's assets without showing any reason other than to force a settlement?

One question was seldom in the foreground: What had become of the old counselors' dictum that "about half the practice of a decent lawyer consists in telling would-be clients that they are damned fools and should stop"? The author of a study of Wall Street firms in the 1950s had concluded that corporate lawyers then possessed enough independence to permit them to serve not only as advisors, but also as conscience to big business. The picture that emerged from a similar study published in 1988 was very different. Three out of four large-firm lawyers could not recollect a single instance in which they had ever even disagreed with a client. Their motto seemed to be: "The client never wants to be told he can't do what he wants to do; he wants to be told how to do it, and it is the lawyer's business to tell him how."

The takeover phenomenon and the savings and loan affair were only the most notorious in a series of developments that have drawn elite law firms out of the trader mode and away from "gentlemen's" ethics. The standard explanations in the legal community emphasize the fierce competition for business among law firms that began when clients started to shop around for the best deal, rather than maintaining their traditional ties with a single firm. Another part of the picture is that corporate clients themselves were undergoing fundamental changes, abandoning their traditional reluctance to sue one another. That led to an increase in the size and prestige of those raider enclaves, litigation departments, in large law firms. The freakish prosperity of the eighties permitted all sorts of excess in terms of salaries for beginners, overstaffing cases, and even interior decoration, as law firms, like the tower-building nobles of San Gimignano, tried to outdo each other in ostentation.

The binge of the eighties was succeeded by the hangover of the nineties, but, as Jacobs says, "Water over the dam carries debris." Many law firms, like many of the corporate clients they served, came under the control of people with a raider cast of mind. But the result was not the emergence of a new raider culture with its characteristic, coherent ethical understandings. The mingling of trader and raider ways, rather, seemed to draw lawyers into a moral quagmire. Old habits and attitudes unraveled, as raider ways spread to areas of professional life where they wrought havoc with relationships that depend on trust. The legal profession here and there began to resemble the Ik tribesmen, neither hunting nor farming, but preying on everyone in sight, including one another. Whence cometh their help?

The field known as "legal ethics" has only a tenuous relation to the systemic difficulties afflicting the legal profession. For one thing, formal codes of ethics never aimed at capturing the full network of understandings that lawyers observe in their dealings with one another, with clients, and with the courts. They merely set forth a small body of fairly obvious minimal duties with which lawyers must comply on pain of discipline or disbarment. Where ethical problems of genuine complexity are concerned, official codes offer little guidance. They are often least helpful where most needed.

The American Bar Association's current Model Rules, adopted in 1983, explicitly recognize that the moral tone of the legal profession depends primarily on a great web of informal understandings. Within the framework of a general obligation to represent the client zealously while remaining within the bounds of the law, a lawyer is free (but not required) to advise clients to comply with the spirit as well as the letter of the law. A lawyer is equally at liberty to press the letter to its limits. If the great web lets go, an individual lawyer is essentially in free fall.

Recent changes in the rules actually seem to go with the flow of systemic problems in the profession rather than helping to counter them. The 1983 Rules, for example, dropped almost all of the language of moral suasion that had permeated earlier codes of lawyer conduct. Just when lawyers were coming under exceptional ethical stress, the Model Rules eliminated such words as "right," "wrong," "good," "bad," "conscience," and "character," and replaced them with words like "prudent," "proper," "permitted." The latest version of the Rules also eliminated a series of helpful discussions that used to follow the cryptic canons. The Preamble to the 1969 Code had emphasized the importance of those "Ethical Considerations": "[T]hey are aspirational in character and represent the objectives toward which every member of the profession should strive. They constitute a body of principles upon which the lawyer can rely for guidance in many specific situations." The reason the Ethical Considerations were dropped, apparently, is the growing lack of consensus within the profession on what is ethical. In other words, the more moral confusion there is, the less guidance one can expect from formal codes.

As they stand, the Model Rules are certainly capacious enough to permit the kind of intelligent flexibility about roles that Jacobs admires and that generalist lawyers seem once to have possessed. But the current rules also lend themselves to a simpler "solution" of complex ethical problems: When in doubt, go with the traditional value of client loyalty. The most hotly debated issue in connection with the 1983 Rules, in fact, was whether a lawyer should be required, rather than merely permitted, to disclose information he has reason to believe necessary to prevent a client from causing death or serious bodily harm to another person. The proponents of mandatory disclosure lost out to the advocates of ironclad client confidentiality.

The apparent advance of the client loyalty ideal at the expense of the independent counselor and court officer roles may mask an even more serious problem: a de facto priority for the lawyer's own personal or political concerns. San Francisco attorney Alan Marks recently broke the taboo on discussing that problem, suggesting in the columns of the *American Bar Association Journal* that ethical rules are mere "showpieces" that leave the most severe ethical dilemmas untouched. The "real" dilemmas, Marks alleged, arise mostly from "the powerful compulsion of self-concern."

Is Marks right? Contingent fees do provide many people with access to justice, but sometimes the fee is so large that the lawyer becomes the real party in interest. Intelligent use of media opportunities can advance a client's cause, but many lawyers who seize them appear to be on personal ego trips. Corporate lawyers have complex loyalties, but many seem more concerned to satisfy the company managers who hire and fire lawyers than to protect the interests of scattered shareholder-owners.

Even more remarkable is the appearance of many lawyers who are *openly* operating on their own account. Often the new grandees portray themselves as rebels against the old notion that law is not a business. Ironically, lawyers' unapologetic embrace of self-interest may have been facilitated by the old mindset that equated "commercialism" and the "morals of the marketplace" with unbridled acquisitiveness. Now that lawyers are increasingly admitting that they want to run their "business as a business," many seem to suppose they are exempt from ordinary decent behavior. Or they imagine that business ethics are something like the full-bore adversarial tactics of criminal defense lawyers. They are like the teenage rat in the *Far Side* cartoon, whose response, when his mother tells him to clean up his room, is: "Criminy! It's *supposed* to be a rat hole!"

What got lost along the way was Lincoln's unpretentious, pragmatic attitude, rooted in the trader understanding that any business, including law business, thrives best on honesty and cooperation—and the companion understanding that a raider's deception for the sake of the task must be carefully limited to certain negotiation and litigation settings.

Academic debunkers of "professionalism," preoccupied with their "discovery" that high-minded lawyers have frequently failed to live up to their professed ideals, have not been helpful in the current period of turmoil. Friendly reminders of practitioners' shortcomings might once have served to puncture the balloon of smug professional self-satisfaction. But the professorial fire brigade has arrived with its pails of cold water just when the embers of professional pride need to be coaxed back to life. The scholarly orgy of debunking has obscured the importance of the facts that such ideals were professed at all, and that debate about them helped to focus the attention of a large, diverse, professional community on the question of what kind of life a lawyer ought to try to live. The old moralistic codes of ethics were often derided in the academy as self-serving attempts to fend off regulation.

But retelling the old stories and exploring their implications for new circumstances helped to orient and reinforce each lawyer's quest for a morally coherent professional life. Today's lawyers wander in an increasingly impersonal, bureaucratized legal world, where neither honesty-based nor loyalty-based systems seem to be operating very well. The families, communities, neighborhoods, and schools that once served as seedbeds and anchors for personal and professional virtues are themselves in considerable disarray. The great web of lawyer's informal understandings hangs in tatters. Today's raw recruits to the knowledge class seldom have a solid base of old world, old WASP, or any other culture to fall back on—and no coherent professional culture to embrace. Emancipated from the old ways, they soldier on, without examples, guidance, or reinforcement.

The legal ethos that is emerging is bound to be very different from a world in which most lawyers, most of the time, were at least oriented toward visions of lawyering that demanded a considerable degree of self-subordination—whether of the raider or trader variety. Just as sexual self-expression has few limits in a culture where chaste behavior is mocked, lawyers' self-interest is apt to run amok when anyone who places client or court above profit is branded a hypocrite or a chump. A lawyer who takes his duties to the court and the legal system seriously may well be at a disadvantage against a less scrupulous adversary. In such circumstances, should we be astonished that short-term self-interest often prevails?

The collision and disintegration of old raider and trader understandings have had personal as well as professional consequences. Transported from their communities of memory to membership in America's deracinated technocrat class, liberated from the networks of old world and old WASP values, many lawyers are now free, self-determining, and miserable. Like the displaced Machiguengas in Mario Vargas Llosa's *The Storyteller*, they have lost their myths about where they came from, who they are, and where they are going. They can no longer make sense of their lives. The stories they heard in law school about independence, public service, and professionalism don't match up with their everyday experiences. Rather than being ethically adaptable in Jacobs' flattering sense, many are merely ethically agile. The patron saint of these lone raiders is not honest, adaptable Abe Lincoln. Nor is it loyal, single-minded Perry Mason. It is the chameleonlike Talleyrand, the all-time champion of reinventing one's self.

CHAPTER 25 • Legal Ethics: Worlds in Collision

# Classical and
# Romantic Judges

*This essay, based on a chapter of my 1994 book, A Nation Under Lawyers,
describes how a new romantic ideal of the judge has replaced
the traditional ideal based on craftsmanship and impartiality.
It appeared in the August 1994 issue of* Commentary.[1]

As LATE AS THE EARLY 1960S, Justice William O. Douglas was widely
regarded as a disgrace to the bench even by many lawyers who shared his
social and economic views. Douglas's contempt for legal craftsmanship was
seen as sloppiness; his visionary opinions were taken as evidence that he was
angling for the presidency; and his solicitude for those he considered under-
dogs was perceived as favoritism.

By the end of the 1960s, however, a new and very romantic ideal of
judging had begun to take shape. In eulogies, tributes, law-review articles,
and legal journalism, judges began to be praised for qualities that would
once have been considered problematic: compassion rather than impartiality, boldness rather than restraint, creativity rather than craftsmanship, and
specific results regardless of the effect on the legal order as a whole. In the
1990s, Douglas would surely have basked in the "Greenhouse Effect"—a
term (named after the *New York Times*'s Linda Greenhouse) for the warm
reciprocity between activist journalists and judges who meet their approval.

This great change was set into motion by the appointment of Earl Warren as Chief Justice in 1953. President Eisenhower's choice of Warren was an
unusual move, for the new Chief Justice had spent almost all his professional
life in electoral politics. After serving as California's attorney general, he
became a power in the state Republican party and then a popular governor.
He was Thomas E. Dewey's running mate in 1948, and a serious contender
for the Republican presidential nomination himself in 1952. Nothing in
Warren's background had prepared him for the fine-gauge work of opinion

---

[1] Mary Ann Glendon, "Partial Justice." *Commentary* 98 (2; August 1994): 22–26,
based on Mary Ann Glendon's, *A Nation Under Lawyers,* (New York: Farrar, Straus,
and Giroux, 1994).

writing. He was impatient with the need to ground a desired outcome in constitutional text or tradition. As described by an admirer, Warren was a man who brushed off legal and historical impediments to the results he felt were right; he was not a "look-it-up-in-the-library" type.

What he was, above all, was a statesman, and although scholars may argue about its foundations in constitutional text and tradition, the Warren Court's decision in *Brown* v. *Board of Education* was indeed an act of statesmanship. Those academics who downplay the importance of *Brown* in the struggle for racial justice have underrated its effects on attitudes about race relations—effects that in turn helped to bring about important political changes like the Civil Rights Act of 1964 and voting-rights legislation. The Warren Court laid its prestige on the line in a bid not only to dismantle official segregation, but to delegitimate racially discriminatory attitudes. That wager was successful. Though racial prejudice has not been eradicated, it has no respectability at all in contemporary American society.

The effects of *Brown* on the legal profession and on the legal order as a whole were another matter. And here it was not Warren but William Brennan, appointed to the Supreme Court by Eisenhower in 1956, who came to incarnate those less salutary effects most fully.

Brennan was of humble origins. The son of Irish immigrants, he made his way to Harvard Law School—encouraged by his trade-unionist father who told him that a lawyer could do a lot for working people. Brennan did go into labor law, but enlisted on the other side of the cause that had meant so much to his father. After some years as a successful corporate practitioner in New Jersey, he became a trial judge and rose in time to the New Jersey Supreme Court. On the U.S. Supreme Court, he became a towering hero to those who shared his view that the Court had not only the power but the duty to promote social and political change.

Described by his biographer, Kim Eisler, as neither the most brilliant nor the best writer on the Court, Brennan during his long tenure may nevertheless have had the most influence on the general direction of its decisions. Few lawyers would disagree with the *New Yorker's* evaluation, on Brennan's retirement in 1990, that he had come "to personify the expansion of the role of the judiciary in American life."

Even toward the end of his career, as the composition and mood of the Court changed, Brennan was often able to beat the odds and further his vision. As portrayed by Bob Woodward and Scott Armstrong in *The Brethren*, "Brennan cajoled in conference, walked the halls constantly and worked the phones, polling and plotting strategy with his allies." In later years, when his colleagues declined to follow him on such excursions as judicially banning capital punishment or abolishing the custom of prayer at the opening of legislative sessions, Brennan went out on the hustings, calling on state courts to take up the cudgels.

In speeches and writings, Brennan encouraged state judges to exercise their powers of constitutional review in new and creative ways. State courts, he pointed out, could interpret their own constitutions so as to provide even more rights than are afforded under the federal Constitution. Like the fox in Aesop's fable, the wily Brennan cajoled whole flocks of jurists into dropping their reserve. "State courts cannot rest," he wrote, "when they have afforded their citizens the full protections of the federal Constitution. State constitutions, too, are a font of individual liberties, their protections often extending beyond those afforded by the Supreme Court's interpretation of federal law."

Unlike many adventurous judges, Brennan had well-developed views of judging and did not mind discussing them. Here he is in a 1988 essay:

> The Constitution is fundamentally a public text—the monumental charter of a government and a people—and a Justice of the Supreme Court must apply it to resolve public controversies. For, from our beginnings, a most important consequence of the constitutionally created separation of powers has been the American habit, extraordinary to other democracies, of casting social, economic, philosophical, and political questions in the form of lawsuits, in an attempt to secure ultimate resolution by the Supreme Court. . . . Not infrequently, these are the issues on which contemporary society is most deeply divided. They arouse our deepest emotions. The main burden of my 29 years on the Supreme Court has thus been to wrestle with the Constitution in this heightened public context, to draw meaning from the text in order to resolve public controversies.

That passage can instructively be compared with views often expressed in the past by Justices Oliver Wendell Holmes and Louis D. Brandeis. Holmes insisted that legislatures, no less than courts, were the ultimate guardians of the liberties and welfare of the people. "About 75 years ago," he said as a very old man, "I learned that I was not God. And so, when the people want to do something I can't find anything in the Constitution expressly forbidding them to do, I say, whether I like it or not, 'Goddammit, let 'em do it.'"

Brandeis for his part emphasized that where vexing social problems were concerned it would often be more advantageous to leave state and local governments free to experiment than to impose uniform and untested federal mandates upon the entire country. The states, he said, were like "laboratories" where innovative approaches to novel problems could be tested and refined or rejected.

Although one of the opinions of which Brennan was proudest was on legislative reapportionment, he maintained an uncharacteristic silence on the role of the elected branches in resolving the issues on which "society is most deeply divided." The reason must be that the way he saw his own life's work, as indicated in the above passage, put him in direct competition with the popular branches. Quoting Justice Robert Jackson, he made no bones

CHAPTER 26 • Classical and Romantic Judges

about his position that, right or wrong, the Court was to have the last word: "The Justices are certainly aware that we are not final because we are infallible; we know that we are infallible because we are final."

Brennan's approach to judging could not be more remote in spirit from Holmes's structural restraint. Nor did Brennan have much use for the prudent avoidance of the appearance of judicial imperialism that was characteristic of the first great shaper of the Court, John Marshall. Brennan did not hesitate to claim, regarding the Court's powers: "The course of vital social, economic, and political currents may be directed."

Energized and prodded to no small degree by Brennan, majorities on the Warren and Burger courts actively pursued a high-minded vision of empowering those individuals and groups they perceived as disadvantaged. When deference to the elected branches served those ends, as in many affirmative-action cases, Brennan deferred as humbly as any classical judge. When the decisions of councils or legislatures got in his way, he invoked expansive interpretations of constitutional language to brush them aside.

While Brennan was not one to let text or tradition stand in the way of a desired result, he knew how to turn his corners squarely. But he did not share the devotion to judicial craftsmanship that characterized the work of colleagues like John Marshall Harlan or Byron White. Nor did he show much concern about the probable side effects of a desired result in a particular case on the separation of powers, federal-state relations, or the long-term health of political processes and institutions. With respect to such matters, he was impatient with what he considered to be abstractions and technicalities.

When it came to compassion, Brennan had plenty for those he made (or wished to make) winners, but he showed little sensitivity toward those he ruled against. His heart went out to Native Americans when a Court majority permitted the federal government to build a road through sacred Indian places on public land. But in striking down a longstanding and successful New York City program providing remedial math and reading teachers to poor, special-needs children in religious schools, Brennan was pitiless. It took a dissent by Justice Sandra Day O'Connor to point out that the majority ruling, written by Brennan, had sacrificed the needs and prospects of 20,000 children from the poorest families in New York, and thousands more disadvantaged children across the country, for the sake of a maximalist version of the principle of separation of church and state.

The new model of bold, assertive judging has also had its exemplars in the lower courts. One federal appellate judge famed for his crusading decisions was the late J. Skelley Wright. Looking back on his role in expanding landlords' liability for the condition of leased premises, he wrote in 1982:

> I didn't like what I saw, and I did what I could to ameliorate, if not eliminate, the injustice involved in the way many of the poor were

required to live in the nation's capital. I offer no apology for not following more closely the legal precedents which had cooperated in creating the conditions that I found unjust.

The romantic ideal also fired the imaginations of judges in the capillaries of the legal system, the sites of the everyday administration of justice
described in *The Federalist* as "the great cement of society." A longtime District of Columbia Superior Court judge, Sylvia Bacon, told the American
Society for Public Administration that "[t]here is a sense among judges that
there are wrongs to be righted and that it is their responsibility to do it." As
for the role of the Constitution and the law in guiding the judge's sense of
right and wrong, Judge Bacon brusquely remarked: "Legal reasons are often
just a cover for a ruling in equity (basic fairness)."

By "fairness," Judge Bacon apparently did not mean anything so prosaic
as keeping an open mind to the arguments, and applying the relevant law
without regard to the identity of the litigants and without regard to a particular outcome. Her notion was more visceral: "Plain and simple sense of outrage by the judge." Such views were no impediment to Judge Bacon's
election to a seat on the American Bar Association's board of governors in
the 1980s.

Yet they would have been anathema to the Founders, for whom impartiality was the sine qua non of judicial justice. Massachusetts, adopting John
Adams's words, built the concept into its Bill of Rights:

> It is essential to the preservation of the rights of every individual, his
> life, liberty, property, and character, that there be an impartial interpre-
> tation of the laws, and administration of justice. It is the right of every
> citizen to be tried by judges as free, impartial, and independent as the
> lot of humanity will admit.

From the early years of the Republic to the present day, every American
judge has taken a vow to carry out his duties without fear or favor:

> I do solemnly swear that I will administer justice without respect to
> persons, do equal right to the poor and to the rich, and that I will
> impartially discharge and perform all the duties incumbent upon me,
> according to the best of my abilities and understanding agreeably to the
> Constitution and laws of the United States, so help me God.

Some critics of the worldview implicit in this oath say that judging
"without respect to persons" can lead to inhumane results by ignoring
important differences—between men and women, rich and poor, black and
white, strong and weak. If the critics had their way, the oath would be
revised to read something like this:

CHAPTER 26 • Classical and Romantic Judges

I affirm that I will administer justice with careful attention to the individual characteristics of the parties, that I will show compassion to those I deem disadvantaged, and that I will discharge my duties according to my personal understanding of the Constitution, the laws of the United States, and such higher laws as may be revealed to me.

Besides, the critics observe, impartiality is often just a mask covering various sorts of bias. They point to historical research that has found more than a little clay on the feet of classical idols. It may well have been Holmes's obnoxious eugenic views, for example, rather than his vaunted restraint, that prompted him to uphold a state statute providing for the forced sterilization of mental patients—with the cruel comment that "three generations of imbeciles are enough."

But are judicial compassion and responsiveness viable substitutes for the elusive ideal of impartiality? Few would dispute that judges should be able to empathize with the people who come before them. But in the early years of this century, adventurous judges were extremely tender-hearted toward big business, while showing little compassion for women and children working long hours in factories.

Let us acknowledge that until someone figures out how to make judges from other than human material, neither classical nor romantic feet will be a pretty sight. The real question, then, is which judicial attributes, systematically cultivated, offer the most protection against arbitrariness and bias.

Whatever one may conclude about the right mix of qualities for the special circumstances of the Supreme Court, it is hard to imagine that the routine administration of justice can benefit from an increase of compassion at the expense of impartiality. A close-knit, relatively homogeneous community can perhaps get along with a system where village elders reach decisions on the basis of their personal sense of fairness and their informed concern for the parties and the community. But that pastoral model cannot serve for an ethnically and ideologically diverse nation where litigants are strangers to the judge and often to each other. Under such conditions, the liberties and fortunes of citizens cannot be left to the mercy of each judge's personal sense of what procedures are fair, what outcome is just, who needs protection, and who deserves compassion.

The combination of subjective judging and an elected judiciary is an especially unhappy one. In the forty states where elections play a role in selecting or retaining some or all judges, the American Judicature Society reports that problems related to campaign advertising and financing are serious and worsening. What does it portend for a judge's impartiality when his election ads look just like a district attorney's: "Tough on Crime"? Or for her independence when she accepts large campaign contributions from lawyers who regularly appear in her court?

For cynics who maintain that judicial independence and impartiality are simply a sham, the logical move is to select judges according to their ideological leanings. But that is a dicey business—and not only because "sensitivity" and "compassion" are easier to fake than intelligence and integrity. The problem with subjective judging is that, sooner or later, the tables are apt to be turned when ambitious judges with the "wrong" ideas ascend to the bench. That is why many journalists and legal academics who once cheered the progress of assertive judging on the Supreme Court had second thoughts as the composition of the Court changed.

But why should the country's response to an old problem flagged by Alexander Hamilton—the scarcity of individuals with the requisite skill and integrity—be to accept a thoroughly politicized judiciary? One alternative that has worked well for some liberal democracies is a meritocratic civil-service judiciary, staffed with graduates of judicial-training academies. But we need not depart so radically from our own traditions. Surely our wise course is to insist on judges who have demonstrated a capacity for self-restraint (structural, interpretive, and personal) as well as a commitment to the time-honored judicial practices that help to promote those qualities.

The relevant skill is to maintain principled continuity in the system, while deciding particular cases in a way that even the losing party can accept as fair. No one is born with that sort of virtuosity. But Anglo-American judges over centuries have developed numerous safeguards against lapses and partiality. Chief among them is the requirement that a judge expose his reasoning in a written opinion. Since a perfectly reasoned opinion may rest on arbitrary premises, a judge is also expected to explain the facts and principles on which each decision is based and to follow those principles consistently in future cases.

Such technical skills in the judiciary are more necessary than ever, given the complexities of current economic and social conditions. Yet the supply of competent judges at all levels is indirectly threatened by several habits associated with adventurous judging.

As every lawyer knows, part of an appellate court's work involves maintaining a reasonable degree of coherence and predictability in the law. If that unglamorous but crucial task is not performed well, the courts falter in their fundamental obligation to decide like cases alike. Practitioners then stumble, too, for they cannot give reliable advice to clients who are trying to plan for the future, or to decide whether to prosecute, defend, or settle claims.

It has, however, become steadily more difficult for appellate judges to ensure reasonable reckonability and coherence in the legal system. Legislatures and administrative agencies rarely take the trouble to fit new statutes and regulations into the framework of existing law. Rather, they leave it up to judges to make some sense of a welter of federal, state, and local enactments that are often conflicting or overlapping—some overly detailed, others airily vague. The intellectual difficulty of many of these cases surpasses anything

CHAPTER 26 • Classical and Romantic Judges

that ever came before Marshall's Court in the early days of the Republic. In consequence, the quality most required of an appellate judge is often a craftsman's art and painstaking care.

Thus it is a cause for concern that specialists in areas like tax, anti-trust, labor, pensions, maritime law, insurance, social security, patents, trademarks, and copyrights increasingly complain of a decline in judicial workmanship.

After all, what will be left of the principle that like cases should be decided alike if every judge feels free to brush aside precedents, statutes, and bargained-for contractual provisions as mere technicalities? What will be the effect on the economy if our present imperfectly functioning system degenerates into a non-system, a chaotic heap of idiosyncratic decisions? Are we really ready for the rank-and-file judiciary to cast off restraints that rested lightly on the shoulders of men like Holmes and Learned Hand? For judges who slip the mailed fist of power into the velvet glove of compassion?

In constitutional cases, romantic judging also exacts a toll on the democratic elements in our form of government. When Warren and Burger court majorities converted the Constitution's safety valves (the Bill of Rights, due process, equal protection) into engines with judges at the controls, they wreaked havoc with grassroots politics. The dismal failures of many local authorities in dealing with racial issues became pretexts for depriving citizens everywhere of the power to experiment with new approaches to a wide range of problems that often take different forms in different parts of the country. Constitutional provisions designed to protect individuals and minorities against majoritarian excesses were increasingly used to block the normal processes through which citizens build coalitions, develop consensus, hammer out compromises, try out new ideas, learn from mistakes, and try again.

Elected officials have offered little resistance to judicial inroads on their powers. On hot issues, they often are only too happy to be taken off the hook by the courts. But each time a court sets aside an action of the political branches through free-wheeling interpretation, self-government suffers a setback. Political skills atrophy. People cease to take citizenship seriously. Citizens with diverse points of view lose the habit of cooperating to set conditions under which all can flourish. Adversarial legalism supplants the sober legalistic spirit that, in the nineteenth century, Alexis de Tocqueville admired in the American people. For, as Abraham Lincoln warned,

> if the policy of the government, upon vital questions, affecting the whole people, is to be irrevocably fixed by decisions of the Supreme Court, . . . the people will have ceased to be their own rulers, having, to that extent, practically resigned their government into the hands of that eminent tribunal.

In retrospect, one can see that the rise of bold judging proceeded for the most part with good intentions. Earlier in the century, state-court judges often had to take the initiative to keep judge-made law abreast of social and economic changes. In the wake of the New Deal, federal judges had to improvise techniques for dealing with regulatory law. Then in *Brown*—and also in the one-man, one-vote cases—the Supreme Court had to exercise statesmanship in addressing legal aspects of the country's most pressing social problems.

The achievements of gifted judges in meeting those challenges made it difficult for some of them—as well as for their less capable colleagues—to resist the impulse to keep on doing justice by their own lights. That those lights were not always powered by authoritative sources was easy to disguise, even from themselves. It was a case of successes leading to temptations, of a good thing taken to extremes.

In finding our way back from these extremes, the beginning of wisdom is to recognize that, whatever the pros and cons of adventurous judging by the Supreme Court on momentous occasions, romantic ideals are a poor guide to how judges throughout the system should comport themselves as a general matter. The unique political role of the nation's highest court may require its members at times to show the sorts of excellence that are traditionally associated with executives or legislators—energy, leadership, boldness. But, day in and day out, those qualities are no substitute for the ordinary heroism of sticking to one's last, of demonstrating impartiality, interpretive skill, and responsibility toward authoritative sources in the regular administration of justice.

As things now stand in the topsy-turvy world of legal journalism, however, a judge will win no plaudits for such heroism, and may even earn contempt for not being interesting enough. When Byron White stepped down from the Supreme Court in 1993, the *New Republic*'s cover story called him "a perfect cipher." Admitting that White was "a first-rate legal technician," a writer for that magazine sneered at him for being "uninterested in articulating a constitutional vision." To that writer, it was evidence of White's "mediocrity" that he was hard to classify as a liberal or a conservative.

What made White hard to classify, of course, were the very qualities that made him an able and conscientious judge—his independence and his faithfulness to a modest conception of the judicial role. His "vision," implicit in nearly every one of his opinions, was not that difficult to discern. As summed up by a former clerk, it was one

> in which the democratic process predominates over the judicial; [and] the role of the Court or any individual justice is not to promote particular ideologies, but to decide cases in a pragmatic way that permits the political branches to shoulder primary responsibility for governing our society. . . . The purpose of an opinion . . . is quite simply to decide the case in an intellectually and analytically sound manner.

Though White's competence, independence, and integrity did not make for lively copy, he was a model of modern neoclassical judging. As for the future, it is heartening that White's replacement, Ruth Bader Ginsburg, took the occasion of a speech shortly after her appointment to embrace the model of the "good judge" as represented by Learned Hand. Quoting Hand's biographer, Justice Ginsburg said:

> The good judge is "open-minded and detached . . . heedful of limitations stemming from the judge's own competence and, above all, from the presuppositions of our constitutional scheme; [the good] judge . . . recognizes that a felt need to act only interstitially does not mean relegation of judges to a trivial or mechanical role, but rather affords the most responsible room for creative, important judicial contributions."

As Justice Ginsburg's former colleague Robert Bork has observed, the key check on judicial authoritarianism will always be the judge's own understanding of the scope and limits of judicial power—and the insistence of a vigilant citizenry on having judges who will resist the temptation to remake the constitutional design for government and who will wholeheartedly comply with the judicial oath's promise to do equal justice without respect to persons.

# CHAPTER 27

# Carl Rowan's
# Thurgood Marshall

*I never suspected when I wrote this review of Carl Rowan's biography
of Thurgood Marshall that two sentences (italicized below) would cost me
a half-year's salary. I had taken a semester-long leave from Harvard on the basis
of a promised grant from the Laurel Foundation, which I knew only as an
environmental protection group. When Laurel reneged on its promise after this review
was published, I was informed that I had offended them because their idea of
protecting the environment included keeping out immigrants and controlling
population growth through abortion. The review appeared
in the March 1, 1993, National Review.[1]*

W HEN THE YOUNG THURGOOD MARSHALL was a law student at Howard University in the early 1930s, he often cut classes to watch former Solicitor General John W. Davis argue cases before the Supreme Court. Davis, then a Wall Street lawyer at the peak of his career, was the leading oral advocate of the day. On those occasions, Marshall later recalled, "I'd ask myself, 'Will I ever, ever . . . ?' and every time I had to answer, 'No, never.'" Davis was his *beau ideal* of a lawyer.

Two decades later, Thurgood Marshall, at the height of his powers, argued and won the most celebrated Supreme Court case of the twentieth century, *Brown* v. *Board of Education*. His adversary: the eighty-year-old John W. Davis. Marshall had been a gracious opponent (forbidding his associates to make snide remarks about Davis) and Davis was noble in defeat (writing a friend that it was good for the country that the Warren Court decision had been unanimous).

By 1954, when the historic school-desegregation case was decided, Marshall's own place in the pantheon of American lawyers was already assured. He was the architect of the legal assault on segregated housing, public accommodations and schools, and on all-white Democratic primaries. In later years, he could look back on winning 29 of the 32 cases he argued

[1] Mary Ann Glendon, "Judgment Day," review of *Dream Makers, Dream Breakers* by Carl Rowan, *National Review* 45 (4; 1 March 1993): 56–59.

before the Supreme Court for the NAACP, 14 of the 19 cases he argued as Solicitor General, and 24 years of service as the first black Justice on the nation's highest tribunal.

Carl Rowan's *Dream Makers, Dream Breakers* recounts in rich detail Marshall's rise from unruly youth to civil-rights hero, master legal strategist, judge on the Second Circuit Court of Appeals, Solicitor General of the United States, and Supreme Court Justice. Like a landscape painter who draws the viewer in by placing human figures in the foreground, Rowan melds history with biography, interspersing his account of Marshall's life and work with events in the struggle for racial justice in which Marshall played such a crucial role. The heroes of the narrative, the "dream makers," include, besides Marshall, Charles Hamilton Houston, Eleanor Roosevelt, Harry Truman, and Earl Warren. Among the villains are Orval Faubus, Strom Thurmond, J. Edgar Hoover, George Wallace, Jesse Helms, and "the most ruthless dream breaker," Richard Nixon.

In its biographical aspect, the book is an unabashed appreciation of the author's long-time friend. As history, it is a straightforward account of the decisions, strategies, struggles, and executive, legislative, and judicial actions that shaped American race relations from the time of Marshall's birth in 1908 to his retirement from the Supreme Court in 1991.

Like the outpouring of tributes that appeared after the Justice's retirement and his recent death, Rowan's book emphasizes that part of Marshall's life (1936 to 1961) devoted to civil-rights activism and strategy, passing rather lightly over his more problematic performance as a Supreme Court Justice. It is left for later biographers to explain why a man who was widely regarded as one of the most talented lawyers of his time was held in relatively low professional esteem as a judge. Rowan seems right to discount law clerks' self-serving criticisms, of the type unearthed by Woodward and Bernstein in their 1979 best-seller, *The Brethren*. Marshall is portrayed there as an indolent and often uncomprehending judge, disdainful of legal technicalities, delegating research and opinion-writing to his clerks, telling them only half in jest, "I'll do whatever Bill [Brennan) does." Rowan's own interviews with Marshall clerks led him to a bottom line not very different from Woodward and Bernstein's—that, though Marshall might have delegated more than most of his brethren, the sentiments and the results were always Marshall's own. Regrettably, as Judge Richard Posner and others have pointed out, the practice of turning work that is properly judicial over to recent law graduates is widespread in the overburdened federal court system. Few judges can now say, as Justice Louis Brandeis once did, "The reason they respect Supreme Court Justices so much is that we are the only people in Washington who do our own work."

The reason that even Marshall's most fervent admirers are expansive concerning his merits as a lawyer while confining themselves to bland generalities about his judging resides in the fact that different branches of the legal profession require different sorts of skills and personal qualities. The traits that are conducive to success in trying cases or arguing appeals are significantly different from those that make for excellence in judging. It must have been difficult for Thurgood Marshall, at age 53, after a lifetime of vigorous advocacy, to begin a second career which required him to renounce the role of impassioned pleader for that of impartial arbiter on the Second Circuit Court of Appeals. His transition was interrupted four years later, moreover, when President Johnson appointed him Solicitor General. Marshall was 59 when he took his seat on the United States Supreme Court.

He carried to that position the qualities that had served him and his causes well—his intelligence, his sense of justice, and the penetrating insight of one who had been excluded from privileges the other judges took for granted. He also brought the skills and mindset of a crusading litigator. Irving Kaufman, Marshall's colleague on the Second Circuit bench, recalls, "My most abiding memory of Thurgood on this court was his ability to infuse his judicial product with the elements of the advocate's craft."

The problem with that blending of roles, though, is that our legal system promises every litigant, rich or poor, black or white, male or female, a judge who (in the words of the judicial oath) will "administer justice without respect to persons" and "impartially discharge" his or her duties "agreeably to the Constitution and laws of the United States." Thurgood Marshall himself had suffered much at the hands of judges who relentlessly advocated their personal visions of the good society.

Rowan provides a revealing glimpse into Marshall's behind-the-scenes advocacy in his discussion of the Court's controversial 1973 abortion decision. According to Rowan, "Marshall became a special advocate, or 'defense attorney,' inside the Court for poor women, black or white, but especially for minority women, who were likely to know both racial discrimination and poverty." Marshall's contribution to *Roe* v. *Wade* is one "that most Americans still don't know about because it took place in that secret Supreme Court world of 'brokering' and gentlemanly power plays." It was Marshall, Rowan recounts, who insisted that the woman's "absolute right" to abortion be protected "way into the second trimester." Remarkably, Rowan maintains that Marshall's collaboration in *Roe* and the abortion cases that followed and expanded on it represents the crowning achievement of his judicial career:

> Most Court watchers never dreamed that Marshall's crowning moments on the Court would involve, not the issue of race, but of any woman's right to make her own decisions as to whether and when she would bring a child into this world. You will not understand Marshall or his world, unless you see how he operated in a political and social milieu that was—and is—poisoned with passions over the abortion

rights of women. The Court records indicate that no Justice ever supported a woman's right to choice as uncompromisingly as Marshall did.

*Apparently Marshall (and Rowan) were unable to discern a sinister side of the
abortion-rights movement: its sibling relationship with the anti-immigration
groups who see abortion and border controls as the major defenses against an
expanding, threatening, welfare-consuming- and non-white-underclass. The full-
page ads of these organizations run a few pages apart in trendy magazines, but
they are linked financially and ideologically.*

In any event, Linda Greenhouse had the order of his distinctions just
right in her *New York Times* obituary: Marshall was a "pillar of the civil-
rights movement, architect of the legal strategy that ended the era of official
segregation, and the first black Justice of the Supreme Court." Rowan seems
to agree, writing that "it is not unreasonable to assume that history will
regard him primarily as 'Mr. Civil Rights.'"

Rowan portrays Marshall in his last years as angry at the course the
Court seemed to be taking. He was bitterly disappointed that *Brown* v.
*Board of Education* and the one-man/one-vote cases had done so little to
wipe out racial injustice. The fact is, though, that Thurgood Marshall, perhaps more than any other civil-rights leader, was responsible for the remarkable achievement of depriving racial prejudice of any respectability
whatsoever in American society. He helped to create a world that John W.
Davis's generation of Southerners had been unable to imagine. The very year
that Marshall retired, a young writer, Melissa Fay Greene, reflected on these
matters in *Praying for Sheetrock*, her moving account of the gradual empowerment of the black community in McIntosh County, Georgia: "Of course,
it is not enough, but it is a beginning. The descendants of the Scottish settlers start to view the descendants of the African slaves, not as aliens in their
midst, and not as servants, but as neighbors, colleagues, partners, fellow
Americans, and increasingly, as leaders."

That same year too, a black Georgian from Pinpoint took the seat vacated
by Thurgood Marshall on the United States Supreme Court. Clarence
Thomas's heroes were not great advocates, but great judges such as Learned
Hand and Benjamin Nathan Cardozo. For Clarence Thomas, the Constitution is not just a bulwark of individual and minority rights, but a remarkable
design for representative government; constitutional text, structure, and tradition are not mere legal technicalities, but the very essence of a regime of
ordered liberty.

With the wildly varying concepts of fairness that currently compete for
ascendancy in our increasingly diverse society, it is more essential today than
ever before to select judges who can resist the temptation to promote partisan causes from the bench. We may therefore, if we are hopeful, look forward to the day when Clarence Thomas earns the same degree of honor as a

judge that Thurgood Marshall achieved as a lawyer. Just as Marshall learned from and transcended Davis, Thomas may help—in ways that Marshall's generation did not imagine—to make America a better, fairer place than it was when Marshall left it.

Meanwhile, it is pleasant to imagine those gracious adversaries Thurgood Marshall and John W. Davis sipping bourbon together and swapping stories in lawyers' Valhalla.

# CHAPTER 28

# Clarence Thomas: Postmodern Judge

*This op-ed piece was prompted by reading criticisms of Justice Thomas at a time when I was studying Eleanor Roosevelt's life, including her battles with her critics. It appeared in the Wall Street Journal on August 7, 1998.*[1]

**O**UTDATED RACIAL ATTITUDES have made it hard for Clarence Thomas to be taken seriously. After his speech to the National Bar Association in Memphis, Tennessee, last week, several old-line African-American leaders once more reviled the youngest justice on the Supreme Court for not being black enough. It must also be dispiriting for Justice Thomas when praise from some supporters in the white conservative establishment sounds mingled with relief that they have found an African-American they can admire.

No doubt it will take a generation more at ease with our multicultural society to fully appreciate this postmodern justice, who is at home with both the old and the new, but prisoner neither to tradition nor fashion. Opponents and supporters who cannot get past Justice Thomas's race have not been paying close attention to the opinions he has produced over the past seven years.

When President Bush appointed him to the high court in 1991, critics labeled him unqualified. It is true that he had been catapulted into a position for which little in his experience had prepared him. Yet he was hardly the first newly appointed justice to have to play catch-up. Some, like the lackluster, insecure Harry Blackmun, never grew into the role at all. But Justice Thomas seems to have buckled down and worked overtime to learn his new job and learn it well.

For his troubles, he is frequently accused of being the alter ego of Antonin Scalia. Implicit in the charge are assumptions never made when other justices vote the same way in a large proportion of cases. No one says that William Rehnquist pulls Sandra O'Connor's strings, or that Ruth Ginsburg and Stephen Breyer are identical twins. Why do you suppose Thomas

---

[1] Mary Ann Glendon, "The Postmodern Justice." *The Wall Street Journal* CCXXXII, 27 (7 August 1998): sec. A:10.

and his predecessor Thurgood Marshall have been described as puppets, respectively, of Scalia and William Brennan?

There are, in fact, intriguing differences between Justice Thomas's and Justice Scalia's approaches to constitutional interpretation even when they reach the same conclusions. In one case, both concluded that the Constitution prohibits Congress from enacting racial preferences. But Justice Scalia characteristically stood on the original meaning of the 14th Amendment text, while Justice Thomas looked to the Declaration of Independence as well, basing his opinion on "the principle of inherent equality that underlies and infuses" our constitutional order.

Justice Thomas's opinions reveal a man who has emerged from his apprenticeship with a distinctive personal style. The hallmarks of that style are lawyerly qualities that, alas, often pass unnoticed by those who focus only on high-profile cases. There are no soliloquies, no mystery passages, no extravagant generalizations. Just careful research, tight reasoning, and total seriousness about the judicial oath to do "justice without respect to persons, to do equal right to the poor and to the rich." Justice Thomas's steady output of workmanlike opinions in tax, employment, property and statutory-interpretation cases marks him as a member of what Judge Learned Hand called the "Society of Jobbists"—honest legal craftsmen who turn their corners squarely.

Anyone who was paying attention to substance during Justice Thomas's confirmation hearings could have learned that he was striving to model himself on great judges like Hand and Henry Friendly, who are seldom remembered for this or that path-breaking decision. Such judges have no illusions of grandeur prompting them to poach on other branches of government; they decide the cases before them according to the laws and the Constitution. They are remembered for their impartiality, restraint, and technical skill.

Much of Justice Thomas's opposition comes from those who admire judges of a different stripe—liberated from legal technicalities, ready to decide cases on the basis of their subjective sense of fairness and careless of the need to ground their decisions in constitutional text, structure, precedent, or tradition.

Justice Thomas's opinions have won respect among his colleagues on the court. He has been assigned to write majority opinions in some of the toughest cases of the past few terms, such as the denial of the appeal of condemned prisoner Joseph O'Dell, and the decision holding that, under certain conditions, states may incarcerate dangerous sex offenders even after their terms have been served. As his work product grows, many lawyers who were once skeptical about his appointment have come to admire his craft. It is fortunate for our complex, diverse republic that Jobbism is better represented on the court today than it was when Thomas's critics were in their heyday. Earl Warren was a good man and a statesman, but few would want to see the nation's courts filled with judges who felt as free as he to sweep aside legal "technicalities." The most ardent devotees of William Brennan's judicial activism would be dismayed to see the judiciary crowded with activist judges with a personal vision of, say, a laissez-faire economy. As the authors of *The Federalist Papers* wisely observed: "Considerate men of every description ought to prize whatever will tend to beget or fortify [integrity and moderation] in the courts; as no man can be sure that he may not be tomorrow the victim of a spirit of injustice by which he may be the gainer today."

It is far too soon to make a general evaluation of a public life that, one hopes, will flourish for many years to come. But I like to think that when historians assess the career of Clarence Thomas, he will remind them in many ways of Eleanor Roosevelt. Yes, Eleanor Roosevelt. When President Truman named Mrs. Roosevelt to America's United Nations delegation, it was over the protests of Senator William Fulbright (D–Ark.) and others who thought that to appoint someone with so little experience in foreign affairs showed disrespect for the institution. Mrs. Roosevelt was as vilified for her progressive views as Justice Thomas has been for his refusal to bow to liberal dogmas.

Her foes, like his, stopped at nothing to try to bring her down, accusing her of communist sympathies at the height of McCarthyism. During the most intensely active period of her public life, she too was threatened with a humiliating public scandal: The wife of a former White House guard threatened to name her as a correspondent in a divorce action on the basis of a series of affectionate letters' Mrs. Roosevelt had written to the man. Though the idea of seeing her letters published gave her excruciating pain, Mrs. Roosevelt faced down her accuser, stating that she had done nothing of which to be ashamed.

Above all, Justice Thomas resembles Mrs. Roosevelt as a figure of towering dignity. At a time when our institutions are under stress, and in a city where there are lamentably few public figures to admire, the postmodern justice quietly goes about his job, making the world a little better for those who will come after him.

# The Continental Advantage in Interpretation

*This essay was a comment on Justice Antonin Scalia's Tanner Lecture*
*at Princeton University titled "Common Law Courts in a Civil Law System:*
*The Role of United States Federal Courts in Interpreting the*
*Constitution and Laws." It was published with Justice Scalia's text,*
*and comments by Gordon Wood, Laurence Tribe, and Ronald Dworkin in*
*A Matter of Interpretation: Federal Courts and the Law.*
*© Princeton University Press. Reprinted by permission of Princeton University Press.[1]*

AS A COMPARATIST WITH A SPECIAL INTEREST in contemporary European law, I could not help but be intrigued by Justice Scalia's use of the "civil law world" as a metaphor for an American legal environment increasingly dominated by enacted, rather than judge-made, law. For my contribution to this symposium, therefore, I offer some reflections on two questions prompted by the Justice's figure of speech: Have civil law lawyers and judges fared any better than we Americans in the maze of twentieth-century legal materials? If so, what can we learn from their experience?

Comparative analysis can often shed light on a problem by throwing into relief those of our own practices that escape attention just because they are so familiar. Statutory interpretation affords a telling, though embarrassing, example. Film buffs will understand if I put it this way: When it comes to dealing with statutes, we American lawyers are like Igor in the scene from *Young Frankenstein* where Gene Wilder as the doctor says: "Perhaps I could do something about your hump"—and Marty Feldman as Igor replies, "What hump?" For decades, eminent scholars, many of them European-trained, have called attention to the primitive state of our skills with legislation. Yet the profession has steadfastly refused to admit that it is textually challenged.

Although more than a century has passed since legislative enactments displaced case law as the principal starting points for legal reasoning, we still operate with craft habits formed in an age when, as Roscoe Pound once put it, a lawyer could count on his fingers the statutes with an enduring effect on

---

[1] Mary Ann Glendon, Comment in *A Matter of Interpretation: Federal Courts and the Law* by Antonin Scalia (Princeton, NJ: Princeton University Press, 1997), 95–114.

private law. To this day, as Justice Scalia complains, American lawyers' chief technical skills are concerned with court decisions. Most of our fellow citizens, no doubt, would be astonished if they knew how little training the average law student receives in dealing with enacted law, or how completely the profession has neglected the art of legislative drafting (the other side of the coin of interpretation).

Some of the leading legal scholars of the twentieth century vainly called attention to these deficiencies—so apparent to anyone familiar with civil law. Pound, for example, wrote:

> [T]he common law has never been at its best in administering justice from written texts. It has an excellent technique of finding the grounds of decision of particular cases in reported decisions of other cases in the past. It has always, in comparison with the civil law, been awkward and none too effective in deciding on the basis of legislative texts.

Karl Llewellyn, even while celebrating the common law tradition, lamented the "unevenness, the jerkiness" of American work with statutes as contrasted with case law. He added, "It is indeed both sobering and saddening to match our boisterous ways with a statutory text against the watchmaker's delicacy and care of a . . . continental legal craftsman. . . ." In his own work as a legislative draftsman on the Uniform Commercial Code and other statutes, he relied heavily on German models.[2]

Nevertheless, decades after the New Deal ushered in the era of administrative law, a 1992 Harvard Law School curriculum committee report admitted: "We teach the basic first-year required program almost without regard to the coming of the regulatory state, and without recognition that statutes and regulations have become the predominant legal sources of our time." That state of affairs prevails in most American law schools, as does the practice of teaching advanced statutory courses mainly through reading court decisions.

What accounts for this persistent deficit? Justice Scalia locates its origin in professional history. It was judges and practitioners who took the lead in developing English law, in contrast to continental Europe where the civil law was developed in important respects by scholars, and was rationalized and systematized at a crucial stage by comprehensive legislative codifications. In England and the United States, so long as court decisions were the principal materials of legal reasoning, common lawyers neither possessed nor required sophisticated skills for interpreting or drafting enacted law. They had a simple set of tools that were adequate for dealing with premodern English legislation—statutes which (unlike European codes) typically did not purport to be complete new sets of authoritative starting points for legal reasoning. English judges, traditionally, treated such statutes as a kind of overlay against

---

[2] Roscoe Pound, "The Formative Era of American Law," in *The Life of the Law*, ed. John Honnold (London: Collier, 1964), 59.

the background of the common law. Accordingly, they tried where possible to construe them so as to blend them into the case law.

The old techniques worked well enough until new forms of enacted law acquired a prominent and permanent place in the legal environment. By mid-twentieth century, however, it was plain to the most astute observers— Roscoe Pound, Karl Llewellyn, Benjamin Cardozo, James M. Landis, Felix Frankfurter—that American lawyers urgently needed to retool for the modern legal world.

In the 1940s and 1950s, momentum for the study of legislation seemed to be building. This was due in part to the influence of talented New Deal lawyers like Frankfurter and Landis who had moved from government to law teaching. During the same period, the National Conference of Commissioners on Uniform State Law, the American Bar Association, and the American Law Institute were undertaking ambitious projects to improve and harmonize law, mainly through legislation. A few treatises and teaching materials on statutory interpretation appeared. Harvard's Henry Hart and Albert Sacks devoted over half of their influential 1958 *Legal Process* materials to legislation, administrative law, and the presentation of differentiated techniques for interpreting new, complex types of statutes. Yet, the field of legislation remained a scholarly backwater.

What nipped the emerging serious study of statutes in the bud? Ingrained professional habits and simple inertia are part of the story. But there was also the double-whammy of the constitutional rights revolution of the 1960s and 1970s, and the anti-regulatory mood of the 1980s. In the heyday of the Warren and Burger courts, scholarship in statutory fields like tax, securities, and labor law gradually fell out of fashion as constitutional law became the glamor subject in the legal academy. The legislative process itself came in for disdain as dramatic civil rights decisions promoted the illusion that social change could be effected through litigation. That illusion deflected reformist energy from ordinary democratic politics. Paul Carrington suggests further reasons why academics have little taste for ordinary politics:

> [O]ne must associate with persons who are not always members of an elite. One must go to meetings and not only talk, but also listen politely, often more than once to the same bad idea. One must study and think about issues and problems that are of immediate concern to others, and not only those issues most attractive to one's own interests. . . . To be effective, one must compromise and accommodate. . . . One must risk the sting of visible defeat. . . . [O]ne must sometimes first win trust by bearing the most unwelcome burdens, performing prosaic tasks that do less honor to one's talents than one might wish. . . .[3]

---

[3] Paul Carrington, "Aftermath," in *Essays for Patrick Atiyah*, ed. P. Cane and J. Stapleton (Oxford: Clarendon Press, 1991), 113, 140.

CHAPTER 29 • The Continental Advantage in Interpretation

Later, advocates of "getting government off our backs" disliked most legislation on principle. Thus, for a variety of reasons, the American legal profession remains disoriented in the "civil law world."

But was it easier for civil lawyers to find their way as strange legislative creations transformed the world of codes? At first glance, it might seem obvious that they would enjoy a methodological advantage. Historically, the civil and common law systems fostered the development of significantly different arrays of professional skills. Just as common lawyers have prided themselves on techniques for dealing with precedent, civil law lawyers have gloried in their methods for drafting and interpreting codes. No shorthand description can do justice to a praxis, but the German scholar Winfried Brugger has provided a succinct summary of the four basic elements of the classical approach: grammatical (sometimes called textual) interpretation, systematic (sometimes called structural) interpretation, historical interpretation, and teleological (sometimes called evolutionary) interpretation.

> In . . . grammatical interpretation, philological methods are used to analyze the meaning of a particular word or sentence. In systematic interpretation, one attempts to clarify the meaning of a legal provision by reading it in conjunction with other, related provisions of the same section or title of the legal text, or even other texts within or outside of the given legal system; thus this method relies upon the unity, or at least the consistency, of the legal world. In historical analysis, the interpreter attempts to identify what the founders of a legal document wanted to regulate when they used certain words and sentences. . . . In teleological analysis, the [other three elements] are only deemed indicative, not determinative, of the contemporaneous purpose of the legal provision or document.[4]

An extensive civil law literature testifies that habits and practices based on those methods have proved less helpful in dealing with modern statutes, ordinances, and decrees than with the codes of an earlier day. Traditional interpretive techniques, developed to deal with relatively comprehensive, coherent, self-contained texts, proved difficult to adapt to laws that did not possess the same degree of conceptual and terminological consistency as the great codifications. In consequence, the civil law systems, like our own, were thrown into interpretive turmoil by new forms of enacted law. Civil law judges were almost as much at sea as their common law counterparts when dealing with hastily cobbled statutes shot through with ambiguities and inconsistencies. As new statutes were piled upon older ones, often with an uncertain or overlapping relation to legislation in other, related, areas, traditional civil law approaches to interpretation were of less and less assistance.

---

[4] Winfried Brugger, "Legal Interpretation, Schools of Jurisprudence, and Anthropology," 42 *American Journal of Comparative Law* (1994): 395, 396–97.

To put the point another way, civil law lawyers no longer inhabit a "civil law world" so far as the materials of legal reasoning are concerned. The word "civil law" connotes, first, private law (property, contracts, torts, family law), and second, the law of the civil codes, which were meant to be complete sets of authoritative starting points for legal reasoning in the private law fields. Those meanings still have an important place in the legal imagination of civilians, but they lost their centrality in continental European practice long ago.

Just as modern regulatory legislation rivaled the importance of judge-made common law in England and the United States, it challenged the predominance of civil codes in continental Europe. Statutes that removed large areas wholly or partially from the coverage of the codes did reinforce the traditional preeminence of enacted law in civil law systems, but they diminished the significance of the codes themselves. France, Germany, and the countries whose legal systems are based on theirs thus remain "civil law" countries only in the sense that their lawyers and judges share a set of habits and practices inherited from a time when the civil code was the heart of the legal system.

To return to the question of comparative advantage, certain features of the civil law systems did aid their transition to the new statutory and administrative environment. Civil lawyers and judges were at least accustomed to taking their bearings from enacted law, and they were in possession of a high degree of expertise in legislative drafting. All European civil law countries, furthermore, had long had separate, specialized courts for disputes involving the state and its agencies. And in some countries, separate court systems for tax, social security, and labor law help to maintain coherence in those specialized regulatory areas.

As in common law countries, the need to interpret a mounting volume of enacted law obliged civil law systems to assimilate a huge and expanding body of court decisions. That, in turn, exposed the Achilles heel of civil law methods: a relative absence of skills in case analysis. Not only has case law been slighted by continental European legal education, but civil law judges have been slow to develop techniques for the reasoned elaboration of precedent. The French legal system, and the many systems modeled on it, were especially handicapped by an exceedingly cryptic judicial opinion style. Civil law systems generally were hobbled by the traditional view of their role as strictly limited to deciding the particular dispute at hand, and their lack of a formal doctrine of stare decisis. That deficit is the civilian counterpart of the common law's weakness with statutes.

Unlike Igor, European jurists have acknowledged their problem. Judges and scholars in Germany were among the first to take measures to develop the skills they lacked. As John P. Dawson wrote in the 1970s: "When the floodtide of case law unexpectedly came, German courts and legal scholars proceeded to train each other in developing navigational skills and direction-finding devices. . . ." The French legal profession was slower to adapt but a

1974 law review article co-authored by the comparatist André Tunc, calling for more facts and reasoning in judicial opinions, has been influential.[5] Another stimulus is the magisterial comparative study by Swiss scholar Thomas Probst showing that an inadequately developed theory and practice of precedent in his home system had led to a loss of predictability and an unacceptably high frequency of violations of the principle that like cases ought to be treated alike. His conclusions to that effect were based on a comparison of overruling decisions handed down by the United States Supreme Court over a 200-hundred-year period with shifts of direction by the Swiss Bundesgericht from 1875 to 1990. According to Probst, the traditional dogmatic conception that a single case has no binding effect has adversely affected judicial opinion writing, scholarly case law analysis, and the integration of case law into the Swiss legal system, with the consequence that similarly situated parties often receive unequal treatment.[6]

Probst therefore called for a rethinking of the role of precedent in the civil law systems. The time has come, he urged, for civil-law scholars and judges to bring the same level of skill and attention to the study of case law that they have traditionally brought to interpretation of enacted law. In the case of judges, that would require fuller exposure of the grounds for their decisions. He exhorted legal scholars, for their part, to develop methodologies that would help to promote more coherence in judicial practice as well as in the materials of legal reasoning as a whole.

In sum, code-based methods of interpretation seem to have provided the civil law systems with a modest advantage in dealing with modern statutory law. In varying degrees, they are on the way to remedying their long-standing deficiency in case law skills.

Turning to constitutional interpretation, the example of the German Constitutional Court suggests that the benefits of code-based methods can be even more substantial in the field of constitutional interpretation than in dealing with modern statutes. That example is significant, for the *Bundesverfassungsgericht* has become the most influential tribunal of its kind in the world.

It might be supposed that the United States, with its 200-year-old Constitution, would be far advanced, relative to younger republics, in the theory and practice of constitutional interpretation. But our Court's first sustained venture in judicial review did not take place until the turn of the twentieth century, when a now discredited series of decisions struck down early social legislation. So far as fair criminal procedures, equal legal treatment, free

5 Adolphe Touffait and André Tunc, "Pour une motivation plus explicite des décisions de justice notamment celles de la Cour de Cassation," 1974 *Revue trimestrielle du droit civil* 487.

6 Thomas Probst, *Die Anderung der Rechtsprechung: Eine rechtsvergleichende, methodologische Untersuchung zum Phanomen der höchrichterlichen Rechtsprechungsänderung in der Schweiz* (civil law) *und den Vereinigten Staaten* (common law) (Basel: Helbing & Lichtenhahn, 1993).

expression, and personal liberties are concerned, the American Supreme Court's experience is comparable in duration to that of its German counterpart—which opened its doors in 1951. In the United States, as in other liberal democracies, the great expansion of constitutional law relating to personal liberties and civil rights has taken place mainly in the half century since World War II ended.

With the era of human rights and constitution-making that began in the late 1940s, civil lawyers found themselves on familiar methodological ground. True, the postwar constitutions were novel in the sense that they brought bills of rights and judicial review to several countries for the first time. But the new constitutions resembled the old codes in key respects—in their careful drafting, in their level of generality, in the mutually conditioning relations among their parts, in the presence of several open-ended clauses, and in their aspiration to be enduring. Traditional techniques of code interpretation therefore quickly became the basis of constitutional hermeneutics in continental civil law systems.

To be sure, consensus on the basics of an approach has not precluded lively controversies over the relative weight to be given to various elements of the method, nor has it resolved the question of how code-based methods are to be supplemented when the text in question is a constitution. The teleological or evolutionary method of construing texts in the light of contemporary circumstances is especially controversial in constitutional law, since the court's "mistakes" cannot be easily corrected. Many European jurists remain nervous about the method's tension with democratic principles, and its potential for abuse.

On the problem of how to adapt traditional methods to the Basic Law of 1949, the views of legal scholar and former Constitutional Court Judge Konrad Hesse have been influential. According to Hesse,

> (1) Each interpretation must support the unity of the constitution. (2) In cases of tension or conflict, the principle of practical concordance must be used to harmonize conflicting provisions.
>
> According to this principle, tension among constitutional provisions and values must be resolved in such a way as to optimize the scope of each. In other words, the judge must not permit one constitutional value to prevail completely over another. (3) All governmental organs must respect the functional differentiation of the constitution, that is, their respective tasks and powers in the separation of powers scheme. (4) Each interpretation must try to create an integrative effect with regard to both the various parties of a constitutional dispute as well as to social and political cohesion. (5) . . . Each interpretation shall attempt to optimize all the aforementioned elements.[7]

---

[7] Summarized by Brugger, "Legal Interpretation," at 398–99.

CHAPTER 29 • The Continental Advantage in Interpretation

In the decisions of the German Constitutional Court on freedom of speech, election law, church-state relations, personal freedoms, equality, and economic liberties, the influence of the grammatical and systematic methods (what Justice Scalia calls textualism) is strong and unmistakeable. The Court has at times been bold in deploying the teleological method, but its boldest decisions, like those of John Marshall, are also among its most prudent. The historical method, in Germany as in other civil law systems, appears to be of less importance than the other three approaches. In continental practice, the historical method is decreasingly employed as a code or Constitution ages. Thus French jurists regard the ideas and intentions of the drafters of the Civil Code of 1804 as almost irrelevant to the decision of present-day cases. As early as 1977, the German Constitutional Court cited the age of the 1949 Basic Law as a reason for declining to accord decisive weight to evidence of the intent of the Framers.

One trait that most conspicuously differentiates the *Bundesverfassungsgericht*'s decisions from those of the American Supreme Court also helps to keep teleological interpretation from running wild. That is the practice of attending consistently to the language and structure of the entire Constitution—to the document as a whole, and to the relationship of particular provisions to one another as well as to the overall design for government. (The Court is aided, it should be noted, by the fact that the Basic Law is a more detailed, integrated, and contemporary document than the U.S. Constitution.)

In the 1930s, Ernst Freund theorized that judicial review, over time, would inevitably subordinate the text and structure of the Constitution to case law. But now that systems of judicial review have been operating for several decades in many liberal democracies, it is apparent that the text and structure need not be thrust so deeply into the background as they have been in the United States. Though recognizing that constitutions are more political and more open-ended than codes, German courts and scholars have found it natural to proceed from close textual analysis in the light of overall structure, to consideration of purpose both in the light of history, and in the light of circumstances as they exist at the time of decision. The text, however, remains the alpha and omega of interpretation. It serves both as the starting point for judicial reasoning and the outer limit on the range of possible results.

When civil lawyers come to American law schools for graduate work, they often express surprise at the degree to which the case method dominates our approach to courses based on enacted law. In particular, they find it hard to understand why constitutional law courses and materials typically begin not with a study of the language and design of the Constitution but with a case (usually *Marbury* v. *Madison*). It was not always thus. According to Paul Carrington, students in early American law schools were required to have a detailed knowledge of the Constitution, and *The Federalist* was often used as a basic text. The foreign students' puzzlement deepens as weeks pass and discussion moves from one case to another, with the Constitution itself glimpsed only in a fragmentary way. One visiting German lawyer told me that an American law professor's response to a student's query about the role of text in constitutional analysis was: "Forget about the text!"

There is no mystery about how we arrived at that state of affairs. At the time of the Founding, as H. Jefferson Powell reminds us, the American Framers were torn "between a global rejection of any and all methods of constitutional construction and a willingness to interpret the constitutional text in accordance with the common law principles that had been used to construe statutes."[8] In the early years of the republic, that tension was temporarily resolved when a consensus developed on a version of originalism. In the *Lochner* era, however, old habits took over. When American judges had to interpret novel types of legislation, and to review them for conformity to the Constitution, they naturally proceeded in the way they knew best.

Their instinct was to fill gaps or ambiguities in the text (statutory or constitutional) with judge-made common law, rather than to search first, as a civil lawyer would, for guiding principles in the structure and design of the instrument. In *Lochner* v. *New York* (1905) and related cases, the Court construed the Constitution in such a way as to harmonize with, rather than displace, a common law background where protection of property rights and freedom of contract were ensconced at the time as leading principles. As Pound put it, "[The common lawyer] thinks of the constitutional checks upon legislation as enacting common-law limitations, and systematically develops those checks in terms of the common law."[9] Oliver Wendell Holmes, Jr., and others protested in vain that the Constitution was not just an overlay on the private law of property and contract.

Even after Holmes' views prevailed in other respects, his methodological point was not fully absorbed. Certainly neither text nor precedent justified the *Lochner* Court in giving property (and freedom of contract to acquire property) the same exalted position in constitutional law that those goods enjoyed in late nineteenth-century common law. On the other hand, to nearly read property out of the Constitution, as the Court later did in cases involving New Deal legislation and takings, was equally indefensible.

In the 1950s and 1960s, the preference for judge-made over enacted law that had been so evident in constitutional interpretation at the turn of the century, came to the fore again as the Supreme Court embarked on a second exciting adventure with judicial review. This time, the Court began treating selected elements of the Bill of Rights as discrete starting points for creative judicial elaboration. Both the Court majority and its academic

---

[8] H. Jefferson Powell, "The Original Understanding of Original Intent," 98 *Harvard Law Review* 885, 887 (1985).
[9] Pound, "Formative Era of American Law," 61.

CHAPTER 29 • The Continental Advantage in Interpretation

admirers in that period studiously ignored what a civil-law approach would have kept in view—that the Constitution is not only a charter of rights, but a design for government which places important limits on both judicial and legislative lawmaking.

As Justice Scalia emphasizes, the Court's free-wheeling approach to constitutional interpretation is a far more serious matter than its careless ways with statutes. For as judicial lawmaking expands, the democratic elements in our republican experiment atrophy. American men and women are not only deprived of having a say on how we order our lives together, but they lose the skills of self-government. Something seems to have gone wrong somewhere—as in that fateful scene where Igor accidentally picked up the wrong specimen jar—the one marked "Beware: Abnormal Brain!"

In 1991, Cass Sunstein ruefully commented in *The New Republic* that "our understanding of constitutional interpretation remains in a primitive state."[10] From a comparative perspective, it would appear that many of our difficulties arise from the frequent omission of steps that civil lawyers perform instinctively. Consider the Court's religion clause jurisprudence, which has been described by scholars of all persuasions, and even by the Justices themselves, as unprincipled, incoherent, and unworkable. As a matter of judicial craftsmanship, it is dismaying to observe how little intellectual effort the Court devoted in the 1940s to the enormously complex issues created by trying to make the establishment language of the First Amendment binding on the states. And how can one account for the consistent failure of Court majorities to recognize what grammatical and structural methods make clear: that the religion language of the First Amendment has a context—in the First Amendment as a whole, the Bill of Rights, and the overall constitutional design? Systematic attention to text and structure would not have produced "one right answer" to thorny interpretive problems in the church-state area, but it would have helped to reduce extreme and atextual outcomes.

At this point, an inquisitive person may be wondering how the civil law disadvantage in dealing with case law has affected constitutional interpretation. The general language of constitutions, after all, necessarily gives rise to a large body of court decisions. As John Dawson's studies have shown, where Germany is concerned Constitutional Court judges have clearly benefited from the experience of an earlier generation of judges on ordinary courts in addressing that problem. In fact, it is difficult to read the German Constitutional Court's decisions without the sense that they stand up better, on the whole, to the traditional criteria by which common lawyers have evaluated judicial work than our own Court's decisions of the same period. The Bundesverfassungsgericht displays impressive skill in maintaining principled continuity in the law, explaining the outcomes of particular cases in ways that can make sense even to the losers and others who disagree, and assuring

---

[10] Cass R. Sunstein, book review, *New Republic* (March 11, 1991): 35.

predictability and stability without foreclosing adaptation to changing social and economic circumstances.

Thus I fear that things here at home may be even worse than Justice Scalia suggests. He is undoubtedly correct as a historical matter that many of our interpretive ills are due to the survival of common law habits in the world of enacted law. But it ought to be said that those habits were good ones, even if ill-adapted to statutory and constitutional interpretation. It is cause for concern, therefore, that they seem to be deteriorating. As Justice Scalia himself points out, *stare decisis* is losing vigor. More ominously, subjective forms of judging in which neither text nor precedent is accorded much respect seem increasingly to be accepted as legitimate.

As for the Supreme Court, it is not at all clear that it really remains attached to common law methods—in the sense of attending in each case to providing a fair resolution of the case at hand, mooring that decision in text and tradition, fairly exposing its reasoning processes, and providing guidance to parties in future cases. Often its rulings look less like the reasoned elaboration of principle than the products of majority vote. At times the Court appears just to be lurching along in irrational and unpredictable fashion, like the monster in the old version of *Frankenstein*. Rather than just being differently abled, American judges and lawyers may be losing the ability to do what they once did best!

Justice Scalia has been more critical of the courts than of the institutions that supposedly exist to nurture and improve legal skills. Yet, as with statutory interpretation, the law schools bear their share of responsibility. Up to about thirty years ago, the typical constitutional law course was heavy on federalism, separation of powers, and the commerce clause, but light on the Bill of Rights. The obvious remedy would have been to teach the whole Constitution from preamble to last amendment—as a design for self-government as well as a charter of rights, and as a text whose parts cannot be understood in isolation from one another. But in the 1960s the emphasis was simply shifted to individual rights. As a result, con law classes have long had the same relation to the Constitution as the Elgin marbles have to the Parthenon. The student sees the professor's prized collection of fragments, but the well-proportioned structure in which these treasures once had their appropriate place is nowhere on display. The Constitution is like a wonder of another world, an ancient temple once used for activities that are no longer much practiced among us—deliberation, voting, local self-government.

In recent years, a diverse and growing group of scholars—such as Akhil Amar, John Hart Ely, Michael McConnell, and Geoffrey Miller—have opened debate on the relationship between our system of limited government and the system of rights that has been at the forefront of constitutional theory in recent years. They are approaching interpretive problems by attending to the overall design of the Constitution and the relationships among its provisions.

CHAPTER 29 • The Continental Advantage in Interpretation

Without neglecting our rights tradition or the principles embodied in two centuries of precedent, they are attempting to restore separation of powers, federalism, and constitutional text and structure to a central and appropriate place in constitutional theory. Those efforts may well bring about improvement in constitutional law teaching, but it is not likely that chaos in the field of constitutional interpretation will diminish any time soon. For if textualism, structuralism, and originalism advance, it can be predicted that selective deployment of textualism, structuralism, and originalism will advance as well. Judges and scholars who have abandoned the notions of principled judging and objective scholarship will not be easily constrained.

That observation brings me to what, in the end, is probably the most important civil law advantage in interpretation: a certain legal culture widely shared by lawyers and judges with diverse personal backgrounds, economic views, and political sympathies. As Dawson's studies showed, "predictability and coherence could not have been maintained in German law in such high degree if a close working partnership had not been maintained between a career judiciary and legal scholars, both highly trained in and firmly committed to the same highly ordered system of legal ideas."[11]

So long as the American legal profession lacks even a minimal consensus that judges, practitioners, and scholars have roles and responsibilities to which personal interests and predilections must be subordinated, Americans sharing Justice Scalia's legal values cannot possibly subscribe to the interpretive techniques (especially the wild-card teleological method) that work reasonably well in many parts of the "civil law world." Our legal culture also explains why many American friends of democratic and rule-of-law values have been driven to espouse what most civil lawyers would regard as excessively rigid forms of textualism. As Dawson put it, "We have much to learn from German law and should be willing to admire the German achievement. It does not follow that we have the means to emulate it."[12]

The subject of democratic values leads me to one last observation. In Justice Scalia's conclusion, he warns that if the public perceives that constitutional interpretation is up for grabs, the Bill of Rights will not long serve to protect important liberties from majority rule. The dreaded "monster" in this part of his story is tyranny of the majority, the same villain as in the tales told by many of the Justice's critics.

Tyranny of the majority does sound alarming. It conjures up visions of peasants with their pitchforks storming the scientist's castle. Small wonder that it is a favorite slogan of those who would prefer to forget that one of the most basic American rights is the freedom to govern ourselves and our com-

---

11 John P. Dawson, "The General Clauses, Viewed from a Distance," 41 *Rabels Zeitschrift* 441, 455 (1977).

12 John P. Dawson, "Unconscionable Coercion: The German Version," 89 *Harvard Law Review* 1041, 1126.

munities by bargaining, education, persuasion, and, yes, majority vote. But is tyranny of the majority really the greatest danger that faces a country when its courts foreclose ordinary politics in one area after another—and when more and more decisionmaking power over the details of everyday life is concentrated in large private and public bureaucracies? Which is more likely: that unruly majorities will have their way, or that the democratic elements in our republican experiment will wither away, while new forms of tyranny by the powerful few take rise? Whom should we fear more: an aroused populace, or the vanguard who know better than the people what the people should want?

Tyranny, as Tocqueville warned, need not announce itself with guns and trumpets. It may come softly—so softly that we will barely notice when we become one of those countries where there are no citizens, but only subjects. So softly that if a well-meaning foreigner should suggest, "Perhaps you could do something about your oppression," we might look up, puzzled, and ask, "What oppression?"

CHAPTER 29 • The Continental Advantage in Interpretation

# Family Law in a
# Time of Turbulence

*This report on major late twentieth-century developments
in Western family law was prepared as a discussion paper
for a Family Policies Congress sponsored by the Social
Trends Institute and held in Rome in April 2004.*[1]

**A**NYONE WHO HAS TRIED to keep track of family law developments in
recent years will understand my use of the word "turbulence" in the title of
this report. My own struggle has lasted for several decades. In the 1960s, several dozens of jurists were commissioned by the Hamburg Max Planck Institute for the Study of Foreign and International Law to begin work on the
preparation of an *International Encyclopedia of Comparative Law*, an ambitious 12-volume project that is finally nearing completion. As successor to
the original editor of the Family Law volume, it was my responsibility in
2003 to update the volume's chapters on family law topics, each prepared by
a different author and each published as a separate monograph, during the
1960s, 1970s, 1980s, and 1990s. That turned out to be an immense undertaking, for those chapters were written during a period of unprecedented
and rapid changes in family behavior, family law, and ideas about marriage
and family life. When work first began on the *Encyclopedia*, a demographic
revolution was just beginning to gather momentum. By the time the last
chapter was completed, family law had been substantially transformed in all
Western legal systems.

This report is organized as follows: Part I briefly recalls the effects on
family life of the demographic revolution that took place in the late twentieth century; Part II summarizes some especially significant general trends in
family law systems in those years; Part III calls attention to some important
differences between the Anglo-American and Romano-Germanic family law
systems; and Part IV offers some tentative observations regarding the three
questions posed by the organizers of this conference.

---

[1] Mary Ann Glendon, "Family Law in a Time of Turbulence," Family Policies Congress,
The Social Trends Institute, Rome, April 2004.

# A REVOLUTION IN BEHAVIOR AND MENTALITIES

Starting in the mid-1960s, in North America, Europe, and Australia, there was an upheaval across the whole set of demographic indicators. It came on so rapidly that it caught even professional demographers by surprise: birth rates and marriage rates fell, while divorce rates, births of children outside marriage, and the incidence of non-marital cohabitation rose to high levels. Louis Roussel of the French National Demographic Institute correctly characterized the changes as widespread, profound, and sudden: widespread, because all "industrialized" nations had been affected to varying degrees; profound, because the changes involved increases or decreases of more than fifty percent; and sudden, because the changes took place in less than twenty years.[2] Along with changes in family behavior came less quantifiable but no less momentous shifts in the meanings that men and women attribute to sex and procreation, marriage, gender, parenthood, kinship relations, and to life itself.

These developments were part and parcel of broader social changes that Francis Fukuyama has described as "The Great Disruption": increased affluence, geographical mobility, the increased labor force participation of women (including mothers of young children), increased control over procreation, and greater longevity.[3] By the end of the 1980s, the major demographic indicators more or less stabilized in the developed countries, but they remained near their new high or low levels, registering only modest rises or declines since then.[4] The legal and social landscape had been utterly transformed. Familiar landmarks had disappeared. We were living in a new world.

With hindsight, it seems evident that those years of turbulence did not provide the most favorable climate for law revision. Nevertheless, many family law systems were completely overhauled, often very hastily, in the 1970s and 1980s.[5] In fact, family law became a testing ground for various ways of re-imagining family relations, and an arena for struggles among competing ideas about individual liberty, human sexuality, marriage and family life. Many unintended consequences, notably a sharp increase in poor, fatherless families, flowed from legal changes that were often presented as merely "adapting the law to social reality." Little thought was given to the idea that law might also help to shape social reality, for better or for worse.

---

[2] Louis Roussel, "Démographie: deux décennies de mutations dans les pays industrialisés," in *Family, State, and Individual Economic Security*, vol. 1, ed. M.–T. Meulders and J. Eekelaar (Brussels: Story Scientia, 1988), 27.

[3] Francis Fukuyama, *The Great Disruption* (New York: Free Press, 1999).

[4] Stephen Bahr, "Social Science Research on Family Dissolution: What it Shows and How it Might be of Interest to Family Law Reformers," 4 *Journal of Law and Family Studies* (2002): 5–6.

[5] See, generally, Mary Ann Glendon, *The Transformation of Family Law* (Chicago: University of Chicago Press, 1989).

(It should be noted that, at the same time, modernization was contributing to the disruption of age-old customs and patterns of family organization in the developing countries as well. Processes of urbanization and economic development that had been spread out over a century in Europe and the United States began occurring at an accelerated pace in other parts of the world as an ever-dwindling proportion of the world's population continued to live in subsistence farming and fishing villages. Many of the ideas that have influenced family law policy in the West have been carried into those fragile situations by globalization and by the activities of Western-based organizations.)

## MAJOR TRENDS IN WESTERN FAMILY LAW

Of the legal developments that have transformed, and continue to shape the course of, Western family law, the following seem particularly laden with implications for the future: (a) the reconceptualization of marriage and the family under the influence of ideas about gender equality, individual rights, and neutrality toward diverse lifestyles; (b) the trend toward lessened State regulation of marriage formation and dissolution as such (for example, fewer restrictions on entry into marriage and fewer obstacles to terminating marriage); (c) legal responses, or non-responses, to developments in biotechnology; and (d) a more adult-centered legal system, despite the rise of "children's rights."

### Reconceptualization of Marriage and the Family

Family law, and public laws affecting the family, are not only systems of rules and procedures—they are also carriers of ideals and symbols that are constitutive of culture.[6] Thus it is of the utmost significance that the "story" the law tells about family life has changed dramatically in recent years. The story now places much more emphasis on the rights of individual family members and less emphasis on family solidarity. Currently, Western legal systems seem to be shifting from treating marriage as a necessary social institution designed to provide the optimal environment for child-rearing, to treating marriage primarily as an intimate relationship between adults. This transition has taken place with little discussion or deliberation concerning the social consequences likely to follow from weakening the connections between marriage as a couple relationship and marriage as a child-raising partnership.

The process of attenuation of legal family ties is manifested in a wide range of developments, for example, abolition or non-enforcement of support obligations among blood relatives except parents and minor children; divorce

---

[6] Mary Ann Glendon, *Abortion and Divorce in Western Law* (Cambridge: Harvard University Press, 1987), 8.

laws permitting either spouse to terminate the relationship without showing grave cause; and emphasis on spousal self-sufficiency after divorce.[7] Marriage has lost much of its former centrality in family law owing to the increased attribution of marriage-like legal effects to various forms of non-marital cohabitation; the equalization of the status of marital and non-marital children; and the widespread withdrawal of legal sanctions against sexual relations outside marriage.

It was only to be expected that the shift of legal emphasis from the family as a group to its individual members would produce an increase in challenges to traditional legal definitions of marriage and the family by individuals and interest groups seeking legal validation of non-traditional lifestyles.

Mention should also be made of the advance of "children's rights." The idea is benign enough when addressed to situations of abuse and neglect, or when it affirms the right of a child to know his or her parents. But in some areas, such as education, the slogan "children's rights" has served as a pretext for transferring decisionmaking authority from parents to the state, and thus has furthered the assault on family solidarity.[8] As a practical matter, moreover, children's rights are regularly subordinated to the desires of adults in the areas that affect them most—namely, their parents' divorce, and the support arrangements after divorce.

### Declining Regulation of Entry into and Exit from Marriage

The widespread transformation of marriage from an institution that could be terminated, if at all, only for grave reasons to an arrangement that can be terminated by either spouse if he or she wishes to do so is so well-known as to require little comment here. There are, of course, important differences among legal systems. Some of the Romano-Germanic nations impose relatively long waiting periods for unilateral no-fault divorce, and some of these nations regulate the economic consequences of divorce so strictly and supervise the agreements of the spouses so closely that the effect may be to make divorce more difficult in practice than it was under the old system of fault grounds.[9]

The gradual abolition of a number of formalities and restrictions in marriage formation law attracted little attention until homosexual activists began to demand that the right to marry be extended to persons of the same sex. The practically universal decriminalization of homosexual behavior has been followed in a very few places by legal recognition of same-sex marriage and in some other places by providing homosexuals with access to legally sanctioned civil unions with many of the effects of marriage. As of 2004, most countries

---

[7] Mary Ann Glendon, *The New Family and the New Property* (Toronto: Butterworths, 1981), 11–97.

[8] Marie-Thérèse Meulders-Klein, "Droits des enfants et responsabilités parentales: quel juste équilibre?" in *La Personne, La Famille, et le Droit* (Brussels: Bruylant, 1999), 345.

[9] Mary Ann Glendon, *The Transformation of Family Law*, 281.

still retained the concept of marriage as a special status reserved for one man and one woman. But the law in this area was in rapid flux:

- *Homosexual marriage.* Only the Netherlands has *legislation* extending *full* marriage rights to same-sex couples. (Belgium's same-sex marriage law forbids adoption by the homosexual partners.) In two Canadian provinces, however, barriers to same-sex marriage have been removed by the *courts*, and the highest court in the U.S. state of Massachusetts issued a decision to the same effect in 2003.[10]

- *Civil Unions.* A number of other jurisdictions have created opportunities for same-sex couples to enter civil unions or registered partnerships with many of the legal effects of marriage, for example, Denmark, France, Germany, Norway, Sweden, Iceland, Finland, the U.S. state of Vermont, and some U.S. municipalities. But most of the European countries stop short where children are concerned—by forbidding such couples to adopt unrelated children, and by barring their access to technologically assisted procreation. The prevailing European approach thus stands in striking contrast to the legal situation in the United States where civil union laws are still rare, but where artificial insemination and *in vitro* fertilization are virtually unregulated, and where most states have long permitted adoption by same-sex couples.[11]

- *Reinforcement of Marriage.* A third group of jurisdictions has adopted legislation or constitutional provisions that reinforce the traditional limitation of marriage to one man and one woman. Poland, Switzerland, and a large majority of U.S. states (38 of 50) have adopted legislation defining marriage as limited to one man and one woman. In the U.S., the federal Defense of Marriage Act (DOMA), passed in 1996, provides that only persons of opposite sexes can be considered as married for purposes of federal law governing such matters as federal income taxes, social security, and immigration.[12]

- *Human Rights Law.* So far as European human rights law is concerned, the European Court of Human Rights stated *in dicta* in 1990 that "marriage" in the meaning of the European Convention on Human

---

[10] *The Netherlands:* Wet wan 21 december 2000 tot wijziging van Boek I van het Burgerlijk Wetboek in verband met de openstelling van het huwelijk voor personen van hetzelfde geschlacht, Stb. 2001, nr. 9; *Belgium*: Loi ouvrant le mariage à des personnes de même sexe et modifiant certaines dispositions du Code civil, Moniteur Belge, 28 février 2003. For *Canada*, see *Halpern* v. *Canada*, 2003 Carswell Ont. 2159 (Ont. C.A., 2003), and *EGALE* v. *Canada*, 2003 Carswell B.C. 1659 (B.C.C.A. 2003); *Massachusetts: Goodridge* v. *Dept. of Public Health*, 798 N.E.2d 941 (Mass. 2003).

[11] See "Developments in the Law—The Law of Marriage and Family," 116 *Harvard Law Review* 1996, 2005 (2003).

[12] Id.

Rights Article 12 (the right to marry) means the union of a man and a woman.[13] Thus far, the Court has declined to find in Articles 8 (equality) and 12 a positive obligation for the state to grant cohabitants a legal status. As recently as 2002, the Court held that a country (France) may deny a homosexual the right to adopt without violating the anti-discrimination provisions of the ECHR, even if the refusal is expressly based on the applicant's homosexuality.[14]

I am in accord with the view expressed by Professor Matlary in her contribution to this conference that the assault on the definition of marriage in the name of equal rights for homosexuals has implications far beyond the small number of persons who are likely to take advantage of same-sex marriage. As she and I saw at the Beijing Women's Conference in 1995, homosexual activist organizations have joined forces with other groups (radical feminism, radical environmentalism, and organizations promoting aggressive population control) to redefine or eliminate words like "marriage," "family," and "motherhood" in international human rights documents.[15] During the 1990s, such groups attempted to use U.N. conferences as offshore manufacturing sites for the creation of new norms, far from democratic accountability and public scrutiny.

## Creation of Relations of Kinship

Perhaps no field of family law was marked by more dramatic developments in the latter part of the twentieth century than that governing the creation of relations of kinship. First, the concept of illegitimacy was abolished in practically all legal systems through legislation, court decisions, or constitutional provisions. Then, advances in biological science made it possible for the first time in history for paternity to be proved with certainty in nearly all cases. No sooner did that happen, however, than the whole concept of filiation was put in question by new reproductive technologies such as artificial insemination, *in vitro* fertilization, and embryo transfer. (Even posthumous procreation has become possible through the use of frozen sperm and embryos.) These practices not only break the link between sexual relations and procreation, but often also sever the relation between biology and parenthood.[16] It is now possible for several different persons to have a plausible claim to being "parents" of the same child: the genetic parents (who provide the

---

13 *Rees* v. *United Kingdom*, ECHR 0009532/81 (1986); *Cossey* v. *United Kingdom*, ECHR 00010843/84 (1990).

14 *Frette* v. *France*, ECHR 00036515/97 (2002).

15 Mary Ann Glendon, "What Happened at Beijing," *First Things* (January 1996): 30–36.

16 M.-T. Meulders-Klein, "Procréations médicalement assistées: à qui appartient l'enfant?" in *Actes des Journées Strasbourgeoises de l'Institut Canadien d'études juridiques supérieures* 1996 (Québec: Editions Yvon Blais, 1997), 61–82.

sperm and egg), the gestational (surrogate) mother who carries the child to birth, and the individual or couple that intends to raise the child.

On the horizon are still more profound changes, as these technologies (where legally allowed to do so) move beyond their original purpose of providing children for infertile couples to include more ambitious aims, such as producing children free of certain defects, and in some cases, producing a child of the desired sex or a child to serve as an organ or bone marrow donor for a sibling. The ever-expanding ability to exercise control over the processes and "products" of human reproduction, and the commercialization of those processes, will affect the very meaning of childhood and parenthood in ways that are difficult to foresee.[17]

### Marginalization of Children in an Adult-Centered World

If one considers the implications for children of the changes in family law that took place in the affluent countries of Europe and North America in the late twentieth century, the outlook is troubling. The law has increasingly ratified many changes in the sexual mores and marriage behavior of large numbers of adults that have transformed the experience of childhood in ways that would have been unimaginable in former times. In the contest between the age-old idea of marriage as an institution mainly for the procreation and raising of children and the idea of marriage as primarily for the benefit of the adult individuals involved, the law increasingly weighs in on the side of individual adults.

The consequences for the children upon whom the human future depends have been drastic: millions of children have been lost to abortion, and an unprecedented proportion of children are spending all or part of their childhoods in fatherless homes, often in poverty. Female-headed families created by divorce, desertion, or single parenthood now constitute the bulk of the world's poverty population. As for intact child-raising families, their standard of living is generally lower than that of childless households, especially if the mother stays home to care for the children.

In sum, the affluent Western nations have been engaged in a massive social experiment—an experiment that has opened many new opportunities and freedoms to adults, but one that has been conducted at the expense of children and future generations.

With declining birth rates, political obstacles to a more child-centered family policy increase. Children are less visible in many societies; adults are less likely to be living with children; and neighborhoods less likely to contain children. As the proportion of childless households grows, the culture becomes ever more adult-centered, and the general level of societal concern for children declines. Political support for measures that might address the

---

[17] See Francis Fukuyama, *Our Posthuman Future: Consequences of the Biotechnology Revolution* (New York: Farrar, Straus & Giroux, 2002).

needs of child-raising families becomes more difficult to rally, in part because policymaking elites in modern societies are disproportionately composed of men and women who are either childless or who see little of their children. As the old saying goes, "Out of sight, out of mind."

## DIVERGENCES WITHIN A COMMON HORIZON

As noted in the conference guidelines, there are significant differences among Western systems. Nevertheless, the overall direction of change in Western family law has been broadly similar everywhere, and most of the differences seem to be differences of degree. It is worth noting, however, that the changes described here tended to originate, and to take extreme forms, in the Nordic countries, the United States, and England. The United States, in particular, is set apart by its relative lack of stringency in assuring either public or private responsibility for the increased cost of caring for dependents associated with changing patterns of family behavior.[18] In the Nordic countries, the state has assumed much of this cost, while the Romano-Germanic systems are more vigorous in enforcing family support obligations.

With the globalization of many aspects of American culture, especially American ideas about rights, it may be important to try to understand why the U.S. model diverges in several respects from both the Nordic and the continental European approaches to family law. One might start with the observation that the "story" about family life encoded in American family law is recognizably related to other American stories—about self-reliance, individual liberty, and tolerance for the great cultural diversity—that are so characteristic of contemporary U.S. society. There seems to be little recognition as yet that, at some point, a society where the legal system gives highest priority to individualistic values will have to come to terms with a larger and larger proportion of the population who put those values above all others—even in family life.

Why the American difference? Modern ideas about individual liberty found hospitable soil quite early in England where free markets in land, the loosening of the connection between family and land, and social mobility based on wealth all emerged sooner than on the European continent. The English also made an early break with a religion whose individual members are conceived of as forming one mystical body, replacing Catholicism with various belief systems that stress the individual and downplay the role of mediating structures.

As for the English colonies that became the United States, there were even fewer obstacles to the spread either of the idea or the practice of individualism on the new continent. A certain restlessness and rootlessness accompanied the westward expansion, and by the early nineteenth century the ideal of the free,

---

[18] See, generally, "Why the American Difference?" in Glendon, *Abortion and Divorce in Western Law,* 112–42.

self-reliant, self-determining individual was so pervasive as to astonish a foreign observer like Tocqueville. In a country where, as he observed, "neither law nor custom holds anyone in one place," individualism was bound to take a somewhat different form than it did in countries where most people still lived their entire lives within a relatively short radius from their birthplace.[19]

One of Tocqueville's rare misjudgments was to overestimate the power of the American family to resist the disintegrating forces that were already at work in nineteenth-century American society. He believed that American women (as the main teachers of children and keepers of orderly, peaceful homes) would play a key role in transmitting the republican virtues of self-restraint and concern for the common good, thus moderating the effects of individual greed, selfishness, and ambition. The fact is, however, that family solidarity in the U.S. began to erode much earlier than is generally supposed. American divorce rates in the "good old days" of the early twentieth century were already at least double, and often triple or quadruple those of any European country at that time.[20]

Some of the differences between common-law and civil-law norms affecting the family seem to have been influenced as well by different types of linkage with political theory. The Anglo-American legal tradition has, to a great extent, absorbed the Hobbesian myth of man in the state of nature as an isolated, self-interested creature of fear and desire, engaged in a perpetual state of war with everyone else, and driven into political society only for the sake of self-preservation. This myth, subjected to devastating critique by Rousseau and others, did not find a parallel reception in continental legal systems where the break with classical political theory and traditional Judeo-Christian views of man was less radical.

Then, in the late nineteenth century, the American legal system welded John Stuart Mill's powerful formulations about individual liberty to its embedded image of the person as essentially solitary. As Dicey recounts in his lectures *On Law and Public Opinion in England,* the essay *On Liberty* "appeared to thousands of admiring disciples to provide the final and conclusive demonstration of the absolute truth of individualism, and to establish on firm ground the doctrine that the protection of freedom was the one great object of wise law and sound policy."[21] Mill's essay (which had more influence on American than on English law) set forth the now-familiar principle: "The only purpose for which power can be rightfully exercised over any member of a civilised community, against his will, is to prevent harm to others."[22] Mill's definition

---

[19] Alexis de Tocqueville, *Democracy in America* (New York: Doubleday Anchor, 1969), 537.

[20] *United Nations Demographic Yearbook 1968* (New York: United Nations, 1968), Table 34.

[21] Albert Vann Dicey, *Lectures on the Relation between Law and Public Opinion in England During the 19th Century,* 2d ed. (London: Macmillan, 1952), 183.

[22] John Stuart Mill, "On Liberty," in *Utilitarianism, Liberty and Representative Government* (New York: Dutton, 1951), 85, 95–96.

CHAPTER 30 • Family Law in a Time of Turbulence

of "harm" was very narrow: He made it clear that by "harm" he meant only direct and immediate harms, thus placing out of bounds any restrictions on liberty based on the probability of adverse indirect or long-term effects. Another striking defect of his famous essay is its failure to consider the cumulative effects of individual choices made by large numbers of people. He did not foresee that lifestyles that once were permissible or affordable only to the wealthy or to artists would one day be democratized, and what effect that would have on society as a whole.

Mill's essay *On Liberty* was enthusiastically embraced by key American legal figures like Supreme Court Justices Oliver Wendell Holmes, Jr., and Louis Brandeis. Their judicial opinions provide sobering illustrations of how the law simplifies and reshapes ideas in the process of incorporating them into its own framework. As Mill's thoughts found their way into legal discourse, several of his nuances were ignored. For example, it is now quite forgotten that Mill's prime examples of improper *grants* of liberty were drawn from family relations, for example, "misplaced notions of liberty prevent moral obligations on the part of parents from being recognised, and legal obligations from being imposed, where there are the strongest grounds for the former always, and in many cases for the latter also."[23] Mill even believed that the right to marry properly could be subordinated to the obligation to pay child support: "The laws which, in many countries on the Continent, forbid marriage unless the parties can show that they have the means of supporting a family, do not exceed the legitimate powers of the State: and whether such laws be expedient or not (a question mainly dependent on local circumstances and feelings), they are not objectionable as violations of liberty."[24] As for divorce, although Mill held that, in principle, one ought to be free to dissolve a marriage at will, he conceded that reliance by one party might change this, and that the interests of children must at least be a factor, if not a bar.

With Mill's own specifications of limits mostly forgotten, the essay *On Liberty* gave impetus to a great expansion of the notion of individual rights in Anglo-American political and legal theory. For Hobbes only life itself, and for Locke only life, property, and a limited concept of liberty were rights, secure as such from the state. But Mill's claim was that a much larger area of human conduct and opinion should be free from both governmental interference and the "soft tyranny" of popular censure. In the United States, these ideas filtered down into popular culture, and legitimated crucial steps in American constitutional law, giving us the "marketplace of ideas," the "clear and present danger" test, the notion of the consenting adult, and "the right to be let alone," which later became the "right of privacy."[25]

---

[23] Id., 219–20

[24] Id., 220.

[25] Mary Ann Glendon, *Abortion and Divorce in Western Law,* 123–24.

Naturally, the legal systems of the European continent were also strongly influenced by modern concepts of individual rights. But rights language, like other languages, has different dialects.[26] In the Romano-Germanic legal traditions, the rights mode of discourse has been modulated to some extent by vestiges of classical and Judeo-Christian notions of man and society. The civil law systems have balanced the emphasis on individual liberty with more attention to social context and individual responsibility. The difference in emphasis is subtle, but its spirit penetrates every detail of the respective legal systems.

At the heart of the difference is a somewhat different concept of human personhood. In legal systems on the French and German model, the image of the person as a free, self-determining individual is tempered by an understanding of man as a being constituted in part by and through his relations with others, for example, the famous statement of the German Constitutional Court that "[t]he concept of man in the Basic Law is not that of an isolated sovereign individual; rather the Basic Law has decided in favor of a relationship between individual and community in the sense of a person's dependence on and commitment to the community, without infringing upon a person's individual value."[27] The individual is envisioned as situated within family and community; his rights are viewed as inseparable from corresponding responsibilities; and liberty and equality are seen as coordinate with solidarity. Though personal values are regarded as higher than social values, they are seen as rooted in them.

That more nuanced understanding of the legal subject pervades court decisions, statutes, social programs, and constitutional texts. For example, the German Constitution gives primacy in Article 1 to the protection of human dignity. Then, in the following articles, it protects a series of individual liberties, and commits the state to protection of marriage and the family. Similarly, the Preamble to the French Constitution provides that "The nation ensures to the individual and the family the conditions necessary to their development." In such documents, the very words "liberty" and "equality" thus resonate quite differently than within the eighteenth-century U.S. Constitution, which is silent both on the subject of the family and on social welfare.

Although the definitions of "marriage" and the "family" are now hotly contested in Europe as in the United States, the presence of specific family protection language in many European constitutions (and in international human rights instruments) still helps to encourage the formation and maintenance of explicit family policy. In the United States, by contrast, there is little explicit family policy at the state or federal level. American family policy is implicit, contained in the details of tax law, employment law, pension and insurance law, social welfare and social security law, and so on. Because

---

[26] Mary Ann Glendon, *Rights Talk: The Impoverishment of Political Discourse* (New York: Free Press, 1991), x–xiii.

[27] Investment Aid Case, 1954 *Bundesverfassungsericht* 7.

it is implicit, it is largely unexamined, and its implications for family life are insufficiently aired and discussed.

Yet another difference between laws affecting the family in the United States and continental Europe concerns the treatment of economic dependency. This is too vast a subject to treat adequately here, but it should be noted that the earlier and more expansive development of the welfare state on the Continent was due, to some extent, to the fact that courts in European countries did not have the power to strike down social legislation as unconstitutional. In the same years when the foundations of the welfare state were being laid in late nineteenth-century France and Germany, the United States Supreme Court was invalidating even modest worker protection laws as violations of constitutional property and contract rights. It was not until the Depression era of the 1930s that the U.S. Supreme Court finally began to uphold labor laws and social security measures.

## RETHINKING FAMILY POLICY

In the wake of the social and legal revolutions sketched above, it seems evident that among the most pressing issues for family policy are those arising from the impaired ability of families to socialize the next generation of citizens, and the *diminished capacity of the family, of government, and of the mediating structures of civil society alike* to furnish care for the very young, the frail elderly, and other dependents. All societies, including the advanced welfare states, still rely heavily on families for the socialization and care of the young, the elderly, the sick, and the severely disabled. But the capacity of families to perform these functions has been dramatically reduced everywhere. In particular, no society has found a substitute for the care, services, and support formerly furnished by the unpaid labor of women. Changes in family structure, in turn, have weakened neighborhood life and the mediating institutions of civil society—social systems that once helped to support and sustain families even as they themselves were once supported and sustained by marriage-based families and volunteer work by women. Frayed connections in one social system have led to unraveling in other systems, and welfare states have been pushed to the edge of crisis.

The same forces that have promoted the rise of the ideal of the free rights-bearing individual have fostered attitudes that make it hard to design and implement family policy—or indeed any policies that look to the long-term common good. In fact, many of the developments that have weakened legal and social family ties are unintended consequences of freedoms that modern men and women prize. No one, for example, wants to roll back the clock on women's rights, but the ideas about women's rights that are now predominant in law were framed with little attention to the needs and desires of women who accord priority to child-raising and who do not accept socialization of child care as a solution. The challenges are thus formidable: How can society take account of children's needs (and the preferences of most mothers) while still providing equal opportunities to women? How can society respond to the needs of persons in broken or dysfunctional families while strengthening, or at least not undermining, the stable families upon which every society depends for the socialization of its future work force and citizenry? How can policymakers develop an adequate response to families currently in distress while attempting to shift probabilities so that fewer families will find themselves in distressed circumstances in the future? When do the advantages for individuals of unprecedented freedom in family matters begin to be outweighed or nullified by the social costs of the cumulative effects of individual choices on social and family life? What makes these dilemmas especially difficult is that their resolution often involves finding a just balance among competing goods.

As Tocqueville foresaw long ago, a certain carelessness about the future appears when the links between generations are broken: "Not only does democracy make men forget their ancestors, but it also clouds their view of their descendants and isolates them from their contemporaries. Each man is forever thrown back on himself alone, and there is danger that he may be shut up in the solitude of his own heart."[28] As he predicted, that mentality has made it difficult for democracies to make and implement long-range plans.

Certainly that seems to be the case with family policy today which, more often than not, emerges from scrambles for entitlements among interest groups rather than from deliberation about the common good. As the proportion of child-raising households declines in the liberal democracies, the priorities of other segments of the population—single or childless adults and the elderly—tend to predominate.

But what would a better family policy look like? What realistic alternatives are there to the libertarian and statist approaches? The problematic for this conference invites us to consider whether the family should or could be treated as a social and legal subject in itself within the framework of subsidiarity (properly understood), rather than merely as a collection of rights-bearing individuals. As the problematic recognizes, that idea immediately encounters the problem of the definition of the family.

So far as family law is concerned, one way of characterizing the trends of the past forty years would be as a steady diminution of legal reinforcement of the bonds among family members, a process spurred on by various interest groups with overlapping agendas. The conference problematic asks the crucial question: "Is it possible to reach a definition of the family that is useful for family policies and that can be, if not unanimously, at least largely shared?" One might start by observing that within contemporary legal systems, the term "family" is often employed with different meanings in different legal

---

[28] Tocqueville, *Democracy in America*, 508.

contexts. A "family" member, for example, may be defined broadly to include unmarried cohabitants where the issue is one of succession to a rent-controlled tenancy, but more narrowly where classification for purposes of immigration is concerned, and still differently in the context of determining who is entitled to inherit a decedent's estate.

Very tentatively, and from the perspective of what might be politically feasible, I would suggest the following three propositions for discussion:

1. The family form that state and society have the greatest interest in promoting is that which provides optimal conditions for child-raising and thus is most important for the common future: the stable child-raising household with a married mother and father present. If this is correct, it is appropriate to single out for encouragement and preferential treatment married couple households where children are being or have been raised—just as it is appropriate to give special treatment to veterans and others who made sacrifices for the common good. This family type may be the best candidate for "treatment as a social and legal subject" with rights that are inherent in it as a relational system.

2. Society and the state also have an interest in other households where children are being raised, but here the interests are of a different kind: the social interest in providing all children with the best possible life-chances and the social interest in responding to the needs of the disadvantaged. But these social goals must be pursued without encouraging the proliferation of suboptimal arrangements. If this is correct, it is appropriate to single out some non-marital child-raising households for special assistance.

3. State and society have little interest in households, marriage-based or not, where children are not being, and have not been, raised. This suggests that perhaps marriage in and of itself should not automatically entitle the spouses to the same benefits accorded to married persons who are raising or who have raised children. That is not to say that society has little interest in encouraging marriage. Quite the contrary: married couples—child-raising or not—model the family-type in which society has the highest interest in promoting, and they serve as linchpins for the "armies of compassion" upon which state and society depend in a myriad of ways.

To conclude this discussion paper: The present legal ordering of the family is composed of the accumulated accidents and inventions of the past. It now appears that the layers that were added in the late twentieth century rested on many questionable assumptions and entailed many unintended adverse consequences, not only for dependent family members, but for the social fabric as a whole. We are now in the process of adding a layer that will reflect whatever intelligence we are able to bring to bear on the difficult issues that confront our societies. How, one wonders, will future generations judge our contributions?

# Human Rights

# Rights in
# Twentieth-Century Constitutions

*In 1991, the University of Chicago Law School held a symposium
to commemorate the Bicentennial of the Bill of Rights.
My contribution, taking a comparative perspective, appeared
in 31 University of Chicago Law Review 1 (1992).[1]*

ALTHOUGH THIS SYMPOSIUM has treated the subject of the Bill of Rights in the welfare state primarily within the context of American constitutional law, it is instructive and appropriate to compare the American experience with the experiences of other liberal democratic welfare states. Indeed, if a symposium on this subject had been held in 1991 at a university anywhere in the world except the United States, its approach to the topic would almost certainly have been cross-national from beginning to end. Most of the participants, no doubt, would have been invited to explore how some countries—for example, Canada, Denmark, France, Germany, Italy, Japan, Norway, and Sweden—have managed, more or less successfully, to remain simultaneously committed to political and civil rights, a well-developed welfare state, and a system of constitutional control of legislative and executive action. There would probably have been a session or two devoted to the transition of the East European countries from socialism to constitutional social democracy. Another major topic would have been how commitments made in international human rights instruments have affected national legal systems. Finally, in all likelihood, there would have been sessions devoted to two special cases: first, England, a welfare state without a bill of rights or a system of judicial review in the modern sense; and second, the United States, a country with a venerable rights tradition, and a strong system of judicial review, but with a minimalist welfare state.

In this article, I cannot present such an extended comparative survey. My goal is rather to advance the proposition that American thinking about rights and welfare would benefit from examining the experiences of other

---

[1] Mary Ann Glendon, "Rights in Twentieth Century Constitutions," *University of Chicago Law Review* 59 (1; Winter 1992): 519–38.

liberal democracies, and to speculate about the insights that might emerge from such a comparative analysis. I concentrate mainly on countries whose experiences seem most relevant to our own: countries at levels of social and economic development comparable to ours; and where welfare states coexist with a strong commitment to individual liberty and the rule of law. I do not claim that we will find abroad any answers to the great questions debated by the participants in this symposium. The benefits I have in mind are, rather, of the type to which the French social historian, Fernand Braudel, was referring when he once said:

> Live in London for a year, and you will not get to know much about the English. But through comparison, and in the light of your surprise, you will suddenly come to understand some of the more profound and individual characteristics of France, which you did not previously understand because you knew them too well.

Taking a cue from Braudel, I will reflect first on some of the "more profound and individual characteristics" of the United States that we often overlook—because we know them so well. I will then consider some of the special difficulties posed by our distinctive experience with respect to both rights and welfare. Finally, I will suggest that heightened awareness of how our country's experience is distinctive can alert us to some opportunities that seem, at least theoretically, to be more available to Americans than to policymakers elsewhere.

## AMERICAN DISTINCTIVENESS

Many of the issues vigorously debated at this symposium owe their very existence to the simple chronological fact that when our Constitution and Bill of Rights were adopted the welfare state as we know it was not even a twinkle in the eyes of the Founding Fathers. Because the overwhelming majority of the world's constitutions have been adopted within the past thirty years, there are few other countries where scholars need to ask questions like: How does our eighteenth-century design for government fit with our modern regulatory state? Does it matter which branches of government take the lead in deciding what adaptations are necessary? Is it a problem that our welfare state, such as it is, continues to develop without any specific constitutional impetus? Or, does the deep structure of the Fourteenth Amendment—say, the idea of "protection"—provide a constitutional lodestar for the welfare state after all?

The age of our Bill of Rights is thus foremost among the features that distinguish the United States with respect to rights and the welfare state. The first ten amendments to the Constitution, backed up by judicial review, were in place long before our legislatures began to attend systematically to the health, safety, and well-being of citizens. In most other liberal democracies, the sequence has been just the reverse. In Canada, France, and Germany, for example, the foundations of the welfare state were in place well before regimes of constitutional rights appeared.

A second distinguishing feature is that the American Constitution, unlike the constitutions of most other liberal democracies, contains no language establishing affirmative welfare rights or obligations. A third factor is the conspicuous unwillingness of American governments to ratify several important international human rights instruments to which all the other liberal democracies have acceded. Finally there is the unusual structure of our welfare state, which, much more than elsewhere, leaves pensions, health insurance, and other benefits to be organized privately, mainly through the workplace, rather than directly through the public sector. I will elaborate briefly on the first three of these factors.

## RIGHTS BEFORE WELFARE

Americans are justly proud of the long tradition of rights protection celebrated in this bicentennial year of the Bill of Rights. We take patriotic satisfaction as well in the fact that, prior to 1945, we were one of very few countries where constitutional rights were protected by the institution of judicial review. However, it is worth recalling that American courts seldom exercised the power of judicial review claimed in *Marbury* v. *Madison* (1803) until the turn of the century, and then the courts deployed the power in a way that may well have impeded the development of the welfare state here for decades. According to James Q. Wilson: "In the first seventy-five years of this country's history, only 2 federal laws were held unconstitutional; in the next seventy-five years, 71 were. Of the roughly 900 state laws held to be in conflict with the federal Constitution since 1789, about 800 were overturned after 1870. In one decade alone—the 1880s—5 federal and 48 state laws were declared unconstitutional." In the *Lochner* era, when the American Supreme Court was engaged in its first sustained adventure with judicial review, legislators in the rest of the industrialized world were busily constructing their infant welfare states on the basis of statutes broadly similar in spirit to those our Court was striking down.

It was not until the active period of constitution-making following World War II that other nations widely adopted bills of rights and institutional mechanisms to enforce them. At that time, the majority of liberal democratic countries opted for variants of a system developed in prewar Austria that has come to be known as the "European model" of constitutional control. The principal feature that distinguishes the "European" from the "American" model is that under the former constitutional questions must be referred to a special tribunal that deals only or mainly with such matters.

Constitutional adjudication is off limits for other courts in such countries. It is only in the United States, and in the relatively small group of countries that have adopted the "American model," that ordinary courts have the power to rule on constitutional questions in ordinary lawsuits. Many nations that have adopted the European model are still further distanced from our system by the fact that constitutional questions may be presented to the constitutional tribunal only by other courts *sua sponte*, or by political authorities, but not by private litigants. A notable exception, with regard to individual standing to bring constitutional complaints, is the Federal Republic of Germany. There, in fact, the bulk of the caseload of the Constitutional Court consists of constitutional complaints by private citizens.

Even among the handful of countries that have adopted a form of the "American model" of judicial review—such as Canada, Japan, and the Republic of Ireland—the United States remains unique. For in those nations, neither the supreme courts nor the lower courts thus far have exercised that power with such frequency and boldness as their American counterparts have exercised at both the state and federal levels. Indeed, to foreigners, the recent burgeoning of state-court constitutionalism and the innovative use of injunctions by federal district courts beginning in the 1960s are two of the most remarkable features of the American legal system. Even if judicial activism in the Supreme Court has subsided somewhat in recent years, the relative readiness of American judges at all levels of jurisdiction to deploy their powers of judical review in the service of a variety of social aims has made the United States a model of a particularly adventurous form of judicial rights protection.

## WHAT COUNTS AS A RIGHT?

The German legal historian Franz Wieacker recently compiled a list he described as representing the "basic inventory" of rights that have been accepted by "most western countries" at the present time. The list included, first and foremost, human dignity; then personal freedom; fair procedures to protect against arbitrary governmental action; active political rights (especially the right to vote); equality before the law; and society's responsibility for the social and economic conditions of its members. An American reader of that list is apt to be struck both by the omission of property rights, and by the inclusion of affirmative welfare obligations. Yet the list cannot be faulted as a description of the law on the books of "most western countries." Welfare rights (or responsibilities) have become a staple feature of postwar international declarations and have been accorded a place beside traditional political and civil liberties in the national constitutions of most liberal democracies. The formulations vary from the bare recitation in the German Basic Law of 1949 that the Federal Republic of Germany is a "social" state (Basic Law Article 20), to detailed lists of specific social and economic rights such as those contained in the constitutions of France, Italy, Japan, Spain, and the Nordic countries. It is the eighteenth-century American Constitution that, with the passage of time, has become anomalous in this respect.

As Gerhard Casper has pointed out, these differences regarding the rights that are accorded constitutional status in various countries are not a mere function of the age of the documents establishing those rights. To a great extent, they are legal manifestations of divergent, and deeply rooted, cultural attitudes toward the state and its functions. Historically, obligations on the part of the state to provide food, work, and financial aid to persons in need were acknowledged even in eighteenth- and nineteenth-century continental European constitutions and codes. And continental Europeans today, whether of the right or the left, are much more likely than Americans to take for granted that governments have affirmative duties to actively promote the well-being of their citizens. The leading European conservative parties, for example, accept the subsidization of child-raising families, and the funding of health, employment, and old age insurance at levels most Americans find scarcely credible. By contrast, it is almost obligatory for American politicians of both the right and the left to profess mistrust of government.

These divergent attitudes toward the state have found constitutional expression in what are sometimes called "negative" and "positive" rights. The American Bill of Rights is frequently described as essentially a charter of negative liberties protecting certain areas of individual freedom from state interference. Judge Posner has succinctly stated the position: "The men who wrote the Bill of Rights were not concerned that the federal government might do too little for the people, but that it might do too much to them." The Supreme Court, while willing to accord procedural due process protection to statutory welfare entitlements, has consistently declined to recognize constitutional welfare rights. Chief Justice Rehnquist's opinion in *DeShaney* v. *Winnebago County Department of Social Services* reaffirms that the Due Process Clause of the Fourteenth Amendment is "a limitation on the State's power to act, not . . . a guarantee of certain minimal levels of safety and security."

These statements contrast markedly with the attitudes of the postwar European constitution-makers who supplemented traditional negative liberties with certain affirmative social and economic rights or obligations. The idea of government underlying the "positive rights" in European constitutions has a complex history. In part, it represents a transposition to the modern state of the feudal notion that an overlord owes protection to his dependents in exchange for their service and loyalty. More proximately, it reflects the programs of the major European political parties—one large group animated by Christian social thought, and another by socialist or social democratic principles. As Casper has observed, it was only natural that peoples accustomed to the notion of a state with affirmative responsibilities would carry that idea forward when they added bills of rights to their constitutions.

CHAPTER 31 • Rights in Twentieth-Century Constitutions

## INTERNATIONAL HUMAN RIGHTS

In view of the longstanding American rights tradition, and the recent history of expansive judicial protection of a broad spectrum of individual and minority rights, the third aspect of American distinctiveness may at first glance seem puzzling. I am referring to the dubious distinction possessed by the United States as the only liberal democracy that has not ratified a number of important human rights instruments, notably the two United Nations Covenants on Civil and Political Rights, and on Economic, Social and Cultural Rights. This reticence, no doubt, is due in large part to our prudent unwillingness to submit to the jurisdiction of international organizations dominated by critics of the United States. But, particularly where economic and social rights are concerned, our reluctance is also attributable to our prevailing ideas about which sorts of needs, goods, interests, and values should be characterized as fundamental rights. Another likely reason is that the American civil litigation system is not well-equipped to handle the potential consequences of characterizing a new set of interests as fundamental rights.

## WELFARE RIGHTS AND WELFARE STATES

The reaction of many Americans to the foregoing contrasts might be that we have little to learn from other nations about welfare, and even less about rights. Others, especially reformers who do not regard American distinctiveness as a badge of honor, might be drawn in the opposite direction, toward viewing the rights or welfare arrangements in other countries as promising models for the United States to follow. Such reform-minded individuals might ask: How have constitutional welfare rights worked out in practice? Do the "experiments" of other nations shed any light on what might have happened here if the Supreme Court had accepted arguments made in the late 1960s and early 1970s that welfare rights could and should be teased out of the language of the Fourteenth Amendment? Though I will conclude that those questions lead almost to a dead end, it is instructive to examine why they do not open an especially fruitful line of inquiry.

As it happens, the contrast between the means of implementation of the American welfare system and other welfare systems is less sharp than it initially appears. Though many countries have included welfare rights or obligations in their constitutions, no democratic country has placed social and economic rights on precisely the same legal footing as the familiar civil and political liberties. In most cases, the drafters have formulated the former somewhat differently from the latter. In some countries, for example, the constitutional welfare language is so cryptic as to be meaningless without extensive legislative specification. More commonly, the constitutions do specifically enumerate various social and economic rights, but present them merely as aspirational political principles or goals to guide the organs of government as they carry out their respective functions. For example, the Swedish Instrument of Government provides, in a section titled "The Basic Principles of the Constitution":

> Art. 2. The personal, economic and cultural welfare of the individual shall be fundamental aims of the activities of the community. In particular, it shall be incumbent on the community to secure the right to work, to housing and to education and to promote social care and security as well as a favorable living environment.

Continental lawyers call such rights "programmatic" to emphasize that they are not directly enforceable individual rights, but await implementation through legislative or executive action, and through budgetary appropriations. Programmatic rights figure prominently in the constitutions of the Nordic countries, as well as in the French, Greek, Italian, and Spanish constitutions.

The most interesting case in some ways is that of Japan, which accepted the American model of judicial review in 1947. In Japan, the catalog of constitutional rights (thanks to the New Dealers in the postwar occupational government) includes much of the "Second Bill of Rights" set forth in Franklin Roosevelt's 1944 State of the Union message. Some of the Japanese welfare rights are not, on their face, programmatic. There is a right to decent minimum subsistence in Article 25, a right to receive an education in Article 26, and a right to work in Article 27. In the drafting process, Article 25 was changed from a purely programmatic provision ("In all spheres of life, the State shall use its endeavors for the promotion and extension of social welfare and security, and of public health"), to a proclamation beginning with unvarnished American-style rights language ("All people shall have the right to maintain the minimum standards of wholesome and cultured living").

The adoption of the 1947 Constitution was quickly followed, however, by a Japanese Supreme Court decision holding that the right to a minimum standard of decent living in Article 25 was programmatic. The government's constitutional welfare obligations, according to that decision, "must, in the main, be carried out by the enactment and enforcement of social legislation. . . . [The] state does not bear such an obligation concretely and materially toward the people as individuals." In the years that followed, the Japanese Supreme Court has maintained the view that the welfare rights in the Constitution do not give rise to judicially enforceable individual rights. In a leading case, *Asahi* v. *Japan,* decided in 1967, the Court held:

> [Article 25 (1)] merely proclaims that it is the duty of the state to administer national policy in such a manner as to enable all the people to enjoy at least the minimum standards of wholesome and cultured living, and it does not grant the people as individuals any concrete rights [citation omitted]. A concrete right is secured only through the

provisions of the Livelihood Protection Law enacted to realize the objectives prescribed in the provisions of the Constitution.

The *Asahi* decision went on to say that government officials would have to determine what constitutes a minimum standard of living under all the circumstances, subject to review for excess or abuse of power. Thus, in Japan, as in the countries where constitutional welfare rights are explicitly programmatic, and as in countries like our own without any constitutional welfare rights at all, the welfare state has been constructed by legislation through ordinary political processes.

At this point, one might well wonder whether the formal differences between the United States and other welfare states have any significance at all. After all, we too have a "program"—spelled out in the New Deal statutes of the 1930s and 1940s, supplemented by Great Society statutes of the 1960s—the cornerstones of our version of the welfare state. Aspiration and implementation are combined, for example, in the Social Security Act of 1935 whose preamble declares that the statute is:

> [t]o provide for the general welfare by establishing a system of Federal old-age benefits, and by enabling the several States to make more adequate provision for aged persons, blind persons, dependent and crippled children, maternal and child welfare, public health, and the administration of their unemployment compensation laws. . . .

Similarly, the Housing Act of 1949 calls for "the realization as soon as feasible of the goal of a decent home and a suitable living environment for every American family. . . ."

Should one conclude, then, that the provisions of modern constitutions, which commit the state to affirmative protection of certain economic and social rights, are of little or no practical consequence? That conclusion seems too strong, if only because such rights at least endow statutes implementing the constitutional "program" with a strong presumption of constitutionality. Moreover, the constitutional status of social and economic rights seems likely to have synergistically reinforced welfare commitments in countries where they are present. Elevating this set of goals to constitutional status has probably played a modest but not a trivial role among the factors that influence the terms, the categories, and the tone of public, judicial, and legislative deliberation about rights and welfare. In countries where constitutional welfare commitments have issued from, or were grafted onto, a well-established welfare tradition, they may well have strengthened that tradition, just as our Bill of Rights both emerged from and buttressed the Anglo-American rights tradition.

Nevertheless there does not appear to be any strict correlation between the strength of constitutional welfare language and the generosity of welfare states, as measured by the proportion of national expenditures devoted to health, housing, social security, and social assistance. For example, the United Kingdom, with no constitutional welfare rights, devotes proportionately more of its resources to social expenditures than its richer "neighbor" Denmark, where rights to work, education, and social assistance are constitutionally guaranteed. Analogous social expenditures consume considerably more of the budget of the Federal Republic of Germany, whose constitution merely announces that it is a "social" state, than they do in Sweden or Italy whose constitutions spell out welfare rights in some detail.

If there is a relationship between the constitutional status of welfare rights and the type and strength of welfare commitments in a given society, it is only a loose relationship of consanguinity, with both the constitution and the welfare system influenced by such factors as the homogeneity or diversity of the population; the degree to which mistrust of government has figured in the country's political history; the vitality of political parties; the health of the legislative process; and the intensity of individualism in the culture. Such speculation leads only to the sort of conclusions that make sociology so unsatisfying to many people. It is difficult to become excited about the idea that a host of mutually conditioning factors, of which the constitutional status of welfare rights may be both cause and consequence, determine in numerous ways the shape of a given country's welfare state—its basic commitments, the priorities among those commitments, the spirit in which it is administered, the degree of support and approval it wins from taxpayers, and the extent to which it disables or empowers those who resort to it.

## WHAT IF . . . ?

Still, a reform-minded American might consider the inconclusiveness of the foregoing analysis a source of encouragement. If the experience of other liberal democracies is any guide, she might contend, according constitutional status to social and economic rights does not seem to cause any harm. At the margin, it may well exert a benign influence on the legislative process and on public deliberation by broadening the range of officially recognized social concerns, heightening their visibility, and underscoring their legitimacy. What a pity, the argument would go, that we have not bolstered the legal status of social and economic rights, either in the forms proposed to the Supreme Court in the 1960s and 1970s, or by ratifying the United Nations Covenant on Social, Economic, and Cultural Rights, as the Carter administration advocated in the 1970s.

It would be risky, in my view, however, to draw those inferences from the foreign experience, for reasons that reside not in the foreign experience but in distinctive American attitudes toward rights. Americans, for better or worse, take rights very seriously. It is not just the term, but the very idea of "programmatic" rights that is unfamiliar and uncongenial to us. It is thus almost inconceivable that constitutional welfare rights, had they appeared in the United States, would have been regarded by the public or treated by the legal community as purely aspirational. An American, hearing of a type of "right" that merely represents a goal or ideal, is apt to react as Mark Twain did when he learned that a preacher was condemning the Devil without giving the Devil the opportunity to confront the witnesses against him. "[It] is irregular," he said; "It is un-English; it is un-American; it is *French!*" Most Americans, like Holmes and Llewellyn, believe that a right-holder should be able to call upon the courts to "smite" anyone who interferes with that right. We take for granted that behind the court's orders to respect that right are sheriffs, marshalls, and the National Guard, if necessary.

As soon as we begin to imagine constitutional welfare rights that are other than programmatic, however, we are headed down a road that no other democratic country has traveled. That does not mean that we cannot make an educated guess about what consequences would be likely to follow if we made such a trip: Recent history suggests that the most directly foreseeable consequence of according constitutional status to social and economic rights would be something that has not occurred in the other liberal democracies—namely, a great increase in the type of litigation that has made Section 1983, since the 1960s, the second most heavily litigated section of the United States Code.

The crucial question for this symposium about that potential increase in federal litigation—a question whose answer is far from clear—is how private damage actions would affect the structure and performance of the welfare state. Some argue that such litigation would "prod" government agencies into action, that it would make them more responsive to the needs of the citizens. But it is at least equally plausible that the costs of defending such litigation, plus the occasional high damage award in Section 1983 actions, would prod financially strapped local providers in the other direction, toward service cutbacks or eliminating some programs altogether. Unfortunately, there is little empirical data to evaluate the utility of private damage actions in promoting improved social services.

Still, comparing the United States to other countries does illuminate the problem. It demonstrates that we Americans place an unusual degree of reliance on our tort system (both ordinary personal litigation and constitutional tort actions) to perform certain social tasks that other advanced nations handle with a more diversified range of techniques—for example, direct health and safety regulation and more comprehensive systems of social insurance. That reliance, in turn, suggests some further questions: Is our tort system really well-suited for all the jobs we presently ask it to do? Do our substantive tort law and our civil litigation system adequately fulfill what is, after all, their principal aim: the assurance of timely, fair, and cost-efficient disposition of legitimate claims, while effectively discouraging frivolous ones? If a major reason for court-centered reform efforts in the United States has been "legislative paralysis," can American legislatures ever be induced to take a proactive role in improving public services in the areas of health, education, and welfare?

## THE UTILITY OF CROSS-NATIONAL COMPARISON

It may seem to follow from the discussion thus far that contrary to what I asserted at the outset, Americans have little to gain from consulting the experience of other nations with rights and welfare. Certainly anyone who looks to comparative studies expecting to find specific models or proposals for domestic law reform is bound to be disappointed, for it is fairly clear that no other country has blazed a trail for the United States to follow. Nevertheless, the experiences of other countries may help us to find our own path by heightening our awareness of indigenous resources that we are inclined to overlook or underrate, because, as Braudel put it, we know them too well.

Beginning in the mid-1970s, economic constraint became an important issue for all advanced welfare states. Even the Nordic countries (whose citizens are as proud of their famous cradle-to-grave welfare systems as we are of our Bill of Rights) began to sense that they were reaching the limits of high taxation and direct public sector provision of services. In that climate, policymakers abroad have begun to gaze with interest at our relatively greater capacity for cooperation between governmental and non-governmental organizations in the areas of health, education, and welfare, and at the ability our sort of federalism gives us to innovate and experiment with diverse approaches to stubborn social problems.

In some cases, tentative efforts at imitation have followed. In the area of industrial relations, some countries have begun to experiment with American-style laws encouraging collective bargaining rather than the direct state regulation of the terms and conditions of employment that has been traditional in continental Europe. Our innovative labor legislation of the 1930s, which has practically fallen into desuetude in the United States, has been seen in France and Germany as the very prototype of "reflexive law" (legal norms that aim at facilitating and structuring private ordering, rather than imposing top-down state regulation). And policymakers abroad have also begun to consider whether some types of social services can be delivered more efficiently and humanely by intermediate associations—churches, unions, community groups, and so on—than by the government. Our voluntary sector, shambles though it may appear to us, is still more vibrant than its counterparts in nations where excessive centralization nearly extinguished non-governmental initiatives in the areas of health, education, and welfare.

Ironically, these American institutions and experiences are attracting interest abroad just at a time when they are showing the effects of long neglect at home. To many Europeans though, the United States represents a rare working example, albeit an imperfect one, of what has come to be known as the principle of "subsidiarity": the notion that no social task should be allocated to a body larger than the smallest one that can effectively do the job. The legal apparatus that promotes and facilitates the subsidiarity principle includes federalism, reflexive legal norms that foster private-ordering, and programs that make use of the mediating structures of civil society to deliver social services.

The reason these aspects of American law are attracting increased attention in highly centralized welfare states is that every country in the democratic world in its own way is experiencing a tension between the two ideals that are linked together in the deceptively bland title of this conference—a regime of rights and a welfare state. Each country is grappling with a set of problems that are in a general way similar: how to provide needed social aid without undermining personal responsibility; how to achieve the optimal mix of markets and planning in a mixed economy; how to preserve a just balance among individual freedom, equality, and social solidarity under circumstances that are constantly changing. The problem of "the Bill of Rights in the Welfare State" is nothing less than the great dilemma of how to hold together the two halves of the divided soul of liberalism—our love of individual liberty and our sense of a community for which we accept a common responsibility.

Below the surface of that dilemma lies a still more serious one. It is that neither a strong commitment to individual and minority rights, nor even a modest welfare commitment like the American one can long be sustained without the active support of a citizenry that is willing to respect the rights of others (not just in the abstract but often at some cost to themselves); that is prepared to accept some responsibility for the poorest and most vulnerable members of society; and that is prepared to take responsibility, so far as possible, for themselves and their dependents. We should make no mistake about the fact that liberal democratic welfare states around the world are now demanding certain kinds of excellence in their citizens to a nearly unprecedented degree. They are asking men and women to possess and practice certain virtues that, even under the best of conditions, are not easy to acquire—respect for the dignity and worth of one's fellow human beings, self-restraint, self-reliance, and compassion.

The questions that seldom get asked, however, are these: Where do such qualities come from? Where do people acquire an internalized willingness to view others with genuine regard for their dignity and concern for their well-being, rather than as objects, means, or obstacles? These qualities do not arise spontaneously in *homo sapiens*. Nor can governments instill them by fear and force. Perhaps there are alternative seedbeds of civic virtue besides vital families, neighborhoods, religious groups, and other communities of memory and mutual aid. If there are, however, history provides scant evidence of them. It is hard to avoid the conclusion that both our welfare state and our experiment in democratic government rest upon habits and practices formed in networks of fragile social structures, structures that are being asked to bear great weight just at a time when they themselves are not in peak condition. The question then becomes: What, if anything, can be done to create and maintain, or at least to avoid undermining or destroying, social conditions that foster the peculiar combination of qualities that are required to sustain our commitments to the rule of law, individual freedom, and a compassionate welfare state?

In a large, heterogeneous nation like the United States, the question is particularly urgent. It has been constantly repeated since Tocqueville famously said it in the 1830s that America is especially well-endowed with moral and cultural resources—with vital local governments, and a variety of associations that stand between citizens and the state. As with our natural resources, however, we have taken our social resources for granted, consuming inherited capital at a faster rate than we are replenishing it. Indeed, like an athlete who develops the muscles in his upper body but lets his legs grow weak, we have nurtured our strong rights tradition while neglecting the social foundation upon which that tradition rests.

We Americans, with our great emphasis in recent years on certain personal and civil rights, have too easily overlooked the fact that *all* rights depend on conserving the social resources that induce people to accept and respect the rights of others. Perhaps it is time, therefore, to take a fresh look at our constitutional framework, and to recall not only that the Bill of Rights is part of a larger constitutional structure, but that its own structure includes more than a catalog of negatively formulated political and civil liberties. As Akhil Amar has pointed out, scholars, litigators, and judges who concentrated single-mindedly in the 1960s and 1970s on judicial protection of individual and minority rights tended to permit other important parts of our constitutional tradition to be obscured. As it happens, those parts of the tradition that have been in the shadows—federalism, the legislative branch, and the ideal of government by the people—have an important bearing on the maintenance of the social capital upon which all rights ultimately depend.

And so, by a long and circuitous route, a cross-national approach to rights and the welfare state points back toward the American Constitution and toward the understanding that individual liberty and strong local institutions need not be at cross-purposes with one another. If America's endangered social environments do indeed hold the key to simultaneously maintaining a liberal regime of rights and a compassionate welfare state, then we must start thinking about how both rights and welfare, as currently conceived, affect those environments. Reflecting upon our own tradition, moreover, should give us pause before indulging the disdain for politics that underlies so much of our current thinking about legal and social policy. For one of the most important lessons of 1789 is the same one the world learned anew in 1989:

CHAPTER 31 • Rights in Twentieth-Century Constitutions

that politics is not only a way to advance self-interest, but to transcend it. That transformative potential of the art through which we order our lives together represents our best hope for living up to our rights ideals and our welfare aspirations in coming years.

# CHAPTER 32

# Law, Communities, and the Religious Freedom Language of the Constitution

*This overly optimistic essay originated as an after-dinner talk given at a bicentennial conference in Philadelphia on the religion language of the First Amendment. I carefully avoided using the conference organizers' term "religion clauses" for, as Richard John Neuhaus had pointed out, and as my co-author Raul Yanes and I had elaborated in "Structural Free Exercise," 90 Michigan Law Review 477 (1991), the First Amendment contains only one religion clause with two mutually reinforcing provisions, not two clauses at odds with each other. This essay appeared in 60 George Washington Law Review 672 (1992).[1] Although confusion still reigns in religion-clause case law, Aguilar v. Felton, criticized here, was over-ruled in Agostini v. Felton (1997).*

LAW AND RELIGION, as many contributors to this symposium have pointed out, are in some ways an uneasy mixture. In his opening remarks at the Bicentennial Conference on the Religion Clauses, Dean Kelley reported that many of the lawyers he had contacted about organizing the conference were skeptical about whether his plan would have a significant legal dimension. Several members of the religious groups he approached had the opposite reaction: They feared the conference would neglect all aspects of the topic except the legal ones. My contribution begins by conceding that there is some basis for the apprehensions of those who sensed that we lawyers might take an excessively narrow view of the proposed subject. After making a few observations about the mental habits that often make it difficult for lawyers to fit religion into their customary modes of analysis, I endeavor to relate these observations to the difficulties that the Supreme Court has had over the years in developing a workable body of religion-clause case law. I conclude by trying to assess the meaning of the Court's decision in the peyote discharge case, *Employment Division* v. *Smith,* in the present period of paradigm change.

---

[1] Mary Ann Glendon, "Law, Communities, and the Religious Freedom Language of the Constitution," *George Washington Law Review* 60 (3; March 1992): 672–84.

# A BLIND SPOT IN LEGAL VISION

There is much evidence that we lawyers have a kind of blind spot, or scotoma as some theologians call it, where religion is concerned. In everyday legal parlance, the "First Amendment," unless otherwise specified, is virtually synonymous with freedom of speech. This routine equation of the First Amendment with speech goes beyond mere verbal shorthand to reveal something about the position lawyers accord to speech in their hierarchy of rights. Professor Laurence Tribe undoubtedly speaks for many in the legal profession when in his treatise on constitutional law he describes the freedom of speech as "the Constitution's most majestic guarantee." To be sure, there is also a large following, especially in the legal academy, for Justice Louis Brandeis' alternative view that "the right to be let alone [is] the most comprehensive of rights and the right most valued by civilized men." One can only surmise where the freedom of religion would rank with those who adhere to such beliefs. But it seems significant that Professor Douglas Laycock's survey of the leading constitutional law casebooks found that their authors accorded relatively little space and attention to Religion Clause issues.

Opinion studies consistently show that free speech is highly valued by the American public, too. But, according to the most recent of these surveys, most American men and women still place freedom of speech exactly where the Framers of the Bill of Rights put it—close to but just behind, the free exercise of religion. In other words, the hierarchy of rights long implicit in works by prominent constitutional law specialists, and in much of the Supreme Court's treatment of religion, differs somewhat from that which is embedded in American culture.

To avoid misunderstanding, let me make it plain that I do not bring up this apparent discrepancy between elite and popular belief systems to suggest that legal elites are to be faulted when they fail to conform to majoritarian sentiment. They perform indispensable service for our society by doing precisely that. Nor do I wish to dwell on the extent to which many members of these elites seem to be lapsing from the independent-mindedness on which they pride themselves into a rather uncritical conformity to the dogmas of knowledge-class culture. Nor do I propose to discuss in this essay the problem of the effect on our democratic political processes of restricting access to the public forum for religiously grounded moral viewpoints on the great issues of our times. Knowledge-class attitudes are relevant to my subject simply because awareness of some of these attitudes helps one to understand better how and why the Supreme Court's Religion Clause case law has reached the point where it is described on all sides as confused, inconsistent, and incoherent.

As an aside, however, I would enter a note of skepticism concerning whether that body of law is really so incomprehensible as it is usually said to be. Admittedly, it is incoherent if one is looking for a reasoned elaboration of principles grounded in constitutional text or tradition, or if one expects to see a sustained collegial effort to discern the underlying values of the religion provisions and effectuate them in a reasonably consistent way. Nevertheless, one can comprehend a good deal about court decisions by examining what judges do as well as what they say, and by comparing fact patterns and outcomes in a line of related cases.

I wish to signal here that one also can learn something about the underlying assumptions of the judges from their silences—what they treat as unimportant or what they choose not to mention at all. Viewed in this way, the Supreme Court's church-state jurisprudence since the First Amendment's religion language began to be made binding on the states is a museum of examples of a pervasive cognitive problem in our legal system. The problem is that although we have a highly developed linguistic and conceptual apparatus for thinking about and dealing with individuals, market actors, and the state, we lack adequate concepts to enable us to consider the social dimensions of human personhood, and the social environments that individual men, women, and children require in order to flourish. I have used the word "communities" in my title as a shorthand way of referring to these matters of context. Sociologists often use more cumbersome expressions like "mediating structures" to refer to groups such as families, neighborhoods, religious groups, and other communities of memory and mutual aid that serve as buffers between the citizen and the state. Psychologists like Urie Bronfenbrenner, who are more inclined to emphasize the role of these primary groups in fostering human development and socialization, sometimes speak of "human ecology." Classical political theory underscored the dependency of good government on the nurture and education of citizens and leaders, and hence on the seedbeds of virtue where character is formed and competence acquired.

Curiously, modern American law has rushed headlong into interdisciplinary relationships with economics and some branches of political science, but has been slow to avail itself of the resources and insights of other bodies of social thought. Legal academics seem to have a preference for what they call the "hard" social sciences, by which they mean forms of inquiry that assume away most of the "irrational," messy, and unpredictable aspects of human behavior that are the subjects of examination by the so-called "soft" social sciences. The new field of chaos science, with its emphasis on probabilistic reasoning in complex, ongoing systems, will change all this perhaps in a generation or two. But at the present time, American courts and legal commentators have difficulty in taking a holistic or ecological view of the relationship between legal and social phenomena. The individual-state-market framework, combined with the relentless present-mindedness that pervades our culture generally, makes it hard for us to take adequate account of any but the immediate implications of much of what we say and do. It is almost as though we had decided to set aside two troublesome factors that threaten to gum up our efforts to devise sensible rules, standards, principles, and policies for a complex, heterogeneous, modern state. Those two elements that are missing from so much contemporary legal thought are "society" and "time."

Ironically, however, the peculiar excellence of the Anglo-American common law tradition over centuries, and what chiefly distinguished it from continental "legal science," was its rejection of simplifying abstractions, its close attention to facts and patterns of facts, and its insistence that judges must not only strive to do justice between the parties before them, but must endeavor to maintain principled continuity with the past and to provide guidance for parties similarly situated in the future. It was this unique combination of phronesis and modest—as distinct from "grand"—theory that enabled England and the United States to develop and maintain a legal order strong enough to weather political and social upheavals, yet flexible enough to adapt and contribute to social change constructively. When we distance ourselves from those ways of thinking, we repudiate much of what is best in our professional tradition. We begin to resemble the late Harvard Professor Thomas Reed Powell's famous caricature of the legal mind as "a mind that can think of something that is inextricably connected to something else without thinking of what it's connected to."

There is no mystery about how we American lawyers acquired the mental habits that prevent us from focusing on the social environments that generate, shape, and transmit the practices that sustain the democratic experiment. For most of our history, there simply was no particular reason for statesmen and scholars to pay special attention to families, neighborhoods, religious groups and other associations, or to the connections among them. These social networks were just there—in abundance, seemingly natural, like gravity, on whose continued existence we rely to keep us grounded, steady, and attached to our surroundings.

Certainly no one can blame the Founders for taking for granted the dense texture of eighteenth-century American society, with its family farms and businesses, its tight-knit communities, and its churches firmly woven into the social fabric. Nor would it be fair to say that the Founders underestimated the importance of the institutions whose durability they assumed. On the contrary, there is much evidence that they counted on families, custom, religion, and convention to help preserve and promote the habits and practices they believed to be required for the success of our experiment in ordered liberty. But it seems not to have occurred to our early leaders that there might come a time when the society's ability to produce virtuous citizens and statesmen would falter. In its social resources, as in its natural resources, the United States seemed endowed with inexhaustible riches.

Things were quite different on the other side of the Atlantic, where the French revolutionaries deliberately set out to try to eliminate every intermediate body standing between citizen and state. In this bicentennial of their founding period, it is appropriate to note that a happy byproduct of all that revolutionary fury directed against the family, the guilds, the Church, and the commune system of local government was to bring into being a great school of social and political thought whose leading figures projected their imaginations toward what might happen when and if society actually did lose its intermediate structures. Edmund Burke, Alexis de Tocqueville, and later Emile Durkheim understood that this could not happen overnight—as the revolutionaries had hoped—but that it could be the long-term consequence of several fateful choices that in themselves seemed benign. What would the world be like, they asked, if nothing stood between the free, self-determining individual and the mighty, sovereign state?

The body of social theory they produced affords a useful perspective from which to consider the United States Supreme Court's religion decisions. For we can now see with hindsight that in the 1940s—when the Court decided to incorporate the religion language of the First Amendment into the Fourteenth Amendment, making it binding on the states—industrialization, urbanization, and our special American history of geographic mobility already had begun to take a certain toll on families and other social structures—even though the more dramatic manifestations of demographic change were still two decades down the road. Our social capital, so to speak, was diminishing a bit.

But we should not fault the authors of the early postincorporation decisions for failing to consider that this country might have been consuming its social capital somewhat faster than it was replenishing it. After all, the Court began to apply the religion language of the First Amendment to the states just at a time when the World War II effort had given the country an extraordinary sense of national unity. The members of the Court had every reason to embark on the incorporation project with a sense of complacency about the crisscrossing networks of associations and relationships that constitute the warp and woof of civil society, When some of those justices—notably Hugo Black and William Douglas—went on to become pioneers in the judicial rights revolution that began in the 1950s, they continued to be somewhat cavalier about cultural foundations. In their zeal to protect certain preferred individual liberties, they seem in retrospect—like the French revolutionaries—to have given little thought to the structures that ultimately sustain a regime of rights. Where, one wonders, did they expect Americans to acquire that ingrained respect for the dignity and worth of others that we now demand from our citizens to a higher degree than ever before? How were citizens of our increasingly diverse country supposed to internalize a sense of concern for their fellow human beings in need that would be strong enough to support the expanded welfare activities of government? To pin so many of their hopes in this regard on the public schools, as some of the judges seem to have done, was to underestimate seriously the extent to which the public schools themselves depended, and still depend, on the support of, and interaction with, families and their surrounding communities.

## INCORPORATION AND THE "WALL OF SEPARATION"

What started out as mere judicial inattention to the role of religious groups in American social ecology seems to have passed over time into a more studied indifference. Purely as a matter of judicial craftsmanship, it is striking in retrospect to observe how little intellectual curiosity most members of the Court demonstrated in the challenge presented by the fact that the First Amendment's religion language was made binding against the states just when state and federal relations were undergoing momentous changes, and when the federal government was rapidly expanding its reach into towns, cities, and local school districts. Incorporation in the 1940s posed an intriguing set of legal-political questions—real brain-teasers that should have called forth every ounce of energy, wit, technical skill, and imagination available to the Court. Yet it is hard to escape the impression in reading the decisions that—regardless of outcomes—important claims and arguments were rather lightly dismissed, and practical implications regularly were ignored. The Court skipped right over formidable interpretive problems that required the kind of attention to language, history, and purposes that its members had lavished on many other parts of the Constitution: Are the establishment and free exercise provisions two separate "clauses," each with its own set of values, and somewhat in tension with one another? Or is there but one religion clause whose establishment and free exercise provisions serve one central value—the freedom of religion? Is free exercise an individual right, or does it also have associational and institutional aspects? Far from grappling seriously with these and other important questions, Court majorities were content for a considerable period of time, in establishment cases, to use the metaphor of the "wall of separation" as a substitute for reasoned analysis. As for free exercise, it seems frequently to have been left on the sidelines of the rights revolution. Indeed, free exercise in the broad sense took something of a battering in this period from Court majorities who gave a very expansive interpretation to the notion of "establishment" without pausing to consider the costs they might be inflicting on the associational aspects of free exercise.

From time to time, various Justices have given us glimpses of the beliefs and assumptions about religion that undergirded their inclination to construe broadly the establishment language in the Religion Clause: beliefs that religion is "inviolately private"; that it is an "individual experience"; and that "religious beliefs worthy of respect are the product of free and voluntary choice." What is troubling about such presuppositions is that they leave out of consideration the free exercise interests of members of religions to which the idea of a worshipping community is central. In addition, as Michael Sandel has pointed out, they fail to respect persons "who regard [themselves] as claimed by religious commitments they have not chosen"—the men and women who experience religious commitment more as a kind of "yoke" or "encumbrance" than as the product of a shopping expedition in the marketplace of ideas.

In the 1970s, Court majorities eventually shifted away from trying to maintain a "high and impregnable" wall of separation in establishment cases. Nevertheless, the Court's generally expansive understanding of what it means to establish religion continued to breed litigation, and to hinder legislative and local experiments with creative use of mediating structures to deliver social services.

Nowhere have the deleterious effects of an excessively narrow view of free exercise and an inflated concept of establishment been more apparent than in the cases involving education. In a judicial pincer movement, one line of decisions requires the public schools to be rigorously secular, while another has struck down most forms of public assistance to parents of private school students who desire to protect their children from a public educational system that is often actively promoting values that are profoundly at odds with the family's religious convictions. The net result has been that a crucial aspect of religious freedom can be exercised only by families wealthy enough to afford private education after paying taxes to support public schools. Nor is private education an entirely safe harbor from intrusive and homogenizing governmental regulation. The Court's 1972 decision in *Wisconsin v. Yoder*, does, of course, give some parents one other option: They can withdraw their children from school altogether. But most families do not even have that alternative, for *Yoder* by its terms is very narrow, and courts have shown no inclination to accept claims that the free exercise provision grounds a right to home-schooling.

All these trends culminated in, and were symbolized by, *Aguilar v. Felton*, the 1985 case in which the Court struck down a Great Society program designed to provide federal aid to educationally deprived children from low-income families. Under the specific program involved in *Aguilar*, public school teachers in New York City furnished remedial services and instruction to poor children with special needs in the city's private schools as well as to public school students. Of the private school children that were helped by this program, 84 percent were in Catholic schools and 8 percent were in Hebrew day schools. After nineteen years of successful operation, six "taxpayers" attacked this program as a violation of the establishment provision of the Religion Clause. Justice William Brennan, in a brief opinion for a five-to-four majority, agreed that it impermissibly entangled church and state. The fatal entanglement arose from a Catch-22 under the *Lemon* test: The program had to be monitored by the school district to assure that the public school teachers did not become involved in advancing religion, but the process of monitoring was itself an impermissible form of state involvement with religion.

Justice Sandra Day O'Connor's dissent in *Aguilar* could serve as an indictment of the Court's general approach to establishment issues from 1947 onward. She chided Justice Brennan for the abstract and perfunctory character of his analysis, for his failure to inquire into the practical operation of the program he struck down, and for his lack of concern with the effects of the Court's decision on the lives and prospects of 20,000 poor special-needs children in New York City—not to mention children in similar programs in other parts of the country. She pointed out that the record did not show a single incident of religious "inculcation" by the public school teachers during the nineteen years that this large-scale program had been in successful operation. She noted, too, that this unblemished history was hardly surprising in view of another undisputed fact: three-quarters of the teachers in the program did not even have the same religious affiliation as the schools in which they taught. Nevertheless, a majority on the Court in *Aguilar* condemned a benign, carefully worked out legislative settlement by mechanically applying an abstract "test."

## EMERGING PATTERNS

It seems fair to observe that until the composition of the Court began to change in the mid-1980s, the decisions under the religion language of the First Amendment showed few signs of giving difficult and important issues the concentrated attention that they needed and deserved. With the departure of Justice Lewis Powell from the Court and his replacement by Justice Anthony Kennedy, a period of paradigm change seemed to be opening. But the Court soon veered alarmingly in the direction of yet another simplistic approach—this time toward reflexive deference to the elected branches of government.

The most serious problem with the emerging deferential approach is that, if applied with the same rigidity as was the old strict separationist approach, it is highly threatening to free exercise concerns, especially where members of small, unpopular, or unconventional religions are involved. The Court's decisions in the Air Force yarmulke case, the prison worship case, and, most recently, the peyote discharge case are troubling in this respect. The problem is not so much the bare results in those cases—reasonable people differ whether some or all of them are justified by strong governmental interests. The problem is the majority's reasoning, or more precisely, its lack of reasoning—its inclination to defer mechanically without examining the governmental interest asserted, and without reckoning the burden to free exercise.

One might imagine that flexible and principled—as opposed to rigid and mechanical—deference could have certain advantages over its predecessors, at least in cases involving claims of establishment. Unlike rigorously separationist approaches, it would not carry overtones of those attitudes Justice Arthur Goldberg once described as "a brooding and pervasive devotion to the secular and a passive, or even active, hostility, to the religious." It would be more sensitive to the significant regional variations that exist in this country, and more respectful of local democratic decisionmaking. It would be apt to facilitate utilization of mediating structures that, as Peter Berger and Richard John Neuhaus have argued, can often deliver social services more efficiently, more economically, and more humanely than the state. And it would be likely to promote an important form of free exercise if it were to facilitate support of parental choice in education. It seems unfortunate that so much attention and energy have been expended for and against prayer in public schools, when more urgent issues are the current state of the public schools themselves and the growing sense of many parents that they are losing the struggle for the hearts and minds of their children.

*Employment Division* v. *Smith,* however, looks very much like a decisive step by a Court majority toward an excessively rigid and deferential approach to church–state issues. I would like to suggest, though, that there is some basis for believing that such a conclusion is premature. In the first place, Justice Scalia's opinion in *Smith* does not unambiguously purport to represent a comprehensive reordering of a body of law that took over forty years to become confused and unworkable. Furthermore, if one takes into consideration the views on religious freedom that have been expressed on various occasions by most of the individual justices who joined in the result in *Smith*, it is hard to believe that this one case represents their last word on a subject to which they have devoted so much thought in dissents and separate concurrences over the years. Keeping in mind that it required decades for the law in this area to achieve its present tangled state, it seems reasonable to expect a few fits and even false starts as the Court strives to work out a better way of dealing with the sensitive and important issues involved in these cases.

Prominent among the elements that one might expect to play a role in the process of developing a more principled and workable approach is Chief Justice William Rehnquist's judicial statesmanship, his attention to history, his often expressed solicitude for the role of religion as a mediating structure, and his approach to federalism. Another is Justice Byron White's longstanding call for a thorough reconsideration of the case law in this area—a process that has not yet taken place. Justice Scalia's fidelity to constitutional text, a text which is no more neutral on the value of religion than it is on the value of free speech or a free press, also may prove pivotal. Yet another factor is Justice Kennedy's alertness to the way in which purported "neutrality" can mask "hostility" to religion, a concern that in many cases cannot be alleviated without some scrutiny of the purpose and effects of laws that appear neutral on their face. A key role undoubtedly will be played by Justice O'Connor. Her willingness to listen, her careful attention to all points of view, her inclination to proceed cautiously case-by-case, her persistence in demanding justification, and her attention to facts and practical consequences, all combine to bring the rich resources of the common law tradition to bear on problems to which the Court in the past has given short shrift.

Possibly, some would say probably, a Court majority will once again, without much deliberation, brush the Religion Clause aside while it pursues an unrelated constitutional agenda. *Smith* may, as many fear, be the decisive step toward a reflexive majoritarianism as simplistic in its way as was the old anti-majoritarianism. But another plausible trajectory seems to be that *Smith* will come to be seen as mainly explicable in relation to a strong national policy relating to a severe social problem. That is, just as *Bob Jones University* v. *United States* is more of an anti-discrimination case than a Religion Clause case, so Smith may turn out to be primarily a drug case—a detour, rather than a landmark, in First Amendment case law. Not every judicial slip gives rise to a long line of progeny.

My hopeful reading of the post-1987 religion cases is that they show a closely divided Court earnestly beginning to struggle with the formidable interpretive difficulties of the Constitution's religion language. The path they are taking may be erratic, but this group of justices is, at least, taking the Religion Clause seriously. Whether they will unite on a workable approach for a pluralistic society, and whether they will restore religion to its rightful place as the first among freedoms, remains to be seen.

# The Illusion of Absolute Rights

*This essay, adapted from my 1991 book, Rights Talk (New York: Free Press, 1991), calls attention to one of the most striking and problematic features of the American rights dialect: our tendency to treat the rights we like as absolute. The essay appeared in the Fall 1991 issue of The Responsive Community.*[1]

A MAN'S HOME IS HIS CASTLE. That maxim (traditionally attributed to Sir Edward Coke) was Marvin Sokolow's defense when he was hauled into a Queens County court by his landlord after his downstairs neighbors had complained about the noise above them. They claimed that their peace and quiet were being destroyed by the Sokolow children, ages two and four. The landlord sought to evict the Sokolows on the basis of a clause in their lease providing that no tenant shall make, or permit any members of his family to make, "disturbing noises" or otherwise interfere with the "rights, comforts, or convenience of other tenants."

In rendering his decision, Judge Daniel Fitzpatrick went right to the heart of the matter. "The difficulty of the situation here," he said, "is that Mr. Sokolow's castle is directly above the castle of Mr. Levin." The judge sympathized with the Levins, a middle-aged working couple who cherished a quiet evening at home after a grueling day in Manhattan. He was understanding about the Sokolows' predicament as well. The judge opined that "children and noise have been inseparable from a time whence the mind of man runneth not to the contrary." He took a dim view, however, of Mr. Sokolow's claim that "This is my home, and no one can tell me what to do in my own home." The judge pointed out the obvious fact that modern apartment-house living brings us into a kind of "auditory intimacy" with our neighbors. Apartment dwellers in urban America are in a different relation with each other than lords and ladies living in an age "when castles were remote, separated by broad moors, and when an intruder had to force moat and wall to make his presence felt within."

---

[1] Mary Ann Glendon, "Absolute Rights": Property and Privacy, *The Responsive Community* (Fall 1991): 12–20.

Though he rejected the notion that Mr. Sokolow had the right to do anything he wanted in his home, the judge did not accept the equally extreme position of the landlord and the Levins that, under the lease, *any* disturbing noise provided grounds for throwing a family out of its apartment. Neither the property interest claimed by the tenant nor the contract language relied on by the landlord could be treated as giving rise to absolute rights. Both were subject to evaluation in the light of reason, and in that light the judge found that the noise made by the Sokolows was neither excessive nor deliberate. Noting that the Christmas season was approaching ("a time for peace on earth to men of good will"), Judge Fitzpatrick announced his solution to the problem: "They are all nice people and a little mutual forbearance and understanding of each other's problems should resolve the issues to everyone's satisfaction."

Nice people all over the United States, like Mr. Sokolow and his neighbors, often deploy the rhetoric of rights as though they and their particular interests trumped everything else in sight. So far as property is concerned, few of us have not maintained at one time or another that "it's mine and I can do what I want with it"—whether the "it" is a flag, a backyard, or our own bodies. If a neighbor complains about our stereo, our noisy party, or our late-night piano practicing, our automatic reaction is apt to be that we have a right to do as we please in our own homes.

In these sorts of situations, like Mr. Sokolow, we often try to clinch the argument by appealing to the ancient property rights of Englishmen, and by invoking these rights in the strongest possible way. Yet this careless manner of speaking cannot be blamed on our English legal inheritance, nor even on the American frontier mentality. Neither in England nor even in Canada (where conditions were historically more similar to ours) is the idea of property or the discourse of rights so extravagant.

The exaggerated absoluteness of our American rights dialect is all the more remarkable when we consider how little relation it bears to reality. There is a striking discrepancy, as the *Sokolow* case illustrates, between our tendency to state rights in a stark unlimited fashion and the commonsense restrictions that have to be placed on one person's rights when they collide with those of another person. On any given day, in courtrooms all over the nation, harried judges use a chastened, domesticated concept of rights when they handle garden-variety disputes. Landlords' contract rights do not extend to evicting tenants for any disturbing noise; but tenants cannot make as much noise as they wish in the enclosed space that belongs to them.

Property, historically the paradigmatic right in England and the United States, has always been subject to reasonable regulation, despite the excited rhetoric that often attends its assertion. How then can we explain the persistence of absoluteness in our property rhetoric, and in our rights rhetoric in general? To find the beginnings of an answer, we must go back to the first great "moment" in the history of rights, when property became the template from which other American rights were cut.

Property acquired its near-mythic status in our legal tradition, in part, because the language and images of John Locke played such a key role in American thinking about government. To show that property rights were "natural" and prepolitical, Locke postulated a "state of nature" in which "every man has a property in his own Person," and in the "Labour of his Body, and the Work of his Hands." When a man "mixed" his labor with something by removing it from its natural state, Locke argued, he made the acorn—or the apple, or the fish, or the deer—his property, "at least where there is enough, and as good left in common for others." The same was true, Locke said, for his appropriation of land by tilling, planting, and cultivating. After spinning this famous tale, Locke went on to his next proposition— namely, that the essential reason human beings submit to government is to safeguard their "property." In a move that was to have great significance for Americans, he announced that he would use the word *property* to designate, collectively, *Lives, Liberties, and Estates.* According to Locke, the preservation of property, in this capacious sense, is "the great and *chief end*" for which men come together into commonwealths.

Locke's property theory entered into a distinctively American property story. It was mediated and reinforced in this respect by William Blackstone's lectures on law that were much more widely read and consulted in the United States than in England. Whereas for Locke property had been a means to an end (constitutional monarchy), it was for Blackstone a good in itself. And what a good! "There is nothing which so generally strikes the imagination and engages the affections of mankind," Blackstone wrote, "as the right of property; or that sole and despotic dominion which one man claims and exercises over the external things of the world, in total exclusion of the rights of any other individual in the universe." In this apostrophe to property, we find no *ifs, ands,* or *buts.* A property owner, Blackstone tells us, rules over what he owns, not merely as a king, but as a despot. Property rights are absolute, individual, and exclusive.

The strong property rights talk of Locke and Blackstone was in the air at the right moment to fuse with certain political factors that helped to make property the cardinal symbol of individual freedom and independence in the United States. Chief among these factors was the uneasiness felt by the Framers of our Constitution concerning the potential threat posed to property rights by popularly elected legislatures. As legal historian Jennifer Nedelsky has put it, the Founding Fathers took property as the "central instance of rights at risk in a republic governed by popularly elected legislatures."

From the very beginning, the absoluteness of American property rhetoric promoted illusions and impeded clear thinking about property rights and rights in general. The Framers' efforts to directly and indirectly protect the

CHAPTER 33 • The Illusion of Absolute Rights

interests of property owners did not, and were not meant to, preclude considerable public regulation of property. The Fifth Amendment expressly recognized the federal eminent domain or "takings" power. In the nineteenth century, the takings authority was liberally invoked, especially at the state level, to promote economic development, and notably to aid railroads in acquiring land. Furthermore, traditional flexible legal limitations on the rights of owners (such as the broad principle that one should not use one's property to inflict harm on others) were routinely applied in the capillaries of private law.

Despite many limitations on property rights in practice, the paradigm of property as a specially important, and very strong, right continued to exert a powerful influence on the law. From the latter years of the nineteenth century up to the 1930s, the Supreme Court repeatedly invoked property rights (in an expansive form) to strike down a series of progressive laws that, taken together, might have served to ease the transition here, as similar legislation did in Europe, to a modern mixed economy and welfare state.

While the Supreme Court was thus according a high level of protection to the interests of owners of productive property, courts at the state level were diligently using the law of trespass to erect a protective shield around another kind of property: the family home. Legal historian Aviam Soifer has written that "the rhetoric surrounding legal doctrine from the middle to the end of the nineteenth century tended to reinforce [beliefs of most white male Americans that they were] entirely free to contract for, hold, and devise property as they saw fit."

The heyday of the absolutist property paradigm in American *law* came to an end more than fifty years ago when the Supreme Court, under heavy pressure to uphold the economic and labor legislation of the Depression and New Deal period, repudiated several earlier cases in which it had sacrificed progressive legislation on the altar of a broad notion of "property."

Nevertheless, the paradigm persists in popular discourse and still occasionally receives lip service even from the Supreme Court. The Court's now-common subordination of property to other rights makes it all the more remarkable that property continues to cast its spell and to entrance the minds of legal scholars as well as laypersons. In America, when we want to protect something, we try to get it characterized as a right. To a great extent, it is still the case that when we *especially* want to hold on to something (welfare benefits, a job) we try to get the object of our concern characterized as a property right.

There are Lockean echoes in the efforts of many persons on both the left and right of the American political spectrum to link "property" with liberty and independence. Each camp, of course, has a different understanding of property. Since land ownership can no longer serve to provide the majority of citizens with a protected sphere, jobs and their associated benefits (especially pensions) are the principal bases for whatever economic security most middle-class people possess. Welfare benefits have become the meager counterpart for a large part of the poverty-level population. As the importance of employment and social assistance for status and security came to be appreciated, Thurman Arnold, Charles Reich, and other legal theorists began to try to reconceptualize jobs and welfare as new forms of property. In the 1960s reformist lawyers launched a campaign to persuade the Supreme Court that welfare benefits, Social Security, and government jobs should be treated as property for constitutional purposes. This effort had only limited success in a series of cases that established that one could not be deprived of welfare benefits and certain other statutory entitlements without an opportunity to be heard. Conservative lawyers, for their part, have had equally modest success in trying to convince the Court that the takings clause should accord more protection to the type of property that interests them—the wealth produced by the free operation of market forces.

Much of the attention the Supreme Court once lavished on a broad concept of property, including the freedom of contract to acquire it, it now devotes to certain other liberties that it has designated as "fundamental." Remarkably, the property paradigm, including the old language of absoluteness, broods over this developing jurisprudence of personal rights. The new right of privacy, like the old right of property, has been imagined by the Court and lawyers generally as marking off a protected sphere that surrounds the individual. Indeed, much of the old property rhetoric has simply been transferred to this new area, and the Court has re-experienced familiar difficulties in working out principled limitations on a right that seemed for a time to have no bounds.

Though the "preferred" rights change from time to time, American legal discourse still promotes careless habits of speaking and thinking about them. Mr. Sokolow spoke for many of us when he claimed that no one could tell him what not to do in his own home. He must have known perfectly well that he could not print dollar bills, raise chickens, commit mayhem, or even have a late-night jam session in his Queens castle. When he spoke as he did, he was not speaking the language of the Founders. Still less was he speaking the language of the early colonists, who accepted much official (and officious) intrusion into their personal lives. The frontier offered more scope, perhaps, for the illusion of absoluteness, but the circumstances of those who opened the West were also conducive to a vivid awareness of human vulnerability and interdependence. Where then does this tough talk come from? Why do we Americans habitually exaggerate the absoluteness of the important rights we legitimately claim?

The starkness of some of the language in the Bill of Rights has helped to legitimate intemperate arguments made by those who have a particular attachment to one of the rights framed in such terms. But stark constitutional formulations alone cannot explain our fondness for absolute rights talk. For property rights appear in the Constitution only in an oblique and implicitly qualified form: "No person . . . shall be deprived of . . . property, without due process of law; nor shall private property be taken for public use, without just compensation." In the case of property, it was not the Fifth Amendment but the Lockean paradigm, cut loose from its context, that became part of our property story as well as of our rights discourse. Blackstone's flights of fancy about property as absolute dominion stuck in American legal imaginations more than his endless boring pages on what property owners really might and might not do with what they owned.

However, neither Lockean rights rhetoric as mediated by Blackstone nor constitutional language can account directly or fully for the illusions of absoluteness that are promoted by American rights talk. Another key piece of the puzzle is the pervasiveness of legal culture in American society. The strong language that Mr. Sokolow and the rest of us so frequently use is remarkably similar to a certain type of lawyers' talk that has increasingly passed into common parlance. A large legal profession, whose most visible members habitually engaged in strategic exaggeration and overstatement, was already having a substantial effect on popular discourse in Alexis de Tocqueville's day. The rank and file of the legal profession, it is true, spend the greater part of their professional lives in the undramatic business of adjusting one person's rights with another's. But we are not only the most lawyer-ridden society in the world, we are also the country in which the lawyer's role is the most adversarial. The careful, precise, professional jargon of the workaday office lawyer appears in popular discourse mainly in caricature ("whereas hereinbefore provided"), while the highly colored language of advocacy flows out to the larger society on the lips of orators, statesmen, and flamboyant courtroom performers. Courtroom law talk, it should be noted, rests on an assumption that is not generally to be commended in civil conversation: that when each of two disputants pushes his or her version of the facts and theory of law to the ethically permissible limit, some third party will be smart enough to figure out from the two distorted accounts what probably happened and how the law should be brought to bear on the case.

What's wrong with a little exaggeration, one might ask, especially in the furtherance of something as important as individual rights? If we always took care to note that rights are qualified, would we not risk eroding them altogether? Well, no. In the first place, no one can be an absolutist for *all* our constitutionally guaranteed rights, because taking any one of them as far as it can go soon brings it into conflict with another. Second, the rhetoric of absoluteness increases the likelihood of conflict and inhibits the sort of dialogue that is increasingly necessary in a pluralistic society. In the common enterprise of ordering our lives together, much depends on communication, reason giving, and mutual understanding. Even the legal profession is beginning to question the utility and legitimacy of the traditional strategic adoption of extreme positions by lawyers. Lawyers, as well as clients, are reckoning the social cost of our unique brand of adversary litigation. How ironic it would be if the American legal profession became more sophisticated about alternative methods of dispute resolution, yet the old hardball litigators' talk lingered on in the rest of society and continued to make it difficult for neighbors and family members to deal with the frictions inherent in everyday living.

Claims of absoluteness have the further ill effect of tending to downgrade rights into the mere expression of unbounded desires and wants. Excessively strong formulations express our most infantile instincts rather than our potential to be reasonable men and women. A country in which we can do "anything we want" is not a republic of free people attempting to order their lives together.

Absoluteness is an illusion, and hardly a harmless one. When we assert our rights to life, liberty, and property, we are expressing the reasonable hope that these good things can be made more secure by law and politics. When we assert these rights in an absolute form, however, we are expressing infinite and impossible desires—to be completely free, to possess things totally, to be masters of our fate and captains of our souls. There is pathos as well as bravado in these attempts to deny the fragility and contingency of human existence, personal freedom, and the possession of worldly goods.

The exaggerated absoluteness of our American rights rhetoric is closely bound up with its other distinctive traits: a near-silence concerning responsibility and a tendency to envision the rights bearer as a lone autonomous individual. Thus, for example, those who contest the legitimacy of mandatory automobile seat belt or motorcycle helmet laws frequently say: "It's my body and I have the right to do as I please with it." In this shibboleth, the old horse of property is harnessed to the service of an unlimited liberty. The implication is that no one else is affected by the exercise of the individual right in question. This way of thinking and speaking ignores the fact that it is the rare driver, passenger, or biker who does not have a child, a spouse, or a parent. It glosses over the likelihood that if the rights bearer comes to grief, the cost of medical treatment, rehabilitation, and long-term care will be spread among many others.

CHAPTER 33 • The Illusion of Absolute Rights

# CHAPTER 34

# John Paul II,
# Letter to Mary Ann Glendon
# and Holy See's Delegation to the
# Fourth World Conference on Women

*Prior to our departure for Beijing, the Holy See Delegation met with John Paul II
and received from him the following letter, dated August 29, 1995. Through this letter,
the Holy See was the first state to respond to Secretary General Boutros Ghali's call
for participating nations to make specific commitments
for the improvement of the condition of women.[1]*

As YOU PREPARE to leave for Beijing, I am happy to meet you, the head of
the delegation of the Holy See to the Fourth World Conference on Women,
and the other members of the delegation. Through you, I extend my best
wishes and prayers to the secretary-general of the conference, to the participant nations and organizations, as well as to the authorities of the host country, the People's Republic of China.

My wishes are for the success of this conference in its aim to guarantee
all the women of the world "equality, development, and peace," through full
respect for their equal dignity and for their inalienable human rights, so that
they can make their full contribution to the good of society.

Over the past months, on various occasions I have drawn attention to
the positions of the Holy See and to the teaching of the Catholic Church on
the dignity, rights, and responsibilities of women in today's society: in the
family, in the workplace, in public life. I have drawn inspiration from the
life and witness of great women within the Church throughout the centuries
who have been pioneers within society as mothers, as workers, as leaders in
the social and political fields, in the caring professions, and as thinkers and
spiritual leaders.

---

[1] John Paul II, letter to Mary Ann Glendon and the Holy See's Delegation to the Fourth
World Conferences on Women, 29 August 1995.

The secretary-general of the United Nations has asked the participating nations at the Beijing conference to announce concrete commitments for the improvement of the condition of women.

Having looked at the various needs of women in today's world, the Holy See wishes to make a specific option regarding such a commitment: an option in favor of girls and young women. Therefore, I call all Catholic caring and educational institutions to adopt a concerted and priority strategy directed to girls and young women, especially to the poorest, over the coming years.

It is disheartening to note that in today's world the simple fact of being a female rather than a male can reduce the likelihood of being born or of surviving childhood; it can mean receiving less-adequate nutrition and health care; and it can increase the chance of remaining illiterate and having only limited access or none at all even to primary education.

Investment in the care and education of girls as an equal right is a fundamental key to the advancement of women. It is for this reason that today I appeal to all the educational services linked to the Catholic Church to guarantee equal access for girls, to educate boys to a sense of women's dignity and worth, to provide additional possibilities for girls who have suffered disadvantage, and to identify and remedy the reasons which cause girls to drop out of education at an early stage.

I appeal to those institutions which are involved in health care, especially primary health care, to make improved basic health care and education for girls a hallmark of their service.

I appeal to the Church's charitable and development organizations to give priority in the allocation of resources and personnel to the special needs of girls.

I appeal to congregations of religious sisters, in fidelity to the special charism and mission given to them by their founders, to identify and reach out to those girls and young women who are most on the fringes of society, who have suffered most, physically and morally, who have the least opportunity. Their work of healing, caring, educating, and of reaching to the poorest is needed in every part of the world today.

I appeal to Catholic universities and centers of higher education to ensure that in the preparation of future leaders in society they acquire a special sensitivity to the concerns of young women.

I appeal to women and women's organizations within the Church and active in society to establish patterns of solidarity so that their leadership and guidance can be put at the service of girls and young women.

As followers of Jesus Christ, who identifies himself with the least among children, we cannot be insensitive to the needs of disadvantaged girls, especially those who are victims of violence and a lack of respect for their dignity.

In the spirit of those great Christian women who have enlightened the life of the Church throughout the centuries and who have often called the

Church back to her essential mission and service, I make an appeal to the women of the Church today to assume new forms of leadership in service, and I appeal to all the institutions of the Church to welcome this contribution of women.

I appeal to all men in the Church to undergo, where necessary, a change of heart and to implement as a demand of their faith a positive vision of women. I ask them to become more and more aware of the disadvantages to which women, and especially girls, have been exposed and to see where the attitude of men, their lack of sensitivity or lack of responsibility, may be at the root.

Once again, through you I wish to express my good wishes to all those who have responsibility for the Beijing conference and to assure them of my support as well as that of the Holy See and the institutions of the Catholic Church for a renewed commitment of all to the good of the world's women.

# CHAPTER 35

# Advancing Women's Freedom and Dignity

*In my first statement at the Beijing Women's Conference, delivered on September 5, 1995, I noted where the Holy See concurred with the draft Platform of Action, but called attention to those areas where the document needed improvement if it were to be responsive to the needs and values of women who dedicate themselves to motherhood and family responsibilities. The 22-member Holy See delegation, mostly composed of women from five continents, was the most ethnically diverse delegation at the conference.[1]*

## THE HOLY SEE'S INTERVENTION AT THE OPENING SESSION OF THE 1995 U.N. WOMEN'S CONFERENCE IN BEIJING

*Madam Chairperson,*

THIS FOURTH WORLD CONFERENCE ON WOMEN, devoted to equality, development and peace, follows a series of International Conferences which will surely mark the international social climate, as we move to the end of this millennium and to the beginning of the new one. From Rio de Janeiro to Vienna, from Cairo to Copenhagen, and now here in Beijing, the community of nations and each single State have been focusing their attention on the significance and the practical consequences of what was affirmed in the first principle of the *Rio Declaration*, namely, that human beings are at the center of the concern for sustainable development.

Today more than ever, our task is to move from aspiration to action. We must see that what has been affirmed at the universal level becomes a reality in the everyday lives of women in all parts of the world. The historical oppression

---

[1] Mary Ann Glendon, "Advancing Women's Freedom and Dignity: The Holy See's Intervention at the Opening Session of the 1995 U.N. Women's Conference in Beijing," The Fourth World Conference on Women, The United Nations, Beijing, 5 September 1995.

of women has deprived the human race of untold resources. Recognition of the equality in dignity and fundamental rights of women and men, and guaranteeing access by all women to the full exercise of those rights, will have far-reaching consequences and will liberate enormous reserves of intelligence and energy sorely needed in a world that is groaning for peace and justice.

During the preparations for this conference, the Holy See has listened carefully to the hopes, fears, and daily concerns of women in various parts of the world and from different walks of life, as well as to their criticisms. Pope John Paul II has directly addressed the concerns of the conference in numerous talks and encounters, especially in his recent personal *Letter to Women*. He has acknowledged the deficiencies of past positions, including those of the Catholic Church, and has welcomed this initiative of the United Nations as an important contribution to a global improvement in the situation of women in today's world.

The delegation of the Holy See, headed by a woman and composed mainly of women with varied backgrounds and experiences, applauds the purpose of the draft Platform of Action to free women at last from the unfair burdens of cultural conditioning that have so often prevented them even from becoming conscious of their own dignity.

The views of the Holy See represent the aspirations of many people, believers of all faiths and non-believers alike, who share the same fundamental vision and wish it to be known. It is only when different viewpoints are sensitively listened to and appreciated that one can arrive at a true discernment of situations and a consensus on how to remedy them.

I will draw attention, therefore, to some of the many points where my delegation concurs with the Platform of Action, while at the same time I will indicate some areas which my delegation feels ought to have been developed in a different manner.

At times in the preparatory process, the Holy See has had strenuously to emphasize that marriage, motherhood, and the family, or the adherence to religious values, should not be presented only in a negative manner. To affirm the dignity and rights of all women requires respect for the roles of women whose quest for personal fulfillment and the construction of a stable society is inseparably linked to their commitments to God, family, neighbor, and especially to their children.

The position of women is linked with the fate of the entire human family. There can be no real progress for women, or men, at the expense of children or of their underprivileged brothers and sisters. Genuine advances for women cannot overlook the inequalities that exist among women themselves. Enduring progress for women must be rooted in solidarity between young and old, between male and female, as well as between those who enjoy a comfortable standard of living with ample access to basic needs and those who are suffering deprivation.

At the same time, it should be clear that promoting women's exercise of all their talents and rights without undermining their roles within the family will require calling not only husbands and fathers to their family responsibilities, but governments to their social duties.

Because so many women face exceptional difficulties as they seek to balance greater participation in economic and social life with family responsibilities, this conference rightly places a high priority on the right of women to effectively enjoy equal opportunities with men in the workplace as well as in the decisionmaking structures of society, especially as they affect women themselves.

Justice for women in the workplace requires in the first place the removal of all forms of the exploitation of women and young girls as cheap labor, all too often at the service of the lifestyles of the affluent. It requires equal compensation for equal work, and equal opportunities for advancement, while addressing also the added responsibilities they may bear as working mothers, and according special attention to the problems of women who are the sole providers for their families.

Furthermore, effective action on behalf of working mothers requires recognition of the priority of human over economic values. If efficiency and productivity are considered the primary goals of society, then the values of motherhood will be penalized. The fear of reinforcing certain stereotypes concerning the roles of women should not prevent this conference from clearly addressing the special challenges and the real life needs and values of those millions of women who dedicate themselves to motherhood and family responsibilities on a full-time basis or who reconcile them with other activities of a social and economic nature. Our societies offer far too little tangible recognition or concrete assistance to those women who are struggling to do a decent job of raising children in economically trying circumstances. For our conference not to face these issues would be to render true equality for the majority of the world's women even more elusive.

The Holy See, at this conference, as it did on the occasion of the World Summit on Social Development, stresses the importance of finding new ways of recognizing the economic and social importance of women's unremunerated work, in the family, in the production and conservation of food, and in a wide range of socially productive work within the community. Women must be guaranteed measures of economic and social security which reflect their equal dignity, their equal rights to ownership of property and access to credit and resources. The effective contribution of women's work to economic security and social well-being is often greater than that of men.

I wish to return now to the fact that so many women today do not have access to those basic rights which belong to them as human beings, to the extent, in fact, as I have said, that they are often even unaware of their own dignity. I return to this theme to indicate some areas of special concern and commitment of the Holy See for the coming years.

It is well-known that the Catholic Church, in its manifold structures, has been a pioneer and leader in providing education to girls in both developed and developing countries and often in areas and cultures where few groups were willing to provide equal educational opportunities to both girls and boys.

Every human person has the right to be helped to make the fullest use of the talents and abilities they possess and thus, as the *Universal Declaration of Human Rights* asserts, "Everyone has the right to education." Universal access to basic education is, indeed, an established goal of all nations. Yet in today's world, of the scandalously high number of persons who are illiterate, over two-thirds are women. Of the millions of children who are not enrolled in basic education, about 70 percent are girls. What is to be said of the situation in which the simple fact of being a girl reduces the likelihood of even being born, of survival, or of then receiving adequate education, nutrition, and health care?

On August 29 last, His Holiness Pope John Paul II committed all of the over 300,000 social, caring, and educational institutions of the Catholic Church to a concerted and priority strategy directed to girls and young women, and especially to the poorest, to ensure for them equality of status, welfare, and opportunity, especially with regard to literacy and education, health and nutrition, and to ensure that they can, in all circumstances, continue and complete their education. The Holy See has made a special appeal to the Church's educational institutions and religious congregations, on their own or as part of wider national strategies, to make this commitment in favor of the girl-child a reality. This is, in fact, a commitment already assumed at the Copenhagen Summit for Social Development, and the Holy See, as on that occasion, places itself side by side with all the governments of the world to work in collaboration with them on such programs of education. More and more it is recognized that investment in the education of girls is the fundamental key to the later full advancement of women.

The question of education is closely linked with the question of poverty and the fact that the majority of those who today live in abject poverty are women and children. Efforts must be strengthened to eliminate all those cultural and legal obstacles which impair the economic security of women. The reasons specific to each region or economic system which render women more likely to bear the heavier burden of poverty must be addressed. No part of the world is without its scandal of poverty which strikes women most. Every society has its specific pockets of poverty, of groups of persons especially exposed to poverty, at times within sight of others whose patterns of consumption and lifestyle are all too often insensitive and unsustainable. The "feminization of poverty" must be of concern to all women. Its social political, and economic roots must be addressed. Women themselves must be in the forefront in the fight against the inequalities among women in today's world through concrete caring and direct solidarity with the poorest among women.

May I draw attention here to the extraordinary work that has been done, and is being done today, by a category of women whose service is so often taken for granted: that of religious sisters. In their communities they have developed innovative forms of female spirituality. From their communities, they have developed forms of solidarity, caring, and leadership for and among women. They are examples of how religious principles are for so many women today a source of inspiration in fostering a new identity for women and a source of perseverance in the service and advancement of women.

The Holy See also recognizes the need to address the urgent specific health care needs of women. It supports the special emphasis of the conference documents on expanding and improving women's health care, especially since so many women in today's world do not even have access to a basic health care center. In such a situation, the Holy See has expressed its concern regarding a tendency to focus privileged attention and resources on the consideration of health problems related to sexuality, whereas a comprehensive approach to the health of all women would have to place greater emphasis on such questions as poor nutrition, unsafe water, and those diseases that afflict millions of women each year, taking a vast toll on mothers and children.

The Holy See concurs with the Platform of Action in dealing with questions of sexuality and reproduction, where it affirms that changes in the attitudes of both men and women are necessary conditions for achieving equality and that responsibility in sexual matters belongs to both men and women. Women are, moreover, most often the victims of irresponsible sexual behavior, in terms of personal suffering, of disease, poverty, and the deterioration of family life. The conference documents, in the view of my delegation, are not bold enough in acknowledging the threat to women's health arising from widespread attitudes of sexual permissiveness. The document likewise refrains from challenging societies that have abdicated their responsibility to attempt to change, at their very roots, irresponsible attitudes and behavior.

The international community has consistently stressed that the decision of parents concerning the number of their children and the spacing of births must be made freely and responsibly. In this context, the Catholic Church's teaching on procreation is often misunderstood. To say that it supports procreation at all costs is indeed a travesty of its teaching on responsible parenthood. Its teaching on the means of family planning is often regarded as too demanding on persons. But no way of ensuring deep respect for human life and its transmission can dispense with self-discipline and self-restraint, particularly in cultures which foster self-indulgence and immediate gratification. Responsible procreation also requires especially the equal participation and sharing of responsibility by husbands, something which will only be achieved through a process of changing attitudes and behavior.

The Holy See joins with all participants in the conference in the condemnation of coercion in population policies. It is to be hoped that the recommendations of this conference to this effect will be adhered to by all nations. It is also to be hoped that, in order to arrive at informed consent, couples will be provided with clear information about all possible health risks associated with family planning methods, especially where these are at an experimental stage or in cases where their use in certain nations has been restricted.

There is clear consensus within the international community that abortion should not be promoted as a means of family planning and that all efforts must be made to eliminate those factors which lead women to seek abortions. Pope John Paul II has emphasized, in speaking of the responsibility for a woman's tragic and painful decision to have an abortion, "before being something to blame on the woman," there are occasions when "guilt needs to be attributed to men and to the complicity of the general social environment."[2] All who are genuinely committed to the advancement of women can and must offer a woman or a girl who is pregnant, frightened, and alone a better alternative than the destruction of her own unborn child. Once again, concerned women must take the lead in the fight against societal practices which facilitate the irresponsibility of men, while stigmatizing women, and against a vast industry that extracts its profits from the very bodies of women, while at the same time purporting to be their liberators.

The conference has, however, rendered a great service by casting a spotlight on violence toward women and girls, violence which may be physical, sexual, psychological, or moral. Much more needs to be done in all our societies to identify the range and the causes of violence against women. The extent of sexual violence in the industrialized nations, as it becomes more evident, comes often as a shock to their populations. The fact of the use, in this twentieth century, of sexual violence as an instrument of armed conflict has stunned the conscience of humanity.

All such forms of violence against women should be condemned, and social policies to eliminate the causes of such violence should be given priority consideration. More must be done to eliminate the practice of female genital mutilation and other deplorable practices such as child prostitution, trafficking in children and their organs, and child marriages. Society must also reach out to all those who have been the victims of such violence, ensuring that justice be applied to the perpetrators of such violence as well as offering victims holistic healing and rehabilitation into society.

The question of violence experienced by women is also linked to those factors which underlie the widespread hedonistic and commercial culture

[2] *Letter to Women,* June 29, 1995, No. 5.

which encourages the systematic exploitation of sexuality and especially reduces women to the role of sex objects. Should the conference not condemn such attitudes it could well be accused of condoning the very root-causes of much violence against women and girls.

Finally, I feel that greater attention could have been drawn to the needs of specific categories of women, especially within changing social and economic environments. I will simply mention here elderly women, who are among those who experience special problems in all our societies.

Madam Chairperson, the title of our conference is "equality, development, and peace." We must move from a vision of human persons looked on as mere instruments or objects to one in which every person can fully realize her or his dignity and full potential. Our century has been a century of unprecedented scientific progress, but one also which has seen horrific conflicts and wars. In the midst of a culture of death, it has been very often women who have safeguarded and promoted a civilization of love, preserving the vestiges of human dignity throughout the darkest days and years. Ignored, underestimated, and taken for granted, the beneficent influence of women has radiated throughout history, enriching the lives of successive generations.

It is to the future that we must now look. The freer women are to share their gifts with society and to assume leadership in society, the better are the prospects for the entire human community to progress in wisdom, justice. and dignified living.

The delegation of the Holy See hopes that this conference and the name of the great city of Beijing will be remembered by history as an important moment in which, by advancing women's freedom and dignity, we will have contributed to building a civilization of love where every woman, man, and child can live in peace, liberty, and mutual esteem with full respect for their rights and responsibilities; a civilization where life and love can flourish; a civilization where the culture of death shall have no dominion. May Almighty God accompany us and sustain us in our task.

# CHAPTER 36

# The Unfinished Journey

*At the closing session of the Beijing Conference, I presented the following assessment of the conference's final documents in keeping with the instruction I had received from Pope John Paul II to affirm what was good in the documents, but to denounce what was false and harmful. The text was published in L'Osservatore Romano (English), September 20, 1995.*[1]

## THE HOLY SEE'S FINAL STATEMENT AT THE FOURTH U.N. WORLD CONFERENCE ON WOMEN, 1995

*Madam President,*

"**W**HEN ONE LOOKS AT THE GREAT PROCESS of women's liberation, one sees that the journey has been a difficult one, with its share of mistakes," but headed toward a better future for women. Those are the words of Pope John Paul II. And he goes on to say: "This journey must go on!" The Holy See delegation joins its voice to his: This great journey must go on!

Women's voyage has been marked by false starts and disappointment, as well as by luminous achievements. There have been times, as in the industrial revolution, when old forms of oppression were exchanged for new, as well as times when intelligence and good will have triumphed.

The documents before us reflect that complex and uneven history of women's search. They are full of promise but often short on concrete commitment, and, in certain respects, one could ask if the long-term consequences will really serve the good of women.

The delegation of the Holy See has worked hard in a constructive way and in a spirit of good will to make the documents more responsive to women. Certainly the living heart of these documents lies in their sections on the needs of women in poverty, on strategies for development, on literacy and education, on ending violence against women, on a culture of peace,

---

[1] Mary Ann Glendon, "This great journey must go on! Holy See's final statement in Beijing," *Osservatore Romano* (Weekly edition in English) (1408; 20 September 1995): 4.

and on access to employment, land, capital, and technology. My delegation is pleased to note a close correspondence between these points and Catholic social teaching.

My delegation would be remiss in its duty to women, however, if it did not also indicate several critical areas where it strongly disagrees with the text.

My delegation regrets to note in the text an exaggerated individualism in which key, relevant provisions of the "Universal Declaration of Human Rights" are slighted—for example, the obligation to provide "special care and assistance" to motherhood. This selectivity thus marks another step in the colonization of the broad and rich discourse of universal rights by an impoverished, libertarian rights dialect. Surely this international gathering could have done more for women and girls than to leave them alone with their rights!

Surely we must do more for the girl-child in poor nations than give lip service to providing access to education, health, and social services while carefully avoiding any concrete commitment of new and additional resources to that end.

Surely we can do better than to address the health needs of girls and women by paying disproportionate attention to sexual and reproductive health. Moreover, ambiguous language concerning unqualified control over sexuality and fertility could be interpreted as including societal endorsement of abortion and homosexuality. A document that respects women's dignity should address the health of the whole woman. A document that respects women's intelligence should devote at least as much attention to literacy as to fertility.

Finally, Madam President, because my delegation is hopeful that out of these documents, which are in some ways at odds with themselves, the good for women will ultimately prevail; it wishes to associate itself with the consensus only on those above-mentioned aspects of the Documents that the Holy See considers to be positive and at the service of the real well-being of women.

Unfortunately, the Holy See's participation in the consensus can be only a partial one because of numerous points in the Documents which are incompatible with what the Holy See and other countries deem favorable to the true advancement of women. These points are indicated in the reservations which my delegation has annexed to this statement.

My delegation is confident that women themselves will overcome the limitations of and bring out what is best in these documents. As John Paul II has so well put it, "The path that lies ahead will be difficult; nevertheless, we must have courage to set out on that path and the courage to go on to the end."

# What Happened
# at Beijing

This report on the Beijing Conference appeared
in the January 1996 issue of First Things.[1]

"**Y**OU ARE GOING TO BEIJING to be witnesses," the Holy See's Under-secretary for State Relations told us as we left for the U.N.'s Fourth World Conference on Women last September—daunting words for our twenty-two member band of fourteen women and eight men from nine countries and five continents. In the turmoil of the next two weeks, however, the idea of being witnesses helped our diverse group to coalesce into a unified team that would work, first, to make the document issued by the conference more responsive to the actual lives of women, and, second—in keeping with the Catholic Church's traditional mission to the poor—to be a voice for the marginalized and voiceless women who can seldom make themselves heard in the corridors of power.

We hoped to avoid the situation that developed at the U.N.'s 1994 Conference on Population and Development in Cairo, where an abortion rights initiative led by a hard-edged U.S. delegation pushed all other population and development issues into the background. The Holy See's efforts to correct that skewed emphasis never got through to the public. For the most part, the press accepted the population lobby's caricature of the Vatican at Cairo as anti-woman, anti-sex, and in favor of unrestrained procreation.

Before the Beijing conference opened, indications were that most nations had little disposition to reopen the fragile consensus that had been reached at Cairo. The idea that abortion was a legitimate tool of population control had been expressly rejected in the Cairo document. The U.S. administration, chastened by the November 1994 elections, was unlikely to openly lead another controversial charge. And in any event, the Beijing conference was not a population conference; its mandate was "Action for Equality, Development, and Peace." On those topics, we believed, the Holy See's positions,

---

[1] Mary Ann Glendon, "What Happened at Beijing," *First Things* 59 (January 1996): 30–36.

drawn from the Church's teachings on social and economic justice, stood a better chance of being heard. Our hopes in that regard were only slightly dimmed by our growing awareness that few media people had a clear idea of the subject and scope of the Beijing conference.

The failure of the press (and even many delegates) to do their homework was understandable. The Beijing documents (a brief Declaration and a long-winded Program of Action) were a 149-page (single-spaced) hodgepodge of the good, the bad, and the silly. To a lawyer's eye, they resembled a sprawling piece of legislation, with slabs of ideological pork interspersed among common-sense provisions and bureaucratic boilerplate. They had been produced, naturally, by a committee, the U.N. Commission on the Status of Women.

The drafting process, through two preparatory conferences, was heavily influenced by population control lobbyists and old-line, hard-line feminist groups. Negotiators from members of the U.N. and its specialized agencies reached agreement fairly easily on the bulk of the provisions, but a large proportion of the draft documents went to Beijing in brackets, signifying that no accord could be reached at the preparatory stage.

From the beginning, the documents were at war with themselves in several respects. Many provisions addressed issues of equal opportunity, education, and development in a sensible way. But reading the drafts overall, one would have no idea that most women marry, have children, and are urgently concerned with how to mesh family life with participation in broader social and economic spheres. The implicit vision of women's progress was based on the model—increasingly challenged by men and women alike—in which family responsibilities are avoided or subordinated to personal advancement. When dealing with health, education, and young girls, the drafts emphasized sex and reproduction to the neglect of many other crucial issues. The overall effect was like the Leaning Tower of Pisa, admirable from some angles, but unbalanced, and resting on a shaky foundation.

The first morning's colorful opening ceremony in the Great Hall of the People was an odd mixture of the sublime and the silly—as though replicating the conference documents. Mistresses of ceremonies who appeared to be on loan from the trade show commissariat presided in sequinned evening gowns over a program that mingled ballet dancers and hula-hula girls, a performance by the Chinese Women's Philharmonic orchestra and a parade of fashions, world-class gymnastics, and a martial arts display where the women vanquished all the men.

That was the last hour of relaxation our delegation had until the conference ended. Our negotiators, four women and three men, worked virtually around the clock for the next two weeks in as many as seven separate, concurrent sessions, dealing with the knotty problems that had been left for resolution in Beijing. The rest of us tried to collect and read reams of conference documents, to maintain a presence of at least two persons in the plenary session, to staff our makeshift headquarters, and to "witness" in our communications with other delegations, the media, and Catholics attending the parallel women's forum in Huairou.

We were heartened by Pakistani Prime Minister Benazir Bhutto's speech in the opening plenary session. Mrs. Bhutto zeroed in on some of the defects in the documents. They were, she said, "disturbingly weak" on the role of the traditional family and on the connection between family disintegration and general moral decay. At a subsequent session, U.S. First Lady Hillary Rodham Clinton was clearly mindful of the Senate's bipartisan resolution instructing American delegates not to denigrate motherhood and the family. She condemned direct coercion in population control programs and made several positive references to women's roles as mothers and family members.

Mrs. Clinton's carefully worded speech was just one of many signs that the U.S. had drastically overhauled its strategy since Cairo. Throughout the Beijing conference, the American delegation avoided taking the initiative on controversial issues. They maintained an appearance of cordiality toward the Holy See, skirting open confrontation in negotiations. Members of the U.S. delegation frequently described the Vatican delegation to the press as "conciliatory"—as though we, not they, had changed since Cairo. Some of the beans were spilled by one American negotiator, after she had piped up briefly in favor of rights based on sexual orientation. Later, she told two members of the Holy See team she had momentarily forgotten that "we were told not to speak out on that one."

In my opening statement, I reaffirmed the positions the Holy See had taken at previous conferences, and called attention to several areas where the Beijing drafts needed to be improved. The documents barely mentioned marriage, motherhood, and the family—except negatively as impediments to women's self-realization and as associated with violence and oppression. The women's health section focussed disproportionately on sexual and reproductive matters, with scarcely a glance toward nutrition, sanitation, tropical diseases, access to basic health services, or even maternal morbidity and mortality. Women's poverty was addressed in narrow terms as chiefly a problem of equality between women and men, slighting the influence of family breakdown and unjust economic structures. I pointed out that without recognition and support of their roles in child-raising, effective equality would remain elusive for far too many women. I concluded with the observation that there can be no real progress for women, or men, at the expense of children or of the underprivileged.

These points seemed so reasonable to us that, in the first few days of the conference, we were confident that they would find wide support. Ominous signs, however, soon appeared. Some delegations from developing countries seemed less independent than at Cairo. Holy See negotiators were often receiving short shrift from chairpersons wielding heavy gavels. The procedural difficulties became acute in sessions dealing with the controversial health sections of the draft. Many otherwise inactive delegations showed up, and the negotiating room became especially crowded and chaotic. At one point, when our negotiator attempted to intervene in support of a bracketed paragraph urging that women be informed of the health risks of promiscuity and certain contraceptive methods, the Chair ruled her out of order on grounds that the Holy See, as a Permanent Observer, did not even have the right to vote. By the time the Chair was forced to retract that mistake, the language in question had been eliminated. The tenor of discussion on the issue is captured by the remark of an Egyptian delegate: "If we start telling women about the harmful effects of contraceptives, they might not use them anymore."

By Thursday of the first week, our negotiators were bringing back news of another unexpected development. A minority coalition, led by the powerful fifteen-member European Union negotiating as a bloc, was pushing a version of the sexual and abortion rights agenda that had been rejected by the Cairo conference. The EU-led coalition was so intent on its unfinished Cairo agenda that it was stalling negotiations on other issues. Equally disturbing, the coalition was taking positions with ominous implications for universal human rights.

Joined by a few other countries (Barbados, Canada, Namibia, South Africa), the EU was opposing the inclusion of key, pertinent principles from U.N. instruments where the nations of the world had recognized certain core rights and obligations as universal. The controversy centered on five crucial areas:

1. To bring the treatment of marriage and the family more into line with women's actual needs and aspirations, the Holy See and other negotiators had proposed references to standard international language. The U.N. Universal Declaration of Human Rights was an obvious source. It makes marriage a fundamental right, and provides that "the family is the natural and fundamental group unit of society and is entitled to protection by society and the state" (Art. 16). The EU coalition not only opposed that language, but pressed to pluralize "family" wherever it appeared in the documents. This move would have been innocent enough if it simply referred to the fact that there is no single form of family organization. But here it seemed intended to place a range of alternative lifestyles on the same legal footing as families founded on kinship or marriage, undermining the legal preferences that many countries accord to child-raising families.

2. Similarly, the coalition contested every effort to include the word "motherhood" except where it appeared in a negative light, even though the Universal Declaration provides that "Motherhood and childhood are entitled to special care and assistance" (Art. 25).

3. The coalition sought to remove all references to religion, morals, ethics, or spirituality, except where religion was portrayed as associated with intolerance or extremism. During one stormy negotiating session on women's health, an EU negotiator even opposed a reference to codes of medical ethics, insisting, astonishingly, that "ethics have no place in medicine." The coalition also objected to a paragraph providing for freedom of conscience and religion in the context of education, in spite of the Universal Declaration's provision that "Everyone has the right to freedom of thought, conscience, and religion . . . [including] freedom, either alone or in community with others and in public or private, to manifest his religion or belief in teaching, practice, worship and observance" (Art. 18).

4. Though the Beijing documents had identified the situation of the "girl child" as a "critical area," the coalition attempted to eliminate all recognition of parental rights and duties from the draft, even rejecting direct quotations from the Convention on the Rights of the Child. They seemed indifferent to the fact that the Universal Declaration and subsequent human rights documents have consistently protected the parent-child relationship from outside intrusion.

5. Finally, the coalition made strenuous efforts to remove references to "human dignity" as used in the Preamble of the Universal Declaration of Human Rights: "[R]ecognition of inherent human dignity and of the equal and inalienable rights of all members of the human family" is the very "foundation of freedom, justice, and peace." They apparently feared that dignity language might legitimate departures from the equality principle. Equality and dignity, however, are inseparable in the Declaration. To eliminate dignity is to undermine the concept that human rights, including equality, belong to all men and women by virtue of their inherent worth as human beings, rather than existing at the whim of this or that political regime.

The EU caucus's assault on key provisions of the universal human rights corpus was something of a mystery. Europe, after all, prides itself on being the cradle and custodian of many of these ideas. More puzzling still, the EU negotiators' stances on these matters were at variance with similar provisions in most of their own national constitutions and with the underlying principles of their own family assistance programs.

In the stark vision promoted by the EU caucus at Beijing, there is no room for the idea that society has a special interest in providing the best possible conditions for raising children. Family life, marriage, and motherhood would be worthy of no more protection than any other ways in which adults choose to order their lives. The girl child, her parents nowhere visible, would be alone with her rights. A document embodying that vision would cast a shadow over programs and policies that provide assistance to child-raising families, just at a time when most countries are already curtailing their social expenditures. A document on women's issues from which all positive references to motherhood and family life were removed would send a discouraging message to women who take pride and satisfaction in family roles.

The EU negotiators' positions can be explained in part by a phenomenon Americans know well—the tendency when arguing for a favorite right to brush aside all other rights and obligations. The EU-led coalition was so single-minded in its determination to seed the Beijing documents with sexual and reproductive rights that it was willing to let important competing values go by the boards. At least that was how it seemed when the Holy See's Ambassador to the U.N., Archbishop Renato Martino, and I met with Christina Alberdi, leader of the European Union caucus, and, later on the same day, with several members of the French delegation. We raised our concerns about human rights issues at both meetings. The delegates and their assistants listened politely, thanked us for our point of view, but were not forthcoming with any explanation.

After several similar encounters, I was reminded of the Cook County criminal courts of the 1960s, when occasionally the rumor would go around the corridors that "the fix was in" on a particular case. I began to wonder whether a blend of sexism and political expediency had induced some governments to regard the women's conference as unimportant in itself, and thus to treat delegation appointments as handy sops to throw to old-line feminists and population control zealots. That would explain the now unmistakable emergence of an unfinished Cairo agenda, the hot pursuit of sexual rights, and the efforts to make sure that parents would not come between their daughters and those who know better than her parents.

While our negotiators struggled to break that impasse, others of us spent many hours talking with representatives of various Catholic organizations who had been attending the women's forum at Huairou. We listened carefully to the different points of view they brought to the documents. One particularly impressive group was the Neo-Catechumens—intelligent, dedicated, lay missionaries who work among the neediest populations in the poorest parts of the world. They had followed the conference closely, and, at the end of the first week, urged the Holy See to reject the documents in their entirety. The Declaration and Program of Action were, in their view, so permeated with a false anthropology, so obsessed with sexuality to the exclusion of other issues, so profoundly subversive of the good for women, that the best way for the Church to witness to the truth would be to denounce them and decline to join the Conference consensus. As matters stood then, that was a live option.

Later that day, several members of our delegation made ourselves available for general discussion with Catholic groups. A glance around the crowded meeting room, however, revealed that the gathering had also drawn several inquisitive journalists, the doyenne of American feminism Betty Friedan, and members of the anti-Catholic, population-control front group that calls itself Catholics for a Free Choice. Few comments from this assembly directly concerned conference issues. The chief preoccupations of most who spoke seemed to be power, sex, and the Catholic Church herself.

A great many critical remarks on decisionmaking power within the Church and the male priesthood came from Catholic women who seemed depressingly unfamiliar with basic principles of religious freedom, with the dynamic feminism of John Paul II, or with the vast range of opportunities for female and lay participation in Church activities, processes, and ministries. Even some women with religious vocations seemed to think of the priesthood as a powerful "job" that ought to be made available on an equal opportunity basis, rather than a calling to humble self-sacrificing service.

Many of those women with whom we met seemed not to realize the number of opportunities for important service going begging because there are not enough women or men with the time, desire, and dedication to help. I urged them to respond to John Paul II's call for women to "assume new forms of leadership in service," noting his simultaneous call to the institutions of the Church "to welcome this contribution of women."

Meanwhile, we had reached conference midpoint, and negotiations were still stalled. It seemed unlikely that the EU caucus's negotiating stances reflected government policy or public opinion in their home countries. On Friday night, we composed a press release calling attention to the conflicts between the positions being taken at Beijing by the EU caucus and settled principles of national and international law.

By Monday, there was a marked change in the negotiating atmosphere. Questions had begun to be posed in European legislatures, including the EU Parliament, concerning what their delegations were up to in faraway Beijing. "Why did you have to bring all this out in the open?" complained one EU delegate who was apparently unfamiliar with the concept of government in the sunshine. Negotiations began moving swiftly, and the text began to change in some key respects. The final documents were rapidly taking shape, section by section, in different negotiating rooms, and seemed to be moving toward something we might be able to accept—at least in part.

The picture in the end was mixed. Many of the best provisions—on women's education, poverty, the environment, and peace—are likely to wither unless supported by major financial commitments and nurtured by well-thought-out programs, while other provisions actually threaten both universal human rights and the well-being of women.

In favor of the Holy See's associating itself with the documents to some extent, nevertheless, there were a number of considerations. The heart of the Program for Action consists of many provisions that are consonant with

Catholic teachings on dignity, freedom, and social justice: those dealing with the needs of women in poverty; with strategies for development, literacy and education; for ending violence against women; for building a culture of peace; and with providing access for women to employment, land, capital, and technology. Other worthwhile provisions concerned the connection between the feminization of poverty and family disintegration, the relation of environmental degradation to scandalous patterns of production and consumption, the discrimination against women that begins with abortion of female fetuses, the promotion of partnership and mutual respect between men and women, and the need for reform of the international economic order. The specific economic recommendations mark a healthy break from the discredited Marxist ideas that once prevailed at U.N. gatherings. Many central ideas, moreover, had been introduced by or with the help of the Holy See over the years (e.g., the emphasis on women's education, and the insistence that the human being must be at the center of concern in development).

Even the worst parts of the draft documents had undergone some improvement, thanks to the efforts of our tireless and talented negotiators, Msgr. Frank Dewane, Patricia Donahoe, John Klink, Msgr. Diarmuid Martin, Janne Matlary, Gail Quinn, and Sheri Rickert. In the preparatory conferences, they had introduced equal educational opportunity for refugees; "general access" for women, as well as "equal access," to education; and the reference to women's roles as peace educators in the family and society. By the end of the conference, they had secured references to relevant universal rights and obligations in all five areas where those concepts had been threatened.

A few swallows, admittedly, do not make a summer. The positive changes tempered the tone of the documents and maintained continuity with the rights tradition that will inform future interpretations. But the documents are still seriously unbalanced. The Cairo principle that abortion must not be promoted as a method of family planning was eventually reaffirmed, but the Cairo language on support for parental rights and responsibilities and respect for religious and cultural values is stronger than in parallel provisions in the Beijing documents.

Though EU efforts to gain inclusion of the phrase "sexual rights" were rebuffed, the final documents do contain ambiguous rights language in the areas of sexuality and fertility. A paragraph in the health section, for example, speaks of women's "right to have control over and decide freely and responsibly on matters related to their sexuality, including sexual and reproductive health, free of coercion, discrimination and violence." The U.S. was well-satisfied with this result, according to a postconference memorandum from Undersecretary of State for Global Affairs Timothy Wirth to members of the American delegation. Wirth's evaluation of the Beijing Platform was that it "met the U.S. government's goals—reaffirm important commitments made at previous international conferences, including human rights of women in reproductive health and rights."

There was no consensus on what the vague new language means beyond the rights to say no and be free of sexual exploitation. By general agreement, it does not cover sexual orientation, Canada's energetic efforts to introduce rights in that area having encountered broad opposition at the conference.

Arguments will no doubt be made that references to women's rights "to control all aspects of their health, in particular their own fertility" implicitly recognize abortion as a human right. Such an interpretation is excluded, however, by Paragraph 107(k), a direct quotation from Cairo, which provides: "Any measures or changes related to abortion within the health system can only be determined at the national or local level according to the national legislative process." This language was necessary in view of the fact that, unlike the United States and China, most countries restrict and strictly regulate abortion. Even nations like Sweden with relatively permissive abortion laws do not follow the U.S. in characterizing abortion as a "right." Paragraph 107(k) contains other language that militates against abortion as a fundamental right: "reduce recourse to abortion," "eliminate the need for abortion," "help avoid repeat abortion." One would hardly say of an important right like free speech, for example, that governments should reduce it, eliminate the need for it, and help avoid its repetition.

Even if there were no such specific language in the Cairo and Beijing documents, it is a basic principle of interpretation that fundamental rights cannot be created or destroyed by implication. Moreover, the Beijing conference had no authority to add to or tinker with the corpus of universal human rights. The U.N. historically has conducted that process with great care and gravity, most recently at the 1993 Human Rights Conference in Vienna. It would indeed be a dark day if human rights could be revised in disorderly negotiating sessions such as those where the Beijing health sections were rammed through.

As at Cairo, the Holy See was concerned that language on sexual and reproductive "health" would be used to promote the quick-fix approach to getting rid of poverty by getting rid of poor people. Much of the foundation money that swirled around the Beijing process was aimed at forging a link between development aid and programs that pressure poor women into abortion, sterilization, and use of risky contraceptive methods. That point has also troubled distinguished non-Catholic observers. In the wake of Cairo, Harvard economist-philosopher Amartya Sen criticized a "dangerous tendency" on the part of developed nations to search for solutions to overpopulation that "treat the people involved not as reasonable beings, allies faced with a common problem, but as impulsive and uncontrolled sources of great social harm, in need of strong discipline." Sen charged that by giving priority to "family planning arrangements in the Third World countries over other commitments such as education and health care," international policy-makers "produce negative effects on people's well-being and reduce their freedoms." In a similar vein, the British medical journal *Lancet* blasted the Beijing documents for a "new colonialism" designed to control rather than liberate women.

The Holy See's position as the conference came to an end was thus a difficult one. The documents had been improved in some respects. But in other ways they were even more disappointing than the Cairo document, which the Holy See had been able to join only partially and with many formal reservations. After an intense session in which members of our delegation shared their views, hopes, doubts, and concerns about the documents, our assessment of their pros and cons was communicated to the Vatican Secretariat of State. On Thursday morning, we received the Holy Father's decision: Accept what is positive, but vigorously reject what cannot be accepted.

Accordingly, the Holy See delegation associated itself in part, with several reservations, with the conference documents. As at Cairo, it reaffirmed its well-known positions on abortion and family planning methods. It could not accept the health section at all. A controversy over the word "gender" that loomed before the conference had been largely defused with a consensus that gender was to be understood according to ordinary usage in the United Nations context. The Holy See, however, deemed it prudent to attach to its reservations a further, more nuanced, statement of interpretation, in which it dissociated itself from rigid biological determinism as well as from the notion that sexual identity is indefinitely malleable. In keeping with the Holy Father's instruction to vigorously reject what was unacceptable, my concluding statement on behalf of the Holy See was sharply critical of the conference documents for the remaining deficiencies that our delegation had tried from the beginning to publicize and remedy.

The most important political lesson to be taken from the Beijing conference is that huge international conferences are not suitable settings for addressing complex questions of social and economic justice or grave issues of human rights. Unfortunately, there is an increasing tendency for advocates of causes that have failed to win acceptance through ordinary democratic processes to resort to the international arena, far removed (they hope) from scrutiny and accountability. The sexual libertarians, old-line feminists, and coercive population controllers can be expected to keep on trying to insert their least popular ideas into U.N. documents for unveiling at home as "international norms."

A number of lingering questions about Beijing merit the attention of investigative reporters. What deals did the affluent nations make with their client states? Why did the EU caucus champion an agenda so far removed from the urgent concerns of most of the world's women? Why did delegates from countries with strong family protection provisions in their constitutions (Germany, Ireland, Italy) not break ranks with the EU when it attacked the spirit of those provisions? Why were the conference documents so skewed from the beginning? Who paid for the voyages of thousands of lobbyists at Huairou whose main interest was not in women's needs and rights, but in controlling women's fertility?

American delegate Geraldine Ferraro's description of the Beijing conference as marking an end to the North-South conflicts that have plagued U.N. conferences in the past was disingenuous. The delegations from affluent countries that battled so boldly at Cairo and Beijing for their ideas about population control and sexual rights were timid as mice when it came to making commitments of resources. In defiance of evidence that economic development and women's education lead to lowered fertility rates, the developed countries made it clear they wanted population control on the cheap. The relative silence of Third World delegates on issues vital to women in their own countries was bewildering. How can one explain that many delegations from poor nations came to sessions involving sexual and reproductive matters with well-prepared position papers, yet were absent or silent when resources and other crucial issues were discussed? Since many of those same delegations entered formal reservations at the end of the conference, chances are the folks back home will never suspect that their representatives did not speak up in negotiations where a few strong voices could have made a difference.

The significance of the Beijing documents should neither be exaggerated nor minimized. The Declaration and Platform are non-binding documents that may or may not serve as international guidelines for the way various private and public actors deal with the issues they cover. The authority of the worst parts of the documents is diminished by their vagueness, their inconsistency with respected international documents, and by the unusually large number of U.N. members who expressed dissent. When 43 of 181 nations present have formally registered serious concerns, it is hard to speak of a consensus. The authority of the constructive sections, on the other hand, is supported by consensus and amplified by their similarity to provisions in documents from other international conferences, most recently the Copenhagen Summit on Social Development.

The significance of Beijing for human rights is mainly in the nature of a warning. As the fiftieth anniversary of the U.N.'s 1948 Universal Declaration of Human Rights approaches, the Beijing conference appears to have been a testing ground for certain ideas and approaches that will be advanced again. We have not seen the last of the effort to make abortion a fundamental right, or of the attempt to depose heterosexual marriage and child-raising families from their traditionally preferred positions. Neither have we seen the last of selective use of rights language to advance an anti-rights agenda— exemplified at Beijing by the emphasis on formal equality at the expense of motherhood's special claim to protection, and by the elimination of most references to religion and parental rights. Worrisome, too, is the trivialization of universally recognized core principles through the attempted addition of vague new rights.

All this is familiar stuff to Americans. At the international level, it is evidence of the continuing colonization of the universal language of human rights by an impoverished dialect that has already made great inroads on political discourse in the United States. Its features include rights envisioned without corresponding individual or social responsibilities; one's favorite rights touted as absolute with others ignored; the rights-bearer imagined as radically autonomous and self-sufficient; and the willy-nilly proliferation of new rights.

That dialect contrasts with the broad, rich, and balanced Universal Declaration where the individual right-bearer's dignity is resoundingly affirmed, but the family is recognized as the basic social unit. In the Universal Declaration, fundamental individual rights are simultaneously affirmed and situated within the social contexts that determine whether rights, freedom, and dignity will become realities: "In the exercise of his rights and freedoms, everyone shall be subject only to such limitations are as determined by law solely for the purpose of securing due recognition and respect for the rights and freedoms of others and of meeting the just requirements of morality, public order and the general welfare in a democratic society."

Not least alarming about the assault on the human rights tradition by powerful actors at Beijing is that it went virtually unreported. As far as the American press was concerned, the human rights story was the Chinese treatment of Harry Wu. To European journalists, it was the failed efforts of a few Islamic countries to authorize opting out of certain equality measures on cultural and religious grounds. The U.S. was correct, of course, to condemn brazen violations of universal rights. The Europeans were right, too, that human rights ought not to be nullified by cultural exceptions. But neither should the catalog of human rights be redefined and expanded to "universalize" the highly individualistic ideologies of modernizing elites. Nor must human rights be sharply separated from the cultural and religious contexts in which rights are rooted and protected. Nor must the corpus of core rights and obligations be casually altered. As memories fade about why it was necessary after World War II to affirm the existence of certain inalienable rights, the citizens of the world must be vigilant to prevent trivialization and dilution of those basic protections of human dignity.

In the end, one may hope that the good in the non-binding Beijing documents will survive and flourish—especially since, as any good feminist would say, they must be seen in context. The context in this case is the framework of the overarching universal human rights tradition.

John Paul II's instruction to his Beijing delegation reflected the approach he has taken on women's issues in his writings. In his 1995 *World*

*Day of Peace* message he noted that "when one looks at the great process of women's liberation," one sees that the journey has been a difficult one, with its "share of mistakes," but headed toward a better future for women and the entire human family. In his recent *Letter to Women*, he added, "This journey must go on!" It is characteristic of this Pope that, in confronting flawed human enterprises of various sorts, he seeks to find and build on what is sound and healthy, while identifying and criticizing what is likely to be harmful to human flourishing.

Looking toward the future, the Pope stressed in his preconference message to Secretary-General Gertrude Mongella that the success of the gathering will depend on whether it will offer a "vision capable of sustaining objective and realistic responses to the struggle and frustration that continue to be a part of all too many women's lives." Ultimately, it is up to concerned citizens, women and men, to bring the seedlings of "equality, development, and peace" to full flower, and to protect them from the encroaching culture of death. Fortunately, we do not garden alone. Not only are we surrounded by a cloud of witnesses, but divine grace is always operating in the world, inviting us to cooperate with it in building the civilization of life and love.

CHAPTER 37 • What Happened at Beijing

# Knowing the Universal Declaration of Human Rights

*After the Beijing Conference, I began to look into the history of the Universal Declaration of Human Rights to see whether that history shed any light on contemporary interpretive controversies. My research yielded many illuminating discoveries, some of which are recounted here, as well as a renewed appreciation of the men and women who contributed to the drafting process. This article, published in the* Notre Dame Law Review, *was a forerunner of my history of the framing of the UDHR:* A World Made New: Eleanor Roosevelt and the Universal Declaration of Human Rights *(New York: Random House, 2001).[1]*

*Interviewer:* Finally, Mrs. Roosevelt, is there any way that students can help to make the Declaration of Human Rights a living document?

*Roosevelt:* Well, I really think the area in which students should function is first of all they should know the Declaration which we agreed that we would strive to implement in our own country.

THE UNITED NATION'S UNIVERSAL DECLARATION of Human Rights of 1948 is the single most important reference point for cross-cultural discussion of human freedom and dignity in the world today. As described in a leading text, "It is the parent document, the initial burst of enthusiasm and idealism, terser, more general and grander than the treaties, in some sense the constitution of the entire movement—the single most invoked human rights instrument." As it reaches its fiftieth anniversary, the Declaration is already showing signs of having achieved the status of holy writ within the human rights movement. Public figures nod briefly in its direction when the occasion arises. Cults have formed around selected provisions. It is widely admired, but little read. The Declaration as a whole is scarcely known.

The loss of, or, more precisely, the failure to acquire a sense of the Declaration as an integral body of principles has facilitated a host of opportunistic

---

[1] Mary Ann Glendon, "Knowing the Universal Declaration of Human Rights," *Notre Dame Law Review* 73 (May–July 1998): 1153–79.

interpretations and uses. The prevailing approach to the rights contained in its thirty articles is a pick-and-choose, cafeteria-style. The sections devoted to traditional political and civil liberties are frequently, but unevenly, invoked. The provisions on social and economic justice are commonly ignored, even by major human rights organizations. The family protection principles have come under direct assault. Though virtually all U.N. members are committed in principle to the proposition that the Declaration's rights are universal, some international actors openly maintain that all rights are relative, others assert the priority of economic interests over human rights, and still others charge that universality is a cover for Western imperialism. The efforts of special interest groups to impose their agendas in the form of rights lend credibility to fears of cultural imperialism.

In its fiftieth year, the universal rights project can evoke, even in the minds of its friends, disquieting thoughts of another ambitious human undertaking: the ill-fated tower built by the men of the Valley of Shinar who wanted their very own staircase to heaven. Were philosophical rights skeptics, such as Michel Villey and Alasdair MacIntyre, right, after all, that something is intrinsically wrong with the universal rights idea? Villey, noting the tensions among several basic rights (e.g., liberty and equality), argued that the whole idea is hopelessly incoherent: "Each of the so-called human rights is the negation of other rights."[2] MacIntyre warned that to combine fragments of different conceptual schemes, resting upon incommensurable moral premises, is a recipe for mischief. Belief in human rights, he scoffed, "is one with belief in witches and unicorns."[3] Garden variety cynics regard the 1948 Declaration as just a hodge-podge of ideas that emerged from deals cut after World War II, with no more coherence than a typical federal statute.

With all the turmoil that surrounds the human rights enterprise, it is natural to wonder whether the design of the Declaration was faulty and the aims of its framers unrealistic. My own current research on the origins of the Declaration, however, has led me to increased admiration for the project of 1948, and for the men and women who dedicated themselves to it. I am struck by the prescience with which the framers anticipated the problems that might arise, and impressed by the safeguards they devised to help minimize future difficulties. I am moved by the vision of the men and women who, after two world wars, which gave them every reason to despair about the human condition, did what they could to help make the world a better and safer place. This essay aims to pay tribute to that vision by taking seriously Mrs. Roosevelt's admonition to "know" the Declaration.

---

[2] Michael Villey, *Les Droits de L'Homme* (Paris: Presses Universitaires de France, 1983), 12–13.

[3] Alasdair MacIntyre, *After Virtue* (London: Duckworth, 1981), 1–21.

## WHAT THE PHILOSOPHERS KNEW

The problem of universality loomed large from the moment the idea of an "international bill of rights" was conceived in the aftermath of World War II. Was it really possible for the fledging United Nations to produce a document acceptable to delegates from fifty-eight countries containing four-fifths of the world's population (twenty-one from the Americas, sixteen from Europe, fourteen from Asia, four from Africa, and three from Oceania)? Six member nations were within the emerging socialist bloc; in eleven, Islamic culture was strong; four countries had a large Buddhist population; and thirty-seven were more or less marked by Judeo-Christian traditions and enlightenment thought. It was by no means certain that a universal declaration of rights was feasible.

In 1946, the United Nations Educational, Scientific, and Cultural Organization (UNESCO) appointed a committee composed of many of the leading thinkers of the day to search for areas of potential agreement among different cultural and philosophical traditions. This blue-ribbon "Committee on the Theoretical Bases of Human Rights" was chaired by Cambridge historian E. H. Carr. University of Chicago philosopher Richard McKeon was the Rapporteur, and Jacques Maritain was one of the most active members. They began by sending an elaborate questionnaire to statesman and scholars in every part of the world. Replies were received reflecting on human rights from Chinese, Islamic, Hindu, and customary law perspectives, as well as from the United States, Europe, and the countries of the socialist bloc. The respondents included such notables as Mahatma Gandhi, Benedetto Croce, Pierre Teilhard de Chardin, and Aldous Huxley. To the Committee's surprise, the lists of basic rights and values they received from their far-flung sources were essentially similar. McKeon's final report recorded their conclusion that it was indeed possible to achieve agreement across cultures concerning certain rights that "may be viewed as implicit in man's nature as an individual and as a member of society."[4]

The Committee members well understood how thin that sort of agreement was. Maritain liked to tell the story of how a visitor to one meeting had expressed astonishment that champions of violently opposed ideologies had agreed on a list of fundamental rights. The man was told, "Yes, we agree about the rights but on condition no one asks us why." Maritain and his colleagues did not regard this lack of consensus on foundations as fatal. The fact that an agreement could be achieved across cultures on several practical concepts was "enough," Maritain wrote, "to enable a great task to be undertaken."[5] Such an agreement, McKeon stressed, would at least provide a

---

[4] Richard McKeon, "The Philosophic Bases and Material Circumstances of the Rights of Man," in *Human Rights: Comments and Interpretations* (New York: UNESCO, 45 n. 16.

[5] Jacques Maritain, "Introduction," ibid., 35 n. 10.

"framework within which divergent philosophical, religious, and even economic, social and political theories might be entertained and developed."[6]

More serious than divergence on the "why" of each right, the philosophers realized, would be the problems of arriving at a common understanding of what the principles meant, of reconciling tensions among the various rights, of integrating new rights, and of incorporating new applications. In that connection, Maritain observed that the document should ideally "cover the scale of values, the key in which, in their practical exercise in social life, the acknowledged rights of man must be harmonized." Everything depends, he continued, on "the ultimate value whereon those rights depend and in terms of which they are integrated by mutual limitations."[7]

McKeon foresaw another problem. Different understandings of the meanings of rights usually reflect divergent concepts of man and of society, which in turn cause the persons who hold those understandings to have different views of reality. Thus, he predicted that "difficulties will be discovered in the suspicions, suggested by these differences, concerning the tangential uses that might be made of a declaration of human rights for the purpose of advancing special interests."[8] That is a philosopher's way of saying, "Watch out, this whole enterprise could be hijacked."

## WHAT THE FRAMERS DID

While the UNESCO Committee was winding up its investigation of the theoretical bases for human rights, the U.N. Commission on Human Rights, headed by Eleanor Roosevelt, was preparing to draft an international bill or declaration. The task that faced the Commission was daunting. Proposals, models, and ideas had poured in from all over the world. How could they ever be analyzed, evaluated, and integrated into a document that the then fifty-eight member nations of the U.N. would find acceptable?

The Commission was set up with eighteen members, with five seats allocated to the representatives of the "great powers"—China, France, the Soviet Union, the United Kingdom, and the United States. The remaining thirteen seats were assigned on a rotating basis to different countries, so that, according to Roosevelt, "there should be due regard to distribution throughout the world, so that . . . there would be no part of the world whose interests would not be considered." The group's very size and scope, however, could easily have led to grave difficulties. The framers might well have ended up like the architects in Pieter Brueghel the Elder's rendition of the Tower of Babel, poring despondently over their plans in the shadow of a crazy pile

---

[6] McKeon, ibid., 35 n. 17.
[7] Maritain, ibid., 5–16, n. 16.
[8] McKeon, ibid., 35 n. 17.

constructed by a consortium, each of whose members had a somewhat different conception of what the whole should look like.

The work in fact got off to a rocky start when the leadership of the Commission (Mrs. Roosevelt, President; China's Peng-chun Chang, Vice-President; and Lebanon's Charles Malik, Rapporteur) appointed itself as the drafting subcommittee. After several delegates protested that the group was insufficiently representative, the membership was expanded to eight by adding the delegates from Australia, Chile, England, France, and the Soviet Union. Happily for the Universal Declaration, this potentially unwieldy assemblage appointed a four-person "working" group. That smaller group, composed of the American, English, French, and Lebanese members, in turn chose to put a single author in charge of the actual drafting process.

The lot fell to one of the most distinguished jurists of the twentieth century. René Cassin had been General Charles de Gaulle's principal legal adviser during World War II, and was entrusted by de Gaulle at war's end with the formidable task of rehabilitating the compromised French administrative system. So far as the Declaration was concerned, it was fortuitous that Cassin was a pioneer of the study of comparative law. He was also experienced in the art of legislative drafting, having drawn up the instruments constituting the government of the Free French during the war.

Cassin's background in a civil law system where drafting skills are highly prized facilitated a response to Maritain's call for a document with a hermeneutical "key." The Preamble and the Proclamation, as well as Articles 1 and 2 of the thirty-article Declaration, belong to what in continental legal terminology is called the "general part." These sections set forth premises, purposes, and principles that guide the interpretation of the specifically enumerated rights in Articles 3 to 27. The Declaration's last three articles, again, contain interpretive guides, contextualizing rights in relation to limits, duties, and the social and political order in which they are to be realized.

When the Declaration emerged from the drafting committee, it was recognizably "civilian" in form and style. Since the civil law tradition then, as now, was the most widely distributed legal tradition in the world, that meant the draft had a familial resemblance, not only to rights declarations in continental European constitutions, but to the constitutions and charters that had appeared or were soon to appear in many Latin American, African, and Asian countries.

The draft was submitted to all U.N. member governments for comments and to the full Human Rights Commission for debate. In the process it went through several revisions. There was no nation, according to Cassin, that did not "usefully contribute to the improvement of the draft through suggestions or criticisms." The fact that representatives from many countries had contributed to its content, plus the broad process of consultation that preceded and accompanied the drafting stage, helped to ease the way for its ultimate adoption by the General Assembly.

Behind the scenes work by Roosevelt must have contributed toward that end as well. Early on she initiated informal meetings among women delegates and found the custom so fruitful that she broadened it. She began getting together with U.N. representatives of different nationalities on a semi-social basis. Malik and Chang, the most scholarly members of her Commission, got to know each other better while bantering about Thomism and Confucianism over tea in Roosevelt's apartment. "I discovered," she wrote in her autobiography, "that in such informal sessions we sometimes made more progress in reaching an understanding of some question before the United Nations than we had been able to achieve in the formal work of our committees." One group, however, remained resolutely aloof from her efforts. "[I]t was difficult to know any Russian well and I suppose the Kremlin planned it that way. It was really impossible to have a private and frank talk with Russian officials.

At the next stage, in July 1948, Cassin and Roosevelt were heartened when the Economic and Social Commission (chaired by Malik) unanimously approved the "final" draft submitted to it by the Human Rights Commission. That removed the last hurdle before submission to the General Assembly. But when the General Assembly began its deliberations on the Declaration in September 1948, the international scene was extremely tense. Relations were worsening between the Soviet Union and the West. The Berlin blockade was a powder keg waiting for a match. Conflict had broken out in Greece and Korea. Small nations were becoming resentful of the influence of the great powers and suspicious of their motives. Cynicism and power politics had taken their toll on the mood of hopefulness in which the human rights project had been launched. A decade later, Roosevelt told an interviewer, "We thought we were presenting such a good draft that there would be very little discussion. We found we were mistaken. In the big committee they argued every word. . . . And so we had some terrible times in Paris."

It took the talents of another extraordinary individual to shepherd the Declaration through the process of deliberation and revision that led up to final adoption in December 1948. That man was Malik, a personable Lebanese philosophy professor whose diplomatic skills were as finely honed as Cassin's legal talents. Malik was a familiar figure on the little gray TV screens of the 1950s. Well-respected among delegates from many different parts of the world, he was frequently elected to leadership positions in the U.N., including membership on the Security Council and the presidency of the General Assembly. During the period leading up to the adoption of the Declaration, he wore many hats, serving as the Human Rights Commission's Rapporteur, an active member of the four-person working group on the draft, and President of the Economic and Social Council to which the Commission reported. When the draft Declaration was ready to be taken to the General Assembly, it was the ubiquitous Malik who chaired the three-person group that steered it through more than eighty stormy meetings in Paris in the fall of 1948.

Malik's fluency in many languages, including Arabic, French, German, and English, enabled him to move easily between East and West, and between large and small nations. He made the most of the fact that the document reflected input from diverse sources, and he took pains to point each country to the places in the Declaration where it could either find its own contributions, or the influence of the culture to which it belonged. At many stages, he was aided by Mrs. Roosevelt, who was a shaper as well as a wielder of the influence of the United States.

The Soviet Union, represented by the intelligent and voluble Professor A. P. Pavlov, made repeated efforts to stall and drag out the process. "[Pavlov] was an orator of great power," Roosevelt recalled, "his words rolled out of his black beard like a river, and stopping him was difficult." With each delay, the prospects for success grew dimmer, to the point where Cassin began to fear that all his work might go for naught. But Malik was up to the challenge. Durward Sandifer, Roosevelt's State Department adviser, described Malik as "the only person I ever knew who succeeded in holding a stopwatch to Pavlov."

Malik directed his arguments to the public and posterity as well as to his fellow delegates. Unlike previous rights declarations which had sprung from particular cultures, he said, the Universal Declaration was "a composite synthesis of all these outlooks and movements and of much Oriental and Latin American wisdom. Such a synthesis has never occurred before in history." The Latin American countries had brought to the process the ideas and experience gained in preparing the 1948 Pan-American Declaration on the Rights and Duties of Man; India had played a key role in advancing the non-discrimination principle, especially with respect to women; the United Kingdom and the United States had shared the wisdom acquired in their long experience with traditional political and civil liberties; the Soviet Union had championed the cause of improving the living conditions of the broad mass of people; the importance of including duties had been emphasized by participants from China, Latin America, the Soviet Union, and France; many smaller countries contributed to the articles on freedom of religion and the rights of the family; the social, economic, and cultural rights had numerous fathers and mothers.

The debates wore on for two months, often lasting late into the night. Finally, on December 10, 1948, in spite of the deteriorating international situation, the Declaration was approved without a single dissenting vote. Malik and Roosevelt received a standing ovation. Clouds loomed on the horizon, however. Eight countries, including the entire socialist bloc, abstained: Byelorussia, Czechoslovakia, Poland, Saudi Arabia, South Africa, the Soviet Union, Ukraine, and Yugoslavia.

Today, when one reads what Cassin, Malik, Maritain, McKeon, Roosevelt, and their colleagues said and wrote many years ago, it is striking that they foresaw nearly every problem their enterprise would encounter—its buffeting from power politics, its dependence on common understandings that would prove elusive, its embodiment of ideas of freedom and solidarity that would be difficult to harmonize, and its vulnerabilty to politicization and misunderstanding. It is of interest, therefore, to see how they attempted to protect it against the most egregious forms of manipulation.

## KNOWING THE DECLARATION

The Universal Declaration, with its thirty short articles, seems at first glance to invite comparison with older rights documents such as the Magna Carta, the French Declaration of the Rights of Man and the Citizen and the first ten amendments to the U.S. Constitution. In recent years, American influence upon the international human rights movement has become so pervasive that the Declaration is now widely read as Americans read the Bill of Rights: as a string of essentially separate guarantees. As we shall see, however, that approach is inappropriate for an organic document like the Declaration. The Declaration is not a list or a "bill," but a set of principles that are related to one another and to certain overarching ideas. It possesses an integrity that has considerable strength when the document is read as it as meant to be read, namely as a whole.

Cassin often compared the Declaration to the portico of a temple. (He had no illusions that the document could be anything more than an entryway to a future where human rights would be respected.) He saw the Preamble, with its eight "whereas" clauses, as the courtyard steps moving by degrees from the recognition of human dignity to the unity of the human family to the aspiration for peace on earth. The general principles of dignity, liberty, equality, and fraternity, proclaimed in Articles 1 and 2, are the portico's foundation blocks. The facade consists of four equal columns crowned by a pediment. The four pillars are: the personal liberties (Articles 3 through 11); the rights of the individual in relation to others and to various groups (Articles 12 through 17); the spiritual, public, and political liberties (Articles 18 through 21); and the economic, social, and cultural rights (Articles 22 through 27). The pediment is composed of the three concluding articles, 28 through 30, which establish a range of connections between the individual and society.

Let us stroll through the portico, noting the relations among its parts, and some of the more interesting architectural details.

The Preamble begins by asserting the dependence of freedom, justice, and peace upon the universal recognition of human dignity and rights. It announces the principal innovation of the Declaration: that human rights are *universal*—belonging to "all members of the human family." In other words, it repudiates the long-standing view that the relation between a sovereign state and its own citizens is that nation's own business.

The Preamble then evokes the circumstances that give rise to the need for universal standards: "[D]isregard and contempt for human rights have resulted in barbarous acts which have outraged the conscience of mankind." It goes on to speak of hopes for a better world where human beings may enjoy what most U.S. readers of the day would have recognized as Franklin Roosevelt's four freedoms: "freedom of speech and belief and freedom from fear and want." It points toward a future when rights will be "protected by the rule of law" and by "the development of friendly relations among nations."

The Preamble then anchors the Declaration firmly in the U.N. Charter:

> Whereas the people of the United Nations have in the Charter reaffirmed their faith in fundamental human rights, in the dignity and worth of the human person and in the equal rights of men and women and have determined to promote social progress and better standards of life in larger freedom.

By expressly including women, by alluding to freedom from want, and by evoking the U.N. Charter's commitment to better standards of life, the Preamble signals from the outset that this document is not just a "universalization" of the traditional eighteenth-century "rights of man," but part of a new "moment" in the history of human rights. In this respect, the Universal Declaration belongs to the family of post-World War II rights instruments that attempted to graft social justice onto the trunk of the tree of liberty. Most of these instruments also bear traces of roots in a past before the first rights moment. In the Declaration, for example, human dignity is said to be "inherent," dignity and rights are "recognized," not conferred; human beings are said to be "born" free and equal, and "endowed" with reason and conscience; the family is "natural" as well as fundamental. (Hence MacIntyre's warning about incommensurable moral premises.) The framers hoped, however, that the graft, the tree, and the roots would nourish one another.

The Preamble is followed by a Proclamation clause which announces the nature of the document. The Declaration is to be "a common standard of achievement for all peoples and nations" toward which "every individual and every organ of society" should "strive" (and by which the conduct of nations and peoples can be measured). The Proclamation implicitly acknowledges the hurdles ahead, stating that "a common understanding" of the Declaration's rights and freedoms "is of the greatest importance for the full realization of this pledge."

The Declaration proper then begins, not with a right, but in civil law fashion, with two introductory general articles. It was at Cassin's insistence that a declaration purporting to be universal should begin with a statement of what all human beings have in common. Thus the first article reads: "All human beings are born free and equal in dignity and rights. They are endowed with reason and conscience and should act toward one another in a spirit of brotherhood." It speaks volumes about the spirit of Cassin, a

World War I veteran of Jewish ancestry who had lost twenty-one relatives in concentration camps, that he insisted on beginning the Declaration with an affirmation of faith in human conscience and rationality. In 1968, that largeness of spirit was recognized when he received the Nobel Peace Prize for his years of work on behalf of human rights.

Article 2's emphatic statement of the anti-discrimination principle underlies the principle of universality. "Everyone" in the Declaration means everyone—"without distinction of any kind."

The Declaration then turns, in Articles 3 to 11, to familiar individual rights that had already received a significant degree of recognition, if not implementation, in various legal systems: rights to life, liberty, and personal security; bans on slavery and torture; rights to legal recognition, equality before the law, effective remedies for violation of fundamental rights, and freedom from arbitrary arrest and detention; and guarantees of fair criminal procedures, presumption of innocence and the principle of non-retroactivity in criminal law.

In Cassin's view, the rights in this first group were mainly directed toward protecting individuals as such from aggression, while the rights in Articles 12 to 17 were more concerned with protecting people in their relations with others and within civil society. His second column includes the right to be free of arbitrary interference with one's "privacy, family, home, or correspondence" and from arbitrary attacks upon one's "honor and reputation"; freedom of movement and the right of return; the right to political asylum; the right to a nationality; provisions on marriage and the family; and the right to own property. This second group of rights is less precisely formulated than the first, leaving larger scope for variation in different social and political contexts.

Article 16, dealing with marriage and the family, is a blend of old and new ideas with varying genealogies. It went far beyond most national legislation of the day with its affirmation of the principle of equal rights between spouses. The idea that the family "is entitled to protection by society and the State," on the other hand, was familiar in many countries as legislative policy, had already appeared in several constitutions, and would shortly appear in many others.

Cassin's third pillar, Articles 18 through 21, covers freedoms of religion and belief in Article 18; opinion, expression, and communication in Article 19; assembly and association in Article 20; and the principle of participatory democratic government in Article 21. Article 18 is noteworthy for its fairly detailed specification of the content of religious freedom. The Human Rights Commission had been on the verge of going forward with a draft that spoke only of conscience and belief, but when Roosevelt interjected that a text protecting religious freedom ought to use the word "religion," that view carried the day. In its final form, Article 18 not only protects religious freedom expressly, but acknowledges the right to manifest one's beliefs in public as well as in private, and "in community with others" (this latter point due to an amendment by Malik to Cassin's more individualistic rendering of the concept).

Apart from the aspiration to universality, the most innovative part of the Declaration was its fourth pillar, Articles 22 through 27, which elevates to fundamental right status several "new" economic, social, and cultural rights. As memories fade, it is sometimes assumed that this collection of rights was included mainly as a concession to the Soviets. The fact is, however, that support for these ideas was very broad-based.

The Declaration's social and economic rights provisions drew from a variety of sources. They contained more than an echo of FDR's proposed "second bill of rights," a legacy which Mrs. Roosevelt "through her very name," according to Malik, "imported into our council chambers."[9] (Officials in the Truman State Department were initially lukewarm toward the idea of social and economic rights, but Mrs. Roosevelt eventually won their backing.) This group of rights also bore a close resemblance to their counterparts in the Preamble of the 1946 French Constitution, the 1948 Bogota Declaration on the Rights and Duties of Man, as well as to the programs of socialist and many Christian political parties. Similar rights would soon appear in most postwar and postcolonial constitutions, sometimes framed as obligations of society and the state. At the international level, similar principles had been recognized by the International Labor Organization.

Much of what is contained in Articles 23 and 24 was already the common stuff of labor legislation in most liberal democracies (decent working conditions including paid vacations and limits on working hours; protection against unemployment; the right to form and join unions). Less widely recognized, however, were Article 23's "right to work" and its "right to equal pay for equal work" without discrimination; Article 25's elevation of social welfare principles into a universal right to decent standard of living; and Article 26's right to education.

Agreement on the relation of the "new" rights to the "old" was much harder to achieve than agreement on their content. According to Cassin, the sessions where the Commission wrestled with that problem were extremely difficult and emotionally charged. England wanted the differences from traditional civil and political liberties to be sharply emphasized. It took the position that the social and economic rights should be handled in an entirely separate document. The Soviet Union, for its part, opposed any measure that would appear to relegate social and economic rights to an inferior rank. Madame Mehta, the Indian representative, pointed out that poorer nations could hope to move only gradually toward making such rights a reality.

Cassin finally resolved the impasse by drafting a "chapeau" or "umbrella" provision, Article 22, which serves as a mini-preamble to the provisions dealing with social, economic, and cultural rights. The chapeau tried to satisfy

---

[9] Charles Habib Malik, Introduction, in O. Frederick Nolde, *Free and Equal: Human Rights in Ecumenical Perspective* (Geneva: World Council of Churches, 1968), 7, 9.

the socialist bloc by making clear that the new rights, like the old, are "indispensable" to human dignity. It responded to the English and Indian concerns by recognizing that the new rights stood on a different footing from the old so far as implementation was concerned. Unlike traditional civil rights, which are protected mainly through access to courts, and political rights, which are secured mainly through constitutional frameworks, the economic and social rights require more official planning for their realization, and are more dependent on each country's economic situation. Accordingly, Article 22 specifies that the economic and social rights are to be realized "in accordance with the organization and resources of each State." It was Mrs. Roosevelt who, in a particularly heated session, came up with the words just quoted that finally permitted agreement to be achieved.

It is a credit to Cassin's skill that the "new" rights were not simply tacked onto but integrated with the more traditional rights that preceded them. Article 22 links the social, economic, and cultural rights to the protection of the individual in such a way that each group of rights sheds interpretive light on the other. The "new" rights are presented as rights of the individual, "indispensable for his dignity and the free development of his personality." The last sentence of Article 26 on parents' rights provides a bridge between the new right to education and the older family protection idea of Article 16. Similarly, Article 27, while recognizing a new "right to participate in the cultural life of the community," looks back to Article 17's property rights through its reference to protecting scientific inventions and literary and artistic creations.

The last three sections of the Declaration, in Cassin's view, constituted the pediment of the portico covering the entire Declaration and making essential links between the individual and society. Like the Preamble and Articles 1 and 2, these three sections bear importantly on the meaning of the document as a whole. They address certain conditions that are prerequisite to the realization of the rights and freedoms enumerated in the Declaration. Once again, a general article serves a kind of mini-preamble to illuminate what follows. Article 28, the invention of Charles Malik, speaks of a right to a certain kind of order: "Everyone is entitled to a social and international order in which the rights and freedoms set forth in this Declaration can be fully realized."

Two necessary features of an order where rights can be realized are then spelled out, but quickly qualified, in Article 29: "Everyone has duties to the community" (but to a certain kind of community, where "the free and full development of his personality is possible"), and everyone's rights are subject to *limitations* (but only "for the purpose of securing due recognition and respect for the rights and freedoms of others and of meeting the just requirements of morality, public order and the general welfare in a democratic society"). A further limit on rights is the subject of Article 30: "Nothing in this Declaration may be interpreted as implying for any State, group, or person any right to engage in any activity or perform any act aimed at the destruction of any of the rights and freedoms set forth herein."

When Cassin described these last three articles as linking the individual and society, he was referring to the way the Declaration handled a problem that had arisen in the drafting process. Where was primary responsibility for implementing human rights to lie? Even if an international enforcement machinery were to be created someday, that could not be the first line of defense. The Soviet representative had insisted that the sentence, "This shall be enforced by the state," be appended to many articles. In the spring of 1948, upon rereading the draft, the Commission members came to the conclusion that a misleading impression had been created. Cassin recalled:

> It was apparent that its provisions repeatedly referred to the role of the State, as if that were the permanent and only agency for the protection and regulation of the rights of man. But man must be envisaged not only in his relations with the State, but with the social groups of all sorts to which he belongs: family, tribe, city, profession, confession, and more broadly the global human community. Amendments were needed in order to remove all ambiguity on this point.

In the view of Cassin and others, it had to be made clear that the responsibility for protecting human rights belonged not only to the nation-states, but to persons and groups below and above the national level. The Declaration was thus ahead of its time in recognizing the importance for human freedom of a wide range of social groups, beginning with families, and extending through the institutions of civil society, nation-states, and international organizations. The Proclamation clause calls not only "all peoples and all nations" but "every organ of society" to promote recognition and observance of human rights. In the main body of the Declaration, individuals are protected in their social as well as political settings. The rights to own property and to participate in important institutions of civil society—religious groups, labor organizations, and families—are guaranteed along with the right to take part in government. The family as such is a subject of human rights protection, to be provided, significantly, "by society" as well as the state (Article 16). Article 28's right "to a social and international order in which the rights and freedoms" of the Declaration can be fully realized is the capstone of this group of provisions.

The Declaration as a whole leaves "no room for doubt," Cassin said in his Nobel speech, "concerning the essential question whether the nations have retained or lost their traditional exclusive jurisdiction over the treatment of their citizens. That national jurisdiction will always be at the base. It will remain primary. But it will no longer be exclusive."

The principal architects of the Declaration believed that the most effective defense of human rights would ultimately be "in the mind and the will of the people." "In the eyes of the Declaration's authors," Cassin wrote, "respect for human rights depends first and foremost on the mentalities of individuals and social groups." Roosevelt mused in a 1958 interview:

> Where, after all, do human rights begin? In small places, close to home—so close and small that they cannot be seen on any maps of the world. . . . Unless these rights have meaning there, they have little meaning anywhere. Without concerned citizen action to uphold them close to home, we shall look in vain for progress in the larger world.

In sum, even a cursory reading of the Declaration in its entirety shows that it is no mere list of rights. In form, as distinct from content, the Declaration is recognizably a product of the drafting tradition that had been brought to its highest degree of refinement in the code-based continental European legal systems. The new rights instruments emerging from that tradition were patterned on the old codes in certain respects—their level of generality, the use of general clauses, the mutually conditioning relations among their parts, and the aspiration to be enduring. It follows that the Declaration is best understood through the methods of interpretation that are associated with that tradition.

The broad elements of those methods can be briefly summarized. The interpreter begins by reading the text as a whole, becoming aware of the interpretive guides that are embedded in it. Ordinarily, the text contains a few general principles that apply to the entire document, supplemented by special principles governing particular sections. Tension or conflict among principles and provisions is approached with a view toward respecting the priorities established in the text, and, if possible, optimizing the scope of each principle involved. Each interpretation should support the unity of the text.

Though there is wide consensus in the civil law world on the elements of an approach to interpretation, that does not preclude lively controversy over specific applications. And, in the case of human rights documents, laden with open-ended general clauses, there is plenty of room for debate as well as for reasoned elaboration of principle. Anticipating the incoherence critique mounted by Villey and others, McKeon tried to put the paradoxes of human rights in a positive light. "[They] are not ambiguities resulting from confusion or contradiction," he argued, "they are productive ambiguities which embody the knowledge and experience men have acquired in the long history of rights, and which provide the beginning points for further advances." The history of human rights is paradoxical because "it embodies concretely all the great antitheses and paralogisms explored by philosophers—the problems of the whole and the part, the universal and the particular, the internal and the external, the apparent and the real."[10]

---

[10] Richard McKeon, *Freedom and History,* ed. Zahava K. McKeon (Chicago: University of Chicago Press, 1990), 490.

Accepting McKeon's characterization, what then is to prevent the interpretation of a document embodying those great tensions from degenerating into utter chaos? Maritain had stressed the need for some "ultimate value whereon those rights depend and in terms of which they are integrated by mutual limitations."

But does the Declaration have such an ultimate value? An obvious candidate is human dignity. Dignity enjoys pride of place in the Declaration: It is affirmed ahead of rights at the very beginning of the Preamble; it is accorded priority again in Article 1; and it is woven into the text at three other key points, connecting the Declaration to the Charter in the fifth clause of the Preamble, introducing the social and economic rights in the "chapeau" (Article 22), and in Article 23's reference to "an existence worthy of human dignity."

The drafters fleshed out the dignity concept by connecting it to a fairly specific image of the human person. Human beings are said to be "endowed with reason and conscience," and they are expected to "act toward one another in a spirit of brotherhood." The Declaration's "everyone" is envisioned as an individual, uniquely valuable in himself. (There are three separate references to the "free development of his personality.") But "everyone" is also portrayed as situated in families, communities, workplaces, associations, societies, cultures, nations, and an emerging international order. In fact, Article 28 tells us that it is in community "alone" that the "free and full development of his personality is possible." Though its main body is devoted to basic freedoms, the Declaration begins and ends with exhortations to solidarity (Articles 1 and 29). Whatever else may be said of him or her, the Declaration's "everyone" is not a lone bearer of rights.

It is instructive to consider, in this connection, the approach that one of the world's most respected constitutional courts has taken to its own dignitarian rights document, approximately contemporaneous with the Universal Declaration. The German Basic Law of 1949, prepared under the watchful eyes of the Allied powers, begins by declaring in Article 1: "The dignity of man shall be inviolable. To respect and protect it shall be the duty of all state authority." In one of its earliest—and most frequently cited—decisions, the German Constitutional Court drew from the Basic Law as a whole a picture of the human person that has informed many subsequent decisions: "The image of man in the Basic Law is not that of an isolated, sovereign individual. The Basic Law resolves the tension between individual and society by relating and binding the individual to society, but without detracting from the intrinsic value of the person." As one commentator puts it, "this implies a departure from classical individualism, but at the same time rejects any form of collectivism."[11]

---

[11] Kurt Sontheimer, "Principles of Human Dignity in the Federal Republic," in *Germany and its Basic Law: Past, Present, and Future*, ed. Paul Kirchhof and Donald Kommers (Baden-Baden: Nomos Verlagsgesellschaft, 1993), 213, 215.

CHAPTER 38 • Knowing the Universal Declaration of Human Rights

Politically savvy, philosophically sophisticated creatures that they were, the Declaration's framers knew that the dignity principle possessed no special immunity to deconstruction, and that no document, however skillfully crafted, was proof against manipulation. Maritain said it best: Whether the music played on the Declaration's thirty strings will be "in tune with, or harmful to, human dignity," will depend primarily on the extent to which a "culture of human dignity" develops.

## REMEMBERING THE DECLARATION

To the disappointment of the framers, the adoption of the Declaration was followed by nearly two decades during which the international human rights project stalled amidst Cold War politics. By 1953, Cassin was complaining bitterly about what he considered to be the "scandalous politicization" of U.N. agencies, especially UNESCO. In his 1968 Nobel acceptance speech, he deplored the delays which he said had been "very prejudicial" to the preparation of covenants to implement the Declaration, and he blamed the "desire of certain powers to delay even modest measures of implementation out of concern for their national sovereignty."

As the Cold War gradually thawed, human rights consciousness did indeed increase. But when the Declaration woke up, so to speak, it was like Rip Van Winkle, who emerged from his long slumber to find himself in a world where no one recognized him. The architects of the Declaration were mostly departed or inactive, and in their place was forming a human rights industry, much influenced by the ideas about rights, both good and bad, that were developed in the American judicial rights revolution. The U.N. itself had grown in size and ambition; its specialized agencies, employing thousands of international civil servants, were surrounded by, and symbiotically intertwined with, various lobbying groups. The Declaration began to be widely, almost universally, read in the way that Americans read the Bill of Rights, that is, as a string of essentially separate guarantees.

By isolating each part from its place in an overall design, that now-common misreading of the Declaration promotes misunderstanding and facilitates misuse. The popular cafeteria approach to the Declaration's rights inevitably means that the devices that were supposed to support the integrity of the document would be ignored. A major casualty has been the Declaration's insistence on the links between freedom and solidarity, just at a time when affluent nations seem increasingly to be washing their hands of poor countries and peoples. As for the aspiration to universality, with 185 flags now flying outside U.N. headquarters, it is natural to wonder whether the idea can withstand the stresses of mutual suspicion and heightened national and ethnic assertiveness.

None of these problems have simple solutions. National interests and healthy economies are important, not only in themselves, but often for the sake of "better standards of living in larger freedom." The language of the Declaration is ambiguous. Principles such as freedom and solidarity *do* sit uneasily with one another. Meanwhile, in the years since 1948, "barbarous acts that outrage the conscience of mankind" have recurred with appalling regularity. Universal human rights remain an elusive dream.

At the present juncture, friends of human rights could do worse than to recall the framers' understandings of what a Declaration calling itself universal can and cannot accomplish. The men and women of 1948 were not naive about politics or human nature. To people who had lived through two world wars, it was evident that "even the noblest and most solemn declarations could not suffice to restore . . . faith in human rights." For the Soviets, that was the end of the matter. After the final vote in the U.N., Andrei Vishinsky contemptuously dismissed the Universal Declaration as just a "collection of pious phrases."

The Declaration's founding fathers and mothers had a vastly different, but no less realistic, outlook. For them, the elusiveness of the goal did not mean it was not worth pursuing with all one's might and main. While not exaggerating the importance of their work, neither did they underestimate the effects that might radiate from a common statement of principles. Malik predicted that the international human rights project would contribute to the formation of a "human rights conscience," and accurately foresaw that it would help to "focus the eyes of the world on the local scene." The Declaration itself is permeated with the realism as well as the hopes of the founders. It recognizes that implementation requires a common understanding that is still far from being achieved; it recognizes that freedom depends on certain social, political, and economic conditions; it anticipates and attempts to forestall the most egregious forms of misinterpretation.

So far as the tension between universal rights and particular traditions is concerned, the Declaration's framework is capacious enough to encompass a degree of pluralism. Philosophers like McKeon and Maritain did not regard recognition of universal rights and respect for particular cultures as irreconcilable. After all, rights emerge from culture, cannot be sustained without cultural underpinnings, and, to be effective, must become part of each people's way of life.

The UNESCO committee theorists did not believe a declaration of universal principles could, or should, lead to completely uniform means of expressing and protecting basic rights. Why should there not be different cultural expressions of the universal human longing for freedom, and different ways of pondering the eternal tensions between freedom and order, the individual and the group? Ideally, each rights tradition would be enriched as it put the principles into practice, and the various experiences of the nations would in turn enrich the understanding of universal rights. With improved communication and with the accumulation of experiences of successful

332 • Mary Ann Glendon

cross-cultural cooperation, they hoped, areas of common understanding would expand. But there would always be, as Maritain put it, different kinds of music played on the same keyboard.

That equanimity concerning different visions of freedom proceeded, no doubt, from modesty concerning the state of human knowledge. "No declaration of human rights will ever be exhaustive or final," Maritain concluded after pondering the history of rights ideas. The dynamic character of the relations among rights, the development of new rights, and new applications of old rights, McKeon added, would constantly "enrich their ambiguity."

One philosopher's fertile ambiguity, of course, is another's fatal flaw. As my own research has progressed, however, I have come to see the Declaration as, on the whole, remarkably well-designed. The flaws in the human rights enterprise are less in its documentary landmarks than in the human person—with all our potential for good and evil, reason and impulse, trust and betrayal, creativity and destruction, selfishness and cooperation. All too familiar with the defects in human nature, the framers nevertheless staked their faith, in Article 1, on "reason and conscience." But they were under no illusions about the precariousness of that wager.

The Declaration thus seems to me less like the Tower of B'abel than like the sculpture by Arnaldo Pomodoro that dominates the plaza outside the U.N. building in New York. A gift from the government of Italy, this marvel consists of an enormous sphere of burnished bronze, perhaps suggesting a globe. The sphere is pleasing to behold, even though it startles with its imperfection. There are deep, jagged cracks in its golden-hued surface, cracks too large to ever be repaired. Perhaps it's cracked because it's flawed (like the broken world), one thinks. Or maybe (like an egg) it has to break in order for something else to emerge. Perhaps both. Sure enough, when one peers into the gashes on its surface, there is another beautiful golden sphere coming along inside. But that one is already cracked, too!

I have no idea what Italy was trying to tell the United Nations! But whatever is going on inside these spheres, it doesn't seem to be all chance and accident. There is a tremendous sense of motion, of dynamism, of potency, of emergent probabilities.

Pomodoro's emerging spheres poignantly evoke the great problem of all politics: To what extent can the probabilities be shifted by reflection and choice, as distinct from the will of the stronger and the blind forces of history and accident? One does not have to be motivated by any love affair with the United Nations to appreciate the importance of a small core of principles to which people of vastly different backgrounds can appeal. To give up on the existence of such principles is to give up on the possibility of cross-cultural deliberation about the human future. It is to give up on the common humanity that makes it possible for people of different cultures to deliberate about how we are to order our lives together in an interdependent world. The framers of the Universal Declaration deserve better, as do the millions of women, men, and children who still lack the essentials for dignified living.

# Foundations of Human Rights: The Unfinished Business

*The more I learned about the circumstances of the framing of the Universal Declaration of Human Rights, the more I realized that the framers had consciously left a crucial task unfinished: demonstrating that fundamental rights could be grounded in the world's major philosophical and religious traditions. This essay appeared in 1999 American Journal of Jurisprudence.[1]*

O VER THE TWO YEARS it took them to draft the 1948 Universal Declaration of Human Rights, the eighteen members of the U.N.'s first Human Rights Commission had surprisingly few discussions of why human beings have rights or why some rights are universal. After the horrors of two world wars, the need for a minimal common standard of decency seemed evident. One of the first tasks assigned to the new Commission chaired by Eleanor Roosevelt was the preparation of an "international bill of rights." The Commissioners, in haste to complete their work before the deepening Cold War made its acceptance by the General Assembly impossible, left the problem of foundations for another day.

At the Commission's first session in January 1947, China's Peng-chun Chang and Lebanon's Charles Malik did try to initiate a discussion of the premises on which such a document might be based. Chang was a Confucian philosopher and educator who had done postgraduate work with John Dewey, and Malik was a philosopher of science who had studied with Alfred North Whitehead and Martin Heidegger. Their suggestions precipitated the Commission's first argument. The Yugoslav, French, and English delegates began to wrangle over the relation between man and society.

Several other Commissioners became impatient with that sort of discussion. They just wanted to get on with the business at hand. After a time, India's Hansa Mehta broke in. She was one of two women on the Commission, a pioneering human rights activist, a crusader against British colonialism,

---

[1] Mary Ann Glendon, "Foundations of Human Rights: The Unfinished Business," *American Journal of Jurisprudence* (1999):1–14.

and an advocate for women's equality. She said, "We are here to affirm faith in fundamental human rights. Whether the human person comes first or the society, I do not think we should discuss that problem now. We do not need to enter into this maze of ideology."[2]

Charles Malik, who had been literally called out of his Beirut classroom and pressed into public service by the government of newly independent Lebanon, had not yet perfected the suave diplomatic style for which he would later become famous. He rebuked Mrs. Mehta as a professor of the old school would chide a student, saying: "Whatever you may say, Madam, must have ideological presuppositions, and no matter how much you may fight shy of them, they are there, and you either hide them or you are brave enough to bring them out in the open and see them and criticize them."[3]

The Commission's Chair, Eleanor Roosevelt, quickly realized that the group would have to concentrate on specifics if the project was to stay on course. She steered the discussion back to the problem of organizing the group's work schedule. Thereafter, the question of foundations surfaced only sporadically. One such occasion was the presentation of a discussion draft by the Secretariat of the U.N. Human Rights Division. Australia's Colonel Roy Hodgson demanded to know what was the philosophy behind the paper: "What principles did they adopt; what method did they follow?"[4] John Humphrey, the Canadian head of the Human Rights Division, replied that the draft "was based on no philosophy whatsoever." It was, he said, merely a collection from existing constitutions of "every conceivable right which the Drafting Committee might want to discuss."[5]

At the very end of the drafting process, and without much discussion, the Commissioners did make a statement about the basis of human rights in the Preamble to the 1948 Declaration. The Preamble's opening line recites that "recognition of the inherent dignity and of the equal and inalienable rights of all members of the human family is the foundation of freedom, justice and peace in the world." The word "dignity" appears at so many key points in the Declaration that many scholars believe it represents the Declaration's ultimate value. Louis Henkin puts it this way: "Eschewing—in its quest for universality—explicit reliance on Divine inspiration or on Natural Rights, the Declaration provided the idea of human rights with a universally acceptable foundation, an *ur* principle, human dignity."[6]

---

2 Verbatim Record, from *The More Important Speeches and Interventions of Charles Malik* (Papers of Charles Malik, Library of Congress, Manuscript Division), 38.

3 Ibid., 44.

4 Human Rights Commission, Drafting Committee, First Session (E/CN.4/AC.1/SR.1, 5).

5 Ibid.

6 Louis Henkin, "The Ideals of Human Rights: Ideology and Aspiration, Reality and Prospect," in *Realizing Human Rights*, S. Power and G. Allison, eds. (New York: St. Martin's Press, 2000), 3, 11.

But inquiring minds must ask what is this "dignity," and what is *its* basis? Its proximate source is easy to locate. The U.N. Charter professes "faith in freedom and democracy," which, according to the Charter, is grounded in another "faith"—"in the inherent dignity of men and women." That is a good deal of faith for a document that eschews divine inspiration. No wonder we find Nobel laureate Czeslaw Milosz musing ruefully about "those beautiful and deeply moving words which pertain to the old repertory of the rights of man and the dignity of the person." Milosz continues, "I wonder at this phenomenon because maybe underneath there is an abyss. After all, these ideas had their foundation in religion, and I am not over-optimistic as to the survival of religion in a scientific-technological civilization. Notions that seemed buried forever have suddenly been resurrected. But how long will they stay afloat if the bottom is taken out?"

Milosz puts the question neatly as only a poet can. Is the universal rights idea merely based on a kind of existential leap of faith? Or does it have some sturdier basis?

Such questions came to the surface when the Universal Declaration celebrated its fiftieth anniversary in 1998 amidst a barrage of attacks upon its aspiration to universality—mainly in the name of cultural relativism. Typically these assaults describe the Declaration as an attempt to universalize a particular "Western" set of ideas and to impose them upon people who were under colonial rule and thus not represented in its creation. The human rights project is dismissed as an instrument of "cultural imperialism" or "neo-colonialism."

An equally common retort is that cultural imperialism is the cry of the world's worst rights violators. That sort of response, however, is obviously inadequate: The allegations of cultural relativism and imperialism could be hypocritical or ideologically motivated, but nevertheless true. I propose therefore to take the accusations seriously.

My conclusions are as follows: (1) The Universal Declaration was an impressively, though imperfectly, multicultural document when it was adopted in 1948. It cannot be dismissed as "Western." (2) The framers of the Declaration did take account of the diversity of cultures by leaving room for a legitimate pluralism in interpreting and implementing its open-ended principles. (3) The danger of human rights imperialism is real, but its source is in the efforts of special interest groups to commandeer human rights for their own purposes, rather than in the Declaration itself. (4) The human rights project will rest on shaky foundations unless and until philosophers and statespersons collaborate on the business that the framers left unfinished.

## IS THE UNIVERSAL DECLARATION "WESTERN"?

Those who label the Universal Declaration "Western" base the claim mainly on two facts: (1) many of the world's peoples, especially those still living under colonial rule, were not represented in the United Nations in 1948, and (2) most of the Declaration's rights first appeared in European and North and South American documents. Those statements are correct, but do they destroy the universality of the Declaration?

Contrary to what is often suggested, the participation by developing countries in the framing of the Declaration was by no means negligible. At the U.N.'s founding conference in San Francisco conference in 1945, it was chiefly the smaller or less developed nations who were responsible for the prominent position of human rights in the U.N. Charter. Within the eighteen-member Human Rights Commission, China's Peng-chun Chang, Lebanon's Charles Malik, the Philippines' Carlos Romulo, and Chile's Hernàn Santa Cruz were among the most influential and active members. It is sometimes said that the educational backgrounds or professional experiences of widely traveled men like Chang and Malik "westernized" them, but their performance in the Human Rights Commission suggests something rather different. Not only did each contribute significant insights from his own culture, but each possessed an exceptional ability to understand other cultures, and to "translate" concepts from one frame of reference to another. Those skills, which can hardly be acquired without substantial exposure to traditions other than one's own, are indispensable for effective cross-cultural collaboration and were key to the adoption of the Declaration without a single dissenting vote in 1948.

The Declaration itself was based on extensive comparative study. The first draft, prepared by the U.N. Secretariat, was accompanied by a 408-page document showing the relationship of each article to provisions of the world's existing and proposed constitutions and declarations. When the Human Rights Commission's second draft was submitted to U.N. members for comment, responses were received from a group of nations that included Brazil, Egypt, India, Mexico, and Pakistan, South Africa, Sweden, and the United States.

Among the 58 Member States represented on the U.N. General Assembly's committee which reviewed the near-final draft in the fall of 1948, there was even greater cultural and ideological diversity. This Committee on Social, Cultural, and Humanitarian Affairs (known as the Third Committee) was chaired by Charles Malik. It included six members from Asia, four from the African continent (Egypt, Ethiopia, Liberia, and South Africa), plus the large Latin American contingent. Six of the "European" members belonged to the communist bloc; Islamic culture was strong in eleven; and four had large Buddhist populations. Over the course of more than one hundred meetings, the members of this large committee went over every word of the draft. Each country's representatives were given, and most of them enthusiastically seized, the opportunity to participate.

At the end of this process, Charles Malik could justly say of the Universal Declaration that "All effective cultures in the world had a creative hand in the shaping of the document. . . ." As Malik put it, "The genesis of each article, and each part of each article, was a dynamic process in which many minds, interests, backgrounds, legal systems and ideological persuasions played their respective determining roles."[7]

It was, of course, true that much of the world's population was not represented in the U.N. in 1948. Large parts of Africa and Asia in particular remained under colonial rule. The defeated Axis powers Japan, Germany, and their allies were excluded. On the other hand, subsequent actions by the non-represented countries suggest that cultural "diversity" had been greatly exaggerated where basic human goods are concerned. Most new nations adopted constitutions resembling the Universal Declaration as soon as they gained independence. Later, nearly all of these countries ratified the two 1966 Covenants based on the Declaration. In 1993, virtually all countries in the world participated in the adoption of the Vienna Human Rights Declaration, which reaffirms the Universal Declaration. It is hard to dismiss this overwhelming endorsement of the principles of the Declaration as a mere vestige of the colonial mentality.

It is unlikely that any other political document in history has ever drawn from such diverse sources, or received the same worldwide, sustained consideration and scrutiny as the Declaration underwent over its two years of preparation. Despite all the wrangling that occurred over specifics, moreover, there was remarkably little disagreement regarding its basic substance. At every stage, even the Communist bloc, South Africa, and Saudi Arabia voted in favor of most of the articles when they were taken up one by one. The biggest battles were political, occasioned by Soviet concerns to protect their national sovereignty.

But what of the second objection mentioned above—the fact that several key ideas in the Declaration were initially described as rights in early modern Europe? On this point, the findings of a UNESCO philosophers' committee, which included Jacques Maritain and University of Chicago philosopher Richard McKeon, are instructive. After surveying leading philosophers and religious thinkers the world over, the UNESCO group discovered to its surprise that a few basic practical concepts of humane conduct were so widely shared that they "may be viewed as implicit in man's nature as a member of society." Freedom, dignity, tolerance, and neighborliness, they found, were highly prized in many cultural and religious traditions.

Nevertheless, the elaboration of these concepts as "rights" was a relatively modern, and European, phenomenon. So, does that give human rights a genetic taint that prevents them from being "universal"? Surely, their origin ought not to be decisive. The question should be not who had the idea first, but whether the idea is a good one; not where the idea was born, but whether

---

[7] Charles Malik, "Introduction," in *O. Frederick Nolde, Free and Equal: Human Rights in Ecumenical Perspective* (Geneva: World Council of Churches, 1968), 12.

it is conducive to human flourishing. Moreover, if a legal-political idea originated in one country but was widely adopted and internalized elsewhere, for
how long and in what sense does it still "belong" to its country of origin? Do
not all vibrant, living cultures constantly borrow from one another?

Consider the civil law tradition that originated in ancient Rome. In
1948 that tradition was, and remains today, the most widely distributed
legal tradition in the world. The form and style of the Declaration gives it a
familial resemblance, not only to rights declarations in many continental
European constitutions, but to the constitutions and charters that had
appeared or were soon to appear in many Latin American, African, and
Asian countries. Does that make all these instruments Roman? The French
Civil Code of 1804 was widely copied by newly independent peoples in
Latin America who admired its clarity and were inspired by its consolidation
of a Revolution which had abolished the old unequal statuses of feudalism.
Does that make the law of all those countries French?

And what does the term "Western" mean anyway, if it is more than an
epithet? The majority of the U.N.'s membership in 1948, perhaps as many
as 37 countries, might have been described as "Western" in the sense of
being influenced by Judeo-Christian traditions and Enlightenment thought.
But how much sense does it make to lump together under a single label a
group that comprises Latin Americans and North Americans, East and West
Europeans, Australians and New Zealanders? By the same token, such broad
concepts as "Asian" or "Islamic" values are not very informative, given the
great variety within traditions. As the Chinese member of the first Human
Rights Commission, P. C. Chang, observed long ago, "Culturally, there are
many 'Easts' and many 'Wests'; and they are by no means all necessarily
irreconcilable."[8]

## HOW CAN THERE BE UNIVERSAL RIGHTS IN DIVERSE CULTURES?

Let us now turn to a more sophisticated version of the cultural relativism critique. Assume that the UNESCO philosophers were right that a few basic
norms of decent human behavior are very widely shared. Even if that is so at
a general level, different nations and cultures attach quite different weights
to these norms. Moreover, different political and economic conditions affect
each nation's ability to bring human rights principles to life. That being so,
what sense does it make to speak of universality?

That version of the cultural relativism critique rests on a false premise
shared by many rights activists and rights skeptics alike. It is the assumption
that universal principles must be implemented in the same way everywhere.

---

[8] P.C. Chang, *China at the Crossroads: The Chinese Situation in Perspective* (London:
Evans, 1936), 124–25.

The Declaration's framers, however, never envisioned that its "common standard of achievement" would or should produce completely uniform practices. P. C. Chang stressed that point in his 9 December 1948 speech to the General Assembly urging adoption of the Declaration. He deplored that colonial powers had tried to impose on other peoples a standardized way of thinking and a single way of life. That sort of uniformity could only be achieved, he said, by force or at the expense of truth. It could never last. Chang and his colleagues on the drafting committee expected the Declaration's rights would be inculturated in various ways, and that over time the corpus of human rights would be enriched by these varied experiences.

The framers of the Universal Declaration also knew it was neither possible nor desirable for the Declaration to be frozen in *time*. They never claimed to have produced the last word on human rights. They expected that new rights would emerge in the future as they had in the past, and that old rights might be reformulated. That did not mean, however, that interpretation was up for grabs. They tried to provide the Declaration with safe passage through such transitions by giving it an interpretive matrix: freedom and solidarity, linked to a thick concept of personhood, and grounded in dignity.

The framers' approach was remembered by at least one distinguished international lawyer on the document's 35th anniversary in 1983. Philip Alston wrote on that occasion, "The Declaration does not purport to offer a single unified conception of the world as it should be nor does it purport to offer some sort of comprehensive recipe for the attainment of an ideal world. Its purpose is rather the more modest one of proclaiming a set of values which are capable of giving some guidance to modern society in choosing among a wide range of alternative policy options."[9]

By the 1970s, however, the original understanding of the Declaration was largely forgotten. And what oblivion had not erased, opportunism was eroding. The abstentions by South Africa and Saudi Arabia from the final vote approving the Declaration had been early warnings of more trouble ahead. South Africa had objected to, among other things, the word "dignity," apparently fearing its implications for the apartheid system it was then constructing. Saudi Arabia had claimed that some of the so-called universal rights, particularly the right to change one's religion, were really just "Western" ideas. In 1948, those were isolated claims. But no sooner was the Declaration adopted than the Cold War antagonists pulled apart and politicized its provisions. That set the stage for further mischief. In 1955, the charge that some rights represented "Western" neo-colonialism resurfaced with particular vehemence at the Bandung conference, where the "non-aligned" nations found unity of a sort in shared resentment of the dominance of a few rich and powerful countries in world affairs.

[9] Philip Alston, "The Universal Declaration at 35," *International Commission of Jurists Review* 30 (1983): 60, 69.

CHAPTER 39 • Foundations of Human Rights: The Unfinished Business

# THE DECONSTRUCTION DERBY

Over the 1960s and 1970s, the Declaration's framers, one by one, were departing from the world stage. The U.N. grew into an elaborate bureaucracy with more than 50,000 employees. Its specialized agencies become closely intertwined with the non-governmental organizations that proliferated as the international human rights movement gained ground in the 1960s and 1970s. That movement in turn was deeply affected by the ideas about rights that predominated in the United States in those days. The movement, like the Declaration itself, attracted many persons and groups who were more interested in harnessing its moral authority for their own ends than in furthering its original purposes.

Another important development, set in motion by the Cold War antagonists, was the nearly universal habit of reading the Declaration in the way that Americans read the Bill of Rights, that is, as a string of essentially separate guarantees. Its dignity-based language of rights began to be displaced by the more simplistic kinds of rights talk that were then making great inroads on political discourse in the United States. Several features of that new, hyper-individualistic dialect had the potential to wreak havoc with the Declaration: rights envisioned without individual or social responsibilities; one's favorite rights touted as absolute with others ignored; the rights-bearer imagined as radically autonomous and self-sufficient; the trivialization of core freedoms by special interests posing as new rights.

Thus, ironically, the charge of cultural imperialism has more credibility than it had in 1948. The global spread of hyper-libertarian, radically individualistic, sound-bite rights ideas has rendered the contemporary international human rights project more vulnerable to the label of "Western" than the Declaration ever was. Launched as a commitment by the nations to compete in advancing human freedom and dignity, the Declaration is now in danger of becoming what its critics have always accused it of being—an instrument of neo-colonialism!

For decades, the seamlessness of the Declaration has been ignored by its professed supporters as well as by its attackers. By isolating each part from its place in the overall design, the now common misreading of the Declaration promotes misunderstanding and facilitates misuse. Nations and interest groups ignore the provisions they find inconvenient and treat others as trumps. A major casualty has been the Declaration's insistence on the links between freedom and solidarity, just at a time when affluent nations seem increasingly to be washing their hands of poor countries and peoples.

For examples of deconstruction in operation, one could do no better than to eavesdrop on the rights babble of the big U.N. conferences of the 1990s. At first glance, the U.N. might seem to be an unlikely forum for the pursuit of law reform. But its agencies and conferences have attracted numerous special interest groups whose agendas have trouble passing muster in ordinary domestic political processes. Over the years, lobbyists of various sorts have acquired considerable influence in the U.N. bureaucracy, whose processes are even less transparent than those of U.S. administrative agencies.

Thus was the stage set for the U.N. and its conferences to become offshore manufacturing sites where the least popular (or least avowable) ideas of special interest groups could be converted into "international norms." These norms, though technically lacking the status of fundamental rights, could then be portrayed at home as universal standards, and imposed on poor countries as conditions for the receipt of aid.

At the U.N.'s 1995 Women's Conference in Beijing, for example, strenuous efforts were made to advance a new human rights paradigm—mainly by representatives from affluent countries. In her speech to a plenary session on the second day of the conference, U.S. First Lady Hillary Rodham Clinton gave high visibility to a misleading slogan. "If there is one message that echoes forth from this conference," she asserted, "it is that human rights are women's rights, and women's rights are human rights."[10] The statement was half true, but only half true. Human rights do belong to everyone. But not every right that has been granted to women by a particular nation-state has gained the status of a human right. The slogan was mainly aimed at universalizing extreme, American-style abortion rights in a world where few countries, if any, go as far as the United States and China in permitting abortions of healthy, viable unborn children.

That there might be some such demolition derby in the Declaration's future was foreseen long ago by Richard McKeon. McKeon realized what every lawyer knows: Practical agreements such as those reached by the U.N. member states in 1948 are achieved only at the price of a certain ambiguity. The framers knew that the same generality that made agreement possible rendered the document vulnerable to misunderstanding and manipulation. In his UNESCO report, McKeon pointed out that different understandings of the meanings of rights usually reflect divergent concepts of man and of society, which in turn cause the persons who hold those understandings to have different views of reality. Thus, he predicted that "difficulties will be discovered in the suspicions, suggested by these differences, concerning the tangential uses that might be made of a declaration of human rights for the purpose of advancing special interests."[11] That was a philosopher's way of saying, "Watch out, this whole enterprise could be hijacked!"

---

[10] Steven Mufson, "First Lady Critical of China, Others on Women's Rights," *Washington Post* (September 6, 1995): A1.

[11] Richard McKeon, "The Philosophic Bases and Material Circumstances of the Rights of Man," in *Human Rights: Comments and Interpretations* (New York: Columbia University Press, 1949), 35, 36.

CHAPTER 39 • Foundations of Human Rights: The Unfinished Business

In sum, the human rights project, launched as a multicultural commitment to compete in advancing freedom and dignity, is now in danger of becoming what its enemies and critics have always accused it of being—an instrument of "Western" cultural imperialism.

That irony did not escape the attention of Calcutta-born, Cambridge economist Amartya Sen. In 1994, just before the U.N.'s Cairo Conference on Population and Development, Sen warned in the *New York Review of Books* that the developed nations were exhibiting a dangerous tendency to approach population issues with a mentality that "treats the people involved not as reasonable beings, allies faced with a common problem, but as impulsive and uncontrolled sources of great social harm, in need of strong discipline." Sen, who won the Nobel Prize for his works on inequality and world hunger, charged that international policymakers, by giving priority to "family planning arrangements in the Third World countries over other commitments such as education and health care, produce negative effects on people's well-being and reduce their freedoms."[12] In short, the whole range of human rights of poor people is at risk when special interests are dressed up as universal rights.

The good news is that as the U.N. enters a period of austerity, the era of big conferences like Cairo and Beijing is probably drawing to a close. The bad news is that the same economic pressures that are putting a damper on huge international gatherings, however, may aggravate the danger of capture of U.N. agencies by well-financed special interests. A case in point is CNN founder Ted Turner's $1 billion "gift" to the U.N. announced in the fall of 1997. Many who look to the U.N. for leadership in humanitarian aid were overjoyed when Mr. Turner announced that his donation was to help "the poorest of the poor." Paid out in installments of $100 million a year for ten years, this infusion of funds would have ranked behind the annual contributions of only the U.S., Japan, and Germany.

The news seemed too good to be true. It was. It soon appeared that the U.N. would not have control over the funds. Rather, its agencies would be required to submit proposals for approval by a foundation headed by a man Mr. Turner chose because "he thinks as I do." The man designated to have the chief say in allocating the Turner millions is former U.S. State Department official Timothy Wirth who spearheaded the aggressive U.S. population control agenda at the 1994 Cairo conference. Wirth has been so zealous in advocating population control that he has even praised China, with its coercive one-child-per-family policy, for its "very, very effective high-investment family planning."[13] As for Mr. Turner, he told a California audience in 1998, that in

[12] Amartya Sen, "Population: Delusion and Reality," *New York Review of Books,* (September 22, 1994): 62.
[13] Quoted in Jeffrey Gedmin, "Clinton's Touchy Feely Foreign Policy," *Weekly Standard* (May 13, 1996): 19, 22.

the post-Cold War world, "The real threat is no longer an army marching on us, it's people infiltrating us, you know, people that are starving."[14]

As its details have unfolded, Mr. Turner's gesture looks less like a gift and more like a take-over bid aimed at U.N. agencies with privileged access to vulnerable populations. The next few years are thus likely to be a time of testing for the U.N. if its prestige and organizational resources are not to be, literally, for sale.

As memories fade about why the nations of the world determined after World War II to affirm certain basic rights as universal, efforts to deconstruct the Universal Declaration and remake it nearer to the heart's desire of this or that special interest group will continue. Whether the relatively rich and complex vision of human rights in the Universal Declaration can withstand the combined stresses of aggressive lobbying, heightened national and ethnic assertiveness, and the powerful, ambiguous forces of globalization is impossible to foresee. Not only U.N. agencies, but the governments of several liberal democracies have become implicated in breaking down the connections among its indivisible rights and deconstructing its core principle, human dignity.

## THE CHALLENGE OF HUMAN RIGHTS

The contest for control of the meaning of the Declaration forcefully reminds us that the framers of the Universal Declaration left the human rights movement with a problem. As John Paul II put it in his Address to the Vatican Diplomatic Corps in January 1989, "[T]he 1948 Declaration does not contain the anthropological and moral bases for the human rights that it proclaims." How, then, can one handle the problem of reconciling tensions among the various rights, or the related problem of integrating new rights from time to time?

Those problems are serious, and have led some thoughtful persons to conclude that the Declaration is hopelessly incoherent. The late Michel Villey, for example, maintained that, "Each of the so-called human rights is the negation of other human rights, and when practiced separately generates *injustices*."[15] Alasdair MacIntyre argues that different rights, borrowed from different traditions, often rest on different, and incommensurable, moral premises.[16]

These problems were not overlooked by Maritain and his colleagues. Maritain noted that, "Where difficulties and arguments begin is in the determination of the scale of values governing the exercise and concrete integration of

---

[14] Ann Bardach, "Turner in 2000?" *New Yorker* (November 23, 1998): 36, 37.

[15] Michel Villey, *Le droit et les droits de l'homme* (Paris: Presses Universitaires de France, 1983), 13.

[16] Alasdair MacIntyre, *After Virtue,* 2d. ed. (Notre Dame, IN: University of Notre Dame Press, 1981).

these various rights."[17] The Declaration, he went on, would need some "ulti-mate value whereon those rights depend and in terms of which they are inte-grated by mutual limitations." That value, explicitly set forth in the Declaration, is human dignity. But as time went on, it has become painfully apparent that dignity possesses no more immunity to hijacking than any other concept. One need only think of current defenses of active euthanasia in terms of "the right to die with dignity." (There is no end, it seems, of pseudo-rights that the stronger are eager to confer upon the weaker whether the latter are willing or not.)

The shift from nature to dignity in modern thinking about the founda-tions of human rights thus entails a host of difficulties. The common secular understandings are that human beings have dignity because they are autonomous beings capable of making choices (Kant), or because of the sense of empathy that most human beings feel for other sentient creatures (Rousseau). But the former understanding has alarming implications for persons of diminished capacity, and the latter places all morality on the frag-ile basis of a transient feeling. Most believers, for their part, would say that dignity is grounded in the fact that human beings are made in the image and likeness of God, but that proposition is unintelligible to nonbelievers.

Moreover, the path from dignity to rights is not clear and straight, even for believers. Brian Benestad has pointed out that the term "dignity of the human person" has two different connotations in Christian teaching—"[it] is *both* a given and an *achievement* or an end to be gradually realized."[18] The Catholic Catechism, he notes, begins its discussion of morality with this quo-tation from Pope Leo the Great: "Christian, recognize your dignity, and now that you share in God's own nature, do not return by sin to your former base condition." But if dignity is a quality to be achieved by strenuous effort to overcome sin and practice virtue, then it is not altogether clear that the dignity of the rights claimant is an adequate basis for human rights. Not every rights claimant, obviously, has made strenuous effort to overcome sin. From a Chris-tian point of view, the resolution of this dilemma may be that human rights are grounded in the obligation of everyone to perfect one's own dignity, which in turn obliges one to respect the "given" spark of dignity of others whatever they may have done with it. In other words, it may be our own quest for dig-nity (individually and as a society) that requires us to refrain from inflicting cruel punishments on criminals, or from terminating the lives of the unborn and others whose faculties are undeveloped or dormant.

In that light, the drafters of the U.N. Charter were prudent to say that human rights rest upon a "faith" in human dignity. It would be a mistake,

[17] Jacques Maritain, "Introduction" in *Human Rights: Comments and Interpretations*, UNESCO ed. (London & New York: Wingate, 1949), 9, 15–16.
[18] Brian Benestad, "What Do Catholics Know about Catholic Social Thought?" in *Keeping Faith*, Patrick Riley, ed. (Front Royal, VA: Christendom Press, 2000), 31–61.

however, to leap from that proposition to the notion that this faith is merely an act of will, an arbitrary choice. All in all, one may say of "dignity" in the Universal Declaration what Abraham Lincoln once said about "equality" in the Declaration of Independence: It is a hard nut to crack. The framers of the Universal Declaration were far from naive about the difficulties that lay ahead. That is evident from many statements in which they acknowledged the priority of culture over law. Though Maritain was not, strictly speaking, a framer, he said it best. Whether the music played on the Declaration's thirty strings will be "in tune with, or harmful to, human dignity," he wrote, will depend primarily on the extent to which a "culture of human dignity develops."[19]

If Maritain, Eleanor Roosevelt, Charles Malik, René Cassin, and others who held this view were right, then a great challenge faces the world's religions, for religion is at the heart of culture. Ultimately it will be up to the religions to demonstrate whether they are capable of motivating their followers to fulfill their own calling to perfect their own dignity, and in so doing to respect the dignity of fellow members of the human family.

---

[19] Jacques Maritain, "Introduction" in *Human Rights: Comments and Interpretations*, UNESCO, ed. (London & New York, Wingate, 1949), 9, 16.

# Catholic Thought and Dilemmas of Human Rights

*My research on the origins of the Universal Declaration of Human Rights disclosed a number of ways in which Catholic Social Teachings had influenced the document as well as how the universal rights idea seemed to have affected the development of the Church's social doctrine. A 1999 symposium at Notre Dame provided the occasion to explore that reciprocal relationship. The essay appeared in* Higher Learning and Catholic Traditions. [1]

THE PARTICIPANTS IN THIS SYMPOSIUM on "Higher Learning and Catholic Traditions" were invited to reflect on whether the Catholic intellectual heritage could offer "unexplored points of view and intellectual models" useful in our respective fields of study. In my case, that invitation arrived when I was in the midst of research on the framing of the United Nations' Universal Declaration of Human Rights (UDHR), and just at a point where I had concluded that Catholic thought might be helpful in resolving four thorny dilemmas that have beset the human rights project from its outset: the dilemmas arising from challenges to its universality, its foundations, its truth claims, and the indivisibility of fundamental rights.

The UDHR was drafted over a two-year period by the U.N.'s first Human Rights Commission, chaired by Eleanor Roosevelt, and was proclaimed by the General Assembly as a "common standard of achievement" in December 1948. Though the great powers of the day attached little importance to that aspirational document, the Universal Declaration surprised everyone by becoming the world's single most important reference point for cross-cultural discussions of human freedom and dignity. It became the polestar of humanity's second great "rights moment," the era of the rights instruments that may be called dignitarian, to distinguish them from their more libertarian eighteenth-century predecessors.

---

[1] Mary Ann Glendon, "Catholic Thought and Dilemmas of Human Rights," in *Higher Learning and Catholic Traditions*, ed. Robert E. Sullivan (Notre Dame, IN: University of Notre Dame Press, 2001), 113–30.

For the entire twentieth century, Catholic social thought and the dignitarian vision of human rights have been closely connected. In this essay, I briefly review some of the ways in which Catholic thought influenced the content of the UDHR, and the manner in which that "gift" was reciprocated when the Church drew upon the Universal Declaration in its Vatican II documents, and in several papal encyclicals. Then, turning to the main subject of this symposium, I suggest that it is time for the flow of ideas to be reversed again as friends of human rights struggle to prevent the Universal Declaration from being pulled apart and politicized beyond recognition.

## CATHOLIC INFLUENCES ON THE UNIVERSAL DECLARATION

Americans, when they read the Universal Declaration, are apt to be struck by its differences from, as well as its similarities to, our own Bill of Rights, especially where its emphasis on family protection and social and economic justice are concerned. Economic conservatives often surmise that the rights to social security, to work, to protection against unemployment, to join trade unions, and to an adequate standard of living were included at the behest of the Soviet Union, and for that reason alone many have refused to take the Declaration seriously as a universal standard. Catholics acquainted with the Church's social doctrine, however, will find more than a few familiar ideas: the emphasis on the "inherent dignity" and "worth of the human person"; the affirmation that the human person is "endowed with reason and conscience"; the recognition of the family as the "natural and fundamental group unit of society" entitled as such to "protection by society and the state"; the insistence that certain economic and social goods are "indispensable" for human dignity; that parents have a prior right to choose the education of their children; and that motherhood and childhood are entitled to "special care and assistance."

These concepts are not prominent in the Anglo-American rights tradition, but neither do they fit neatly with Marxist-Leninist rights theory which makes the state the sole source and guarantor of rights.

Where, then, did these ideas come from? In the manner of legal drafters everywhere, the framers of the UDHR derived most of the content of its thirty articles from existing models—constitutions and rights instruments that the staff of the U.N. Human Rights Division had collected from all over the world.

The provisions listed above were based mainly on early twentieth-century continental European and Latin American constitutions, and from the document that became the 1948 Pan-American (or Bogota) Declaration of the Rights and Duties of Man. The ideas they embodied were standard features of the dignitarian family of rights instruments, and they are part of what sets that family apart both from positivist state socialism and the more individualistic, liberty-based constitutions of the Anglo-American world.

But how did this constellation of ideas find its way into so many twentieth-century constitutions? The proximate answer to that question is: mainly through the programs of political parties. The social and economic rights were promoted by Social-Democratic, Labor, and Christian parties alike, while rights pertaining to the family and the protection of the mediating structures of civil society were more attributable to Christian political and labor organizations.

But where did Christian parties and unions get *their* ideas about the family, work, civil society, and the dignity of the person? The proximate answer to that is: mainly from *Rerum Novarum* (1891) and *Quadragesimo Anno* (1931) in which Leo XIII and Pius XI, respectively, rethought the Enlightenment, the eighteenth-century revolutions, socialism, and the labor question in the light of Scripture, tradition, and the Church's experience as an "expert in humanity."

Even before World War II drew to a close, voices were raised in several quarters in favor of including some sort of human rights provision in an eventual peace treaty. Among them was that of Pope Pius XII, who, in his June 1, 1941 radio address, called for an international bill recognizing the rights that flowed from the dignity of the person. Against that background, it is easy to see how the dignitarian rights tradition found its way into many national legal systems and ultimately into the Universal Declaration.

Contrary to what is now widely believed, the UDHR's social and economic justice provisions also had very broad support—including from the United States until the Eisenhower administration reorganized the State Department and asked for Eleanor Roosevelt's resignation from the Human Rights Commission. (There were, to be sure, heated disputes over the precise formulation of those ideas and the manner in which they were to be implemented.) The most zealous promoters of social and economic goods in the particular form in which they entered the Declaration were from the Latin American countries, then the largest single group of countries in the United Nations.

The family-related provisions also had broad support in the drafting process. They were already present in many Latin American and continental European constitutions, and were thus quite familiar to René Cassin, the French Jewish lawyer who was one of the chief drafters of the Declaration. It was Cassin who introduced most of this material into the draft, where it was expanded and refined by many others over a two-year period. The main defender of this group of ideas was Lebanon's Charles Malik, the most formidable intellectual on the drafting committee. I was struck, in reading U.N. records, to see Malik's use of terms like "intermediate associations" of civil society, and his emphatic preference for the term "person" rather than "individual." Later, I had the opportunity to ask Malik's son where his father, a member of the Greek Orthodox faith, had acquired his ideas about the social dimension of personhood, and the importance of mediating structures. The answer was: from *Rerum Novarum* and *Quadragesimo Anno*. Charles Malik was one of the first of an impressive line of non-Catholic intellectuals who have found a treasure trove of ideas in Catholic social teaching.

Besides those direct influences on the drafting process, there were several indirect channels through which Catholic thought reached the framers of the UDHR. The National Catholic Welfare Conference (forerunner of the National Conference of Catholic Bishops) had an observer at practically every session of the Human Rights Commission. And both Cassin and Malik were acquainted with Jacques Maritain, who was one of the most active members of a committee that UNESCO had appointed to study the theoretical foundations of human rights.

When the draft Declaration was submitted for one last review to a large committee composed of representatives from all 58 U.N. member nations, the Latin Americans were again among the most active participants, offering many amendments and refinements. The Canadian lawyer who was then serving as the Director of the U.N. Division of Human Rights did not like this time-consuming development at all. In his memoirs, John Humphrey referred to the Latin American efforts to bring in ideas from the 1948 Pan-American Declaration as "the Bogota Menace." Of the group's Cuban spokesman, he said, "Highly intelligent, Guy Perez Cisneros used every procedural device to reach his end. His speeches were laced with Roman Catholic social philosophy, and it seemed at times that the chief protagonists in the conference room were the Roman Catholics and the communists, with the latter a poor second." In his private diaries, Humphrey gave somewhat freer vent to his feelings. There, he described Cisneros as a man who "combines demagogy with Roman Catholic social philosophy," and said that the Cuban "should burn in hell" for holding up the proceedings with his numerous calls for amendments.[2]

There were of course many other influences on the Universal Declaration, but as the foregoing discussion indicates, it is no mere coincidence that its implicit vision of personhood, its attention to the mediating structures of civil society, its dignitarian character, and its insistence on the links between freedom and social justice so closely resemble the social teachings of Leo XIII and Pius XI. In later years, that influence was reciprocated.

## THE INFLUENCE OF THE UNIVERSAL HUMAN RIGHTS IDEA ON CATHOLIC SOCIAL THOUGHT

There is an intriguing sentence in the part of René Cassin's memoirs where he describes the efforts of the Human Rights Commission to secure support from as many nations as possible when the Declaration was presented for adoption by the U.N. General Assembly at its Paris session in the fall of

---

[2] *On the Edge of Greatness: The Diaries of John Humphrey,* ed. A. J. Hobbins, Vol. I (Montreal: McGill University Libraries, 1994), 87.

1948. According to Cassin, the Commission was aided on several occasions by the "discreet personal encouragements" of the Papal Nuncio in Paris, one Angelo Roncalli. The future John XXIII must have agreed with Maritain and other Catholic thinkers that there was value in discussing certain human goods as rights, even though the language of rights could never be the mother tongue of Christians. For when he became pope, he described the UDHR as "an act of the highest importance."[3]

Many Catholics were surprised, and some were even shocked, at the extent to which the documents of Vatican II, and John XXIII's encyclicals *Pacem in Terris* and *Mater et Magistra* seemed to effect a shift from natural law to human rights. I agree with those who regard this shift as more rhetorical than theoretical, an effort on the part of the Church to make her own teachings intelligible to "all men and women of good will." But with that shift came significant risks, and the need to be very clear about the fact that the Church did not always use terminology in the same way it was used in secular circles. Passages like the following from *Pacem in Terris*, for example, may sound like the Universal Declaration, but are grounded in Christian anthropology, and conditioned by Christian understandings of what rights are *for*:

> Beginning our discussion of the rights of man, we see that every man has the right to life, to bodily integrity, and to the means which are necessary and suitable for the proper development of life; these are primarily food, clothing, shelter, rest, medical care, and finally the necessary social services. Therefore a human being also has the right to security in cases of sickness, inability to work, widowhood, old age, unemployment, or in any other case in which he is deprived of the means of subsistence through no fault of his own (11).

Vatican II, we now know, only marked the beginning of the Church's appropriation of modern rights talk. One of the Council Fathers, Karol Wojtyla of Krakow, would travel even further along that road when he became John Paul II. He has often praised the Universal Declaration of Human Rights, calling it "a real milestone on the path of the moral progress of humanity," and "one of the highest expressions of the human conscience of our time." As Avery Dulles has written, "Of all the popes in history, none has given so much emphasis to human rights as John Paul II."[4]

Critics of these developments have rightly noted their risks, but they have often failed to notice four important facts about the Church's use of rights language. First, the rights tradition into which the Church has tapped is the dignitarian tradition which she herself had already done so much to

---

[3] *Pacem in Terris*, 143.

[4] Avery Dulles, *Human Rights: The United Nations and Papal Teaching* (New York: Fordham University Press, 1999), 4.

shape, not the highly individualistic, libertarian tradition which we Anglo-Americans often take as the only or the best way of thinking about rights. "The Catholic doctrine of human rights," Father Dulles points out, "is not based on Lockean empiricism or individualism. It has a more ancient and distinguished pedigree."[5]

Second, in no sense did the Church uncritically adopt even the dignitarian vision as her own. Already in *Gaudium et Spes*, the Council Fathers warned that the movement to respect human rights "must be imbued with the spirit of the Gospel and be protected from all appearance of mistaken autonomy. We are tempted to consider our personal rights as fully protected only when we are free from every norm of divine law; but following this road leads to the destruction rather than to the maintenance of the dignity of the human person." Similarly, in *Pacem in Terris*, John XXIII noted that, "Some objections and reservations . . . were raised regarding certain points in the declaration, and rightly so (144)." Everything the Church says about human rights is conditioned by their foundation in the dignity that attaches to the person made in the image and likeness of God, and everything is oriented to the end of the common good, defined in *Gaudium et Spes* as "the sum of those conditions of social life by which individuals, families and groups can achieve their own fulfillment in a relatively thorough and ready way." (74).

Third, the new terminology of rights is closely connected to traditional teachings concerning obligations. The Church is concerned as much about the souls of those who disregard the dignity of others as she is for those to whom obligations are owed.

Finally, the most distinctive feature of the Church's posture toward the modern human rights project has been encouragement, accompanied by constructive but pointed criticism. Thus, for example, when John Paul II sent his good wishes on the occasion of the fiftieth birthday of the Declaration, he warned that "[c]ertain shadows hover over the anniversary, consisting in the reservations being expressed in relation to two essential characteristics of the very idea of human rights: their *universality* and their *indivisibility*."[6]

## THE JOURNEY CONTINUES: POTENTIAL CONTRIBUTIONS OF CATHOLIC LEARNING TO THE DILEMMAS OF UNIVERSALITY, INDIVISIBILITY, FOUNDATIONS, AND TRUTH

The fact is that "certain shadows" have hovered over the universal rights idea from the beginning. Can any rights really be said to be universal in a constantly changing world composed of many different cultures? Can freedom really coexist with a broad array of rights to social security? What is the basis

---

[5] Ibid., 12.
[6] "World Day of Peace Message, 1999," 3.

for human rights? Is belief in human rights just a leap of faith? In the remainder of this essay, I suggest some ways in which Catholic thinkers could be especially helpful with four persistent dilemmas facing the human rights project—particularly if they can deepen, develop, and communicate the wisdom the Church has gleaned through the ages concerning: inculturation, solidarity, subsidiarity, and the ability of the properly formed human mind to progress toward knowledge of objective truth.

## Universal Rights in Diverse Cultures

Let us begin with the challenge posed to universality by cultural diversity. The claim that every human being is entitled to certain basic rights simply by virtue of being human has come under increasing attack from a variety of directions. To take one prominent example, the standard response of China's leaders, when criticized for rights violations, is that all rights are relative. A number of Islamic governments and leaders of some developing countries have taken the position that some so-called universal rights are just masks for cultural imperialism aimed at imposing "Western" or "Judeo-Christian" ideas on the rest of the world. Meanwhile, in the West it has become fashionable to deny that there is any such thing as a universally valid proposition about human beings or human affairs.

None of these challenges can be lightly dismissed. Certainly it is no answer to simply assert, as does the U.N.'s 1993 Vienna Human Rights Declaration, that the universality of these rights is "beyond question."

The long Catholic experience in the dialectic between universal principles and diverse cultures provides encouraging evidence, though, that universality need not entail homogeneity, and that pluralism does not necessarily entail relativism. The history of inculturation of the Christian faith in many different societies also shows that the common understanding of core truths can be enriched by the accumulation of a variety of experiences in living those truths.

John Paul II, in his 1995 Address to the fiftieth General Assembly of the United Nations, applied that body of knowledge to the dilemma of the universality of human rights. Universal rights and particular cultures, he said, cannot be radically opposed. After all, rights emerge from culture; rights cannot be sustained without cultural underpinnings; and rights, to be effective, must become part of each people's way of life. Different cultures, he went on, are "but different ways of facing the question of the meaning of personal existence." Thus there can be a "legitimate pluralism" in forms of freedom, with different means of expressing and protecting basic rights, provided "that in every case the levels set for the whole of humanity by the Universal Declaration are respected."[7] As Jacques Maritain nicely put it long ago, there could be many different kinds of music played on the Declaration's thirty strings.[8]

---

[7] "World Day of Peace Message, 1999," 3.

[8] Jacques Maritain, *Man and the State* (Chicago: University of Chicago Press, 1951), 106.

From centuries of evangelization efforts, and from her dialogue with political philosophy, the Church has absorbed another important lesson about human affairs: that personal formation is essential to cultural formation and that no program for advancing the common good is secure unless it rests on firm cultural foundations. Indeed, John Paul II sounds much like Alexis de Tocqueville when he points out that "[o]nly when a culture of human rights which respects different traditions becomes an integral part of humanity's moral patrimony shall we be able to look to the future with serene confidence," or when he says that "the dignity of the individual must be safeguarded by custom before the law can do so."[9]

The bottom-up approach to protecting human dignity in Catholic thought corresponds perfectly with the understanding of universality shared by the principal architects of the Universal Declaration: Mrs. Roosevelt, René Cassin, Charles Malik, and the Chinese philosopher-diplomat Peng-chun Chang. The records of their deliberations are replete with statements showing that they never intended that its common standard of achievement would or should produce completely uniform practices. One of the most pointed examples occurs in Chang's speech urging the U.N. General Assembly to adopt the Declaration. The peoples of the world, he said, had had enough of the sort of uniformity that colonial powers once sought to impose on them—a standardized way of thinking and a single way of life. That sort of uniformity could only be achieved by force or at the expense of truth. It could never last.

By contrast, today's human rights activists, influenced more than they realize by American legal ideas that came into vogue in the 1960s, tend almost instinctively to think in terms of legalistic, top-down solutions, and to forget about the primacy of culture. The numbers of international lawyers who recall the wisdom of the framers are diminishing. One such, however, is Philip Alston, who wrote on the UDHR's 35th anniversary that, "The Declaration does not purport to offer a single unified conception of the world as it should be nor does it purport to offer some sort of comprehensive recipe for the attainment of an ideal world. Its purpose is rather the more modest one of proclaiming a set of values which are capable of giving some guidance to modern society in choosing among a wide range of alternative policy options."[10]

## Indivisibility

I hope I have said enough to indicate some ways in which Catholic experience might be helpful to the dilemma of reconciling universality of human rights with cultural diversity. A second dilemma arises from the perennial tension between certain rights, for example, between freedom and social security. The 1948 Declaration, like the Catholic social doctrine which

[9] "Address to the Diplomatic Corps, 1989," 7.
[10] Philip Alston, "The Universal Declaration at 35: Western and Passé or Alive and Universal," *International Commission of Jurists Review* 30 (1983): 60–61.

influenced it in this respect, insists on the mutual dependence between political and civil rights on the one hand, and social justice on the other. The rights it contains are said to be indivisible.

No sooner was the ink dry on the UDHR, however, than the Cold War antagonists put asunder what the framers had joined together. The Eisenhower State Department dismissed the social and economic provisions as "socialistic," while their Soviet counterparts derided the traditional eighteenth-century rights as "bourgeois."

What began as expediency hardened into habit. Today, the Declaration is almost universally approached by friend and foe alike as Americans approach the Bill of Rights, that is, as a kind of menu from which one can pick-and-choose according to one's taste. The more affluent countries (and even the major human rights organizations which are based in such countries) concern themselves hardly at all with the articles relating to social and economic justice. Meanwhile, leaders of some developing countries ignore political and civil liberties in favor of social and economic rights, or insist that human rights are luxuries that need to be put on hold for the sake of national security or economic development. Without devaluing the good work the international human rights movement has done for victims of torture and discrimination, it must also be said that this case-and-controversy oriented movement has nearly lost sight of the fact that the Universal Declaration embodies a wider, integrated conception of rights. The movement itself needs to be reminded of the fact that "when the violation of any fundamental human right is accepted without reaction, all other rights are placed at risk."

One of the most pressing challenges for friends of the universal human rights idea, therefore, is to reunite the two halves of the divided soul of the Declaration—its commitment to human liberty and its acknowledgment of a single human family for which all bear a common responsibility.

In a development that few would have anticipated fifty years ago, it is the Catholic Church that has become the principal institutional defender in the world today of the Universal Declaration as an integrated whole. There is no way to exaggerate the importance of the presence of the Holy See in the U.N. in keeping alive the connection between freedom and solidarity—at a time when affluent nations seem increasingly to be washing their hands of poor countries and peoples. Time and again, John Paul II has challenged those who would emphasize individual liberty, but neglect social justice. In his speech to the U.N. on its fiftieth anniversary, for example, he said: "Inspired by the example of all those who have taken the *risk of freedom*, can we not recommit ourselves also to taking the *risk of solidarity*—and thus the *risk of peace?*" The pleas of this Pope on behalf of social justice go largely unreported, yet they are at least as deeply challenging and far more "judgmental" than anything this Pope has ever said about human sexuality. Consider, for example:

CHAPTER 40 • Catholic Thought and Dilemmas of Human Rights

The distinctive mark of the Christian, today more than ever, must be love for the poor, the weak, the suffering. Living out this demanding commitment requires a total reversal of the alleged values which make people seek only their own good: power, pleasure, the unscrupulous accumulation of wealth. . . . A society of genuine solidarity can be built only if the well-off in helping the poor, do not stop at giving from what they do not need. . . . Those living in poverty can wait no longer: They need help now and so have a right to receive immediately what they need.[11]

Strongly worded as are these calls to solidarity from the pen of John Paul II, they are mild in comparison to what Jacques Maritain wrote in the UNESCO philosophers' volume on human rights:

It is an irony stained with blood to think that . . . the atheist ideology [of socialism] is a heritage from the most "bourgeois" representatives of the bourgeoisie, who, after calling on the god of the Deists that they might base their own demands on the natural law, rejected that God and the God of the Christians alike when they were come to power and sought to free the all-embracing exercise of proprietary rights from the shackles of the natural law, and to close their ears to the cry of the poor.[12]

Again, it is important to note that much confusion exists about the relation of Catholic social thought to similar-sounding secular ideas. The Church teaches solidarity as a virtue which relates to the perfection of the individual, by inclining us to overcome sources of division within ourselves (personal sin) and within society ("structural sins"). The virtue of solidarity is thus inseparable from personal reform and requires constant practice. It can hardly be equated with crude mandates for state-directed programs for redistributing wealth or restructuring institutions, nor with the kind of solidarity that exalts the group over the individual. But it is highly compatible with the intent of UDHR framers like Chang who maintained that the principal goal of the Declaration should be "to build up better human beings," and Charles Malik who wrote that "Men, cultures and nations must first mature inwardly" before human rights can be a reality.

With regard to the formidable problem of how to move from the principle of solidarity to its practical implementation under diverse social and political conditions, the Church of course has no specific models to propose. In this area where the state of human knowledge is not far advanced, and practically everything remains to be done, she does, however, have several potentially fruitful insights. Her principle of subsidiarity, for example, is already implicit in the Universal Declaration, as is her understanding that

---

[11] "World Day of Peace Message, 1997," 8.

[12] Jacques Maritain, "On the Philosophy of Human Rights," in *Human Rights: Comments and Interpretations* (New York: Columbia University Press, 1949), 72, 76.

freedom and justice have conditions. Though subsidiarity is attracting increasing attention from political thinkers, it is an idea that needs to be deepened and developed. And what would be more fitting than that Catholic thinkers should take the initiative in clarifying and developing this potentially useful concept?

That, of course, would require Catholic thinkers to become familiar with their own social tradition, in emulation of Charles Malik. In this connection, it seems appropriate to mention the recent lament of the American bishops that, "our social doctrine is not shared or taught in a consistent and comprehensive way in too many of our schools, seminaries, religious education programs, colleges and universities."[13]

Catholics would also have to come to terms with the sad fact that, just as "certain shadows" have fallen over the UDHR's link between freedom and social justice, so a shadow has fallen over the connection between Catholic social thought and the moral teachings that undergird it. All too many Catholics seem to want the preferential option for the poor without attending to the habits and conditions that make such a commitment sustainable. All too many others seem to resist the teaching that living the whole Christian faith means living the option for the poor.

## The Dilemma of Foundations

A third area where Catholic thinkers might benefit the human rights project concerns some business that the drafters of the Universal Declaration left unfinished—namely, the problem of supplying firm foundations for the practical consensus they had achieved on human rights. The framers of the Declaration forged ahead, under pressure of time, on the basis of that consensus. The surprisingly similar lists of fundamental principles the UNESCO philosophers and the U.N. Human Rights Division discovered in their cross-national surveys gave them confidence that foundations could be supplied, but they had to leave the demonstration for another day. It had been easy for representatives of different religions and cultures to agree on the rights, Jacques Maritain famously said, so long as no one asked why.

Today, however, the problem of foundations has acquired new urgency. The close of the Cold War has seen a surge of bloody regional and ethnic conflicts that have impaired the sense of unity of the human family. Economic and technological developments have brought new risks that human beings will be treated as instruments or objects. Fashionable philosophies deny the existence of truth or the ability of the human mind to grasp it. As Dulles points out, "Without a sound basis in philosophical anthropology, the human rights tradition can be easily dismissed or perverted."[14]

---

[13] U.S. Bishops, *Sharing Catholic Social Teaching* (Washington, DC: U.S.C.C., 1998), 3.
[14] Dulles, *Human Rights,* 17.

The inadequacy of much contemporary thinking about the foundations of human rights is exemplified by Michael Ignatieff's recent article in the *New York Review of Books*. Posing the question of why we should "believe that human beings should not be beaten, tortured, coerced, indoctrinated, or in any way sacrificed against their will," Ignatieff replies that this ethic "derives from our own experience of pain and our capacity to imagine the pain of others." Apparently unaware that he has reproduced almost word for word Rousseau's argument for compassion as the basis of morality, Ignatieff also fails to realize that the shakiness of that foundation has long since been exposed. Empathy is just a feeling, and a transient one at that. It yields easily, as Rousseau himself conceded, to self-preservation and, one might add, to self-interest. Something sturdier is needed to engender the habits that impel people to respect the dignity of others—and to set the conditions under which human rights will be respected.

The time thus seems overdue to provide the universal rights idea with a more secure philosophical basis. Vaclav Havel seems to have had some such project in mind when he proposed on the Declaration's fiftieth anniversary that the United Nations undertake "a quest for a common denominator of spiritual values uniting the different cultures of our present world."[15] The UNESCO philosophers' committee long ago realized, however, that the quest for a single foundation of human rights would almost certainly prove fruitless. They concluded that "the members of the United Nations share common convictions upon which human rights depend, but . . . that those common convictions are stated in terms of different philosophic principles and on the background of divergent political and economic systems."[16]

As Ralph McInerny has explained, Maritain and his colleagues were proceeding on the assumptions that common appreciations of the human good are embedded in diverse traditions, and that they can be formulated abstractly in such a way as to enable all concerned to stand on principle—even though the principles on which they stand are different.[17] That line of thinking seems similar to what John Paul II must have had in mind when he told the Vatican Diplomatic Corps in 1998 that it is now the task of "the various schools of thought—especially communities of believers—to tackle the job of furnishing the legal framework governing the rights of mankind with a moral foundation" (7).

At last, after fifty years, those assumptions are being tested. Serious investigations are taking place into the ways in which the world's cultural,

[15] Vaclav Havel, "On the 50th Anniversary of Human Rights Declaration," Czech News Agency, March 16, 1998.
[16] UNESCO Committee on the Theoretical Bases of Human Rights, Final Report, in *Human Rights: Comments and Interpretations,* 258–59.
[17] Ralph McInerny, "Natural Law and Human Rights," *American Journal of Jurisprudence* 36 (1991): 1, 14.

philosophical, and religious traditions have affirmed the unity of the human family and the universality of certain basic human goods that have been cast in modern times as fundamental rights.

As Catholic scholars join in that endeavor, no doubt they will find their own thinking about human dignity deepened and enriched in the process. Christians, we are told in *Centesimus Annus*, are obliged not only to bring light to the world, but also to remain open to discover "every fragment of truth . . . in the life experience and in the culture of individuals and nations" (46). As Alasdair MacIntyre has reminded us, a living tradition is distinguished not only by its continuity, but by its dynamism. And, I would add, a great tradition is distinguished not only by what it can contribute to the world's stock of wisdom, but by its ability borrow judiciously from other stores.

It will be good news if, as the framers and UNESCO philosophers predicted, the Declaration's principles can be shown to be deeply rooted in the world's major philosophical and religious traditions and thus in the shared history of the human race. Documenting that proposition would improve the chances for a truly universal dialogue about how we are to order our lives together on this conflict-ridden, but interdependent planet. But sooner rather than later, any such dialogue will have to confront the challenges of historicism and relativism.

## The Dilemma of Truth

If there are no common truths to which all men and women can appeal, then there are no human rights, and there is little hope that reason and choice can prevail over force and accident in the realm of human affairs. It is one thing to acknowledge, with St. Paul, that the human mind can glimpse Truth only as though a glass darkly (I Corinthians 13:12), and quite another to deny the existence of truth altogether. Hannah Arendt has warned of the grave practical implications of everyday nihilism, arguing persuasively that "the ideal subject of totalitarian rule is not the convinced Nazi or the convinced communist, but people for whom the distinction between fact and fiction (for example, the reality of experience) and the distinction between true and false (for example, the standards of thought) no longer exist."[18] John Paul II puts it this way: "[T]he root of modern totalitarianism is to be found in the denial of the transcendent dignity of the human person. . . ."[19]

But we postmoderns must ask—how do we know what is true? Here, again, is an area where practically everything remains to be done. I would only point out that in the world today, where relativism and historicism rule the secular academy, the Catholic Church, again to the surprise of many, has stepped forward as an unabashed defender of reason, notably with the

---

[18] Hannah Arendt, *The Origins of Totalitarianism,* 2d ed. (New York: Meridian Books, 1958), 474.

[19] *Centesimus Annus,* 44.

remarkable encyclical *Fides et Ratio*. Hers is not the calculating reason of Hobbes in the service of the passions, nor the narrow scientific rationalism of the French self-proclaimed *Lumières*, but rather the dynamic, recurrent, and potentially self-correcting processes of human knowing.

It does not seem too much to hope that this may be the moment for Catholic universities to be true to their highest calling by preserving the dynamic interaction between tradition and the spirit of free inquiry that is not, alas, enjoying its finest hour in secular American universities. The time is ripe, I believe, to ponder carefully the work of religious thinkers, like Jesuit philosopher Bernard Lonergan, who take modern historical consciousness and the diversity of cultures seriously, but who find the basis for objectivity in "the dynamic unity of the human mind in its related and recurrent operations."[20]

## CONCLUSION

I trust that my confidence in the unexplored potential of Catholic intellectual traditions will not be understood as unbridled Catholic triumphalism. As John Paul II himself reminds us, the Church approaches the Third Millennium "on her knees," painfully aware of the ways in which her sons and daughters through history have fallen short in thought, word, and deed. Much of what her intellectual tradition has to offer was learned painfully after mistakes and sad experiences.

On the other hand, there is such a thing as exaggerated self-criticism. At a time and in a culture where religion, reason, and human rights alike are under siege from so many directions, I believe those of us who are teachers do a great disservice if by our words or our silence we contribute to the myth that the history of Christianity in general and Catholicism in particular is a history of patriarchy, worldliness, or exclusion of people or ideas. We have inherited a great tradition of free inquiry and fearless engagement with ideas. We should rejoice in that tradition—and resolve to use it!

---

[20] Matthew L. Lamb, "Divine Transcendence and Eternity: The Early Lonergan's Recovery of Thomas Aquinas as a Response to Father McCool's Question," in *Continuity and Plurality in Catholic Theology: Essays in Honor of Gerald A. McCool, SJ*, ed. Anthony J. Cernera (Fairfield, CT: Sacred Heart University Press, 1998), 75–76.

# Charles Malik and the
# Universal Declaration

*Among the "greatest generation" of diplomats in the early United Nations,*
*none was more remarkable than Lebanon's Charles Malik. On the fiftieth anniversary*
*of the UDHR, I traveled to Beirut to pay tribute to his role in its framing, and later wrote*
*this introduction to his selected writings,* The Challenge of Human Rights:
Charles Malik and the Universal Declaration,
*edited by his son, Habib C. Malik.* [1]

THIS VOLUME OF WRITINGS by Charles Malik represents a major contribution to the understanding of the rise of the universal human rights idea in
the years after the Second World War. Though no individual had a greater
role in shaping, and securing consensus for, the U.N.'s 1948 Universal Declaration of Human Rights, and though none of the framers reflected in
greater depth on the dilemmas of human rights, Malik's many speeches and
essays have not been readily available. Now, thanks to Habib Malik, a distinguished scholar in his own right, the published reflections of this great
twentieth-century philosopher-diplomat have been collected from far-flung
sources—and supplemented with excerpts from private papers and diaries.
The result is a treasure trove of material.

An additional reason to celebrate the appearance of this volume is that it
will help to reacquaint the world with the life and achievements of one of
the truly extraordinary figures of twentieth-century diplomacy. In the 1950s,
the Lebanese Ambassador to the United States and the United Nations was
one of the best-known men on the international stage. At one time or
another, Malik held nearly all the major posts in the U.N., including a rotating seat on the Security Council and the Presidency of the General Assembly. During the period covered by most of the writings in this book, he
served as Rapporteur of the U.N. Human Rights Commission, which he
later chaired.

---

[1] Mary Ann Glendon, Introduction to *The Challenge of Human Rights: Charles Malik*
*and the Universal Declaration*, ed. by Habib Malik (Oxford: Charles Malik Foundation, 2000), 1–9.

One of the first tasks entrusted to that Commission was that of framing an "international bill of rights." That presented the Commissioners with quite a challenge—for then, as now, political "realists" did not believe there were any universal principles of human decency. Then, as now, many held to the view that Thucydides attributes to the Athenian generals at Melos: "Right is only a question between equals in power. The strong do what they can while the weak suffer what they must." To some, the horrors of two world wars only served to confirm that position.

Nevertheless, the Commissioners set out to find a set of principles so basic that every nation and culture might accept them as a common yard-stick, and a framework for further progress. Four members of the Human Rights Commission played such important roles in bringing that difficult task to a successful conclusion that they deserve to be called "founding parents" of the Universal Declaration. Eleanor Roosevelt, the Commission's chair, possessed the prestige and political skills that enabled her to influence the policy of, as well as to represent, the country that had emerged most powerful from the War. The craftsmanship of René Cassin, who had been General Charles de Gaulle's wartime legal advisor, made the text an inte-grated whole, rather than a mere list of rights. China's delegate, the immensely learned P. C. Chang, facilitated consensus with his talent for "translating" concepts from one culture to another. But I believe the histori-cal record shows that it was Charles Malik the philosopher who, more than any other framer, helped to reinforce the Declaration's claim to being uni-versal; and Charles Malik the master diplomat who, more than any other individual, helped to assure its adoption without a single dissenting vote in the turbulent fall of 1948, a time when the General Assembly was deeply divided over Palestine, the Cold War, and many other issues.

## THE CONTRIBUTIONS OF MALIK THE PHILOSOPHER

At the initial session of the Human Rights Commission in January 1947, Malik's insistence on probing beneath the surface of things precipitated the Commission's first big argument—but also brought a fundamental issue out in the open. Fresh from the academy, the young philosophy teacher some-times sounded rather pompous as he lectured his elders. When we say "human rights," he pointed out, we are raising the fundamental question: What is man? When we disagree on human rights, we are really disagreeing about the nature of the person. Is he merely a social being, like a bee or an ant? Is he merely an animal with biology governing his destiny? Is he just an economic being, a rational calculator of self-interest? Malik boldly proposed that the Commission accept as a guiding principle for its work that the human person is more important than any group to which he may belong. In the heated discussion that followed, the communist delegates predictably reacted by proclaiming the superiority of the common interest, as embodied in the State, over individual claims. Mrs. Roosevelt predictably rose to the defense of the rights of the "individual." While Malik welcomed Mrs. Roosevelt's support, he took pains to differentiate his own nuanced view of human personhood from Anglo-American-style individualism. The person, as Malik used that term, was neither Marx's "species being" nor the lone rights-bearer of Hobbes or Locke or American frontier legends. Malik saw man as uniquely valuable in himself, but as constituted in part by and through his relationships with others—his family, his community, his nation, and his God. He thus challenged not only members of the Soviet bloc who wanted to subordinate the person to the State, but also the more individualistic Westerners on the Commission. In the end, Malik's view won the support of the Chinese and Latin American delegates, and prevailed. That helped to assure that the Universal Declaration would be neither collectivist nor radically individualist.

In the course of those discussions, Malik also brought another crucial distinction to the fore: that between society and the State. In the vein of social thinkers like Alexis de Tocqueville and Edmund Burke, Malik insisted on the political importance of the many associations and institutions of civil society that stand between the individual and the State—families, religious groups, professional associations, and so on. It is due in no small part to Malik's vigilance that the Declaration explicitly protects these mediating structures.

The records of those early meetings reveal that Malik had not yet perfected the suave diplomatic style for which he would later become famous. For example, when India's Hansa Mehta urged the Commissioners to concentrate on practical questions without entering into an "ideological maze," Malik tartly chided her: "Everything you say, Madam, must have ideological presuppositions, and no matter how much you may fight shy of them, they are there, and you either hide them or you are brave enough to bring them out in the open and see them and criticize them." Later, Malik the diplomat would have responded more tactfully, keeping in mind India's vote.

Those arguments provided an advance warning of the difficulties that would beset the diverse 18-member Commission over the two-year period of its work on the Declaration. The alliance between Russia and the United States was crumbling. Malik and Chang, by all accounts, dominated the group intellectually, but their philosophical orientations often pulled them in different directions. Moreover, the Commissioners were divided on the Palestine question—with Mrs. Roosevelt and Cassin (who had lost several relatives in concentration camps) supporting a Jewish homeland, while Carlos Romulo of the Philippines was strongly opposed, and Malik was emerging as a leading spokesman of the Arab League.

Still, it was Cassin, wholeheartedly supported by Malik, who insisted from the beginning that a declaration purporting to be universal ought to affirm the unity of the human family. Later on, when that idea was dropped from Article 1, Malik succeeded in gaining its inclusion in an even stronger form in the Preamble. Malik was also the principal defender of Article 1's affirmation that human beings are "endowed with reason and conscience."

## THE CONTRIBUTIONS OF MALIK THE DIPLOMAT

Much more could be said about Malik's contributions as a philosopher to the framing of the Declaration, but his achievements as a diplomat were perhaps even more impressive, considering that he was never fully comfortable in the world of politics. So let us move forward to June 1948, when the Human Rights Commission completed its work on the draft Declaration. There could not have been a worse time to begin the process of trying to get the Declaration adopted by the U.N. General Assembly. That was the month of the Berlin blockade, which marked the definitive collapse of the postwar alliance between the Russia and the West. Nearly all observers agreed that with the deteriorating international situation, the Declaration would be dead if it were not adopted soon. But in order to come before the General Assembly, it had first to be approved by the Economic and Social Council (ECOSOC). Unlike the Human Rights Commission, ECOSOC was filled with hard-boiled, hard-nosed practitioners of Realpolitik, and the Declaration was expected to face strong opposition there.

But the new President of ECOSOC, elected a few months earlier, was none other than young Charles Malik. And in the summer of 1948, to the astonishment of many, ECOSOC gave the document its unanimous approval.

There was still another big hurdle to be cleared, though, before the Declaration could come before the General Assembly. That was the requirement of approval by the General Assembly's own Committee on Social, Economic and Cultural Affairs (known as the Third Committee). It was a large body composed of 58 members, one from each U.N. member state. In the fall of 1948, when the Third Committee convened for the final round of review, the person who was elected by secret ballot to its chair was, again, none other than Charles Malik.

How can one explain this meteoric rise of a man who felt himself profoundly unsuited for public life? Malik's diaries all through this period show that he felt like an alien in the world of politics—isolated, without allies or intellectual companions. He often referred to "the loneliness of Lebanon" in a way that suggests it was a metaphor for his own sense of isolation. But at a certain point, he seems to have turned his loneliness into a source of inner strength, which probably contributed to the sense that many in the U.N. had of Malik's independence. John Humphrey, the Canadian Director of the U.N. Secretariat's Human Rights Division, for example, referred in his memoirs to Malik as "one of the most independent people ever to sit on the Commission." And when the *New York Herald Tribune* reported Malik's election to the presidency of ECOSOC, the article said that his popularity was "based on his personal U.N. record despite criticisms from some sources that Lebanon, as a member of the Arab bloc defying the U.N. decision to partition Palestine, should not be singled out at this time for one of the U.N.'s highest honors."

The Third Committee meetings in the fall of 1948 tested all of Malik's hard-won diplomatic skills. The Committee was so large, and its members so unfamiliar with the Declaration, that it took over eighty meetings to go over it, arguing over every word and line. The meetings stretched out over October and November—perilously close to the General Assembly's December adjournment date.

Malik was under severe pressure from several different directions. The Soviet bloc was trying to kill the project by prolonging the debates until the General Assembly disbanded. Knowing this, Mrs. Roosevelt and many other members of the Human Rights Commission wanted to cut short debate and rush the matter to a vote. At the same time, however, the many representatives who were unfamiliar with the Declaration had a legitimate desire to be fully informed and to have their say.

Malik knew it was risky to let the discussion drag on. His judgment, however, was that the risk had to be taken. Perhaps only someone like Malik from a small, newly independent country could understand how important it was that each participant should have a sense of personal involvement in the Declaration. He was farsighted enough to realize that a sense of "ownership" on the part of many cultures would not only improve the Declaration's chance of adoption but, more importantly, would promote its lasting reception among the nations.

Finally, at the end of November, the Third Committee approved the text of the Declaration with seven abstentions, but with no nay votes. That practically assured that the Declaration would obtain the required two-thirds vote in the General Assembly. Both Santa Cruz and Humphrey gave Malik the lion's share of credit for successfully steering the draft through the Committee shoals.

The problem at that stage was to secure the largest majority possible in the General Assembly. For any "no" votes at all would undermine the document's claim to be a universal standard. Once again, Malik rose to the challenge. His speech presenting the Declaration to the General Assembly was perfectly tailored to the occasion. He pointed each country to the places where it could find its own contributions or the contribution of the culture to which it belonged. He explained that, unlike previous declarations of rights which had sprung from particular cultures, the Universal Declaration was something new in the world. It was a composite synthesis of all previous thinking about rights. Due to the variety of its sources, he said, the Declaration had been "constructed on a firm international basis wherein no regional philosophy or way of life was permitted to prevail."

Malik then reviewed the history of the document, its "negative roots" in the atrocities of the recent War, and its "positive roots" in the common aspirations summed up so well for the World War II generation by Franklin Roosevelt's "Four Freedoms" (freedom of speech and belief, freedom from fear and want). He reminded the Assembly that the Declaration represented the first step toward fulfillment of the U.N. Charter's promise to protect human rights. To be sure, it would need to be supplemented with measures of implementation, but even without these, Malik concluded, it would "serve as a potent critic of existing practice" and would "help to transform reality." How right he was! Though the non-binding Declaration was regarded by the Great Powers as of little importance, its "merely" moral force later eclipsed in significance the Covenants that were adopted to implement its provisions.

Of Malik's speech, Santa Cruz later wrote: "He gave a detailed account of the whole long process of elaboration of the instrument that was being discussed. No one was able to do it with such authority, not only because of the responsibilities he had assumed in the process, but also by virtue of his lucid intelligence and his extraordinary talent for explanation."

Today, one sometimes hears it said among critics who challenge the universality of the Declaration that the educational backgrounds of Commission members like Chang and Malik "westernized" them. But the performance of such persons in the Human Rights Commission suggests something rather different. Highly intelligent persons like Malik and Chang, whose education or professions had taken them abroad, were able not only to contribute insights from their own cultures, but had exceptional abilities to understand other cultures and to render concepts from one frame of reference in terms that were intelligible to others. Those skills, which can hardly be acquired without substantial exposure to traditions other than one's own, are indispensable for any cross-cultural collaboration, and were essential for the success of the Declaration. Multi-ethnic Lebanon, in Malik's youth, had been a crucible for the formation of such talents.

As everyone now knows, the General Assembly adopted the Declaration on December 10, 1948, 48–0, with eight abstentions (the Soviet bloc plus Saudi Arabia and South Africa), and no nays. Less remembered, but equally significant, is that 23 of its 30 articles were approved without any abstentions whatsoever when the General Assembly took a preliminary vote on each article separately.

In his first major speech after that historic date, Malik spoke of the challenges facing the universal rights idea. Even then, he saw that they were deeper than the challenges posed by Marxism. The problems to be surmounted were, he said, threefold. They involved finding the proper relationship between the person and society; striking an appropriate balance between freedom and social security; and achieving a shared understanding of the nature and origin of human rights. It is evidence of the quality of his mind that those challenges he posed over fifty years ago remain with us after the fall of the Soviet regime—and that they are as acute today as they were then.

As for how Malik was thinking about his own transition from philosopher to diplomat at the height of his political career, his papers suggest that he seems finally to have accepted his new role, but only as something he was obliged to carry "as a chastening cross." I believe one can see in a diary entry about a meal in an unsanitary restaurant a metaphor for his feelings about politics. After returning from dinner that night, he wrote: "The whole place was disgustingly dirty. The cook in front of us touching everything with his hands—the meat, the potatoes, the bread, the waffle, the pieces of butter, the dollars and silver change, and finally with his dirty hands wiping his face. I ate the waffle." Just as he overcame his distaste and ate the waffle, so he remained in the political jungle. By 1949, he had not only made his personal peace with his uncomfortable vocation, but he also showed in his public speeches that he had come to understand how important it is for persons of moral conviction to be active in public life.

In 1987, as Charles Malik approached his death, the outlook for the universal rights idea must have seemed bleak. Yet, amazingly, just two years after he died, the Declaration's principles were rallying points for the movements that brought down the seemingly indestructible totalitarian regimes of Eastern Europe. In the years that have followed the demise of European communism, the Declaration has become the single most important reference point in the world for cross-cultural discussions of human freedom and dignity. Today, the Declaration's aspiration to universality is still under threat from many directions. But, thanks in great part to Charles Malik, the document possesses a number of features that will aid it in its struggle to survive. It is, for example, hard to sustain the accusation that the Declaration is a "Western" document when one looks at the wide participation that he helped to assure.

As a man of faith, Charles Malik must have known that many of the fruits of his labors would ripen only after he had gone to his rest, and that nothing good that he did would ever be lost or in vain. There is much unhappiness and loneliness in his diary, but no despair.

In this respect, it is interesting to compare Malik with another great twentieth-century philosopher–politician, Max Weber, whose writings include the famous pair of essays, "Politics as Vocation" and "Science as Vocation." Like Malik, Weber was torn between philosophy and politics. Like Malik, Weber suffered considerable discontent in the vocation that made him famous (though, in his case, he was a renowned thinker yearning to be a man of action). As with Malik, there is much anguish in Weber's writings. But there the resemblance ends. For Weber's anguish was that of a man determined to live without God, while Malik's was that of a man who felt, more keenly than most, the distance that separates us from God. As the writings in this volume testify, Charles Malik, who often thought he was laboring in darkness, was endowed with a special gift for bringing light to a troubled world.

CHAPTER 41 • Charles Malik and the Universal Declaration

# CHAPTER 42

# John P. Humphrey and the Universal Declaration of Human Rights

*The contributions of Canadian lawyer John Humphrey to the UDHR have received relatively little recognition. Yet it was Humphrey, in his capacity as first Director of the U.N.'s Human Rights Division, who wrote the first draft of the Declaration, not René Cassin as some French writers have claimed. This essay appeared in the Journal of the History of International Law.[1]*

IN HIS CAPACITY as the first Director of the United Nations Human Rights Division, John Peters Humphrey was one of the key figures in the framing of the 1948 Universal Declaration of Human Rights. It was Humphrey who wrote the first draft of the UDHR, buttressing its aspiration toward universality by drawing on sources from many different legal cultures. Both during the drafting process and after the adoption of the Declaration, Humphrey and his staff provided essential continuity, backup, and staying power for the often-embattled U.N. Human Rights Commission. Yet today his name is little known outside Canada. The present essay, which grows out of research on the making of the Declaration, aims to pay tribute to this "forgotten framer" by recalling some of the ways Humphrey helped to set conditions for a better future on our increasingly conflict-ridden, yet interdependent planet.

Even as an orphan boy in New Brunswick, John Humphrey dreamed of helping "to make the world a better place." He wanted to make a difference. And so he did. As head of the U.N. Human Rights Division, he played a key role in what he called "a great adventure"—the enterprise of getting the U.N.'s human rights program off the ground and drafting the Universal Declaration. One of the first decisions taken by the United Nations after its founding was to ask the U.N. Human Rights Commission, chaired by Eleanor Roosevelt, to frame an "international bill of rights." That was a daunting challenge—for then, as now, there was substantial doubt in several quarters concerning the existence of universal principles of human decency.

---

[1] Mary Ann Glendon, "John P. Humphrey and the Drafting of the Universal Declaration of Human Rights," *Journal of the History of International Law,* 20. 2 (1 February 2000): 250–60.

Then, as now, many "realists" held to the view that Thucydides attributes to the Athenian generals at Melos: "Right is only a question between equals in power. The strong do what they can while the weak suffer what they must."

The horrors of two world wars had confirmed many people in that harsh outlook. But fortunately there were others—including Humphrey—who believed that some principles of human decency are so basic that every nation and culture could accept them as a common yardstick. That faith was sorely tested, however, when the 18 members of the first Human Rights Commission tried to put those principles into words. They were a remarkable group of people, with strong convictions and strong personalities. The story of the making of the UDHR in 1947 and 1948 is thus, to a large extent, the story of how a highly diverse collection of men and women worked together, against daunting odds, to make the idea of an international human rights standard a reality.

With the exception of Eleanor Roosevelt, most of the members of that first Human Rights Commission are now little remembered. Yet they included some of the most able and colorful public figures of their time. The Commission's Lebanese Rapporteur, Charles Malik, a philosophy professor turned diplomat, was the chief spokesman for the Arab League during the Palestine crisis, and would later hold many key posts in the U.N., including the presidency of the General Assembly. The French member, René Cassin, was an ardent Zionist, who had served as Charles de Gaulle's wartime legal adviser, and who would receive the Nobel Peace Prize in 1968 for his varied contributions to human rights. Nationalist China's Peng-chun Chang, the vice-chairman of the Commission, was a leading educator turned diplomat who had also achieved renown as a poet and playwright. General Carlos Romulo of the Philippines had won a Pulitzer prize for his prewar articles predicting the end of colonialism. Mrs. Hansa Mehta was a veteran of India's struggle for independence and a tireless advocate for women's equality. Alexei Pavlov, nephew of the famed conditioned-reflex scientist, was a powerful orator who, we now know, was under instructions from Moscow to obstruct and delay the proceedings. Chile's Hernàn Santa Cruz was an aristocratic man of the left who shared John Humphrey's determination to include social and economic rights in the Declaration along with traditional political and civil liberties.

One wonders whether this motley crew could have managed to surmount their linguistic, cultural, political, and personal differences to produce a document of broad applicability without the capable, behind-the-scenes staff work supervised by John Humphrey. Humphrey worked closely with the Commission throughout the entire period of the preparation of the Universal Declaration, and was present at nearly every Commission meeting. Well in advance of the Commission's first meeting in January 1947, he began assembling documentation on all existing human rights instruments.

Not surprisingly, it became evident in that first session that a draft declaration could not be produced by the full 18-member Commission. The members thus unanimously approved a resolution that a "preliminary draft" should be prepared by the three officers of the Commission (Roosevelt, Chang, and Malik) "with the assistance of the Secretariat" (Humphrey and his staff) for submission at the Commission's second session. A factor in this decision seems to have been that all three officers were based near enough to U.N. headquarters to be available for regular meetings.

Eager to get started, Mrs. Roosevelt invited Chang, Malik, and Humphrey to tea at her Washington Square apartment on the weekend following the Commission's adjournment. As she recalled in her memoirs,

> They arrived in the middle of a Sunday afternoon, so we would have plenty of time to work. It was decided that Dr. Humphrey would prepare the preliminary draft, and as we settled down over the teacups, one of them made a remark with philosophical implications, and a heated discussion ensued. Dr. Chang was a pluralist and held forth in charming fashion on the proposition that there is more than one kind of ultimate reality. The Declaration, he said, should reflect more than simply Western ideas and Dr. Humphrey would have to be eclectic in his approach. His remark, though addressed to Dr. Humphrey, was really directed at Dr. Malik, from whom it drew a prompt retort as he expounded at some length the philosophy of Thomas Aquinas. Dr. Humphrey joined enthusiastically in the discussion, and I remember that at one point Dr. Chang suggested that the Secretariat might well spend a few months studying the fundamentals of Confucianism![2]

Humphrey, then a forty-year-old lawyer who had built a solid reputation as an international legal scholar at McGill University, seems to have been thrilled by the responsibility entrusted to him. He began working on the draft right away. On February 21, 1947, he permitted himself to preen a bit in a letter to his older sister Ruth: "I am now playing the role of a Jefferson, because it is I who have responsibility for drawing up the first draft of the International Bill of Rights. I have been working on it for three days now."[3] In later years, the scrupulous Humphrey took pains to acknowledge that the Declaration "had no father in the sense that Thomas Jefferson was the father of the Declaration of Independence," because "literally hundreds of people . . . contributed to its drafting."[4] It is a pity that Humphrey did not live to learn that his role was very similar to that of Jefferson after all—for recent research has revealed that the Declaration of Independence had no single author,

---

[2] Eleanor Roosevelt, *On My Own* (New York: Harper, 1958), 77.
[3] John P. Humphrey, unpublished letter of February 21, 1947 (McGill University Achives, reprinted with permission of Humphrey's literary executor, A. J. Hobbins, Associate Director of Libraries, McGill University).
[4] John P. Humphrey, *No Distant Millennium: The International Law of Human Rights* (Paris: UNESCO, 1989), 149.

either! Pauline Maier's Pulitzer Prize-winning book on the making of the Declaration of Independence demonstrates that Thomas Jefferson drew upon many "earlier documents of his own and other people's creation." Maier concludes that "considering its complex ancestry and the number of people who actively intervened in defining its text, the Declaration of Independence was the work not of one man, but of many."[5] That the same is true of the UDHR is one of the most important supports of its claim to universality.

The decision to entrust the first draft to Humphrey made good sense. Humphrey was well-grounded in both civil and common law, and fluent in French and English. He and his multinational staff had been collecting and studying pertinent material from all over the world, including proposals, models, and drafts that were continuously arriving from governments, nongovernmental organizations, and private individuals far and wide. Roosevelt, Malik, and Chang had been taken aback by the sheer volume of this material when they first met with Humphrey. Malik later confessed that they had felt "completely lost; we had no conception of how to proceed with the task entrusted to us."[6]

While Humphrey was plunging ahead with his new assignment, however, some people had grown dissatisfied with the composition of the drafting committee. Among them was France's Cassin, even though he had been one of the sponsors of the resolution to establish a drafting committee composed of the three officers.[7] Years later in his memoirs, apparently forgetting his own initial position, Cassin described as "deplorable" the decision to entrust the first draft to a small group that included "no European, nor any representative of Latin America, nor anyone from the peoples' republics."[8] Moscow, too, was displeased that its delegate had gone along with an arrangement that included "no European." The Soviet Union, joined by France, asked the Commission's parent body, the U.N. Economic and Social Council, to expand the committee. When Mrs. Roosevelt learned of this, she oiled the squeaky wheels by adding five more members on her own initiative—from Australia, Chile, the United Kingdom, and, of course, Cassin and the Soviet delegate.[9]

The first meeting of the new eight-person drafting team was set for June 1947. By that time, Humphrey and his cadre of assistants at the U.N. Secretariat had spent four months preparing a draft declaration, and studying all the world's existing constitutions and rights instruments, as well as the vari-

---

[5] Pauline Maier, *American Scripture: Making the Declaration of Independence* (New York: Alfred Knopf, 1997), 98–99.

[6] "The Universal Declaration of Human Rights," speech delivered by Charles Malik at the American University of Beirut, January 5, 1949 (Malik Papers, Library of Congress, Manuscript Collection), 7.

[7] Human Rights Commission, First Session, Summary Records (E/CN.4/SR.12, 2).

[8] René Cassin, *La Pensée et l'Action* (Boulogne-sur-Seine: Editions Lalou, 1972), 107.

[9] *U.N. Weekly Bulletin* (June 17, 1947): 639.

ous suggestions that had poured in to the Secretariat.[10] Aiming for comprehensiveness, Humphrey borrowed freely from two models that were themselves based on worldwide surveys: a draft of a transnational rights declaration then being deliberated in Latin America by the predecessor of the Organization of American States, and a "Statement of Essential Human Rights" produced on the basis of a comparative study sponsored by a U.S. legal group, the American Law Institute.[11] After poring over all this material, Humphrey came up with a list of 48 items that represented, in his view, the common core of the documents and proposals his staff had collected. He had done so, he said, with a view toward including "every conceivable right which the Drafting Committee might want to discuss."[12]

That 48-article draft provided the Drafting Committee with a distillation of nearly two hundred years of efforts to articulate the most basic human goods and values in terms of rights. It contained the "first generation" political and civil rights found in British, French, and American revolutionary declarations of the seventeenth and eighteenth centuries: protections of life, liberty and property; and freedoms of speech, religion, and assembly. It also included the "second generation" economic and social rights found in late nineteenth- and early twentieth-century constitutions, such as those in Sweden, Norway, Russia, and various countries in Latin America: rights to work, education, and basic subsistence. Each draft article was followed by an extensive annotation detailing its relationship to rights instruments then in force in the U.N.'s Member States. All told, there were over 400 pages of commentary prepared by Humphrey's staff.[13] The U.N. proudly announced that it had produced "the most exhaustive documentation on the subject of human rights ever assembled."[14]

Although the Soviet Union had taken the initiative in demanding an expanded committee, it was their representative who first bowed to reality after a few days of mulling over this mountain of material. At the June 1947 Drafting Committee meeting, the Soviet delegate suggested the creation of a smaller four-person "working group" composed of René Cassin, Charles Malik, the U.K. representative Geoffrey Wilson, and Mrs. Roosevelt.[15] His

---

[10] John Hobbins, "René Cassin and the Daughter of Time: The First Draft of the Universal Declartion of Human Rights," 2 *Fontanus* 7 (Montreal: McGill University, 1989), 22; *U.N. Weekly Bulletin* (June 17, 1947): 639.

[11] John P. Humphrey, *Human Rights and the United Nations: A Great Adventure* (Dobbs Ferry, NY: Transnational Publishers, 1984), 31–32. See also, *U.N. Weekly Bulletin* (June 17, 1947): 639.

[12] Human Rights Commission, Drafting Committee, First Session, Verbatim Record of June 9, 1947 Meeting (Charles Malik Papers, Library of Congress, Manuscript Division).

[13] Ibid. See also, E/CN.4/AC.1/3/Add. 1.

[14] "International Bill of Rights to be Drafted," *U.N. Weekly Bulletin* (June 17, 1947): 639.

[15] Human Rights Commission, Drafting Committee, First Session (E/CN.4/AC.1/SR.6, 2).

proposal was accepted, and the working group was instructed "to suggest a logical arrangement of the articles of the Draft Outline supplied by the Secretariat" and "a redraft of the various articles in the light of the discussions of the Drafting Committee."[16]

The request for a "logical arrangement" was made because Humphrey had deliberately confined himself to listing what seemed to him the most widely accepted "justiciable" rights gathered from his varied sources.[17] Some of the Commissioners sensed, however, that if people were to make sense of these ideas and how they fit together, more was needed. The working group, convinced that the document would have greater unity if the revisions were handled by a single drafter, asked Cassin "to undertake the writing of a draft Declaration based on those articles in the Secretariat outline which he considered should go into such a Declaration."[18] Cassin was well-equipped for the job, having been schooled in the continental legal tradition where important documents are typically constructed with great attention to the relation among their parts, and to providing interpretive guides.

With the assistance of Émile Giraud, a French international lawyer who had been working with Humphrey on the Secretariat draft, Cassin revised the draft over a single weekend.[19] He preserved most of the substantive content of Humphrey's draft, but added a preamble, followed by what is known in continental legal terminology as a "General Part"—a set of introductory principles to guide the interpretation of the specific provisions that followed. The rights themselves were then arranged according to the logic of the general principles, proceeding from those belonging to persons as such to the rights of persons in social and political relationships. The draft which Humphrey had loosely organized by topic began to take on a more organic structure, a beginning, middle, and end.[20]

A comparison of the two drafts, however, shows that Cassin introduced very little new content. Johannes Morsink's estimate that "over three-quarters of the Cassin draft was taken from Humphrey's first draft" seems to me to be fair.[21] Though the document underwent many further changes as it wound through the committee process over the next year and half, most of the ideas

---

[16] Human Rights Commission, Report of the Drafting Committee, First Session (E/CN.4/21, 3–4).

[17] Humphrey, *Human Rights,* 44.

[18] Id. at 4.

[19] Hobbins, "René Cassin," 12.

[20] A Secretariat memorandum describes the arrangement of articles in Humphrey's draft as follows: two preliminary articles, articles on liberties ("individual," "public," and "remedies"), articles on social rights, two articles on equality, two general dispositions on implementation. Human Rights Commission, Drafting Committee (E/CN.4/AC.1/7, 6).

[21] Johannes Morsink, *The Universal Declaration of Human Rights: Origins, Drafting, and Intent* (Philadelphia: University of Pennsylvania Press, 1999), 8.

in Humphrey's draft ultimately found their way into the Universal Declaration, as did the "logical arrangement" contributed by Cassin.

## THE AUTHORSHIP ISSUE

A regrettable dispute developed many years later over the question of who had written the "first" draft of the Universal Declaration. It was not exactly a paternity dispute since neither Cassin nor Humphrey ever claimed to be the "author" of the Declaration.[22] When Cassin was in his seventies, though, he gave a speech in which he asserted that he had had "sole responsibility" for the "first draft," referring to Humphrey's contribution only as "an excellent basic documentary work."[23] This counterfactual claim, which Cassin repeated in a 1968 article, was puzzling, but not without historical precedent. To this day, no one has been able to explain why Alexander Hamilton, in his old age, claimed authorship of several of *The Federalist Papers* that were actually written by James Madison![24]

Some of Cassin's admirers made matters worse by calling him the "father" of the Declaration in various writings.[25] In 1958, the U.N. itself helped to perpetuate that myth by permitting the French government to organize a display of Cassin's handwritten redraft in the lobby of U.N. headquarters on the occasion of the Declaration's tenth anniversary.[26] That display, without any accompanying explanation, must indeed have been wounding to the hard-working and generally self-effacing Director of the U.N. Human Rights Division. Finally, some writers downplayed Humphrey's role to such an extent that he felt obliged to set the record straight in his memoir.[27]

---

[22] Humphrey, in fact, expressly disclaimed authorship. Humphrey, *Human Rights,* 43.

[23] Cassin, "Historique de la Déclaration Universelle," reprinted in *La Pensée et l'Action,* 108: "[J]e fus chargé par mes collègues de rediger, sous ma seule responsabilité, un premier avant-projet."

[24] Clinton Rossiter, "Introduction," to Alexander Hamilton, James Madison, John Jay, *The Federalist Papers* (New York: Mentor, 1961), x–xi.

[25] Marc Agi's 1998 biography, *René Cassin 1887–1976,* is misleadingly subtitled *Père de la Déclaration Universelle des droits de l'homme.* In the text, Agi concedes that Cassin was not the "sole father" of the Declaration and correctly notes that the Declaration is a "collective work." Agi claims too much for the man he justly admires, however, when he says that "in comparison with what other persons brought to the project in their individual capacity, [Cassin] was its principal animating spirit" (229–30). Similar claims are made by Geoffrey Best, "Whatever Happened to Human Rights?" 16 *Review of International Studies* 3 (1991).

[26] Humphrey, *Human Rights,* 43.

[27] Id., 42–43. Some writers have stated, incorrectly, that Cassin was Rapporteur of the Human Rights Commission, a mistake apparently based on the fact that he was made Rapporteur of the small working group on the declaration at the Commission's Geneva meeting. Gérard Israël, René Cassin (Paris: Desclée de Brouwer, 1990),

That Humphrey wrote the first draft, and that Cassin's draft was a revision of Humphrey's is clear from the official U.N. records.[28] Some confusion resulted, perhaps, from the frequent use of the term "outline" to describe Humphrey's work. As Humphrey pointed out, Cassin "in many cases merely prepared a new French version of the official United Nations translation, and when this was translated back into English the result seemed further removed from the original than it really was."[29] Independent reviews of the record by a number of scholars, however, confirm the sequence of events beyond any doubt. On June 17, 1947, for example, we find Mrs. Roosevelt saying, "Now we come to Mr. Cassin's draft, which has based itself on the Secretariat's comparative draft."[30] Cassin himself acknowledged in the Drafting Committee that "it is always the Secretariat's draft which should be considered the basic source of the Committee's work."[31]

Unfortunately, the myth that Cassin was the principal architect of the Universal Declaration of Human Rights not only scants the roles of other key individuals such as Humphrey, Malik, and Chang, but it undermines the claim to universality of a document that drew on many sources from a variety of cultures and legal traditions.

To give each man his due, one might say that Humphrey's work was to Cassin's as Tycho Brahe's was to Johannes Kepler's. Just as Kepler could not have had his paradigm-breaking insight into the movements of the planets without Tycho's meticulous records, so Cassin could not have produced, over a weekend, an integrated document of worldwide application without Humphrey's distillation of the essence from the material he had collected. But just as Tycho was unable to see in his own data what Kepler saw, Humphrey had simply compiled a list of rights, loosely grouped under categories, while Cassin's arrangement brought out the relations among them. Cassin's revisions made the document a more integrated whole (like a civil

---

186–87. Disregarding Humphrey's role, Israël mentions only that Cassin was "greatly aided" by the "documentation" that the Secretariat assembled.

[28] My examination of the records confirms Humphrey's account of the process in all material respects. Other scholars have previously come to the same conclusion. See the careful examination of the evidence and the detailed chronology in Hobbins, "René Cassin." Johannes Morsink's research finds that Humphrey's draft was "both the first and the most basic draft of the Universal Declaration." Morsink, *Universal Declaration*, 6.

[29] Humphrey, *Human Rights*, 43. For a scholarly appreciation of John Humphrey and his distinguished legal career, see R. St. J. MacDonald, "Leadership in Law: John P. Humphrey and the Development of the International Law of Human Rights," 29 *Canadian Yearbook of International Law* 3 (1991). Humphrey and his work are becoming better known, thanks to the many highly informative articles, cited herein, by historian A. J. Hobbins, the editor of the Humphrey papers and diaries.

[30] Human Rights Commission, Drafting Committee, First Session, Verbatim Record, June 17, 1947 meeting (Charles Malik Papers, Library of Congress, Manuscript Division).

[31] Human Rights Commission, Drafting Committee (E/CN.4/AC.1/SR.3, 5).

law code), rather than a mere list or "bill" of rights in the Anglo-American sense. But it was Humphrey's broad-based research that established the basis for a credible claim of universal applicability.

## SOCIAL AND ECONOMIC RIGHTS IN THE UDHR

One of Humphrey's most important contributions was his decision to include social and economic rights in his draft. That part of the UDHR is still so foreign to mainstream Anglo-American legal thinking that many people today assume that those articles were included at the instance of, or as a concession to, the Soviets. The real story, now nearly forgotten, is quite different. Humphrey based the articles in question on provisions already in effect in a great many countries. Some of these were longstanding, with ancestors in early continental instruments such as Frederick the Great's Prussian General Code (which provided that the State was obliged to provide food, work, and wages for all who could not support themselves, and relief for the poor who were unable to work); the Norwegian Constitution of 1814 (obliging "the authorities of the State to create conditions which make it possible for every person who is able to work to earn his living by his work"); and various French Constitutions from the revolutionary period to the 1946 Constitution of the Fourth Republic. Several articles on these subjects could also be found in the draft Latin American declaration of rights and duties, inspired in part by Christian social thought and in part by the Mexican socialist revolution.

Though the specific details of these provisions were to prove a continuing source of heated controversy within the Commission, no nation opposed them in principle. On the Drafting Committee, it was the Chilean Hernàn Santa Cruz who was their most consistently zealous promoter. Cassin, too, was strongly in favor. In the United Kingdom, the ruling Labor Party acquiesced, although the draft proposals submitted by that country dealt only with civil and political rights. As for the U.S., the Truman State Department fully backed Mrs. Roosevelt in supporting the new group of rights. Similar ideas, after all, had been embodied in the constitutionlike statutes of Franklin Roosevelt's New Deal—the National Labor Relations Act and the Social Security Act. And Roosevelt had even proposed a "second bill of rights" in his 1944 State of the Union speech, summing up the social and economic goals embodied in New Deal legislation.[32] The U.S. position changed drastically after the election of Republican Dwight Eisenhower to the Presidency in 1952, but that is a story for another day.

Humphrey himself, like Santa Cruz, was an enthusiast for the second-generation rights. His diary reveals, however, that his support became more nuanced as he came to believe that moral responsibility was prior to solidarity.

[32] Franklin Delano Roosevelt, State of the Union Message (January 11, 1944), in *1944–45 The Public Papers and Addresses of Franklin D. Roosevelt* (1950), 32.

Shortly before the Declaration was adopted, he wrote in his diary. "[M]oral bankruptcy is the reason for our failure to organize peace. I once thought that socialism could fill this moral gap; but now, although I still remain a socialist, I know better. For socialism is a technique and nothing more. What we need is something like the Christian morality without the tommyrot."[33]

Humphrey's draft of the UDHR, in fact, placed significantly greater emphasis on responsibility than the final version adopted in December 1948. He had suggested that the Preamble state "That man does not have rights only; he owes duties to the society of which he forms a part." His Article 1 included this language: "Everyone . . . must accept his just share of such common sacrifices as may contribute to the common good." In the UDHR as adopted, those ideas were reduced to the following language in the next-to-last article: "Everyone has duties to the community in which alone the free and full development of his personality is possible . . ." (Art. 29). With hindsight, it seems regrettable that the emphasis on duty advocated by Humphrey, Peng-chun Chang, several Latin American delegates, and distinguished consultants like Mohandas Gandhi, did not hold. The Declaration's scanty attention to responsibilities still gives pause to many persons concerned with "human co-existence."

## THE "GREAT ADVENTURE" CONTINUES

In the autumn of 1948, the draft Declaration was ready for presentation to the U.N. General Assembly. John Humphrey recalled the political atmosphere that fall as "charged to the point of explosion by the Cold War with irrelevant recriminations coming from both sides."[34] He and other proponents of the UDHR believed that with the deteriorating international situation, the Declaration would be effectively dead if it were not adopted by the time the General Assembly adjourned in December. But before the General Assembly could vote, the document had to be approved by its Committee on Social, Economic, and Cultural Affairs (known as Committee Three). This was a large committee with 58 members, one from each country in the U.N. Most of the delegates had never seen the Declaration before and it took two long months and over eighty meetings for them to complete their review. The Soviet bloc fully exploited the situation, making strenuous efforts to prolong the Committee Three debates until the General Assembly adjourned. During these debates, Humphrey found the silent role of an international civil servant almost unbearably frustrating. "Sitting next to the Chairman, and both professionally and emotionally involved, I wished at times that I were a delegate. . . . There were times when I felt that I must speak if only to set the record straight."[35]

[33] Humphrey, *On the Edge of Greatness,* 39.
[34] Humphrey, *Human Rights,* 66.
[35] Id., 71.

Finally, on December 7, 1948, the draft, with some revisions, was approved by the Third Committee for submission to the General Assembly. There were no votes against it, but seven countries recorded abstentions at this stage—the six members of the Soviet bloc and, to the dismay of John Humphrey, Canada. The Canadian position, ostensibly having to do with federal-provincial relations, was quickly reversed, but not before Canada had taken considerable public relations flak for its move.[36] The indignant Humphrey stated in his memoirs, "I had no doubt whatsoever that this quick change in position was dictated solely by the fact that the government did not relish the company in which it found itself."[37] Three days later, the General Assembly approved the UDHR without a single dissenting vote. The Soviet bloc continued to abstain, joined by South Africa and Saudi Arabia.

Though the adoption of the UDHR was undoubtedly a great landmark in the history of human rights, the Soviet abstentions foreshadowed the cloud that was to hang over the work of the Human Rights Commission for the remainder of John Humphrey's tenure at the U.N. As the years passed, he became increasingly discouraged not only by the two great powers' resistance to the slightest intrusion on their national sovereignty, but by the lowered priority accorded to human rights in the U.N. during the Dag Hammarskjold years. Humphrey had strongly supported the idea of "completing" the Universal Declaration with a binding Covenant, but deplored the decision to have two separate covenants reflecting Cold War divisions—one for political and civil rights, the other for social and economic rights.[38] Though torn by misgivings, he remained at his post until 1966, struggling to keep the program alive. As his friend, biographer and literary executor John Hobbins put it, "Prior to 1952, Humphrey worked for love of his job and a belief in what the U.N. was doing. After this, he appears to have stayed on from a sense of duty to protect the programme and the division from an unfriendly world."[39]

Humphrey retired from the Secretariat at age 61 after twenty years of service, and returned to law teaching at McGill. He remained active in the cause of human rights, helped to establish the Canadian branch of Amnesty International, championed the cause of Korean comfort women, wrote his memoirs, and lived to the ripe old age of 89.

---

[36] Archival research by William A. Schabas suggests that "provincial jurisdiction was little more than a pretext for federal politicians who wanted to avoid international human rights commitments," 43 *McGill Law Journal* 403 (1998). See also, A. J. Hobbins, "Eleanor Roosevelt, John Humphrey and Canadian Opposition to the Universal Declaration of Human Rights," 53 *International Journal* (Spring 1998): 325.

[37] Humphrey, *Human Rights,* 72.

[38] Id., 165–66.

[39] A. J. Hobbins, "René Cassin and the Daughter of Time: The First Draft of the Universal Declaration of Human Rights," 2 *Fontanus* 10 (1989).

On more than one occasion, John Humphrey had expressed the belief that "every individual can make some contribution to the development of the [human] race, and that he lives on as it were in that contribution."[40] Humphrey's influence on the course of events was, by any standard, exceptional. Certainly he deserves to be ranked with Eleanor Roosevelt, Charles Malik, Peng-chun Chang, and René Cassin as one of the key "founding parents" of the Universal Declaration of Human Rights. The boy from New Brunswick did indeed help to change the world for the better.

---

[40] See Hobbins, "Human Rights," 153; and John Humphrey's Letter of September 30, 1928 to his sister Ruth in A. J. Hobbins, "'Dear Rufus . . .': A Law Student's Life at McGill in the Roaring Twenties, from the Letters of John P. Humphrey," 44 *McGill Law Journal* 753, 775 (1999).

# The Forgotten Crucible:
# The Latin American Influence on
# the Universal Human Rights Idea

*One of the most important parts of the history of the modern human rights project that I discovered in my excavations was the story of the key roles played by Latin Americans, a story little remembered even in their countries of origin. This account of the Latin American influence appeared in 16 Harvard Human Rights Journal 27 (2003).[1]*

**W**ITH THE PASSAGE OF TIME and the deaths of all the main participants, the origins of the post-World War II international human rights project have been obscured by forgetfulness and myth. The polestar of that movement, the 1948 Universal Declaration of Human Rights, is widely regarded as merely a compendium of classical Western political and civil liberties, with its provisions relating to the family and to social and economic justice routinely ignored, even by major human rights organizations. Yet those provisions, based in large part on Latin American models, played a key role in helping the UDHR to gain wide acceptance among diverse cultures. Indeed, Latin American diplomats, documents, and traditions had such a profound influence both on the decision to include human rights protection among the purposes of the U.N. and on the content of the Universal Declaration that I believe it is fair to refer to Latin America as the forgotten crucible of the universal human rights idea.

## LATIN AMERICAN INFLUENCES ON THE U.N. CHARTER
In April 1945, when delegates from fifty countries gathered in San Francisco to put the finishing touches on a proposed charter for the United Nations, representatives of the Latin American and Caribbean nations arrived with a common plan to work for the inclusion of an international bill of rights. That idea

---

[1] Mary Ann Glendon, "The Forgotten Crucible: The Latin American Influence on the Universal Human Rights Idea." *Harvard Human Rights Journal* 16 (Spring 2003): 27–30.

was far from the minds of the Allied leaders who called the conference. Their draft proposal for the new organization had been negotiated in a much more exclusive meeting a few months earlier at Dumbarton Oaks. What Churchill, Roosevelt, and Stalin wanted was a collective security arrangement for the postwar period, and it was only after they had settled everything that was most important to them that they announced a meeting where the rest of the Allies could have a say. The "Big Three" do not seem to have contemplated that the San Francisco conference would produce major changes in their design. As Churchill had put it to Roosevelt and Stalin at Yalta, when discussing the extent to which "smaller powers" should participate in the peace process, "The eagle should permit the small birds to sing and care not wherefore they sang."[2] The idea of human rights ranked so low among the priorities of the major powers that they mentioned it only once, briefly, in their draft charter.

Among the delegates who came to the U.N. founding conference, however, were several who had a more expansive vision of the new organization, a vision that included protection of human rights. The twenty-nation Latin American contingent, as the single largest bloc, was in a position to press the issue.[3] They were well-suited for that role by experience as well as numbers, for they had been engaged for some time in thinking about human rights at the supranational level. As early as 1938, with war impending, the Inter-American Conference, the predecessor of the Organization of American States, adopted a "Declaration in Defense of Human Rights" at its eighth international meeting in Lima, Peru. That Declaration stated that when recourse is had to war in any region of the world, "respect [should] be given to those human rights not necessarily involved in the conflict, to humanitarian sentiments and to the spiritual and material inheritance of civilization."[4] At the same conference, three forward-looking resolutions were adopted: one condemning racial and religious persecution, one in favor of women's rights, and one on freedom of association for workers.[5] In February and March 1945, just before the San Francisco gathering, the Inter-American Conference held a meeting in Mexico City where they decided to begin drafting a Pan-American declaration of rights and duties.[6] With an eye

---

[2] Quoted in Charles E. Bohlen, *Witness to History, 1929–1969* (New York: Norton, 1973), 181. Churchill was recalling these lines from Shakespeare's *Titus Andronicus*, Act. 2, Scene 4: "The eagle suffers little birds to sing/And is not careful what they mean thereby."

[3] The countries represented were Argentina, Bolivia, Brazil, Chile, Columbia, Costa Rica, Cuba, Dominican Republic, Ecuador, El Salvador, Guatemala, Haiti, Honduras, Mexico, Nicaragua, Panama, Paraguay, Peru, Uruguay, and Venezuela.

[4] *International Conferences of American States, First Supplement, 1933–1940* (Washington, DC: Carnegie Endowment for International Peace, 1943), 245.

[5] Id., 238.

[6] *International Conferences of American States, Second Supplement, 1942–1954* (Washington, DC: Pan American Union, 1958), 102.

toward San Francisco, they also resolved to seek inclusion of a transnational declaration of rights in the U.N. Charter.[7]

That surge of regional interest in supranational human rights grew out of efforts at the national level by several Latin American countries to establish constitutional democracies where rights of citizens would be legally protected. The 1940s, according to Hector Gros Espiell, vice-president of the Inter-American Court of Human Rights, were "a moment of idealistic optimism and democratic euphoria."[8] As Johannes Morsink puts it, "In their joint reaction to the Great Depression and to the absolutism of both right and left, they all (or almost all) hit a democratic stretch at the same time."[9] Cuba, for example, adopted a democratic constitution in 1940, and voted out its corrupt leader Fulgencio Batista in 1944. Within eight years, Batista would return to power with the aid of the military and would suspend all constitutional guarantees. The Batista regime in turn was overthrown by Fidel Castro in 1959. But in 1945, Cuba was enjoying a brief interlude of political hope and promise. She sent an eloquent young democrat, 30-year-old Guy Pérez Cisneros, to be her representative at the San Francisco meeting.

As soon as the San Francisco proceedings got underway, Panama submitted a draft declaration of human rights (complete with rights to education, work, health care, and social security).[10] Delegates from Chile, Cuba, and Mexico joined Panama in waging an unsuccessful fight to have that declaration incorporated into the U.N. Charter. In a more productive effort, the Latin coalition joined forces with delegates from newly independent countries like the Philippines and Lebanon, and with observers from Catholic, Protestant, and Jewish religious groups, civic associations, and labor organizations, to try to make sure the Charter would at least proclaim a serious commitment to the protection of human rights.

The reaction of the major powers to those initiatives ranged from coolness on the part of the United States to outright hostility on the part of the Soviet Union and colonial nations like France and Britain. But in May 1945 two developments gave a decisive boost to the movement for raising the profile of human rights in the Charter. First, the conference members were shocked by the photographs that began to arrive from the newly liberated concentration camps in Europe. Second, and no doubt related to those revelations, the

---

[7] Id., 93–94.

[8] Hector Gros Espiell, "La Declaración Americana: Raíces Conceptuales y Políticas en la Historia, la Filosofía y el Derecho Americano," *Revista Instituto Interamericano de Derechos Humanos,* Número Especial (San José, Costa Rica, 1989), 41, 44.

[9] Johannes Morsink, *The Universal Declaration of Human Rights: Origins, Drafting, and Intent* (Philadelphia: University of Pennsylvania Press, 2000), 130.

[10] The draft was the product of cross-national collaboration conducted under the auspices of the American Law Institute, "Statement of Essential Rights," in American Law Institute, *Seventy-Fifth Anniversary 1923–1998* (Philadelphia: American Law Institute, 1998), 267, 269.

386 • Mary Ann Glendon

United States dropped its opposition to the idea of creating a U.N. Human Rights Commission.[11] By the time the conference ended in June 1945, principles of human rights had been inserted into the U.N. Charter in seven places, including a provision establishing a commission on human rights.[12]

## LATIN AMERICAN INFLUENCES ON THE DRAFTING OF THE UNIVERSAL DECLARATION OF HUMAN RIGHTS

Latin American delegates remained active on the human rights front when the U.N. got up and running. One of the first tasks the new organization assigned to its Human Rights Commission, chaired by Eleanor Roosevelt, was the preparation of what was then referred to as an international bill of rights.[13] The idea was that the Commission should produce a set of common standards that would serve as a kind of yardstick by which all countries could measure their own and each others' progress toward making human rights a reality. The 18-member Commission was reasonably well-suited for that assignment, in the sense that it had been constituted with a view toward cultural and political diversity. Three of the 18 seats were given to Latin American countries: one to Chile, one to Uruguay, and one to Panama. The other seats were held by Australia, Belgium, China, Egypt, France, India, Iran, Lebanon, Philippines, the United Kingdom, the United States, and four Eastern bloc members: Byelorussia, the Soviet Union, the Ukraine, and Yugoslavia.

That very heterogeneity, however, posed daunting challenges. Not least of these was that no one really knew whether there were any rights with a plausible claim to acceptance in all the cultures of the world, or if so what they might be.[14] As an initial step, the Human Rights Commissioners asked the

---

[11] M. Glen Johnson, "The Contributions of Eleanor and Franklin Roosevelt to the Development of International Protection of Human Rights," 9 *Human Rights Quarterly* 26 (1987).

[12] U.N. Charter, Preamble and Articles 1, 13, 55, 62, 68, 76.

[13] For detailed histories, see Mary Ann Glendon, *A World Made New: Eleanor Roosevelt and the Universal Declaration of Human Rights* (New York: Random House, 2001); and Morsink, *The Universal Declaration of Human Rights.*

[14] To examine those questions, UNESCO appointed a committee of philosophers, including some, such as Jacques Maritain and Benedetto Croce, who were prominent in the West, and others belonging to Confucian, Hindu, and Muslim traditions. The philosophers in turn sent a questionnaire to other leading thinkers all over the world—from Mahatma Gandhi to Teilhard de Chardin. In due course, the committee reported that, somewhat to their surprise, the responses they received had indicated that there were a number of principles of basic decency that were widely shared—though not always formulated in the language of rights. Gandhi, for example, recommended framing a bill of duties. The Committee's report, the questionnaire, and several responses are collected in *Human Rights: Comments and Interpretations* (London: Wingate, 1949).

SECTION IV • Human Rights

Director of the U.N.'s Human Rights Division, the Canadian international lawyer John Humphrey to prepare a first draft.[15] Humphrey began by having his staff conduct a complete survey of the world's existing rights documents, together with all the proposals that had been submitted to the U.N. Following on their initiative at San Francisco, the first three governments to submit proposed bills of rights were Panama, Chile, and Cuba.[16] After studying the material he had received and collected—over four hundred pages—Humphrey took as his principal models the Panamanian and Chilean submissions.[17]

The Panamanian-sponsored document was the same proposal that Latin American delegations had unsuccessfully put forward at San Francisco.[18] It was the product of a cross-national study conducted in 1942 and 1943 under the auspices of the American Law Institute, an organization of U.S. judges, practitioners, and academics dedicated to the improvement of the law. With assistance from the ALI, a multinational committee had consulted experts from "Arabic, British, Canadian, Chinese, French, pre-Nazi German, Italian, Indian, Latin American, Polish, Soviet Russian and Spanish" countries and cultures in order to ascertain to what extent there could be worldwide agreement respecting rights.[19] In 1944, reporting that it had "found a very large measure of agreement which, in view of its multinational make-up, was most encouraging," the committee produced a "Statement of Essential Human Rights" that they believed to have a claim to acceptance "by men of good will in all nations."[20] It was this Statement that Panama's Foreign Minister, Ricardo Alfaro, a member of the drafting group, had proposed for inclusion in the U.N. Charter. In their preface, the drafters took pains to emphasize: "This is not a statement made by the American Law Institute, which is composed exclusively of United States citizens. It is a statement by a committee representing many different nations."[21]

The Chilean draft was the work-in-progress commissioned by the Mexico City Inter-American Conference in 1945, a preliminary version of the American Declaration of the Rights and Duties of Man.[22] Its authors, too,

[15] A. J. Hobbins, "René Cassin and the Daughter of Time: The First Draft of the Universal Declaration of Human Rights," 2 *Fontanus* 7 (Montreal: McGill University Library Publications, 1989).
[16] Morsink, *Universal Declaration of Human Rights,* 131.
[17] John P. Humphrey, *Human Rights and the United Nations: A Great Adventure* (Dobbs Ferry, NY: Transnational Publishers, 1984), 31–32. See also, *U.N. Weekly Bulletin* (June 17, 1947): 639.
[18] Statement of Essential Human Rights Presented by the Delegation of Panama, A/148, 24 October 1946; E/HR/3.
[19] "Statement of Essential Rights," in *Seventy-Fifth Anniversary 1923–1998* (Philadelphia: American Law Institute, 1998), 267, 269.
[20] Id., 267.
[21] Id.
[22] Draft Declaration of the International Rights and Duties of Man, 8 January 1947, E/CN.4/2.

had consulted a wide variety of sources, including an early version of the Statement of the ALI group.[23] Dated December 31, 1945, the draft was signed by a four-person committee that included Felix Nieto del Rio who represented Chile at the first meeting of the U.N. Human Rights Commission.[24] The American Declaration, often known as the Bogotá Declaration, became the world's first international human rights declaration when it was adopted on April 30, 1948, at Bogotá, Columbia.[25]

Morsink's line-by-line comparison of the Panamanian- and Chilean-sponsored drafts with the first draft of the Universal Declaration led him to conclude that "Humphrey took much of the wording and almost all of the ideas for the social, economic, and cultural rights of his first draft" from those two proposals.[26]

What made the Latin American-sponsored drafts such important sources for Humphrey and the Human Rights Commission was their compatibility with a broad range of cultures and philosophies represented in the United Nations. No small part of that wide appeal was due to the fact that several elements of Latin American legal traditions resonated with non-Western traditions. As I have described elsewhere, the modern language of rights from the outset developed two main branches.[27] The differences were ones of degree, but their spirit had penetrated every corner of the societies affected. One branch, influenced by the rhetoric of the American revolution and by early modern Anglo-American thinkers, placed greater emphasis on individual liberty and property than on equality and fraternity (or, as we would say today, solidarity). This dialect was infused with a good deal of mistrust of government. The other dialect was more influenced by the continental European branch of the Enlightenment where the break with classical, biblical, feudal, and Roman-law thinking about man and government had been less complete. Continental rights documents had more room for equality and fraternity along with liberty; they often explicitly tempered rights with duties and limits; and they generally presented government in a positive light as a guarantor of rights and protections for the needy.

[23] Gros Espiell, "La Declaración Americana," 48.

[24] The other signers were Francisco Campos, Charles Fenwick, and Antonio Gómez Robledo. Ibid., 45.

[25] The American Declaration of the Rights and Duties of Man can be found in *Basic Documents on Human Rights*, Ian Brownlie, ed. (Oxford: Clarendon Press, 1994), 489. The Bogota conference where the Declaration was adopted was the scene of a violent far-left demonstration (known as the Bogotazo) in which 5,000 persons lost their lives. Among the participants in the Bogotazo was the young Fidel Castro. Claudio F. Benedi, *Human Rights: The Theme of Our Times* (St. Paul: Paragon House, 1997), 38.

[26] Morsink, *Universal Declaration of Human Rights*, 131.

[27] Mary Ann Glendon, *Rights Talk: The Impoverishment of Political Discourse* (New York: Free Press, 1991), 20–46; *Abortion and Divorce in Western Law: American Failures, European Challenges* (Cambridge: Harvard University Press, 1987), 112–34.

When Latin American nations gained independence in the nineteenth century, those two strains converged, and merged with an older, more universalist, natural law tradition. The result was a distinctively Latin American form of rights discourse. Paolo Carozza has traced the roots of that discourse to a distinctive application, and extension, of Thomistic moral philosophy to the injustices of Spanish conquests in the New World.[28] The key figure in that development seems to have been Bartoloméo de las Casas, a sixteenth-century Spanish bishop who condemned slavery and championed the cause of Indians on the basis of a natural right to liberty grounded in their membership in a single common humanity.[29] "All the peoples of the world are humans," Las Casas wrote, and "all the races of humankind are one."[30] According to historian Brian Tierney, Las Casas and other Spanish Dominican philosophers laid the groundwork for a doctrine of natural rights that was independent of religious revelation "by drawing on a juridical tradition that derived natural rights and natural law from human rationality and free will, and by appealing to Aristotelian philosophy."[31] Carozza has built on Tierney's work to show how an identifiably Latin American understanding of human rights emerged from the fusion of the teachings of Dominican opponents of slavery and conquest with French revolutionary ideas, United States constitutionalism, and the Pan-American vision of the Liberator, Símon Bolívar.

Upon independence, most of the new nations in South and Central America retained their European-style legal systems based on civil codes, but adopted constitutions inspired by the U.S. founding documents, the rhetoric of the French Revolution, and a natural law tradition to which the idea of the common humanity of all persons was central. These constitutions were less libertarian than the U.S. model and bore no trace of the anti-clericalism that characterized French models. Later, in the first half of the twentieth century, many Latin American countries supplemented their constitutions with protections for workers and the poor. Though conventional history treats Latin American constitutionalism as merely derivative of American and European models, it is more accurately regarded as representing a distinctive fusion of moral and political traditions. The insistence on the correlation between human rights and duties, for example, has been a characteristic feature of Latin American political philosophy and constitutional law since

---

[28] Paolo Carozza, "From Conquest to Constitutions: Retrieving a Latin American Tradition of the Idea of Human Rights," 25 *Human Rights Quarterly* 281 (2003).

[29] Brian Tierney, *The Idea of Natural Rights: Studies on Natural Rights, Natural Law and Church Law, 1150–1625* (Atlanta: Scholars Press, 1997), 272–73.

[30] Id., 273.

[31] Tierney describes Las Casas as having initiated a new language of natural rights through "a systematic grafting of the juridical language of Roman and canon law onto Aquinas's teaching on natural law." Id., 287.

the beginning of the nineteenth century.[32] The universalizing, internationalist dimension of this heritage was furthered by the Inter-American Conference, established in 1890.

In view of that background, it is not surprising that Humphrey found the Panamanian- and Chilean-sponsored drafts especially useful resources for a U.N. declaration that aspired to be universally applicable. In the first place, by emphasizing the importance of the family, and that rights are subject to duties and limitations, both drafts resonated with several non-Western as well as continental European traditions.[33] Second, they were both based on extensive cross-national research with the aim of finding acceptance from a large group of countries that are far from homogeneous. And third, they were prime examples of the modern constitutional trend to combine "first generation" political and civil liberties with "second generation" rights relating to social justice. Though many other cultures contributed to the Universal Declaration of Human Rights, the U.N. document bears unmistakable marks of the strong influence of the same ideas and sources that helped to shape the 1948 American Declaration of the Rights and Duties of Man.[34]

When Humphrey finished the initial draft of the UDHR, he turned it over to the Human Rights Commission, which appointed an eight-member

---

[32] Gros Espiell, "La Declaración Americana," 53.

[33] For example, "The fulfillment of duty by each individual is a prerequisite to the rights of all. Rights and duties are interrelated in every social and political activity of man. While rights exalt individual liberty, duties express the dignity of that liberty." Preamble, American Declaration of the Rights and Duties of Man.

[34] An emphasis on human dignity, for example, is pervasive in both documents, and both begin by sounding the theme of liberty, equality, and fraternity (solidarity):

*UDHR, Article 1:* All human beings are born free and equal in dignity and rights. They are endowed with reason and conscience and should act toward one another in a spirit of brotherhood.

*ADRDM, Preamble:* All men are born free and equal, in dignity and in rights, and, being endowed by nature with reason and conscience, they should conduct themselves as brothers and sisters.

Both documents also recognize the importance of the family:

*UDHR, Article 16 (3):* The family is the natural and fundamental group unit of society and is entitled to protection by society and the State.

*ADRDM, Article 6:* Every person has the right to establish a family, the basic element of society, and to receive protection therefor.

Both recognize a right to social security:

*UDHR, Article 22:* Everyone as a member of society has the right to social security and is entitled to the realization through national effort and international cooperation and in accordance with the organization and resources of each State of the economic, social and cultural rights indispensable for his dignity and the free development of his personality.

drafting committee to continue the work. A key member of that subcommittee was Hernán Santa Cruz who succeeded Nieto del Rio as Chile's representative on the HRC after the first meeting. Contrary to what many suppose today, it was Santa Cruz, far more than any Soviet bloc representative, who was the Commission's most zealous promoter of social and economic rights. Indeed, Morsink has concluded, in his study of the origins of the Declaration, that the social and economic rights in the Declaration are mainly derived from the traditions of "Latin American socialism."[35]

---

*ADRDM, Article 16:* Every person has the right to social security which will protect him from the consequences of unemployment, old age, and any disabilities arising from causes beyond his control that make it physically or mentally impossible for him to earn a living.

Both recognize a worker's right to remuneration that assures a decent existence for himself and his family:

*UDHR, Article 23 (3):* Everyone who works has the right to just and favorable remuneration ensuring for himself and his family an existence worthy of human dignity, and supplemented, if necessary, by other means of social protection.

*ADRDM, Article 14 (2):* Every person who works has the right to receive such remuneration as will, in proportion to his capacity and skill, assure him of a standard of living suitable for himself and for his family.

Both accord special protection to motherhood and childhood:

*UDHR, Article 25 (3):* Motherhood and childhood are entitled to special care and assistance.

*ADRDM, Article 7:* All women during pregnancy and the nursing period, and all children have the right to special protection, care and aid.

Both expressly state that people have duties as well as rights:

*UDHR, Article 29 (1):* Everyone has duties to the community in which alone the free and full development of his personality is possible.

*ADRDM, Preamble:* The fulfillment of duty by each individual is a prerequisite to the rights of all. Rights and duties are interrelated in every social and political activity of man. While rights exalt individual liberty, duties express the dignity of that liberty.

Both expressly state that rights have limits:

*UDHR, Article 29 (2):* In the exercise of his rights and freedoms, everyone shall be subject only to such limitations as are determined by law solely for the purpose of securing due recognition and respect for the rights and freedoms of others and of meeting the just requirements of morality, public order and the general welfare in a democratic society.

*ADRDM, Article 28:* The rights of man are limited by the rights of others, by the security of all, and by the just demands of the general welfare and the advancement of democracy. The texts of the Universal Declaration and the American Declaration can be found in *Basic Documents on Human Rights,* 21–27 and 489–94, respectively.

[35] Morsink, *Universal Declaration of Human Rights,* 131.

That the rights in question owe much to Latin American models is clear, but whether those models are best described as socialist depends on what one means by socialist. By the 1940s, social and economic rights had found their way into the constitutions of many Latin American and continental European countries, via the programs of socialist, social democratic, labor, Christian democratic, and Christian social parties.[36] Except in Mexico, which adopted a socialist constitution in 1917, the particular formulations of rights in Latin America—with their emphasis on the family, religion, and the dignity of the person—are significantly at odds with Marxist anthropology and with state socialism.

One feature that set most twentieth-century Latin American rights documents apart from Marxist models was their resemblance to two influential papal encyclicals that grounded social justice in respect for human dignity: the 1891 encyclical *Rerum Novarum*, and *Quadragesimo Anno*, published on the fortieth anniversary of *Rerum Novarum*. As Michael Novak has observed, "Unless one understands the Catholic intellectual traditions of southern Europe and Latin America, one cannot really enter the horizon of Latin American intellectual discourse. Many Latin Americans do not think of themselves as Catholic at all, and many may be quite irreligious. But even the irreligious have become used to expressing themselves within the horizon of Latin Catholic history."[37] In *Rerum Novarum*, Pope Leo XIII deplored that "workingmen have been given over, isolated and defenseless, to the callousness of employers and the greed of unrestrained competition," and gave a ringing endorsement to workers' rights on the basis of human dignity.[38] At the same time, he vigorously rejected state socialism as a remedy for grave social ills.[39] Forty years later, Pius XI observed that his predecessor's dignitarian approach to rights had played a role—via Christian political parties, labor organizations, and social action groups—in shaping social legislation enacted after the Great War. He noted that "there has arisen a new branch of jurisprudence unknown to earlier times, whose aim is the energetic defense of those sacred rights of the workingman which proceed from his dignity as a man," and he reaffirmed the duty to provide for the needy, the right to form and join unions, the right to an adequate wage for the worker and his

---

[36] At least ten Latin American countries rewrote their constitutions in the 1940s; five others did so in the 1930s; and two had done so in the first quarter of the twentieth century, according to Morsink, *Universal Declaration of Human Rights*, 130. On the constitutionalization of social and economic rights, see Mary Ann Glendon, "Rights in Twentieth Century Constitutions," 59 *University of Chicago Law Review* 519 (1992).

[37] Michael Novak, *This Hemisphere of Liberty: A Philosophy of the Americas* (Washington, DC: American Enterprise Institute, 1992), 1.

[38] Pope Leo XIII, *Rerum Novarum: Encyclical Letter on Capital and Labor* (May 15, 1891) in 2 *The Papal Encyclicals 1878–1903*, ed. Claudia Carlen (Ann Arbor, MI: Pierian Press, 1990), 241, paras. 2, 31–38.

[39] Id., paras. 11–12.

family, and the need to avoid the "double dangers" of extreme individualism and collectivism.[40]

The contributions to the UDHR of Hernán Santa Cruz, the principal advocate of social and economic rights on the Human Rights Commission, were in keeping with that tradition. Santa Cruz was an aristocratic man of the left, a member of the Chilean Popular Front, and a close friend from boyhood of the ill-fated Salvatore Allende, but he was seldom aligned with the socialist bloc in the U.N. His vision of human rights—melding freedom, dignity, and social justice—is well-captured in the following amendment proposed by Chile to the UDHR's Article 3 on the right to life: "Unborn children, incurables, the mentally retarded, and the insane have the right to life. Every human being has the right to enjoy living conditions that permit him to live in dignity and develop his personality normally. Persons who cannot provide for their own needs have the right to be supported and maintained."[41] Santa Cruz was unsuccessful in his efforts to have unborn children recognized in the Declaration as members of the human family, but no one played a greater role than he in securing recognition for the rights of "[p]ersons who cannot provide for their own needs."

## LATIN AMERICANS IN THE DEBATES LEADING TO APPROVAL OF THE UDHR BY THE GENERAL ASSEMBLY

In the autumn of 1948, the Human Rights Commission presented its draft declaration for review by the U.N.'s Committee on Social, Humanitarian, and Cultural Affairs, a large body composed of representatives from all (then-58) member nations. Approval by that group was a necessary step before the Declaration could be presented for a final vote in the General Assembly. The Latin American countries were still the largest single group in the U.N., and their delegates were eager to bring the experience gained in preparing the Bogotá Declaration to bear on the U.N.'s human rights project. So proud were they of the newly minted American Declaration, that many backed a movement spearheaded by Cuba to send the draft U.N. Declaration to a committee to be compared line-by-line with the American document. When that idea was rejected, several Latin American delegates began offering amendments aimed at conforming the U.N. draft to the Bogotá Declaration.

This activity, though it produced a number of important last-minute changes to the UDHR, produced alarm among many of the Declaration's

---

[40] Pope Pius XI, *Quadragesimo Anno: Encyclical Letter on Reconstruction of the Social Order* (May 15, 1931) in 3 *The Papal Encyclicals 1903–1939*, 421, paras. 12, 22, 28, 46, 120.

[41] E/CN.4/21, 59; and E/CN.4/2. See also, Mary Ann Glendon, *A World Made New: Eleanor Roosevelt and the Universal Declaration of Human Rights* (New York: Random House, 2001), Appendix 3, 282.

supporters, for it unwittingly aided Soviet efforts to delay the proceedings. Among those who feared that the Declaration's chance of approval would be dead forever if it were not adopted at the 1948 session was John Humphrey. In his memoir, referring to the Latin American initiatives as "the Bogotá Menace," Humphrey recalled his feelings of frustration as the "[h]ighly intelligent, Perez Cisneros used every procedural device to reach his end. His speeches were laced with Roman Catholic social philosophy, and it seemed at times that the chief protagonists in the conference room were the Roman Catholics and the communists, with the latter a poor second."[42] In Humphrey's private diaries, published after his death, he describes Perez Cisneros as a man who "combines demagogy with Roman Catholic social philosophy," remarking that the Cuban "should burn in hell, but he will probably go down in history as a great defender of freedom."[43]

Fortunately, Hernán Santa Cruz, who sympathized both with Humphrey's sense of urgency and with the aims of his fellow Latin Americans, was in a position to intervene effectively. As a member of the drafting committee, he was able to point out to delegates who were seeing the UDHR for the first time how much of the document had in fact been based on the preparatory work for the Bogotá Declaration.[44]

The persistence of the Latin American delegates did result, however, in significant additions to the UDHR in the course of debates that stretched out over October and November 1948. On the motion of Minerva Bernardino of the Dominican Republic, the Preamble was amended to emphasize that the Declaration's rights belong to women as well as men. At the instance of Perez Cisneros, the reference to the needs of families was inserted in Article 23(3) on the right to just remuneration. On the motion of Ecuador, Article 9 was amended to include protection against arbitrary exile. And at Mexico's behest, a new article (Article 8) was added adopting the Latin American institution known as the *amparo* (the right to an effective remedy for acts in violation of fundamental rights).

The importance of the Latin American contributions was officially recognized on December 9, 1948, when Charles Malik, as Rapporteur of the U.N.'s Human Rights Commission, presented the draft Universal Declaration of Human Rights to the General Assembly for its vote.[45] Malik began

---

[42] John P. Humphrey, *Human Rights and the United Nations,* 65–66.

[43] *On the Edge of Greatness: The Diaries of John Humphrey,* vol. 1, A.J. Hobbins, ed. (Montreal: McGill University Libraries, 1994), 87.

[44] Santa Cruz's account can be found in his memoir, *Cooperar o Perecer: el dilemma de la comunidad mundial,* vol. 1 (Buenos Aires: Grupo Editor Latinoamericano, 1984), 184–93. See also, Committee on Social, Humanitarian, and Cultural Affairs, Ninety-first Meeting, October 2, 1948, *U.N. Summary Records,* 49.

[45] "Speech of Thursday 9 December 1948," in *The Challenge of Human Rights: Charles Malik and the Universal Declaration,* ed. Habib C. Malik (Oxford: Charles Malik Foundation, 2000), 117.

by describing the document as something new in the world, a synthesis of all existing rights traditions. He then proceeded to point the Member States to places in the Declaration where they could either find their own contributions or the influence of the cultures to which they belonged. After noting that a great number of proposals for an international bill of rights had been submitted from all over the world, he singled out the Panamanian, Chilean, and Cuban drafts for special mention. He recognized Hernán Santa Cruz for having "kept alive in our mind the great humane outlook of his Latin American world"; "Mr. Cisneros of Cuba and Mr. Carrera de Andrade of Ecuador [who] contributed from the great fund of their erudition and high idealism"; "the keen legal logic of Mr. de Aréchaga of Uruguay"; and noted that "credit must go to Miss Minerva Bernardino of the Dominican Republic" for the mention of the equal rights of men and women in the Preamble.

On the following day, the Universal Declaration was adopted by the U.N. General Assembly without any dissenting votes (although the Soviet bloc, Saudi Arabia, and South Africa recorded abstentions). As Malik noted, many nations contributed to that impressively, if imperfectly, multicultural document. The Latin American contributions, however, were among the major factors that helped it to avoid extremes of individualism or collectivism, and to become the principal model for the majority of rights instruments in the world today. Neither a U.S.-style nor a Soviet-style document could have commanded a consensus from a United Nations that included representatives from so many different cultures.

## CONCLUSION

As this brief survey demonstrates, the efforts of Latin Americans were instrumental in securing a place for human rights in the U.N. Charter, in providing models for the Human Rights Commission in its drafting process, and in endowing the UDHR with broad cross-cultural appeal. It is desirable to retrieve what Latin Americans brought to the human rights project, not only for the sake of giving credit where credit is due, but because the expansive vision that inspired so many post-World War II rights instruments is currently at risk of being displaced by narrowly individualistic and libertarian interpretations.[46] I need to emphasize, however, that I have only excavated the top layer of a story that needs to be more fully explored. My hope is that Latin American thinkers and statespersons will soon recover this part of their heritage in its fullness, not only for the sake of their own democratic experiments, but for the sake of the human rights movement. In 1948, they

---

[46] See Glendon, *Rights Talk: The Impoverishment of Political Discourse* (New York: Free Press, 1991).

CHAPTER 43 • Latin American Influence on the Universal Human Rights Idea

helped to prevent the Universal Declaration from falling into the excesses of individualism or collectivism. Now that the UDHR has become the single most important reference point for discussions of human rights in international settings today, Latin America may once again help friends of human rights to realize the full promise of the Declaration's vision of human dignity.

# Catholicism in a Time of Turmoil

# CHAPTER 44

# Why I'm Still a Catholic

*When my friends Kevin and Marilyn Ryan asked me to be one of the contributors to their 1998 collection of essays, Why I am Still a Catholic, my reaction to the title was the same as that of another contributor, Fr. Andrew Greeley: "That's easy: I love being Catholic." Pressed to say more, I reflected on the pre-Vatican II Church of my childhood, the excitement of encountering the Catholic philosophers as a university student, and the privilege of living in a time of inspiring popes.[1]*

I AM ALWAYS AMAZED when I read of Catholics of my generation who complain that they felt stifled in the Church of the 1950s. For me, as a girl in a small Massachusetts hill town, pre-Vatican II Catholicism was a window opening out to the wide world that lay beyond the Berkshires. Its ceremonies spoke to me of a history before Plymouth Rock, and its liturgy linked me to every living Catholic on earth. The words and gestures of the Latin Mass connected us parishioners of St. Agnes to villagers in places where it never snowed, to inhabitants of great cities like Rome and New York, and to our own ancestors buried in faraway lands. The rituals; the sacramentals; the crimson, green, and purple vestments; the stories of saints and apostles relieved the drabness of everyday life in the land the pilgrims made. The Church enabled the sons and daughters of mill workers and mill owners alike to find themselves in the rich tapestry of world history, and in the unfolding mystery of salvation. Small-town life in former times was sometimes stifling, but Catholicism was liberating. It enlarged the spirit, gave wings to the imagination, and lent meaning to suffering.

A stranger driving through Dalton on Route 9 might well have taken our little white church for a Protestant meeting house. It was a graceful wooden building of the type often seen on New England village greens. But anything more than a superficial glance would have told you that there was something special about it. The steeple was topped with a cross rather than a weathervane; there was a stained glass window, rather than a clock, over the

---

[1] Mary Ann Glendon, "A Woman's Place," in *Why I Am Still a Catholic*, ed. Kevin and Marilyn Ryan (New York: Riverhead Books, 1998), 198–210.

entrance. The interior was crowded with statues and pictures that prompted little children to ask questions: Why does St. Agnes have a lamb? Why is Theresa carrying red roses? What are those men doing to Jesus? That old wooden church has long since been replaced with a modern brick structure, but in my memory it is as lovely as Chartres.

Directly across from St. Agnes on Main Street was the First Congregational Church, an imposing gray granite structure. As the child of a mixed marriage between an Irish Catholic and a Yankee Congregationalist, I was fully immersed in both cultures—destined, I suppose, to be a comparatist. My mother's parents, Julia and Theodore Pomeroy, went out of their way to support her in her promise to raise her children as Catholics. My grandmother Pomeroy gave me a rosary for my first communion and a little book about different religions called *One God*.

By the 1950s, the Dalton Congregational Church functioned mainly, but vibrantly, as a social organization. The Congregationalism of those days bore not a trace of its stern puritan origins, but the church was a beehive of fraternal and charitable activities. Unlike the Catholics who took the obligation to attend Sunday Mass very seriously, most of the town's Protestants confined their church attendance to Christmas, Easter, weddings, and funerals. My mother's relatives were typical in that they rarely attended services, but the women were active in the church's many social clubs. Protestant church ladies organized a never-ending round of events and benefits that the whole town, Catholic and Protestant alike, thoroughly enjoyed: bake sales, potluck suppers, white elephant sales, talent shows, clambakes, and so on. In the war years, these good women knitted socks for our soldiers. After the war, they packed care packages for the children of Europe. During Lent, Congregational families saved spare change in little calico sacks to be brought to church on Easter and sent to some worthy charity.

The groups and events at St. Agnes' Church had a very different focus. There were no suppers, no sales, no shows, but many novenas, recitations of the rosary, Benedictions, and Adorations of the Blessed Sacrament. In the war years, we prayed for our soldiers and for the conversion of the bad guys. Afterward, we prayed for the conversion of Russia. During Lent, we prayed and fasted, confessed our sins, did penance and tried to amend our lives. Exactly contrary to the oft-asserted theological distinction, Dalton's Protestants were virtuosos of good works; the Catholics were virtuosos of faith.

The Catholic Church was, of course, not the only window through which one could glimpse the great world of people, places, events, and ideas beyond the Housatonic River Valley. There was also *Time* magazine which came every week, and the Dalton Public Library. It was through a *Time* article on Graham Greene that I first became aware of a more intellectual side of Catholicism. I do not recall what it was about that article that impelled me, at the age of 11 or 12, not only to read all of Graham Greene's novels that I could find, but to seek out works by the other authors mentioned in the article, Evelyn Waugh and Fyodor Dostoevsky. But that began a series of life-long "friendships" with a circle of writers who took religion very seriously. T. S. Eliot and Gerard Manley Hopkins were soon added and promoted to the head of that list.

Curiosity led me to other books that some of the authors I liked seemed to treat as very important. Thus, works by Freud, Marx, and Darwin were duly checked out of the Dalton Public Library. Only once in my high school years did the librarian call my mother to see whether I had permission to read something. My mother must have thought *From Here to Eternity* was inspirational reading, because she told the librarian to go ahead and give it to me. That entertaining novel about the pre-World War II army certainly expanded my vocabulary, but did not do much for my spiritual or intellectual development!

As for Freud, Marx, and Darwin, the former two enabled me to torment my brother with accusations of having an Oedipus complex, and to annoy my parents with disquisitions on the exploitation of man by man. By the 1950s, Darwin's evolutionary theory was uncontroversial in our milieu, and Darwinism as a proselytizing ideology was still unknown. In the period when I was becoming dimly aware of the pretensions of psychological, economic, and biological theories to become total philosophies, I was fortunate to come across an essay in our local newspaper by Theodore Hesburgh, then the president of Notre Dame. One sentence jumped out at me and it is no exaggeration to say that it had a transformative effect on my life. "When you encounter a conflict between science and religion," he wrote, "you're either dealing with a bad scientist or a bad theologian."

It was a joy many years later to have the opportunity to thank Father Ted personally for that gift. That single sentence from a newspaper column not only helped me on the perilous journey from childhood beliefs to adult faith, but it also served to channel some of my adolescent rebelliousness toward a dialectical and critical engagement with the natural and human sciences (not that I didn't find other ways to be a pest to my parents, brother, and sister.)

I count it among my blessings that a full scholarship enabled me to pursue that engagement at the University of Chicago. Indeed, improbable as it may seem, the University of Chicago deserves a good deal of credit for "why I am still a Catholic." Though Robert Maynard Hutchins was no longer its president when I entered, the core "great books" curriculum he had installed was still in place. Hutchins himself had a great respect for the Catholic Church, once referring to it somewhat enviously as having "the longest intellectual tradition of any institution in the world." He, Mortimer Adler, and their colleagues drew freely from that tradition in constructing Chicago's mandatory core of courses. Not only did Catholic students at the University of

Chicago become acquainted with our own greatest thinkers, but we observed that those thinkers were honored by the best Chicago teachers. Works by Augustine and Aquinas were taught by the likes of Richard Weaver, Leo Strauss, and Richard McKeon. Catholic luminaries like Jacques Maritain and Martin D'Arcy were frequent visiting lecturers. Wags of the day used to joke that the University of Chicago was the university where Jewish professors taught Thomas Aquinas to Marxist students.

I like to think that, thanks to Father Hesburgh and St. Thomas, I absorbed a little of the confident approach to knowledge that enabled Thomas to engage the minds of the ancient Greeks without the slightest worry that his faith would be unsettled. Thomas understood the intellect as a gift from God—a gift whose use not only need not threaten faith, but that may advance the ability of each new generation to know, love, and serve the Creator in this world. Paradoxically, the same Chicago education that reinforced a critical and dialectical approach to learning, helped to put an intellectual platform under the religious habits and practices I had acquired in Dalton.

Like many Catholics of my generation, however, I entered the 1960s with a livelier appreciation of the spiritual and intellectual riches of my religion than of its social mission. The Second Vatican Council and the encyclicals *Mater et Magistra* and *Pacem in Terris* thus came as a revelation and an inspiration. In the mid-60s, I was a young lawyer practicing in a large Chicago firm, but active in the pro bono defense of indigent prisoners and in the burgeoning civil rights movement. But I did not really connect my public service activities to my Catholicism. In the Dalton of my childhood, after all, it had been the Protestants who were most conspicuously involved in various social causes. When my sister Julia and I traveled to the March on Washington where Reverend King gave his famous "I Have a Dream" speech, it was with a group organized by the Unitarian Church in Pittsfield. As Vatican II unfolded, however, I realized that Catholic social thought had been sorely neglected in my education. I came to understand that my religious experience thus far had been rather self-centered—overly aesthetic and intellectual.

In the three decades that have passed since the Second Vatican Council, Catholic social teaching has come into its own, attracting increased interest and study from non-Catholics and Catholics alike. We American Catholics are more aware than ever of the 300,000 educational, health care, and relief agencies that the Church maintains around the world, serving mainly the earth's poorest inhabitants.

As a law teacher specializing in international and comparative legal studies, I have watched with pride as the post-Vatican II Church has developed into the world's most influential institutional champion of social justice in international settings. As a Permanent Observer at the U.N., the Holy See adopted a distinctive approach to the human rights that were declared fundamental in the Universal Declaration of Human Rights of 1948. Most

U.N. members have taken a "cafeteria" attitude to the human rights menu, with some favoring the traditional political and civil liberties, and others focusing on the newer social and economic rights. The Holy See, for its part, has consistently affirmed both human freedom and solidarity.

The idea that social justice can and must be harmonized with traditional political and civil liberties has been the touchstone of the Holy See's advocacy in the U.N., as well as a central theme of the social encyclicals of John Paul II. Amidst the tug-and-pull of special interests and power politics, the Church has stood clearly, and often alone, for all the freedoms that flow from the common principle of the innate dignity of creatures made in the image and likeness of God. (Needless to say, those of us American Catholics who are passionately convinced of the rightness of that stance find it somewhat difficult to fit into conventional American political categories!)

On the fiftieth anniversary of the founding of the U.N. in 1995, John Paul II took the occasion to remind the nations that the promises they made in the wake of the horrors of World War II are mutually reinforcing. He celebrated the freedoms of which the liberal democracies are rightly proud, saying that humanity has been "inspired by the example of all those who have taken the risk of freedom." But then he asked: "Can we not recommit ourselves also to taking the risk of solidarity—and thus the risk of peace?"

Thanks to the flowering of Catholic social thought, I am not only "still" a Catholic, but an enthusiastic Catholic. Thanks to John Paul II, I am a Catholic who is immensely proud of her Church and its role in the modern world.

I should say, too, that this seems to me to be a tremendously exciting time to be a Catholic woman. When I hear women complain about "sexism" in the Church, I always want to ask "Compared to what other institution?" Back in the 1950s, Flannery O'Connor gave what I consider to be the perfect response to a friend who asked her how she could belong to a Church that treated women as second-class citizens. "Don't say the Church drags around this dead weight," wrote O'Connor, "just the Rev. So&So drags it around, or many Rev. So&Sos. The Church would just as soon canonize a woman as a man and I suppose has done more than any other force in history to free women."

Alas, many contemporary Catholics are unaware of the ways in which the advance of Christianity strengthened the position of women in the ancient world. When we read the Apostolic Writings today, we can easily overlook how radically Our Lord departed from the customs of his time when he befriended a variety of women, including public sinners. It is striking how many important conversations Jesus had with women, and how many of his teachings were first confided to his female friends. Even his disciples were puzzled by his taboo-shattering behavior. One day, for example, when they had left him alone at Jacob's well, they returned to find him talking with a Samaritan woman. Jews did not ordinarily socialize with Samaritans. Moreover, we are told, "They marveled that he was speaking with a woman." And this particular woman was a Wife of Bath-like character who had had five husbands and was living with a man to whom she was not married! But through her tale of an encounter at the well with a man "who knew everything I had ever done" many Samaritans became followers of Jesus.

As for the early Church, one can only stand in awe of her countercultural accomplishments where women and the family were concerned. It still boggles my mind, as a student of law and society, to think that the Church succeeded in gaining wide acceptance for the novel idea that marriage was indissoluble—in cultures where men had always been permitted by custom to put aside their wives! She also succeeded in introducing the ideal of monogamy in societies where polygamy had been the norm. In her rules governing separation from bed and board, she introduced standards of marital fidelity and decent treatment of wives that were unknown to the secular law. Later, despite pressures from princes and merchants, the Council of Trent stood firm against marriages arranged without the consent of the spouses.

Not even Flannery O'Connor guessed, however, that the Church would one day become one of the world's most vigorous advocates of the freedom and dignity of women. Vatican II set that process in motion with a few cryptic statements, rich in implications. The Council said that political and economic orders should extend the benefits of culture to everyone, aiding both women and men to develop their gifts in accordance with their innate dignity. (*Gaudium et Spes,* 1). And in their *Closing Message,* the Council fathers proclaimed: "The hour is coming, in fact has come, when the vocation of women is being acknowledged in its fullness, the hour in which women acquire in the world an influence, an effect and a power never hitherto achieved."

That the Church would be more than a passive observer of women's progress along those lines became clear in the 1970s when she emerged as a vigorous proponent in international settings of social and economic justice for women, especially poor women, refugee women, migrant women, and mothers everywhere. In international debates, she has avoided ideological extremes, combining respect for women's roles in the family with full support of women's aspirations for participation in economic, social, and political life.

As of the time of this writing in the late 1990s, it is already clear that one of the many significant achievements of the papacy of John Paul II has been to give increased life and vigor to the Second Vatican Council's fertile statements on women. In a remarkable series of writings, he has meditated more deeply than any of his predecessors on the roles of women and men in the light of the word of God. *Mulieris Dignitatem* (1988), which contains the main theological basis for his messages to women, labels discrimination against women as sinful, and repeatedly emphasizes that there is no place in the Christian vision for oppression of women. The tone of all these writings to and about women is dialogical. Their author invites women to help him and the Church to reflect upon the quest for equality, freedom, and dignity in the light of the faith—in the context of a changing society where the Church and the faithful are faced with new and complex challenges.

As time went on, the Pope embraced the cause of women's rights in ever-more specific terms. His *Apostolic Letter to Women* prior to the 1995 Beijing Women's Conference stated: "[T]here is an urgent need to achieve real equality in every area: equal pay for equal work, protection for working mothers, fairness in career advancements, equality of spouses with regard to family rights and the recognition of everything that is part of the rights and duties of citizens in a democratic State." A few months later, he urged all Catholic educational, health care and relief organizations to adopt a priority strategy for girls and young women, especially the poorest, with a special emphasis on education. He pointedly included in this strategy the education of boys "to a sense of women's dignity and worth." In the same document, he made a special appeal that will challenge women and clergy alike for years to come: He appealed to women of the Church "to assume new forms of leadership in service . . . and to all institutions of the Church to welcome this contribution of women."

The vocabulary of these writings came as a surprise to many. In aligning himself with women's quest for freedom, the Pope adopted much of the language of the women's movement, even calling for a "new feminism" in *Evangelium Vitae*. In his 1995 *World Day of Peace Message*, he observed that, "When one looks at the great process of women's liberation," one sees that the journey has been a difficult one, with its "share of mistakes," but headed toward a better future for women. In his 1995 *Apostolic Letter to Women*, he added: "This great journey must go on!"

No one who reads the Pope's writings to and about women can fail to be impressed by the evident love, empathy, and respect John Paul II holds for womankind. This is especially manifest in his compassionate words to unwed mothers and women who have had abortions. The image that comes through is of a man who is comfortable with women, and who listens attentively to their deepest concerns. After meeting with the Pope prior to the Beijing conference, Secretary-General Gertrude Mongella told reporters, "If everyone thought as he does, perhaps we wouldn't need a women's conference."

Where women's changing roles are concerned, the Pope's writings contain no trace of the dogmatism that often characterizes the rhetoric of organized feminism and hidebound conservatives alike. He affirms the importance of biological sexual identity, but he is no biological determinist. Indeed, how could he be—since our religion requires us to strive constantly to rise above mere culture and biology to "put on the new man" (so to speak)? The writings of this sophisticated and thoughtful Pope give no comfort to those who believe men's and women's roles are forever fixed in a static pattern. On the contrary, he has applauded the assumption of new roles by women, and deplored the degree to which "cultural conditioning" has been an obstacle to women's advancement. (*Apostolic Letter to Women,* 1995).

Unfortunately, many Catholics receive their information about these matters second or third hand, often from dissenters. Many are unaware of the Holy Father's ongoing dialogical reflections about the roles of women, and of the role of the Holy See as a defender of women's interests in society. Many women, like Flannery O'Connor's correspondent long ago, complain that the Church has been slow to examine her own structures and the behavior of her own representatives in the light of the Holy Father's meditations. A glance at recent developments, however, shows that significant changes have occurred under his leadership. More importantly for the long run, he has provided a powerful impetus toward further and deeper transformations. Squarely confronting past injustices and the problem of all the "Rev. So&Sos" throughout history, he has written: "And if objective blame [for obstacles to women's progress], especially in particular historical contexts, has belonged to not just a few members of the Church, for this I am truly sorry. May this regret be transformed, on the part of the whole Church into a renewed commitment of fidelity to the Gospel vision." *(Apostolic Letter to Women).*

Modeling this resolve in his own sphere, John Paul II has taken a number of steps to raise the level of participation of religious and laywomen at all levels of the Church. In 1995, in the Letter he presented to the Holy See Delegation on the eve of our departure for Beijing, he appealed in strong terms to "all men in the Church to undergo, where necessary, a change of heart and to implement, as a demand of their faith, a positive vision of women. I ask them to become more and more aware of the disadvantages to which women, and especially girls, have been exposed and to see where the attitude of men, their lack of sensitivity or lack of responsibility may be at the root." The following year, he reiterated his call upon all the institutions of the Church to welcome the contributions of women, saying, "It is . . . urgently necessary to take certain concrete steps, beginning by providing room for women to participate in different fields and at all levels, including decision-making processes, above all in matters which concern women themselves." (*Vita Consecrata,* 1996). He himself has made an unprecedented number of appointments of lay and religious women to pontifical councils and academies, providing an example for cardinals, bishops, and other priests throughout the world.

Those who take a legalistic, formal approach to the study of institutions can easily underestimate the profundity of the changes that are presently underway. The issue of women's ordination is apt to loom large in a formalist's thinking. But an organization's formal rules can give a very misleading picture of the actual status of women within the group. One need only think of the United Nations as an example of an organization whose practice has fallen far short of its official commitment to sexual equality! In the Catholic Church, by the same token, the tradition of an exclusively male priesthood has in practice been accompanied by an extraordinary increase in female participation in the life of the Church since Vatican II.

The changes from the Church I knew in the 1950s are striking. All over the world, lay and religious women currently are serving in many roles that were formerly confined mainly or exclusively to priests, men, and boys. Pastoral and ministerial roles today are more open than ever to women. Indeed, the Church in many places desperately needs and seeks the contributions of laymen and -women in these areas. Perhaps not since the first century A.D. have women been so actively and visibly involved in the life of the people called together by Jesus Christ.

As for leadership roles, I know of no religious group that ordains women that comes close to the Church's outstanding record in promoting women's progress. The Church's health care system, the second largest in the world, is managed almost entirely by dynamic Catholic women executives (mainly religious sisters). Catholic women, religious and lay, are superintendents, principals, and trustees in the world's largest provider of private elementary and secondary education. Women are high-ranking officers in Catholic colleges and universities. (And let us not forget that the Church long ago pioneered in women's education, opening up opportunities for young women in countries where others paid little or no attention to girls' intellectual development.) In other words, there seems to be no correlation at all between the ordination of women and the advancement of women within a given religious organization. The Catholic Church has no comparative need to apologize in this regard

Church agencies also compare favorably, where progress for women is concerned, to large secular institutions such as corporations, governmental bureaucracies, universities, and the United Nations. The larger and more powerful these are, the slower they seem to remain in accepting the contributions of women, especially at higher levels. Unlike many secular institutions, moreover, the Church does not expect laywomen to sacrifice their family lives. When Dr. Janne Matlary, a member of the Holy See's Beijing delegation, announced she had to return to Norway before the end of the conference because her youngest child was having difficulty adjusting to kindergarten, she left with blessings and good wishes. Many a woman's progress in the business world has been permanently impaired by resolving such a conflict in favor of her family. But the Church takes a different view. John Paul II subsequently appointed Dr. Matlary to the Pontifical Council on Justice and Peace.

All in all, the Church seems to have entered a period of great vitality for women (and laypeople) who are willing and able to "think with the Church" as she enters the new millennium.

Has the Church done enough to conform its own structures to the principle that men and women are equal partners in the mystery of redemption?

Of course not. Flannery O'Connor had it right. When her proto-feminist friend railed against the Church's shortcomings, O'Connor replied, "[W]hat you actually seem to demand is that the Church put the kingdom of heaven on earth right here now."

Today, a Catholic woman impatient with the pace of change might consider asking herself: Where in contemporary society do I feel most respected as a woman, whatever my chosen path in life? What body of thought takes most seriously my deepest concerns? What organization speaks most clearly on behalf of all women, including those in poverty? Catholic mothers might consider asking as well: Where do I feel most supported and encouraged in the difficult task of raising children under today's conditions? For my own part, I cannot think of any institution that surpasses the Catholic Church in these respects.

Finally, no reflection concerning what binds me to the Church would be complete without mention of my friend and teacher Joseph Flanagan, the longtime chairman of the Boston College philosophy department. Father Flanagan loped into my law school office one day in 1976 and asked me to join an interdisciplinary group that was working on a new core curriculum. Among the many benefits I received from being associated with that remarkable collection of scholars was an exposure to the path-breaking thought of Bernard Lonergan. Just as Thomas Aquinas performed an inestimable service for the theology of his day by assimilating the best of ancient and contemporary thought, Lonergan has laid the foundations for a twenty-first century theology that both learns from and challenges the modern natural and human sciences. For many years, I had the exceptional good fortune of reading and discussing Lonergan's works with Father Flanagan. It was a kind of second Sunday School that opened new intellectual horizons for me and, I like to think, endowed me with a bit of Ignatian spirituality.

So, why am I still a Catholic? By the grace of God, and aided by many relatives, friends, and teachers—some of them dead for centuries, several of them non-Catholic. Thank you, Martin Francis Glendon, for keeping the faith of your forebears. Thank you, Sarah Pomeroy Glendon, for the Protestant rectitude that kept you faithful to your promise to raise your children as Catholics. Thank you, Holy Mother Church, for not dumbing down your demands to suit the culture, and for holding us sinners to a high standard. Thank you, Edward Lev, for our comradely marriage in which, like my mother, you supported the Catholic upbringing of our children. Thank you, Lord, for the utterly inestimable gift of faith, and for the privilege of having lived in the time of John Paul the Great.

# Contrition in the
# Age of Spin Control

*As the Jubilee Year 2000 approached, Pope John Paul II sorrowfully recollected many ways
in which Christians had sinned against God and their fellow human beings.
This essay, prompted by concern that these expressions of sorrow
were not always received in the spirit in which they were given,
appeared in the November 1999 issue of First Things.[1]*

IT CAN HARDLY HAVE ESCAPED the notice of persons interested in religion
and public life that there has been a good deal of public sorrow expressed
lately concerning errors or misdeeds committed by representatives or members of the Catholic Church at various times in history. Recently, a diligent
Italian journalist counted no less than ninety-four instances where the Pope
himself has acknowledged the mistakes and sins of Christians in connection
with, among other things, the Crusades, the Inquisition, persecution of
Jews, religious wars, Galileo, and the treatment of women.

This penitential activity is linked to Pope John Paul's 1994 apostolic letter, *Tertio Millennio Adveniente,* where he suggests that the period leading up
to the Third Millennium be regarded as "a new Advent," a time for examination of conscience: "It is appropriate that as the Second Millennium of Christianity draws to close, the Church should become more fully conscious of the
sinfulness of her children, recalling all those times in history when they
departed from the spirit of Christ and his Gospel, and, instead of offering to
the world the witness of a life inspired by the values of faith, indulged in ways
of thinking and acting that were truly forms of counter-witness and scandal."

The Pope's evocations of historical wrongdoing have been instructive.
They are direct, to-the-point, and aimed toward what he sometimes calls the
"healing of memories." In every way, they reflect the wisdom and largeness
of spirit that are characteristic of his writings and speeches.

Yet, when the Pope presented his plan for a premillennial public expression of sorrow to the College of Cardinals, some news stories reported that

[1] Mary Ann Glendon, "Contrition in the Age of Spin Control," *First Things* 77 (November 1997): 10-12.

many cardinals had grave misgivings about the idea. Whether or not that rumor is well-founded, the Pope did anticipate possible criticisms of his plan. He pointed out in *Tertio Millennio Adveniente* that while "the Church is holy because of her incorporation into Christ," she is "always in need of being purified," and thus "does not tire of doing penance." He reminded his readers that acknowledging the weaknesses of the past is an act of honesty and courage which helps to strengthen our faith, which alerts us to face today's temptations and challenges."

It would be hard to dispute those propositions. So why should anyone be nervous about a program of purification aimed at healing historical resentments and evangelizing contemporary men and women? My own uneasiness has nothing to do with what the Pope has said, and everything to do with the way in which the expressions of regret he calls for may be manipulated by spin doctors who are no friends of the Church; indeed by persons for whom no apology will ever be enough until Catholics apologize themselves into non-existence.

My anxiety level escalates when I think of these acknowledgments of past sins in the light of Gertrude Himmelfarb's chilling account of the current state of historical scholarship. History is always an amalgam of fact and myth. But historians seem increasingly to have turned from the search for fact toward free-wheeling, imaginative reconstructions of events. All too many are strategically reinventing history in the service of various agendas. As an elderly Boston lawyer recently remarked to me, "It's getting to be tough times for the dead."

As for the popular image of the Church in history, it must be hard for Catholics brought up on movies and TV to avoid the impression that their Church holds a special niche in some historical hall of shame.

Add to this that most people hear of official expressions of regret as filtered through the news media. Thus, though the Pope himself is careful to speak of sin or error on the part of the Church's members or representatives, rather than the Church in its fullness, that important theological distinction is almost always lost in the transmission.

Sometimes the distinction is deliberately obscured, as in the article on the papacy and the Holocaust in the April 7, 1997, *New Yorker* magazine. Author James Carroll begins with what at first appears to be an appreciation of John Paul II's special relationship with the Jewish people. He recounts the well-known facts: Wojtyla's bravery as a young man in Nazi-occupied Poland, his grief over the Holocaust, his denunciations of anti-Semitism, his establishment of diplomatic relations with Israel, his historic visit to the Rome synagogue, his sympathy to demands for withdrawal of the convent at Auschwitz, and his sorrowful admissions that "many Christians" were responsible for Jewish suffering.

Acknowledging John Paul II's exemplary record and enormous popularity, Carroll pretends to lament that the present pontificate is nevertheless "tainted." The "tragedy" of the present pontificate, according to ex-priest Carroll, is that the Pope stopped short of "indicting the Church itself." He quotes dissenting theologian Hans Küng's dismissive remark on the Pope's expressions of sorrow: "This Pope likes to make some kind of confession." For Küng, no confession will do until the Pope endorses the bizarre view that Küng himself holds, namely, that "it [is] no longer possible to say the Nazis were responsible without saying the Church is co-responsible." Carroll also complains that John Paul II has not condemned Pius XII by name, as Carroll does in a simplistic, selective account of the role of the papacy during the Holocaust.

Not only is it not enough for the Pope to admit that "many Christians" sinned against Jews—nor that he has said the Church "always acknowledges as her own her sinful sons and daughters"—Carroll even objects to the Pope's mention of acts of heroism by individual Catholics in saving Jews. As for the *New Yorker*, it published this one-sided attack without requiring Carroll to give so much as a hint of the case against ascribing collective guilt to the entire mystical body of Christ. Did it occur to them that they might not get the whole story from one of the corps of Catholics and ex-Catholics who specialize in sniping at the Church? Did it raise any editorial eyebrows that Carroll relied so heavily on a notoriously disgruntled theologian?

Carroll's (and Küng's) real target seems to be the institution of the papacy, and their point of entry the doctrine of papal infallibility. If it was "the Church" and Pius XII that erred or sinned, they suggest, the doctrine cannot stand. But surely both of them recall enough theology to know that none of the historical errors or misdeeds of which they complain fall within the scope of the infallibility doctrine. As Flannery O'Connor once succinctly put it:

> Christ never said that the Church would be operated in a sinless or intelligent way, but that it would not teach error. This does not mean that each and every priest won't teach error, but that the whole Church speaking through the Pope will not teach error in matters of faith.

Whether that crucial point is intentionally obscured, or simply overlooked, the effect is apt to be the same. Some of the faithful begin to wonder: "If the Church was wrong about so many things in the past, maybe she is wrong about what she is teaching now." This is another reason why public acknowledgments of past errors have given rise to anxiety in some quarters of the Church.

Consider, in that connection, the apology contained in the Pope's 1995 *Apostolic Letter to Women*. There, after deploring various affronts to women's dignity throughout the ages, John Paul II says, "If objective blame, especially in particular historical contexts, has belonged to not just a few members of the Church, for this I am truly sorry."

CHAPTER 45 • Contrition in the Age of Spin Control

I think it is fair to say that that gracious apology has not met with an equally gracious reception in circles wedded to the idea that the Church is a sexist institution. I was surprised, when I took the job of heading the Holy See delegation to the Beijing women's conference, at the number of people who asked me how I could represent an institution that treats women as second-class citizens. When I hear these knee-jerk accusations of sexism in the Church, I always want to ask: "Compared to what other institution?" Wasn't it the Church that gained wide acceptance for the novel idea that marriage was indissoluble—in societies where men had always been permitted by custom to put aside their wives? That fostered the rise of strong, self-governing orders of women religious in the Middle Ages? That pioneered in women's education in countries where most other institutions paid scant attention to girls' intellectual development? No one with the slightest knowledge of history could deny that the advance of Christianity has strengthened the position of women.

In recent years the Holy See has emerged in international settings as one of the world's most vigorous proponents of social and economic justice for women. The Church has been one of the very few international actors to insist both on respect for women's roles in the family, and on support for women's aspirations for full participation in economic and social life.

To all this, the gender police think they have a slam-dunk response: The Church is sexist because it refuses to ordain women. This is not the place for a full discussion of complementarity and the universal call to holiness in relation to ordination. Let's just ask: How does the position of women in the Catholic Church compare with the position of women in churches that ordain women? Strangely, many people who are obsessed with the ordination issue seem uninterested in the vast and increasing array of pastoral and ministerial roles, once reserved to priests, that are now being performed by women. For the gender police, who make no bones about being preoccupied with power, these expanded opportunities for service do not signify. They want to know about "leadership" positions. Leaving aside the inappropriateness of analogizing the Church to business or governmental institutions, let us consider that question on its own terms. Who runs the second largest health care system in the world? Has it not long been managed almost entirely by dynamic Catholic women executives (mainly religious sisters)? Who runs the world's largest system of private elementary and secondary education? Has it not long been largely run by Catholic women, religious and lay, as teachers, principals, and superintendents? (Incidentally, where did the idea come from that you have to be ordained to be a leader? I expect that the Archbishop of Calcutta is a very capable administrator, but was Mother Teresa less a leader than he?)

Moreover, John Paul II seems determined to push the Church further and faster along these lines. He has repeatedly appealed to women "to assume new forms of leadership in service . . . and to all institutions of the

Church to welcome this contribution of women." Practicing what he preaches, he has made an unprecedented number of appointments of lay and religious women to pontifical councils and academies.

If the question is whether the Catholic Church has done enough to conform her own structures to the principle that men and women are equal partners in the mystery of redemption, it is clear from his writings that John Paul II would be the first to say no. My point here is that though the Church may fall short of her *own* aspirations, she can hold her head high in comparison to *other* institutions so far as her long record of respect for the dignity and freedom of women is concerned.

That journalists turn a blind eye to this record brings me back to the general problem of public expressions of contrition in the age of spin. It seems to me that Catholic laypeople have a significant responsibility to help make sure that public penitential activities are kept in proper perspective. Often it is the laity who will be in the best position to see when sincere expressions of regret are being opportunistically exploited by persons or groups who are only too eager to help the Church rend her garments and to heap more ashes on the heads of Catholics. Often it will be the laity who are in the best position to set the record straight.

That means, for one thing, recalling that when we sinners ask forgiveness, we are addressing ourselves, first and foremost, to God. (As we say in the Act of Contrition, "but most of all because I have offended Thee, my God.") Expressions of sorrow over past shortcomings do not require abasing ourselves before others, and certainly not before persons who are unwilling to admit any misdeeds of their own. Many historical memories will not be healed until there has been mutual forgiveness.

Setting the record straight also means challenging those who, innocently or deliberately, seek to erase the distinction between the Church and her sinful children. When Flannery O'Connor ran into the likes of Carroll and Küng in the 1950s, she pointed out:

> What you actually seem to demand is that the Church put the kingdom of heaven on earth right here now. Christ was crucified on earth and the Church is crucified by all of us, by her members most particularly, because she is a church of sinners. . . . The Church is founded on Peter who denied Christ three times and couldn't walk on the water by himself. You are expecting his successors to walk on the water.

Truly, it is right that we confess our sins and do penance. We never "tire of repenting" because we and our pilgrim Church are on a trajectory—climbing Jacob's Ladder, striving to "put on the new man," trying to be better Christians today than we were yesterday. Probably the best way to show that we are moving forward on that trajectory is simply, as the Pope says, to "offer to the world the witness of a life inspired by the values of faith."

CHAPTER 45 • Contrition in the Age of Spin Control

But so far as our public acts of repentance are concerned, let us be vigilant to prevent them from being hijacked and exploited. Let us join with our sisters and brothers of other faiths to resist all those who peddle the poison of collective guilt. Let us make sure our expressions of sorrow are never permitted to denigrate the role of the Church in history as an overwhelmingly positive force for peace and justice. And above all, let us remember what they are not: They are not apologies for being Catholic.

# CHAPTER 46

# Witness to Hope

This review of George Weigel's magisterial Witness to Hope:
The Biography of Pope John Paul II appeared in
L'Osservatore Romano on September 29, 1999.[1]

GEORGE WEIGEL'S BIOGRAPHY of John Paul II is a panoramic tapestry of a book. General readers will be swept along by the dramatic life story of the man who triggered the revolution of consciousness that led to the collapse of European communism, prepared the Catholic Church to meet the challenges of the twenty-first century, and touched the lives of hundreds of millions of women and men with his televised messages and worldwide pilgrimages. Scholars will admire the finely stitched research that sustains this sweeping narrative. Most importantly, *Witness to Hope* provides an introduction to the theological context without which the pontificate of John Paul II cannot be understood.

Many writers have been fascinated by this Pope's role as a shaper of world events, but most have shown little comprehension of the philosophical and religious commitments that undergird his decisions and actions. Hence the common tendency to analyze this papacy in merely political terms, and even, Weigel notes, to treat it as one whose "Act I," the struggle against communism, gives way to an "Act II," where the Pope rejects many aspects of the new freedom he helped to bring about. Of such interpretations, the Pope once remarked, "They try to understand me from the outside. But I can only be understood from the inside."

To interpret John Paul II "from the inside," however, requires a biographer with a rare combination of qualities. Such a person must be well-grounded not only in Catholic thought, but in modern secular philosophies, politically sophisticated, independent of mind, yet able to "think with the Church." Happily, George Weigel, the author of the first fully developed argument that the Polish Pope had played a crucial role in the demise of the Soviet Empire *(The Final Revolution)*, possesses all those qualifications plus a

---

[1] Mary Ann Glendon, review of *Witness to Hope: The Biography of Pope John Paul II* by George Weigel, *Osservatore Romano* (Weekly edition in English), no. 1610 (29 September 1999): 9.

gift for explaining without simplifying that any theologian would envy. The result is a portrait both of a towering "witness to hope" and of the Catholic Church as she enters the third millennium.

*Witness to Hope* is not, as Weigel takes pains to point out, an official or "approved" biography. However, the author's many personal discussions with the Pope and his closest associates, his interviews with men and women who knew Karol Wojtyla at every stage of his life from boyhood onward, and his access to many hitherto unpublished documents make it likely that this book will be the standard reference on its subject.

The principal task that Weigel set himself was to understand how John Paul II came to his convictions, how he deepened them, and how he learned to express, defend, and bear witness to them. While fulfilling that aim admirably, Weigel does not neglect the view "from the outside." He identifies eight achievements that guarantee John Paul II's pontificate a special place in history: his revitalization of the papacy; his development of the full implications of Vatican II, thereby setting the Church's course for many years to come; his role in the peaceful defeat of totalitarian regimes; his clarification of the moral challenges facing free societies; his placement of ecumenism at the heart of Catholicism; his dedication to progress in the Church's relations with Judaism; his commitment to the dialogue with Islam; and his success in using modern means of transportation and communication to reach hearts and minds in every part of the world.

The person behind those achievements appears in Weigel's study as a complex modern man—an intellectual with a warm appreciation of popular piety; a mystic who is also an avid sportsman; a celibate who celebrates human sexuality and has many women friends; a Pole with deep sensitivity toward Jews and Judaism; a man of profound interiority with an exceptional public presence. As Weigel points out, no pope in living memory has ever brought to his office such extensive pastoral experience, nor such intimate familiarity with the everyday problems of ordinary laymen and laywomen.

Bishop Wojtyla's singular qualities were already evident at the Second Vatican Council. Yves Congar noted at the time that: "His personality dominates. Some kind of animation is present in his person, a magnetic power, prophetic strength, full of peace, and impossible to resist." In the discussions on *Gaudium et Spes*, Congar was struck by the fact that Wojtyla had insisted on a point made by no one else—the need for the modern Church to consider views that conflicted with her own. That eagerness to learn from others was a hallmark of the future Pope's thought. For him, as for Thomas Aquinas, "Be not afraid" meant being bold enough to look for truth wherever some fragment of it might be found, and that meant engaging with science, secular philosophy, and other religions.

To this lay reader, Weigel's most impressive achievement is his demonstration of the continuities among pastor "Wujek's" hands-on ministry in

Poland; philosopher Wojtyla's work on *The Acting Person*; the literary Wojtyla's plays and poems; and Pope John Paul II's encyclicals and speeches. The thread that runs through them all is the Pope's vision of the human person as an actor in the drama of salvation. From his early days as a pastor to his unforgettable worldwide pilgrimages, he has electrified young people, in particular, with that vision. To women and men in all walks of life, he has preached that we are not adrift at the mercy of forces beyond our control, but are moral agents who constitute ourselves, for better or worse, with every action we take and every choice we make.

The movement of all history is dramatic, he teaches, and the great struggle of any life is to move from the "person-I-am now" to the "person-I-am-called-to be." Each person's life is a process of seeking and questioning, but we do not seek in a void because at the center of the human drama is Jesus Christ "whose entry into the human condition and whose conquest of death means that hope is neither a vain illusion nor a defensive fantasy constructed against the fear at the heart of modern darkness."

The Pope's historic speech on his return to Poland in June 1979 ("perhaps the greatest sermon of his life") was, Weigel suggests, a popular rendition of *The Acting Person*, readily intelligible to believers and non-believers alike. In contrast to Marxism's materialistic reduction of humanism, the native son held up the Church's social doctrine "in which men and women were not the victims of impersonal historical or economic forces, but the artisans of society, economy, and politics."

When an older, frailer John Paul II traveled to another closed society nearly two decades later, he exhorted Cubans in the same manner. "You are not victims," he told the crowds, "You are and must be the principal agents of your own personal and national history." Time and again, on these and other occasions, John Paul II has portrayed individual human beings, and all humanity throughout history, as travelers on a journey where every step counts, either helping to build the civilization of life and love or collaborating with the culture of death. His ability to communicate that vision has helped countless men and women to take the high road.

Weigel movingly describes how the 1981 assassination attempt, illnesses, and age have taken their toll on the man who for so long exuded exceptional physical vitality. From 1994 on, with complications from hip surgery and the diagnosis of a form of Parkinson's disease, "the way of the Cross would ever more visibly mark the pontificate of John Paul II." Yet, the increasingly infirm Pope has retained his special gift for communicating with young people, his prodigious work habits, and his uncanny knack of giving everyone in a room the sense he is looking right at them. Under the pressure of aging publicly, he seems to be teaching the rest of us how to walk that path with dignity. At times, as Weigel notes, he exhibits "an even more palpable sense of command" than in his more physically vigorous days. One thinks in this connection of his great 1995 U.N. speech, where he issued this challenge to the nations: "Inspired by the example of all those who have taken the risk of freedom, can we not recommit ourselves also to taking the risk of solidarity—and thus the risk of peace?"

Weigel makes clear with dozens of examples that John Paul II's pontificate cannot be divided into two "Acts," but is all of one piece. The same concern for the dignity of the person, and the same dedication to genuine human liberation, have impelled the Pope to speak out against whatever reduces human beings to objects or instruments, whether in rich countries or poor, dictatorships or democracies. "The papacy," says Weigel, "has been a one-act drama, although different adversaries have taken center stage at different moments in the script." Throughout it all, John Paul II has been "a courageous pastor determined to speak truth to power."

That steadfastness in defending human dignity whether it is threatened by political repression or rampant materialism is nowhere more evident than in the Church's surprising emergence in recent years as the world's foremost institutional defender of the universality and indivisibility of fundamental human rights. John Paul II's leadership in making the Church a "voice for the voiceless" in international settings is so important that it would, I believe, have merited separate mention on Weigel's list of the great achievements of this papacy.

One cannot, obviously, do justice in a brief review to a work as comprehensive as *Witness to Hope*. I would be remiss, however, if I did not at least mention Weigel's brilliant elucidation of another important theme of this papacy: the Pope's conviction that culture, more than military or economic power, is the driving force of history. When Weigel turns from John Paul II's theology to his social encyclicals, he enters more controversial territory. Not every faithful Catholic will agree with Weigel's interpretations of the meaning of these much-discussed teachings, or of their relation to one another, but all should find his analyses intelligent and challenging.

Lest anyone think this papal biography by a loyal son of the Church is the literary equivalent of an air-brushed studio portrait, I should mention that Weigel seems to have taken to heart the quotation from Melchior Cano that he describes as "the watchword" of his project: "Peter has no need of our lies or flattery. Those who blindly and indiscriminately defend every decision of the supreme Pontiff are the very ones who do most to undermine the authority of the Holy See—they destroy instead of strengthening its foundations." Most of Weigel's criticisms relate to the fact that Karol Wojtyla, whether as pastor, bishop, cardinal, or pope, was never a micro-manager. That lack of close supervision, Weigel concedes, was probably the price to be paid for the benefits of a papacy with great intellectual creativity and public impact.

At the conclusion of this richly detailed, carefully documented book, Weigel steps back to sum up what, to him, is the meaning of this extraordinary pontificate: "If the Church of the future knows John Paul II as 'John Paul the Great', it will be for this reason: At another moment of peril, when barbarians of various sorts threatened civilization, a heroic figure was called from the Church to meet the barbarian threat and propose an alternative. In the case of Pope Leo the Great, the barbarians in question were Attila and his Huns. In the case of Gregory the Great, the barbarians were the Lombards. In the case of John Paul II, the barbarism threatening civilization has been a set of . . . defective humanisms that, in the name of humanity and its destiny, create new tyrannies and compound human suffering."

Recently, after Weigel delivered a speech on his research at the Pope John XXIII Seminary in Massachusetts, a seminarian asked Weigel how he personally had been affected by writing the biography of the Pope. Weigel responded that he had been deeply changed by the experience. That is easy to believe—just as it is easy to believe that many readers will be changed by the opportunity this splendid biography provides to know John Paul II "from the inside."

# The Hour of the Laity

*This essay, written at the height of the crisis brought on by revelations of clerical sexual misconduct, appeared in the November 2002* First Things.[1]

THROUGHOUT THE TWENTIETH CENTURY, leaders of the Catholic Church implored laymen and -women with increasing urgency to be more active as Catholics in society, and—since Vatican II—to become more involved in the internal affairs of the Church. The earlier call found a warm response among Catholic Americans in the 1930s, 1940s, and 1950s. But as Catholics gained in affluence and influence, the lay apostolate has suffered, while new opportunities for service in the institutional Church have gone begging. No wonder that John Paul II, with his history of close collaboration with laymen and -women, often refers to the laity as a "sleeping giant." For decades, the giant has seemed lost in the deep slumber of an adolescent. Now that the sleeper is beginning to stir—roused by media coverage of clerical sexual misconduct— it is beginning to look as though the Leviathan has the faith I.Q. of a pre-adolescent. Can this be the long-awaited "hour of the laity"?

The current resurgence of interest in lay organization suggests that the time is ripe to explore what has happened to American Catholics' understanding of the lay vocation over the years during which they made unprecedented economic and social advances. Are the sixty-three million or so Catholics who comprise over one-fifth of the U.S. population evangelizing the culture, as every Christian is called to do, or is the culture evangelizing them?

Since poets and novelists often help us to see things afresh, I propose to approach that question through a lens borrowed from an acute literary observer of the modern world. The protagonist of Mario Vargas Llosa's *The Storyteller* is arguably not a person, but a group—a nomadic tribe of rainforest-dwellers. To outsiders, they are known as the Machiguengas, but they call themselves the people-who-walk. The reader never meets the Machiguengas face-to-face; we only hear of them from a narrator who is trying to find out whether the tribe still exists. We learn that from time immemorial, the stories and traditions of the people-who-walk were remembered, enriched, and

---

[1] Mary Ann Glendon, "The Hour of the Laity," *First Things* 127 (November 2002): 23–29.

handed down by *habladors*—storytellers. These stories helped the tribe to maintain its identity—to keep on walking no matter what, through many changes and crises. But as the rainforest gave way to agriculture and industry, the Machiguengas scattered. For a time, their *habladors* traveled from one cluster of families to another and kept them bound together. The storytellers "were the living sap that circulated and made the Machiguengas into a society, a people of interconnected and interdependent beings." But anthropologists think that the storytellers eventually died out, that the Machiguengas were absorbed into cities and villages, and that their stories survive only as entertainment. The narrator suspects otherwise, and the drama of the novel comes from his effort to find out whether it is really true that a mysterious red-haired stranger has become the *hablador* of the Machiguengas so that they will not lose their stories and their sense of who they are.

That problem—the problem of how a dispersed people remembers who it is and what constitutes it as a people—lies at the heart of the challenges confronting the *Ecclesia* (which may be translated as "the people-called-together") in America. Catholics are constituted as a people by the story of the world's salvation, and part of that story requires them to be active in the world, spreading the Good News wherever they are. The people-called-together are called to witness, and to keep on witnessing no matter what, in and out of season. How well have American Catholics done at keeping that story alive through the crises, changes, temptations, and opportunities they encountered in the mission territory that is the United States?

From the beginning, Catholic settlers in North America were strangers in a Protestant land. At the time of the Founding, several states had established Protestant churches. Congregationalism, for example, was the official religion of Massachusetts until 1833, and in many New England towns the Congregational meeting house was the seat of town government as well as the place of Sunday worship. Nevertheless, when Alexis de Tocqueville surveyed the American social landscape in 1831, he predicted that Catholics would flourish there. The growing Catholic presence would prove beneficial for the young nation's experiment in self-government because, he argued, their religion made them "the most democratic class in the United States"—since it imposes the same standards on everyone, rich and poor, and it leaves its followers free to act in the political sphere.

The French visitor, farsighted as he often was, never suspected that a storm was gathering as he wrote those words. He failed to detect the anti-Catholicism that would fuse with nativism and erupt into violence as Catholic immigrants arrived from Europe in ever-increasing numbers. In 1834, an angry mob in Boston (the city he had regarded as America's most civilized) burned an Ursuline convent to the ground while police and firemen stood by and watched. Three years later, arsonists destroyed most of Boston's

Irish quarter. Similar atrocities were repeated across the country. But the expanding economy demanded cheap labor, and the immigrants kept arriving from Ireland, Italy, Germany, French Canada, and Eastern Europe. By the turn of the century, the Roman Catholic Church was the country's largest and fastest growing religious community, with twelve million adherents.

Struggling for survival in a hostile environment, the immigrant Catholics built their own separate set of primary and high schools, hospitals, and colleges. Picking up on the American penchant for associating, they formed countless fraternal, social, charitable, and professional organizations. Protestants had the Masons and the Eastern Star, Catholics had the Knights of Columbus and the Daughters of Isabella. Through dogged effort and sacrifice, they constructed, in historian Charles Morris's words, "a virtual state-within-a-state so Catholics could live almost their entire lives within a thick cocoon of Catholic institutions." From their neighborhood bases in northern cities, the newcomers used democratic political processes to win political power at the state and local level. But when the Catholic governor of New York ran for president in 1928, virulent anti-Catholicism broke out again. Al Smith's resounding defeat reinforced the Catholic sense of separateness through the 1930s, 1940s, and 1950s.

Interestingly, the period when Catholic Americans were most separate was the time when they were most active—as Catholics—in the world. In 1931, on the fortieth anniversary of the historic social encyclical *Rerum Novarum*, Pius XI called for Catholic action to counter the transformation of society along Communist or Fascist lines. "Nowadays," he wrote in *Quadragesimo Anno*, "as more than once in the history of the Church, we are confronted with a world which in large measure has almost fallen back into paganism." He told the lay faithful that they must "lay aside internal quarrels" so that each person could play his role "as far as talents, powers and station allow" in a peaceful but militant struggle for "the Christian renewal of human society." Laypersons were to be "the first and immediate apostles" in that struggle, he said. The response of Catholics in this country was all that the pope could have wished. They were instrumental in curbing Communist influence in the labor movement, and they made the Democratic party in the urban North into the party of the neighborhood, the family, and the workingman.

The Spanish philosopher George Santayana, who taught at Harvard in the early twentieth century, was intrigued by the contrast between what he perceived as a buoyant, optimistic American culture and the ancient Catholic faith with its "vast disillusion about this world and minute illusions about the next." He wrote in 1934 that Catholics in the U.S. had no serious conflicts with their Protestant neighbors because "[t]heir respective religions pass among them for family matters, private and sacred, with no political implications." If Santayana had spent less time in Cambridge and more in Boston, he would have realized that the Catholicism of urban immigrant communities was not at all "private"; it was merely enclosed in the neighborhoods. Those were the decades when lay Catholics were intensely involved, as Catholics, in the parish, the workplace, and the precinct. It was also a time when the people-called-together was blessed with an abundance of storytellers. In parochial schools, at Mass and devotions, and around their kitchen tables, Catholics were constantly reminded of who they were, where they came from, and what their mission was in the world.

But as St. Paul told the Corinthians, "The world as we know it is always passing away." As Catholics climbed up the economic and social ladder, they left the old neighborhoods for the suburbs. Parents began sending their children to public schools and to non-Catholic colleges. Vocations to religious life declined. Geographic and social mobility scattered Catholic communities of memory and mutual aid as relentlessly as agriculture and industry pushed back the rainforest of the Machiguengas. By the 1960s, the nation-within-a-nation had dissolved and the diaspora had begun.

The people-called-together thus embarked on what Morris well describes as "the dangerous project of severing the connection between the Catholic religion and the separatist . . . culture that had always been the source of its dynamism, its appeal, and its power." The transition was symbolized by the election to the presidency of a highly assimilated Catholic, John F. Kennedy, who matched the nativists in the vigor of his denunciation of public aid to parochial schools. The 1960 election taught ambitious descendants of immigrants that all doors could be open to them so long as they were not too Catholic.

Two years later came the opening of the Second Vatican Council, the Church's historic effort to meet the challenges of bringing the gospel to the structures of the modern, increasingly secularized, world. The Council fathers, realizing that the cooperation of the laity would be crucial, sent strongly worded messages to laymen and -women, reminding them that they are the front line of the Church's mission in society, and that, wherever they find themselves, they must strive to "consecrate the world itself to God." But events underway in the United States and other affluent countries would make it harder than ever for such messages to get through. The breakdown in sexual mores, the rise in family disruption, and the massive entry of mothers of young children into the labor force amounted to a massive social experiment, an unprecedented demographic revolution for which neither the Church nor the affected societies were prepared.

In those turbulent years, pressures intensified for Catholics to treat their religion as an entirely private matter, and to adopt a pick-and-choose approach to doctrine. Many of their *habladors*—theologians, religious educators, and clergy—succumbed to the same temptations. In that context, it was not only difficult for the strong demands of Vatican II to be heard; the messages that did get through were often scrambled. In an important sense, all the most divisive controversies of the postconciliar years were about how far Catholics can go in adapting to the prevailing culture while remaining Catholic.

Though American society was rapidly becoming more secular, certain cultural elements of Protestantism remained as strong or stronger than ever: radical individualism, intolerance for dissent (redirected toward dissent from the secular dogmas that replaced Christianity in the belief systems of many), and an abiding hostility to Catholicism. For the upwardly mobile Catholic, assimilation into that culture thus meant acquiescing in anti-Catholicism to a degree that would have astonished our immigrant ancestors. But that is what all too many of us did. In the 1970s, Andrew Greeley observed that, "of all the minority groups in this country, Catholics are the least concerned about their own rights and the least conscious of the persistent and systematic discrimination against them in the upper reaches of the corporate and intellectual worlds."

In this observation, as in his early warnings about child abuse and the growth of a homosexual subculture among the clergy, Father Greeley was on the mark. I regret to say that I was a case in point until my consciousness was raised by my Jewish husband. In the 1970s, when I was teaching at Boston College Law School, someone took down all the crucifixes from the walls one summer. Though the majority of the faculty at the time was Catholic and the dean was a Jesuit priest, not one of us entered a protest. When I told my husband, he was shocked. He said, "What's the matter with you Catholics? There would be an uproar if anyone did something like that with Jewish symbols. Why do Catholics put up with that kind of thing?" That was a turning point for me. I began to wonder: Why do we Catholics put up with that sort of thing? Why did we get so careless about the faith for which our ancestors made so many sacrifices?

In many cases, the answer lies simply in the desire to get ahead and be accepted. But for most Catholics of the American diaspora, I believe the problem is deeper: They no longer know how to talk about what they believe or why they believe it. The people-called-together have lost their sense of who they are and what they were called to do.

And they seem to have lost a lot of mail as well. How many laypeople, one wonders, have read any of the letters that popes have addressed to them over the years? For that matter, how many Catholics can give a sensible account of basic Church teachings on matters as close to them as the Eucharist and human sexuality, let alone the lay apostolate? If few can do so, it is not for lack of communications from Rome. Building on *Rerum Novarum* and *Quadragesimo Anno*, the fathers of Vatican II reminded the lay faithful that it is their particular responsibility "to evangelize the various sectors of family, social, professional, cultural and political life."

These have been constant themes of Pope John Paul II. In *Solicitudo Rei Socialis*, to take just one example, he renewed the call to the social apostolate, emphasizing "the preeminent role" of the laity in protecting the dignity of the person, and asking "both men and women . . . to be convinced of . . . each one's individual responsibility, and to implement–by the way they live as individuals and as families, by the use of their resources, by their civic activity, by contributing to economic and political decisions and by personal commitment to national and international undertakings—the measures inspired by solidarity and love of preference for the poor." He spelled out the implications of the lay vocation for contemporary Americans with great clarity in Baltimore in 1995: "Sometimes witnessing to Christ will mean drawing out of a culture the full meaning of its noblest intentions. . . . At other times, witnessing to Christ means challenging that culture, especially when the truth about the human person is under assault."

Now that the "sleeping giant" is beginning to show signs of regaining Catholic consciousness, the Church is going to have to reckon with the fact that the most highly educated laity in its history has forgotten a great deal about where it came from. Meanwhile, as with any emerging mass movement, activists with definite ideas about where they would like it to go are eager to capture the giant's strength for their own purposes. In recent months, American Catholics have heard vague but strident calls for "structural reform," for lay "empowerment," and for more lay participation in the Church's internal "decision making." Dr. Scott Appleby, for example, told the American bishops in Dallas that, "I do not exaggerate by saying that the future of the Church in this country depends on your sharing authority with the laity."

There has also been much talk about the need for a more independent American Catholic Church. "Let Rome be Rome," said Dr. Appleby. Then there is Governor Frank Keating, chosen by the bishops to head their National Review Board, who proclaimed, astonishingly, at his first press conference that, with respect to the role of the laity, "Martin Luther was right." The Voice of the Faithful, an organization, formed in 2002 by Boston suburbanites, states as its mission: "To provide a prayerful voice, attentive to the spirit, through which the faithful can actively participate in the governance and guidance of the Catholic Church." (One has to wonder just what spirits had been consulted when a leader of that group boasted excitedly to the *Boston Globe* that "the mainstream Catholics, all sixty-four million of them" were speaking through Voice of the Faithful's convention this past July.)

There is nary a sign, thus far, that these spokesmen have a sense of the main job the Gospels tell Christians they were placed on earth to do. Even the late Basil Cardinal Hume, hardly a reactionary in Church matters, took pains to caution an earlier reform-minded group, the Common Ground Initiative, against "the danger of concentrating too much on the life within the Church." "I suspect," he said, "that it is a trick of the Devil to divert good people from the task of evangelization by embroiling them in endless controversial issues to the neglect of the Church's essential role, which is mission."

By leaving evangelization and the social apostolate out of the picture, many lay spokespersons are promoting some pretty basic misunderstandings: that the best way for the laity to be active is in terms of ecclesial governance; that the Church and her structures are to be equated with public agencies or private corporations; that she and her ministers are to be regarded with mistrust; and that she stands in need of supervision by secular reformers. If those attitudes take hold, they will make it very difficult for the Church to move forward through the present crisis without compromising either her teachings or her constitutionally protected freedom to carry out her mission.

Much of that careless talk simply reflects the fact that, with the decline of Catholic institutions, the actual experience of the lay apostolate has disappeared from the lives of most Catholics—along with the practical understanding of complementarity among the roles of the different members of the mystical body of Christ. It is only common sense that most of us laypeople are best equipped to fulfil our vocations primarily in the places where we live and work. It is because we are present in all the secular occupations that the Vatican II fathers emphasized our "special task" to take a more active part, according to our talents and knowledge, in the explanation and defense of Christian principles and in the application of them to the problems of our times. John Paul II elaborated on that theme in *Christifideles Laici*, pointing out that this will be possible in secularized societies only "if the lay faithful will know how to overcome in themselves the separation of the gospel from life, to again take up in their daily activities in family, work, and society, an integrated approach to life that is fully brought about by the inspiration and strength of the gospel." Those are the main messages of all those letters that most of us have not read or answered. Those are the messages that are notably absent from the statements of spokespersons for the lay groups that have formed over the past few months.

As memories of the lived experience of lay apostolate faded, the lay ministry expanded in the post-Vatican II years. It is not surprising, therefore, that many Catholics came to believe that the principal way to be active as Catholics is to participate in the internal life of the Church. Those who began clamoring for more such participation in 2002 seem unaware that they are battering on an open door. The Church has long been beseeching lay men and women to come forward and assume positions at all levels. No one should complain, however, if bishops and priests are reluctant to give posts of responsibility to dissenters who want to use such positions to change basic church teachings. No good shepherd will invite wolves to look after his flock.

Needless to say, the Church will need to undertake far-reaching reforms in order to move beyond the present crisis, and many of the recent calls for reform are coming from well-intentioned men and women. Most Catholics are deeply and rightly concerned about the recent revelations of clerical sexual abuse; they want to do something about the havoc wrought by unfaithful priests; and they are grasping at the slogans that are in the air. But slogans about "structural reform" and "power-sharing" did not come from nowhere. Aging members of the generation of failed theories—political, economic, and sexual—have seized on the current crisis as their last opportunity to transform American Catholicism into something more compatible with the spirit of the age of their youth. It is, as Michael Novak puts it, their last chance to rush the wall.

Southern writers such as Flannery O'Connor and Walker Percy saw where those warped visions could lead American Christianity long before most of the rest of us did. The anti-hero of O'Connor's *Wise Blood* sets himself up as a preacher of the Church of Christ Without Christ. Percy's 1971 novel, *Love in the Ruins*, is set in some not-too-distant future when the American Catholic Church has split into three pieces: the patriotic Catholic Church with headquarters in Cicero, Illinois, where "The Star Spangled Banner" is played at the elevation of the Host; the Dutch Reformed Catholic Church founded by several priests and nuns who left to get married; and "the Roman Catholic remnant, a tiny scattered flock with no place to go." While matters happily have not reached that point, it is noteworthy that the two most salient themes of self-appointed lay spokespersons during the 2002 crisis have been in those directions: the desire for a more American Church free of hierarchical authority, and the desire for a do-it-yourself magisterium free of hard teachings regarding sex and marriage.

Meanwhile, like Paul of old, John Paul II keeps sending those pesky letters reminding what he generously calls the faithful that Christians must not conform to the spirit of the age, but must seek to do what is good, pleasing and perfect in the sight of God. For the umpteenth time, he explains that, "It is not a matter of inventing a 'new program.' The program already exists: it is the plan found in the gospel and in the living Tradition; it is the same as ever." One might think those messages would at least be picked up and amplified by those Catholics whose profession it is to figure out how to mediate the truths that are "ever ancient and ever new" under changing social conditions. But the fact is that far too many American Catholic theologians, trained in non-denominational divinity schools, have received little grounding in their own tradition. Far too many religious education materials are infused with the anger and disappointments of former priests and sisters who went to work in religious publishing because their training suited them for little else. Far too many bishops and priests have ceased to preach the Word of God in its unexpurgated fullness, including the teachings that are most difficult to follow in a hedonistic and materialistic society.

Derelictions on the part of so many *habladors* have left far too many parents poorly equipped to contend with powerful competitors for the souls of their children—the aggressively secular government schools and an entertainment industry that revels in debasing everything Catholic. I do not mean to suggest that failures of theologians, religious educators, bishops and priests excuse the lapses of the laity. What I do mean to suggest is that we are in the midst of a full-blown formation crisis.

Fr. Richard John Neuhaus has said that the crisis of the Catholic Church in 2002 is threefold: fidelity, fidelity, and fidelity. He is right to stress that lack of fidelity has brought the Church in America to a sorry pass. But it also needs to be said that we are paying the price for another three-dimensional disaster: formation, formation, and formation (formation of our theologians, of our religious educators, and thus of parents).

The wordsmiths of the culture of death have been quick to exploit that weakness in the Church that has consistently been their most feared and powerful enemy. Thirty or so years ago, they came up with one of the most insidious slogans ever invented: "Personally, I'm opposed to (fill-in-the-blank), but I can't impose my opinions on others." That slogan was the moral anesthesia they offered to people who are troubled about moral decline, but who do not know quite how to express their views, especially in public settings. Only in recent years have some Catholics, Protestants, and Jews stepped forward to point out that when citizens in a democratic republic advance religiously grounded moral viewpoints in the public square, they are not imposing anything on anyone. They are proposing. That is what is supposed to happen in our form of government—citizens propose, they give reasons, they deliberate, they vote. It is a sinister doctrine that would silence only those moral viewpoints that are religiously based. But the anesthesia was very effective in silencing the witness of countless good men and women. And of course the slogan was a bonanza for cowardly and unprincipled politicians.

At this point, a person aware that faith illiteracy has always been common might ask, "What's so urgent about formation now?" The answer is that poor formation presents a special danger in a society like ours where Catholics have lost most of their old support networks, and where education in other areas is relatively advanced. If religious education falls short of the general level of secular education, Christians run into trouble defending their beliefs—even to themselves. They are apt to feel helpless when they come up against the secularism and relativism that are so pervasive in the general culture.

It is ironic, given their rich intellectual heritage, that so many Catholics feel unable to respond even to the simplistic forms of secular fundamentalism that are prevalent among America's semi-skilled knowledge class. Traditionally, it has been one of the glories of their faith that Catholics can give reasons for the moral positions they hold—reasons that are accessible to all men and women of good will, of other faiths, or of no faith. Long ago, St. Thomas Aquinas wrote: "Instruct those who are listening so that they will be brought to an understanding of the truth envisaged. Here one must rely on arguments which probe the root of truth and make people know how what is said is true; otherwise, if the master decides a question simply by using sheer authorities, the hearer will . . . acquire no knowledge or understanding and will go away empty." St. Thomas inspired Bartolomeo de las Casas, who denounced slavery and proclaimed the full humanity of aboriginal peoples in the sixteenth century, without direct reliance on Revelation. Princeton's Robert George does the same today, in his philosophical defense of human life from conception to natural death. Recently, Dr. John Haas, the president of the National Catholic Bioethics Center, met with a well-known scientist who is engaged in human cloning. In the course of that meeting, the researcher told Dr. Haas that he had been raised an evangelical Protestant, but that at a certain point, "I knew I had to make a choice between religion and science, and I chose science." Dr. Haas' response, of course, was, "But you don't have to choose," and, like the good evangelist that he is, he began to expound the teaching of *Fides et Ratio*. A meeting that was supposed to last thirty minutes went on for hours.

John Paul II urges Catholics to emulate such examples when he says in *Novo Millennio Ineunte*: "For Christian witness to be effective, especially in . . . delicate and controversial areas, it is important that special effort be made to explain properly the reasons for the Church's position, stressing that this is not a case of imposing on nonbelievers a vision based on faith, but of interpreting and defending the values rooted in the very nature of the human person." To explain the reasons, however, means that one must know the reasons. "Be not afraid" does not mean "Be not prepared."

The time is overdue for Catholics (not only in America) to recognize that we have neglected our stewardship duties toward the intellectual heritage that we hold in trust for future generations. The question of why have we failed to keep that tradition abreast of the best human and natural science of our times—as St. Thomas did in his day—would be a subject for another occasion. Suffice it to note here that, in the twentieth century, that was the project of Bernard Lonergan and others, but the job has had few takers. Andrew Greeley's diagnosis is harsh: "American Catholicism," he says, "did not try intellectualism and find it wanting; it rather found intellectualism hard and decided not to try it."

Perhaps Greeley is too severe, but it is hard to disagree with theologian Frederick Lawrence when he says that "the Church's current activity in the educational sphere is not making sufficiently manifest how the basic thrust of Catholic Christianity is in harmony with full-fledged intellectualism, let alone that intellectual life is integral to the Church's mission." Lawrence goes on to say, "The Church today needs to proclaim loud and clear that understanding the natural order of the cosmos in the human and subhuman sciences, and in philosophy and theology, is part of appreciating God's cosmic Word expressed in creation. It is part and parcel of the fullness of the Catholic mind and heart."

American Catholics need to rededicate themselves to the intellectual apostolate, not only for the sake of the Church's mission, but for the sake of a country that has become dangerously careless about the moral foundations on which our freedoms depend. Tocqueville was right that Catholicism can be good for American democracy, but that can only happen if Catholicism is true to itself.

Is it possible that the scandal-induced surge of lay activity in 2002 foreshadows a season of authentic reform and renewal? If one is hopeful, one can discern here and there some encouraging signs. A number of newly formed lay associations, for example, are said to be forming study groups to read church documents, encyclicals, and the Catechism. The most promising sign of better times ahead, however, is the growing generation of unapologetically Catholic young people, including many young priests, who have been inspired by the heroic life and teachings of John Paul II.

Meanwhile, the world as we know it is still passing away. The demographic landscape of the United States is once again being transformed by immigration, this time mainly from the South. The vast majority of these newcomers have been formed in the Catholic cultures of Central and South America and the Caribbean. True, many of them have lost their story, but even so, they tend to have a Catholic way of imagining the real, of looking at the human person and society. At present rates, the United States will soon be the country with the third largest Catholic population in the world, after Brazil and Mexico. In the spring of 2002, while members of Boston's Voice of the Faithful were debating church finances and governance, Boston's Latino Catholics were holding prayer vigils to affirm the solidarity of all the members of the mystical body of Christ—men and women, rich and poor, clergy and laity, and, yes, victims and abusers.

Wherever the sons and daughters of the American Catholic diaspora are to be found, one thing is certain. The people-called-together are searching for the stories that will help them make sense of their lives. The woman on the bus who pores over the astrological chart in the morning paper is looking for meaning. The professor worshiping this or that ideological idol is looking for a creed to live by and for. The opinion polls telling us that most Americans believe the country is in a moral decline, yet do not feel they can "impose" their morality on others, testify to the confusion that afflicts good people in times when "the best lack all conviction, while the worst are full of passionate intensity."

What if the scattered Catholic faithful were to remember and embrace the heritage that is rightly theirs? What if they were to rediscover the newness of their faith and its power to judge the prevailing culture? What an awakening that would be for the sleeping giant! As John Paul II likes to tell young people: "If you are what you should be—that is if you live Christianity without compromise—you will set the world ablaze!"

CHAPTER 47 • The Hour of the Laity

Is it fanciful to think that the people-called-together could rediscover the dynamic newness of their faith in their dispersed condition? Members of the Church's great lay organizations around the world do not think so. Even as mobility has sapped the vitality of many parishes, there has been a great upsurge—mostly outside the U.S. thus far—of lay associations, formation programs, and ecclesial movements. These groups, so varied in their charisms, so rich in storytellers, are providing a way for Catholics to stay in touch with each other and with their tradition under diaspora conditions. John Paul II has recognized the remarkable accomplishments of these groups in the area of formation, and has urged his brother bishops and priests to take full advantage of the potential they afford for personal and ecclesial renewal.

Until recently, like most American Catholics, I was relatively unaware of the extent and variety of these movements. It was only through serving on the Pontifical Council for the Laity that I came to know groups like Communion and Liberation, the Community of St. Egidio, Focolare, the Neo-Catechumenate Way, Opus Dei, and Regnum Christi, and became acquainted with many of their leaders and members. What a contrast between these groups that work in harmony with the Church and organizations that define their aims in terms of power! It is no surprise that the more faithful and vibrant the great lay organizations are, the more they are vilified by dissenters and anti-Catholics. But attacks do not seem to trouble them, for they know who they are and where they are going.

Finally, one of the great blessings of having a papacy and a magisterium is that they help to assure that the story of the people-called-together will be preserved, even in the most trying times. In Vargas Llosa's *The Storyteller*, an outsider comes to the dispersed Machiguengas, a man who loves the people-who-walk and their stories so much that he becomes their *hablador*. He is often on the road, traveling from family to family, bringing news from one place to the next, "reminding each member of the tribe that the others are alive, that despite the great distances that [separate] them, they still [form] a community, [share] a tradition and beliefs, ancestors, misfortunes, and joys." Among the many reasons to rejoice in the long pontificate of John Paul II is that, like the greatest of *habladors*, he has kept the story of his people radiantly alive, carrying it to every corner of the earth in one of humanity's darkest times.

# A Generation Searching

*In preparation for the 2005 World Youth Day, the Pontifical Council for the Laity held a youth forum in March 2004 at Rocca di Papa on "Witnessing to Christ in the University World." My difficult assignment—to present a composite portrait of today's university students—prompted these reflections.[1]*

SINCE MOST OF YOU ARE STUDENTS, I am sure you know what it is like to be assigned to write a paper in a field where you are not an expert. So I think you can imagine my reaction when the Council for the Laity asked me to give a talk titled "University Students Today: Portrait of a New Generation." I was honored, but a bit daunted.

## WHAT THE SOCIAL SCIENTISTS SAY

I began my assignment the way you probably would. I went to the library to find out what the social scientists tell us. There I found that there is an enormous literature about the young men and women who were born after 1979, who came of age with the new century, and who for that reason are sometimes called the Millennials. In fact, no generation has been more studied than the cohort sometimes also known as Generation Y.

The social science data tells us that you are blessed in many ways. We are told that you are the best-educated generation in history. More young people from more diverse backgrounds are attending universities than ever before (although large gaps still exist between affluent and developing countries, and between rich and poor within the more affluent countries). Girls in particular have never had more opportunities to develop their full human potential.

A circumstance that has given a decisive stamp to your age group is that you and the personal computer grew up together. The first computers for homes, offices, and schools were introduced by IBM in 1981, and you are skilled with them in a way that few of your elders will ever be. Another blessing many of you enjoy is that—thanks to improved longevity—no generation has ever had the opportunity to know their grandparents for so long a time.

---

[1] Mary Ann Glendon, "A Generation Searching," Witnessing to Christ in the University World, The Pontifical Council for the Laity, Rocca di Papa, 31 March 2004.

In certain other respects, however, Generation Y bears unusual burdens. Probably nothing has had more profound influence on the hopes and fears of your generation than the social revolution that took place between the mid-1960s (when most of your parents were the age you are now) and the 1980s when most of you were born. Beginning in the 1960s, birth rates and marriage rates plummeted in the affluent nations of North America, Europe, Japan, and Australia. At the same time, divorce rates rose steeply, as did the rates of births outside marriage, and the incidence of non-marital cohabitation. The scale and speed of these phenomena were unprecedented—with increases or decreases of more than 50 percent in less than twenty years. When these rates finally stabilized at their new, high levels toward the end of the 1980s, we found ourselves on a social landscape that was utterly and completely transformed. Customary understandings that had governed human sexual behavior for millennia were not only widely disregarded, but openly rejected.

With hindsight, we can see that the changes in behavior and ideas that took place in those years amounted to nothing less than a massive social experiment. Though few realized it at the time, it was an experiment that was conducted largely at the expense of children. We now understand what should have been obvious all along—that when the behavior of adults changes, the environments in which children grow up are changed as well.

By giving priority to adults' quest for personal fulfillment, society changed the whole experience of childhood: More children than ever before grew up in households without fathers. More were left in non-parental care at younger ages. Little thought was given to what these changes might mean for children, or for the future of the societies most affected.

Some of you may have heard reflections on that subject by Father Tony Anatrella, the psychoanalyst who addressed this gathering last year. According to him, the changing experience of childhood has had an adverse effect on the ability of many young people to have trust in others, and even on their ability to have hope for the future. He was rather harsh in his criticism of the generation that came of age in the 1960s. He claimed that while they, like all parents, wanted their children to be happy, many failed to teach their children "the basic rules of social life, the customs that are the treasures of a people, and the Christian life that has been the matrix of diverse civilizations."

The story in the developing world is different, but changes in family life there have been equally rapid and profound. Industrialization, urbanization, and globalization have accelerated the disruption of age-old customs and patterns of family organization. In many countries, the process of industrialization that had been spread out over a century in the West was accomplished in little more than a decade. In some parts of the world, children have been robbed both of their childhood and their parents by the ravages of AIDS—or by violent ethnic and political strife.

That is the sort of information I found when I looked to see what social scientists tell us about Generation Y. But as a university teacher, a mother, and a grandmother, I felt that something was missing. I wanted to know more about what young people themselves make of their situations as they prepare to assume responsible positions in an era of turbulent changes wrought by globalization, conflict, and widespread disruption of family life. And I wanted to know more about how Catholic university students, in particular, see themselves.

## SOME VOICES OF YOUNG CATHOLICS

So to try to get a sense of your own hopes and fears for the future, I asked some colleagues and friends who deal with young Catholics in universities and youth organizations to circulate a little questionnaire for me. Here are two of the questions I asked: What social developments do you most hope for in your lifetime, and what do you fear the most? What developments do you most hope for in your personal life, and what do you fear the most?

What was most striking about the replies I received from Catholic students all over the world was the similarity in the way these young men and women expressed their personal hopes and fears. From the Philippines to Kenya, from Europe to North and South America, the students mainly spoke of hopes for three things: hope to find the right person to marry and found a family with; hope for work that is satisfying as well as rewarding; and the hope to be able to help to bring about positive changes in society, which many express as building the civilization of love. Their chief anxieties concerned their ability to realize these hopes. Thus, one young Spaniard wrote, "I look forward to marriage and the birth of each one of my sons and daughters, and I hope to find the kind of job that will enable me to better society. What I fear are the same things, because these are the most important decisions in my life and I fear choosing in the wrong way." Along the same lines, a German student wrote, "I hope for a great family life and for the kind of work that will enable me to return some of what God has given me, but I fear not finding the right person to spend the rest of my life with."

Anna Halpine, a remarkable Catholic activist who founded the World Youth Alliance five years ago when she was still in her 20s, summed up the reaction of her co-workers to my questions this way: "Our experience is that all young people are searching for meaning and purpose to their lives. Once this has been established, once they recognize the profound dignity that they possess, they are in a position to extend this to others. Before this cornerstone has been laid, they are unable to give any proposal to the world and any rationale to their own existence."

Last year, the Director of the European branch of the World Youth Alliance, Gudrun Lang, gave a speech to the European Parliament where she described her contemporaries this way: "It is my generation that is the first to experience what it means to live in a more or less 'value-free' continent. It is we who witness a society of broken families—you are aware of what that entails for the individual, the spouses, the children, and all the people around them. It is we who witness a society of convenience at all costs: killing our own children when they are still unborn; killing our older relatives because we don't want to give them the care, the time and the friendship that they need." She went to say, "Many young people I work with have experienced this loss of respect for the inviolable dignity of every member of the human family. Our own families are broken, our own relatives are lonely, and many do not see a meaning in life." But at the same time, she noted the emergence of a determination to change things for the better. Her generation, she said, has "experienced the ideologies of the second half of the past century put into legislation—and we are not happy with them."

## THE QUEST FOR MEANING IN THE POSTMODERN UNIVERSITY

What emerges from these data and impressions, it seems to me, is a portrait of a generation that is searching—a generation of young men and women who want something better for themselves and their future children than has been handed on to them; a generation that is exploring uncharted territory and finding little guidance from its elders. It is only to be expected that, for many members of Generation Y, the search for meaning takes on special urgency when they enter the university, a place traditionally dedicated to the unrestricted quest for knowledge and truth.

What better place than a university, one might think, to pursue one's quest for meaning. What better place to learn how to make balanced and reliable judgments. What better place to acquire skill in distinguishing between what is important and what is trivial. What better place to learn to discern what is harmful even it if seems attractive, and what is true even if defending it makes you unpopular or leads you to martyrdom.

But if those are your hopes, you are apt to be disappointed in many of today's universities. For universities themselves seem to be losing their sense of purpose and meaning. As a young woman from the United States put it in her answer to my questionnaire: "If I could sum up what has been drilled into my generation's minds in one word, that word would be 'tolerance.' While this has resulted in us being pretty nice people, it has also produced in my opinion a generation that has little concept of objective morality or truth. We are equipped with few guidelines for judging right and wrong." A young woman who teaches in Kenya wrote that university students there "need role models and something to believe in and they search for these desperately. There is a constant clash between how their parents brought them up and what society is offering them." Sad to say, the postmodern university seems even to be losing its vaunted regard for tolerance of diverse opinions—at least where religiously grounded moral viewpoints are concerned, and especially if those viewpoints are Christian.

Thus we find ourselves in a curious situation where all too many of the most highly educated men and women in history have a religious formation that remains at a rather primitive level. Have you noticed how many well-educated Catholics seem to be going through life with a kindergarten-level apprehension of their own faith? How many of us, for example, have spent as much time deepening our knowledge of the faith as we have on learning to use computers! I must admit that when I read in the Holy Father's letters to the laity that we are supposed to fearlessly "put out into the deep," I can't help thinking there should be a footnote to the effect that: "Be not afraid" doesn't mean "Be not prepared." When Our Lord told the apostles to put out into the deep, he surely didn't expect them to set out in leaky boats. When he told them to put down their nets, he didn't expect those nets to be full of holes!

This brings me to the most important point I wish to make today: I want to suggest to you that *poor formation represents a special danger in a society like ours where education in other areas is so advanced.* In contemporary society, if religious formation does not come up to the general level of secular education, we are going to run into trouble defending our beliefs—even to ourselves. We are going to feel helpless when we come up against the secularism and relativism that are so pervasive in our culture and in the university. We are going to be tongue-tied when our faith comes under unjust attack.

When that happens, many young Catholics drift away from the faith. Countless young men and women today have had an experience in the university comparable to that which caused the great social theorist Alexis de Tocqueville to lose his faith two hundred years ago at the height of the Enlightenment. All through his childhood, Tocqueville had been tutored by a pious old priest who had been trained in a simpler era. Then, at the age of sixteen, he came upon the works of Descartes, Rousseau, and Voltaire. Here is how he described that encounter in a letter to a friend many years later:

> I don't know if I've ever told you about an incident in my youth that marked me deeply for the rest of my life; how I was prey to an insatiable curiosity whose only available satisfaction was a large library of books. . . . Until that time my life had passed enveloped in a faith that hadn't even allowed doubt to enter. . . . Then doubt . . . hurtled in with an incredible violence. . . . All of a sudden I experienced the sensation people talk about who have been through an earthquake when the ground shakes under their feet, as do the walls around them, the ceilings over their heads, the furniture beneath their hand, all of nature before their eyes. I was seized by the blackest melancholy and then by an extreme disgust with life, though I knew nothing of life. And I was

almost prostrated by agitation and terror at the sight of the road that remained for me to travel in this world.

What drew him out of that state, he told his friend, were worldly pleasures to which he abandoned himself for a time. But his letters testify to a lifelong sadness at his incapacity for belief. How many young Catholics have fallen into those same pitfalls when they had to make the difficult transition from their childhood faith to a mature Christianity? Tocqueville at least was confounded by some of the greatest minds in the Western tradition. But many of our contemporaries are not even equipped to deal with simplistic versions of relativism and skepticism!

Some young men and women, like Tocqueville, may spend their whole lives in a kind of melancholy yearning. Others may start to keep their spiritual lives completely private, in a separate compartment sealed off from the rest of their lives. Still others imitate the chameleon, that little lizard who changes his color to blend in with his surroundings. When parts of their Christian heritage don't fit with the spirit of the age, the chameleon just blocks them out.

How many of these lost searchers, I wonder, might have held their heads high as unapologetic Catholics if somewhere along the way they had become acquainted with our Church's great intellectual tradition and her rich treasure house of social teachings? Today, in the age of John Paul II, there are really no good excuses for ignoring the intellectual heritage that provides us with resources to meet the challenges of modernity. No Catholic who takes the trouble to tap into that heritage has to stand tongue-tied in the face of alleged conflicts between faith and reason or religion and science.

In *Novo Millennio Ineunte*, the Holy Father has a message that is highly relevant to the topic of this conference on "Witnessing to Christ in the University." "For Christian witness to be effective," he writes, "it is important that special efforts be made to explain properly *the reasons* for the Church's position, stressing that it is not a case of imposing on non-believers a vision based on faith, but of interpreting and defending the values rooted in the very nature of the human person." (51)

Three implications of those wise words need to be spelled out:

First, those of us who live in pluralistic societies have to be able to give our reasons in terms that are intelligible to all men and women of good will, just as St. Paul had to be "a Jew to the Jews, and a Greek to the [pagan] Greeks." Fortunately, we have great models of how to do that in Catholic social teaching, and in the writings of John Paul II.

Second, we who labor in the intellectual apostolate need to keep our intellectual tradition abreast of the best human and natural science of our times, just as St. Thomas Aquinas did in his day.

And third, because we live in a time when our Church is under relentless attack, we need to be equipped to defend her. That does not mean we have to react to every insult no matter how slight. But we do need to learn to have and to show a decent amount of pride in who we are.

There is nothing wrong with taking pride in our Church's intellectual tradition—a tradition that predates and outshines the impoverished secularism that is stifling thought in many leading universities. There is nothing wrong with taking pride in our Church's record as the world's foremost institutional voice opposing aggressive population control, abortion, euthanasia, and draconian measures against migrants and the poor. *At a time, and in a culture, where Christianity is under assault from many directions, Catholics do a great disservice when they do not contest the myth that the history of Christianity in general and Catholicism in particular is a history of patriarchy, worldliness, persecution, or exclusion of people or ideas.*

As a university teacher and a parent myself, I am acutely aware of how difficult it is to "witness to Christ in the university." Thus, I was delighted to read last month of the Holy Father's proposal to the bishops of Paris for the creation of "schools of faith" at the university level. After all, why should religious education cease just at the point when faith is apt to be faced with its most serious challenges—and just when many young men and women are for the first time away from home? It seems to me that the Church needs to follow her sons and daughters to the university. She needs to find ways to accompany them on that dangerous journey toward a mature Christianity. There are many ways this could be accomplished. In many places, the great lay organizations are already present to university students—they have done wonderful work, showing that formation and fellowship go hand in hand. But much more can and must be done along these lines.

## THE ANSWER TO THE QUESTION
## THAT IS EVERY HUMAN LIFE

To sum up, then: I would suggest that the "Y" in Generation Y might stand for yearning—yearning, questioning, searching, and refusing to be satisfied with easy answers. No one has understood this better than Pope John Paul II—and that, I suspect, is one of the reasons why young people love him so much and why the World Youth Days have been such a transformative experience for so many. As he wrote in *Tertio Millennio Adveniente*, "Christ expects great things from young people. . . . Young people, in every situation, in every region of the world do not cease to put questions to Christ: they meet him and they keep searching for him in order to question him further. If they succeed in following the road which he points out to them, they will have the joy of making their own contribution to his presence in the next century and in the centuries to come, until the end of time: 'Jesus Christ is the same yesterday, today, and for ever'" (58). Jesus Christ is the answer to the question that is every human life.

CHAPTER 48 • A Generation Searching

It only remains for me to thank you for the opportunity to be with you today. What a difference you Catholic university students are going to make in the world! We don't yet know how each one of you will respond to your baptismal callings to holiness and evangelization. But we do know that there is no shortage of work to be done in the vineyard. There are families to be nurtured; intellectual frontiers to be explored; young minds to be taught; the sick to be cared for; the poor to be lifted up; and the faith to be handed on to future generations. My wish for you is that the Lord will multiply you, and that each one of you will touch thousands of lives.

# Index

## A

abortion
anthropology of, 160, 162–63, 165
Beijing Women's Conference (1995)
and, 106, 300, 308–9, 343
Cairo Conference on Population and
Development (1993), 301, 304,
306, 308, 344
Catholic Church on women's rights
and, 294, 300
clinics, attacks on, 165–66
dependency-welfare crisis and, 141
immigration opponents and, 216,
345
Marshall, Thurgood, on, 215–16
motives behind pro-life and pro-
choice positions on, 161–62
parental rights and duties, 305, 308
protection of vulnerable persons
and, 110, 162
*Roe* v. *Wade* (1973), 157, 158, 162,
163, 165, 215–16
RU-486, 160
for sex-selection purposes, 158, 160
social welfare and, 159, 160, 161, 165
terminology used in debate on,
165–66
Tribe, Lawrence, and, 157–63
of viable fetuses, 158, 162

*Webster* v. *Reproductive Health
Services* (1989), 157, 158
and women's liberty, 110, 161, 162,
163
absolute rights, concept of, 279–85
Abzug, Bella, 108
Ackerman, Bruce, 121
*The Acting Person,* Karol Wojtyla, 417
Adams, John, 207
Adler, Mortimer, 401
adoption of children by same-sex
couples, 241
African Americans. *See also* civil rights
movement
Thomas, Clarence, opinion regarding,
219–21
Agi, Marc, 376n25
*Agostini* v. *Felton* (1997), 269
agricultural and small town life, 83–89
*Aguilar* v. *Felton* (1985), 269, 275–76
Alberdi, Christina, 306
Alfaro, Ricardo, 387
Allende, Salvatore, 393
Alston, Philip, 341, 356
Amar, Akhil, 234
ambition and pride *(thymos),* 146, 149
American Bar Association, 199–200,
225
American Civil Liberties Union, 181

American Judicature Society, 208
American Law Institute, 28, 174, 225, 375, 387–88
Amis, Martin, 115
Amnesty International, 381
*amparo,* 394
Anatrella, Tony, 434
Anthony, Susan B., 105, 108
anthropology (study of human nature)
  abortion and, 160, 162–63, 165
  absolutist view of rights and, 285
  at Beijing Women's Conference (1995), 300, 304
  culture of 1950s and roots of hyper-individualism, 95
  democracy's cultural underpinnings and effects of hyper-individualism, 72, 126, 130
  *eros,* pursuit of knowledge as form of, 145, 147, 149
  family law and U.S. notions of individualism, 244–48
  of *The Federalist Papers,* 39, 59, 145–51
  of human rights, 343
  John Paul II on, 46, 57, 59
  Mill's concept, influence on American law of, 245–46
  moral structure of freedom and, 57–59
  passive subjects or instrumental rationalists, humans treated as, 141
  religion, private and individualized vs. communitarian view of, 274–75
  *thymos* or "spiritedness" (pride and ambition), role of, 146, 149
  Universal Declaration on Human Rights' need for, 359
  U.S. hyper-individualist view of human rights and, 342
Appleby, Scott, 426

Arab League, 365, 372
Archer, Margaret, 141
Archimedes, 18
Aréchaga, Eduardo Jiminez de, 395
Arendt, Hannah, 72, 361
Aristotle, 14, 92, 389
Armstrong, Scott, 204
Arnold, Thurman, 283
Arrow, Kenneth, 138
*Asahi* v. *Japan* (1967), 261–62
assisted suicide movement, 110, 141, 346
Attila the Hun, 419
Auchincloss, Louis, 197
Augustine of Hippo, 402
Australia and Universal Declaration on Human Rights, 319, 374, 386
Austrian origins of continental model of judicial review, 257
authority and community, relationship between, 95–97

**B**

babyboomers
  dependency-welfare crisis and aging of, 138
  parental authority and community in 1950s, 95–97
Barbados delegates to Beijing Women's Conference (1995), 304
Bartok, Bela, 23
Batista, Fulgencio, 385
Beijing Women's Conference (1995)
  anthropology of, 300, 304
  Holy See delegation
    activities of, 302–3, 306–7
    final statement of, 299–300
    instructions to, 312–13
    opening address of, 291–97, 303
    position taken by Holy See on final documents, 310
  Catholic organizations represented at, 306–7

Catholic power structure critiqued
at, 307
colonialism at, 309–10, 311
EU delegation, 304–6, 307, 308,
310–11
family law and, 242
final documents, 310–12
John Paul II and, 287–89, 300, 307,
312–13, 405–6, 411–12
negotiation process at, 303–7
opening events, 302–3
population control lobbyists and
abortion proponents at, 302,
304, 306–10, 343
reports on conduct and outcomes,
105–8, 301–13
U.N. Commission on Status of
Women, document prepared by,
107, 302
Universal Declaration on Human
Rights and, 294, 304–5
U.S. delegation, 303, 308
Belgium and Universal Declaration on
Human Rights, 386
Bellah, Robert, 63
Bellow, Saul, 134
Benedi, Claudio F., 388n25
Benestad, Brian, 346
Berger, Peter L., 75n24, 128, 277
Bernardino, Minerva, 394, 395
Bernstein, Carl, 214
Bhuto, Benazir, 303
Bill of Rights. *See* civil rights
movement; constitutional law;
constitutional rights in welfare state;
human rights; individual
amendments, e.g. Fifth Amendment
birth control
abortion as means of, 308
Beijing Women's Conference (1995)
and, 106, 304
health ramifications of, 159–60,
296, 304

RU-486, 160
birth rate
democracy, cultural underpinning
of, 67–68
dependency-welfare crisis and, 137,
140
family law affected by demographic
change, 238, 243
Bismarck, Otto von, 137
Black, Hugo, 273
Blackmun, Harry, 162, 219
Blackstone, William, 281, 284
Bloom, Allen, 35, 38
*Bob Jones University* v. *United States*
(1983), 278
Bogota (Pan-American) Declaration on
the Rights and Duties of Man
(1948), 321, 325, 350, 383, 384,
387–88, 390, 394
Bohlen, Charles E., 384n2
Bolivár, Simon, 389
Bork, Robert, 212
Borries, Reimer von, 29
Bottum, J., 115
Brahe, Tyco, 378
Brandeis, Louis B., 194, 205, 214, 246,
270
Braudel Fernand, 19, 100, 256, 265
Brazil and Universal Declaration on
Human Rights, 338
Brennan, William J., Jr., 154, 204–6,
221, 275
Breyer, Stephen, 219
Brigid of Kildare, 134–35
Britain. *See* England
Bronfenbrenner, Uri, 271
Bronzeville neighborhood, Chicago,
93–94
Brooklyn Dodgers, suit over use of
name of, 187
*Brown* v. *Board of Education* (1954),
185, 186, 204, 211, 216
Brueghel, Peter, the Elder, 318

Brugger, Winifried, 226, 229n7
Buchanan, Patrick, 127
Buddhism, 317, 338
Burger, Warren, E., and Burger Court,
    11, 206, 210, 225
Burke, Edmund, 273, 365
Bush, George H. W., 219
Byelorussia and Universal Declaration
    on Human Rights, 321, 386

C

Cairo Conference on Population and
    Development (1993), 301, 304,
    306, 308, 344
Callahan, Daniel, 157, 160–61
Campos, Francisco, 388n24
Canada
    absolute rights, concept of, 280
    Beijing Women's Conference (1995)
        delegates, 304
    constitutional rights in welfare
        states, 255, 257, 258
    homosexual marriage in, 241
    Universal Declaration on Human
        Rights and, 381
Cano, Melchior, 418
Cardozo, Benjamin Nathan, 14, 216,
    225
Carozza, Paolo, 389
Carr, E. H., 317
Carrera de Andrade, Jorge, 395
Carrington, Paul, 12, 225, 230
Carroll, James, 410–11, 413
Carter, Jimmy, 99, 263
Carter, Stephen, 133
case law. See common law and case law
    methodology, and also specific cases,
    e.g. Brown v. Board of Education
Casey v. Planned Parenthood (1992), 41
Casper, Gerhard, 17, 259
Cassin, René, and Universal
    Declaration on Human Rights
authorship controversy, 377–79

Catholic thought and, 351–53, 356
creation of, 319–27, 330
foundations of, 347
Humphrey, John P., and, 372–79
Malik, Charles, and, 364, 365
second draft of, 376–77
Castro, Fidel, 385, 388n25
Catherine the Great, 35
Catholic Church. See also John Paul II;
    Vatican II; individual papal
    documents, e.g. Centesimus Annus
American Catholicism, 132, 421,
    422–25, 431
Beijing Women's Conference and
    (See Beijing Women's
    Conference)
child sex abuse scandal, 421, 425,
    427
dignitarian rights concept espoused
    by, 56, 353–54, 361
familiarity of Catholic thinkers with
    own social tradition, need for,
    359
laity, participation of (See lay
    apostolate)
papal infallibility, 411
penitence, expressions of, 409–14
political policies or models not
    prescribed by, 51
power structure of, 307, 406,
    426–27
pre-Vatican II Catholicism, author's
    experience of, 399–402
reason and rationality, as defender
    of, 361–62
revitalization of social teaching by
    Vatican II, 402–3
social sciences and social thought of,
    50–51
U.N., Holy See as permanent
    observer at, 402–3
Universal Declaration on Human
    Rights and (See Universal
    Declaration on Human Rights)

women and, 403–8, 411–13
women's ordination, issue of, 307,
    406, 412
Catholics for a Free Choice, 307
*Centesimus Annus* (1991), 45–47, 50
centralization of government and
    power, effects of, 10, 62, 66, 70, 75,
    127, 128, 180
Chang, Peng-chun
    Catholic social thought and
        Universal Declaration, 356, 358
    creation of Universal Declaration,
        319, 320
    foundation of Universal Declaration,
        335, 338, 340, 341
    Humphrey, John P., and, 372–74,
        378, 380, 382
    Malik, Charles, and, 364, 365, 367
Chicago
    culture and society in the 1950s and
        today, 91–97
    financial district and city hall,
        191–92
child custody and support law
    industrial revolution affecting, 66
    recent reforms in, 172–74
childcare
    Beijing Women's Conference (1995)
        barely mentioning, 105–8, 292,
        302–5
    communitarian aspects of, 128
    democracy, cultural underpinnings
        of, 68, 128
    dependency-welfare crisis and,
        137–41
    family law's need to address new
        problems of, 248–51
    gender-based income gap and work-
        family dilemma, 108–9
    "just stay home" argument, critique
        of, 109
children
    adoption by same-sex couples, 241

Catholic child sex abuse scandal,
    421, 425, 427
Convention on the Rights of the
    Child, 305
    marginalization of, 139, 243–44
    parental rights and duties, 95–97,
        305, 308
    rights of, 240
children born outside marriage
    democracy, cultural underpinnings
        of, 68–69
    equalization of status of marital and
        non-marital children, 240, 242
Chile
    U.N. Charter and, 385
    Universal Declaration on Human
        Rights and, 319, 338, 374, 386,
        387, 390, 391, 395
China
    abortion rights in, 309, 343
    population control in, 344
    Universal Declaration on Human
        Rights and, 318, 321, 386
*Christifideles Laici* (1988), 426
Churchill, Winston, 384
civic religion and meaning of flag, 155
civic republicanism of Michael Sandel,
    125–30
civil law methodology, advantages of,
    223–35
    constitutional interpretation,
        228–35
    statutory interpretation, 223–28
        in common law/case law
            tradition, 224–26
        skills sets of lawyers from civil
            law tradition, 226–29
civil law tradition and Universal
    Declaration on Human Rights, 319,
    328, 340, 389
Civil Rights Act of 1964, 185, 186, 204
civil rights movement
    American respect for law and, 179

*Brown* v. *Board of Education* (1954),
  ramifications of, 185, 186, 204,
  211, 216
exaggerated notions of power of law,
  185–86
legislation regarding, 185, 186, 204
Marshall, Thurgood, and, 214, 216
segregation and community,
  relationship between, 93
civil society and democracy in America.
  *See* democracy in America, cultural
  underpinnings of
civil unions, 240–42
classical vs. romantic judicial values. *See*
  romantic vs. classical judicial values
Clinton, Hillary Rodham, 303, 343
Clinton, William, 119
code-based legal methodologies. *See*
  civil law code methodology,
  advantages of
cognitive theory, 18
Cohen, Morris, 66
Coke, Edward, 5, 7, 279
Cold War and Universal Declaration on
  Human Rights, 320, 330, 335, 341,
  342, 357, 359, 381–82
colonialism
  at Beijing Women's Conference
    (1995), 309–10, 311
  soft tyranny of mass media, 72
  and Universal Declaration on
    Human Rights, 337–40
commerce. *See* economics and commerce
common law
  civil law methodology's advantages
    over (*See* civil law methodology,
    advantages of)
  creativity and tradition in American
    law, relationship between, 4–6
  rejection of simplifying abstractions
    by, 272
  U.S. inheritance of British tradition
    of, 224–25

Communion and Liberation, 432
communism. *See* socialism
communitarianism
  Etzioni's communitarian platform,
    119
  Galston's communitarian liberalism,
    119–23
  religion, private and individualized
    vs. communitarian view of,
    274–75
  Sandel's liberal communitarianism,
    125–30
community and democracy in America.
  *See* democracy in America, cultural
  underpinning of
Community of St. Egidio, 432
comparative law
  advantages of studying, 15–22
  author's background and, 400
  constitutional rights (*See*
    constitutional rights in welfare
    states)
  European civil law system compared
    to common law/case law system
    (*See* civil law code methodology,
    advantages of)
  human rights, 20, 246–47
  Rheinstein, Max, contributions of,
    17, 19, 20, 24, 29–30
Confucianism, 85, 320, 335, 373,
  386n14
Congar, Yves, 416
constitutional law. *See also* Supreme
  Court, U.S.
  civil law methodology, advantages
    of, 228–34
  communitarian aspects of, 126
  religious freedom (*See* freedom of
    religion in U.S constitution)
  romantic vs. classical values in
    (*See* romantic vs. classical judicial
    values)
  speech, freedom of (*See* free speech)

state judges' exercise of power of
  constitutional review, 205
strict vs. liberal construction, 205–7
textualism, structuralism, and
  originalism, 230–31, 234
welfare states and human rights
  (*See* welfare states, constitutional
  rights in)
contingent fees, ethical problems
  related to, 200
contraception. *See* birth control
Convention on the Rights of the Child,
  305
corruption, individual and systemic,
  196–97
Cortes, Ernesto, 185
Cox, Archibald, 83
creativity and tradition in American
  law, relationship between, 3–14
  common law, 4–6
  in constitutional law, , 11
  critical theory, influence of, 11–13
  history and etymology of concept of
    creation, 3
  Holmes and realist legal theory,
    7–10
  industrial revolution, effect on law
    of, 10
  statutory and regulatory law,
    revolution of, 9–11
  three traditions of American law, 4, 6
Critchfield, Richard, 83–89
critical theory, 11–13, 169
Croce, Benedetto, 317, 386n14
cross-disciplinary studies. *See*
  interdisciplinary studies
Cuba
  U.N. Charter and, 385
  Universal Declaration on Human
    Rights and, 387, 395
culture and morality
  in economic survival strategies,
    77–81

constitutional rights in welfare
  states,
  underpinnings of, 266–67
democracy in America,
  underpinnings of (*See* democracy
  in America, cultural
  underpinnings of)
of family and divorce law, 167–75
flag-burning and values associated
  with flag, 153–55
law's founding in, 188
legal ethics (*See* legal ethics)
legalism of American culture (*See*
  legalism and litigiousness in
  American life)
as rooted in rural life, 85, 86–87
in suburban life
  Elmhurst, Illinois, 94–95
  women's history and, 101–2
culture of death, 429
Currie, David, 17, 19–20
Cutler, Lloyd, 159
Czechoslovakia and Universal
  Declaration on Human Rights, 321

# D

Daley, Richard J., 196
D'Arcy, Martin, 402
Darwin, Charles, 19, 401
Dasgupta, Partha, 139
Davis, John W., 213, 216, 217
Dawson, John P., 19, 227, 232
Dawson, William, 93
de Gaulle, Charles, 319, 364, 372
death, culture of, 429
Defense of Marriage Act (DOMA), 241
democracy
  in extended territory with diverse
    population, 121, 146, 148
  Plato's ideal size of *polis* for
    cultivation of, 88
democracy in America, cultural
  underpinnings of, 61–75

beginnings of modern democratic era, 62–75
during industrial era, 65–66, 101
in period following World War II, 65–66
in era of globalization, 70–73
anthropology of Federalist Papers and, 148, 151
constitutional rights in welfare states, 266–67
Galston's communitarian liberalism, 119–23
Lasch on, 100
rural/small town life and, 88–89
Sandel's civic republicanism, 125–30
soft tyranny of mass media, 72
special need of democratic republic for certain kinds of excellence, 120
structural checks on majoritarianism, 58, 64
Tocqueville on, 61–67, 69, 72, 73, 88, 120–22, 267, 273
Wolfe's invocation of, in *A Man in Full*, 118
women's history and, 68, 71, 100–2
demographic change
democracy in America, cultural underpinnings of
industrial era, 66
post-World War II, 67–69, 127
dependency-welfare crisis and, 137–41
family law affected by, 237, 238–39
Generation Y and, 434
in rural and small town life, 84–85
turmoil caused by, ix–x
*Demoiselles of Avignon,* Picasso, 9
Denmark. *See also* Nordic countries
civil unions in, 241
constitutional rights in welfare states, 255, 263
Descartes, René, 5, 437

*DeShaney* v. *Winnegabo County Department of Social Services* (1989), 259
Dewey, John, 335
Dewey, Thomas E., 203
dialogue form, use of, 78–79
Dicey, Albert Vann, 245
Diderot, Denis, 34
dignitarian basis for human rights
Bogota Declaration compared with U.N. Declaration, 390n34
Catholic espousal of, 56, 353–54
libertarian rights concepts vs., 56–58, 300, 305
in U.N. Charter, 337, 346–47
in Universal Declaration on Human Rights, 329, 336–37, 346–47, 390n34, 396
work and (*See* work, dignity of)
disabled and sick, care of
democracy, cultural underpinning of, 68
family law's need to address new problems of, 248
diverse populations
democracy's viability, 121, 146, 148
family law and, 244
legalism and litigiousness in American life, 182–83, 190
universality of Universal Declaration on Human Rights amongst, 337, 340–41, 355–56
divorce
decline in regulation of entry into and exit from marriage, 240–42
democracy, cultural underpinnings of, 61, 67–68, 127
dependency-welfare crisis and, 137, 140
early Church and, 404
in early twentieth century America, 245
family law and demographic revolution in, 238, 240–42

during industrial revolution, 66
law (*See* family law)
Wolfe's invocation of, in *A Man in Full,* 117
work-family dilemma and, 109
domestic violence, 296
Dominican Republic and Universal Declaration on Human Rights, 394, 395
Donati, Pierpaolo, 141
Dostoevsky, Fyodor, 401
Douglas, William O., 203, 273
Drobnig, Ulrich, 21
Duden, Konrad, 30
Dulles, Avery, 13, 353, 354, 359
Durkheim, Emile, 273
Dworkin, Ronald, 121, 223

# E

economics and commerce. *See also* work, dignity of
civic consequences, 126
family law and, 239, 248
feminism and, 102–3
*A Man in Full,* Wolfe, portrayal of Atlanta in, 115
trader vs. raider survival strategies (*See* trader vs. raider ("commercial" vs. "guardian") survival strategies)
women's dependence on male breadwinner, industrial intensification of, 66, 101
ECOSOC (U.N. Economic and Social Council), 320, 366–67
Ecuador and Universal Declaration on Human Rights, 394, 395
education. *See also* knowledge, pursuit of; schools
cultural (*See* culture and morality)
women and girls' access to, 288, 294, 300, 308
Edwards, Harry, 16

*EGALE* v. *Canada* (2003), 241n10
Egypt and Universal Declaration on Human Rights, 338, 386
Ehrenhalt, Alan, 75n25, 91–97
Einstein, Albert, 23
Eisenhower, Dwight D., 203, 204, 351, 357, 379
elderly, care of
assisted suicide movement, 110, 141, 346
democracy, cultural underpinnings of, 68
dependency-welfare crisis and, 137–41
family law's need to address new problems of, 248
protection of vulnerable persons, 110, 141
work-family dilemma and, 109–10
Eliot, T. S., 9, 21, 115, 401
Elmhurst, Illinois, 94–95
Ely, John Hart, 234
*Employment Division* v. *Smith* (1990), 269, 277–78
England
absolute rights, concept of, 280
constitutional rights in welfare states, 255, 263, 379
family law in, 171, 174
property rights in, 280–81
Universal Declaration on Human Rights, 318, 319, 321, 326, 335, 374, 379, 386
U.S. inheritance of common law tradition of, 224–25
Enlightenment, 33–35
Erasmus, Desiderius, 4, 6
eros, pursuit of knowledge as form of, 145, 147, 149
ethics. *See* culture and morality
Ethiopia and Universal Declaration on Human Rights, 338
Etzioni, Amitai, 119

European continent
  civil law tradition
    methodological advantages of
      (*See* civil law code
      methodology, advantages of)
    Universal Declaration on Human
      Rights and, 319, 328, 340,
      389
    family law in, 244–48 (*See also*
      family law: comparative study of)
European Union (EU) delegation to
  Beijing Women's Conference (1995),
  304–6, 307, 308, 310–11
euthanasia, 110, 141, 346
*Evangelium Vitae* (1995), 405

**F**

family law. *See also* divorce; marriage
  child custody and support law
    industrial revolution affecting, 66
    recent reforms in, 172–74
  comparative study of
    Anglo-American vs. Romano-
      Germanic systems, 244–48
    demographic change, effect on
      family law of, 237, 238–39
    modern trends, 239–44
    problems and possible solutions,
      248–51
  as cultural education, 167–75
  decline in regulation of entry into
    and exit from marriage, 240–42
  definition of family, 249–50
  definition of marriage, 242
  demographic change, effect on
    family law of, 237, 238–39
  economic issues of, 239, 248
  homosexuality and, 240–42
  kinship relations, changes in creation
    of, 242–43
  "no-fault" divorce laws, 25–26, 184,
    188, 240
  recent reforms in, 172–74

reconceptualization of marriage and
  family, 239–40
reinforcement of one man, one
  woman marriage, laws providing
  for, 247–48
reproductive technologies,
  ramifications of, 231, 242–43
Rheinstein, Max, influence of,
  25–26
technically-assisted procreation,
  ramifications of, 231
ubiquity of law and legal language in
  American life, 167–68
welfare of children as aim of, 172,
  174
family life
  at Beijing Women's Conference
    (1995), 105–8, 292, 302–5
  Bogota Declaration compared with
    U.N. Declaration, 390–391n34
  Catholic support for, 407
  Chicago in the 1950s and authority
    in, 95
  civil institutions dependent upon,
    139, 140–41
  democracy, cultural underpinnings
    of, 61, 67–69, 71, 128
  industrial revolution affecting, 66,
    101
  single parents (*See* single-parent
    families)
  Universal Declaration on Human
    Rights on, 324, 390–391n34,
    394
  in Wolfe's *A Man in Full*, 116–17
  work-family dilemmas
    means of resolving, 111–13
    society-wide nature of, 108–11
family planning. *See* birth control
farm and small town life, 83–89
Faubus, Orval, 214
*The Federalist Papers*
  anthropology of, 39, 145–51

creativity, tradition, and the law, 6
forces establishing good government, debate as to, 59, 126
Hamilton's claim of authorship of some of Madison's contributions, 377
on judiciary, 221
as law school text, 230
on legalism and aptitude for self-government, 179
Felstiner, William, 168–72, 174
*The Feminine Mystique,* Friedan, 102
feminism. *See also* women and women's work
abortion and issues of women's liberty, 110, 161, 162, 163
Beijing Women's Conference (1995) and, 105–8, 302, 306, 310
Lasch's critique of, 102–3
"old-style" 1970's feminism, critique of, 107–8, 110, 140
Fermi, Enrico, 23
Fermi, Laura, 23, 31
Ferraro, Geraldine, 311
fertility technologies, ramifications of, 231
*Fides et Ratio* (1998), 362, 430
Fifth Amendment, 282, 284
Finland, civil unions in, 241. *See also* Nordic countries
First Amendment. *See* free speech, and entries at freedom of religion
Fish, Charles K., 83–89
flag-burning and values associated with flag, 153–55
Focolare, 432
formation. *See* education; Generation Y; knowledge, pursuit of; lay apostolate; schools
Fourteenth Amendment, 220, 259, 260, 273
Fourth World Conference on Women. *See* Beijing Women's Conference

France
anticlericalism, 389
Beijing Women's Conference (1995) delegates, 306
civil law system, advantages of, 227–28, 230
civil unions in, 241
constitutional rights in welfare states, 255, 257, 259, 261, 265, 379
dependency-welfare crisis, 138
family law, anthropology of, 247
French Revolution
cultural institutions attacked by, 62, 272–73
Rousseau's influence on, 35
U.N. Charter, Latin American push to include human rights in, 385
Universal Declaration on Human Rights and, 318, 319, 321, 325, 335, 374, 379, 386
uprisings of 1848, Tocqueville on, 179
welfare state, beginnings of, 248
Frankfurter, Felix, 11, 225
Frederick II of Prussia (Frederick the Great), 35, 379
free speech
constitutional law, civil law methodologies applied to, 230
flag-burning as, 153–55
importance given to, 270
terminology used in abortion debate, 166
Freedman, Haskell C., 167, 175
freedom
family law and U.S notions of, 244–48
John Paul II's concept of moral structure of, 55–59
Mill's concept, influence on American law of, 245–46
Roosevelt's four freedoms, 323, 368

freedom of religion in Universal
Declaration on Human Rights, 324
freedom of religion in U.S constitution,
269–78
deference to governmental interests,
emerging pattern of, 276–77
grammatical structure of clause, 269,
274
legal blind spot regarding, 270–74
local jurisdictions, expansion of
federal government, 274
possible future approaches, 277–78
primacy of, 270
private and individualized view of
religion, 274–75
schools and education programs,
cases involving, 275–76
secularism and hostility to religion,
277
"wall of separation" approach to
establishment provisions, 274–76
French Revolution
cultural institutions attacked by, 62,
272–73
Rousseau's influence on, 35
*Frette* v. *France* (2002), 242n14
Freud, Sigmund, 103, 401
Freund, Ernst, 230
Fried, Charles, 83
Friedan, Betty, 102, 108, 307
Friedman, Lawrence, 167–68, 186
Friendly, Henry, 220
Fukuyama, Francis, 139, 145–51, 238,
243n17
Fulbright, William, 221
fundamentalism, rise of, 88

# G

Galston, William, 119–23
Gandhi, Mahatma, 317, 380, 386n14
*Gaudium et Spes* (1965), 354, 404
Gauss, Karl Friedrich, 18
Geertz, Clifford, 26–27

Generation Y, 433–40
defined, 433
demographic change of later
twentieth century affecting, 434
goals and aspirations of, 435–36
John Paul II and, 438, 439
meaning, quest for, 436–39
social scientists on, 433–35
George, Robert, 430
Germany
Beijing Women's Conference (1995)
delegates, 311
civil law system, advantages of, 227,
228–34
civil unions in, 241
constitutional rights in welfare
states, 255, 257, 258–59, 263,
265
dependency-welfare crisis, 138
dignitarian rights concept in
constitutional law of, 329
family law, anthropology of, 247
U.N., initial exclusion from, 339
U.S.-German relations after World
War II, Rheinstein's contributions
to, 30–31
welfare state, beginnings of, 248
Ginsberg, Ruth Bader, 212, 219
Giraud, Emile, 376
Glazer, Nathan, 63
Glendon, Martin Francis, 408
Glendon, Sarah Pomeroy, 408
globalization and cultural
underpinnings of democracy, 70–73
Goldberg, Arthur, 276
Golden Rule, Rousseau's espousal of
principles of, 42, 346, 360
Gómez Robledo, Antonio, 388n24
Goodman, Ellen, 127
government. *See* politics and
government
Great Britain. *See* England
Great Society programs, 262, 275

Greece
    civil war in, 320
    constitutional rights in welfare
        states, 261
Greeley, Andrew, 399, 425, 430
Greene, Graham, 400–1
Greene, Melissa Fay, 216
Greenhouse, Linda, and "Greenhouse
    Effect," 203, 216
Greenspan, Alan, 138
Gregory the Great, 419
Gros Espiell, Hector, 385, 388n23,
    389n32
"guardian" survival strategy. See trader
    vs. raider ("commercial" vs.
    "guardian") survival strategies

**H**

Haas, John, 430
*Halpern v. Canada* (2003), 241n10
Halpine, Anna, 435
Hamilton, Alexander, 145–50, 209,
    377
Hand, Learned, 188, 212, 216, 220
Hansberry, Lorraine, 93
Harlan, John Marshall, 206
Hart, Henry, 225
Harvard Law School curriculum,
    statutory law in, 11, 224
Havel, Vaclav, 360
health of women. See women's health
Hegel, Georg Wilhelm Friedrich, 36,
    150
Heidegger, Martin, 335
Helms, Jesse, 214
Henkin, Louis, 336
Hesburgh, Theodore, 131–32, 133,
    401–2
Hesse, Konrad, 229
Higgins, George, 110
Himmelfarb, Gertrude, 410
Hinduism, 28, 317, 386n14
historical scholarship, state of, 410

Hobbes, Thomas, 5, 22, 35, 36, 37, 41,
    145, 245, 246
Hobbins, A. J., 375n10, 378n29,
    381n39, 382n40, 387n15
Hodgson, Roy, 336
Holmes, Oliver Wendell, Jr., ix, 5,
    7–10, 205–6, 231, 246, 264
homosexuality
    Beijing Women's Conference (1995)
        and, 300, 303, 309
    clerical subculture of, 425
    family law and, 240–42
Hoover, J. Edgar, 214
Hopkins, Gerard Manley, 401
Housing Act (1949), 262
Houston, Charles Hamilton, 214
human nature. See anthropology
human rights. See also individual rights,
    e.g. free speech
    absolute rights, concept of, 279–85
    anthropology affecting, 343
    Catholic adoption of modern rights
        talk, 352–54
    children's rights, concept of, 240
    civil law system, advantages of, 229
    comparative studies of, 20, 246–47
    defining, 258–59
    different understandings of, 55–58,
        247, 331–32, 340–41
    dignitarian basis for (See dignitarian
        basis for human rights)
    fundamental or primary rights,
        changing concepts of, 270, 283
    indivisibility in Universal
        Declaration (See Universal
        Declaration on Human Rights)
    international agreements, 255, 260,
        263
    John Paul II on, 355, 356, 357–58,
        360
    Latin America and (See Latin
        America)
    libertarian basis for, 56–58, 300, 305

marriage, right of, 241–42
negative and positive rights, 17, 56, 259
social and economic rights (*See* social welfare; welfare states, constitutional rights in)
U.N. Commission on, 318–19, 335, 338, 349, 371–73, 386
U.N. Universal Declaration on (*See* Universal Declaration on Human Rights)
universal standard for, 317, 322–23, 337
in U.S. (*See* United States)
U.S. concepts of "right to be let alone" and "right of privacy," 58, 246, 283
human sciences. *See* social sciences
Hume, Basil, 426
Humphrey, Hubert, 126
Humphrey, John P., and Universal Declaration on Human Rights, 371–82
adoption of, 380–81
authorship controversy, 377–79
career after passage of, 381–82
Catholic social thought and, 352
first draft/outline, 373–76
foundations of, 336
Latin American human rights tradition and, 375, 380, 387–88, 390, 394
on Malik, 366, 367
on Pérez Cisneros, 352, 394
U.N. Human Rights Commission and, 371–73
welfare rights in, 379–80
Hutchins, Robert Maynard, 132, 401
Huxley, Aldous, 317
hyper-individualistic view of human person. *See* anthropology

**I**

Iceland, civil unions in, 241
Ignatieff, Michael, 360
Ik tribe of Uganda, 79, 196
immigration opponents, population control, and abortion rights, 216, 345
imperialism, cultural. *See* colonialism
inculturation of universal rights regime, 340–41
India and Universal Declaration on Human Rights, 321, 325, 326, 338, 386
individualism. *See* anthropology
indivisibility of rights in Universal Declaration. *See* Universal Declaration on Human Rights
Industrial Areas Foundation, 185
industrial revolution
cultural underpinnings of democracy in America affected by, 65–66, 101
family life, effect on, 66, 101
legal system in America affected by, 10
Inter-American Conference (now Organization of American States), 384, 387
interdisciplinary studies
advantages of, 15–22
Rheinstein, Max, contributions of, 26–27, 28
social science and law, 271–72
social sciences and Catholic social thought, dialogue between, 50
international human rights agreements, 255, 260, 263
Investment Aid Case (1954, Germany), 247n27
investment banking scandal, 196–97
Iran and Universal Declaration on Human Rights, 386

Ireland
    Beijing Women's Conference (1995)
        delegates, 311
    constitutional rights in welfare
        states, 258
Islam, 28, 85, 312, 317, 338, 340, 355,
    386n14, 416
Italy
    Beijing Women's Conference (1995)
        delegates, 311
    constitutional rights in welfare
        states, 255, 259, 261
    United Nations, Pomodoro's
        sculpture presented to, 332

**J**

Jackson, Robert, 205
Jacobs, Jane, 77–81, 191–201. *See also*
    trader vs. raider ("commercial" vs.
    "guardian") survival strategies
Japan
    constitutional rights in welfare
        states, 255, 258, 259, 261–62
    United Nations, initial exclusion
        from, 339
Jay, John, 145, 148–50
Jefferson, Thomas, 86, 373–74
Jenner, Albert, 192
Jews, John Paul II's expressions of
    penitence regarding persecution of,
    409, 410–11
John XXIII, 50, 353, 354
John Paul II
    anthropology of, 46, 57, 59
    Beijing Women's Conference, letter
        to, 287–89, 300, 307, 312–13,
        405–6, 411–12
    biography of, 415–19
    on dignity of human person, 361
    on dignity of work, 103
    as "the Great", 419
    on human rights, 355, 356, 357–58,
        360

lay apostolate encouraged by, 406–7,
    421, 425–26, 428, 430–32
moral structure of freedom
    according to, 55–59
penitence, expressions of, 409–14
Pontifical Academy of Social
    Sciences, establishment and
    purpose of, 49–51, 138
on recognition of existence of
    objective truth, 72–73
social encyclicals of, 403
social sciences challenged in
    *Centesimus Annus* by, 45–47
United Nations, 1995 address to, 355
on Universal Declaration on Human
    Rights, 345, 354
Vatican II and, 353, 416
on women's rights, 287–89, 294, 300,
    307, 312–13, 404–6, 411–13
on young people, 438, 439
Johnson, Lyndon B., 215
Joseph II of Austria, 35
Jubilee Year 2000, 409
judicial review
    and human rights, 230, 255, 256,
        257–58
    local ordinances and, 83–84
    Supreme Court's use of, 9, 11, 65
judiciary
    and elected branches of government,
        185–87, 205–6, 210–11
    litigation vs. judging skills, 215
    romantic vs. classical values of
        (*See* romantic vs. classical judicial
        values)
    and statesmanship, 204, 211
    oath taken by, 207–8

**K**

Kant, Immanuel, 36, 42, 346
Kaufman, Irving, 215
Kennedy, Anthony, 276, 277
Kennedy, John F., 424

Kepler, Johannes, 378
Keynes, John Maynard, 126
King, Martin Luther, 402
knowledge, pursuit of
  anthropology of *The Federalist Papers*
    and, 145–51
  *eros*, as form of, 145, 147, 149
  lay apostolate and, 425–26, 429–31
  moral structure of freedom and, 59
  multidisciplinary study and the
    "Aha" moment, 17–18, 20
  Rheinstein, Max, 24–25
  Thomas Aquinas' approach to, 132,
    408, 429–30
Koestler, Arthur, 18n1, 19
Korean War, 179, 320
Kramer, Hilton, 9
Kuhn, Thomas, 3, 19, 21
Küng, Hans, 411, 413

**L**

*L.A. Law,* 181
labor. *See* work, dignity of
Lamb, Matthew L., 362n20
Landis, James M., 11, 225
las Casas, Bartoloméo de, 389, 430
Lasch, Christopher, 99–104
Lasch-Quinn, Elizabeth, 99–100,
  103–4
Latin America and human rights,
  383–96
  Bogota (Pan-American) Declaration
    on the Rights and Duties of Man
    (1948), 321, 325, 350, 383, 384,
    387–88, 390, 394
  distinctive discourse, origins of, 389,
    392
  U.N. Charter, 383–86
  Universal Declaration on Human
    Rights
    approval of, 393–95
    Catholic social thought and,
      350–52, 392–93

creation of, 319, 321
drafting of, 386–93
foundations of, 338, 340
Humphrey, John P., and, 375,
  380, 387–88, 390, 394
Laurel Foundation, 213
law. *See also* specific cases, e.g. *Brown
  v. Board of Education*
  American penchant for (*See* legalism
    and litigiousness in American
    life)
  civil law system
    advantages of methodology (*See*
      civil law methodology,
      advantages of)
    Universal Declaration on Human
      Rights and, 319, 328, 340,
      389
  common law (*See* common law)
  comparative (*See* comparative law)
  constitutional (*See* constitutional
    law)
  creativity and tradition in (*See*
    creativity and tradition in
    American law, relationship
    between)
  cultural underpinnings of democracy
    and, 74
  divorce and family (*See* family law)
  judicial branch (*See* judicial review;
    judiciary; Supreme Court, U.S.)
  natural law (*See* natural law)
  preventive (*See* preventive law)
  reason and rationality in
    family law, 168–72
    Holmes' denigration of, 7–10
  Rheinstein, Max, influence of,
    23–31
  Rousseau on, 39
  social sciences and, 271–72
  statutory law revolution, 9–11,
    223–26
  tort system, 264

Lawrence, Frederick, 430
lay apostolate, 421–32
    Catholic America and, 421, 422–25,
        431
    ecclesiastical structures and, 426–27
    John Paul II's encouragement of,
        406–7, 421, 425–26, 428,
        430–32
    knowledge, pursuit of, 425–26,
        429–31
    organizations for, 426, 431
    role of, 426–28
    Vatican II's encouragement of, 421,
        424–25, 427
    women's involvement in, 406–7,
        412
Laycock, Douglas, 270
Lebanon. *See also* Malik, Charles
    Palestine, U.N. decision to partition,
        367
    U.N. Charter, 385
    Universal Declaration on Human
        Rights and, 319, 336, 338, 386
legal ethics
    professional ethics of lawyers,
        174–75
    professional pride, 200–1
    self-interest, 200–1
    systemic and individual corruption
        in, 196–97
    tenuous relation of Model Rules to
        actual problems, 199–200
    trader vs. raider survival strategies in
        (*See* trader vs. raider
        ("commercial" vs. "guardian")
        survival strategies)
legal sociology, contributions of Max
    Rheinstein to, 23–31
legalism and litigiousness in American
    life, 177–90
    absolutist view of rights and, 284
    adversarial stance encouraged by,
        180–81, 184–85, 190

breakdown of non-legal behavioral
    constraints and, 181–84
diversity of population and, 182–83,
    190
exaggerated notions of power of law,
    185–87
family law, 167–68
historical development of, 178–80
importance of culture as foundation
    of law, 188
"law talk," in U.S. 178, 184–85
mass media and, 180–81, 183, 184
role of law in culture, 188–90
Tocqueville on, 167–68, 177–79, 210
Leo XIII, 50, 351, 352, 392
Lev, Edward R., 191, 408, 425
Lévi-Strauss, Claude, 74
liberalism
    anthropology of, 46
    freedom, libertarian concept of,
        56–58
    Galston's communitarian liberalism,
        119–23
    Rousseau's critique of, 39
    Sandel's liberal communitarianism,
        125–30
Liberia and Universal Declaration on
    Human Rights, 338
libertarian vs. dignitarian rights
    concepts, 56–58, 300, 305
liberty. *See* freedom
Liebmann, George, 74–75
Lincoln, Abraham, 12, 149, 193–95,
    200, 201, 210, 347
litigiousness. *See* legalism and
    litigiousness in American life
Llewellyn, Karl, 26, 27, 225, 264
local government, 10, 62, 66, 70, 75,
    83–84, 112–13, 127, 128, 180, 274
*Lochner v. New York* (1905), 231
Locke, John, 35, 36, 37, 145, 246, 281
Lonergan, Bernard J. F., x, 362, 408
Luther, Martin, 41, 426

# M

Macchiavelli, Niccoló, 22, 35, 145
Macedo, Stephen, 120
MacIntyre, Alasdair, 4, 6, 120, 121,
    316, 345
Madison, James, 39, 145, 146, 148–50,
    377
Maier, Pauline, 374
Mailer, Norman, 115
Maitland F. W., 5
Malik, Charles
    appreciation of, 363–69
    Catholic thought and Universal
        Declaration, 351–52, 356, 359
    creation of Universal Declaration,
        319–21, 325, 326, 331
    death of, 369
    as diplomat, 366–69
    foundations of Universal
        Declaration, 335, 336, 338, 339,
        347
    Humphrey, John P., and, 372–75,
        378, 382
    Latin American delegates and
        Universal Declaration, 394–95
    as philosopher, 335, 364–66, 369
Malik, Habib, 361, 363
Malinvaud, Edmond, 51
A Man in Full, Wolfe, 115–18
Mann, Thomas, 23
Mansfield, Harvey C., Jr., 121
Marbury v. Madison (1803), 230, 257
Maritain, Jacques
    Catholic social thought and
        Universal Declaration, 352, 355,
        358, 360
    creation of Universal Declaration,
        317, 318, 319, 321, 331–32,
        386n14
    foundations of Universal
        Declaration, 345–46, 347
    on Rousseau, 42
marriage. See also divorce; family law;

family life
    at Beijing Women's Conference
        (1995), 105–8, 292, 302–5
    definition of, 242
    democracy, cultural
        underpinnings of, 67–68, 127
    demographic changes in, 238–39
    dependency-welfare crisis and,
        139
    early Church and, 404
    homosexuality and, 240–42
    non-marital cohabitation rise in,
        68, 238, 240, 250, 434
    reinforcement of one man, one
        woman marriage, laws
        providing for, 247–48
    right to marry, 241–42
    Universal Declaration on Human
        Rights on, 324
Marshall, John, 230
Marshall, Thurgood, 179, 213–17, 220
Martin, Diarmuid, 308
Martin, Judith (Miss Manners), 77,
    182
Marx, Karl, 12, 36, 401
Marxism. See socialism
masculinity as theme of Wolfe's A Man
    in Full, 115–16
mass media
    at Beijing Women's Conference,
        302, 307, 310–11, 312
    judges, romantic vs. classical values
        regarding, 211
    legal ethics of use of, 200
    legalism and litigiousness in American
        life and, 180–81, 183, 184
    penitence, interpretation of Catholic
        expressions of, 409–14
    soft tyranny of, 72
Massachusetts: Goodridge v. Dept. of
    Public Health (2003), 241n10
Mater et Magistra (1961), 50, 353, 402
Matlary, Janne, 242, 308, 407

Max Planck Institute, 237
McCarthyism, 221
McConnell, Michael, 234
McInerny, Ralph, 360
McKeon, Richard, 317, 318, 321, 328–29, 331, 339, 343, 402
media. *See* mass media
Mehta, Hansa, 325, 335, 336, 365, 372
Meulders-Klein, Marie-Thérèse, 240n8, 242n16
Mexico
    U.N. Charter and, 385
    Universal Declaration on Human Rights and, 338, 394
Michelman, Kate, 161
Mill, John Stuart, 245–46
Miller, Geoffrey, 234
Milosz, Czeslaw, 337
Minow, Martha, 175
Miss Manners (Judith Martin), 77, 182
Mongella, Gertrude, 313, 405
Montesquieu, Charles-Louis de Secondat, Baron de, 35, 145
morality. *See* culture and morality
"morning after" pill (RU-486), 160
Morris, Charles, 423, 424
Morsink, Johannes, 376, 385, 387n16, 388, 391
Mother Teresa, 412
mothers and motherhood. *See also* childcare; family life; single-parent families; women, women's rights, and women's work
    at Beijing Women's Conference (1995), 105–8, 292, 302–5
    Bogota Declaration compared with U.N. Declaration, 390–391n34
    Catholic support for, 407
    Universal Declaration on Human Rights on, 324, 390–391n34, 394
    work-family dilemmas
        means of resolving, 111–13
        society-wide nature of, 108–11

Motley, Constance Baker, 187
*Mulieris Dignitatem* (1988), 404
multidisciplinary studies. *See* interdisciplinary studies
Muslim traditions, 28, 85, 312, 317, 338, 340, 355, 386n14, 416

## N

Namibian delegates to Beijing Women's Conference (1995), 304
National Catholic Welfare Conference (predecessor of U.S. Conference of Catholic Bishops), 352
National Conference of Commissioners on Uniform State Law, 225
National Labor Relations Act, 379
natural law
    Latin American rights tradition and, 389
    Maritain on, 358
    Rousseau's rejection of, 37, 43
negative and positive rights, 17, 56, 259
neighborhoods as cultural underpinning of democracy, 61, 68–69
Neo-Catechumenate Way, 307, 432
Netherlands, homosexual marriage in, 241
Neuhaus, Richard John, 75n24, 128, 269, 277, 429
New Deal, 10, 11, 66, 224, 231, 261, 262, 282, 379
New England town meeting, 64, 83, 88, 112–13, 180
Nieto del Rio, Felix, 388, 391
Nietzsche, Friedrich, 35, 148
nihilism. *See* relativism and skepticism
Nisbet, Robert, 63
Nixon, Richard, 179, 214
"no-fault" laws, 25–26, 184, 188, 198, 240
non-marital cohabitation rise in, 68, 238, 240, 250, 434

Nordic countries. *See also* Denmark;
Finland; Norway; Sweden
community ties in, 75
constitutional rights in welfare
states, 259, 265
family law in, 244
Norway. *See also* Nordic countries
civil unions in, 241
constitutional rights in welfare
states, 255, 379
Universal Declaration on Human
Rights, 375, 379
Notre Dame commencement address
(1996), 131–35
Novak, Michael, 392, 428
*Novo Millennio Ineunte* (2001), 430,
438

## O

objective truth. *See also* relativism and
skepticism
and cultural underpinnings of
democracy, 72–73
freedom, relationship to, 55, 58–59
and Universal Declaration of
Human Rights, 259, 361–62
O'Connor, Flannery, 403, 404, 406,
408, 411, 413, 428
O'Connor, Sandra Day, 206, 219, 276,
277
one-man, one-vote cases, 211, 216
Opus Dei, 432
Organization of American States
(formerly Inter-American
Conference), 375, 384, 387

## P

*Pacem in Terris* (1963), 50, 353, 354,
402
Pakistan
Bhuto, Benazir, at Beijing Women's
Conference (1995), 303

Universal Declaration on Human
Rights, 338
Palestine, partition of, 367
Pan-American (Bogota) Declaration on
the Rights and Duties of Man
(1948), 321, 325, 350, 383, 384,
387–88, 390, 394
Panama
U.N. Charter and, 385
Universal Declaration on Human
Rights and, 386, 387, 390, 395
Pangle, Thomas, 121, 145–51
papacy. *See* Catholic Church, and
individual popes (e.g. John XXIII)
and papal documents (e.g.
*Centesimus Annus*)
parental rights and duties
in 1950s, 95–97
at Beijing Women's Conference
(1995), 305, 308
"participant-observer" anthropological
method, 84
Pasteur, Louis, 18
Pavlov, Alexei P., 321, 372
*The People's Court,* 180, 183
Percy, Walker, 166, 428
Pérez Cisneros, Guy, 352, 385, 394,
395
perfectibility, Rousseau's concept of, 36,
43
personal injury law, 186
personhood, concepts of. *See*
anthropology
Pfaff, William, 69n13
Philippines
U.N. Charter, 385
Universal Declaration on Human
Rights, 338, 386
Picasso, Pablo, 9, 21
Pius XI, 351, 392, 393n40, 423
Pius XII, 351, 411
Planned Parenthood, 41, 165–66
Plato, 35, 64–65, 79, 88, 146, 190

Podhoretz, John, 115
Poland, marriage law in, 247
politics and government
    centralization, effects of, 10, 62, 66,
        70, 75, 127, 128, 180
    Church not providing policy or
        models for, 51
    erosion of cultural institutions,
        political ramifications of, 69 (*See
        also* democracy in America,
        cultural underpinnings of)
    "guardian" vs. "commercial" (raider
        vs. trader) survival strategies,
        77–81
    judicial usurpation of elected
        branch's powers, 185–87, 205–6,
        210–11
    legalism in America and, 179–80
    local (*See* local government)
    moral structure of freedom, John
        Paul II's concept of, 55–59
    public role of religion, 122, 131–35
    religion clause cases, deference to
        governmental interests in, 276–78
    Rousseau's influence on, 35–40
    Supreme Court, statesmanship role
        of, 204, 211
    Universal Declaration on Human
        Rights, duties of states in, 327
    welfare state, dependency crisis in,
        137–41
    work-family dilemmas, means of
        resolving, 111–13
Pomodoro, Arnaldo, 332
Pontifical Academy of Social Sciences,
    49–51, 137–41
poor, preferential option for, 134, 159,
    359
population control
    abortion as means of, 308
    Beijing Women's Conference (1995),
        lobbyists at, 302, 304, 306–10,
        343

Cairo Conference on Population and
    Development (1993), 301, 304,
    306, 308, 344
immigration opponents and
    abortion rights advocates, ties
    between, 216, 345
Western approach to developing
    nations as to, 309, 344
positive and negative rights, 17, 56,
    259
Posner, Richard, 188–89, 214, 259
Pound, Roscoe, 26, 223, 225, 231
poverty, 137, 294–95, 303, 309–10
Powell, H. Jefferson, 231
Powell, Lewis, 276
Powell, Thomas Reed, 272
President's Council on Bioethics, 138
preventive law
    creativity and tradition in, 6
    litigation vs., 170–71
pride and ambition *(thymos)*, 146, 149
privacy
    religion, private and individualized
        vs. communitarian view of,
        274–75
    right of privacy and "right to be let
        alone," 58, 246, 283
Probst, Thomas, 228
the procedural state, 125
Progressivism, 126

## Q

*Quadragesimo Anno* (1931), 351, 352,
    392, 393n40, 423
Quinn, Gail, 308

## R

Rabel, Ernst, 24, 27
racism and racial attitudes. *See also* civil
    rights movement
Thomas, Clarence, opinion regarding,
    219–21

raider vs. trader. *See* trader vs. raider
  ("commercial" vs. "guardian")
  survival strategies
*A Raisin in the Sun,* Hansberry, 93
rationality. *See* reason and rationality
Rawls, John, 121
Reagan, Ronald, 83
realist legal theory of Oliver Wendell
  Holmes, Jr., 7–10
reason and rationality
  Catholic Church as defender of,
    361–62
  everyday life, Lasch on
    rationalization of, 100
  faith and, enlightened approach to,
    132
  *The Federalist Papers,* reason and
    human nature according to,
    145–51
  John Paul II's challenge to social
    sciences in *Centesimus Annus,* 47
  in law
    in family law, 168–72
    Holmes' denigration of reason
      and tradition in, 7–10
  Rousseau's elevation of sentiment
    over, 33–34, 36, 37–38, 40–42
*Rees* v. *United Kingdom* (1990), 242n13
reflexive law, 265
Regnum Christi, 432
Rehnquist, William H., 155, 219, 259,
  277
Reich, Charles, 283
Reich, Robert, 127
relativism and skepticism
  critical theory, 11–13
  democracy, cultural underpinnings
    of, 72–73
  historical scholarship, state of, 410
  John Paul II's challenge to social
    sciences in *Centesimus Annus,*
    46–47

Universal Declaration on Human
  Rights
  cultural relativism critique of,
    337, 340–41, 355–56
  foundation of, 259, 361–62
religion
  Beijing Women's Conference (1995)
    and, 305, 308
  civic religion and meaning of flag,
    155
  democracy, cultural underpinnings
    of, 61, 65, 69, 122, 129–30, 132
  Lasch on moral effects of, 103
  private and individualized view of,
    274–75
  public role of, 122, 131–35
  reason, faith, and pursuit of
    knowledge, enlightened approach
    to, 132
  as rooted in rural life, 85, 87–89
  Rousseau on, 40–41
  secularism and hostility to, 277
  social change and decline of, 85, 88
  suburban church established in
    Elmhurst, Illinois, 94–95
  Universal Declaration on Human
    Rights on, 324
  U.S. guarantees regarding (*See*
    freedom of religion in U.S
    constitution)
  in Wolfe's *A Man in Full,* 116–17
reproductive health of women as
  addressed at Beijing Women's
  Conference (1995), 106, 295–96,
  300, 303, 304, 308, 309
reproductive rights. *See also* abortion;
  birth control; population control
  at Beijing Women's Conference (1995),
  300, 306, 308–9
reproductive technologies, ramifications
  of, 231, 242–43
*Rerum Novarum* (1891), 50, 351, 352,
  392, 423

Rheinstein, Max
  biographical information, 23–24
  comparative law, contributions to,
    17, 19, 20, 24, 29–30
  as German-American intermediary
    after World War II, 30–31
  legal sociology in America, influence
    on, 23–31
"right to die" movement, 110, 141, 346
rights. *See* civil rights movement;
  entries at constitutional; human
  rights
*Rio Declaration,* 291
Rockwell, Norman, 153, 155
*Roe* v. *Wade* (1973), 157, 158, 162,
  163, 165, 215–16
Roman Catholic Church. *See* Catholic
  Church
Roman empire, Wolfe's invocation of,
  in *A Man in Full,* 117–18
Romano-Germanic countries
  civil law tradition
    methodological advantages (*See*
      civil law methodology,
      advantages of)
    Universal Declaration on Human
      Rights and, 319, 328, 340, 389
  family law in, 244–48 (*See also*
    family law: comparative study of)
  romantic vs. classical judicial values,
    203–12
    coherence and predictability of law,
      problem of maintaining, 209–11
    differences in, 203
    Douglas, Warren, and Brennan,
      judgeships of, 203–6
    elected judiciary, special problems
      of, 208
    impartiality as chief virtue, 207–9
    Marshall, Thurgood, as romantic
      judge, 214–17
    strict vs. liberal construction of
      constitutional issues, 205–7

Thomas, Clarence, craftsmanship of,
  219–21
Romanticism
  creativity, concept of, 3
  Rousseau's influence on, 41
Romulo, Carlos, 338, 365
Roncalli, Angelo (later John XXIII),
  353
Roosevelt, Eleanor
  Catholic thought and Universal
    Declaration, 349, 351, 356
  controversy over appointment as
    delegate to U.N., 221
  drafting of Universal Declaration,
    315, 318–21, 324, 325
  foundations of Universal
    Declaration, 335, 336, 347
  Humphrey, John P., and, 371–75,
    378, 379, 382
  Malik, Charles, and, 364, 365, 367
  requested to resign from U.N.
    Human Rights Commission, 351
  Rowan, Carl, on, 214
  social welfare rights in Universal
    Declaration and, 379
  Thomas, Clarence, compared, 221
Roosevelt, Franklin D., 261, 323, 368,
  379, 384
Rosenberg, Gerald, 186
Rossiter, Clinton, 376n24
Rousseau, Jean-Jacques, 33–43
  biographical information, 33–35
  on empathy and human dignity, 42,
    346, 360
  originality, or lack thereof, 41
  perfectibility, concept of, 36, 43
  political thought of, 35–40
  reason vs. sentiment in, 33–34, 36,
    37–38, 40–42
  on religion, 40–41
  Tocqueville's discovery of, 437
  writings of, 33, 34–35
Roussel, Louis, 67–68, 238

Rowan, Carl, 213–17
RU-486, 160
rural and small town life, 83–89
Russian revolution, 65
Rutland, Vermont, rural and small
    town life in, 83–89
Ryan, Kevin and Marilyn, 399

## S

St. Nicholas of Tolentine Parish,
    Chicago, 92–93
same-sex marriage, 240–42
Samuelson, Robert J., 184
Sandel, Michael, 121, 125–30
Santa Cruz, Hernàn, 338, 367, 368,
    372, 379, 391, 393, 394, 395
Santayana, George, 423
Sarat, Austin, 168–72, 174
Saudi Arabia and Universal Declaration
    on Human Rights, 321, 339, 341,
    381, 395
savings and loan scandal, 196–97
Scalia, Antonin
    on advantages of civil law code
        methodology, 223–24, 230,
        233–34
    religion clause and, 277
    Thomas, Clarence, and, 219–20
schools
    Chicago in the 1950s and authority
        in, 95
    children's legalism in, 178, 181
    democracy, cultural underpinning
        of, 69, 70, 128
    freedom of religion cases involving,
        275–76
    Notre Dame commencement
        address (1996), 131–35
Scott, Dred, 165
Second Vatican Council. See Vatican II
secularism
    and hostility to religion, 277
    rise of, 88

seedbeds of civil virtue. See democracy in
    America, cultural underpinnings of
segregation and community,
    relationship between, 93
Sen, Amartya, 309, 344
Seneca, 117
sex-selection abortions, 158, 160
sexual behavior
    Catholic child sex abuse scandal,
        421, 425, 427
    democracy, cultural underpinnings
        of, 67, 72
    dependency-welfare crisis and, 139
    lawyers' embrace of self-interest
        compared to lack of modern
        limits on, 201
    responsibility for consequences of,
        160
    women's rights and, 295, 297, 300,
        304, 306, 308–9, 310
sexual orientation. See homosexuality
Shaffer, Mary, 194–95
Shaffer, Thomas L., 174–75, 194–95
Sharp, Malcolm, 30
Shays, Daniel, and Shays' Rebellion,
    112
Shils, Edward, 28
Shklar, Judith, 42
sick and disabled, care of
    democracy, cultural underpinning
        of, 68
    family law's need to address new
        problems of, 248
Silverglate, Harvey, 166
single-parent families
    democracy, cultural underpinning
        of, 68–69
    dependency-welfare crisis and, 137,
        139
    special assistance needed for, 250
    in Wolfe's A Man in Full, 116
skepticisim. See relativism and
    skepticism

small town and rural life, 83–89
Smith, Adam, 22
Smith, Al, 423
social improvements, threats posed by.
    *See* threats posed by genuine social
    improvements
social regulation. *See* culture and
    morality
social sciences
    creativity and tradition in
        (*See* creativity and tradition in
        American law, relationship
        between)
    on Generation Y, 433–35
    John Paul II's challenge in
        *Centesimus Annus* to, 45–47
    and law, 271–72
    Pontifical Academy of Social
        Sciences, establishment and
        purpose of, 49–51
    Rheinstein, Max, influence of,
        23–31
Social Security Act (1935), 262, 379
social welfare. *See also* welfare states
    abortion and, 159, 160, 161, 165
    absolutist view of rights to, 283
    demographics of dependency-welfare
        crisis, 137–41
    Universal Declaration on Human
        Rights as to, 323, 325–26, 379–80
socialism
    anthropology of, 46
    Humphrey on, 380
Socrates, 190
*Solicitudo Rei Socialis* (1987), 51,
    425–26
Sontheimer, Kurt, 329n11
South Africa
    Beijing Women's Conference (1995)
        delegates, 304
    Universal Declaration on Human
        Rights, 321, 338, 339, 341, 381,
        395

Soviet Union
    Cold War, 320, 330, 335, 341, 342,
        357, 359, 381–82
    John Paul II and collapse of, 415
    Russian revolution, 65
    U.N. Charter, Latin American push
        to include human rights in, 385
    Universal Declaration on Human
        Rights and, 318, 319, 321, 325,
        327, 374, 375, 380–82, 386, 395
Spain and constitutional rights in
    welfare states, 259, 261
speech and thought, freedom of. *See*
    free speech
Spinoza, Baruch, 35
Stael, Madame de, 41
Stalin, Joseph, 384
Stanton, Elizabeth Cady, 105
statutory law revolution, 9–11, 223–29
Stevens, John Paul, 154–55
Stiglitz, Joseph, 138
Stoicism, in Wolfe's *A Man in Full*,
    117–19
*The Storyteller*, Mario Vargas Llosa, 201,
    421–22, 432
Strauss, Leo, 402
Stravinsky, Igor, 9, 21
structuralism as form of constitutional
    interpretation, 234
subsidiarity, principle of
    Catholic social thought and
        Universal Declaration on Human
        Rights, 355, 358, 359
    constitutional rights in welfare states
        and, 266
    cultural underpinnings of democracy
        and, 75
    family law and, 249
    reawakening of political interest in,
        128
suburban life and culture
    Elmhurst, Illinois, 94–95
    women's history and, 101–2

suicide, assisted, 110, 141, 346
Sunstein, Cass R., 232
Supreme Court, U.S. *See also*
    constitutional law, and individual
    cases, e.g. *Brown* v. *Board of
    Education*
    judicial review as used by, 9, 11, 65
    one-man, one-vote cases before, 211,
        216
    religion clause, difficulties with (*See*
        freedom of religion in U.S.
        Constitution)
    romantic vs. classical values on (*See*
        romantic vs. classical judicial
        values)
    statesmanship required of, 204, 211
Sweden. *See also* Nordic countries
    abortion rights in, 309
    civil unions in, 241
    constitutional rights in welfare
        states, 255
    Universal Declaration on Human
        Rights, 338, 375
Switzerland
    civil law system, advantages of, 228
    reinforcement of one man, one
        woman marriage, laws providing
        for, 247

**T**

takeover phenomenon, effect on law
    firms of, 196–97
Talleyrand, Charles de, 201
technically-assisted procreation, 231,
    242–43
Teilhard de Chardin, Pierre, 317,
    386n14
Tenth Amendment, 112
Teresa of Calcutta (Mother Teresa), 412
*Tertio Millennio Adveniente* (1994),
    409–10, 439
Teubner, Gunther, 20
*Texas* v. *Johnson* (1989), 153–55

textualism in constitutional
    interpretation, 230, 234
Thomas Aquinas and Thomism, 49,
    132, 373, 389, 402, 408, 429–30
Thomas, Clarence, 216–17, 219–21
thought and speech, freedom of. *See*
    free speech
Thurmond, Strom, 214
*thymos* or "spiritedness," 146, 149
Tierney, Brian, 389
Tocqueville, Alexis de
    on Catholicism in America, 422, 431
    on creativity and tradition, 6–7
    on cultural underpinnings of
        democracy in America, 61–67,
        69, 72, 73, 88, 120–22, 267, 273
    on family structure in America, 245
    on French uprisings of 1848, 179
    on intergenerational relations, 249
    Jacobs, Jane, compared, 77, 79
    John Paul II reminiscent of, 356
    on legalism of American culture,
        167–68, 177–79, 210
    loss of faith by, 437–38
    Malik, Charles, compared, 365
    New England town meeting
        admired by, 113
    on public role of religion, 122
    Rousseau and, 39, 49
    on soft vs. hard tyranny, 61–67, 69,
        72, 73, 235
tort system, U.S. reliance on, 264
Toulmin, Stephen, 3
trade. *See* economics and commerce
trader vs. raider ("commercial" vs.
    "guardian") survival strategies
    honesty as chief virtue of trader
        mentality, 193
    in investment banking and savings
        and loan scandals, 196–97
    in law and legal ethics, 80, 191–201
    mingling of raider with trader
        ethics, 196–99

misplaced fear of
commercialization, 195–96
"old WASP/gentleman's ethic" vs.
"old world ethic", 194–95, 201
professional pride, 200–1
self-interest, 200–1
tenuous relation of model ethics
codes to actual problems,
199–200
as two separate schools of legal
ethics, 192–95
loyalty as chief virtue of raider
mentality, 193, 200
in politics and government, 77–81
tradition and creativity. *See* creativity
and tradition in American law,
relationship between
Trent, Council of, 404
Tribe, Lawrence, 83, 154, 157–63, 223,
270
Truman, Harry, 179, 214, 221, 379
Tunc, André, 228
Turner, Ted, 344–45
Twain, Mark, 264

# U

Ukraine and Universal Declaration on
Human Rights, 321, 386
UNESCO, 317, 330, 331, 339, 340,
352, 358, 359, 361, 386
United Kingdom. *See* England
United Nations
Cairo Conference on Population and
Development (1993), 301, 304,
306, 308, 344
Charter
dignitarian basis of, 337, 346–47
Latin American contribution to,
383–86
non-Western contributions to,
338
Universal Declaration on Human
Rights anchored in, 323

Commission on Human Rights,
318–19, 335, 338, 349, 371–73,
386
Commission on Status of Women,
document prepared by, 107, 302
Committee on Social, Economic,
and Cultural Affairs, 380
Committee on Theoretical Bases of
Human Rights, 317–18, 339,
352, 358, 359, 361, 386n14
Convention on the Rights of the
Child, 305
Covenant on Civil and Political
Rights, 260
Covenant on Economic, Social, and
Cultural Rights, 260, 263
Economic and Social Council
(ECOSOC), 320, 366–67
Fourth World Conference on
Women (*See* Beijing Women's
Conference)
Holy See as permanent observer at,
402–3
on human rights (*See* Universal
Declaration on Human Rights)
John Paul II's 1995 address to,
55–59, 355
special interest groups, 343–45
Vienna Human Rights Conference
(1993), 309, 339, 355
United States
abortion rights in, 309, 343
anthropology of founders of, 39, 59,
145–51
Beijing Women's Conference (1995),
delegation to, 303, 308
Catholicism in, 132, 421, 422–25,
431
Cold War, 320, 330, 335, 341, 342,
357, 359, 381–82
creativity and tradition involved in
founding of, 6 (*See also* creativity
and tradition in American law,
relationship between)

cultural underpinnings of democracy
in (*See* democracy in America,
cultural underpinnings of)
Enlightenment influences on
founders of, 35
as experiment, 148
flag-burning and values associated
with flag, 153–55
German-American relations after
World War II, Rheinstein's
contributions to, 30–31
homosexual marriage and civil
unions in, 241
human rights as viewed in
absolutist approach, 279–85
constitutional rights in welfare
states, 255, 256–58, 260,
263–65
hyper-individualist anthropology,
342
international agreements not
ratified by U.S., 260, 263
property rights, 280–83
United Nations, influence of
Latin America regarding,
385–86
Universal Declaration on Human
Rights, 318, 319, 321, 338,
342, 386
legalism and litigiousness in (*See*
legalism and litigiousness in
American life)
reinforcement of one man, one
woman marriage, laws providing
for, 247
Rousseau's influence on founders of,
39
tort system, reliance on, 264
ubiquity of law and legal language in
American life, 167–68
Universal Declaration on Human
Rights and, 318, 319, 321, 338,
342, 386

Universal Declaration on Human
Rights
abstentions from, 321, 381
adoption of, 320–22
Humphrey, John P., and, 380–81
Latin American delegates and,
393–95
anthropology, need for, 359
authors of and contributors to (*See*
Cassin, René; Chang, Peng-chun;
Humphrey, John P.; Malik,
Charles; Maritain, Jacques;
Roosevelt, Eleanor)
Beijing Women's Conference (1995)
and, 294, 304–5, 311–12
Catholic social thought and,
349–62, 402–3
future potential contributions of,
354–62
influence of Church on Universal
Declaration, 350–62
influence of Declaration on
Vatican II and Church
generally, 352–54
Latin American influence,
350–52, 392–93
civil law tradition and, 319, 328,
340, 389
Cold War and, 320, 330, 335, 341,
342, 357, 359, 381–82
contemporary interpretation of,
330–33
deconstruction and misuse of,
342–45
dignitarian rights concept of, 329,
336–37, 346–47, 390n34, 396
drafting, modification, and passage
of, 318–22
duties and responsibilities in, 321,
326–27, 354, 380, 391n34
foundations of, 335–47
Catholic social thought and,
359–61

dignitarian basis for, 346–47
need for, 345–47
objective truth, 259, 361–62
reasons for not initially
establishing, 335–37
importance of, 315–17, 349, 396
indivisibility of rights in
Catholic social thought and,
356–59
deconstruction and misuse,
342–45
structure, content, and import of,
322–30
Latin America and (See Latin
America)
moral structure of freedom in, 56,
57
objective truth required for
foundation of, 259, 361–62
states, duties of, 327
structure, content, and import of,
322–30
Theoretical Bases of Human Rights,
U.N. Committee on, 317–18,
339, 352, 358, 359, 361
U.N. Charter, anchoring in, 323
universality
cultural relativism and, 337,
340–41, 355–56
need for, 317, 322–23
Western vs. multicultural origins
of Declaration's rights, 337–40
welfare rights in, 323, 325–26,
379–80
women's rights in, 321, 323, 394,
395
Updike, John, 115, 117
urban culture
Chicago in the 1950s and today,
91–97
family law and demographic
revolution, 239
rural life vs., 85, 87, 88

Uruguay and Universal Declaration on
Human Rights, 386, 395
utilitarianism, 58

**V**

Vallin, Jacques, 139
Vargas Llosa, Mario, 201, 421–22, 432
Vatican II
author's experience of Church and,
402–3
John Paul II and, 353, 416
lay apostolate encouraged by, 421,
424–25, 427
Universal Declaration on Human
Rights influencing, 352–54
Vermont, rural and small town life in,
83–89
Vienna Human Rights Conference and
Declaration (1993), 309, 339, 355
village and rural life, 83–89
Villey, Michel, 316, 328, 345
violence against women and girls, 296
Vishinsky, Andrei, 331
Vita Consecrata (1996), 406
Voltaire, 35, 437
voting rights. See also civil rights
movement
one-man, one-vote cases before
Supreme Court, 211, 216
Voting Rights Act, 185, 204

**W**

Wallace, George, 214
Wallace v. Jaffree (1985), 41
Walzer, Michael, 127
Wapner, Joseph A., 180, 183
Warren, Earl, and Warren Court, 11,
203–4, 206, 210, 213, 214, 220,
225
Waugh, Evelyn, 401
Weaver, Richard, 402
Weber, Max, 26–29, 369

*Webster* v. *Reproductive Health Services* (1989), 157, 158
Weigel, George, 415–19
welfare states. *See also* social welfare
dependency crisis in, 137–41
family law and worker protections, 248
welfare states, constitutional rights in, 255–68
cultural underpinnings of, 266–67
defining rights, 258–59
distinctiveness of U.S. regarding, 256–58
economic constraints, 265
European and American models of, 247–58
international human rights agreements, 255, 260, 263
judicial review and, 255, 256, 257–58
resistance to constitutionalization of welfare rights, 263–65
significance of formal differences between, 260–63
White, Byron, 206, 211–12, 277
Whitehead, Alfred North, 335
Wieacker, Franz, 258
Wilson, Geoffrey, 375
*Wilson, James Q.,* 257
Wirth, Timothy, 308, 344
*Wisconsin* v. *Yoder* (1972), 275
*Witness to Hope,* George Weigel, 415–19
Wojtyla, Karol (later John Paul II), 353, 410, 415–19
Wolfe, Tom, 115–18
women, women's rights, and women's work. *See also* abortion; birth control; childcare; elderly, care of; family life; feminism; marriage; entries at reproductive; sexual behavior; women's health
caretaking roles, change in, 68, 137, 139–40

Catholic Church and, 403–8, 411–13
Catholic ordination, issue of, 307, 406, 412
democracy, cultural underpinnings of, 68, 71, 100–2
domestic violence, 296
economic dependence, 66, 101–2
education, women and girls' access to, 288, 294, 308
family law and, 248–49
Fourth World Conference on (*See* Beijing Women's Conference)
John Paul II on, 287–89, 294, 300, 307, 312–13, 404–6, 411–13
Lasch's theory of, 99–104
poverty of women, 137, 294–95, 303, 309–10
sexual behavior and sexual rights, 295, 297, 300, 304, 306, 308–9, 310
Universal Declaration on Human Rights on, 321, 323, 394, 395
women's health
Beijing Women's Conference and, 106, 295–96, 300, 303, 304, 308, 309
birth control and, 159–60
Catholic concern with, 288
defined for purposes of abortion law, 158
Wood, Gordon, 223
Woodward, Bob, 204, 214
work, dignity of
applicability to work-family dilemma, 108–11
gender gap in wages, 108–9
John Paul II on, 103
Lasch on, 103
women and (*See* women, women's rights, and women's work)
World Summit on Social Development, 293

World Youth Alliance, 435
World Youth Day address, 433–40. *See
also* Generation Y
Wright, J. Skelley, 206–7
Wu, Harry, 312

## Y

Yankelovich, Daniel, 182
Yeats, William Butler, 9
*Young Frankenstein,* 223
Yugoslavia and Universal Declaration
on Human Rights, 321, 335, 386